Étienne Davodeau

THE INITIATES

A Comic Artist and a Wine Artisan
Exchange Jobs

ISBN 9781561637034
Library of Congress Control Number: 2012953818
© Futuropolis 2011
© NBM 2013 for the English translation
Translation by Joe Johnson
Lettering by Ortho
Printed in China
1st printing January 2013

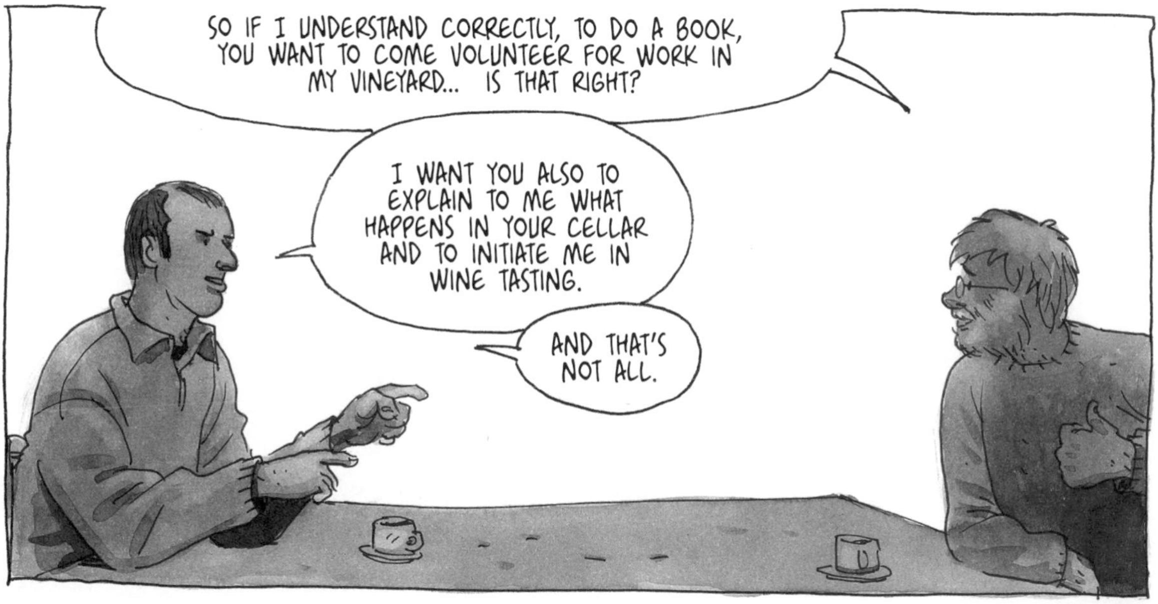
SO IF I UNDERSTAND CORRECTLY, TO DO A BOOK, YOU WANT TO COME VOLUNTEER FOR WORK IN MY VINEYARD... IS THAT RIGHT?
I WANT YOU ALSO TO EXPLAIN TO ME WHAT HAPPENS IN YOUR CELLAR AND TO INITIATE ME IN WINE TASTING.
AND THAT'S NOT ALL.

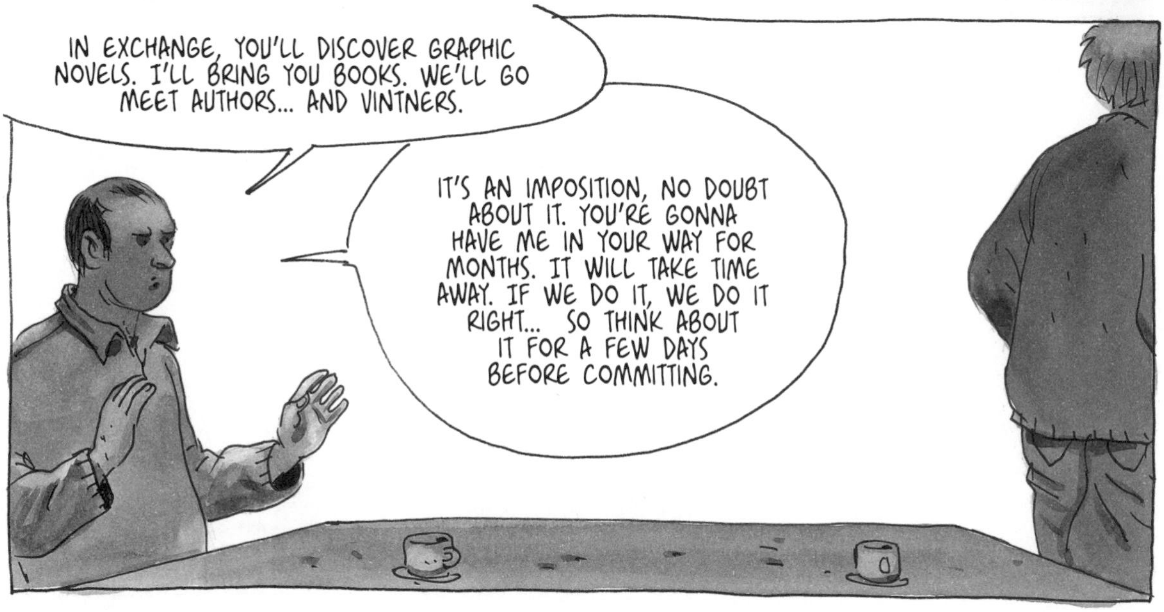
IN EXCHANGE, YOU'LL DISCOVER GRAPHIC NOVELS. I'LL BRING YOU BOOKS. WE'LL GO MEET AUTHORS... AND VINTNERS.
IT'S AN IMPOSITION, NO DOUBT ABOUT IT. YOU'RE GONNA HAVE ME IN YOUR WAY FOR MONTHS. IT WILL TAKE TIME AWAY. IF WE DO IT, WE DO IT RIGHT... SO THINK ABOUT IT FOR A FEW DAYS BEFORE COMMITTING.

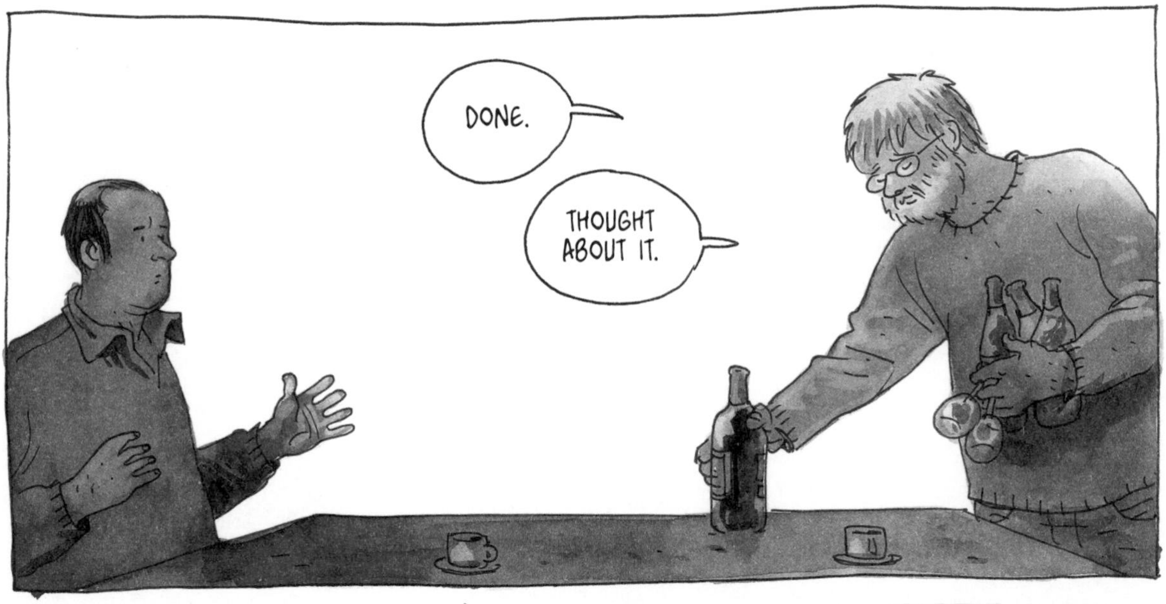
DONE.
THOUGHT ABOUT IT.
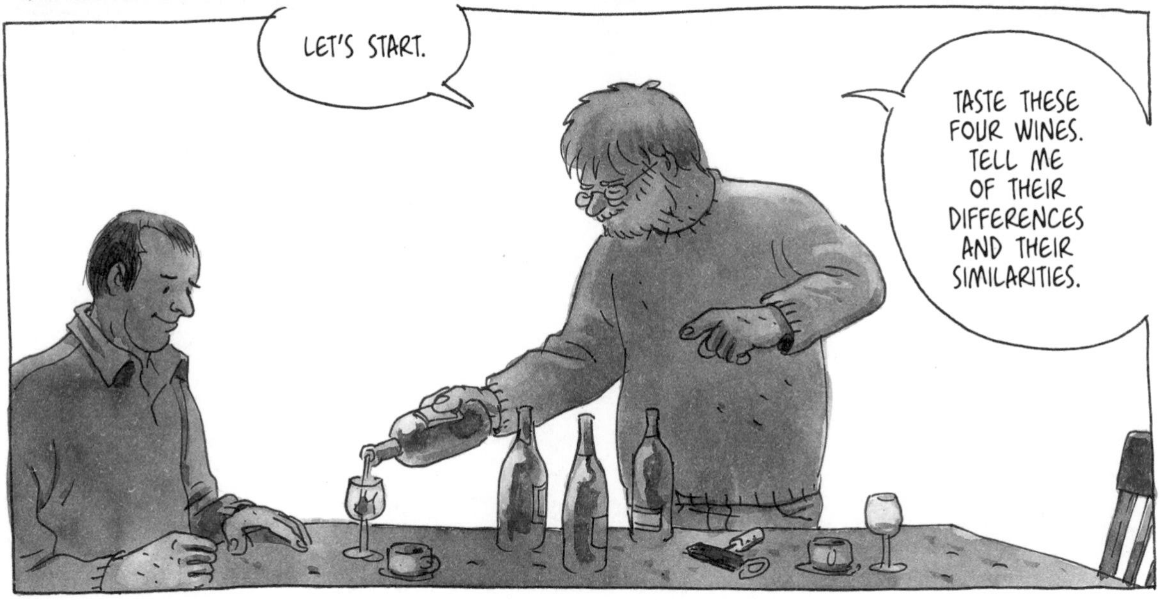
LET'S START.
TASTE THESE FOUR WINES. TELL ME OF THEIR DIFFERENCES AND THEIR SIMILARITIES.
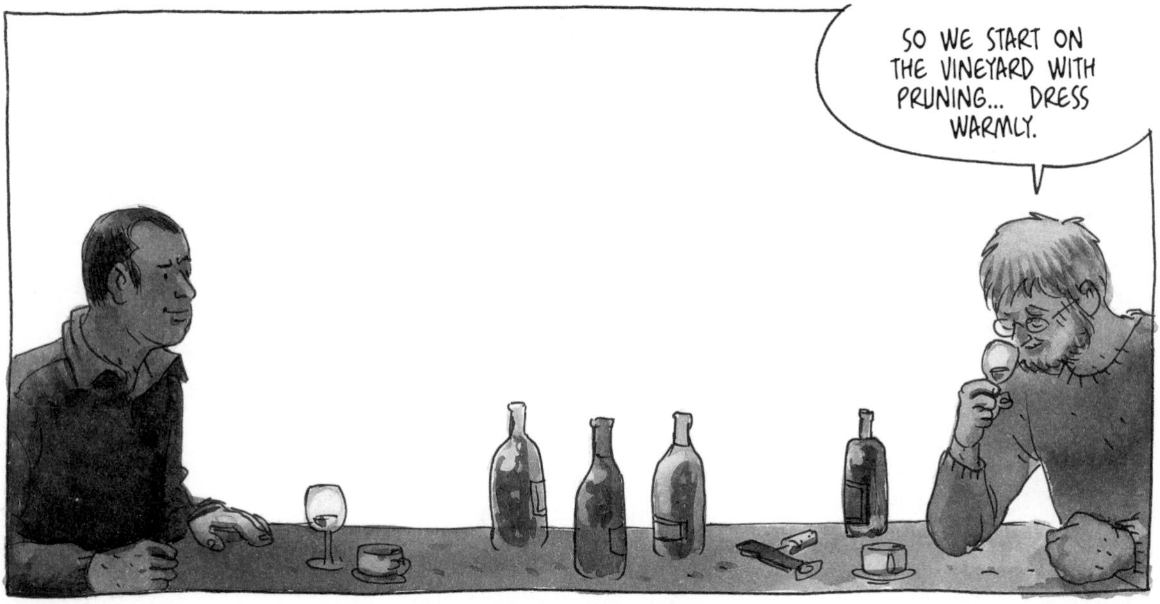
SO WE START ON THE VINEYARD WITH PRUNING... DRESS WARMLY.

CHAPTER ONE   # TO PRUNING, THEN
(PLUS ONE BELGIAN PRINTING)

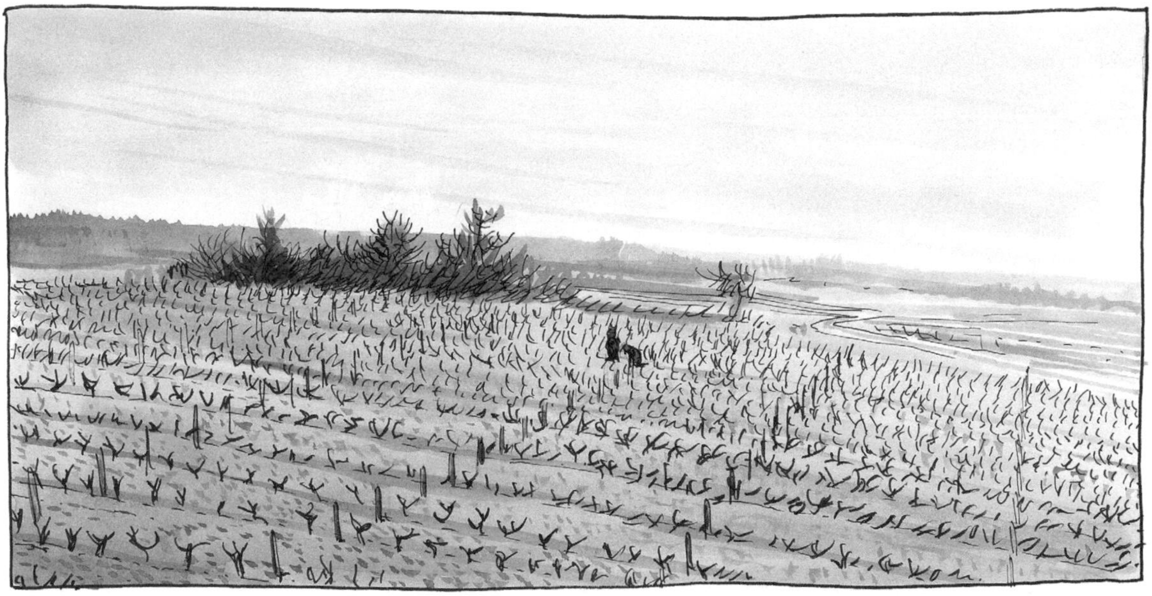

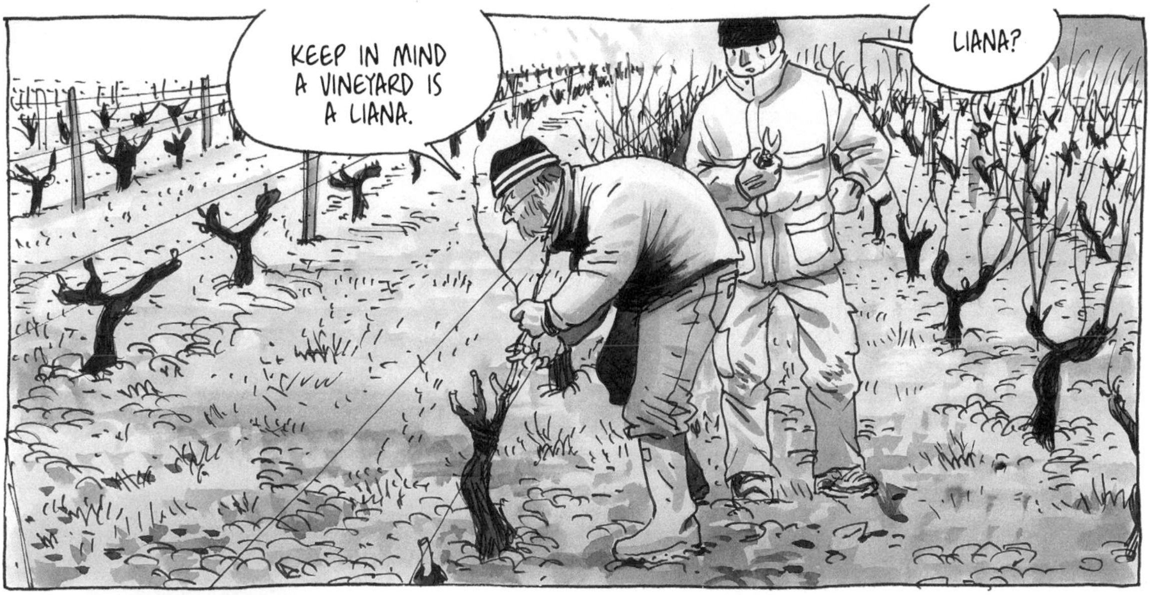
KEEP IN MIND A VINEYARD IS A LIANA.
LIANA?

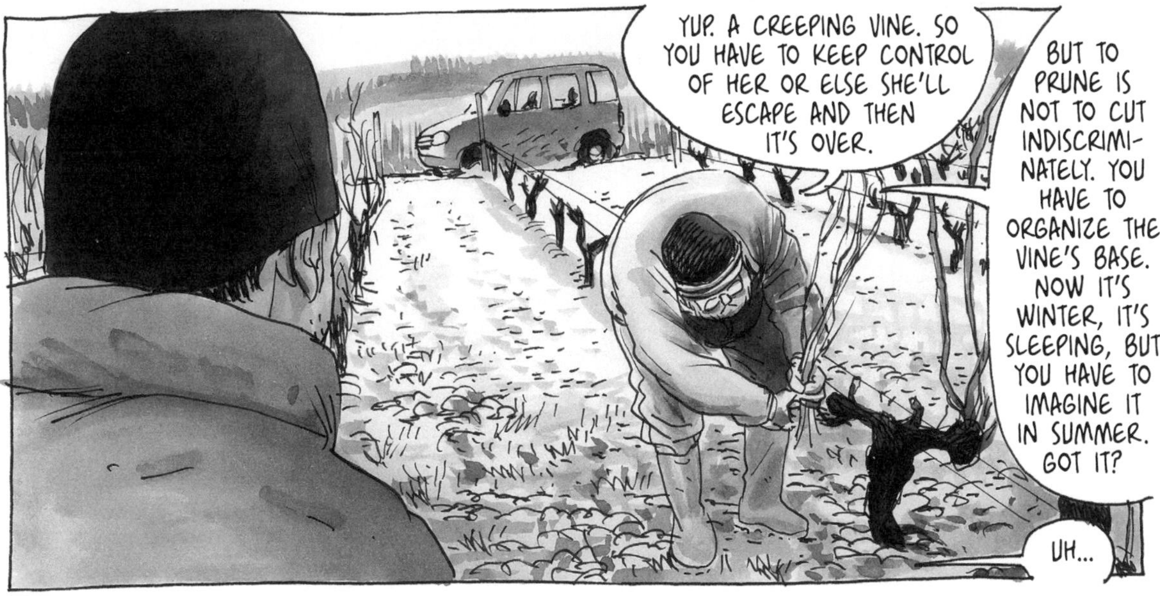
YUP. A CREEPING VINE. SO YOU HAVE TO KEEP CONTROL OF HER OR ELSE SHE'LL ESCAPE AND THEN IT'S OVER.
BUT TO PRUNE IS NOT TO CUT INDISCRIMI-NATELY. YOU HAVE TO ORGANIZE THE VINE'S BASE. NOW IT'S WINTER, IT'S SLEEPING, BUT YOU HAVE TO IMAGINE IT IN SUMMER. GOT IT?
UH...

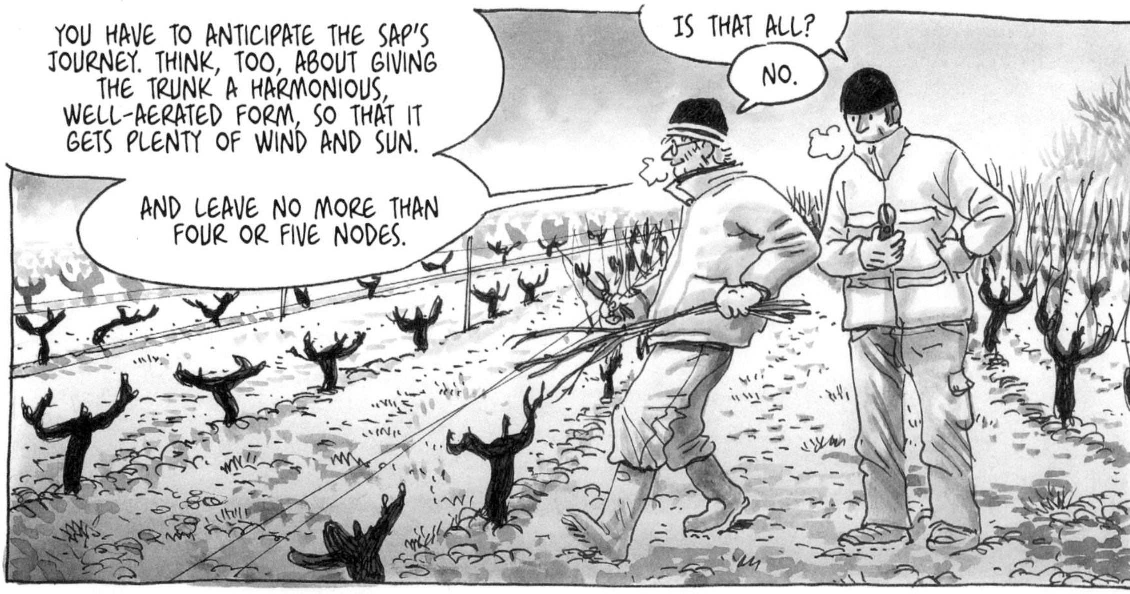
YOU HAVE TO ANTICIPATE THE SAP'S JOURNEY. THINK, TOO, ABOUT GIVING THE TRUNK A HARMONIOUS, WELL-AERATED FORM, SO THAT IT GETS PLENTY OF WIND AND SUN.
AND LEAVE NO MORE THAN FOUR OR FIVE NODES.
IS THAT ALL?
NO.
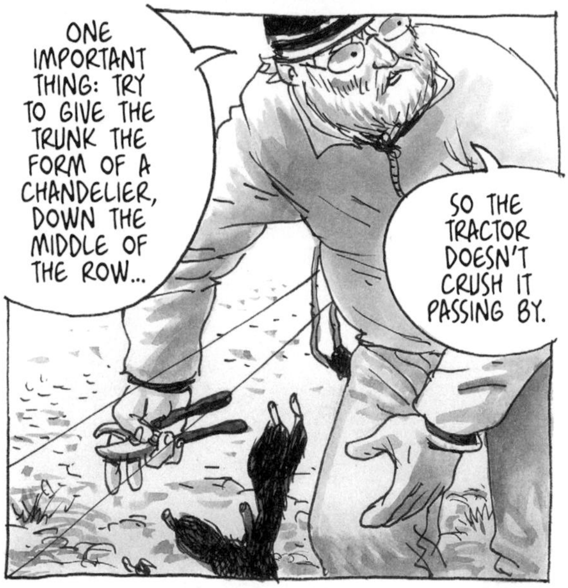
ONE IMPORTANT THING: TRY TO GIVE THE TRUNK THE FORM OF A CHANDELIER, DOWN THE MIDDLE OF THE ROW...
SO THE TRACTOR DOESN'T CRUSH IT PASSING BY.
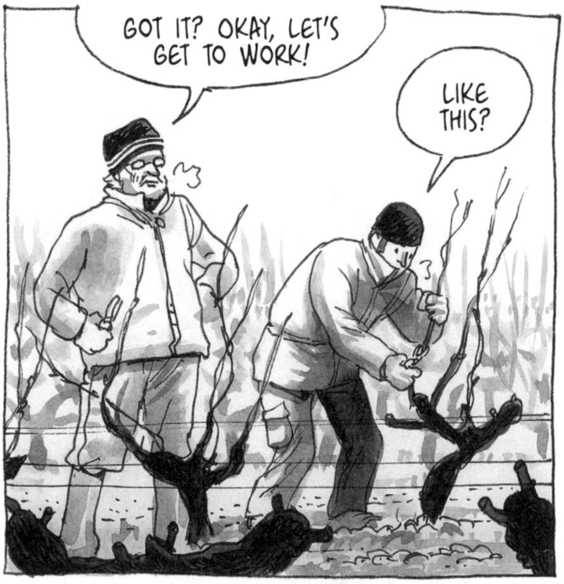
GOT IT? OKAY, LET'S GET TO WORK!
LIKE THIS?
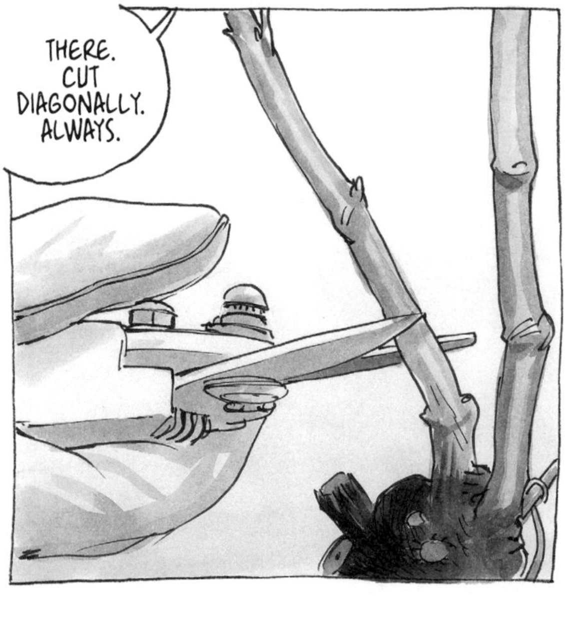
THERE. CUT DIAGONALLY. ALWAYS.
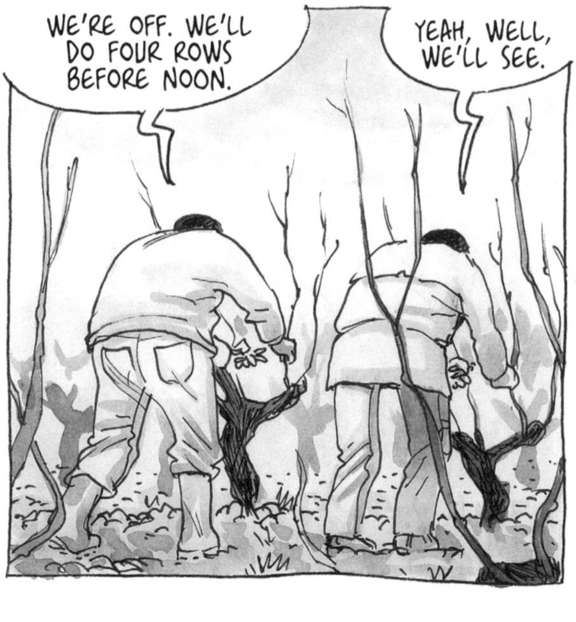
WE'RE OFF. WE'LL DO FOUR ROWS BEFORE NOON.
YEAH, WELL, WE'LL SEE.

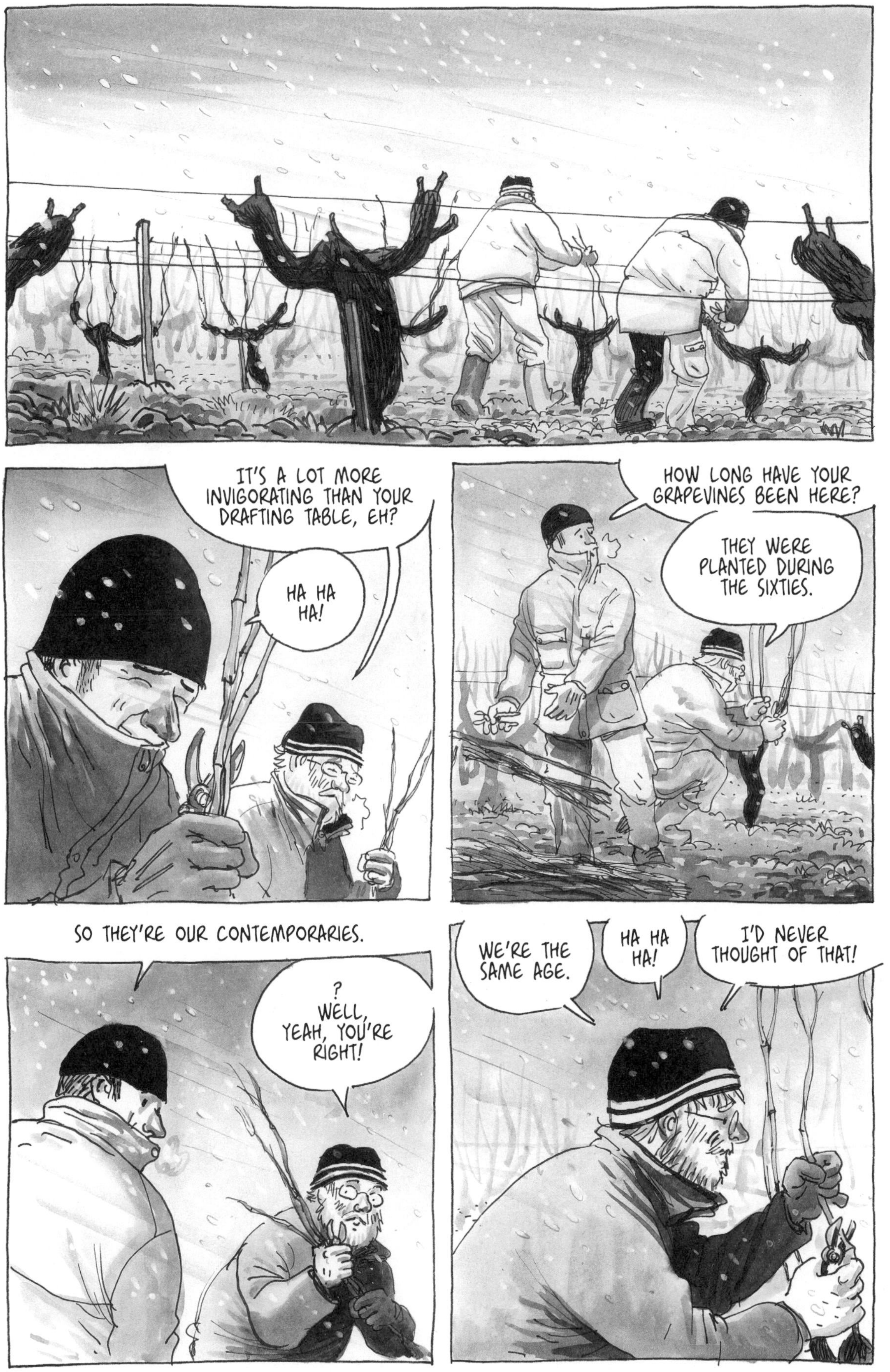
IT'S A LOT MORE INVIGORATING THAN YOUR DRAFTING TABLE, EH?
HA HA HA!
HOW LONG HAVE YOUR GRAPEVINES BEEN HERE?
THEY WERE PLANTED DURING THE SIXTIES.
SO THEY'RE OUR CONTEMPORARIES.
? WELL, YEAH, YOU'RE RIGHT!
WE'RE THE SAME AGE.
HA HA HA!
I'D NEVER THOUGHT OF THAT!

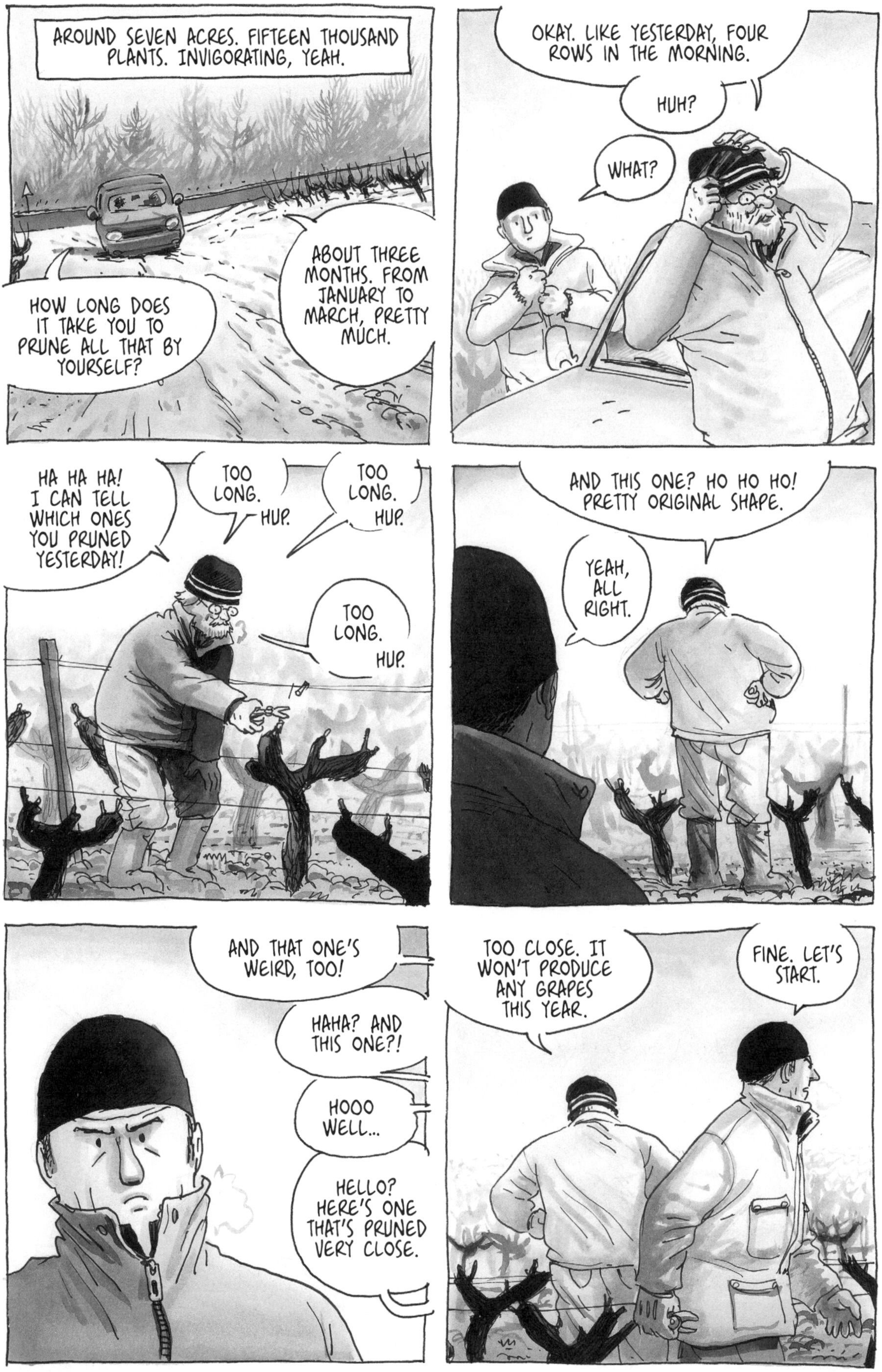
AROUND SEVEN ACRES. FIFTEEN THOUSAND PLANTS. INVIGORATING, YEAH.
HOW LONG DOES IT TAKE YOU TO PRUNE ALL THAT BY YOURSELF?
ABOUT THREE MONTHS. FROM JANUARY TO MARCH, PRETTY MUCH.
OKAY. LIKE YESTERDAY, FOUR ROWS IN THE MORNING.
HUH?
WHAT?
HA HA HA! I CAN TELL WHICH ONES YOU PRUNED YESTERDAY!
TOO LONG. HUP.
TOO LONG. HUP.
TOO LONG. HUP.
AND THIS ONE? HO HO HO! PRETTY ORIGINAL SHAPE.
YEAH, ALL RIGHT.
AND THAT ONE'S WEIRD, TOO!
HAHA? AND THIS ONE?!
HOOO WELL...
HELLO? HERE'S ONE THAT'S PRUNED VERY CLOSE.
TOO CLOSE. IT WON'T PRODUCE ANY GRAPES THIS YEAR.
FINE. LET'S START.

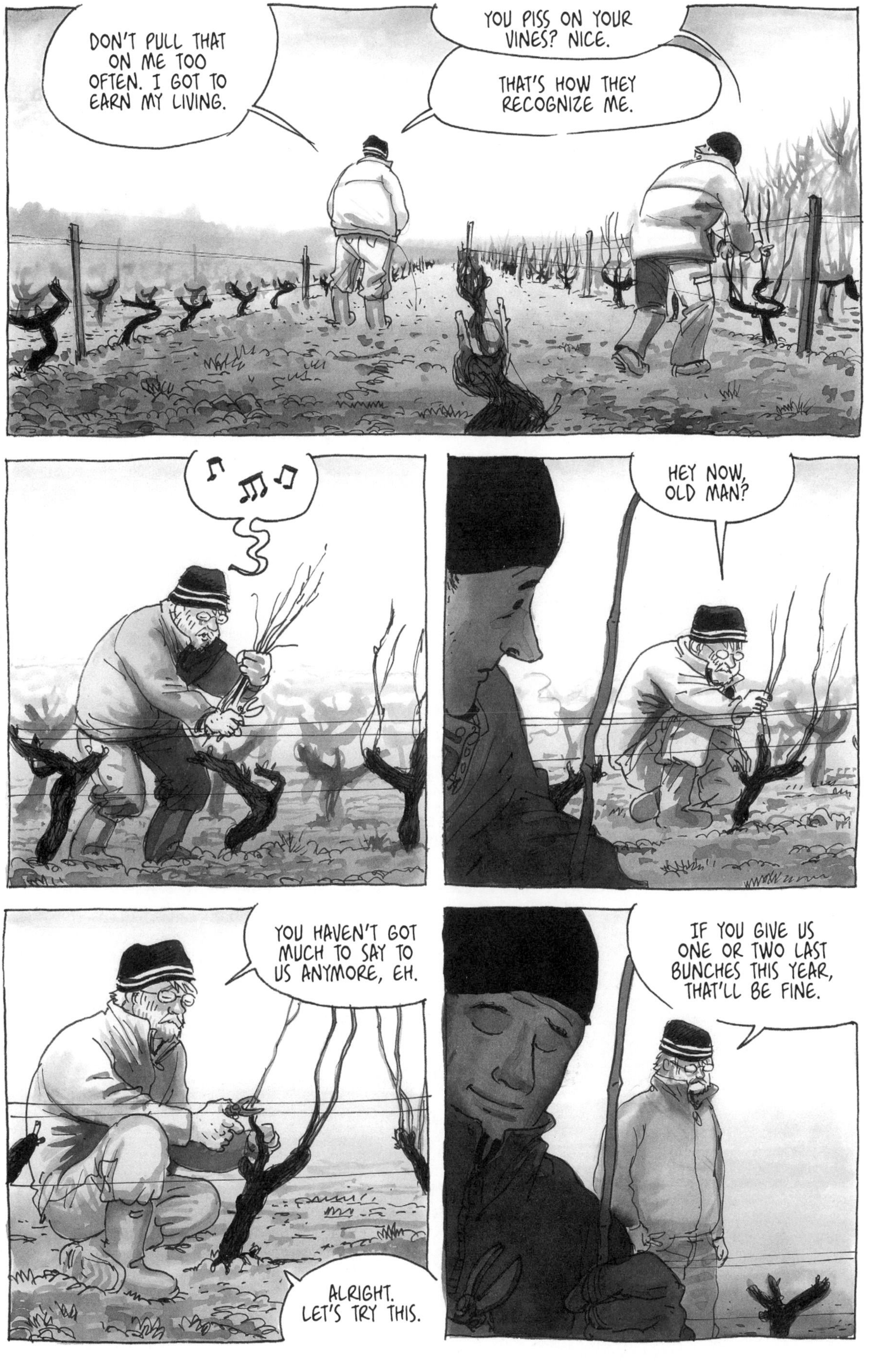
DON'T PULL THAT ON ME TOO OFTEN. I GOT TO EARN MY LIVING.
YOU PISS ON YOUR VINES? NICE.
THAT'S HOW THEY RECOGNIZE ME.
HEY NOW, OLD MAN?
YOU HAVEN'T GOT MUCH TO SAY TO US ANYMORE, EH.
ALRIGHT. LET'S TRY THIS.
IF YOU GIVE US ONE OR TWO LAST BUNCHES THIS YEAR, THAT'LL BE FINE.

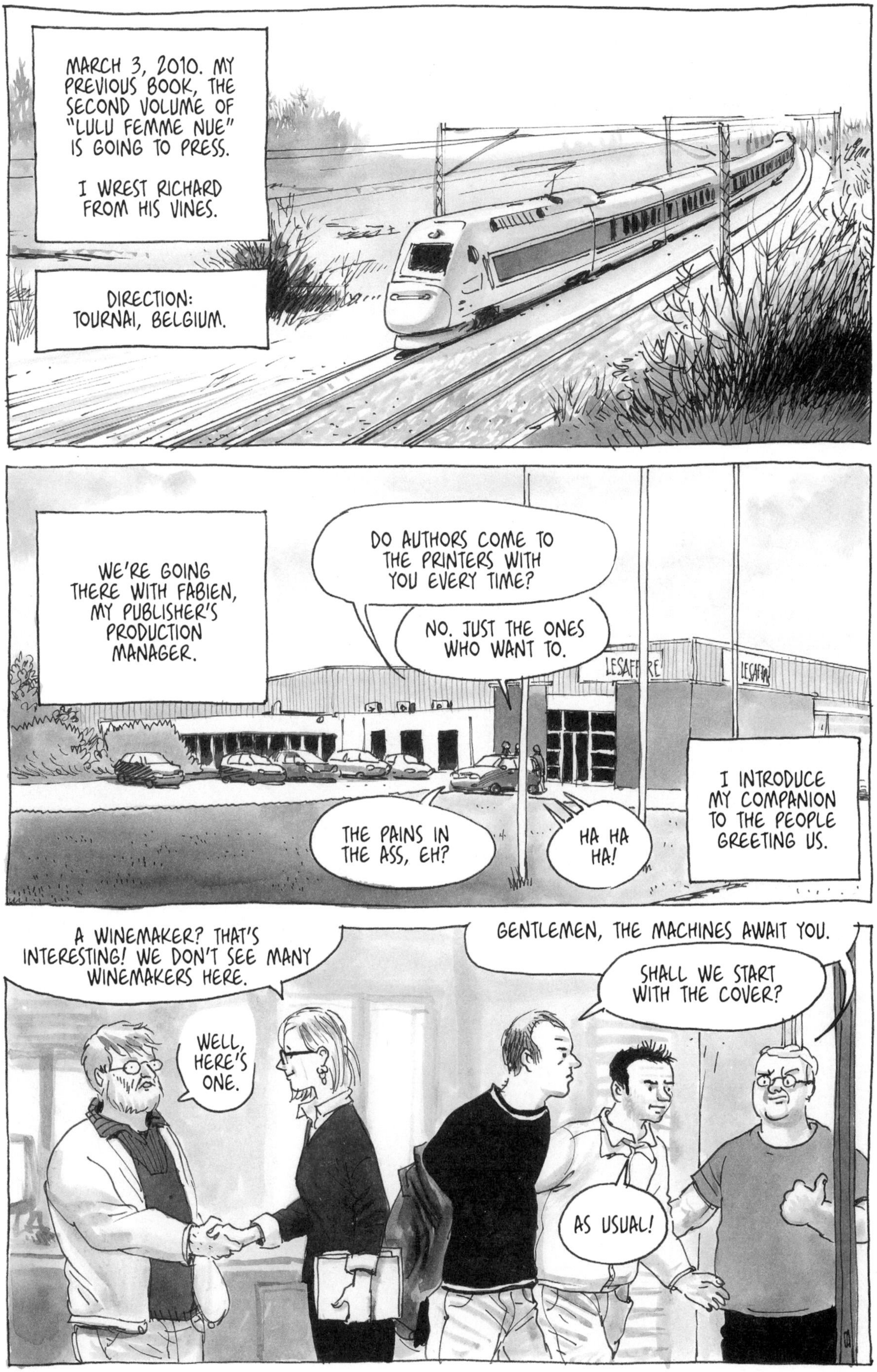
MARCH 3, 2010. MY PREVIOUS BOOK, THE SECOND VOLUME OF "LULU FEMME NUE" IS GOING TO PRESS.
I WREST RICHARD FROM HIS VINES.
DIRECTION: TOURNAI, BELGIUM.
WE'RE GOING THERE WITH FABIEN, MY PUBLISHER'S PRODUCTION MANAGER.
DO AUTHORS COME TO THE PRINTERS WITH YOU EVERY TIME?
NO. JUST THE ONES WHO WANT TO.
THE PAINS IN THE ASS, EH?
HA HA HA!
I INTRODUCE MY COMPANION TO THE PEOPLE GREETING US.
A WINEMAKER? THAT'S INTERESTING! WE DON'T SEE MANY WINEMAKERS HERE.
WELL, HERE'S ONE.
GENTLEMEN, THE MACHINES AWAIT YOU.
SHALL WE START WITH THE COVER?
AS USUAL!

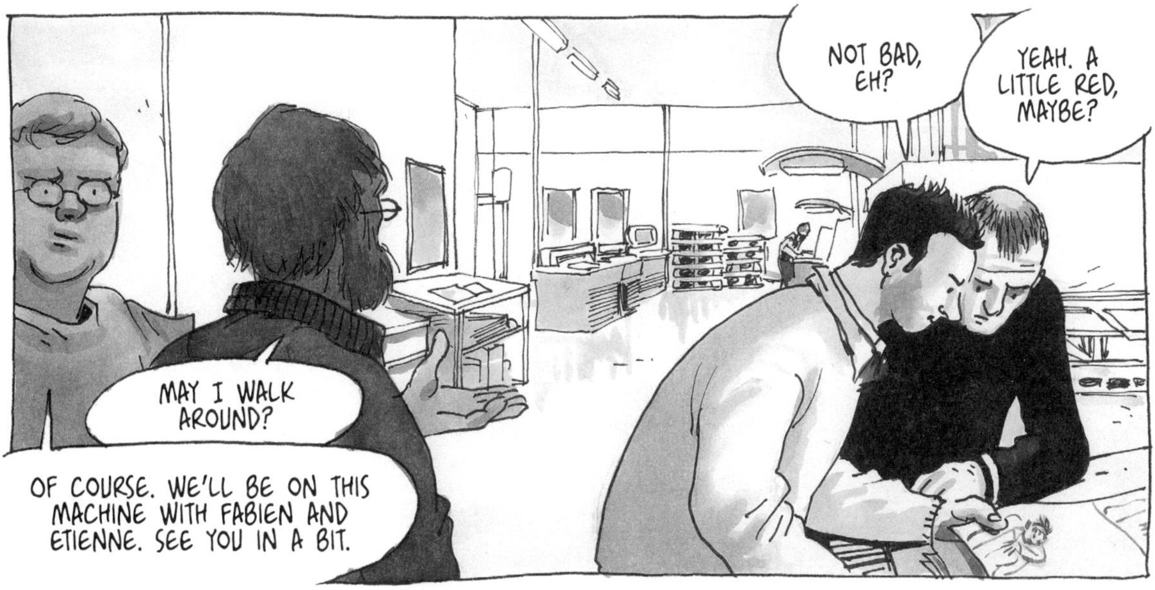
MAY I WALK AROUND?
OF COURSE. WE'LL BE ON THIS MACHINE WITH FABIEN AND ETIENNE. SEE YOU IN A BIT.
NOT BAD, EH?
YEAH. A LITTLE RED, MAYBE?

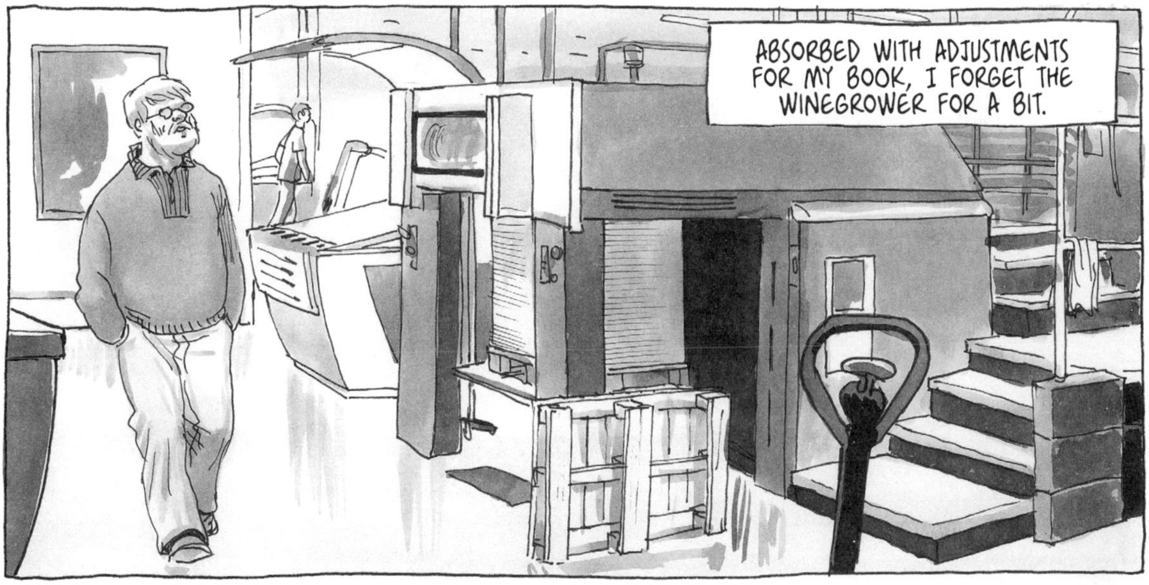
ABSORBED WITH ADJUSTMENTS FOR MY BOOK, I FORGET THE WINEGROWER FOR A BIT.

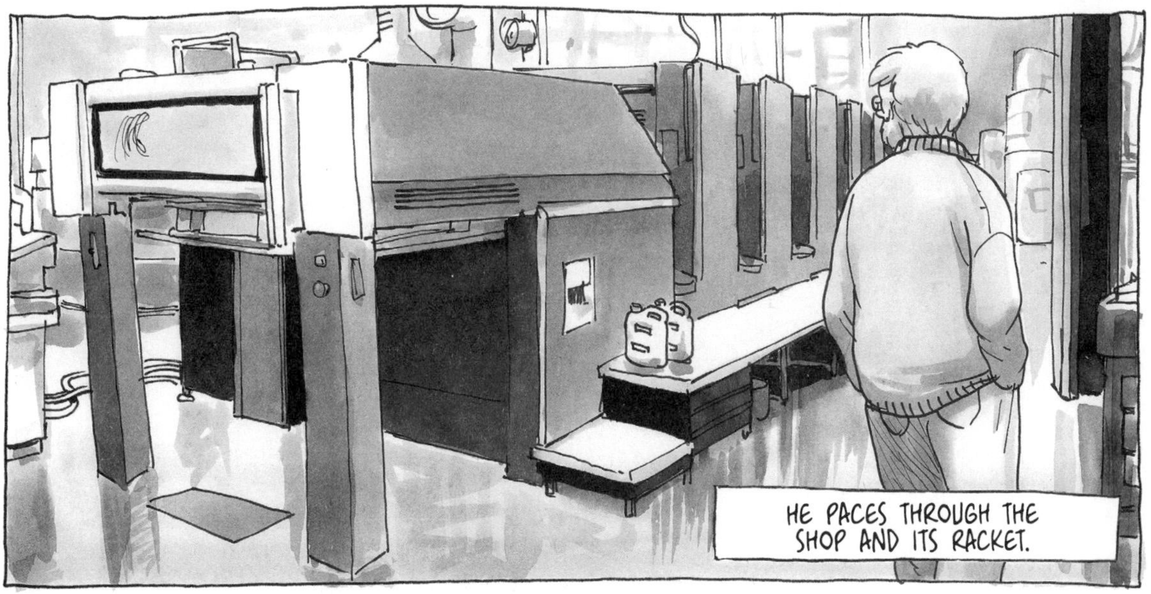
HE PACES THROUGH THE SHOP AND ITS RACKET.

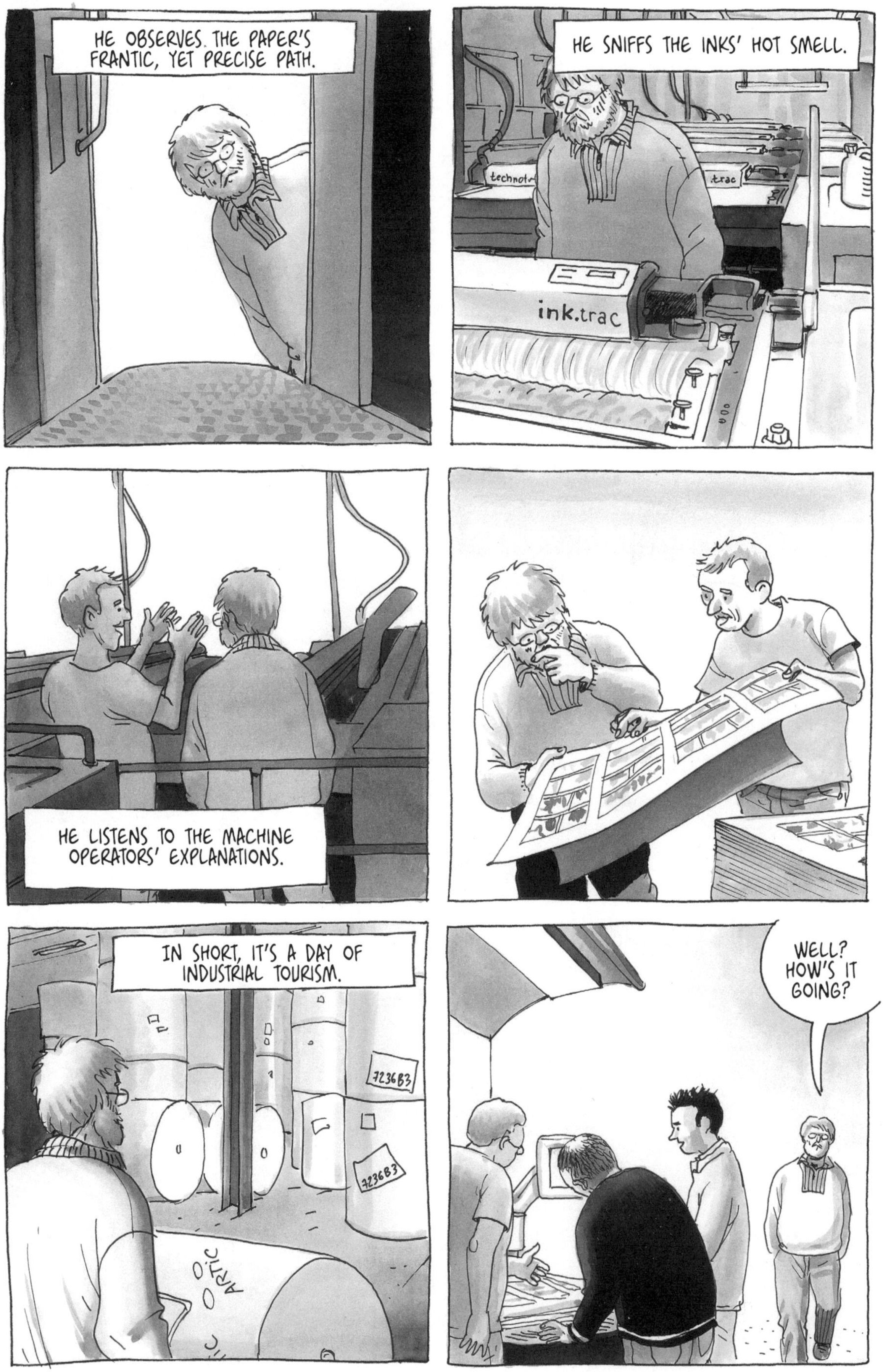
HE OBSERVES THE PAPER'S FRANTIC, YET PRECISE PATH.
HE SNIFFS THE INKS' HOT SMELL.
ink.trac
HE LISTENS TO THE MACHINE OPERATORS' EXPLANATIONS.
IN SHORT, IT'S A DAY OF INDUSTRIAL TOURISM.
7236B3
7236B3
WELL? HOW'S IT GOING?

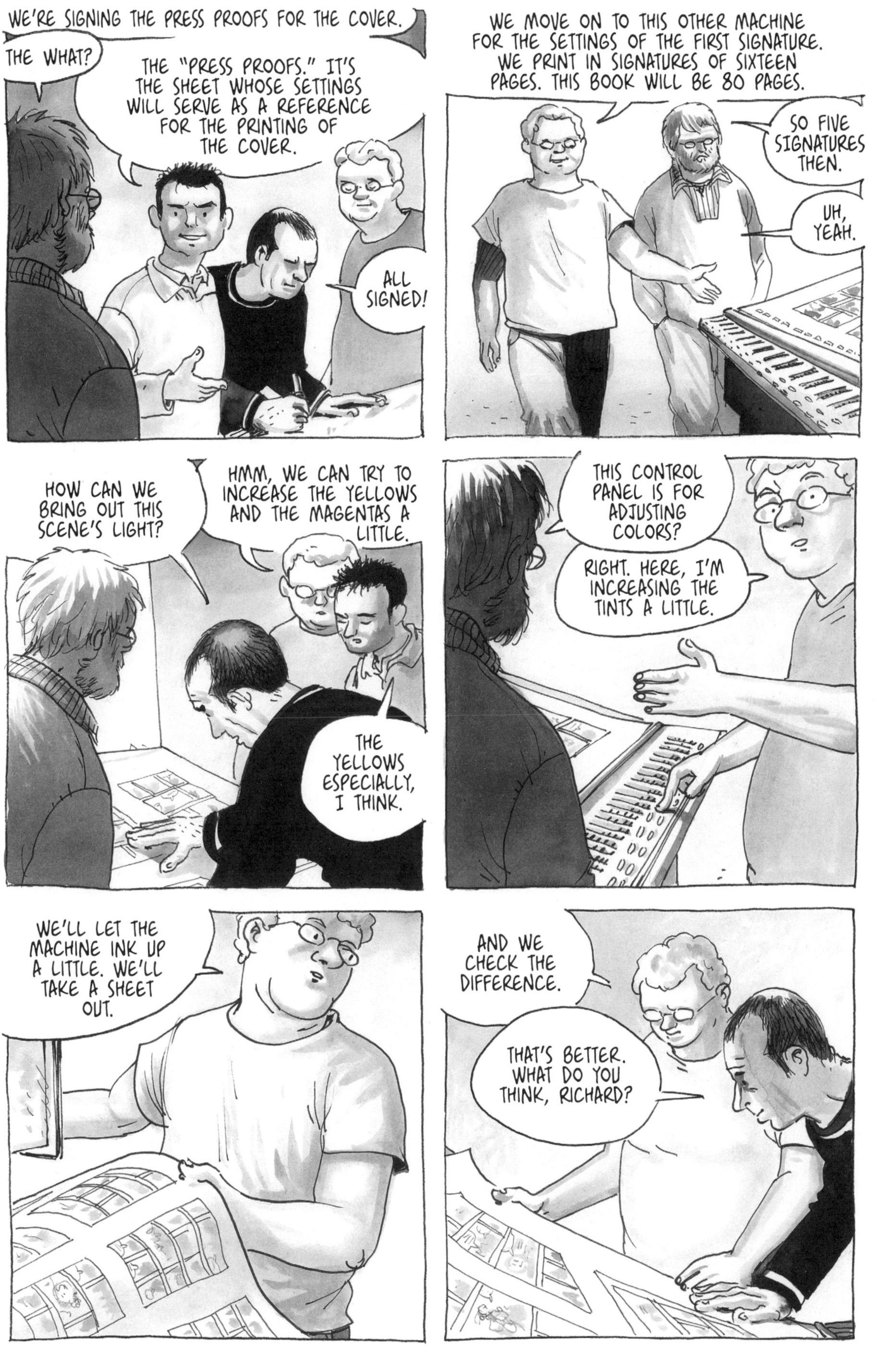
WE'RE SIGNING THE PRESS PROOFS FOR THE COVER.
THE WHAT?
THE "PRESS PROOFS." IT'S THE SHEET WHOSE SETTINGS WILL SERVE AS A REFERENCE FOR THE PRINTING OF THE COVER.
ALL SIGNED!
WE MOVE ON TO THIS OTHER MACHINE FOR THE SETTINGS OF THE FIRST SIGNATURE. WE PRINT IN SIGNATURES OF SIXTEEN PAGES. THIS BOOK WILL BE 80 PAGES.
SO FIVE SIGNATURES THEN.
UH, YEAH.
HOW CAN WE BRING OUT THIS SCENE'S LIGHT?
HMM, WE CAN TRY TO INCREASE THE YELLOWS AND THE MAGENTAS A LITTLE.
THE YELLOWS ESPECIALLY, I THINK.
THIS CONTROL PANEL IS FOR ADJUSTING COLORS?
RIGHT. HERE, I'M INCREASING THE TINTS A LITTLE.
WE'LL LET THE MACHINE INK UP A LITTLE. WE'LL TAKE A SHEET OUT.
AND WE CHECK THE DIFFERENCE.
THAT'S BETTER. WHAT DO YOU THINK, RICHARD?

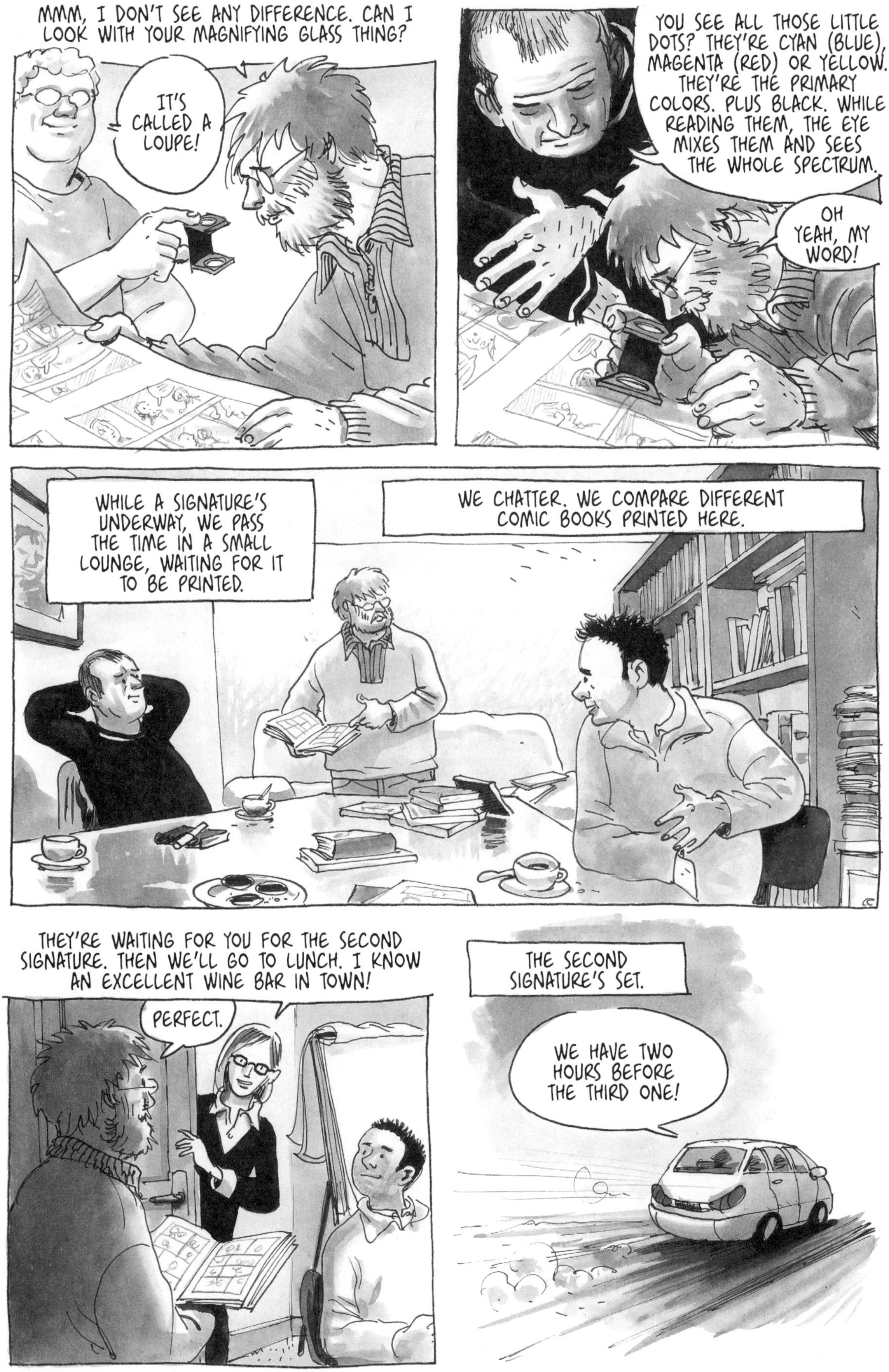
MMM, I DON'T SEE ANY DIFFERENCE. CAN I LOOK WITH YOUR MAGNIFYING GLASS THING?
IT'S CALLED A LOUPE!
YOU SEE ALL THOSE LITTLE DOTS? THEY'RE CYAN (BLUE), MAGENTA (RED) OR YELLOW. THEY'RE THE PRIMARY COLORS. PLUS BLACK. WHILE READING THEM, THE EYE MIXES THEM AND SEES THE WHOLE SPECTRUM.
OH YEAH, MY WORD!
WHILE A SIGNATURE'S UNDERWAY, WE PASS THE TIME IN A SMALL LOUNGE, WAITING FOR IT TO BE PRINTED.
WE CHATTER. WE COMPARE DIFFERENT COMIC BOOKS PRINTED HERE.
THEY'RE WAITING FOR YOU FOR THE SECOND SIGNATURE. THEN WE'LL GO TO LUNCH. I KNOW AN EXCELLENT WINE BAR IN TOWN!
PERFECT.
THE SECOND SIGNATURE'S SET.
WE HAVE TWO HOURS BEFORE THE THIRD ONE!

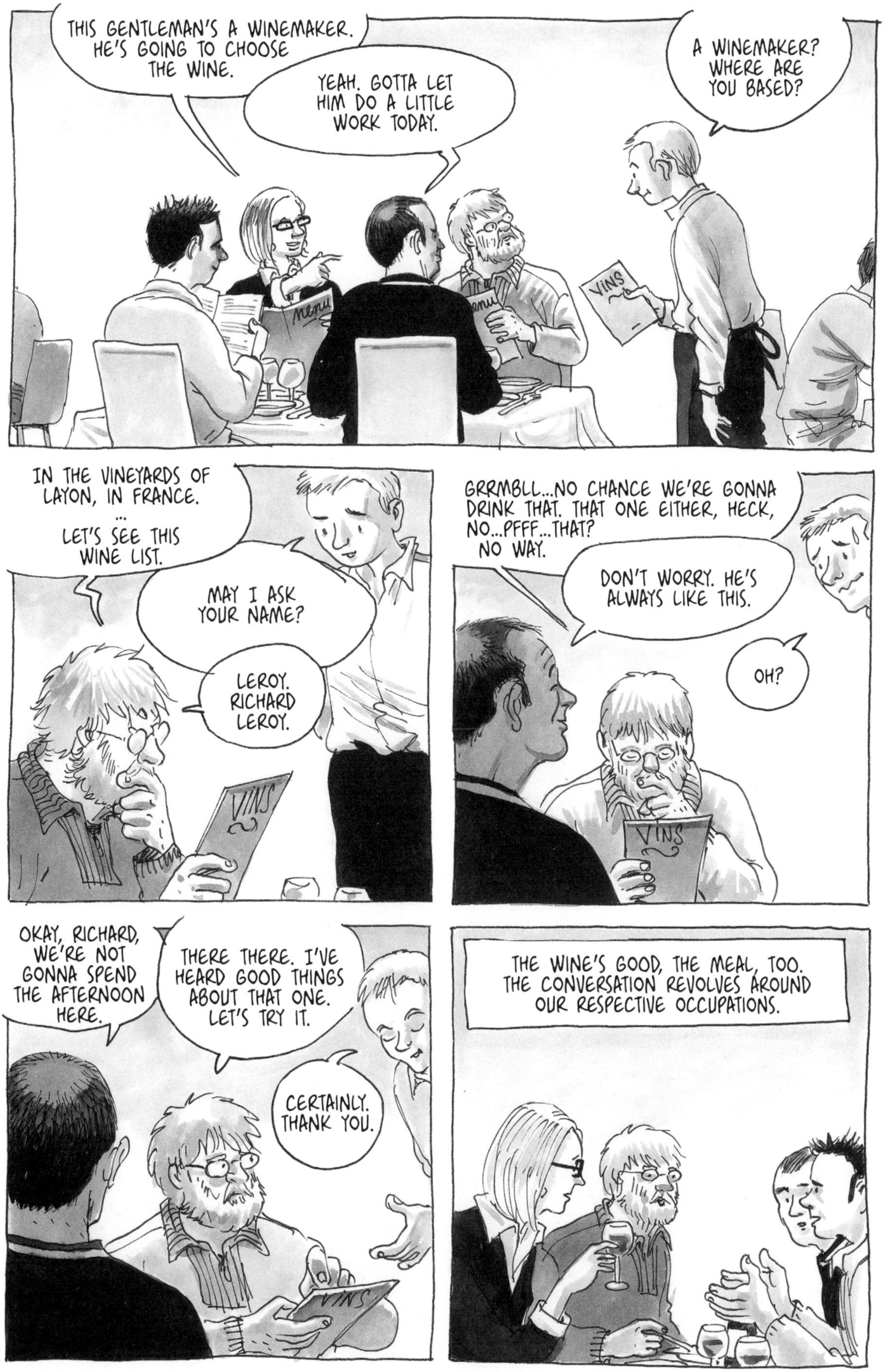
THIS GENTLEMAN'S A WINEMAKER. HE'S GOING TO CHOOSE THE WINE.
YEAH. GOTTA LET HIM DO A LITTLE WORK TODAY.
A WINEMAKER? WHERE ARE YOU BASED?
MENU
VINS
IN THE VINEYARDS OF LAYON, IN FRANCE. ... LET'S SEE THIS WINE LIST.
MAY I ASK YOUR NAME?
LEROY. RICHARD LEROY.
VINS
GRRMBLL...NO CHANCE WE'RE GONNA DRINK THAT. THAT ONE EITHER, HECK, NO...PFFF...THAT? NO WAY.
DON'T WORRY. HE'S ALWAYS LIKE THIS.
OH?
VINS
OKAY, RICHARD, WE'RE NOT GONNA SPEND THE AFTERNOON HERE.
THERE THERE. I'VE HEARD GOOD THINGS ABOUT THAT ONE. LET'S TRY IT.
CERTAINLY. THANK YOU.
VINS
THE WINE'S GOOD, THE MEAL, TOO. THE CONVERSATION REVOLVES AROUND OUR RESPECTIVE OCCUPATIONS.

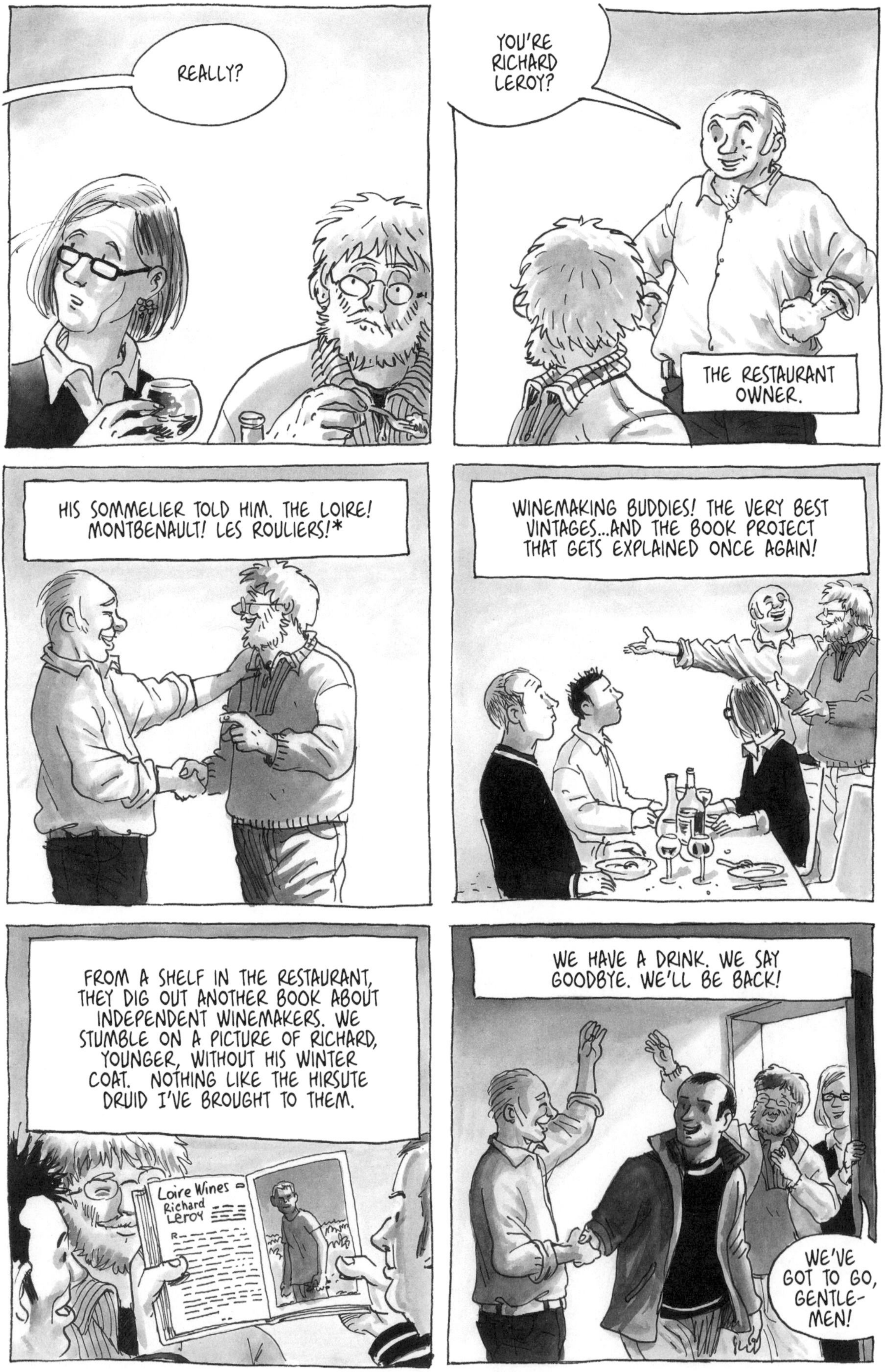
REALLY?
YOU'RE RICHARD LEROY?
THE RESTAURANT OWNER.
HIS SOMMELIER TOLD HIM. THE LOIRE! MONTBENAULT! LES ROULIERS!*
WINEMAKING BUDDIES! THE VERY BEST VINTAGES...AND THE BOOK PROJECT THAT GETS EXPLAINED ONCE AGAIN!
FROM A SHELF IN THE RESTAURANT, THEY DIG OUT ANOTHER BOOK ABOUT INDEPENDENT WINEMAKERS. WE STUMBLE ON A PICTURE OF RICHARD, YOUNGER, WITHOUT HIS WINTER COAT. NOTHING LIKE THE HIRSUTE DRUID I'VE BROUGHT TO THEM.
Loire Wines
Richard Leroy
WE HAVE A DRINK. WE SAY GOODBYE. WE'LL BE BACK!
WE'VE GOT TO GO, GENTLE-MEN!

*WINES PRODUCED BY LEROY AT MONTBENAULT IN THE LOIRE VALLEY.

...ESPECIALLY IF WE WANT TO SHOW YOU THE BINDING SHOP.

I'VE BEEN AUTHORING BOOKS FOR ALMOST TWENTY YEARS AND I'VE NEVER HAD A CHANCE TO SEE THAT.

YOU'RE NOT VERY CURIOUS.

THIS WAY, PLEASE.

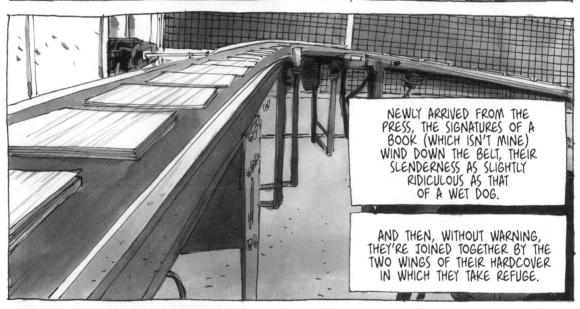

NEWLY ARRIVED FROM THE PRESS, THE SIGNATURES OF A BOOK (WHICH ISN'T MINE) WIND DOWN THE BELT, THEIR SLENDERNESS AS SLIGHTLY RIDICULOUS AS THAT OF A WET DOG.

AND THEN, WITHOUT WARNING, THEY'RE JOINED TOGETHER BY THE TWO WINGS OF THEIR HARDCOVER IN WHICH THEY TAKE REFUGE.

AND THERE.

AN AUTONOMOUS, PERMANENT AND, FRANKLY, SLIGHTLY MAGICAL OBJECT, THE BOOK IS SUDDENLY THERE BEFORE OUR EYES.

STACKED, PACKAGED, IT DISAPPEARS TOWARDS ITS DESTINY, WHICH ONE HOPES WILL BE INCARNATED BY A READER'S HANDS.

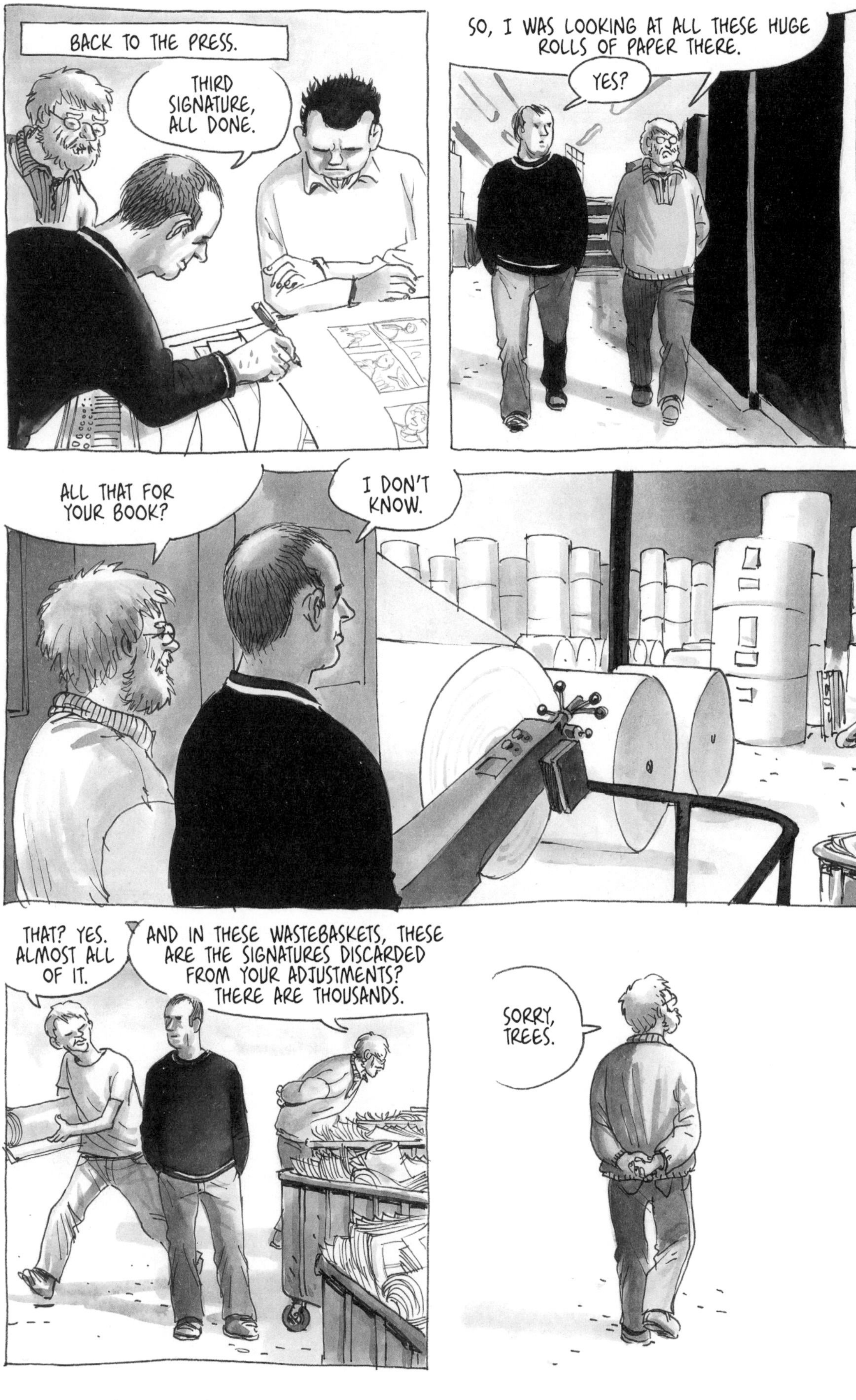
BACK TO THE PRESS.
THIRD SIGNATURE, ALL DONE.
SO, I WAS LOOKING AT ALL THESE HUGE ROLLS OF PAPER THERE.
YES?
ALL THAT FOR YOUR BOOK?
I DON'T KNOW.
THAT? YES. ALMOST ALL OF IT.
AND IN THESE WASTEBASKETS, THESE ARE THE SIGNATURES DISCARDED FROM YOUR ADJUSTMENTS? THERE ARE THOUSANDS.
SORRY, TREES.

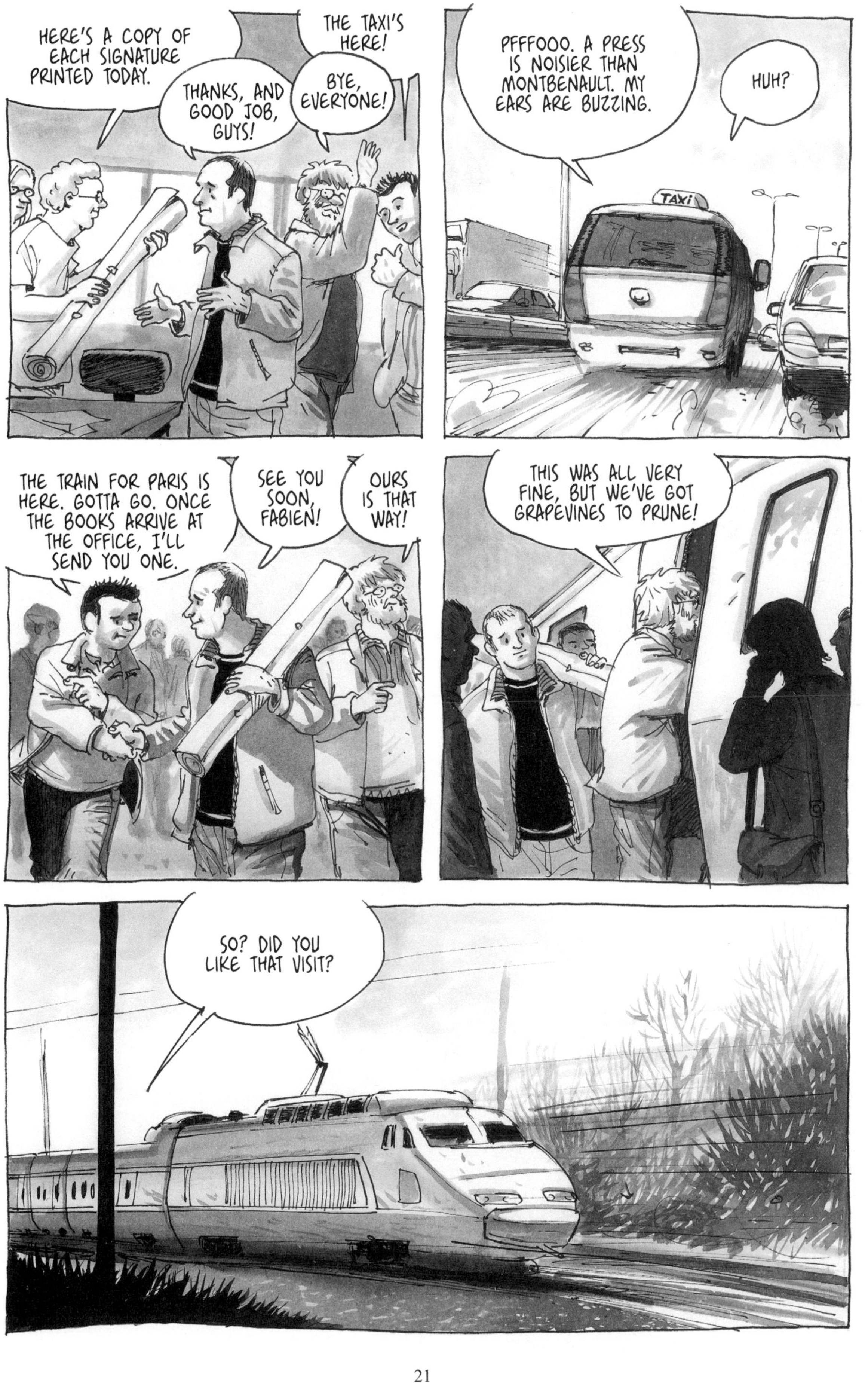
HERE'S A COPY OF EACH SIGNATURE PRINTED TODAY.
THANKS, AND GOOD JOB, GUYS!
THE TAXI'S HERE!
BYE, EVERYONE!
PFFFOOO. A PRESS IS NOISIER THAN MONTBENAULT. MY EARS ARE BUZZING.
HUH?
TAXI
THE TRAIN FOR PARIS IS HERE. GOTTA GO. ONCE THE BOOKS ARRIVE AT THE OFFICE, I'LL SEND YOU ONE.
SEE YOU SOON, FABIEN!
OURS IS THAT WAY!
THIS WAS ALL VERY FINE, BUT WE'VE GOT GRAPEVINES TO PRUNE!
SO? DID YOU LIKE THAT VISIT?

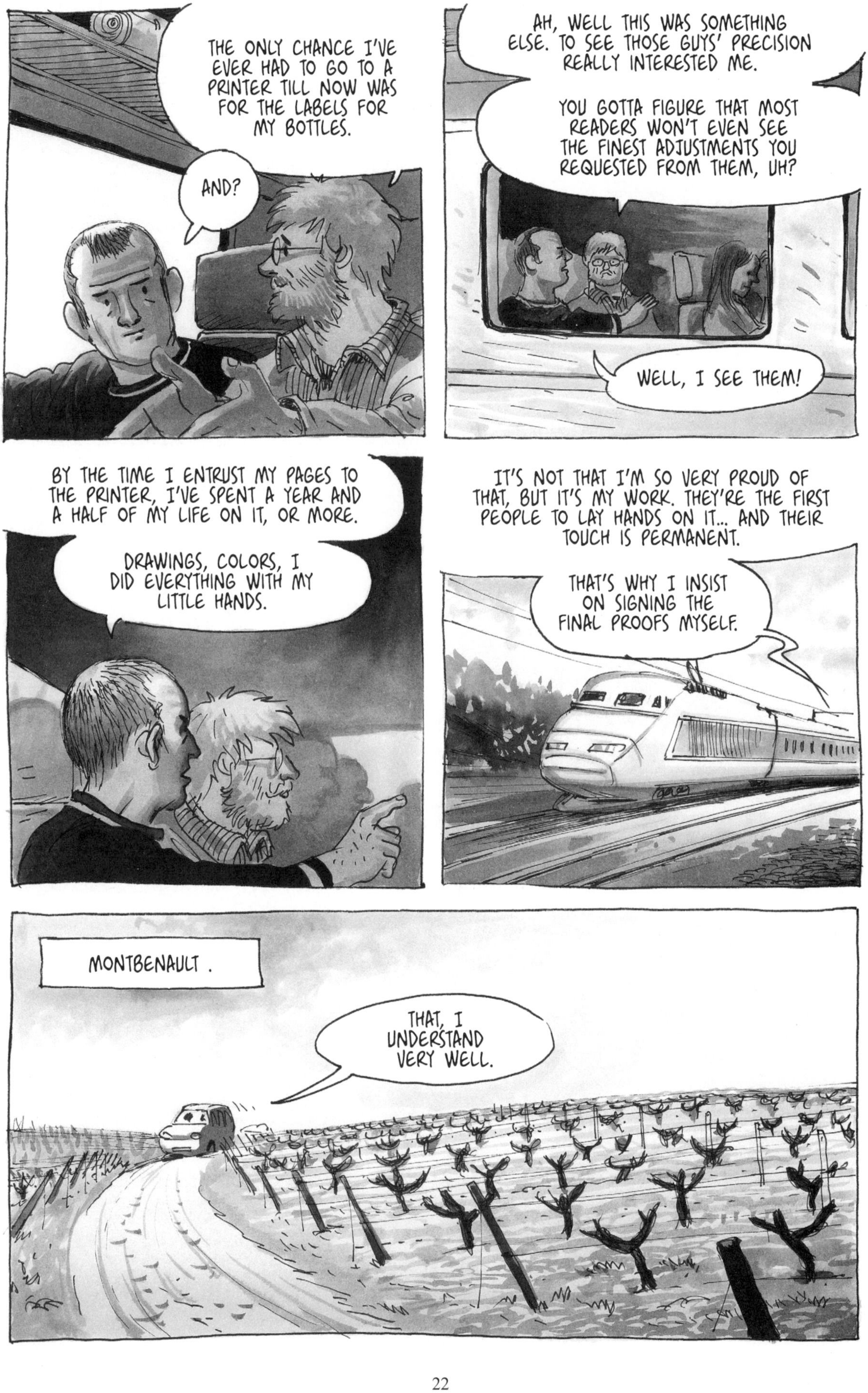
THE ONLY CHANCE I'VE EVER HAD TO GO TO A PRINTER TILL NOW WAS FOR THE LABELS FOR MY BOTTLES.
AND?
AH, WELL THIS WAS SOMETHING ELSE. TO SEE THOSE GUYS' PRECISION REALLY INTERESTED ME.
YOU GOTTA FIGURE THAT MOST READERS WON'T EVEN SEE THE FINEST ADJUSTMENTS YOU REQUESTED FROM THEM, UH?
WELL, I SEE THEM!
BY THE TIME I ENTRUST MY PAGES TO THE PRINTER, I'VE SPENT A YEAR AND A HALF OF MY LIFE ON IT, OR MORE.
DRAWINGS, COLORS, I DID EVERYTHING WITH MY LITTLE HANDS.
IT'S NOT THAT I'M SO VERY PROUD OF THAT, BUT IT'S MY WORK. THEY'RE THE FIRST PEOPLE TO LAY HANDS ON IT... AND THEIR TOUCH IS PERMANENT.
THAT'S WHY I INSIST ON SIGNING THE FINAL PROOFS MYSELF.
MONTBENAULT.
THAT, I UNDERSTAND VERY WELL.

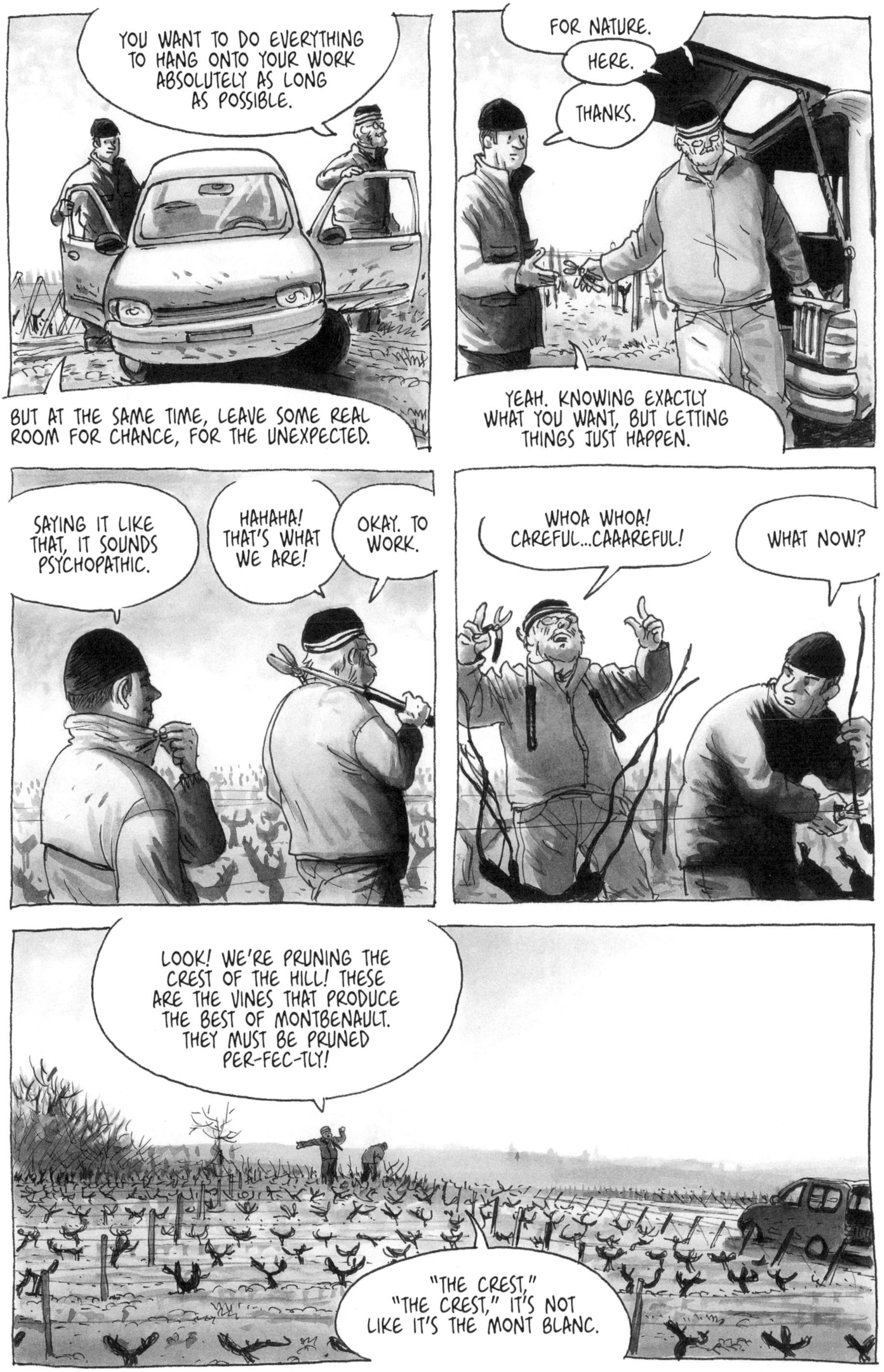
YOU WANT TO DO EVERYTHING TO HANG ONTO YOUR WORK ABSOLUTELY AS LONG AS POSSIBLE.
BUT AT THE SAME TIME, LEAVE SOME REAL ROOM FOR CHANCE, FOR THE UNEXPECTED.
FOR NATURE.
HERE.
THANKS.
YEAH. KNOWING EXACTLY WHAT YOU WANT, BUT LETTING THINGS JUST HAPPEN.
SAYING IT LIKE THAT, IT SOUNDS PSYCHOPATHIC.
HAHAHA! THAT'S WHAT WE ARE!
OKAY. TO WORK.
WHOA WHOA! CAREFUL...CAAAREFUL!
WHAT NOW?
LOOK! WE'RE PRUNING THE CREST OF THE HILL! THESE ARE THE VINES THAT PRODUCE THE BEST OF MONTBENAULT. THEY MUST BE PRUNED PER-FEC-TLY!
"THE CREST," "THE CREST," IT'S NOT LIKE IT'S THE MONT BLANC.

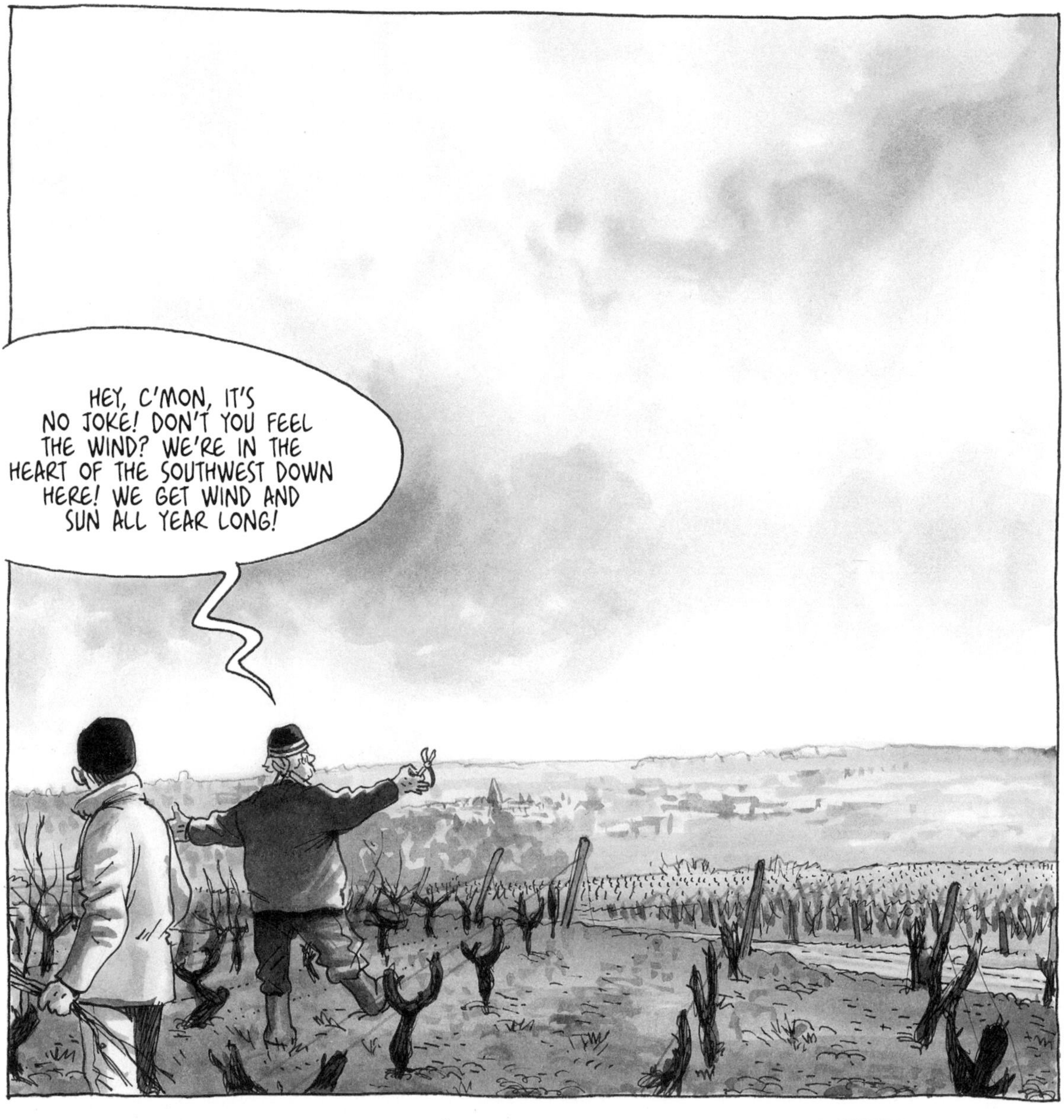
HEY, C'MON, IT'S NO JOKE! DON'T YOU FEEL THE WIND? WE'RE IN THE HEART OF THE SOUTHWEST DOWN HERE! WE GET WIND AND SUN ALL YEAR LONG!

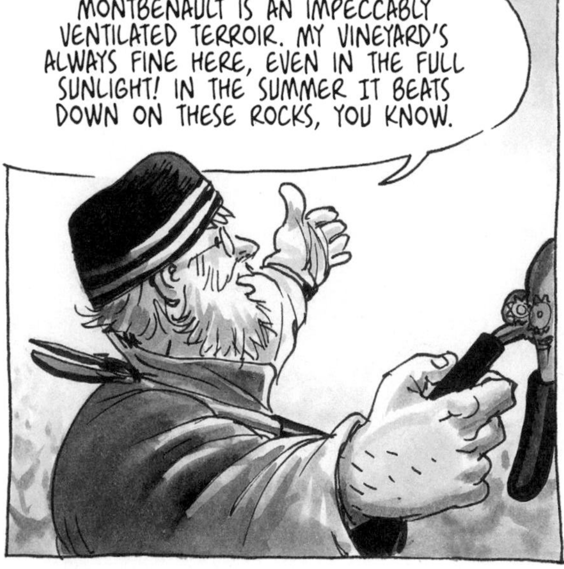
MONTBENAULT IS AN IMPECCABLY VENTILATED TERROIR. MY VINEYARD'S ALWAYS FINE HERE, EVEN IN THE FULL SUNLIGHT! IN THE SUMMER IT BEATS DOWN ON THESE ROCKS, YOU KNOW.

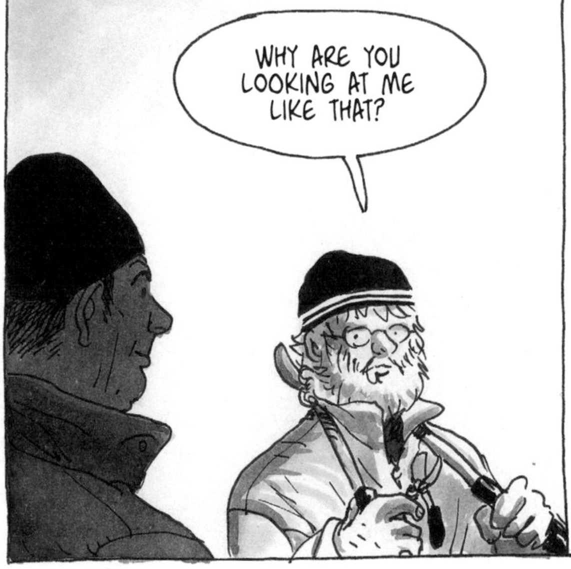
WHY ARE YOU LOOKING AT ME LIKE THAT?

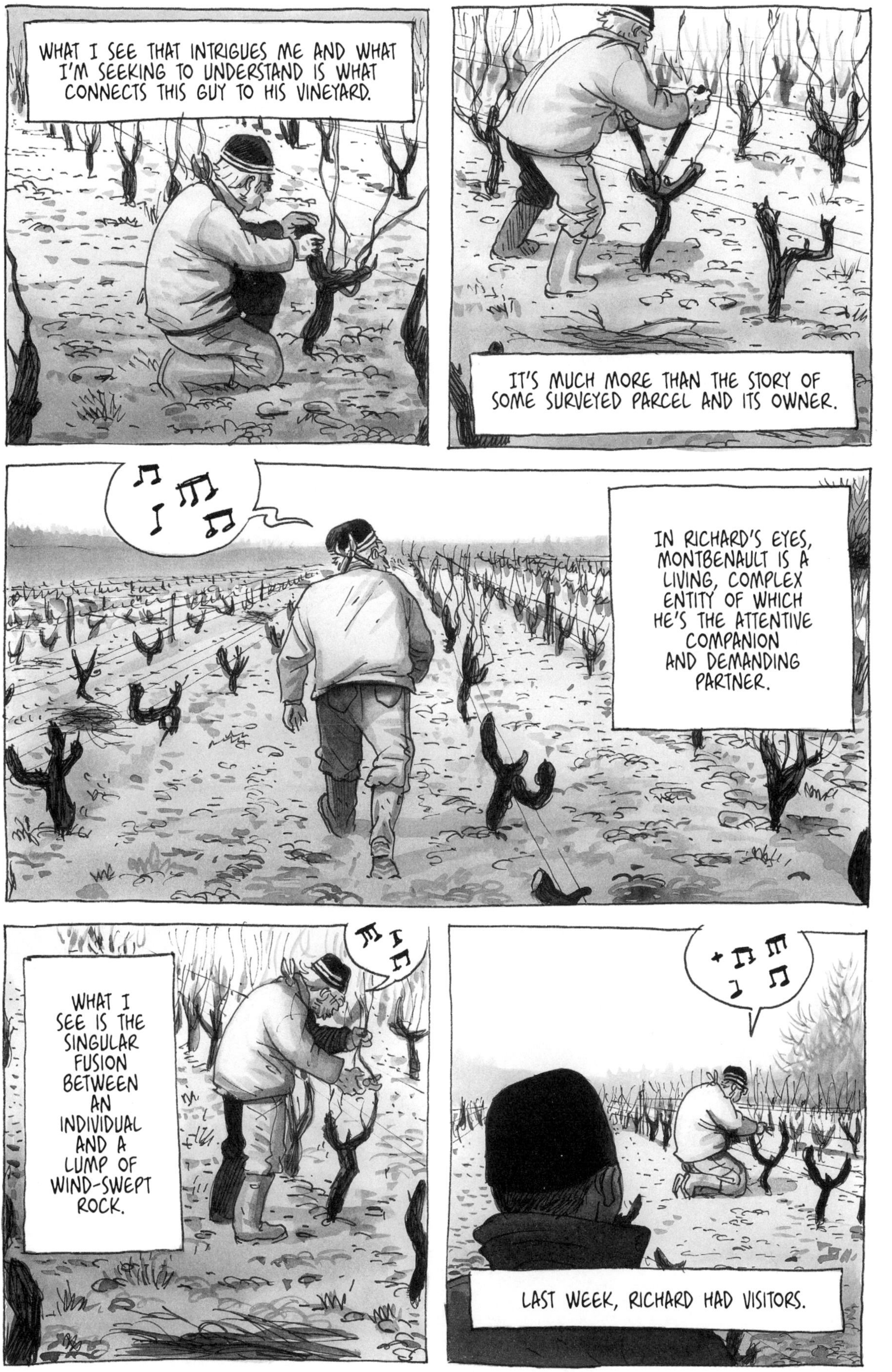
WHAT I SEE THAT INTRIGUES ME AND WHAT I'M SEEKING TO UNDERSTAND IS WHAT CONNECTS THIS GUY TO HIS VINEYARD.
IT'S MUCH MORE THAN THE STORY OF SOME SURVEYED PARCEL AND ITS OWNER.
IN RICHARD'S EYES, MONTBENAULT IS A LIVING, COMPLEX ENTITY OF WHICH HE'S THE ATTENTIVE COMPANION AND DEMANDING PARTNER.
WHAT I SEE IS THE SINGULAR FUSION BETWEEN AN INDIVIDUAL AND A LUMP OF WIND-SWEPT ROCK.
LAST WEEK, RICHARD HAD VISITORS.

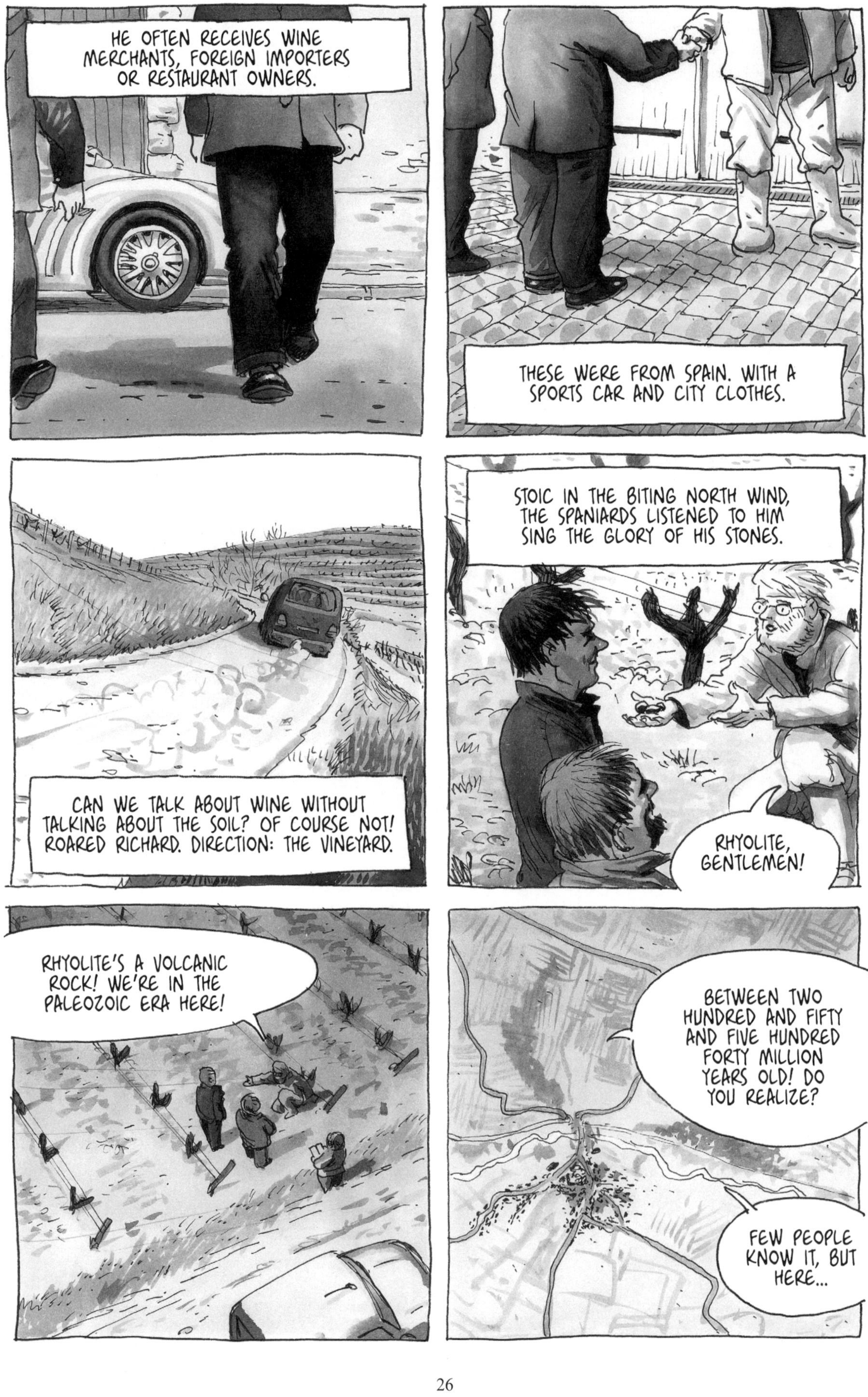
HE OFTEN RECEIVES WINE MERCHANTS, FOREIGN IMPORTERS OR RESTAURANT OWNERS.
THESE WERE FROM SPAIN. WITH A SPORTS CAR AND CITY CLOTHES.
CAN WE TALK ABOUT WINE WITHOUT TALKING ABOUT THE SOIL? OF COURSE NOT! ROARED RICHARD. DIRECTION: THE VINEYARD.
STOIC IN THE BITING NORTH WIND, THE SPANIARDS LISTENED TO HIM SING THE GLORY OF HIS STONES.
RHYOLITE, GENTLEMEN!
RHYOLITE'S A VOLCANIC ROCK! WE'RE IN THE PALEOZOIC ERA HERE!
BETWEEN TWO HUNDRED AND FIFTY AND FIVE HUNDRED FORTY MILLION YEARS OLD! DO YOU REALIZE?
FEW PEOPLE KNOW IT, BUT HERE...

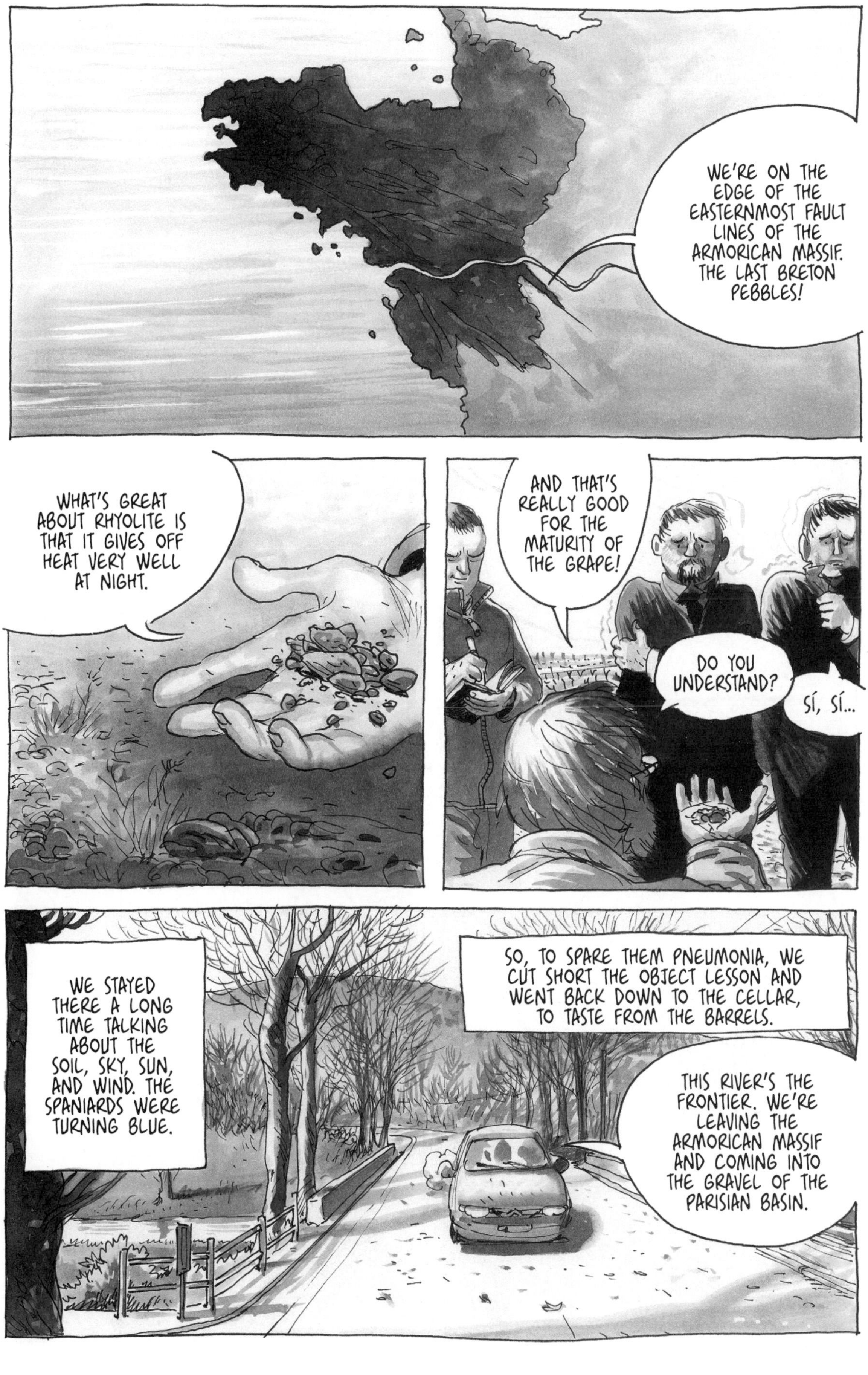
WE'RE ON THE EDGE OF THE EASTERNMOST FAULT LINES OF THE ARMORICAN MASSIF. THE LAST BRETON PEBBLES!
WHAT'S GREAT ABOUT RHYOLITE IS THAT IT GIVES OFF HEAT VERY WELL AT NIGHT.
AND THAT'S REALLY GOOD FOR THE MATURITY OF THE GRAPE!
DO YOU UNDERSTAND?
SÍ, SÍ...
WE STAYED THERE A LONG TIME TALKING ABOUT THE SOIL, SKY, SUN, AND WIND. THE SPANIARDS WERE TURNING BLUE.
SO, TO SPARE THEM PNEUMONIA, WE CUT SHORT THE OBJECT LESSON AND WENT BACK DOWN TO THE CELLAR, TO TASTE FROM THE BARRELS.
THIS RIVER'S THE FRONTIER. WE'RE LEAVING THE ARMORICAN MASSIF AND COMING INTO THE GRAVEL OF THE PARISIAN BASIN.

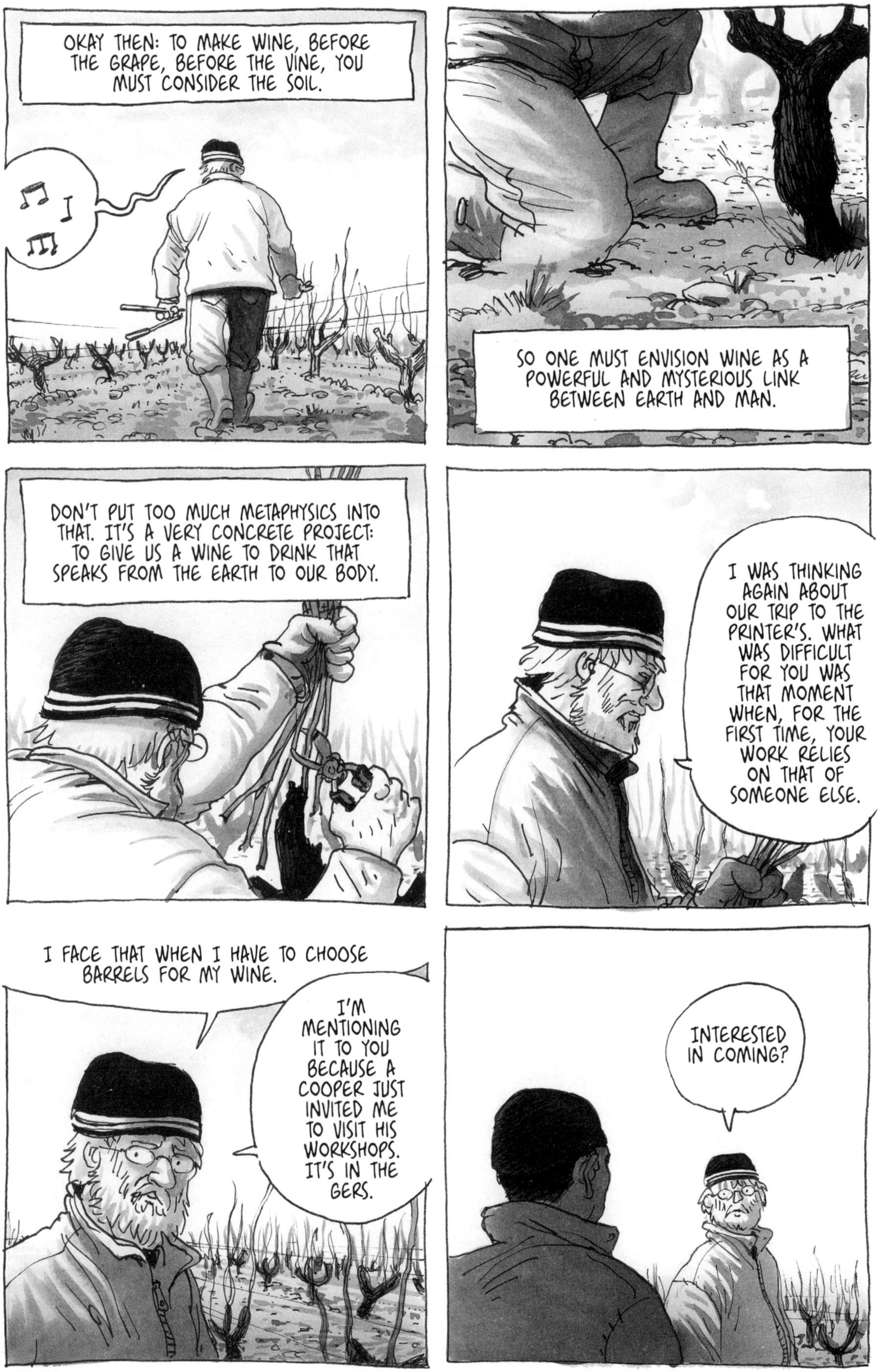
OKAY THEN: TO MAKE WINE, BEFORE THE GRAPE, BEFORE THE VINE, YOU MUST CONSIDER THE SOIL.
SO ONE MUST ENVISION WINE AS A POWERFUL AND MYSTERIOUS LINK BETWEEN EARTH AND MAN.
DON'T PUT TOO MUCH METAPHYSICS INTO THAT. IT'S A VERY CONCRETE PROJECT: TO GIVE US A WINE TO DRINK THAT SPEAKS FROM THE EARTH TO OUR BODY.
I WAS THINKING AGAIN ABOUT OUR TRIP TO THE PRINTER'S. WHAT WAS DIFFICULT FOR YOU WAS THAT MOMENT WHEN, FOR THE FIRST TIME, YOUR WORK RELIES ON THAT OF SOMEONE ELSE.
I FACE THAT WHEN I HAVE TO CHOOSE BARRELS FOR MY WINE.
I'M MENTIONING IT TO YOU BECAUSE A COOPER JUST INVITED ME TO VISIT HIS WORKSHOPS. IT'S IN THE GERS.
INTERESTED IN COMING?

CHAPTER TWO WOOD

BUT WE'VE GOT VINES TO PRUNE ONCE WE GET BACK, UH?

YEAH, YEAH.

TELL ME ABOUT YOUR BARRELS.

MY BARRELS, HA HA HA! SIX HOURS ON THE ROAD WON'T BE ENOUGH.

DO YOU ALWAYS BUY THEM NEW?

ALWAYS. OR BARRELS OF A WINE.

"OF A WINE"?

FROM A GOOD YEAR.

THEN I KEEP THEM AS LONG AS THEY'RE GOOD. IT'S NOT COMPLICATED.

MEANING?

OH, FOUR OR FIVE YEARS, NOT MORE.

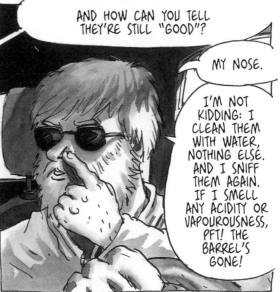

AND HOW CAN YOU TELL THEY'RE STILL "GOOD"?

MY NOSE.

I'M NOT KIDDING: I CLEAN THEM WITH WATER, NOTHING ELSE. AND I SNIFF THEM AGAIN. IF I SMELL ANY ACIDITY OR VAPOUROUSNESS, PFT! THE BARREL'S GONE!

AND WHAT DO YOU EXPECT OUT OF THIS VISIT?

OH! LIKE YOU AT THE PRESS. TO MAKE SURE THE GUY WHO'S AFFECTING MY WORK WON'T SPOIL IT.

SO YOU'RE LOOKING FOR NEUTRAL BARRELS.

HMM...IT'S MORE COMPLICATED THAN THAT. THE BARREL'S A VERY GOOD TOOL IN WINE MAKING, BUT ITS WOOD MUSTN'T LEAVE TOO MUCH OF A MARK ON MY WINE. I'M LOOKING FOR...LET'S SAY...AN ACTIVE AND BENEVOLENT NEUTRALITY, OK?

GOTCHA.

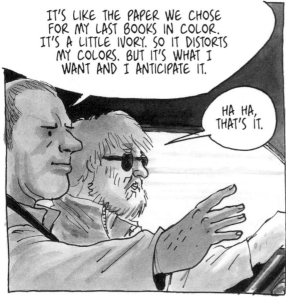

IT'S LIKE THE PAPER WE CHOSE FOR MY LAST BOOKS IN COLOR. IT'S A LITTLE IVORY. SO IT DISTORTS MY COLORS. BUT IT'S WHAT I WANT AND I ANTICIPATE IT.

HA HA, THAT'S IT.

HEH HEH...

THESE ANALOGIES ARE FUNNY.

I WORK SO MUCH IN MY VINEYARDS BUT THEN I JUST LET THE WINE DO ITS OWN THING IN THE BARRELS. SO THEY GOTTA BE EXCELLENT.

SO THIS COOPER'S INVITATION IS VERY MUCH ABOUT BUSINESS, UH.

BUT I DON'T WANT TO HEAR ANY TALK OF "BANG FOR THE BUCK," I WANT QUALITY. PERIOD.

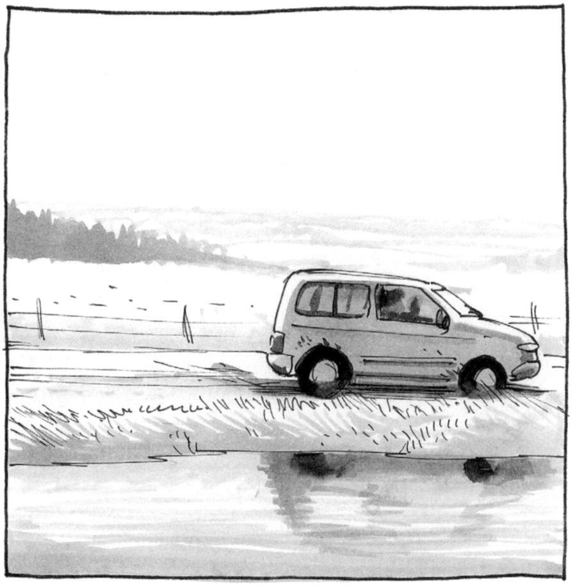

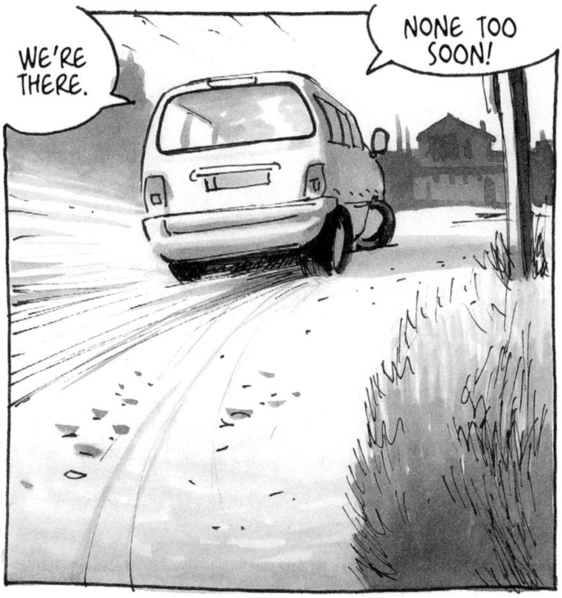
WE'RE THERE.
NONE TOO SOON!

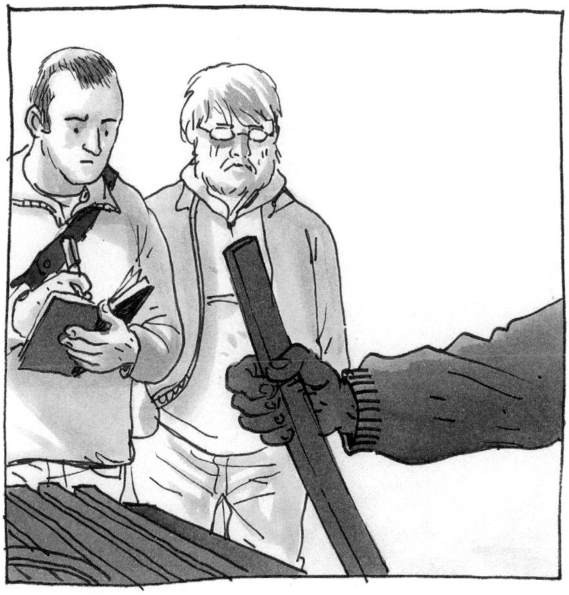

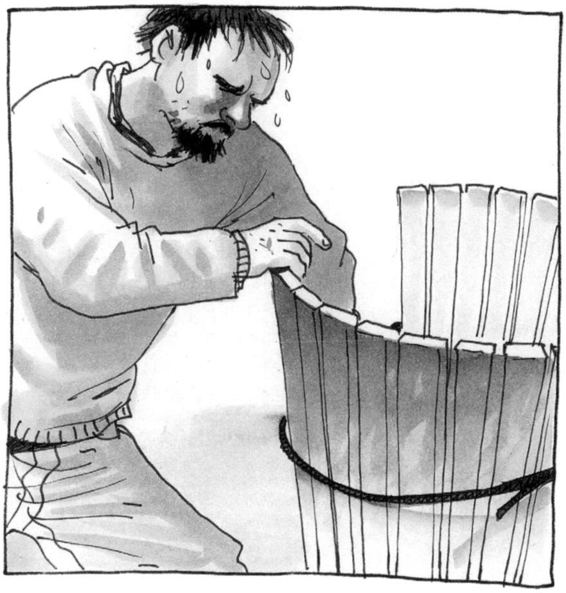

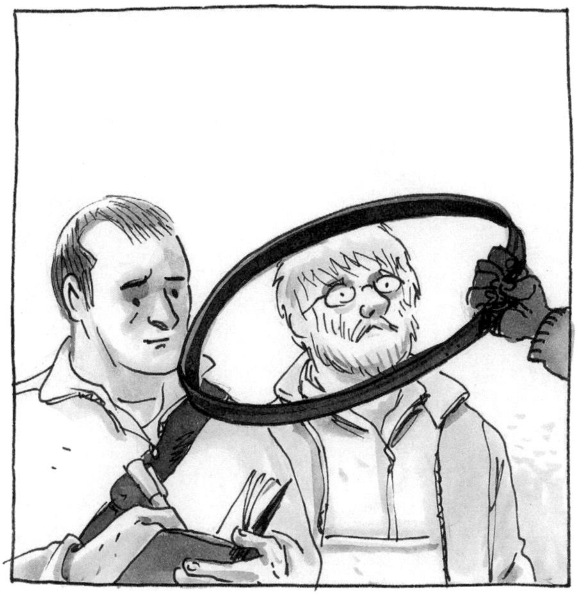

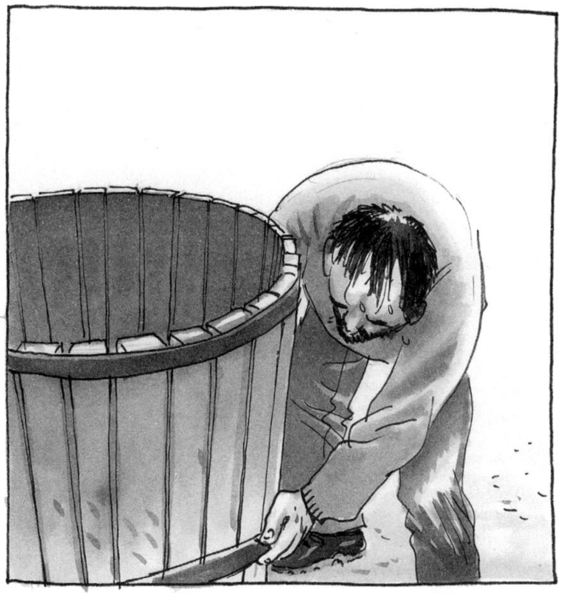

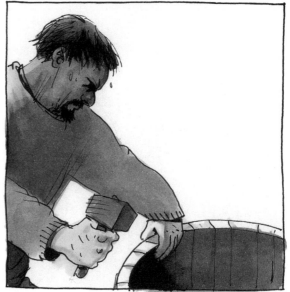

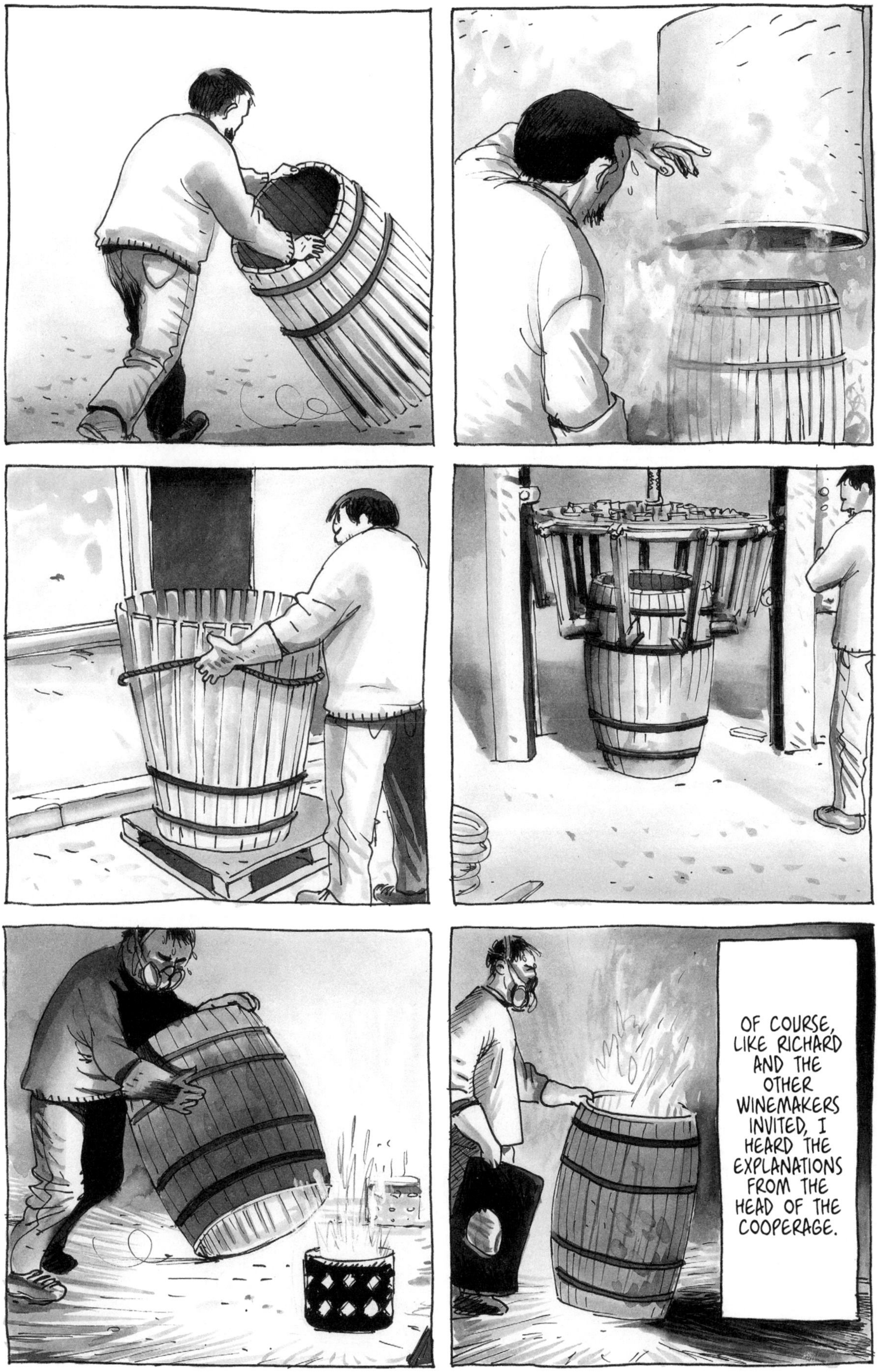
OF COURSE, LIKE RICHARD AND THE OTHER WINEMAKERS INVITED, I HEARD THE EXPLANATIONS FROM THE HEAD OF THE COOPERAGE.

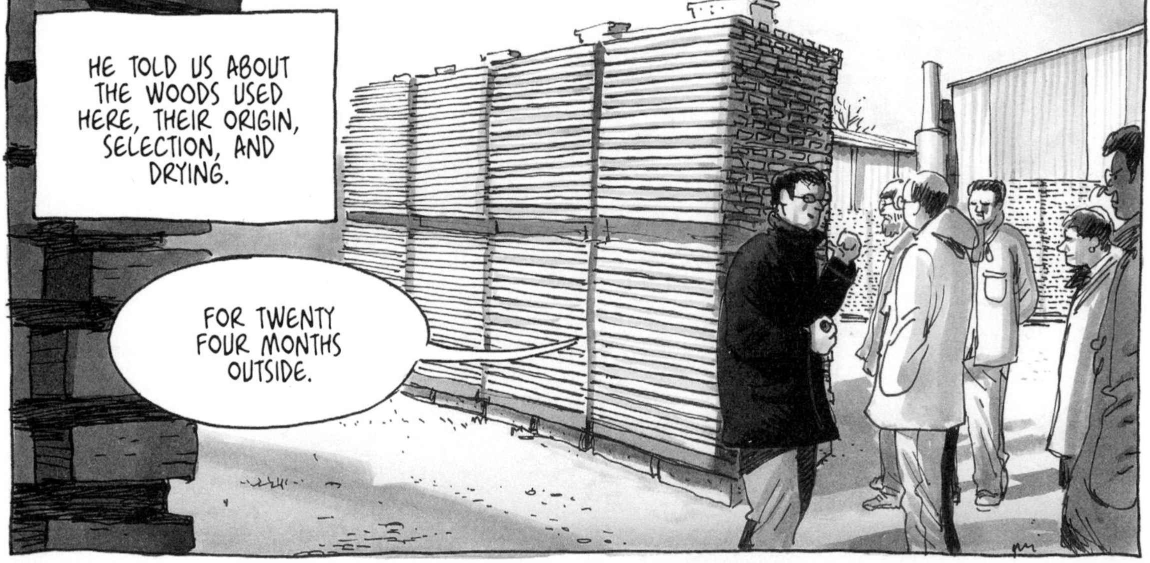
HE TOLD US ABOUT THE WOODS USED HERE, THEIR ORIGIN, SELECTION, AND DRYING.
FOR TWENTY FOUR MONTHS OUTSIDE.

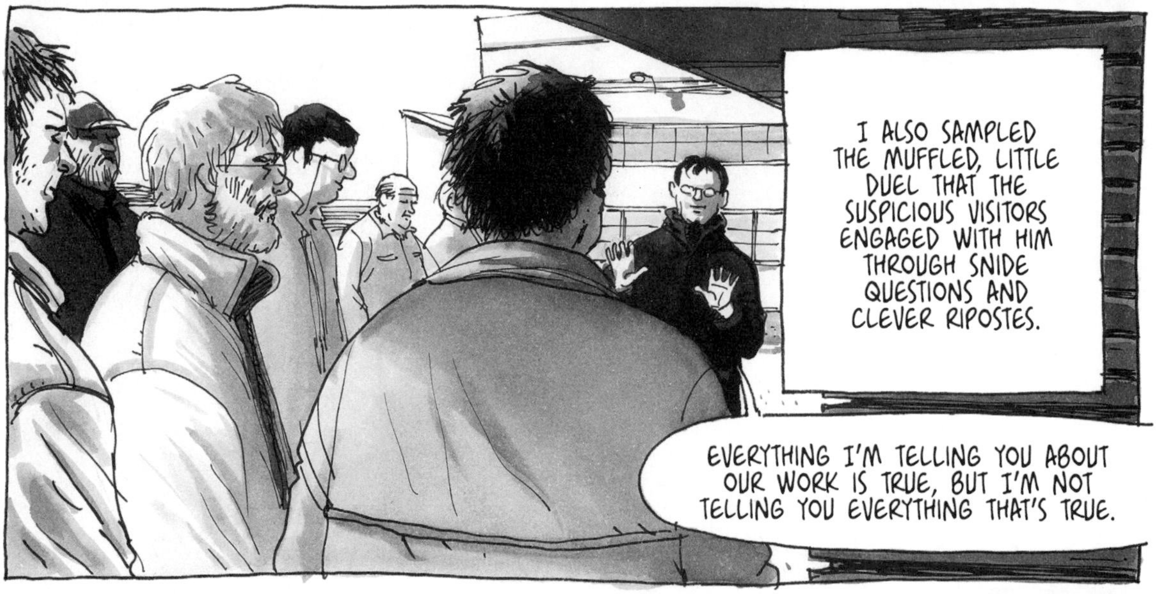
I ALSO SAMPLED THE MUFFLED, LITTLE DUEL THAT THE SUSPICIOUS VISITORS ENGAGED WITH HIM THROUGH SNIDE QUESTIONS AND CLEVER RIPOSTES.
EVERYTHING I'M TELLING YOU ABOUT OUR WORK IS TRUE, BUT I'M NOT TELLING YOU EVERYTHING THAT'S TRUE.

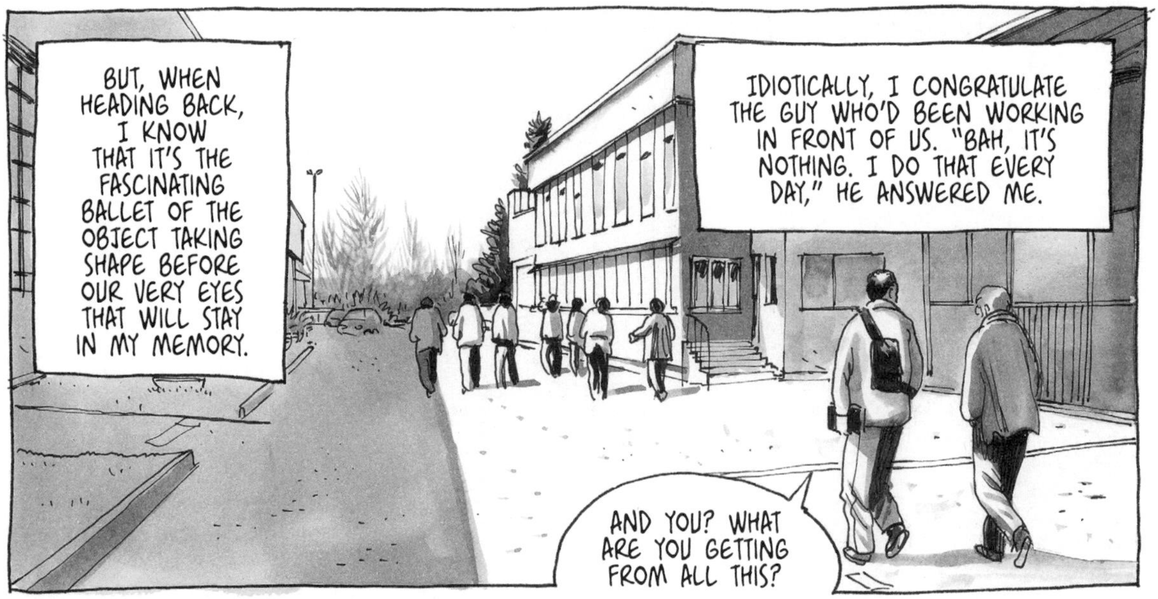
BUT, WHEN HEADING BACK, I KNOW THAT IT'S THE FASCINATING BALLET OF THE OBJECT TAKING SHAPE BEFORE OUR VERY EYES THAT WILL STAY IN MY MEMORY.
IDIOTICALLY, I CONGRATULATE THE GUY WHO'D BEEN WORKING IN FRONT OF US. "BAH, IT'S NOTHING. I DO THAT EVERY DAY," HE ANSWERED ME.
AND YOU? WHAT ARE YOU GETTING FROM ALL THIS?

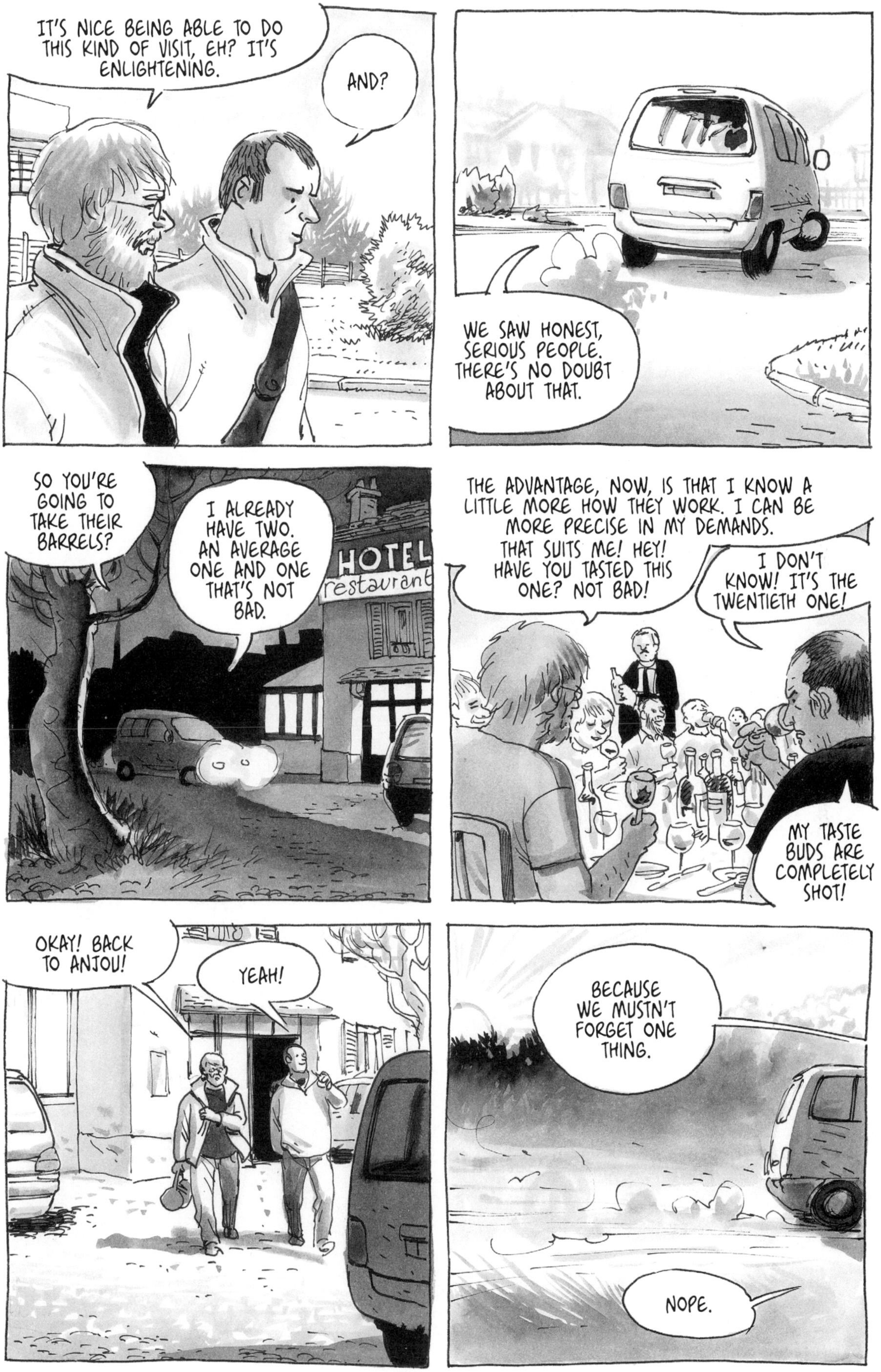
IT'S NICE BEING ABLE TO DO THIS KIND OF VISIT, EH? IT'S ENLIGHTENING.
AND?
WE SAW HONEST, SERIOUS PEOPLE. THERE'S NO DOUBT ABOUT THAT.
SO YOU'RE GOING TO TAKE THEIR BARRELS?
I ALREADY HAVE TWO. AN AVERAGE ONE AND ONE THAT'S NOT BAD.
HOTEL
restaurant
THE ADVANTAGE, NOW, IS THAT I KNOW A LITTLE MORE HOW THEY WORK. I CAN BE MORE PRECISE IN MY DEMANDS.
THAT SUITS ME! HEY! HAVE YOU TASTED THIS ONE? NOT BAD!
I DON'T KNOW! IT'S THE TWENTIETH ONE!
MY TASTE BUDS ARE COMPLETELY SHOT!
OKAY! BACK TO ANJOU!
YEAH!
BECAUSE WE MUSTN'T FORGET ONE THING.
NOPE.

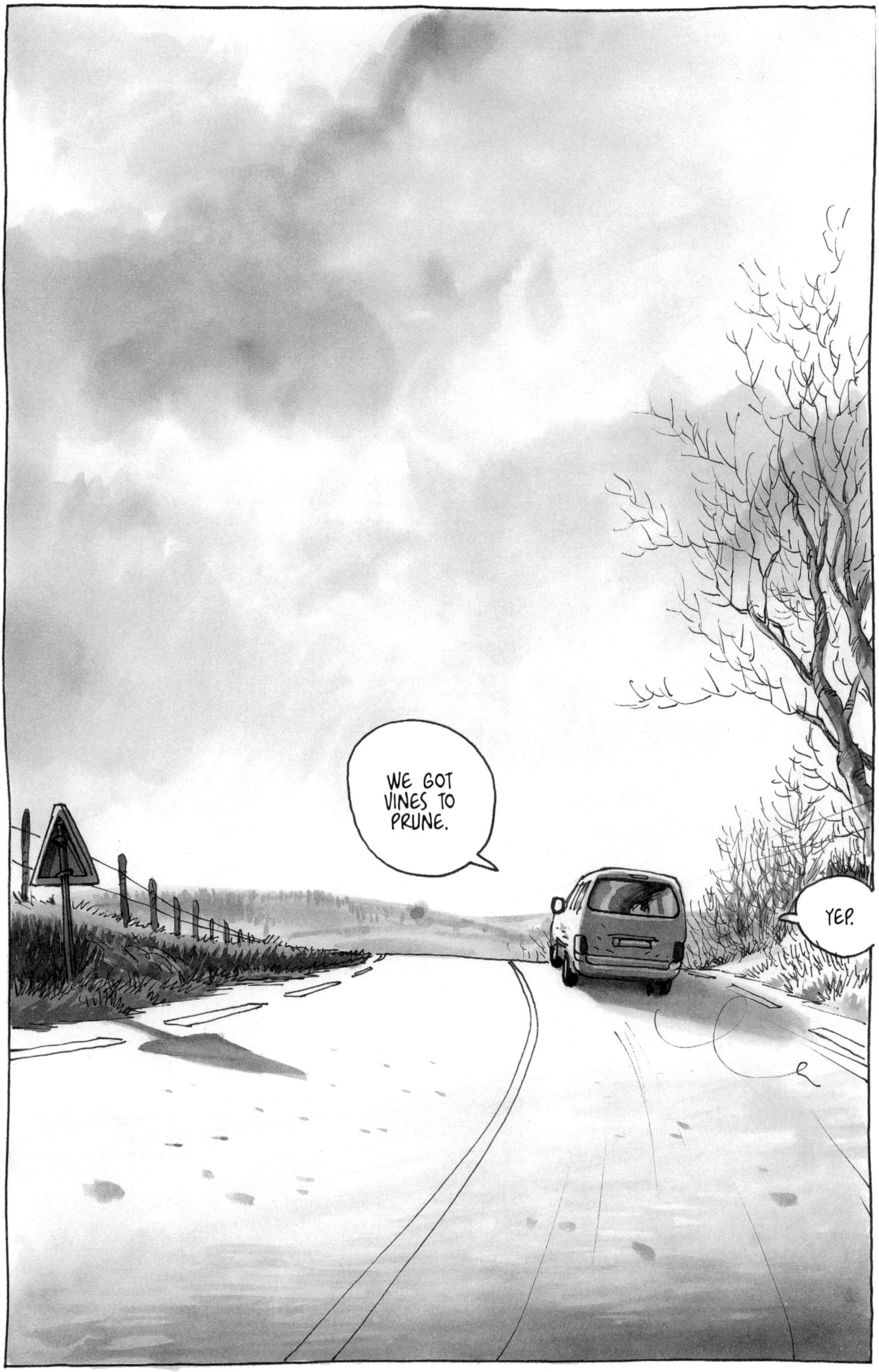
WE GOT VINES TO PRUNE.
YEP.

CHAPTER THREE

JEAN-PIERRE
(AND JIMI, AND WOLFGANG AMADEUS, AND A FEW OTHERS)

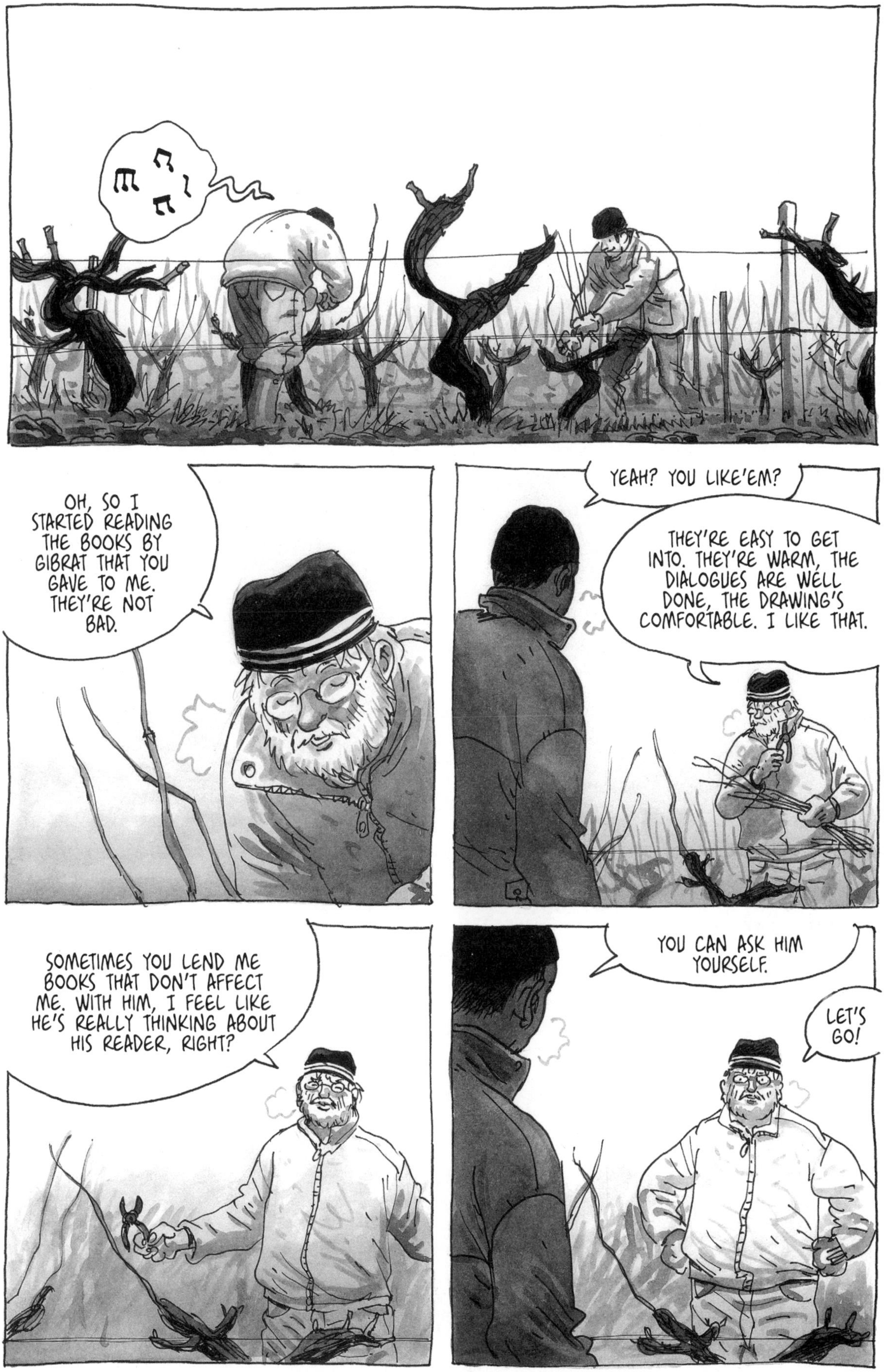
OH, SO I STARTED READING THE BOOKS BY GIBRAT THAT YOU GAVE TO ME. THEY'RE NOT BAD.
YEAH? YOU LIKE'EM?
THEY'RE EASY TO GET INTO. THEY'RE WARM, THE DIALOGUES ARE WELL DONE, THE DRAWING'S COMFORTABLE. I LIKE THAT.
SOMETIMES YOU LEND ME BOOKS THAT DON'T AFFECT ME. WITH HIM, I FEEL LIKE HE'S REALLY THINKING ABOUT HIS READER, RIGHT?
YOU CAN ASK HIM YOURSELF.
LET'S GO!

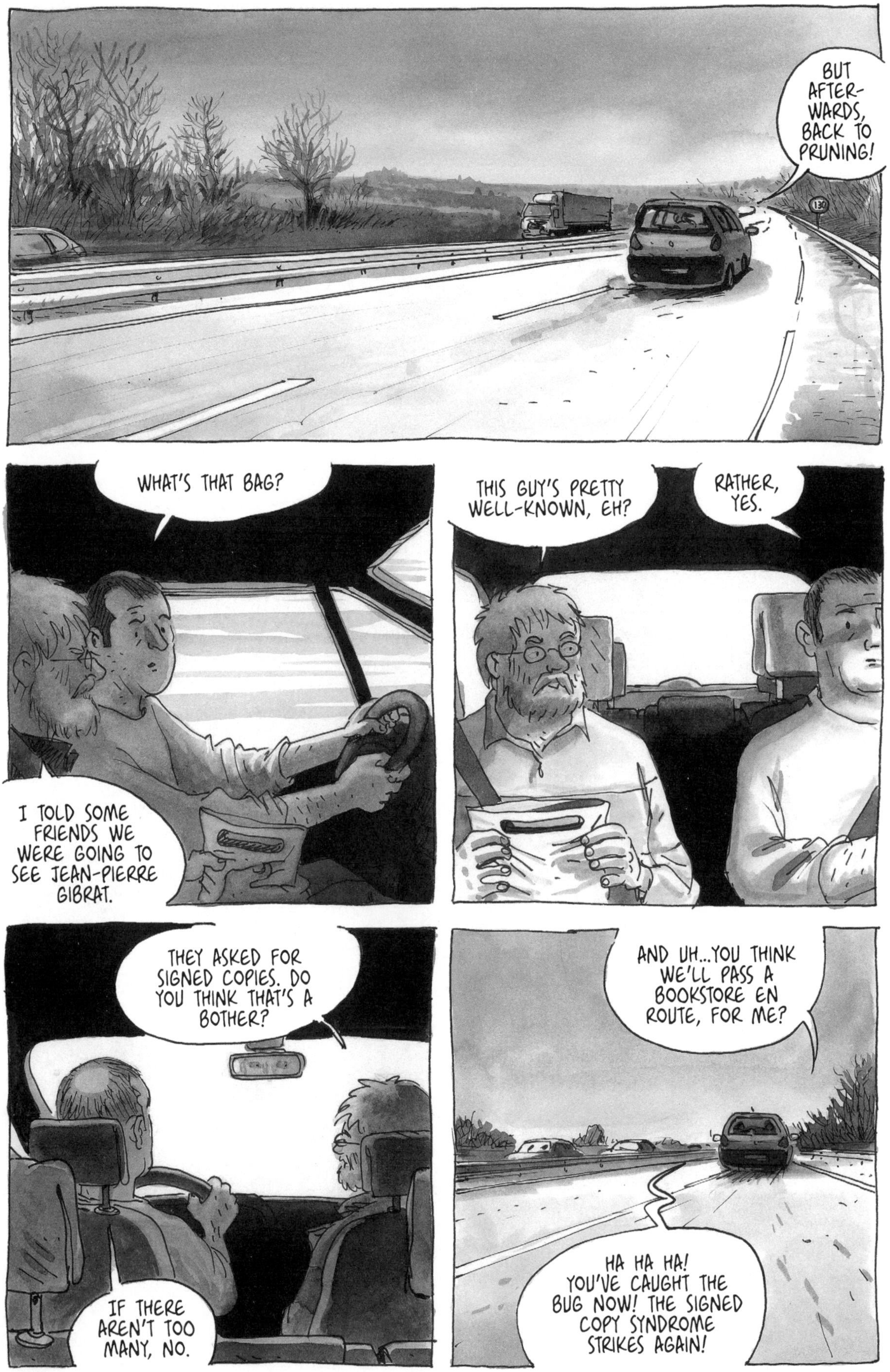
BUT AFTER-WARDS, BACK TO PRUNING!
WHAT'S THAT BAG?
I TOLD SOME FRIENDS WE WERE GOING TO SEE JEAN-PIERRE GIBRAT.
THIS GUY'S PRETTY WELL-KNOWN, EH?
RATHER, YES.
THEY ASKED FOR SIGNED COPIES. DO YOU THINK THAT'S A BOTHER?
IF THERE AREN'T TOO MANY, NO.
AND UH...YOU THINK WE'LL PASS A BOOKSTORE EN ROUTE, FOR ME?
HA HA HA! YOU'VE CAUGHT THE BUG NOW! THE SIGNED COPY SYNDROME STRIKES AGAIN!

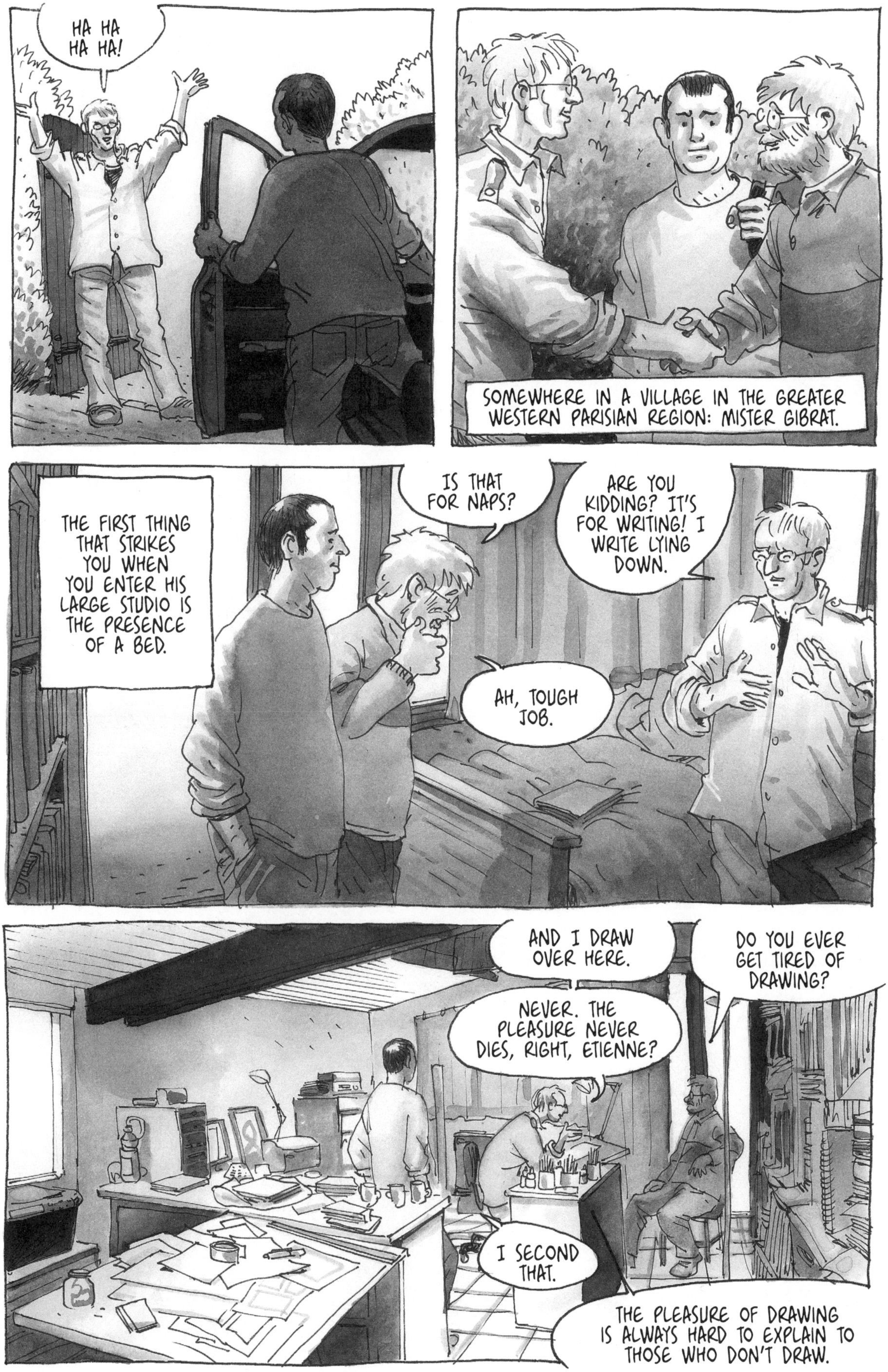
HA HA
HA HA!
SOMEWHERE IN A VILLAGE IN THE GREATER WESTERN PARISIAN REGION: MISTER GIBRAT.
THE FIRST THING THAT STRIKES YOU WHEN YOU ENTER HIS LARGE STUDIO IS THE PRESENCE OF A BED.
IS THAT FOR NAPS?
ARE YOU KIDDING? IT'S FOR WRITING! I WRITE LYING DOWN.
AH, TOUGH JOB.
AND I DRAW OVER HERE.
NEVER. THE PLEASURE NEVER DIES, RIGHT, ETIENNE?
DO YOU EVER GET TIRED OF DRAWING?
I SECOND THAT.
THE PLEASURE OF DRAWING IS ALWAYS HARD TO EXPLAIN TO THOSE WHO DON'T DRAW.

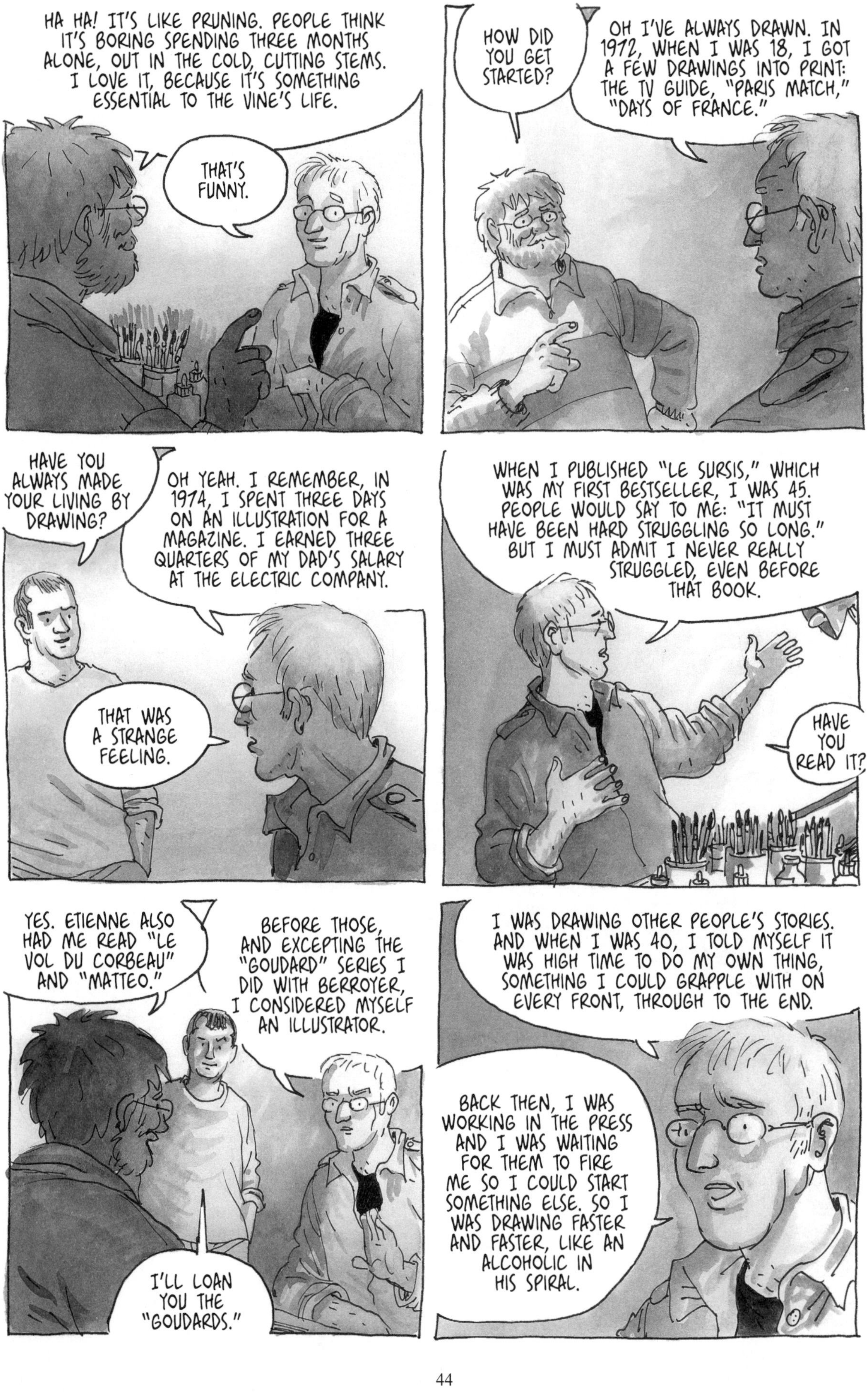
HA HA! IT'S LIKE PRUNING. PEOPLE THINK IT'S BORING SPENDING THREE MONTHS ALONE, OUT IN THE COLD, CUTTING STEMS. I LOVE IT, BECAUSE IT'S SOMETHING ESSENTIAL TO THE VINE'S LIFE.
THAT'S FUNNY.
HOW DID YOU GET STARTED?
OH I'VE ALWAYS DRAWN. IN 1972, WHEN I WAS 18, I GOT A FEW DRAWINGS INTO PRINT: THE TV GUIDE, "PARIS MATCH," "DAYS OF FRANCE."
HAVE YOU ALWAYS MADE YOUR LIVING BY DRAWING?
OH YEAH. I REMEMBER, IN 1974, I SPENT THREE DAYS ON AN ILLUSTRATION FOR A MAGAZINE. I EARNED THREE QUARTERS OF MY DAD'S SALARY AT THE ELECTRIC COMPANY.
THAT WAS A STRANGE FEELING.
WHEN I PUBLISHED "LE SURSIS," WHICH WAS MY FIRST BESTSELLER, I WAS 45. PEOPLE WOULD SAY TO ME: "IT MUST HAVE BEEN HARD STRUGGLING SO LONG." BUT I MUST ADMIT I NEVER REALLY STRUGGLED, EVEN BEFORE THAT BOOK.
HAVE YOU READ IT?
YES. ETIENNE ALSO HAD ME READ "LE VOL DU CORBEAU" AND "MATTEO."
BEFORE THOSE, AND EXCEPTING THE "GOUDARD" SERIES I DID WITH BERROYER, I CONSIDERED MYSELF AN ILLUSTRATOR.
I'LL LOAN YOU THE "GOUDARDS."
I WAS DRAWING OTHER PEOPLE'S STORIES. AND WHEN I WAS 40, I TOLD MYSELF IT WAS HIGH TIME TO DO MY OWN THING, SOMETHING I COULD GRAPPLE WITH ON EVERY FRONT, THROUGH TO THE END.
BACK THEN, I WAS WORKING IN THE PRESS AND I WAS WAITING FOR THEM TO FIRE ME SO I COULD START SOMETHING ELSE. SO I WAS DRAWING FASTER AND FASTER, LIKE AN ALCOHOLIC IN HIS SPIRAL.

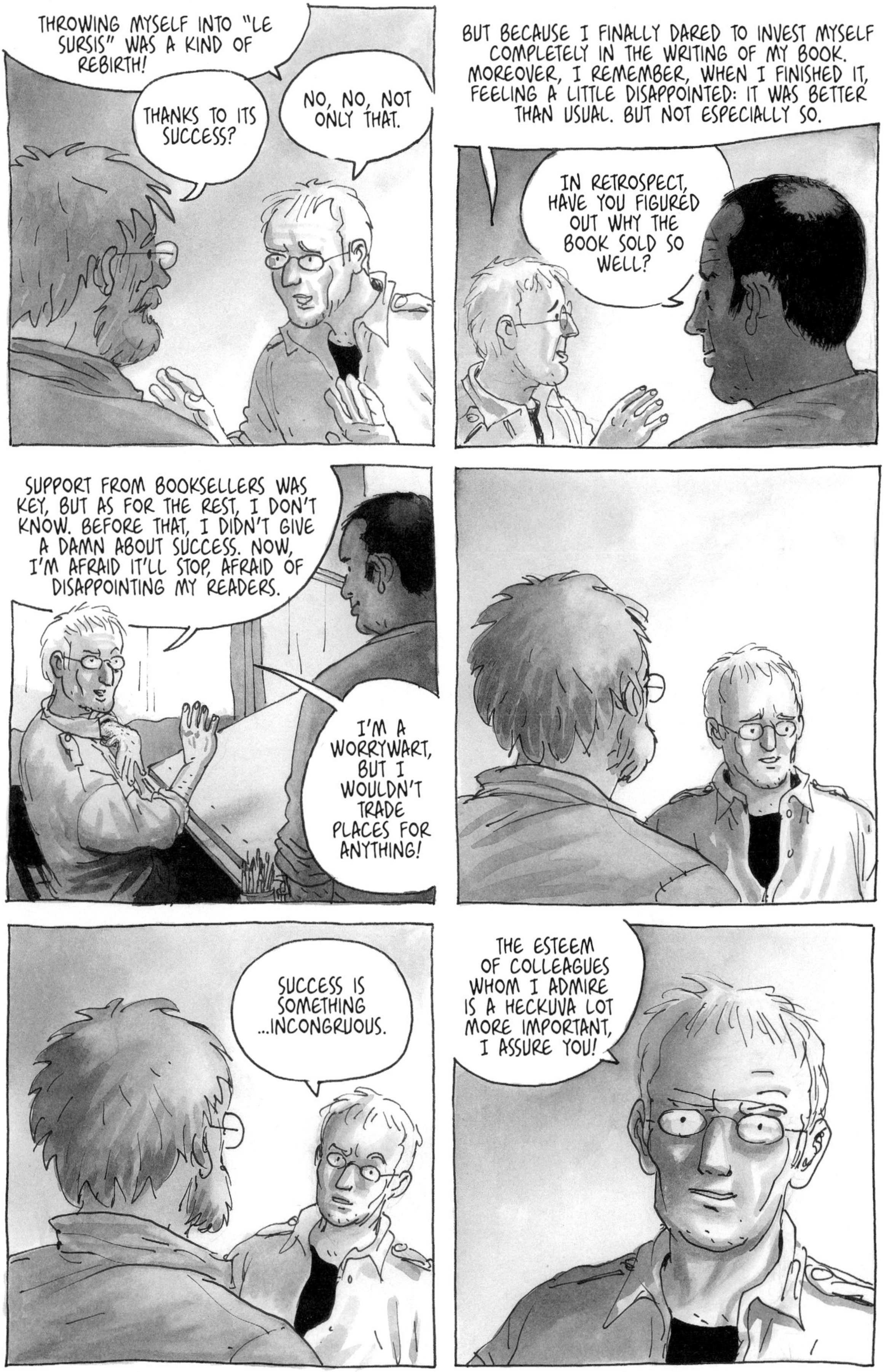
THROWING MYSELF INTO "LE SURSIS" WAS A KIND OF REBIRTH!
THANKS TO ITS SUCCESS?
NO, NO, NOT ONLY THAT.
BUT BECAUSE I FINALLY DARED TO INVEST MYSELF COMPLETELY IN THE WRITING OF MY BOOK. MOREOVER, I REMEMBER, WHEN I FINISHED IT, FEELING A LITTLE DISAPPOINTED: IT WAS BETTER THAN USUAL. BUT NOT ESPECIALLY SO.
IN RETROSPECT, HAVE YOU FIGURED OUT WHY THE BOOK SOLD SO WELL?
SUPPORT FROM BOOKSELLERS WAS KEY, BUT AS FOR THE REST, I DON'T KNOW. BEFORE THAT, I DIDN'T GIVE A DAMN ABOUT SUCCESS. NOW, I'M AFRAID IT'LL STOP, AFRAID OF DISAPPOINTING MY READERS.
I'M A WORRYWART, BUT I WOULDN'T TRADE PLACES FOR ANYTHING!
SUCCESS IS SOMETHING ...INCONGRUOUS.
THE ESTEEM OF COLLEAGUES WHOM I ADMIRE IS A HECKUVA LOT MORE IMPORTANT, I ASSURE YOU!

WHY DOES A BOOK REACH ITS READERS OR NOT? WHAT MAKES THE VALUE OF AN AUTHOR? IT'S VERY MYSTERIOUS! I LIKE BOOKS AND AUTHORS WHO HAVE A STRONG IDENTITY...

AND I THINK THAT WHAT MAKES OUR IDENTITY, AMONG OTHER THINGS, IS OUR FAULTS. YOU HAVE TO UNDERSTAND AND ACCEPT THEM. IT'S LIKE YOUR MUG: A SUPPOSEDLY FLAWLESS FACE IS DULL, IT ANNOYS EVERYONE.

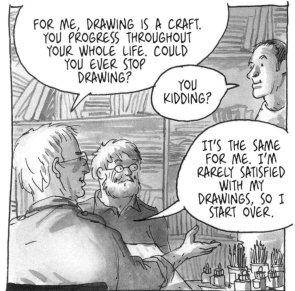

FOR ME, DRAWING IS A CRAFT. YOU PROGRESS THROUGHOUT YOUR WHOLE LIFE. COULD YOU EVER STOP DRAWING?

YOU KIDDING?

IT'S THE SAME FOR ME. I'M RARELY SATISFIED WITH MY DRAWINGS, SO I START OVER.

WRITING'S DIFFERENT. YOU NEVER KNOW WHERE YOU'RE HEADED.

THAT MUST SCARE THE CRAP OUT OF YOU.

EXACTLY. BUT SOMETIMES, AFTER WRITING SOMETHING, I TELL MYSELF, "HEY, I'D LIKE THAT, IF SOMEBODY ELSE HAD WRITTEN IT."

BEING ABLE TO SEE THAT, FROM TIME TO TIME, IS A PLEASURE!

THAT'S INTERESTING. I DON'T SEPARATE THE ACT OF DRAWING AND WRITING AS MUCH AS YOU.

OH YEAH?

MAYBE IT'S BECAUSE YOU'RE MORE OF AN ARTIST THAN ME.

WHAT ARE YOUR FAULTS IN DRAWING?

MY LINE. I FIND IT...ILL-DEFINED. HAVE YOU READ ANY BOOKS BY JUILLARD?

UH...

YES. YOU READ "THE BLUE NOTEBOOK."

OH YEAH! NOT BAD!

THERE'S A FELLOW WHO HAS THE GIFT. A BOX OF MATCHES DRAWN BY JUILLARD IS WORTH THE EFFORT!

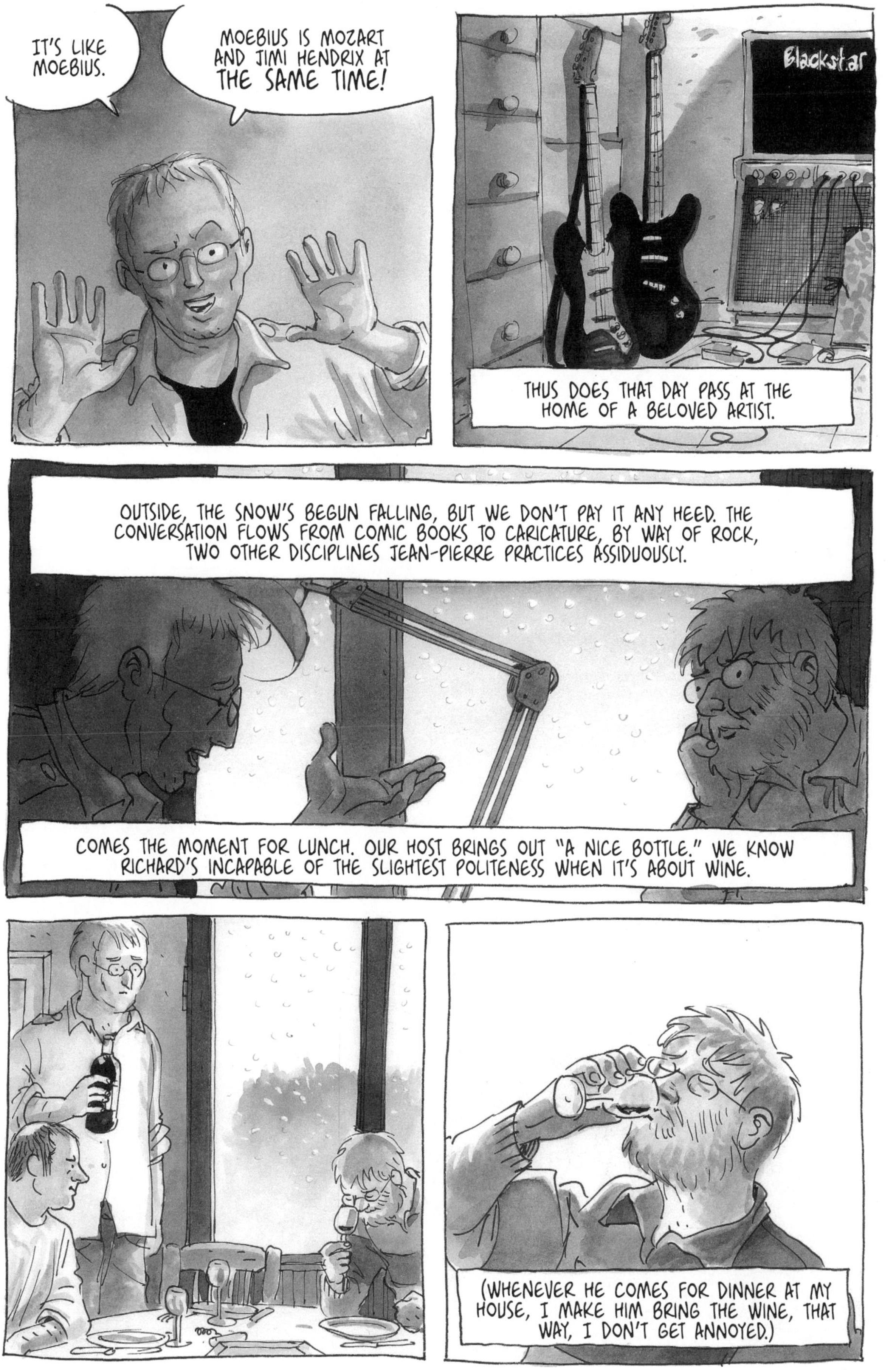
IT'S LIKE MOEBIUS.
MOEBIUS IS MOZART AND JIMI HENDRIX AT THE SAME TIME!
Blackstar
THUS DOES THAT DAY PASS AT THE HOME OF A BELOVED ARTIST.
OUTSIDE, THE SNOW'S BEGUN FALLING, BUT WE DON'T PAY IT ANY HEED. THE CONVERSATION FLOWS FROM COMIC BOOKS TO CARICATURE, BY WAY OF ROCK, TWO OTHER DISCIPLINES JEAN-PIERRE PRACTICES ASSIDUOUSLY.
COMES THE MOMENT FOR LUNCH. OUR HOST BRINGS OUT "A NICE BOTTLE." WE KNOW RICHARD'S INCAPABLE OF THE SLIGHTEST POLITENESS WHEN IT'S ABOUT WINE.
(WHENEVER HE COMES FOR DINNER AT MY HOUSE, I MAKE HIM BRING THE WINE, THAT WAY, I DON'T GET ANNOYED.)

SsssSCHHLLuuuuRRPR

IT'S A BORDEAUX AND IT'S GOOD. IT'S DENSE, IT'S MATURE... NOT BAD!

AAAH...

HERE'S SOMETHING THAT COUNTS: FEELING THE DEVOTION AND PLEASURE FELT BY THE GUY WHO MADE THE WINE... OR THE BOOK.

ABSHOLUTELY!

FOR EXAMPLE, I'VE NEVER READ THE BEST-SELLING "LARGO WINCH," BUT YOU SENSE THAT THE ARTIST IS SINCERE IN THAT GENRE. SO, I RESPECT IT.

BUT SINCERITY ISN'T ALWAYS ENOUGH.

EXACTLY!

RIGHT!

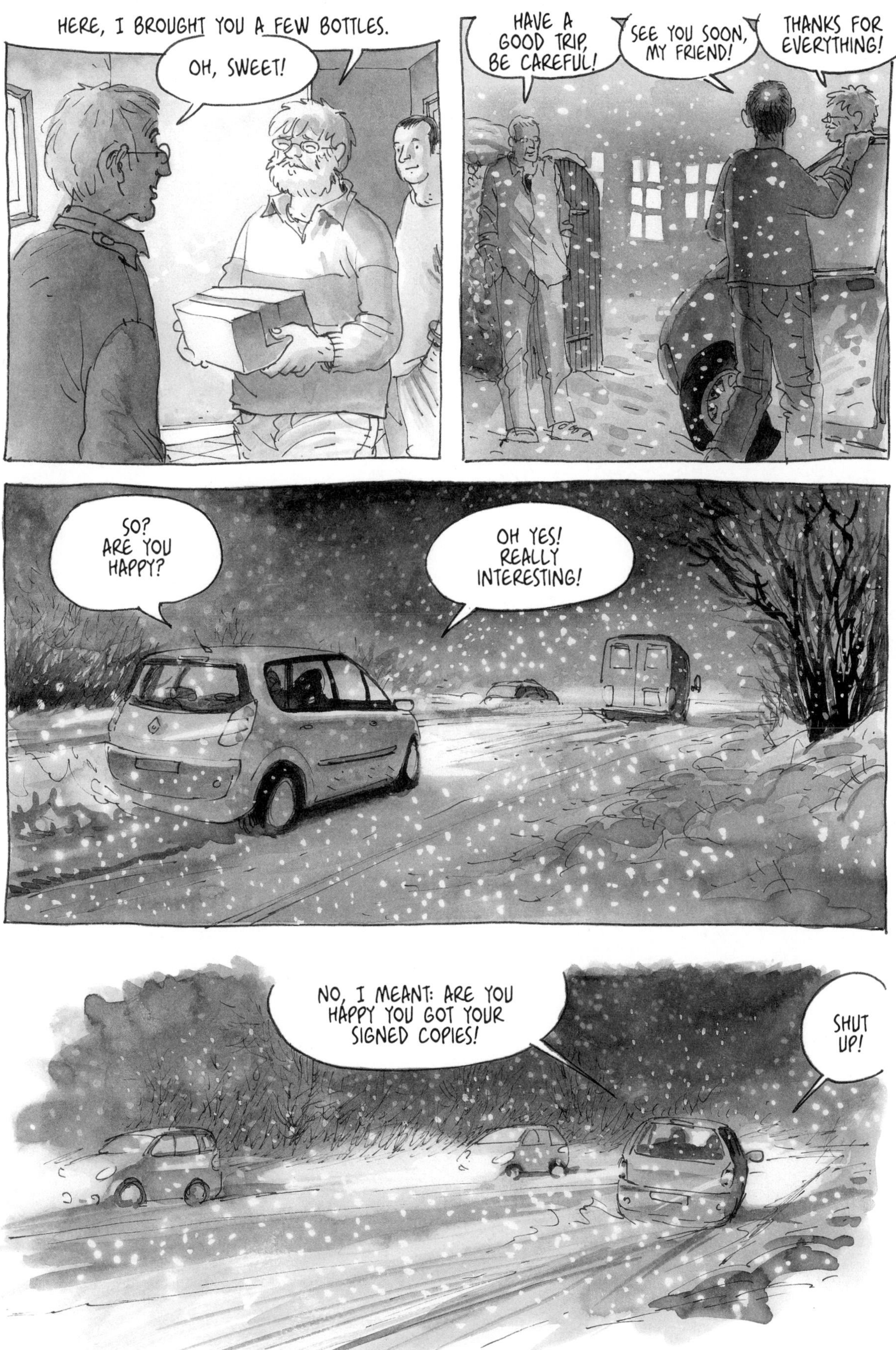
HERE, I BROUGHT YOU A FEW BOTTLES.
OH, SWEET!
HAVE A GOOD TRIP, BE CAREFUL!
SEE YOU SOON, MY FRIEND!
THANKS FOR EVERYTHING!
SO? ARE YOU HAPPY?
OH YES! REALLY INTERESTING!
NO, I MEANT: ARE YOU HAPPY YOU GOT YOUR SIGNED COPIES!
SHUT UP!

CHAPTER FOUR

THE ART OF THE PORTRAIT AND ITS VICISSITUDES, OR "THE THEORY OF THE BEAK"

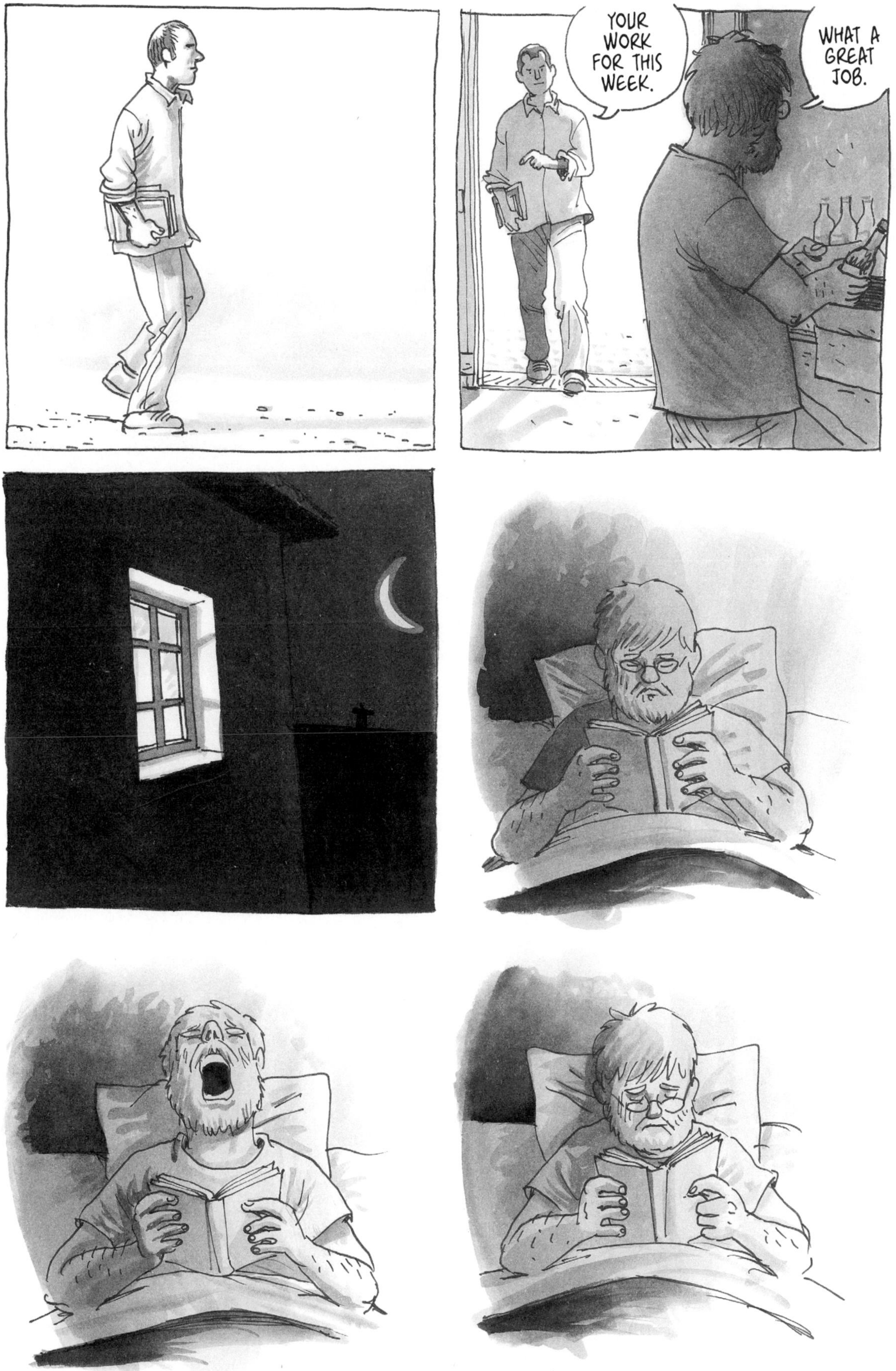
YOUR WORK FOR THIS WEEK.
WHAT A GREAT JOB.

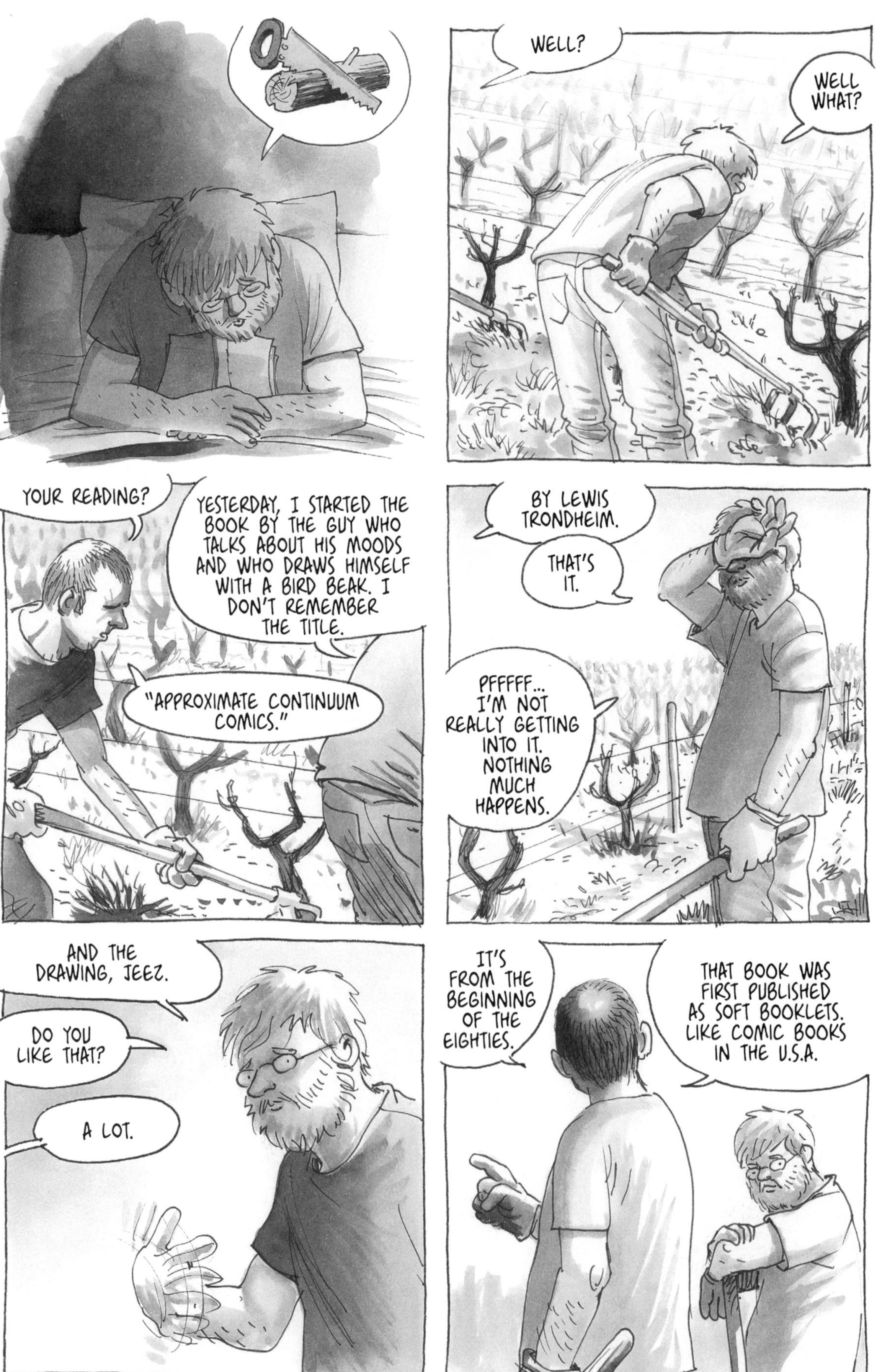
WELL?
WELL WHAT?
YOUR READING?
YESTERDAY, I STARTED THE BOOK BY THE GUY WHO TALKS ABOUT HIS MOODS AND WHO DRAWS HIMSELF WITH A BIRD BEAK. I DON'T REMEMBER THE TITLE.
"APPROXIMATE CONTINUUM COMICS."
BY LEWIS TRONDHEIM.
THAT'S IT.
PFFFFF... I'M NOT REALLY GETTING INTO IT. NOTHING MUCH HAPPENS.
AND THE DRAWING, JEEZ.
DO YOU LIKE THAT?
A LOT.
IT'S FROM THE BEGINNING OF THE EIGHTIES.
THAT BOOK WAS FIRST PUBLISHED AS SOFT BOOKLETS. LIKE COMIC BOOKS IN THE U.S.A.

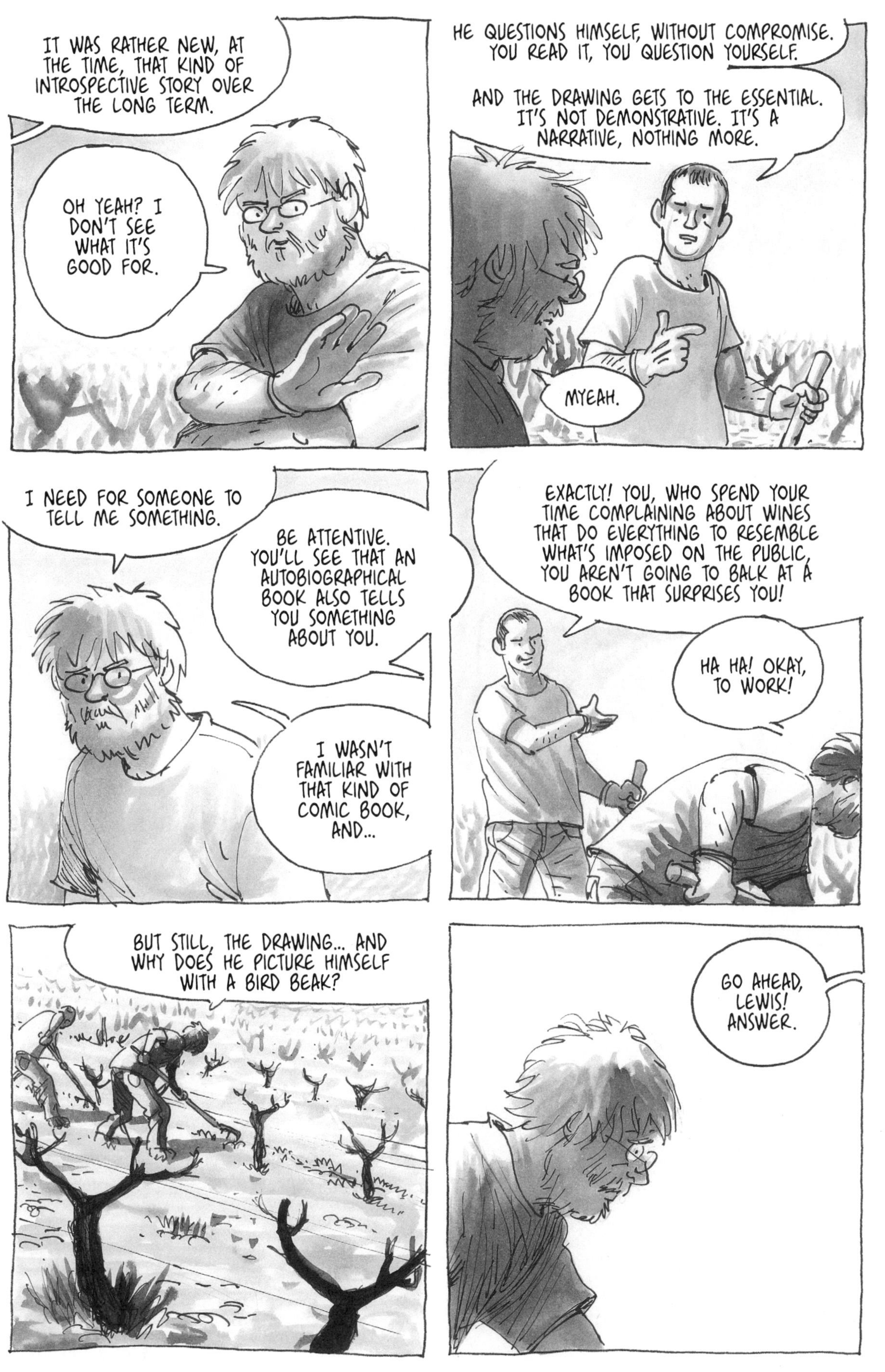
IT WAS RATHER NEW, AT THE TIME, THAT KIND OF INTROSPECTIVE STORY OVER THE LONG TERM.
OH YEAH? I DON'T SEE WHAT IT'S GOOD FOR.
HE QUESTIONS HIMSELF, WITHOUT COMPROMISE. YOU READ IT, YOU QUESTION YOURSELF.
AND THE DRAWING GETS TO THE ESSENTIAL. IT'S NOT DEMONSTRATIVE. IT'S A NARRATIVE, NOTHING MORE.
MYEAH.
I NEED FOR SOMEONE TO TELL ME SOMETHING.
BE ATTENTIVE. YOU'LL SEE THAT AN AUTOBIOGRAPHICAL BOOK ALSO TELLS YOU SOMETHING ABOUT YOU.
I WASN'T FAMILIAR WITH THAT KIND OF COMIC BOOK, AND...
EXACTLY! YOU, WHO SPEND YOUR TIME COMPLAINING ABOUT WINES THAT DO EVERYTHING TO RESEMBLE WHAT'S IMPOSED ON THE PUBLIC, YOU AREN'T GOING TO BALK AT A BOOK THAT SURPRISES YOU!
HA HA! OKAY, TO WORK!
BUT STILL, THE DRAWING... AND WHY DOES HE PICTURE HIMSELF WITH A BIRD BEAK?
GO AHEAD, LEWIS! ANSWER.

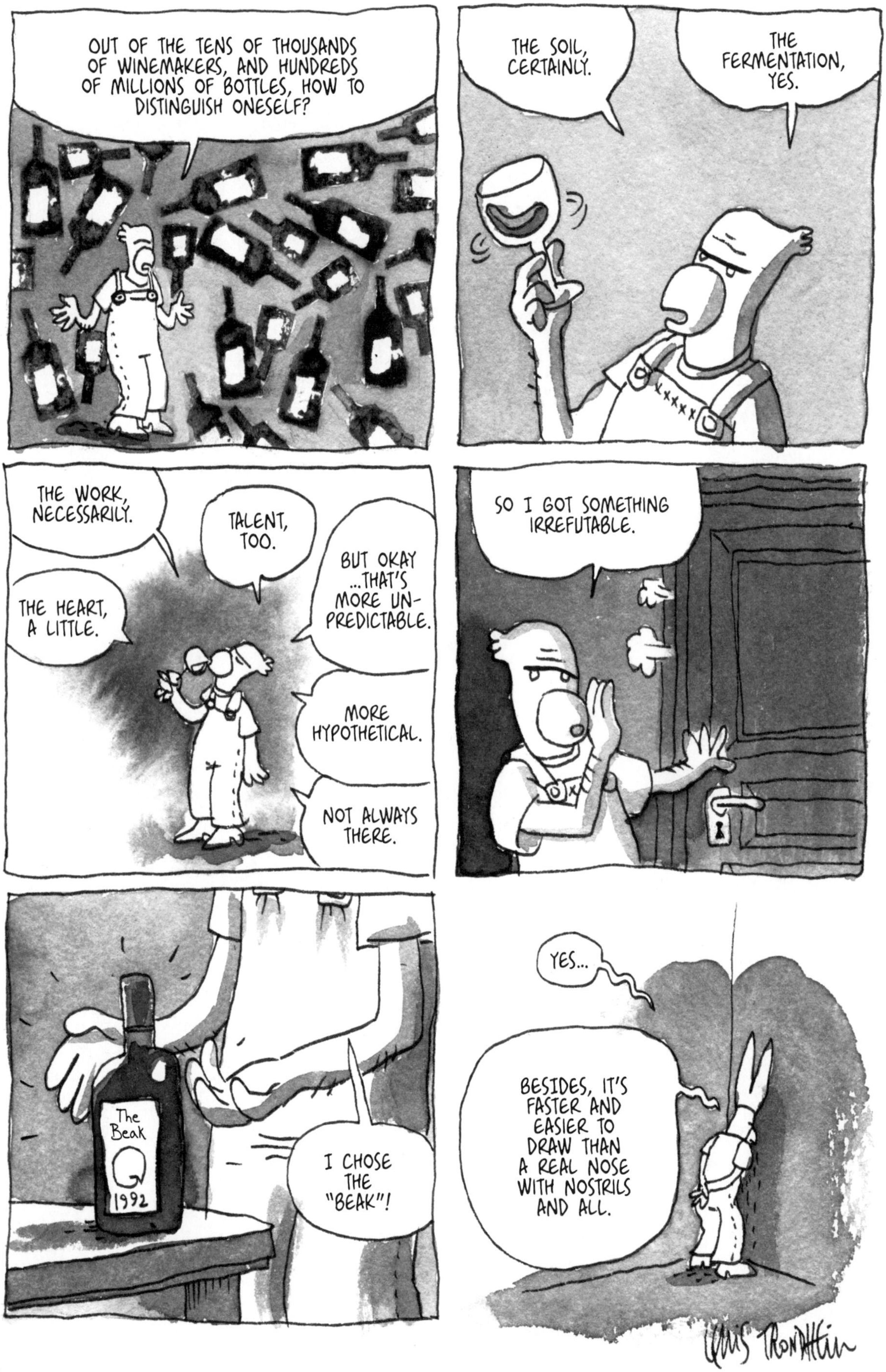
OUT OF THE TENS OF THOUSANDS OF WINEMAKERS, AND HUNDREDS OF MILLIONS OF BOTTLES, HOW TO DISTINGUISH ONESELF?
THE SOIL, CERTAINLY.
THE FERMENTATION, YES.
THE WORK, NECESSARILY.
TALENT, TOO.
THE HEART, A LITTLE.
BUT OKAY ...THAT'S MORE UN-PREDICTABLE.
MORE HYPOTHETICAL.
NOT ALWAYS THERE.
SO I GOT SOMETHING IRREFUTABLE.
The Beak 1992
I CHOSE THE "BEAK"!
YES...
BESIDES, IT'S FASTER AND EASIER TO DRAW THAN A REAL NOSE WITH NOSTRILS AND ALL.

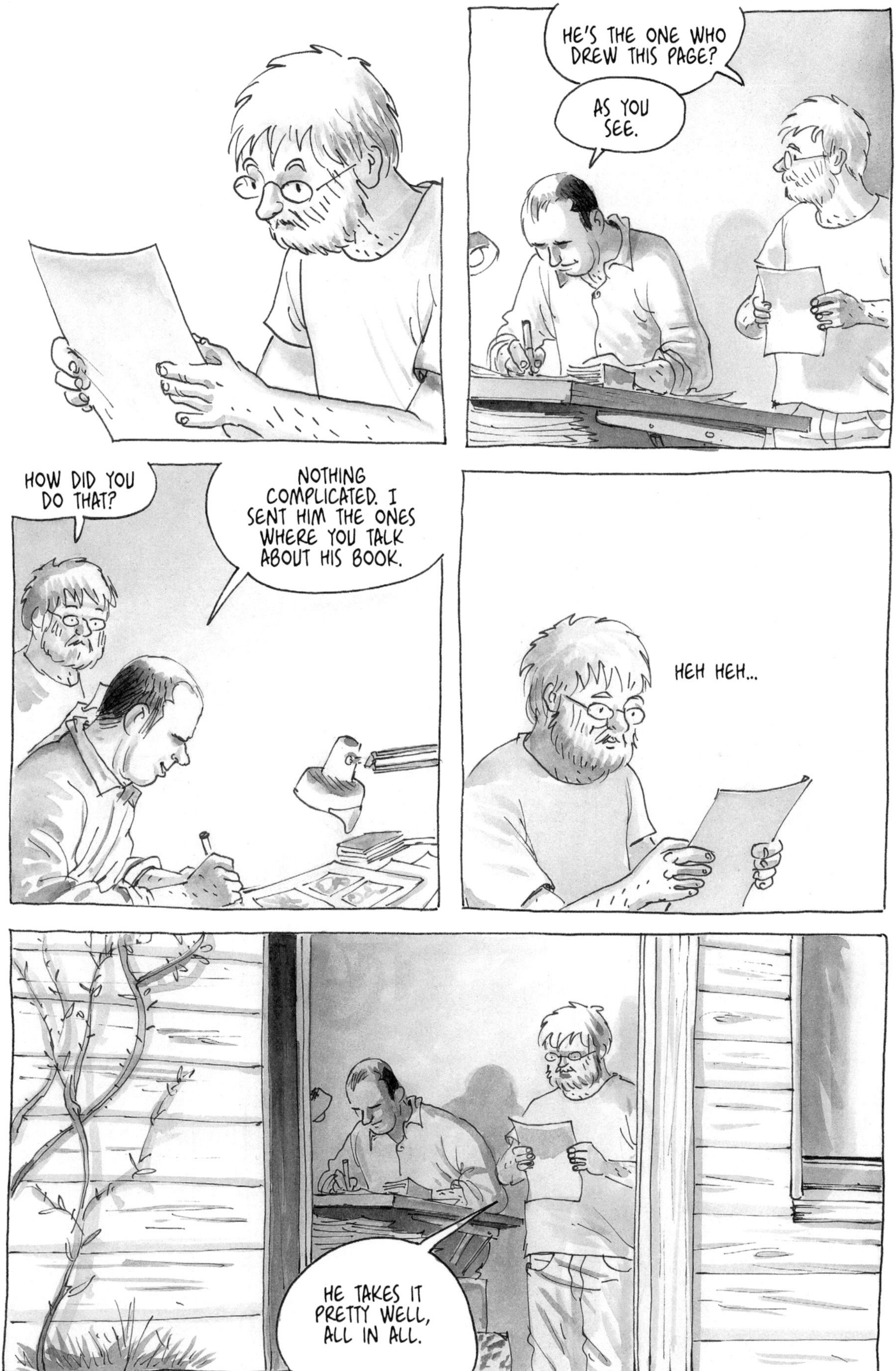

HE'S THE ONE WHO DREW THIS PAGE?
AS YOU SEE.
HOW DID YOU DO THAT?
NOTHING COMPLICATED. I SENT HIM THE ONES WHERE YOU TALK ABOUT HIS BOOK.
HEH HEH...
HE TAKES IT PRETTY WELL, ALL IN ALL.

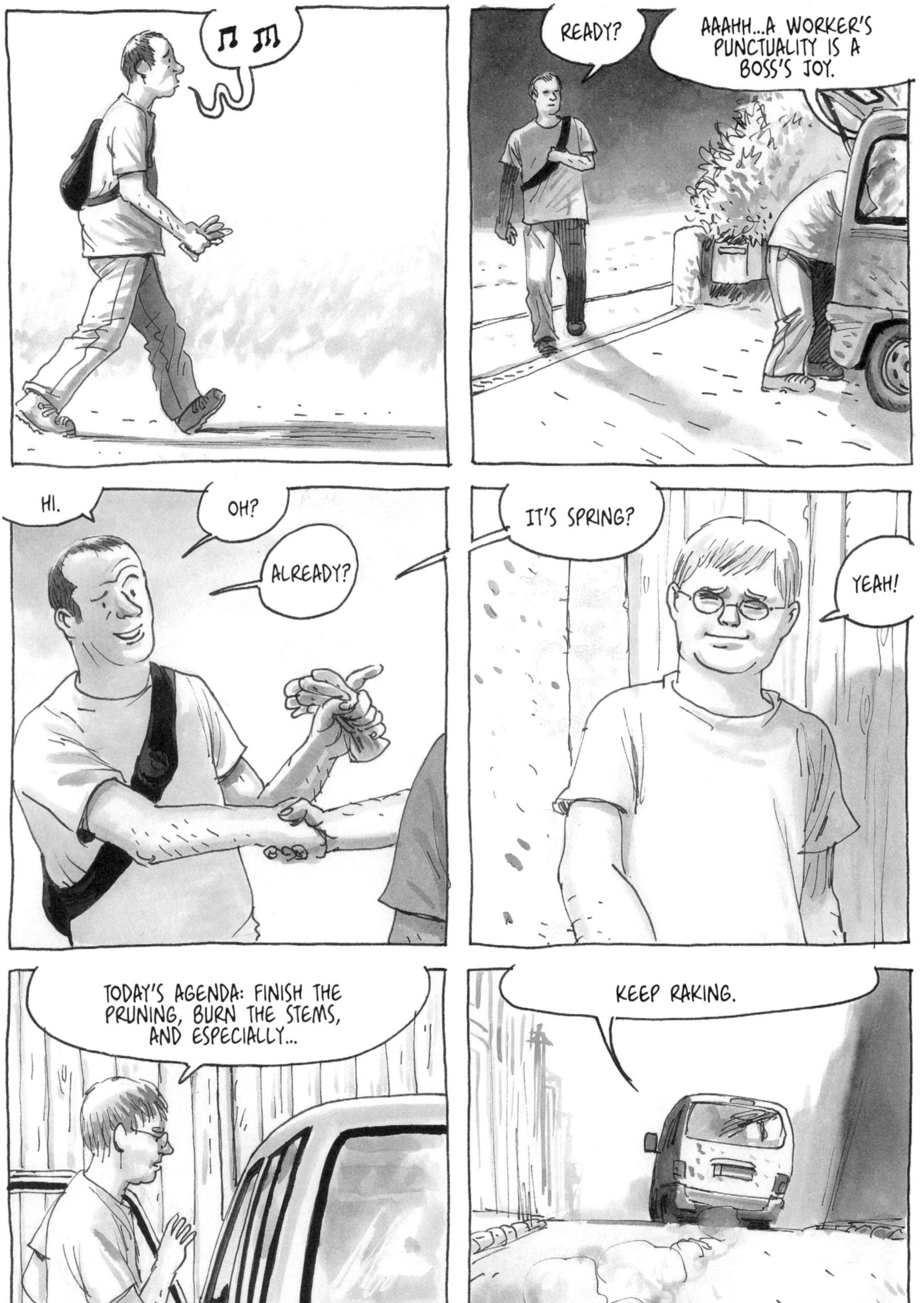
READY?
AAAHH...A WORKER'S PUNCTUALITY IS A BOSS'S JOY.
HI.
OH?
ALREADY?
IT'S SPRING?
YEAH!
TODAY'S AGENDA: FINISH THE PRUNING, BURN THE STEMS, AND ESPECIALLY...
KEEP RAKING.
YES, YES. THAT'S REALLY HIM.

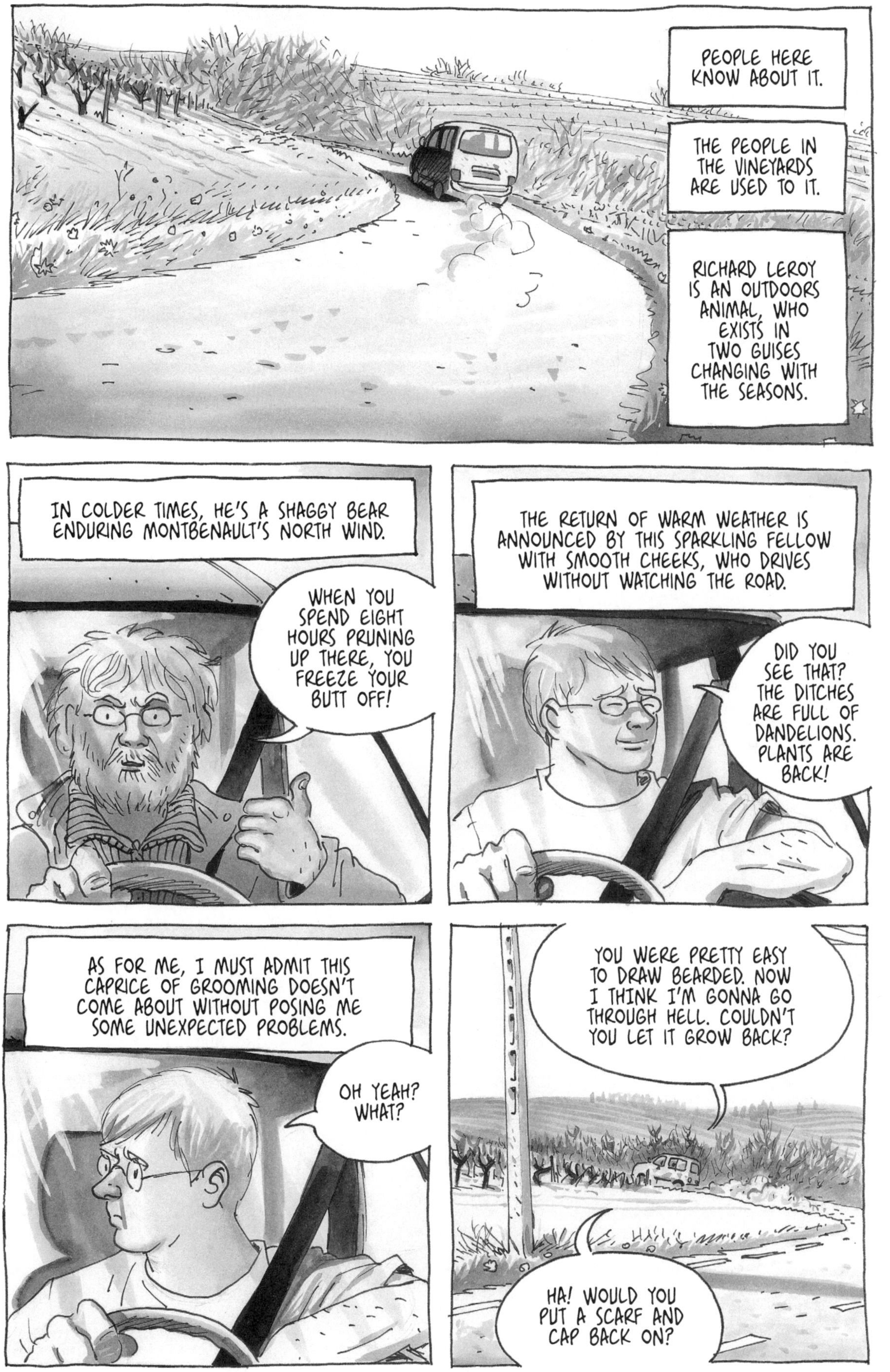
PEOPLE HERE KNOW ABOUT IT.
THE PEOPLE IN THE VINEYARDS ARE USED TO IT.
RICHARD LEROY IS AN OUTDOORS ANIMAL, WHO EXISTS IN TWO GUISES CHANGING WITH THE SEASONS.
IN COLDER TIMES, HE'S A SHAGGY BEAR ENDURING MONTBENAULT'S NORTH WIND.
WHEN YOU SPEND EIGHT HOURS PRUNING UP THERE, YOU FREEZE YOUR BUTT OFF!
THE RETURN OF WARM WEATHER IS ANNOUNCED BY THIS SPARKLING FELLOW WITH SMOOTH CHEEKS, WHO DRIVES WITHOUT WATCHING THE ROAD.
DID YOU SEE THAT? THE DITCHES ARE FULL OF DANDELIONS. PLANTS ARE BACK!
AS FOR ME, I MUST ADMIT THIS CAPRICE OF GROOMING DOESN'T COME ABOUT WITHOUT POSING ME SOME UNEXPECTED PROBLEMS.
OH YEAH? WHAT?
YOU WERE PRETTY EASY TO DRAW BEARDED. NOW I THINK I'M GONNA GO THROUGH HELL. COULDN'T YOU LET IT GROW BACK?
HA! WOULD YOU PUT A SCARF AND CAP BACK ON?

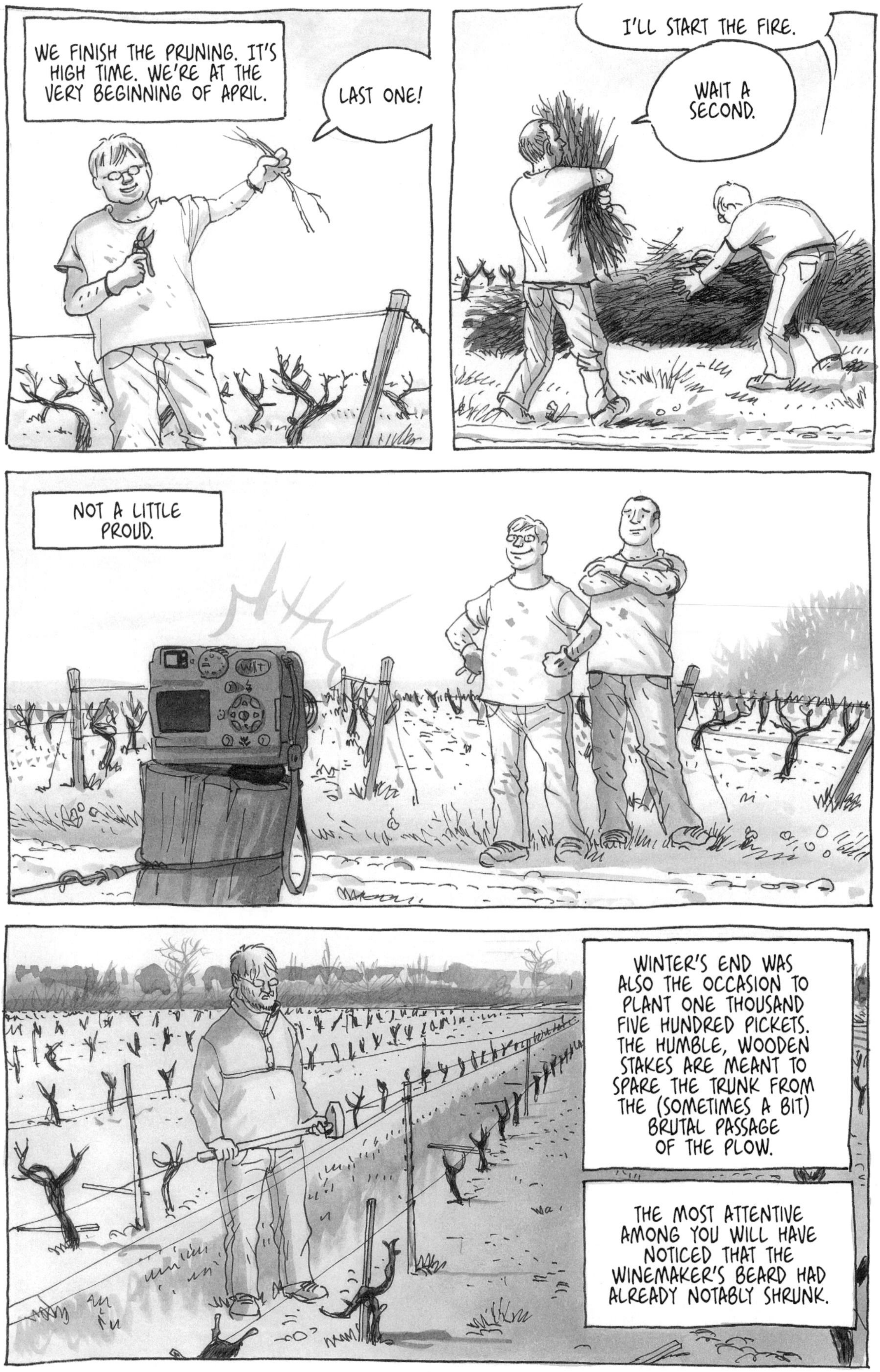
WE FINISH THE PRUNING. IT'S HIGH TIME. WE'RE AT THE VERY BEGINNING OF APRIL.
LAST ONE!
I'LL START THE FIRE.
WAIT A SECOND.
NOT A LITTLE PROUD.
WINTER'S END WAS ALSO THE OCCASION TO PLANT ONE THOUSAND FIVE HUNDRED PICKETS. THE HUMBLE, WOODEN STAKES ARE MEANT TO SPARE THE TRUNK FROM THE (SOMETIMES A BIT) BRUTAL PASSAGE OF THE PLOW.
THE MOST ATTENTIVE AMONG YOU WILL HAVE NOTICED THAT THE WINEMAKER'S BEARD HAD ALREADY NOTABLY SHRUNK.

IT'S THE SIGN THAT SPRING WAS APPROACHING. IT WAS TIME, THEREFORE, TO REPLACE MONTBENAULT'S "MISSING" ONES. A HUGE JOB.

IN THOSE CASES, THE SOLUTION CONSISTS IN CALLING UPON WINEMAKERS OF BOTH SEXES SHARING THE SAME CONCEPTION OF WINE.

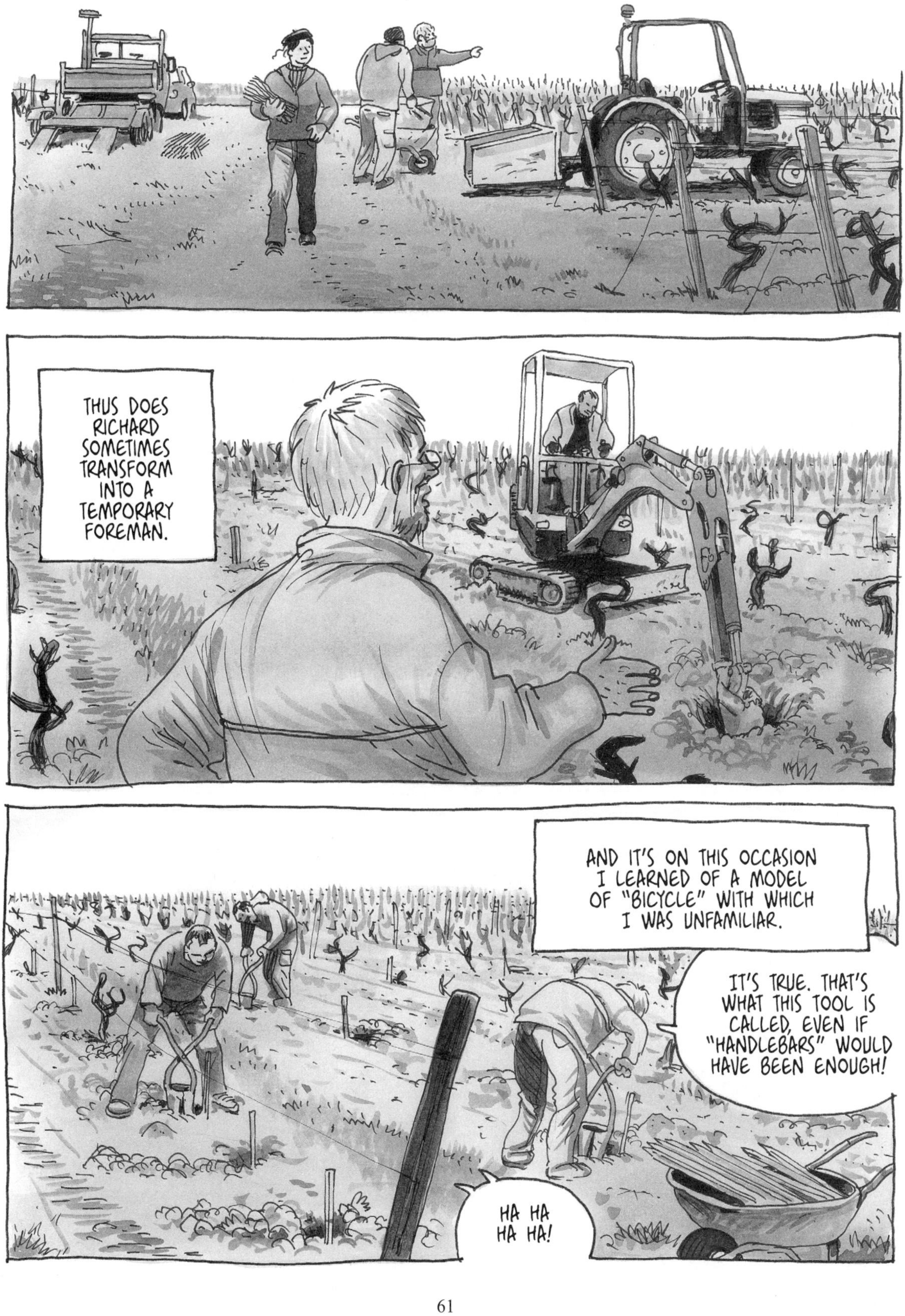
THUS DOES RICHARD SOMETIMES TRANSFORM INTO A TEMPORARY FOREMAN.
AND IT'S ON THIS OCCASION I LEARNED OF A MODEL OF "BICYCLE" WITH WHICH I WAS UNFAMILIAR.
IT'S TRUE. THAT'S WHAT THIS TOOL IS CALLED, EVEN IF "HANDLEBARS" WOULD HAVE BEEN ENOUGH!
HA HA HA HA!

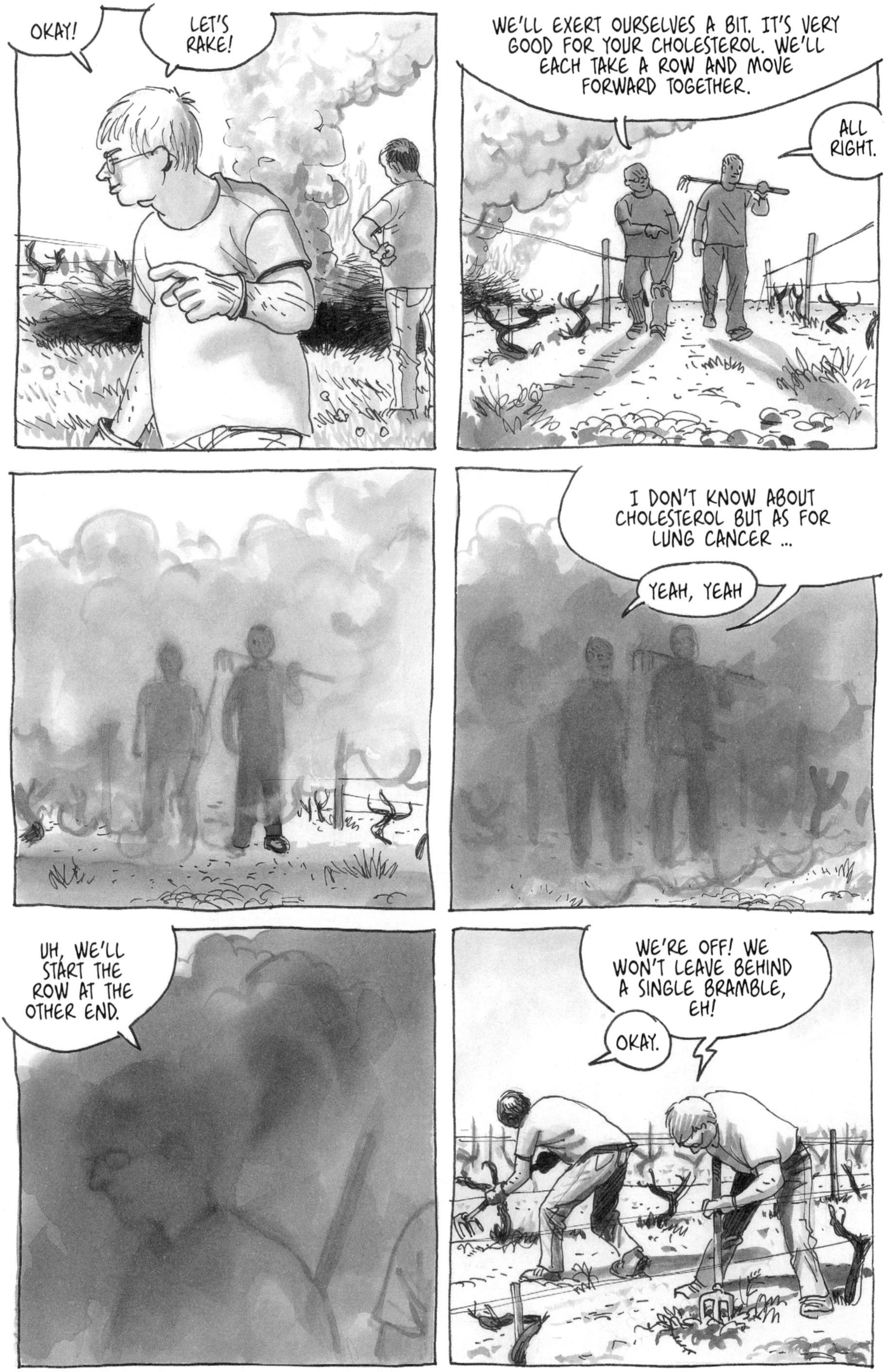

OKAY!
LET'S RAKE!
WE'LL EXERT OURSELVES A BIT. IT'S VERY GOOD FOR YOUR CHOLESTEROL. WE'LL EACH TAKE A ROW AND MOVE FORWARD TOGETHER.
ALL RIGHT.
I DON'T KNOW ABOUT CHOLESTEROL BUT AS FOR LUNG CANCER ...
YEAH, YEAH
UH, WE'LL START THE ROW AT THE OTHER END.
WE'RE OFF! WE WON'T LEAVE BEHIND A SINGLE BRAMBLE, EH!
OKAY.

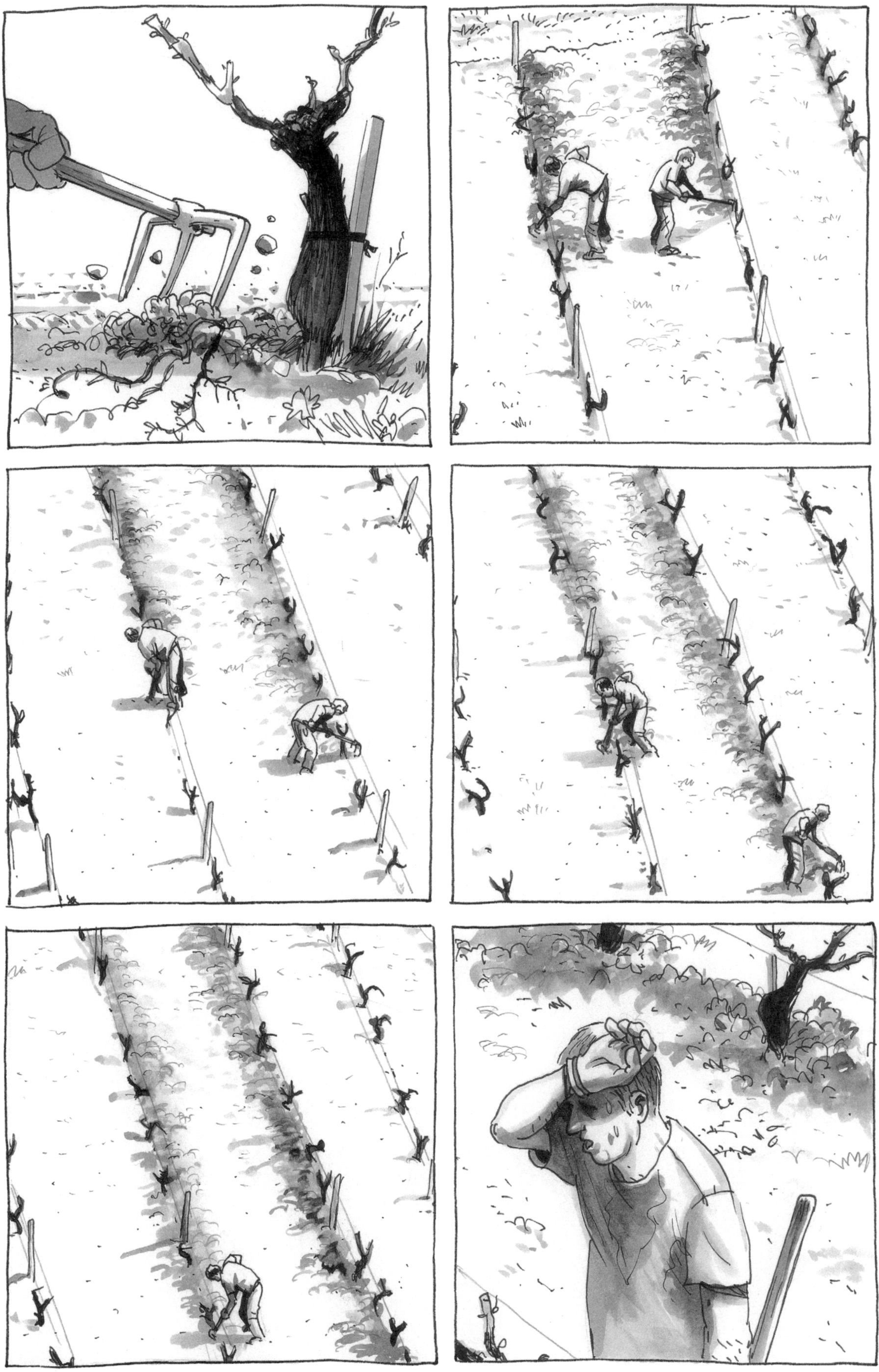

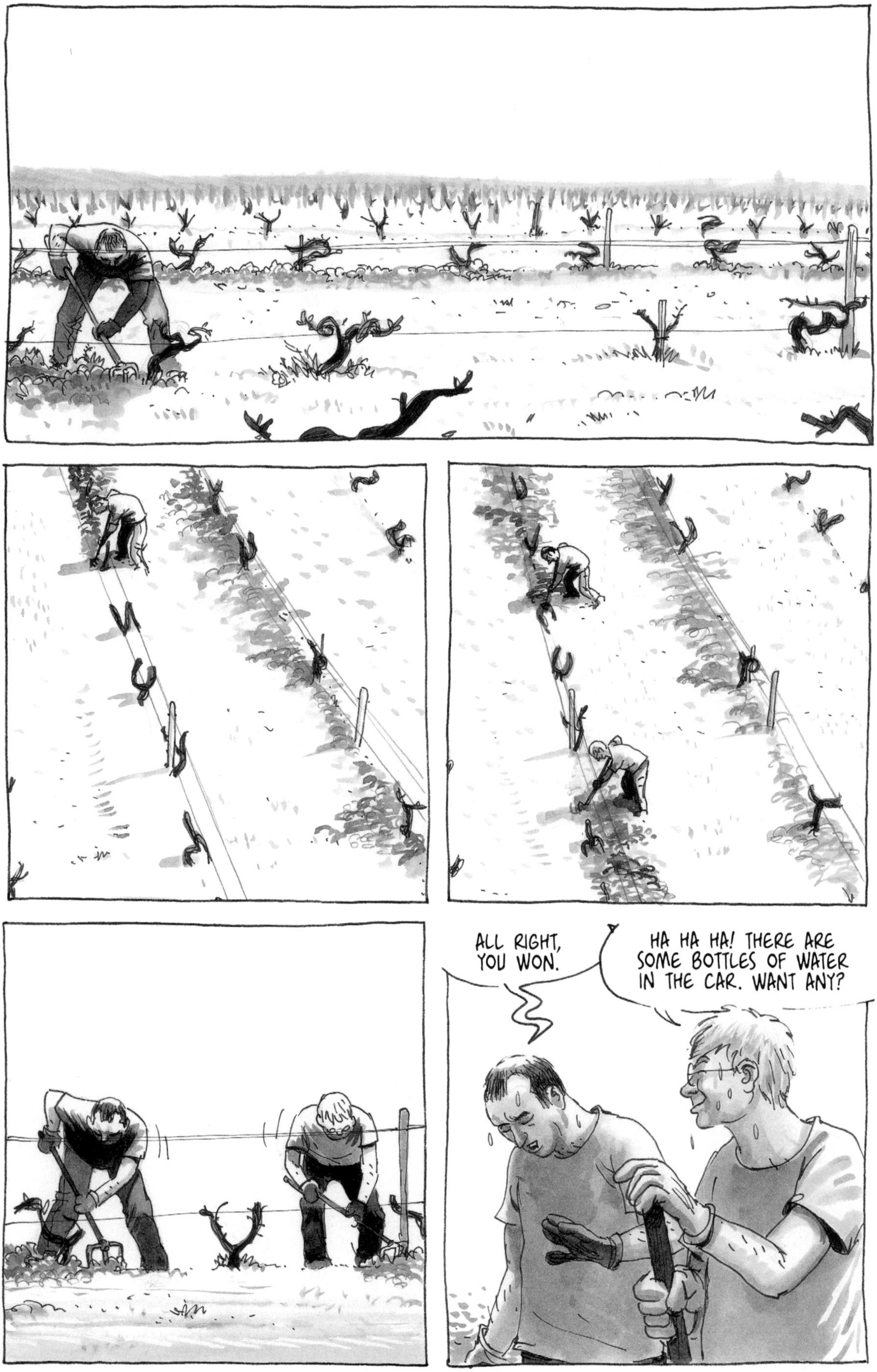
ALL RIGHT, YOU WON.
HA HA HA! THERE ARE SOME BOTTLES OF WATER IN THE CAR. WANT ANY?

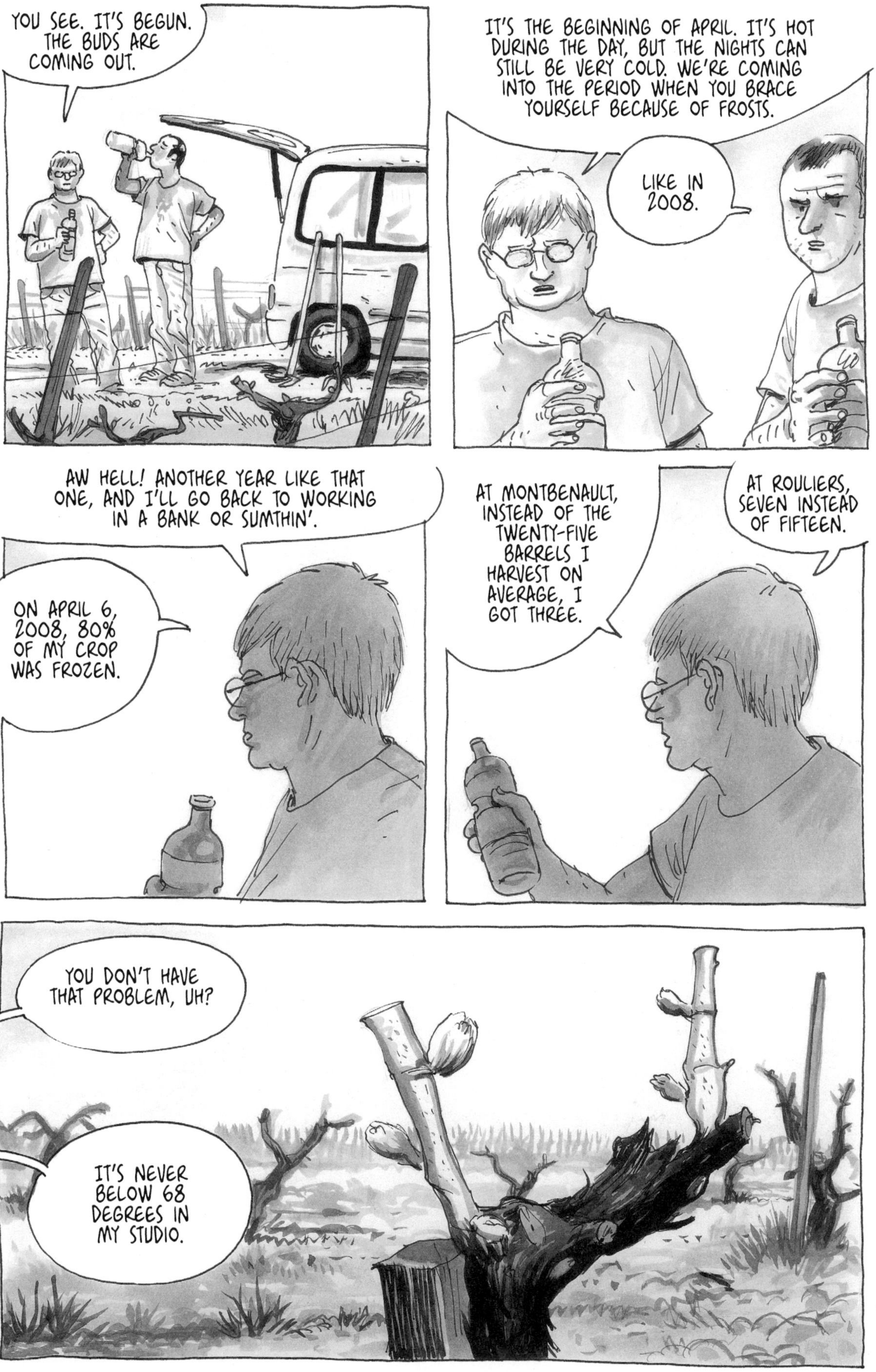
YOU SEE. IT'S BEGUN. THE BUDS ARE COMING OUT.
IT'S THE BEGINNING OF APRIL. IT'S HOT DURING THE DAY, BUT THE NIGHTS CAN STILL BE VERY COLD. WE'RE COMING INTO THE PERIOD WHEN YOU BRACE YOURSELF BECAUSE OF FROSTS.
LIKE IN 2008.
AW HELL! ANOTHER YEAR LIKE THAT ONE, AND I'LL GO BACK TO WORKING IN A BANK OR SUMTHIN'.
ON APRIL 6, 2008, 80% OF MY CROP WAS FROZEN.
AT MONTBENAULT, INSTEAD OF THE TWENTY-FIVE BARRELS I HARVEST ON AVERAGE, I GOT THREE.
AT ROULIERS, SEVEN INSTEAD OF FIFTEEN.
YOU DON'T HAVE THAT PROBLEM, UH?
IT'S NEVER BELOW 68 DEGREES IN MY STUDIO.

CHAPTER FIVE   WHAT GOES WITHOUT
SAYING

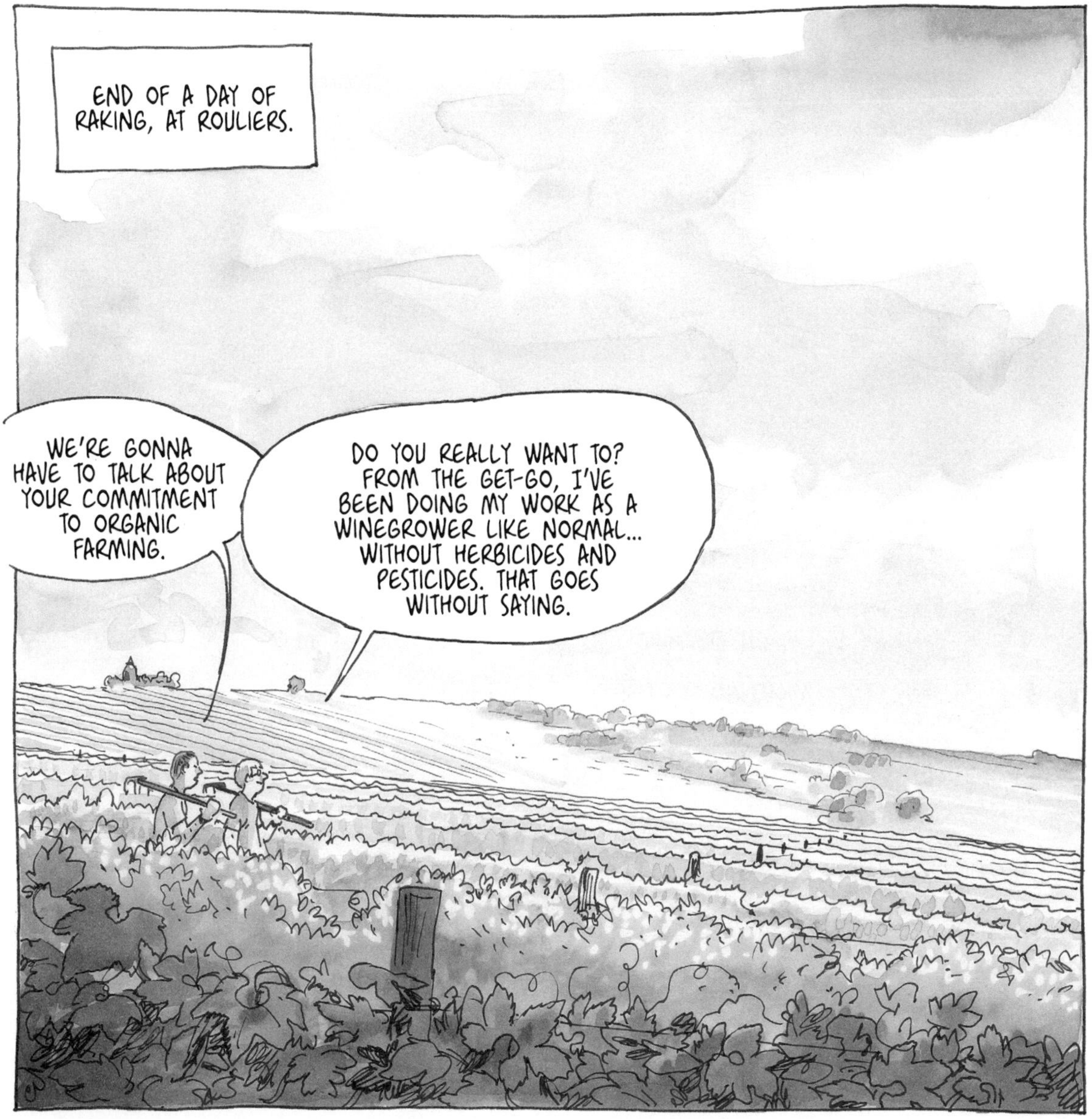
END OF A DAY OF RAKING, AT ROULIERS.
WE'RE GONNA HAVE TO TALK ABOUT YOUR COMMITMENT TO ORGANIC FARMING.
DO YOU REALLY WANT TO? FROM THE GET-GO, I'VE BEEN DOING MY WORK AS A WINEGROWER LIKE NORMAL... WITHOUT HERBICIDES AND PESTICIDES. THAT GOES WITHOUT SAYING.

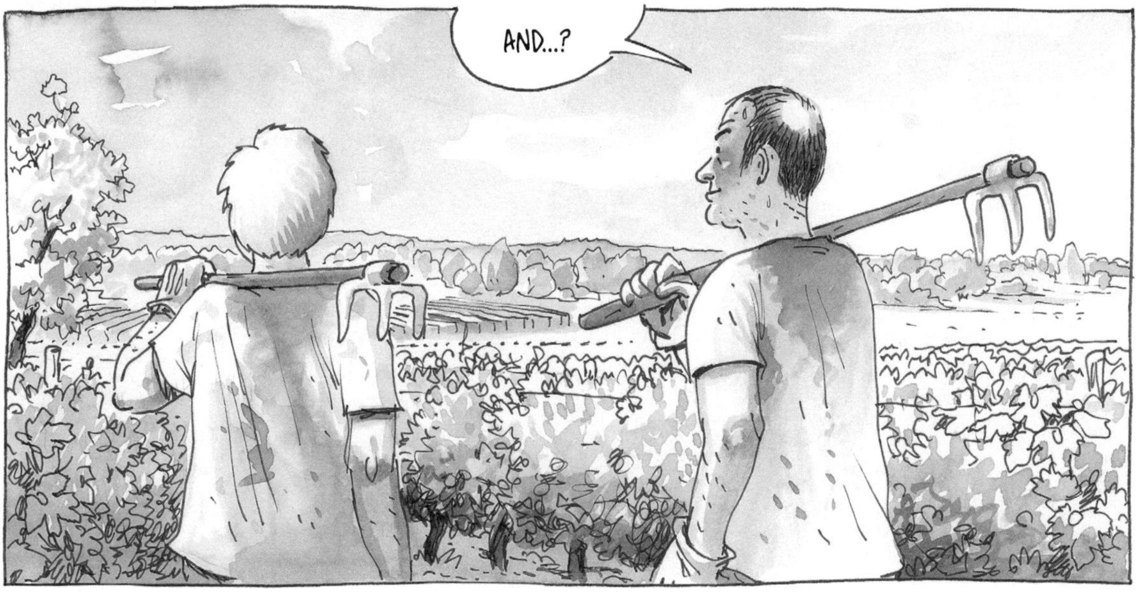
AND...?

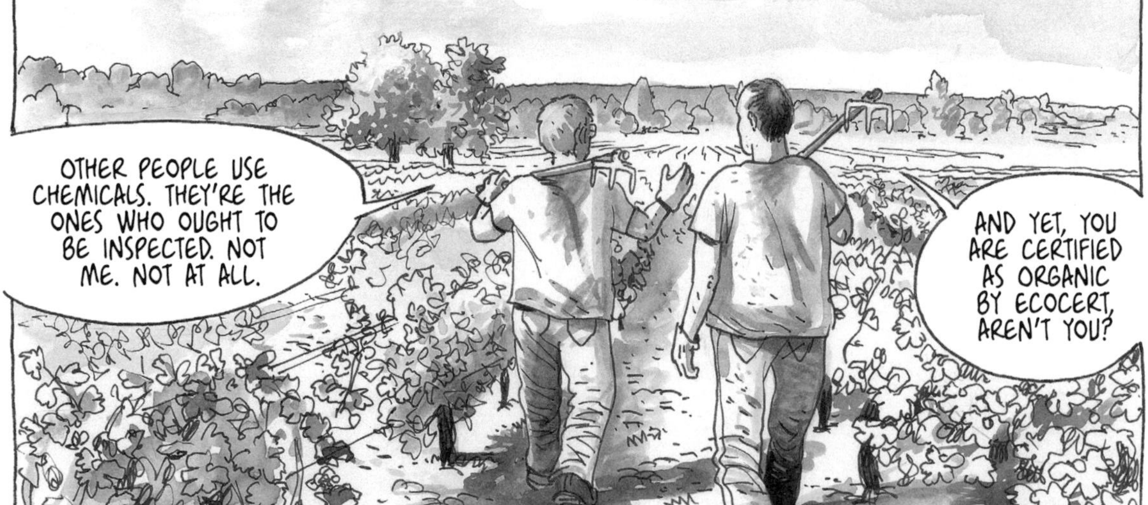
OTHER PEOPLE USE CHEMICALS. THEY'RE THE ONES WHO OUGHT TO BE INSPECTED. NOT ME. NOT AT ALL.
AND YET, YOU ARE CERTIFIED AS ORGANIC BY ECOCERT, AREN'T YOU?

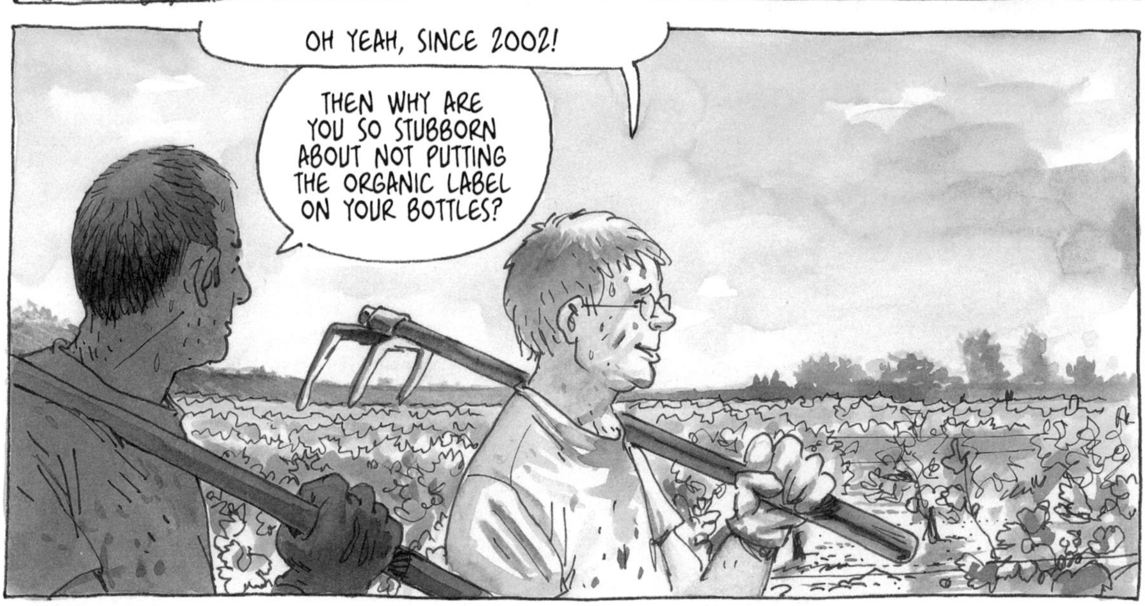
OH YEAH, SINCE 2002!
THEN WHY ARE YOU SO STUBBORN ABOUT NOT PUTTING THE ORGANIC LABEL ON YOUR BOTTLES?

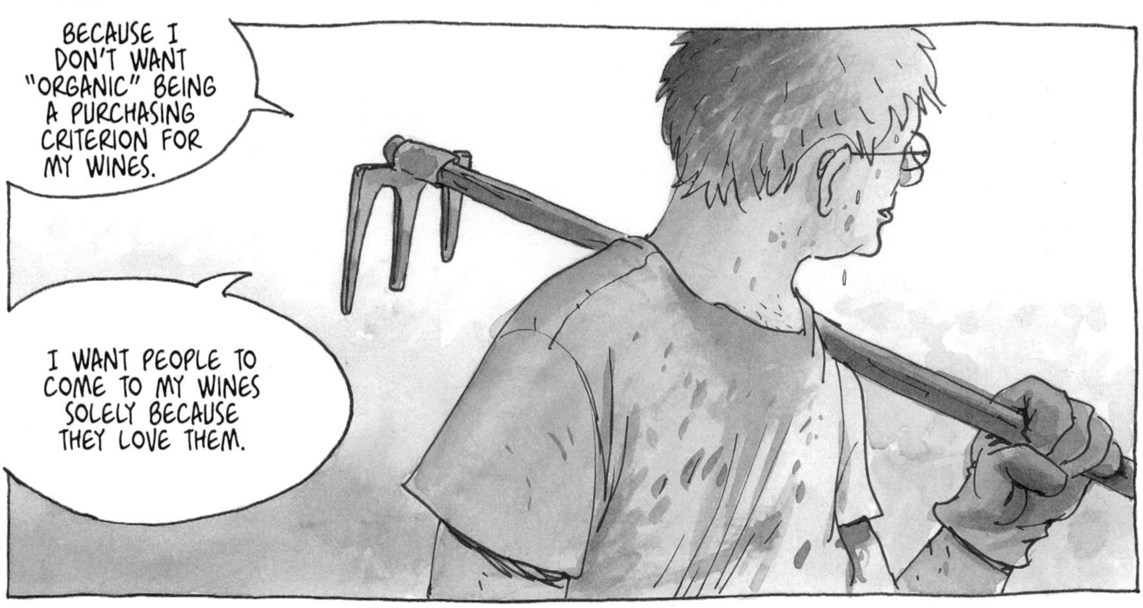
BECAUSE I DON'T WANT "ORGANIC" BEING A PURCHASING CRITERION FOR MY WINES.
I WANT PEOPLE TO COME TO MY WINES SOLELY BECAUSE THEY LOVE THEM.

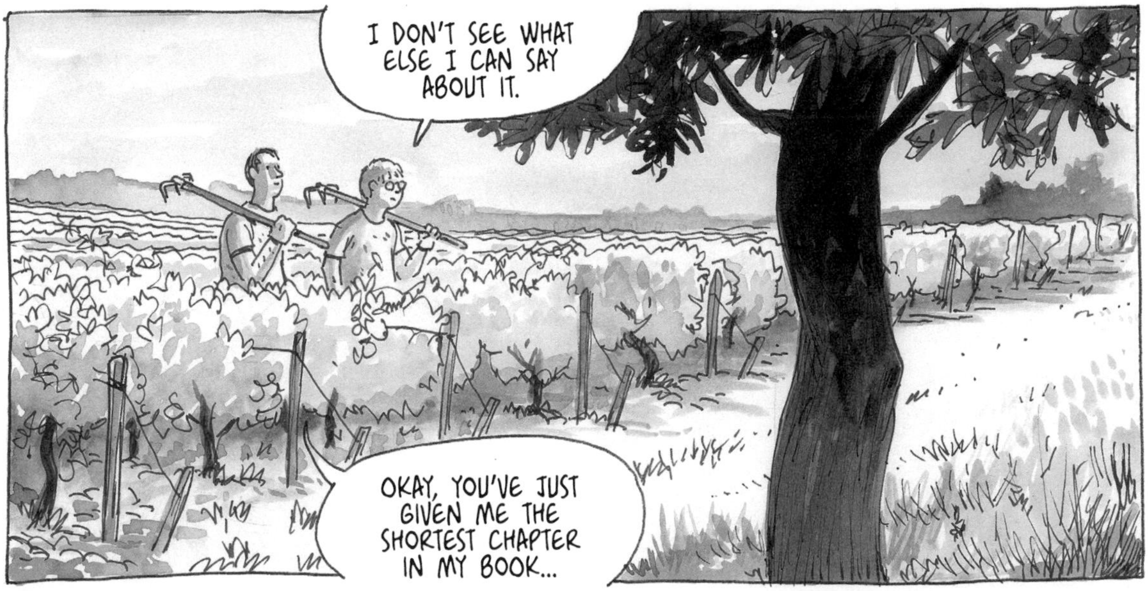
I DON'T SEE WHAT ELSE I CAN SAY ABOUT IT.
OKAY, YOU'VE JUST GIVEN ME THE SHORTEST CHAPTER IN MY BOOK...

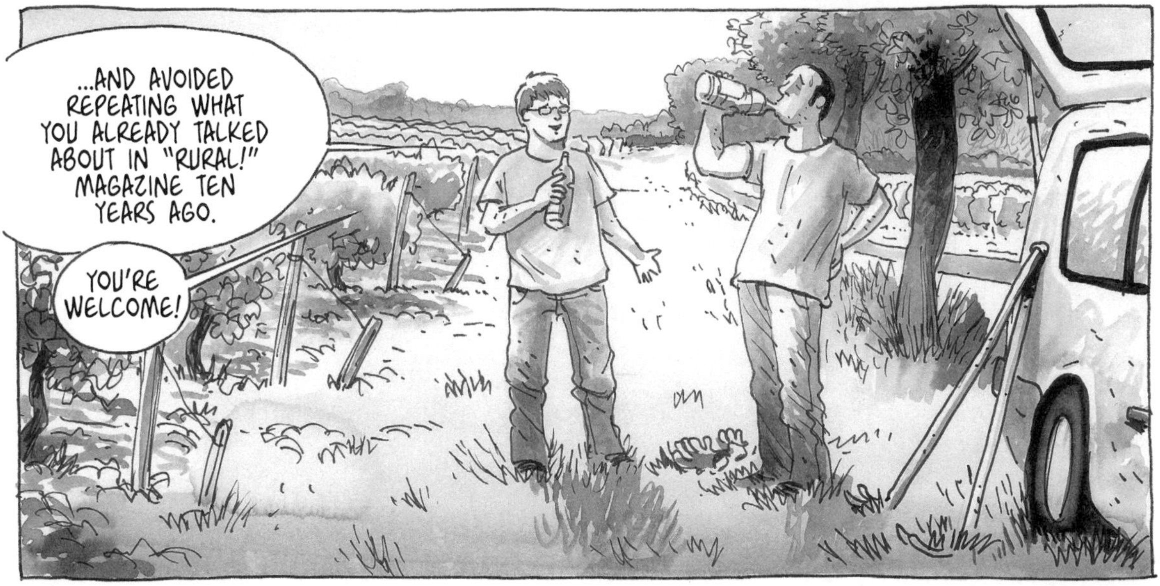
...AND AVOIDED REPEATING WHAT YOU ALREADY TALKED ABOUT IN "RURAL!" MAGAZINE TEN YEARS AGO.
YOU'RE WELCOME!

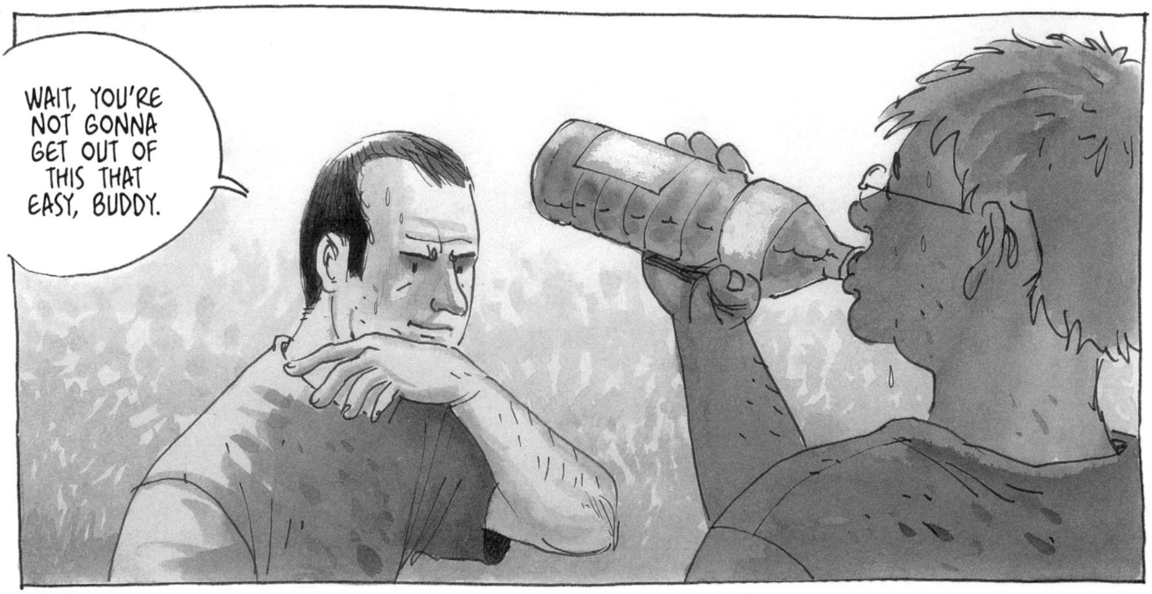
WAIT, YOU'RE NOT GONNA GET OUT OF THIS THAT EASY, BUDDY.

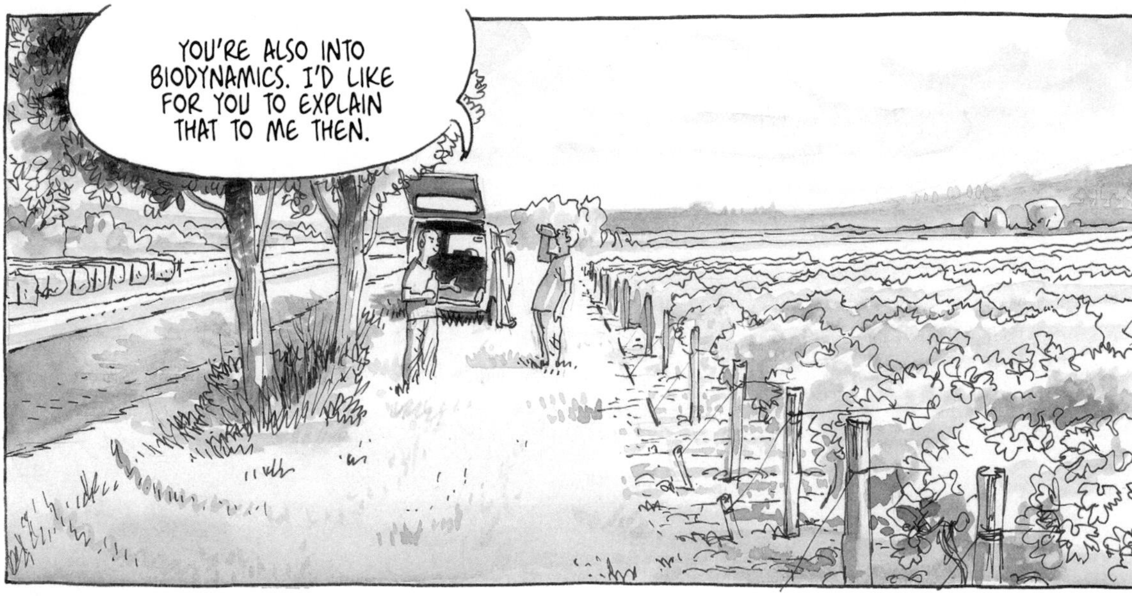
YOU'RE ALSO INTO BIODYNAMICS. I'D LIKE FOR YOU TO EXPLAIN THAT TO ME THEN.

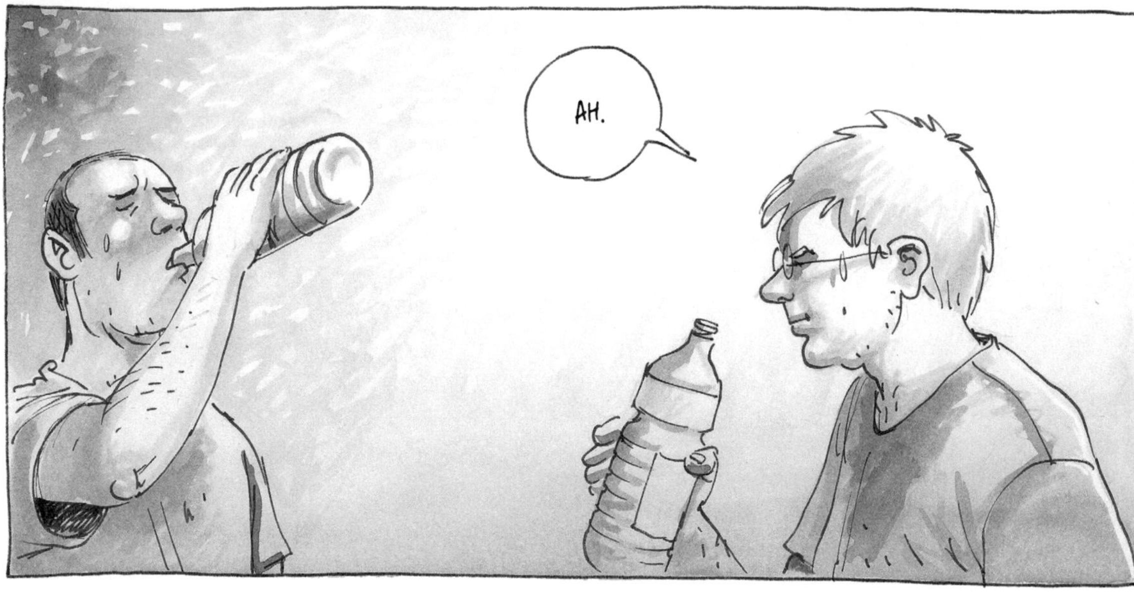
AH.

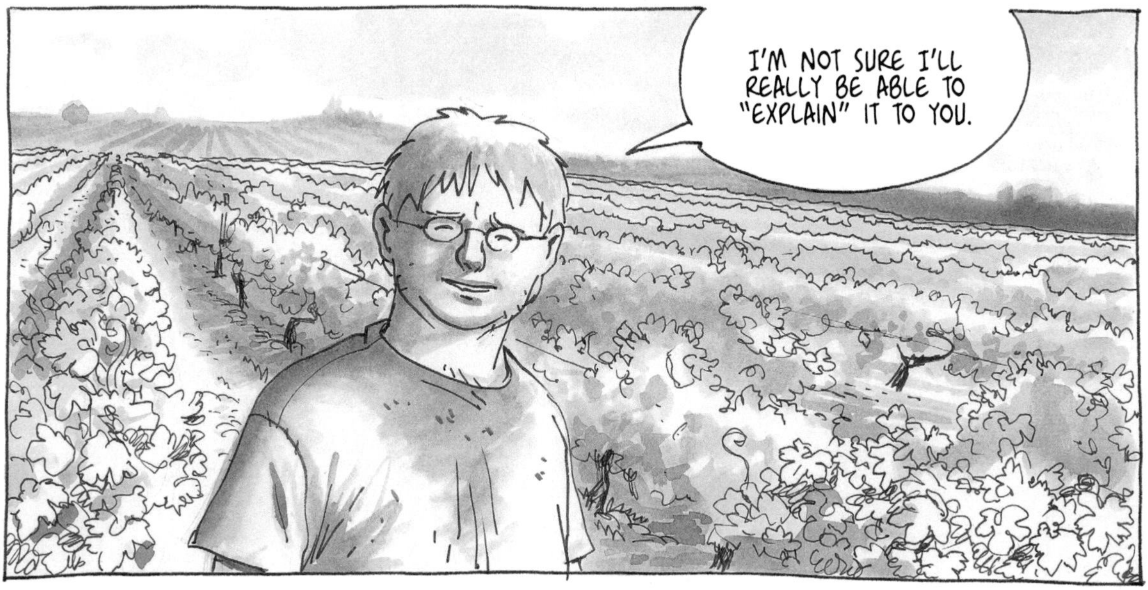
I'M NOT SURE I'LL REALLY BE ABLE TO "EXPLAIN" IT TO YOU.

CHAPTER SIX IN PRAISE OF MANURE

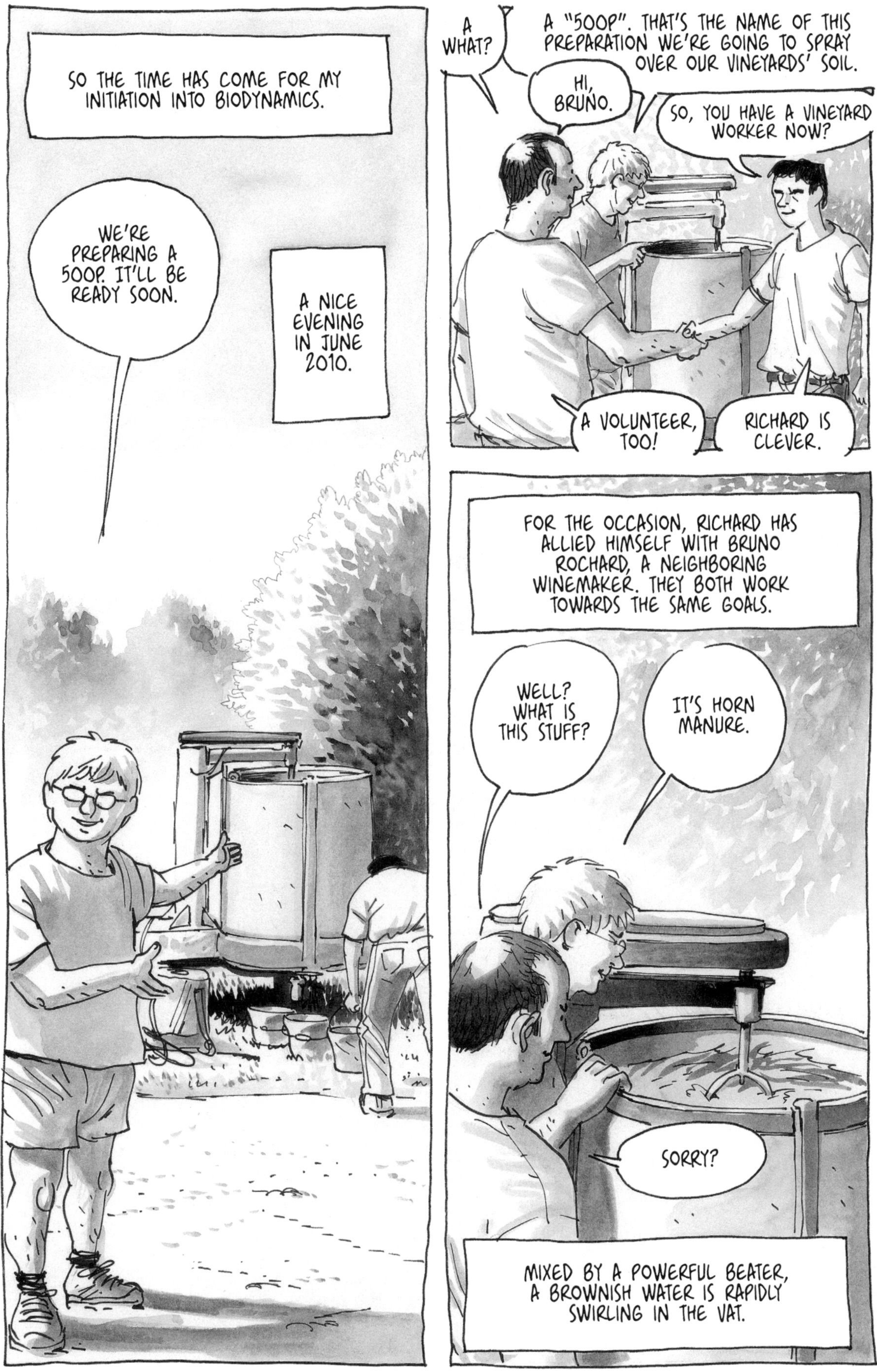
SO THE TIME HAS COME FOR MY INITIATION INTO BIODYNAMICS.
WE'RE PREPARING A 500P. IT'LL BE READY SOON.
A NICE EVENING IN JUNE 2010.
A WHAT?
A "500P". THAT'S THE NAME OF THIS PREPARATION WE'RE GOING TO SPRAY OVER OUR VINEYARDS' SOIL.
HI, BRUNO.
SO, YOU HAVE A VINEYARD WORKER NOW?
A VOLUNTEER, TOO!
RICHARD IS CLEVER.
FOR THE OCCASION, RICHARD HAS ALLIED HIMSELF WITH BRUNO ROCHARD, A NEIGHBORING WINEMAKER. THEY BOTH WORK TOWARDS THE SAME GOALS.
WELL? WHAT IS THIS STUFF?
IT'S HORN MANURE.
SORRY?
MIXED BY A POWERFUL BEATER, A BROWNISH WATER IS RAPIDLY SWIRLING IN THE VAT.

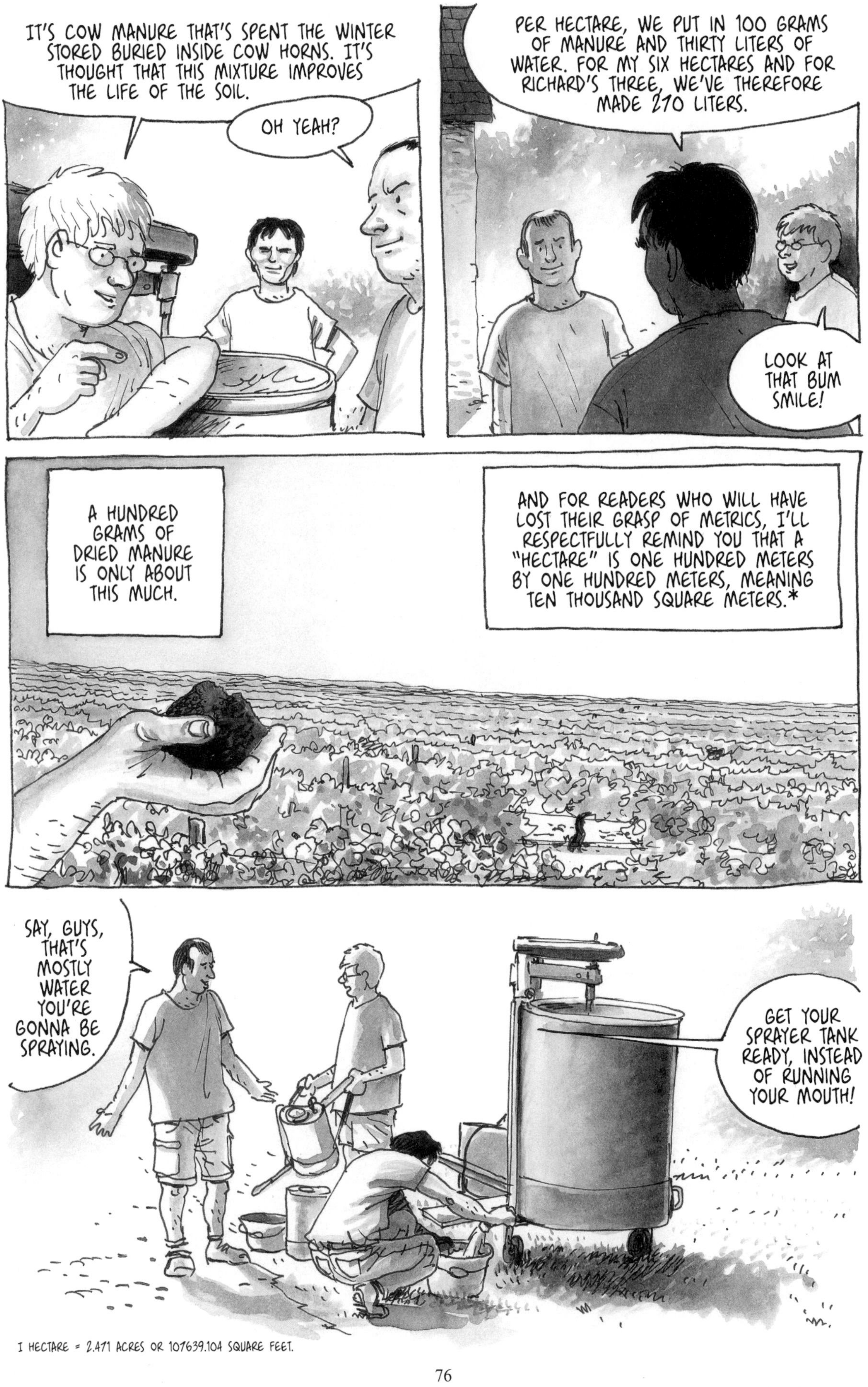
IT'S COW MANURE THAT'S SPENT THE WINTER STORED BURIED INSIDE COW HORNS. IT'S THOUGHT THAT THIS MIXTURE IMPROVES THE LIFE OF THE SOIL.
OH YEAH?
PER HECTARE, WE PUT IN 100 GRAMS OF MANURE AND THIRTY LITERS OF WATER. FOR MY SIX HECTARES AND FOR RICHARD'S THREE, WE'VE THEREFORE MADE 270 LITERS.
LOOK AT THAT BUM SMILE!
A HUNDRED GRAMS OF DRIED MANURE IS ONLY ABOUT THIS MUCH.
AND FOR READERS WHO WILL HAVE LOST THEIR GRASP OF METRICS, I'LL RESPECTFULLY REMIND YOU THAT A "HECTARE" IS ONE HUNDRED METERS BY ONE HUNDRED METERS, MEANING TEN THOUSAND SQUARE METERS.*
SAY, GUYS, THAT'S MOSTLY WATER YOU'RE GONNA BE SPRAYING.
GET YOUR SPRAYER TANK READY, INSTEAD OF RUNNING YOUR MOUTH!

1 HECTARE = 2.471 ACRES OR 107639.104 SQUARE FEET.

THERE. IT'S FULL.

IT HAS A REAL IMPACT, YOU KNOW. IT TRULY REVITALIZES THE SOIL!

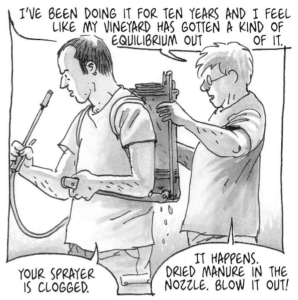

I'VE BEEN DOING IT FOR TEN YEARS AND I FEEL LIKE MY VINEYARD HAS GOTTEN A KIND OF EQUILIBRIUM OUT OF IT.

YOUR SPRAYER IS CLOGGED.

IT HAPPENS. DRIED MANURE IN THE NOZZLE. BLOW IT OUT!

FFLLFP

IN THE END, THIS DILUTION SUITS ME.

OKAY THEN, HOW DOES IT HAVE SUCH AN EFFECT?

LISTEN, I USE A TRACTOR, TOO. I USE IT ALMOST EVERY DAY.

BUT DON'T ASK ME HOW IT WORKS. I HAVEN'T GOT A CLUE!

MMM YEAH, I NOTICE THAT, ON THIS SUBJECT, YOU'RE SHOWING A PRUDENCE I'VE NOT OBSERVED SO FAR.

I'M NOT "PRUDENT" ABOUT THE PRINCIPLE OF BIODYNAMICS.

I'M "PRUDENT" ABOUT MY EXPERTISE IN BIODYNAMICS.

IS THERE ANY DIFFERENCE BETWEEN A WINE COMING FROM A VINE CULTIVATED ORGANICALLY ONLY AND A WINE CULTIVATED ON BIODYNAMICS? HAVE YOU DONE ANY TESTS?

NAH. MY VINEYWARD'S TOO LITTLE FOR THAT. BUT...

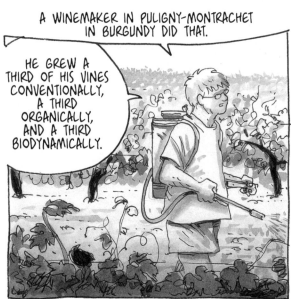

A WINEMAKER IN PULIGNY-MONTRACHET IN BURGUNDY DID THAT.

HE GREW A THIRD OF HIS VINES CONVENTIONALLY, A THIRD ORGANICALLY, AND A THIRD BIODYNAMICALLY.

AND?

ME, A DRINKER, I FOUND THE THIRD ONE A HECKUVA LOT RICHER, MORE VIBRANT!

THAT'S IT. I WAS CONVINCED EMPIRICALLY. DON'T ASK ME FOR ANY TECHNICAL EXPLANATIONS.

VIBRANT WINES! THAT'S WHAT WE'RE LOOKING FOR OUT OF THIS PRACTICE AND THERE'S THIS, TOO: SPRAYING WITH A TRACTOR WOULD BE A LOT EASIER, BUT DOING IT BY HAND IS A MOMENT OF PRIVILEGE. BEING SO CLOSE TO THE VINE IS A PLEASURE!

I AGREE! IN FRANCE, BIODYNAMICS IS ABOUT THIRTY YEARS OLD. IT'S OLDER IN NORTHERN EUROPE, BUT THE IMPORTANT WORD IS THIS: WE'RE **SEARCHING**.

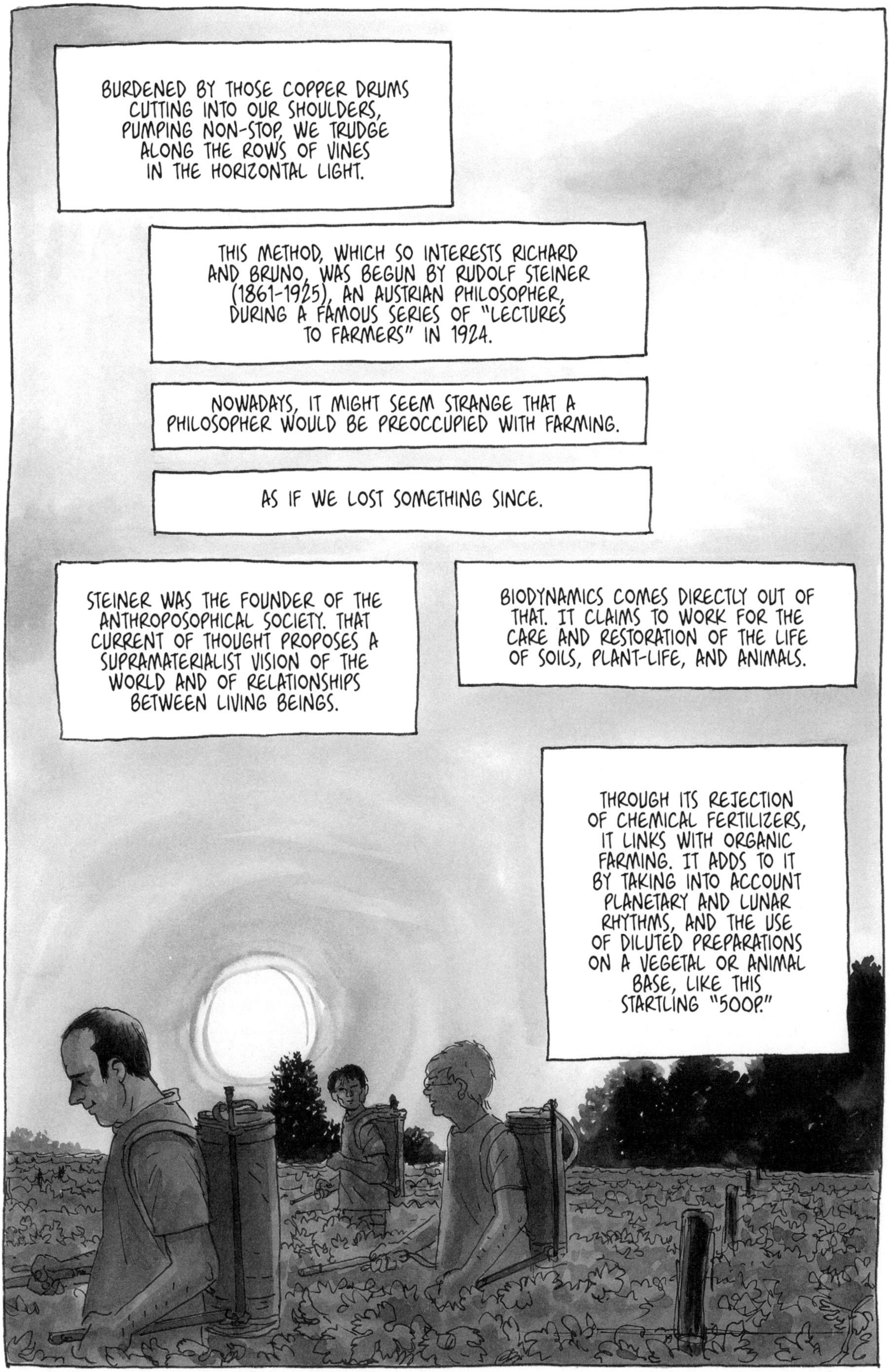
BURDENED BY THOSE COPPER DRUMS CUTTING INTO OUR SHOULDERS, PUMPING NON-STOP, WE TRUDGE ALONG THE ROWS OF VINES IN THE HORIZONTAL LIGHT.
THIS METHOD, WHICH SO INTERESTS RICHARD AND BRUNO, WAS BEGUN BY RUDOLF STEINER (1861-1925), AN AUSTRIAN PHILOSOPHER, DURING A FAMOUS SERIES OF "LECTURES TO FARMERS" IN 1924.
NOWADAYS, IT MIGHT SEEM STRANGE THAT A PHILOSOPHER WOULD BE PREOCCUPIED WITH FARMING.
AS IF WE LOST SOMETHING SINCE.
STEINER WAS THE FOUNDER OF THE ANTHROPOSOPHICAL SOCIETY. THAT CURRENT OF THOUGHT PROPOSES A SUPRAMATERIALIST VISION OF THE WORLD AND OF RELATIONSHIPS BETWEEN LIVING BEINGS.
BIODYNAMICS COMES DIRECTLY OUT OF THAT. IT CLAIMS TO WORK FOR THE CARE AND RESTORATION OF THE LIFE OF SOILS, PLANT-LIFE, AND ANIMALS.
THROUGH ITS REJECTION OF CHEMICAL FERTILIZERS, IT LINKS WITH ORGANIC FARMING. IT ADDS TO IT BY TAKING INTO ACCOUNT PLANETARY AND LUNAR RHYTHMS, AND THE USE OF DILUTED PREPARATIONS ON A VEGETAL OR ANIMAL BASE, LIKE THIS STARTLING "500P."

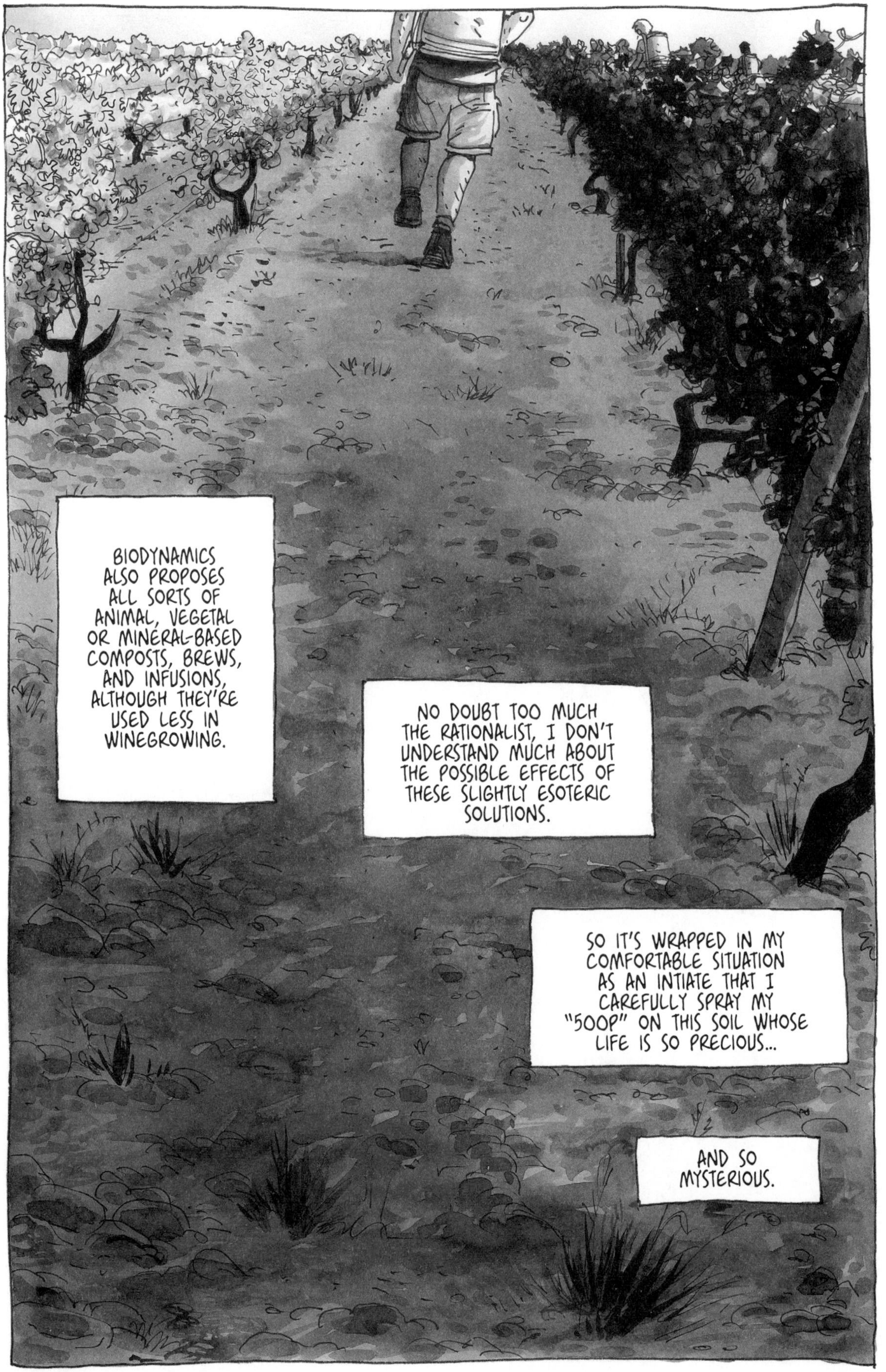
BIODYNAMICS ALSO PROPOSES ALL SORTS OF ANIMAL, VEGETAL OR MINERAL-BASED COMPOSTS, BREWS, AND INFUSIONS, ALTHOUGH THEY'RE USED LESS IN WINEGROWING.
NO DOUBT TOO MUCH THE RATIONALIST, I DON'T UNDERSTAND MUCH ABOUT THE POSSIBLE EFFECTS OF THESE SLIGHTLY ESOTERIC SOLUTIONS.
SO IT'S WRAPPED IN MY COMFORTABLE SITUATION AS AN INTIATE THAT I CAREFULLY SPRAY MY "500P" ON THIS SOIL WHOSE LIFE IS SO PRECIOUS...
AND SO MYSTERIOUS.

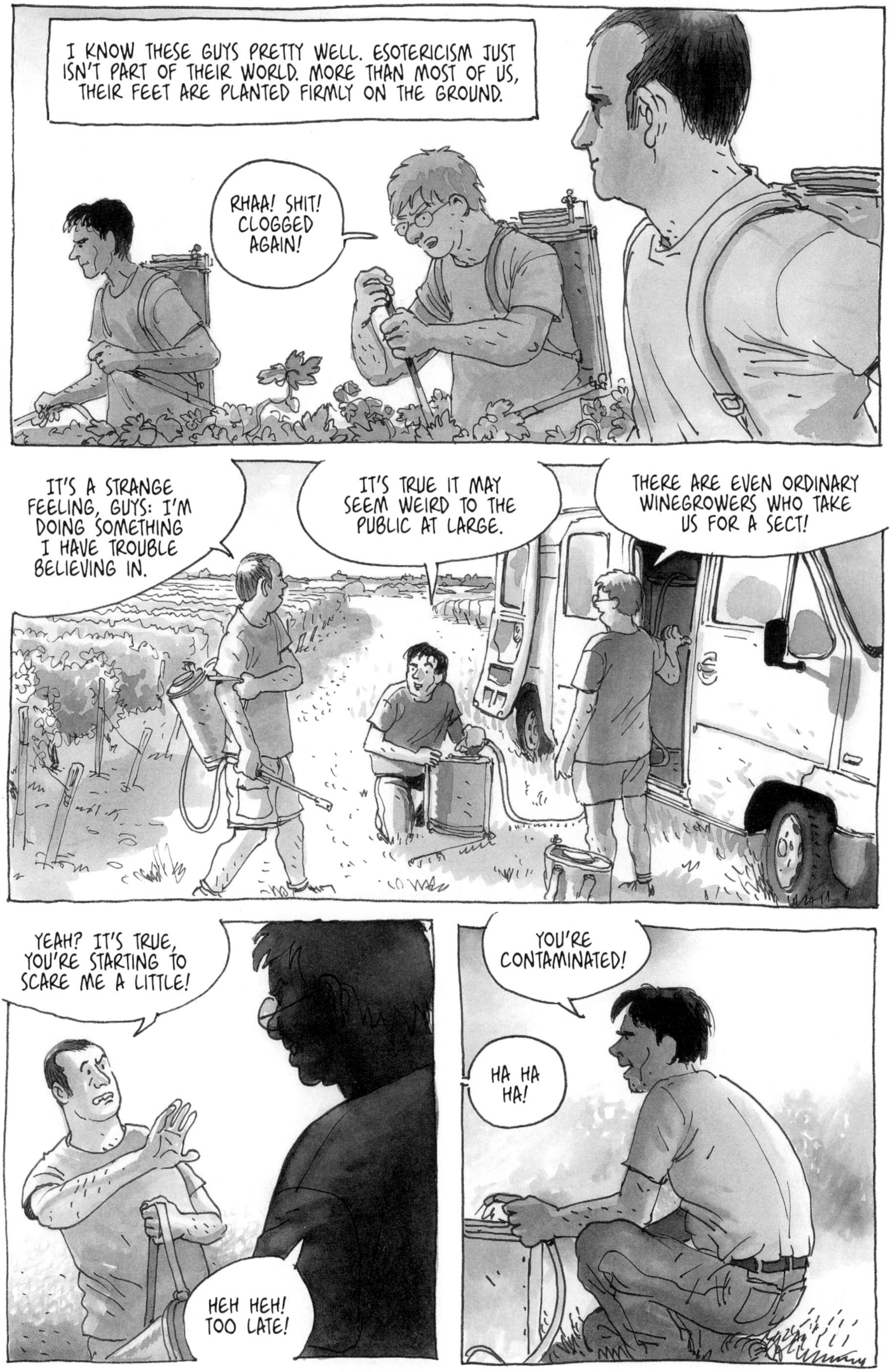
I KNOW THESE GUYS PRETTY WELL. ESOTERICISM JUST ISN'T PART OF THEIR WORLD. MORE THAN MOST OF US, THEIR FEET ARE PLANTED FIRMLY ON THE GROUND.
RHAA! SHIT! CLOGGED AGAIN!
IT'S A STRANGE FEELING, GUYS: I'M DOING SOMETHING I HAVE TROUBLE BELIEVING IN.
IT'S TRUE IT MAY SEEM WEIRD TO THE PUBLIC AT LARGE.
THERE ARE EVEN ORDINARY WINEGROWERS WHO TAKE US FOR A SECT!
YEAH? IT'S TRUE, YOU'RE STARTING TO SCARE ME A LITTLE!
HEH HEH! TOO LATE!
YOU'RE CONTAMINATED!
HA HA HA!

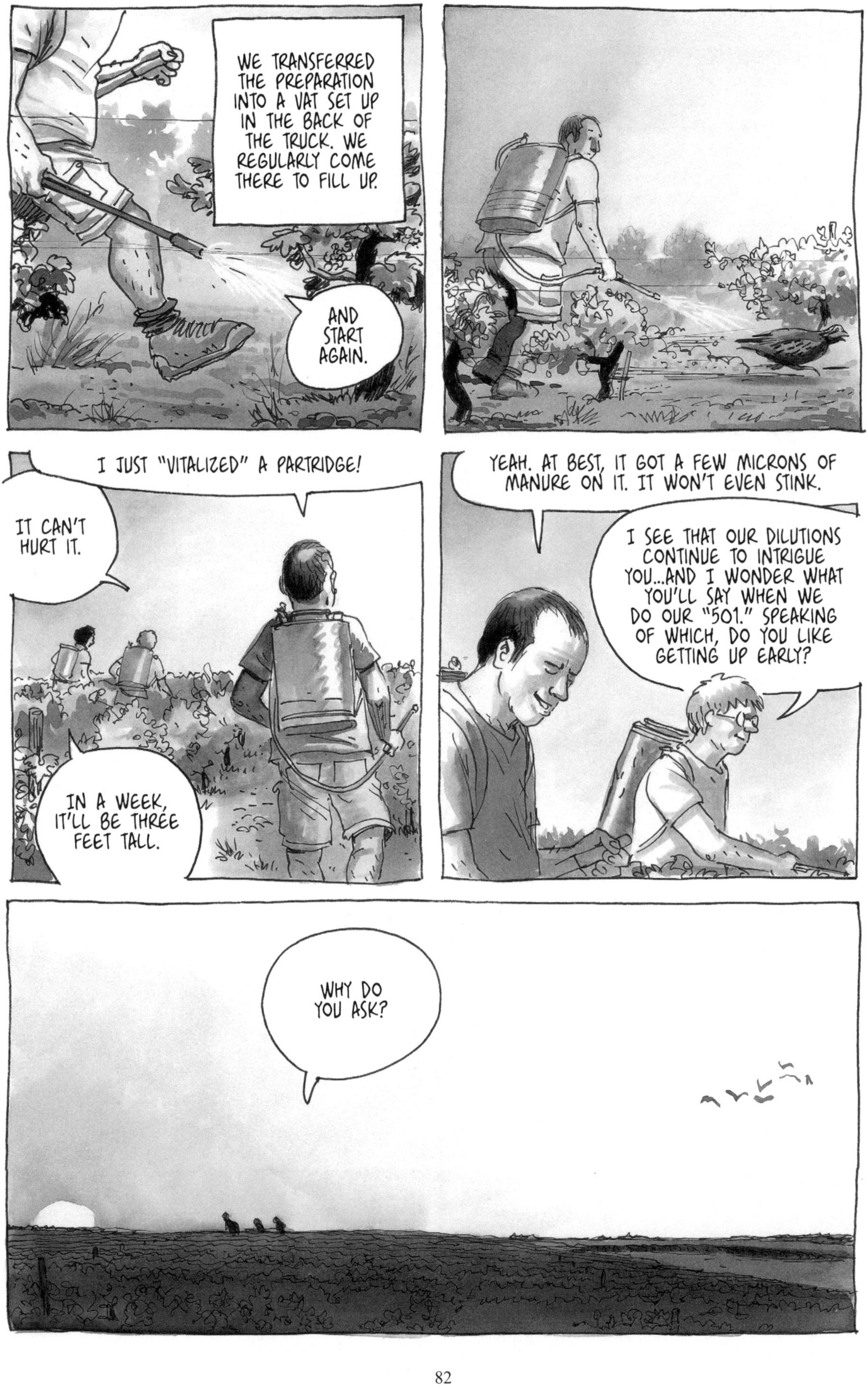
WE TRANSFERRED THE PREPARATION INTO A VAT SET UP IN THE BACK OF THE TRUCK. WE REGULARLY COME THERE TO FILL UP.
AND START AGAIN.
I JUST "VITALIZED" A PARTRIDGE!
IT CAN'T HURT IT.
IN A WEEK, IT'LL BE THREE FEET TALL.
YEAH. AT BEST, IT GOT A FEW MICRONS OF MANURE ON IT. IT WON'T EVEN STINK.
I SEE THAT OUR DILUTIONS CONTINUE TO INTRIGUE YOU...AND I WONDER WHAT YOU'LL SAY WHEN WE DO OUR "501." SPEAKING OF WHICH, DO YOU LIKE GETTING UP EARLY?
WHY DO YOU ASK?

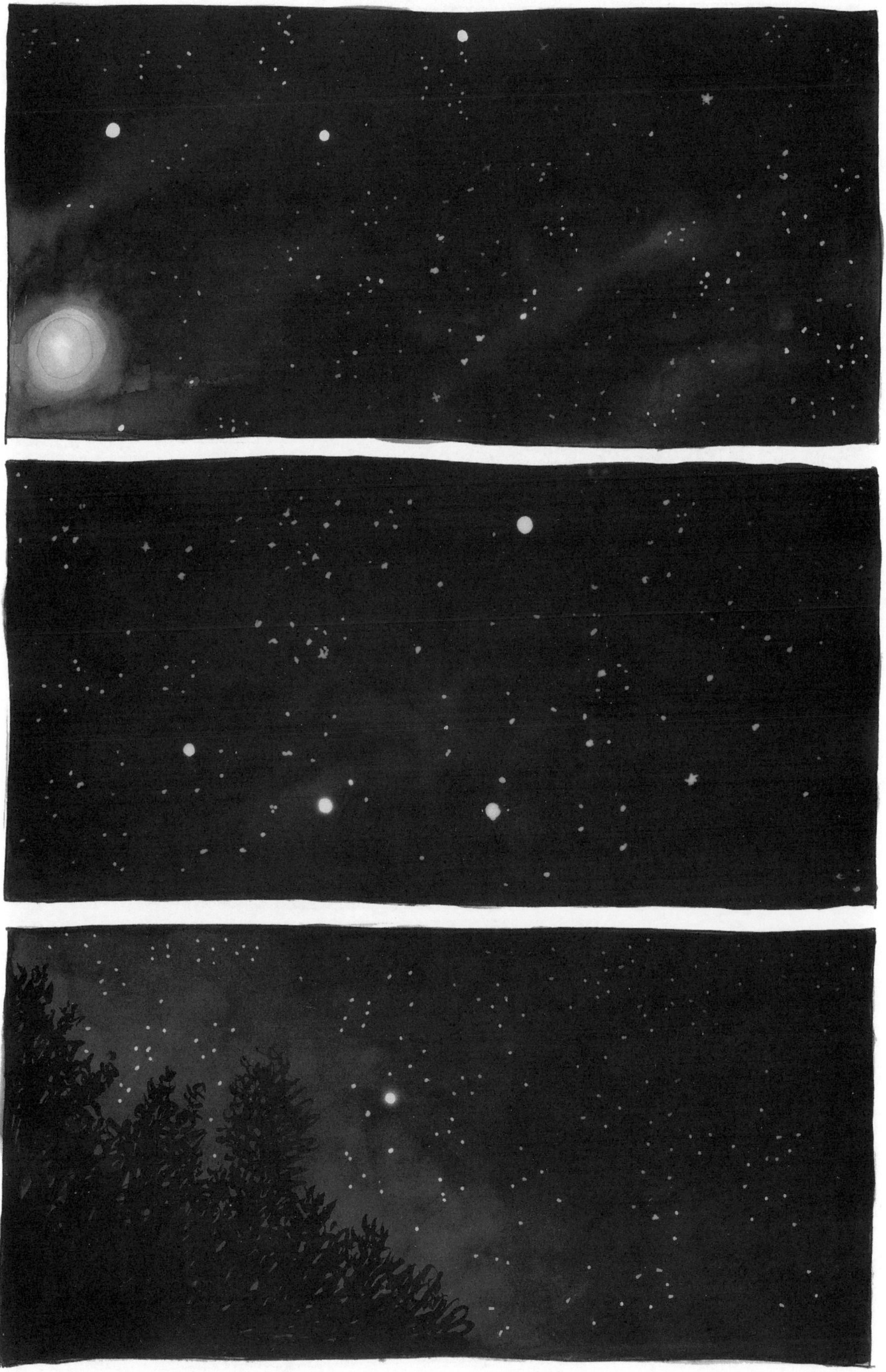

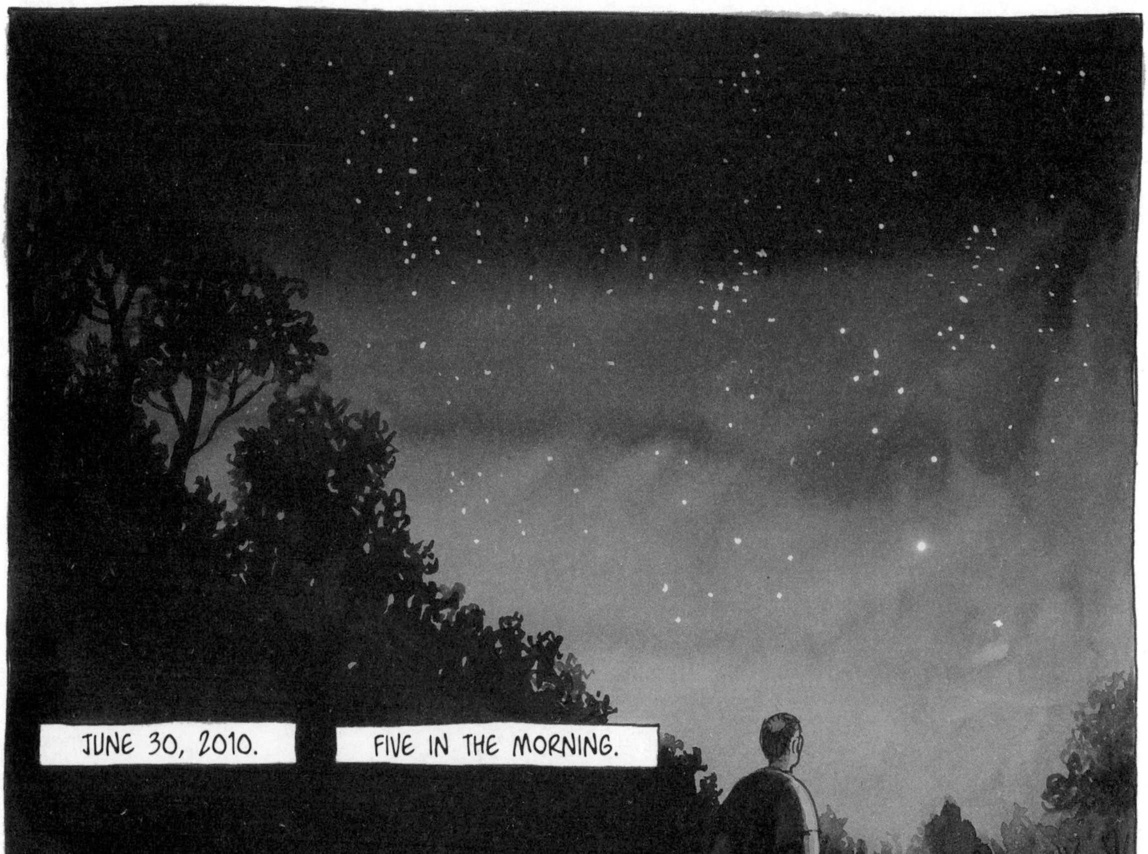
JUNE 30, 2010.
FIVE IN THE MORNING.

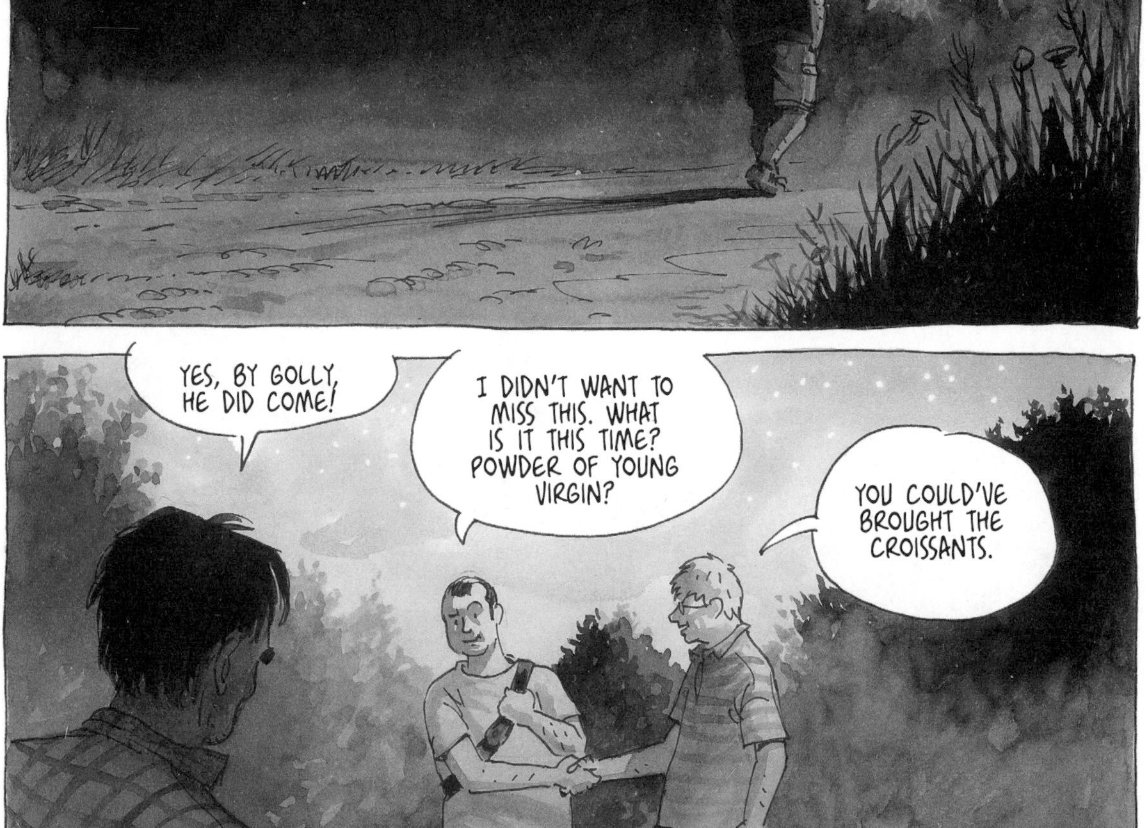
YES, BY GOLLY, HE DID COME!
I DIDN'T WANT TO MISS THIS. WHAT IS IT THIS TIME? POWDER OF YOUNG VIRGIN?
YOU COULD'VE BROUGHT THE CROISSANTS.

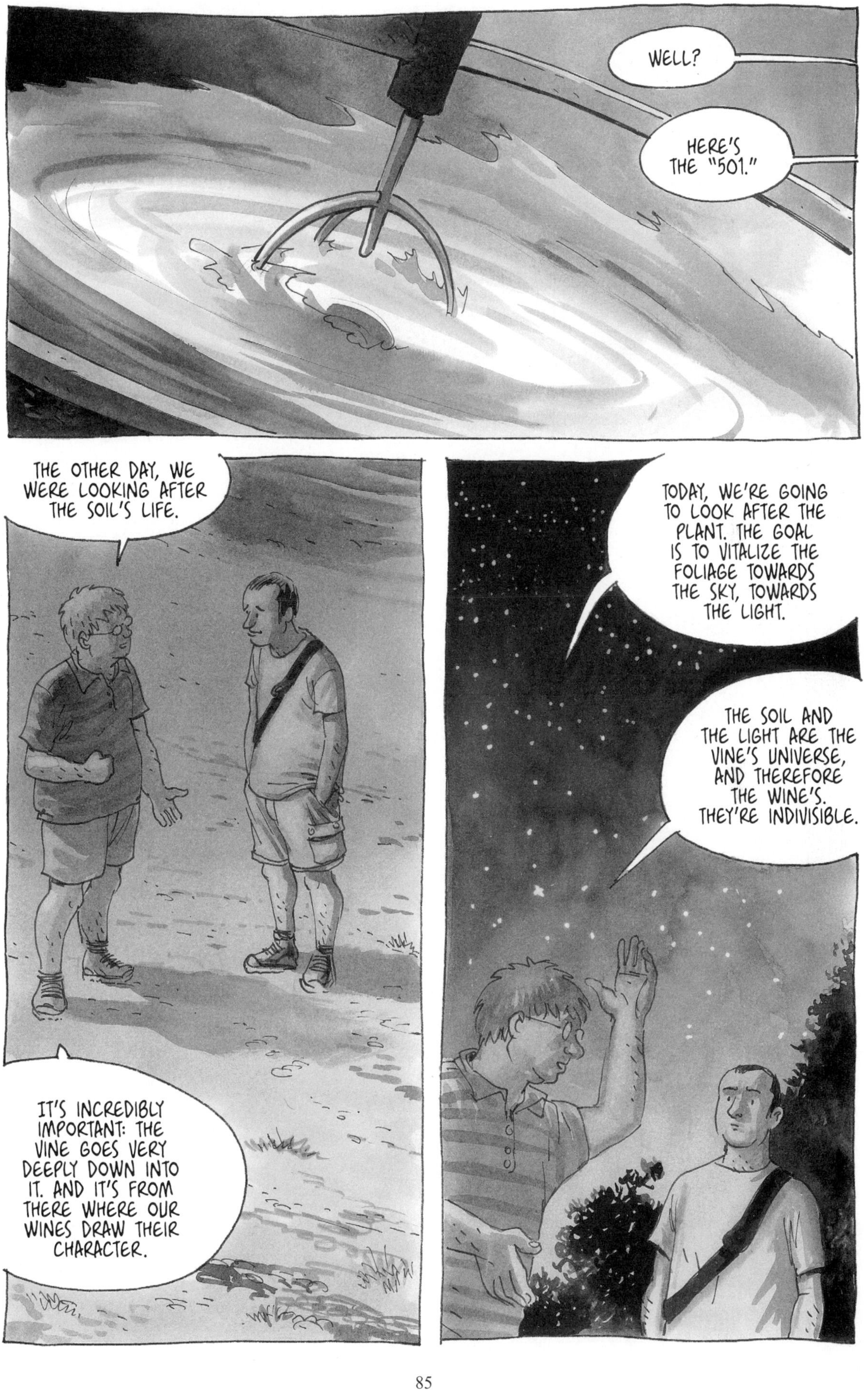

WELL?
HERE'S THE "501."
THE OTHER DAY, WE WERE LOOKING AFTER THE SOIL'S LIFE.
IT'S INCREDIBLY IMPORTANT: THE VINE GOES VERY DEEPLY DOWN INTO IT. AND IT'S FROM THERE WHERE OUR WINES DRAW THEIR CHARACTER.
TODAY, WE'RE GOING TO LOOK AFTER THE PLANT. THE GOAL IS TO VITALIZE THE FOLIAGE TOWARDS THE SKY, TOWARDS THE LIGHT.
THE SOIL AND THE LIGHT ARE THE VINE'S UNIVERSE, AND THEREFORE THE WINE'S. THEY'RE INDIVISIBLE.

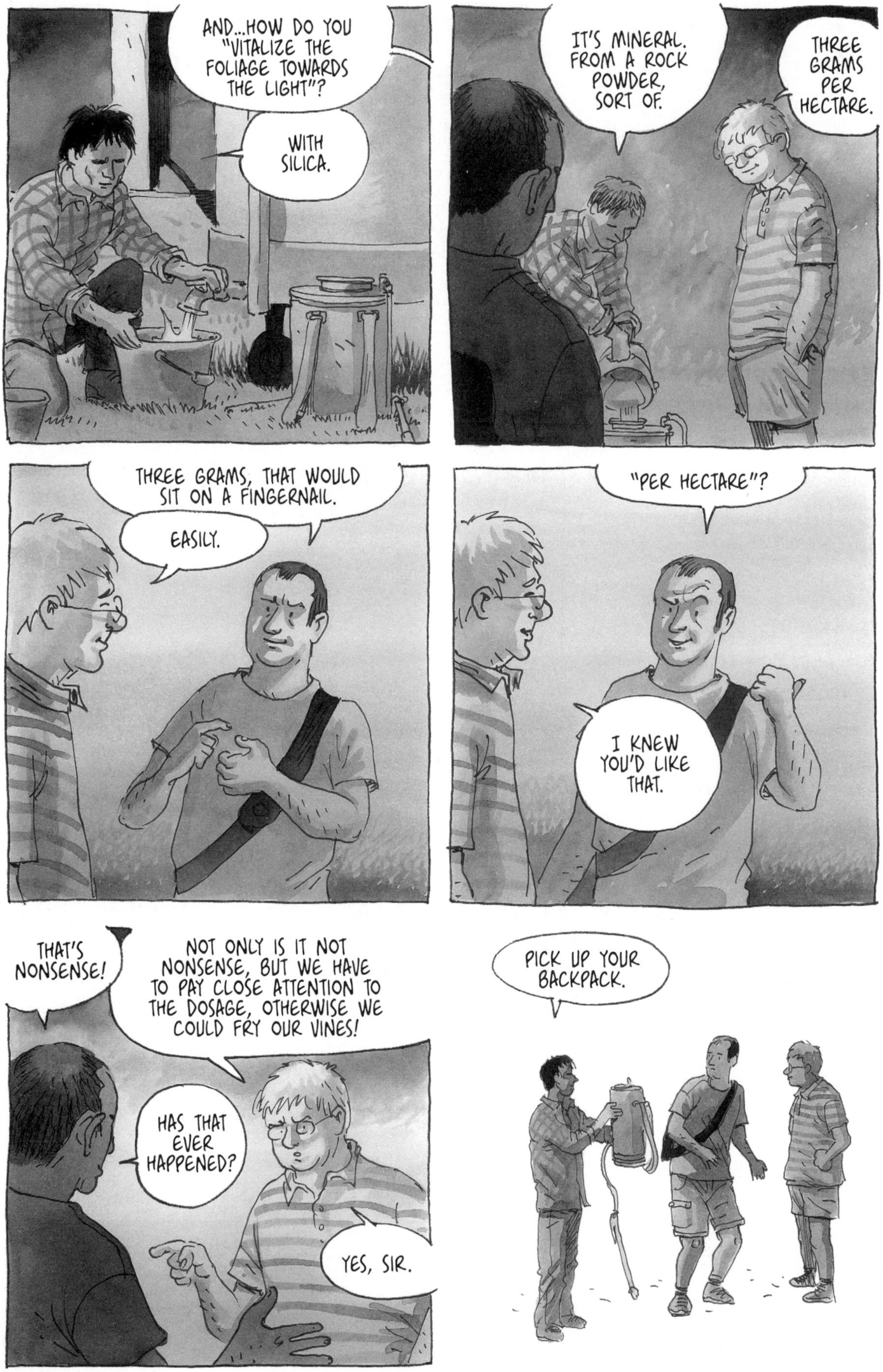
AND...HOW DO YOU "VITALIZE THE FOLIAGE TOWARDS THE LIGHT"?
WITH SILICA.
IT'S MINERAL. FROM A ROCK POWDER, SORT OF.
THREE GRAMS PER HECTARE.
THREE GRAMS, THAT WOULD SIT ON A FINGERNAIL.
EASILY.
"PER HECTARE"?
I KNEW YOU'D LIKE THAT.
THAT'S NONSENSE!
NOT ONLY IS IT NOT NONSENSE, BUT WE HAVE TO PAY CLOSE ATTENTION TO THE DOSAGE, OTHERWISE WE COULD FRY OUR VINES!
HAS THAT EVER HAPPENED?
YES, SIR.
PICK UP YOUR BACKPACK.

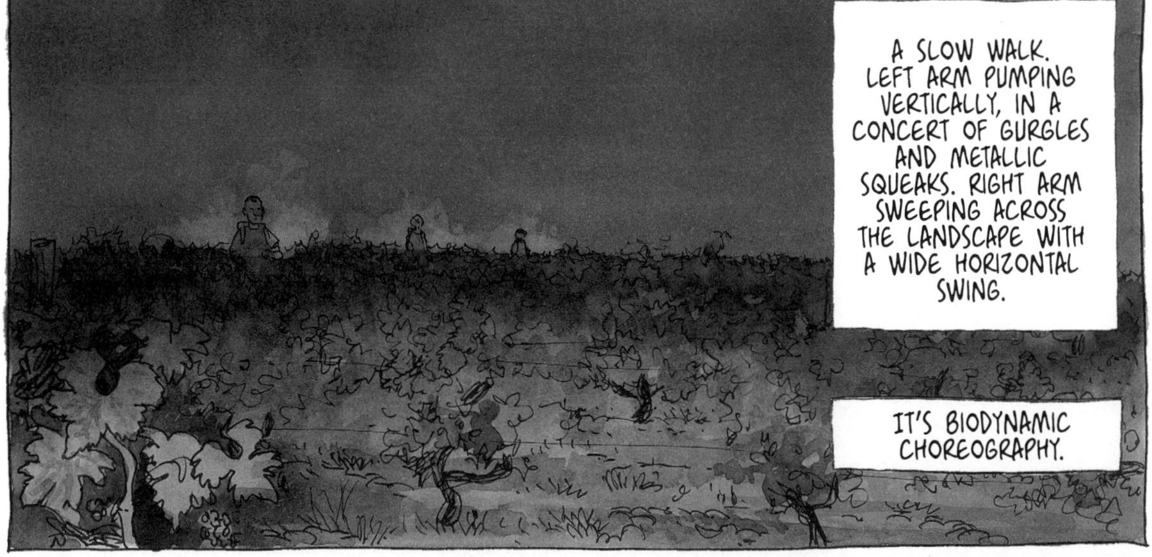
A SLOW WALK. LEFT ARM PUMPING VERTICALLY, IN A CONCERT OF GURGLES AND METALLIC SQUEAKS. RIGHT ARM SWEEPING ACROSS THE LANDSCAPE WITH A WIDE HORIZONTAL SWING.
IT'S BIODYNAMIC CHOREOGRAPHY.
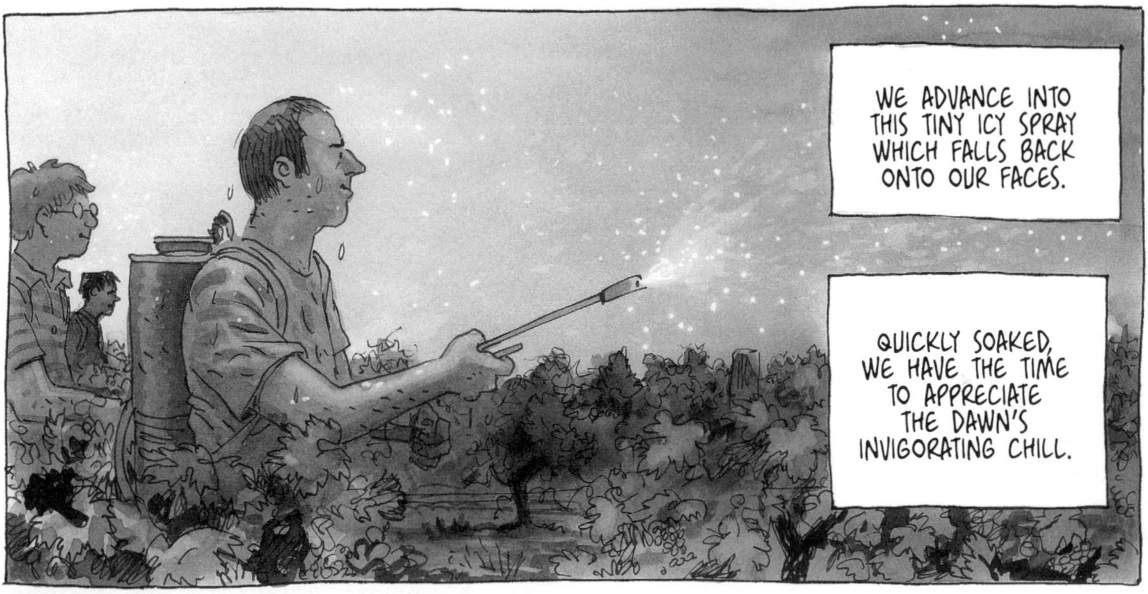
WE ADVANCE INTO THIS TINY ICY SPRAY WHICH FALLS BACK ONTO OUR FACES.
QUICKLY SOAKED, WE HAVE THE TIME TO APPRECIATE THE DAWN'S INVIGORATING CHILL.
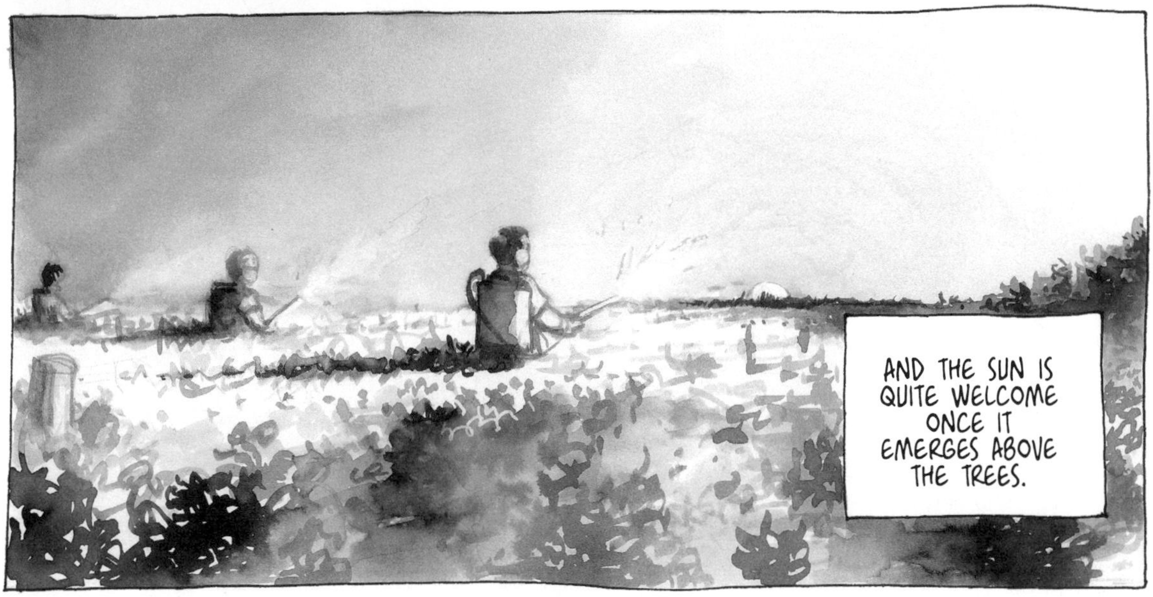
AND THE SUN IS QUITE WELCOME ONCE IT EMERGES ABOVE THE TREES.

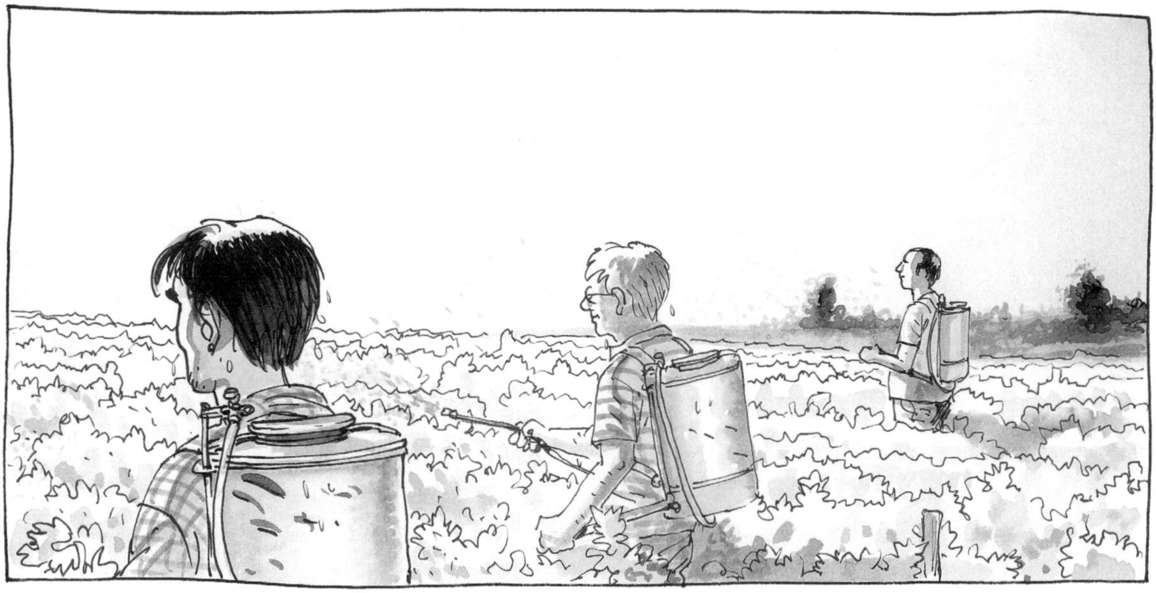

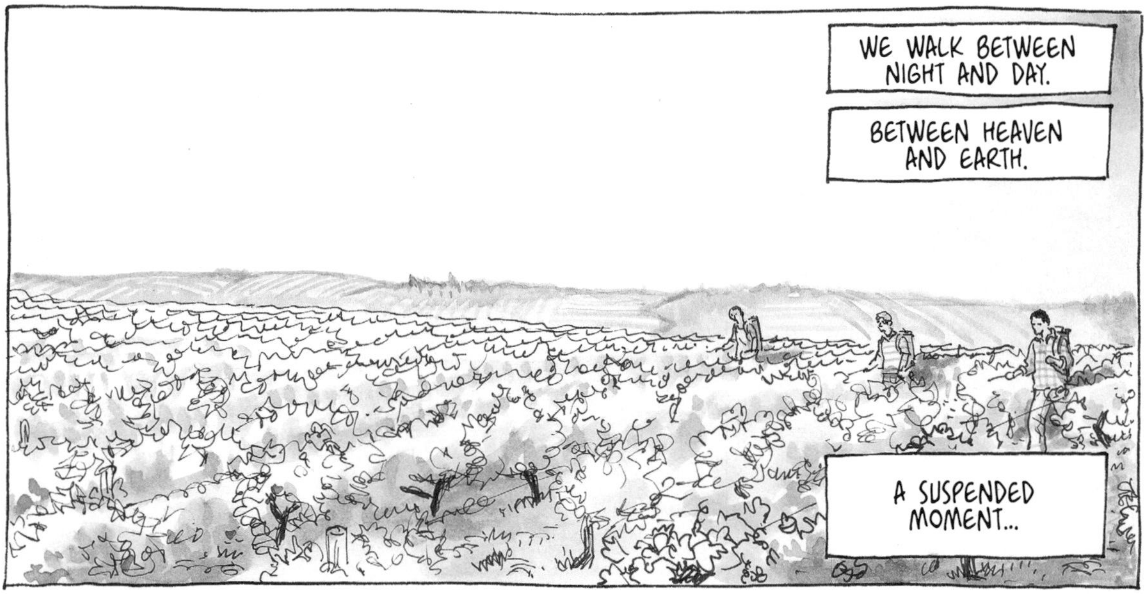
WE WALK BETWEEN NIGHT AND DAY.
BETWEEN HEAVEN AND EARTH.
A SUSPENDED MOMENT...

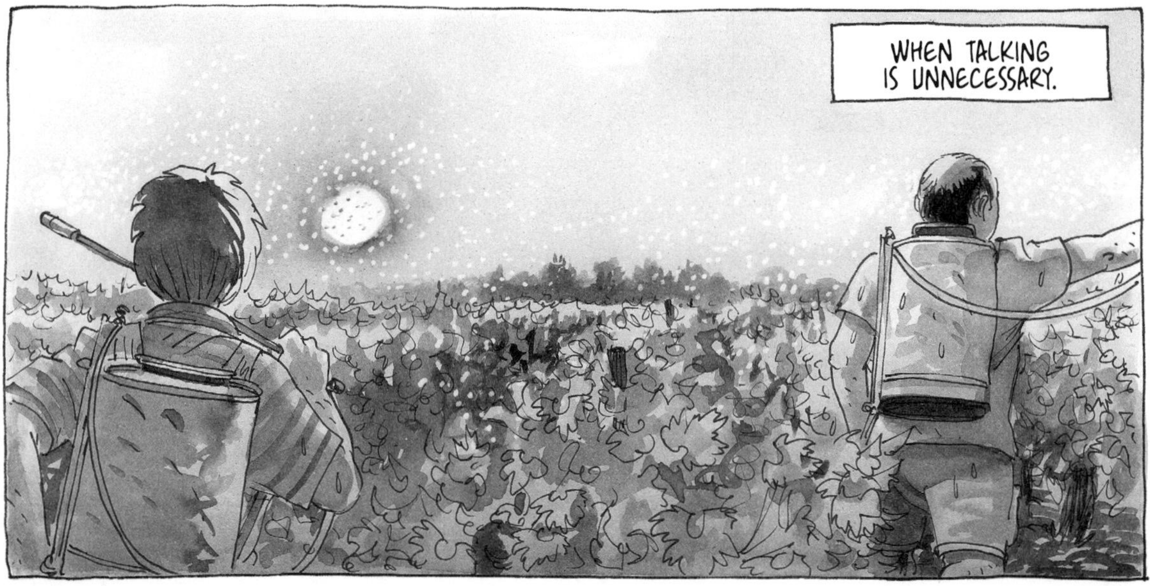
WHEN TALKING IS UNNECESSARY.

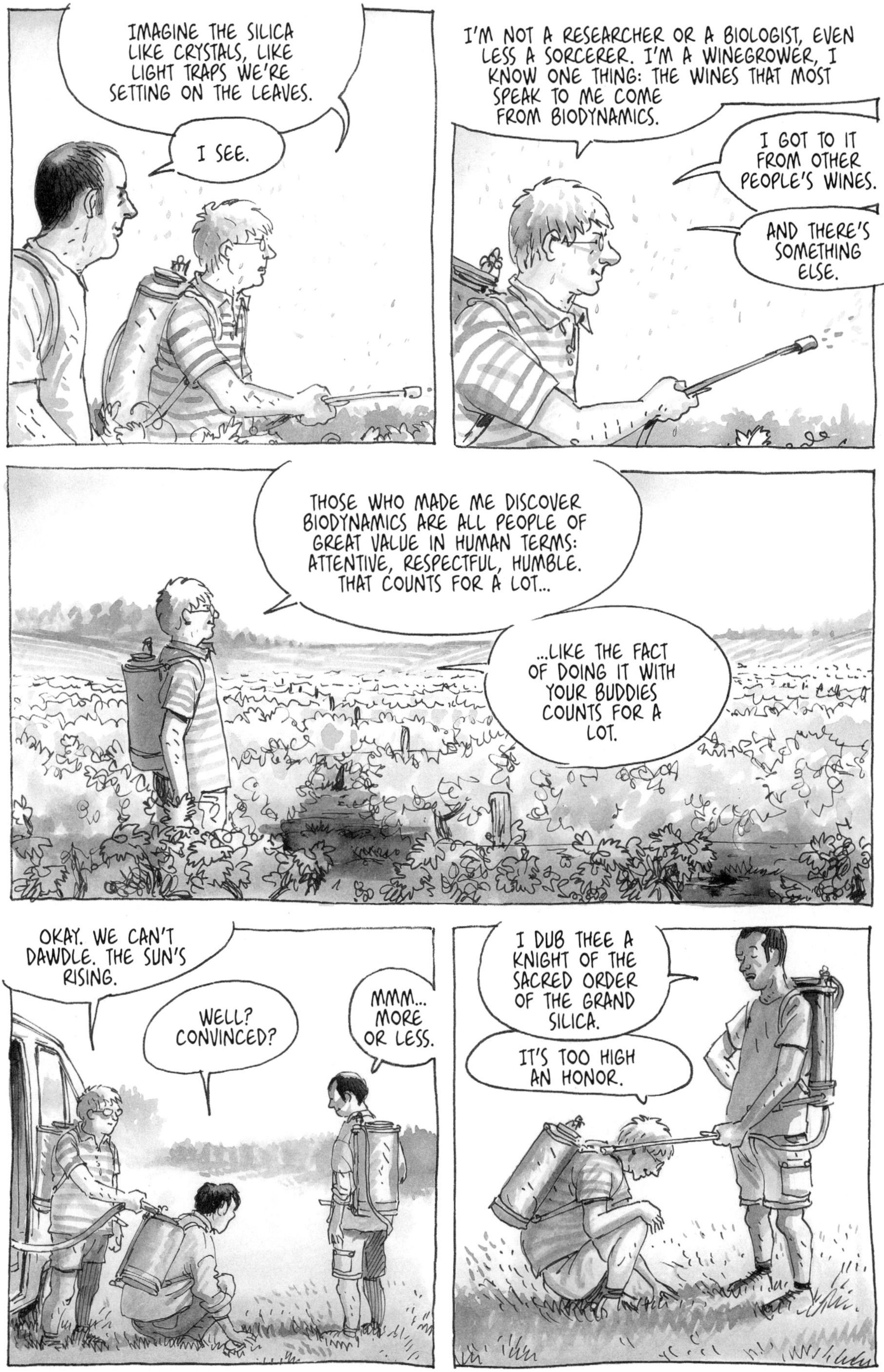
IMAGINE THE SILICA LIKE CRYSTALS, LIKE LIGHT TRAPS WE'RE SETTING ON THE LEAVES.
I SEE.
I'M NOT A RESEARCHER OR A BIOLOGIST, EVEN LESS A SORCERER. I'M A WINEGROWER, I KNOW ONE THING: THE WINES THAT MOST SPEAK TO ME COME FROM BIODYNAMICS.
I GOT TO IT FROM OTHER PEOPLE'S WINES.
AND THERE'S SOMETHING ELSE.
THOSE WHO MADE ME DISCOVER BIODYNAMICS ARE ALL PEOPLE OF GREAT VALUE IN HUMAN TERMS: ATTENTIVE, RESPECTFUL, HUMBLE. THAT COUNTS FOR A LOT...
...LIKE THE FACT OF DOING IT WITH YOUR BUDDIES COUNTS FOR A LOT.
OKAY. WE CAN'T DAWDLE. THE SUN'S RISING.
WELL? CONVINCED?
MMM... MORE OR LESS.
I DUB THEE A KNIGHT OF THE SACRED ORDER OF THE GRAND SILICA.
IT'S TOO HIGH AN HONOR.

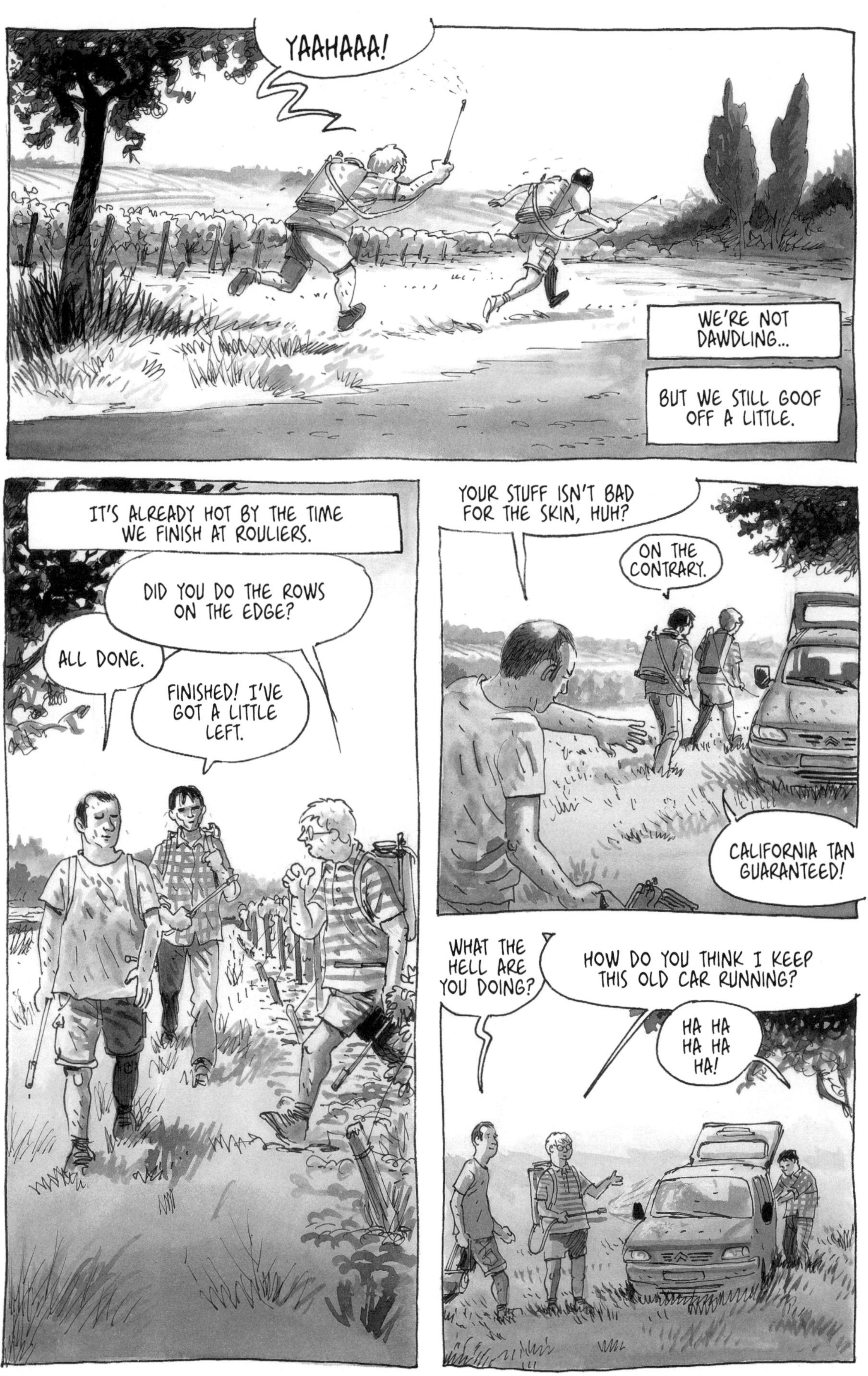
YAAHAAA!
WE'RE NOT DAWDLING...
BUT WE STILL GOOF OFF A LITTLE.
IT'S ALREADY HOT BY THE TIME WE FINISH AT ROULIERS.
DID YOU DO THE ROWS ON THE EDGE?
ALL DONE.
FINISHED! I'VE GOT A LITTLE LEFT.
YOUR STUFF ISN'T BAD FOR THE SKIN, HUH?
ON THE CONTRARY.
CALIFORNIA TAN GUARANTEED!
WHAT THE HELL ARE YOU DOING?
HOW DO YOU THINK I KEEP THIS OLD CAR RUNNING?
HA HA HA HA HA!

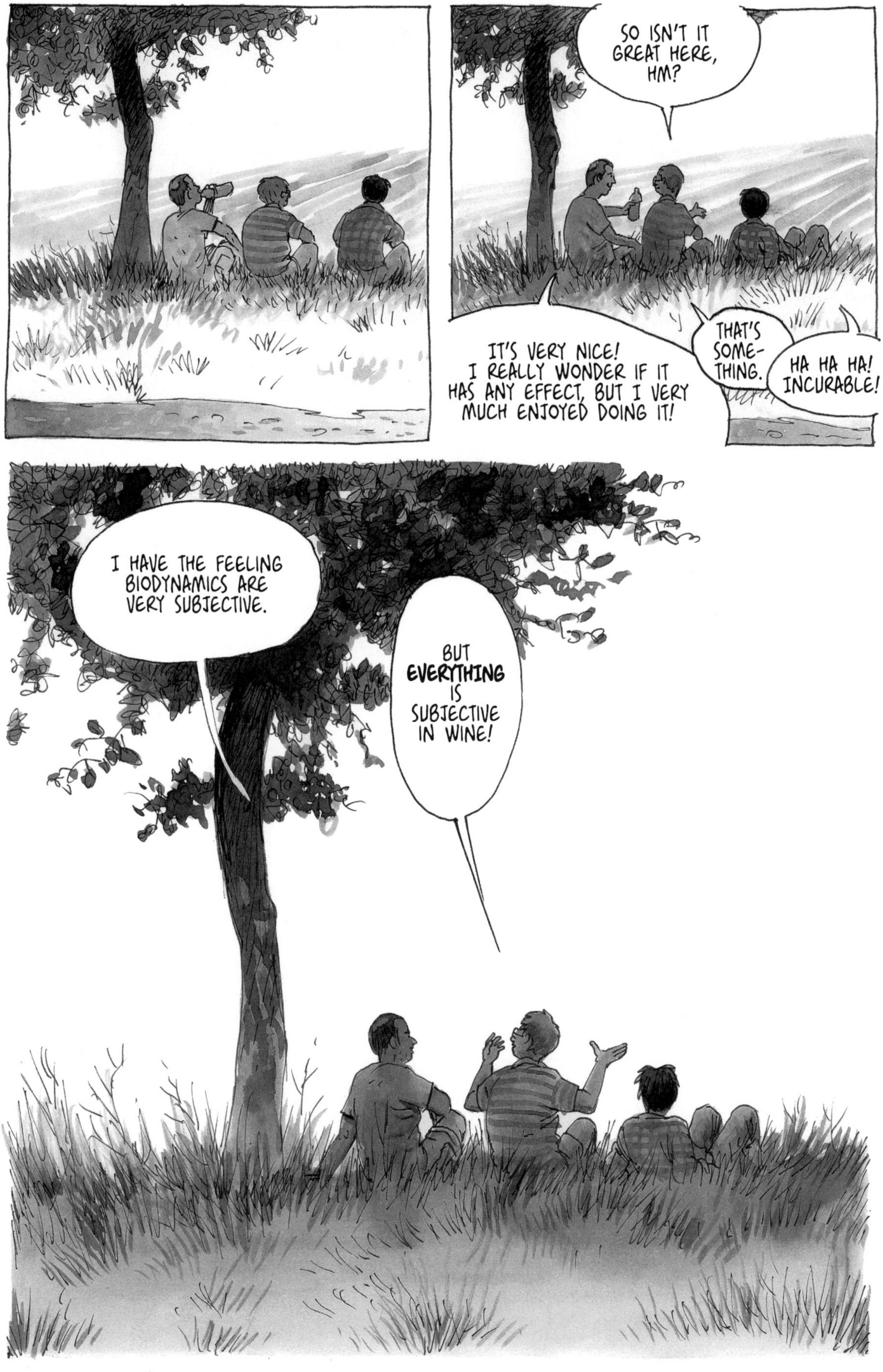
SO ISN'T IT GREAT HERE, HM?
IT'S VERY NICE! I REALLY WONDER IF IT HAS ANY EFFECT, BUT I VERY MUCH ENJOYED DOING IT!
THAT'S SOME-THING.
HA HA HA! INCURABLE!
I HAVE THE FEELING BIODYNAMICS ARE VERY SUBJECTIVE.
BUT **EVERYTHING** IS SUBJECTIVE IN WINE!

CHAPTER SEVEN

A QUESTION OF PROXIMITY

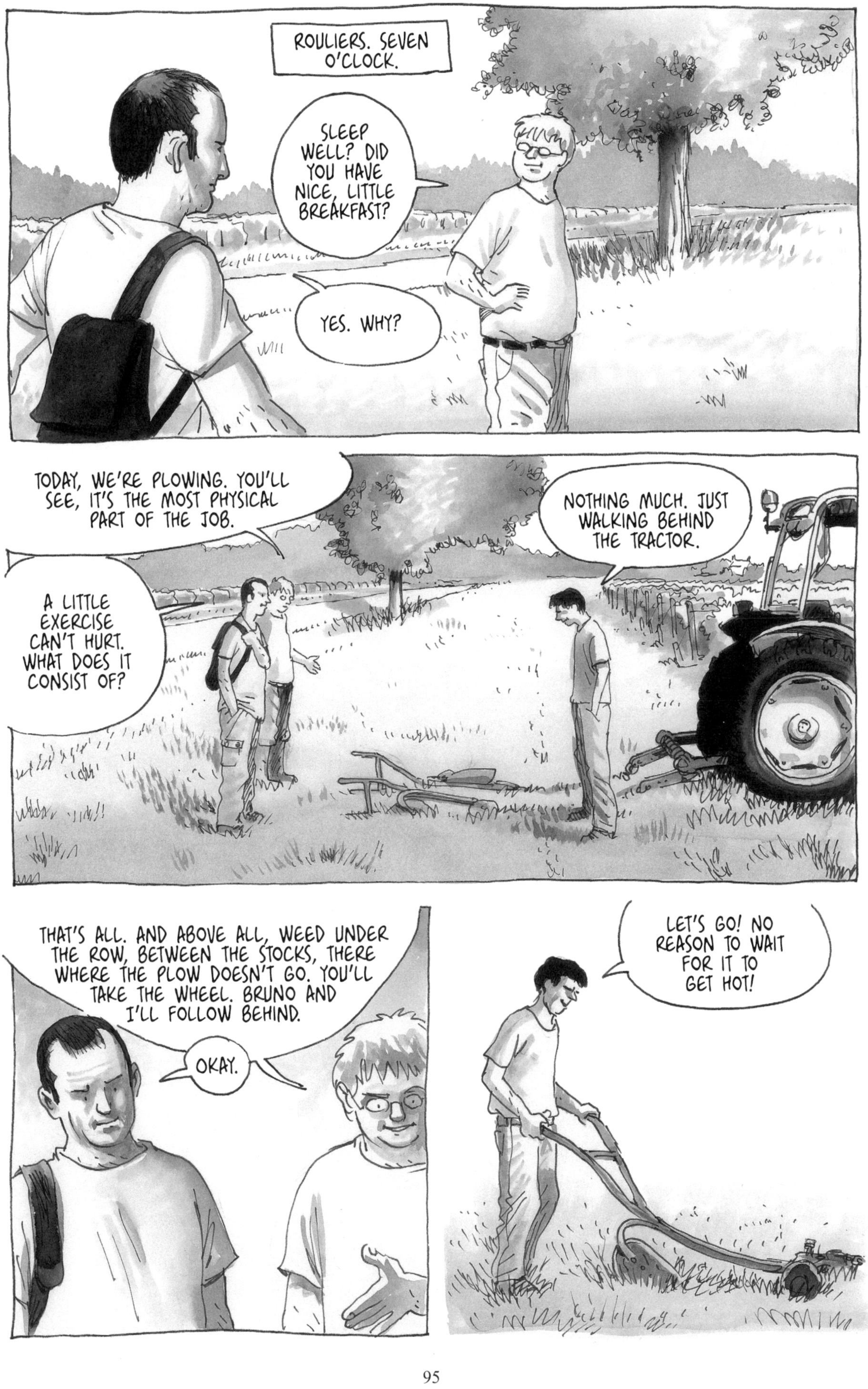
ROULIERS. SEVEN O'CLOCK.
SLEEP WELL? DID YOU HAVE NICE, LITTLE BREAKFAST?
YES. WHY?
TODAY, WE'RE PLOWING. YOU'LL SEE, IT'S THE MOST PHYSICAL PART OF THE JOB.
A LITTLE EXERCISE CAN'T HURT. WHAT DOES IT CONSIST OF?
NOTHING MUCH. JUST WALKING BEHIND THE TRACTOR.
THAT'S ALL. AND ABOVE ALL, WEED UNDER THE ROW, BETWEEN THE STOCKS, THERE WHERE THE PLOW DOESN'T GO. YOU'LL TAKE THE WHEEL. BRUNO AND I'LL FOLLOW BEHIND.
OKAY.
LET'S GO! NO REASON TO WAIT FOR IT TO GET HOT!

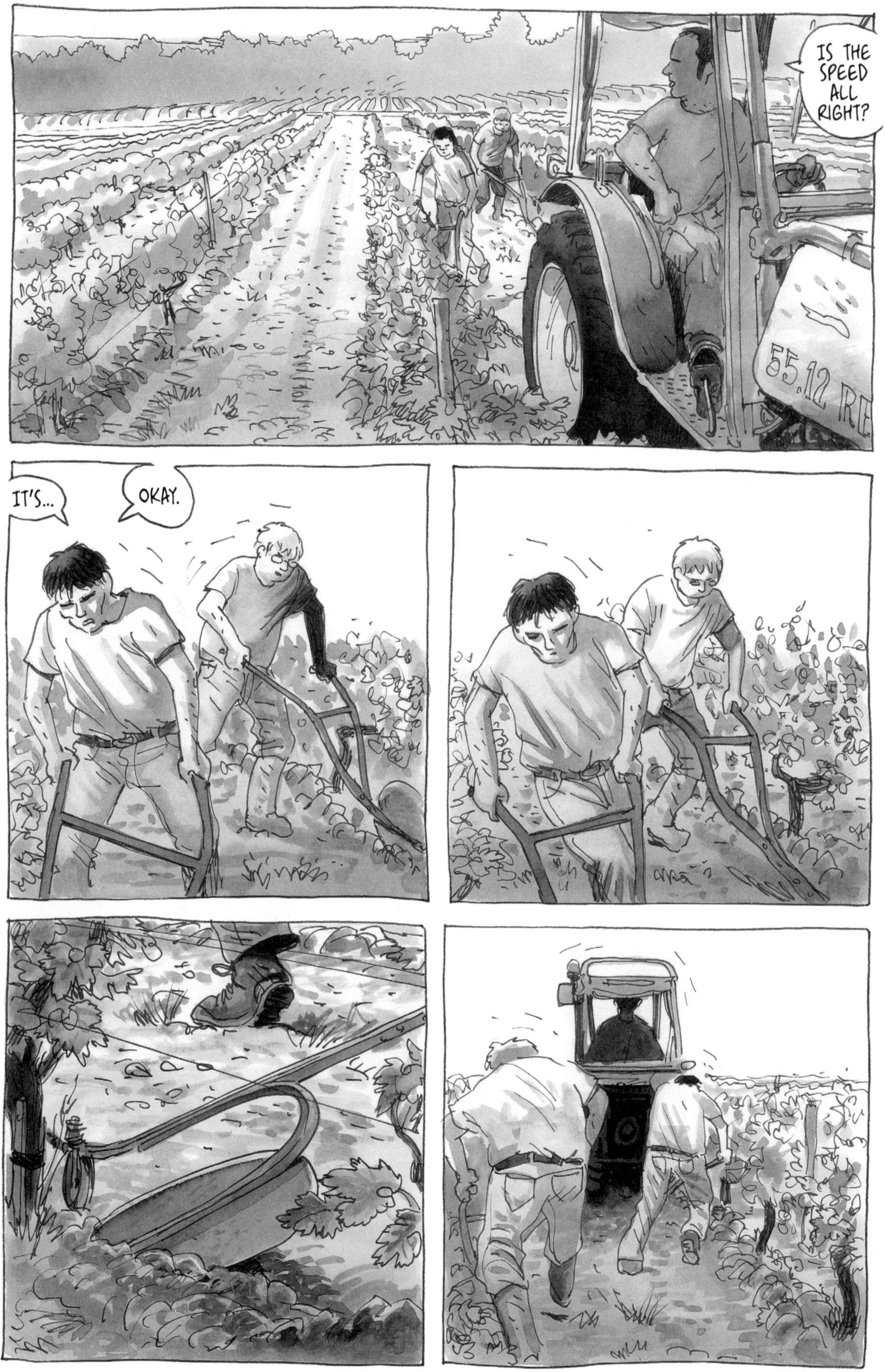
IS THE SPEED ALL RIGHT?
55.12 RE
IT'S...
OKAY.

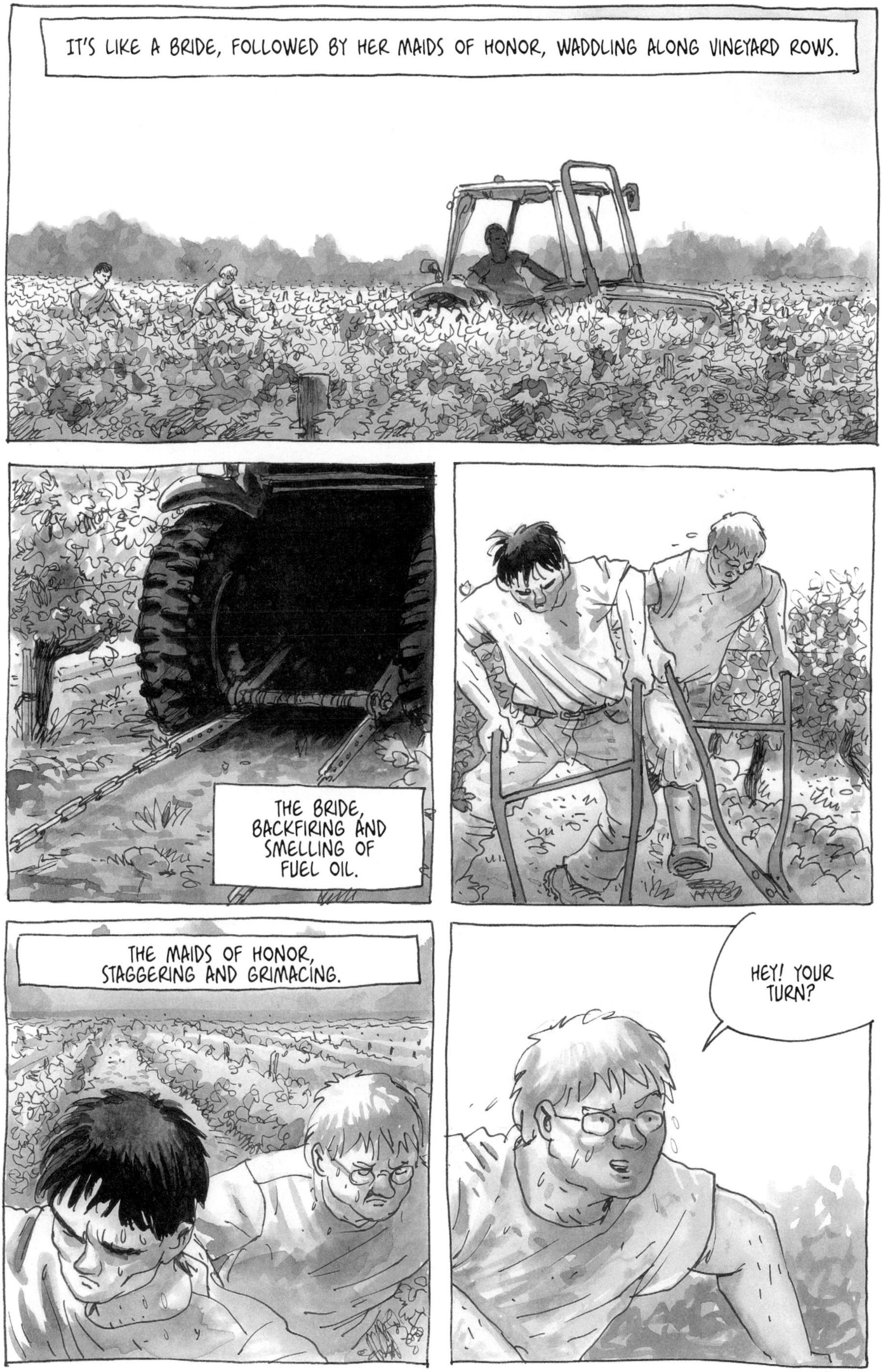
IT'S LIKE A BRIDE, FOLLOWED BY HER MAIDS OF HONOR, WADDLING ALONG VINEYARD ROWS.
THE BRIDE, BACKFIRING AND SMELLING OF FUEL OIL.
THE MAIDS OF HONOR, STAGGERING AND GRIMACING.
HEY! YOUR TURN?

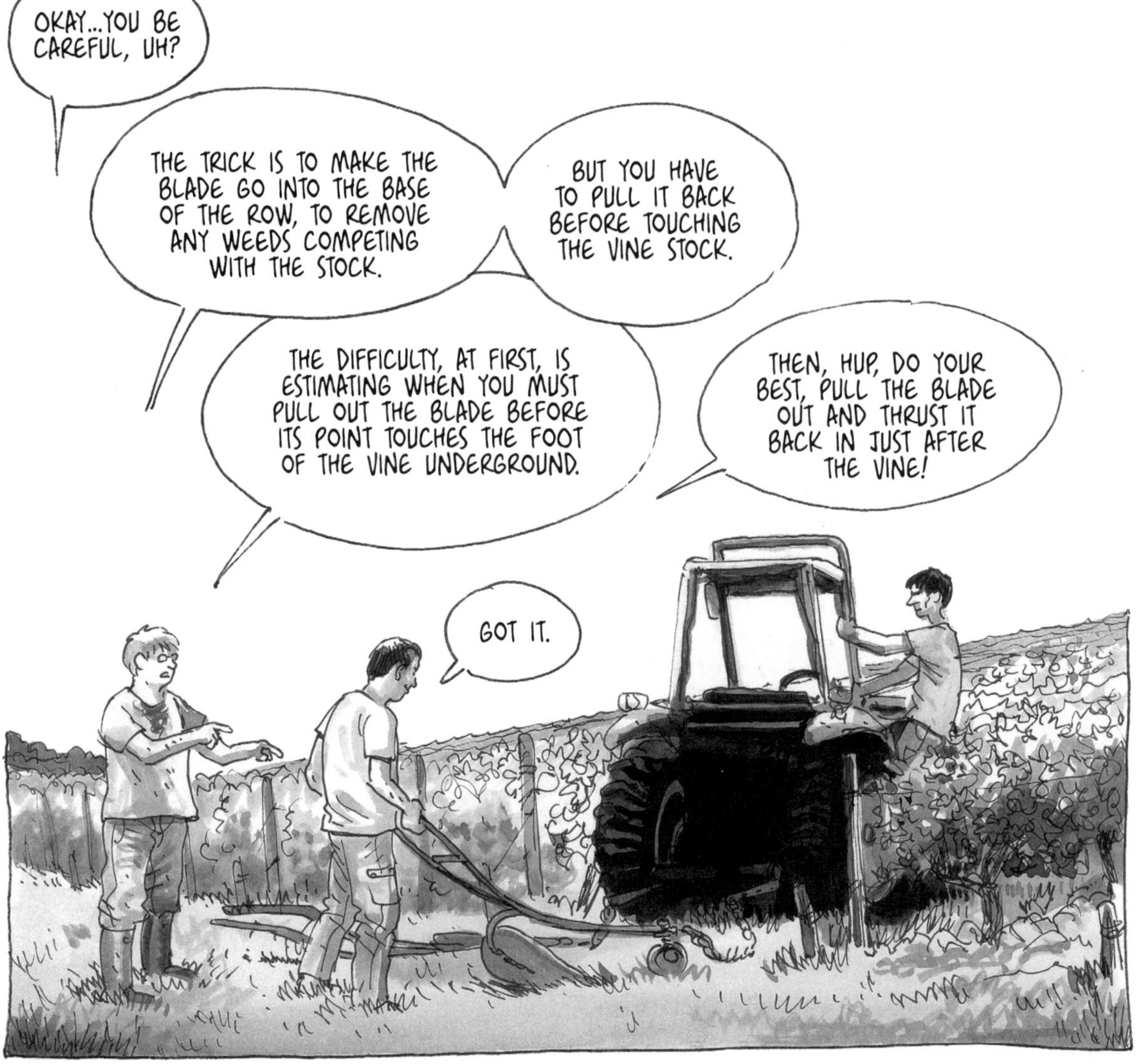
OKAY...YOU BE CAREFUL, UH?
THE TRICK IS TO MAKE THE BLADE GO INTO THE BASE OF THE ROW, TO REMOVE ANY WEEDS COMPETING WITH THE STOCK.
BUT YOU HAVE TO PULL IT BACK BEFORE TOUCHING THE VINE STOCK.
THE DIFFICULTY, AT FIRST, IS ESTIMATING WHEN YOU MUST PULL OUT THE BLADE BEFORE ITS POINT TOUCHES THE FOOT OF THE VINE UNDERGROUND.
THEN, HUP, DO YOUR BEST, PULL THE BLADE OUT AND THRUST IT BACK IN JUST AFTER THE VINE!
GOT IT.

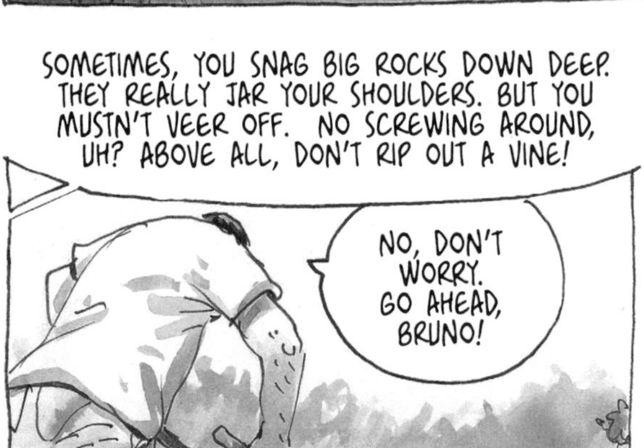
SOMETIMES, YOU SNAG BIG ROCKS DOWN DEEP. THEY REALLY JAR YOUR SHOULDERS. BUT YOU MUSTN'T VEER OFF. NO SCREWING AROUND, UH? ABOVE ALL, DON'T RIP OUT A VINE!
NO, DON'T WORRY. GO AHEAD, BRUNO!

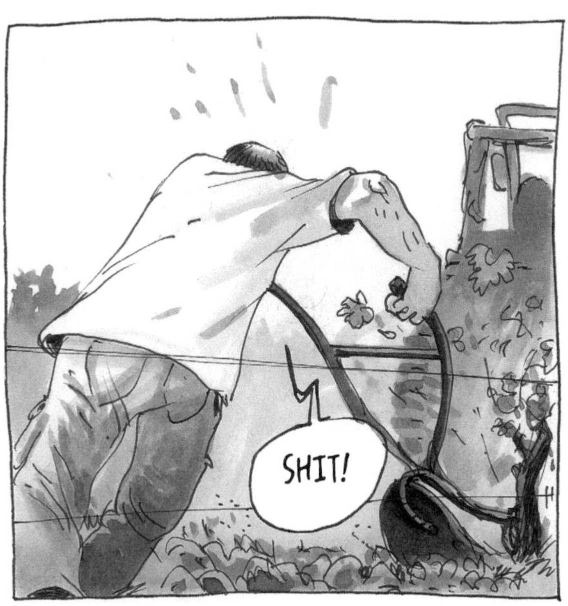
SHIT!

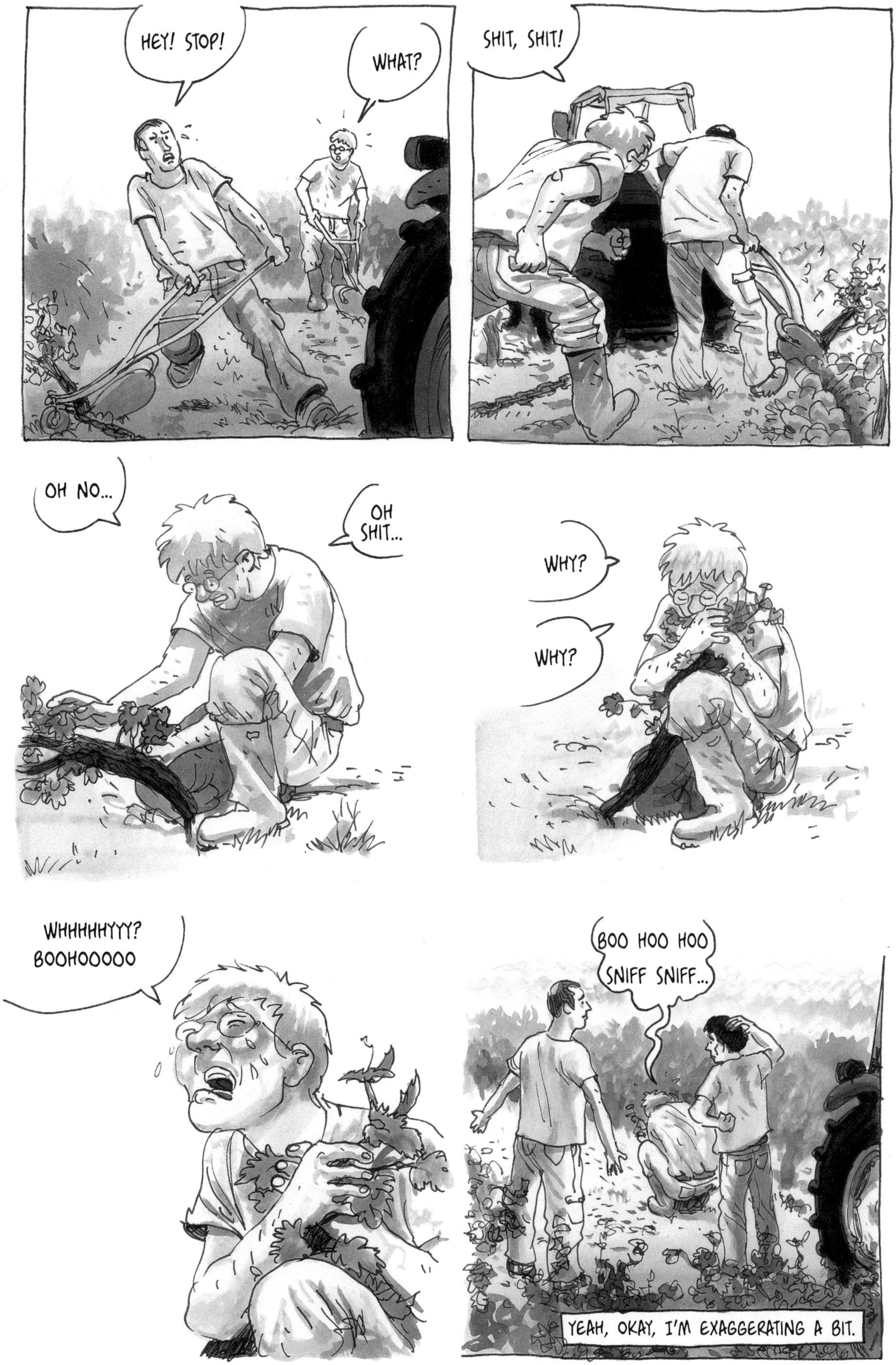
HEY! STOP!
WHAT?
SHIT, SHIT!
OH NO...
OH SHIT...
WHY?
WHY?
WHHHHHYYY? BOOHOOOOO
BOO HOO HOO SNIFF SNIFF...
YEAH, OKAY, I'M EXAGGERATING A BIT.

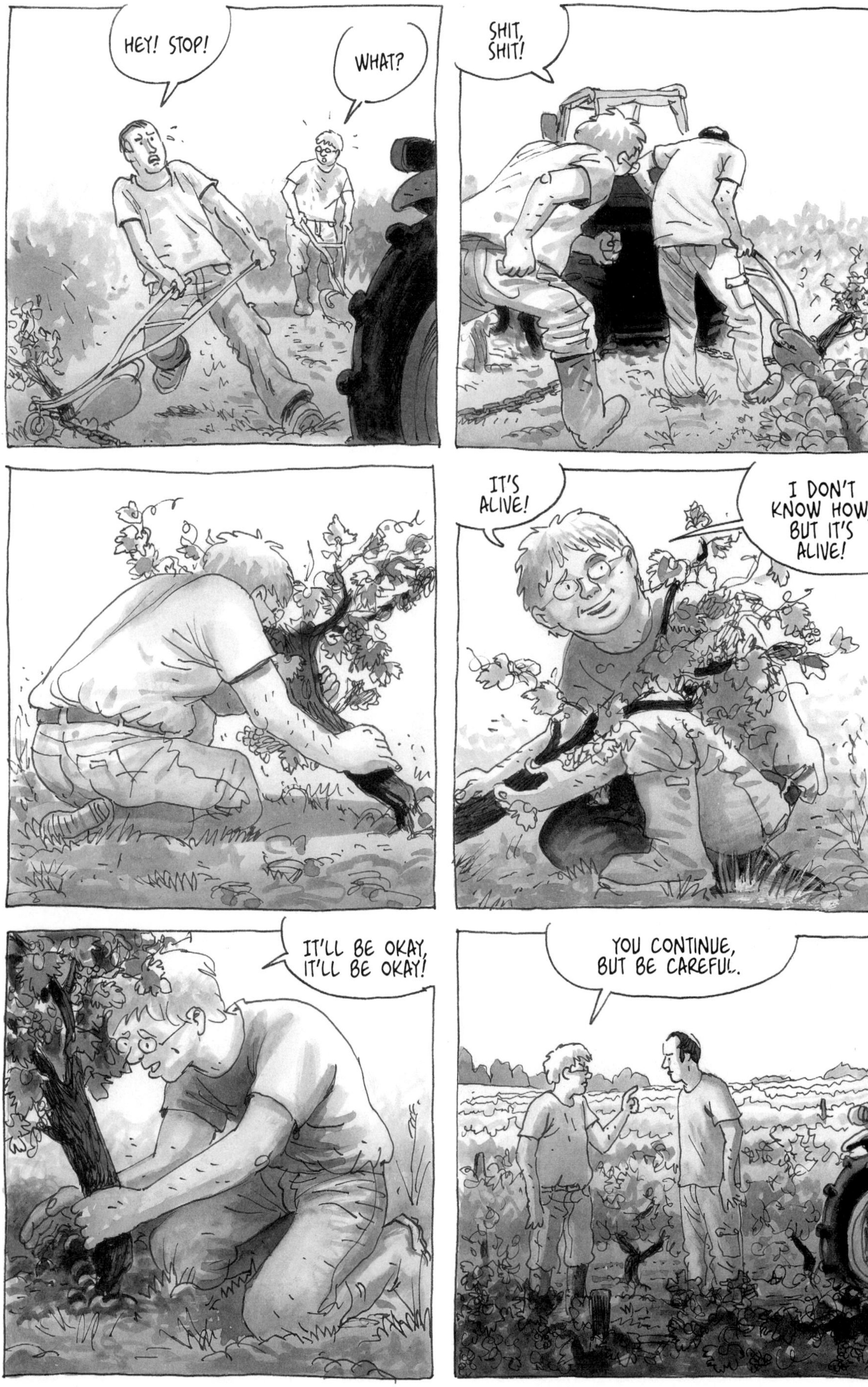
HEY! STOP!
WHAT?
SHIT, SHIT!
IT'S ALIVE!
I DON'T KNOW HOW, BUT IT'S ALIVE!
IT'LL BE OKAY, IT'LL BE OKAY!
YOU CONTINUE, BUT BE CAREFUL.

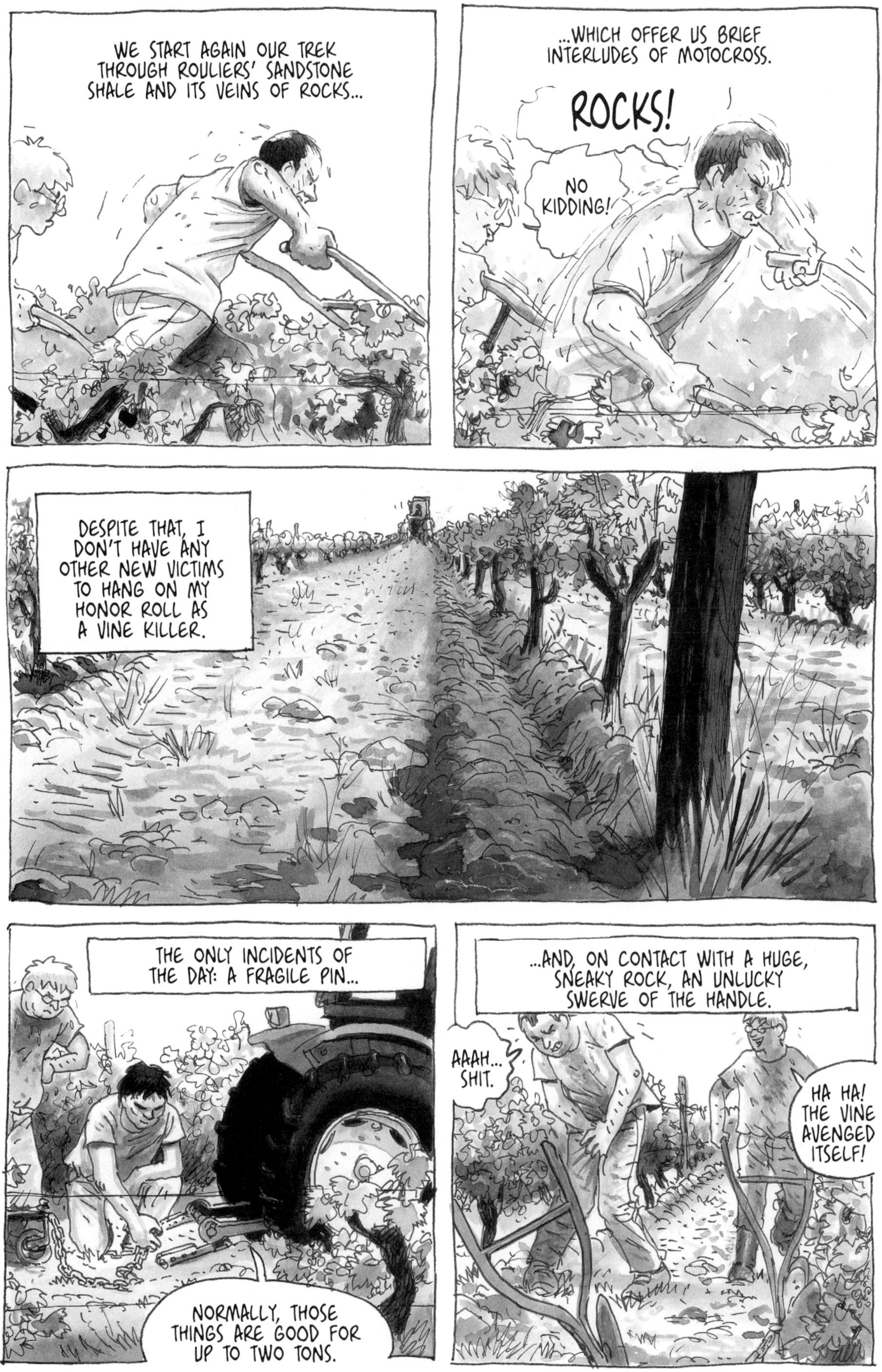
WE START AGAIN OUR TREK THROUGH ROULIERS' SANDSTONE SHALE AND ITS VEINS OF ROCKS...
...WHICH OFFER US BRIEF INTERLUDES OF MOTOCROSS.
ROCKS!
NO KIDDING!
DESPITE THAT, I DON'T HAVE ANY OTHER NEW VICTIMS TO HANG ON MY HONOR ROLL AS A VINE KILLER.
THE ONLY INCIDENTS OF THE DAY: A FRAGILE PIN...
NORMALLY, THOSE THINGS ARE GOOD FOR UP TO TWO TONS.
...AND, ON CONTACT WITH A HUGE, SNEAKY ROCK, AN UNLUCKY SWERVE OF THE HANDLE.
AAAH... SHIT.
HA HA! THE VINE AVENGED ITSELF!

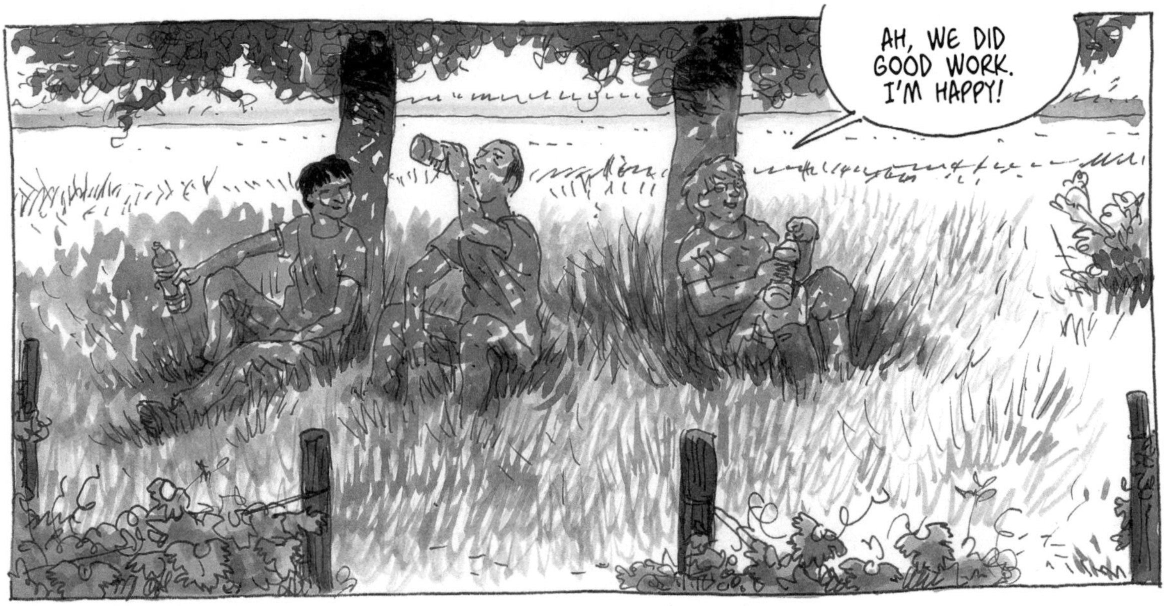
AH, WE DID GOOD WORK. I'M HAPPY!

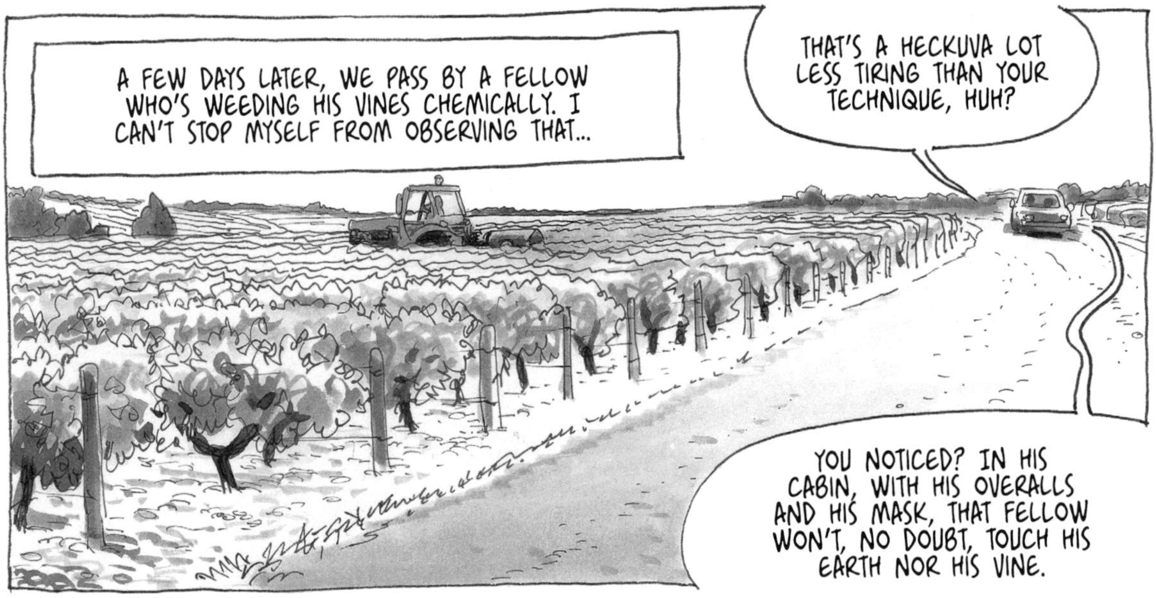
A FEW DAYS LATER, WE PASS BY A FELLOW WHO'S WEEDING HIS VINES CHEMICALLY. I CAN'T STOP MYSELF FROM OBSERVING THAT...
THAT'S A HECKUVA LOT LESS TIRING THAN YOUR TECHNIQUE, HUH?
YOU NOTICED? IN HIS CABIN, WITH HIS OVERALLS AND HIS MASK, THAT FELLOW WON'T, NO DOUBT, TOUCH HIS EARTH NOR HIS VINE.

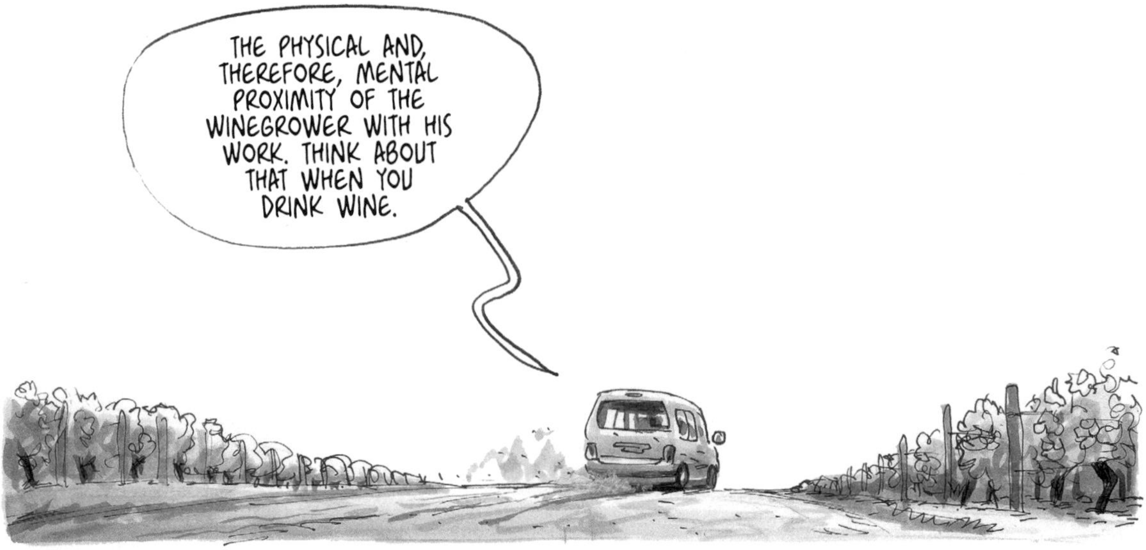
THE PHYSICAL AND, THEREFORE, MENTAL PROXIMITY OF THE WINEGROWER WITH HIS WORK. THINK ABOUT THAT WHEN YOU DRINK WINE.

CHAPTER EIGHT   NEW YORK
MONTBENAULT
NEW YORK

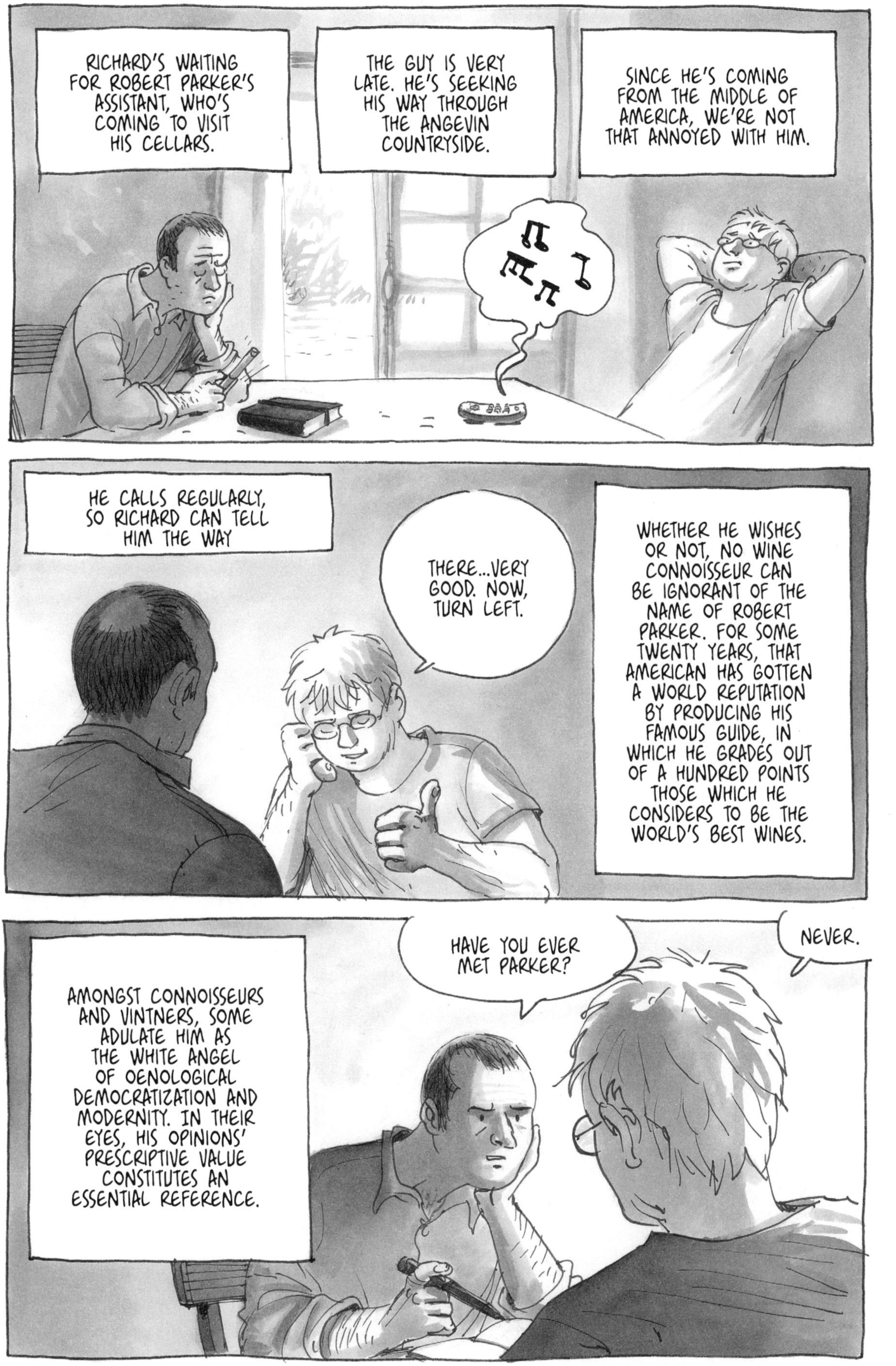
RICHARD'S WAITING FOR ROBERT PARKER'S ASSISTANT, WHO'S COMING TO VISIT HIS CELLARS.
THE GUY IS VERY LATE. HE'S SEEKING HIS WAY THROUGH THE ANGEVIN COUNTRYSIDE.
SINCE HE'S COMING FROM THE MIDDLE OF AMERICA, WE'RE NOT THAT ANNOYED WITH HIM.
HE CALLS REGULARLY, SO RICHARD CAN TELL HIM THE WAY
THERE...VERY GOOD. NOW, TURN LEFT.
WHETHER HE WISHES OR NOT, NO WINE CONNOISSEUR CAN BE IGNORANT OF THE NAME OF ROBERT PARKER. FOR SOME TWENTY YEARS, THAT AMERICAN HAS GOTTEN A WORLD REPUTATION BY PRODUCING HIS FAMOUS GUIDE, IN WHICH HE GRADES OUT OF A HUNDRED POINTS THOSE WHICH HE CONSIDERS TO BE THE WORLD'S BEST WINES.
AMONGST CONNOISSEURS AND VINTNERS, SOME ADULATE HIM AS THE WHITE ANGEL OF OENOLOGICAL DEMOCRATIZATION AND MODERNITY. IN THEIR EYES, HIS OPINIONS' PRESCRIPTIVE VALUE CONSTITUTES AN ESSENTIAL REFERENCE.
HAVE YOU EVER MET PARKER?
NEVER.

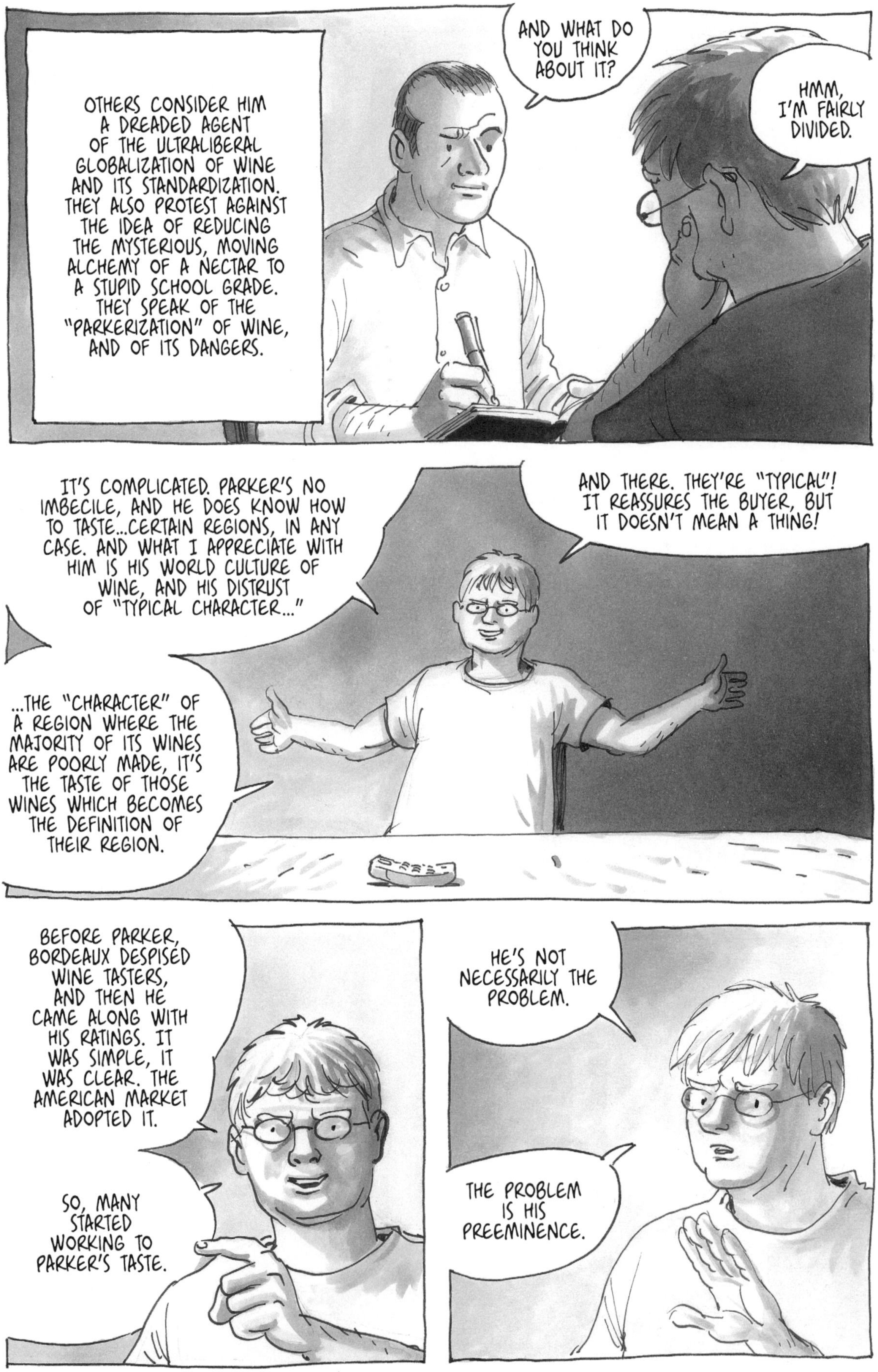
OTHERS CONSIDER HIM A DREADED AGENT OF THE ULTRALIBERAL GLOBALIZATION OF WINE AND ITS STANDARDIZATION. THEY ALSO PROTEST AGAINST THE IDEA OF REDUCING THE MYSTERIOUS, MOVING ALCHEMY OF A NECTAR TO A STUPID SCHOOL GRADE. THEY SPEAK OF THE "PARKERIZATION" OF WINE, AND OF ITS DANGERS.
AND WHAT DO YOU THINK ABOUT IT?
HMM, I'M FAIRLY DIVIDED.
IT'S COMPLICATED. PARKER'S NO IMBECILE, AND HE DOES KNOW HOW TO TASTE...CERTAIN REGIONS, IN ANY CASE. AND WHAT I APPRECIATE WITH HIM IS HIS WORLD CULTURE OF WINE, AND HIS DISTRUST OF "TYPICAL CHARACTER..."
...THE "CHARACTER" OF A REGION WHERE THE MAJORITY OF ITS WINES ARE POORLY MADE, IT'S THE TASTE OF THOSE WINES WHICH BECOMES THE DEFINITION OF THEIR REGION.
AND THERE. THEY'RE "TYPICAL"! IT REASSURES THE BUYER, BUT IT DOESN'T MEAN A THING!
BEFORE PARKER, BORDEAUX DESPISED WINE TASTERS, AND THEN HE CAME ALONG WITH HIS RATINGS. IT WAS SIMPLE, IT WAS CLEAR. THE AMERICAN MARKET ADOPTED IT.
SO, MANY STARTED WORKING TO PARKER'S TASTE.
HE'S NOT NECESSARILY THE PROBLEM.
THE PROBLEM IS HIS PREEMINENCE.

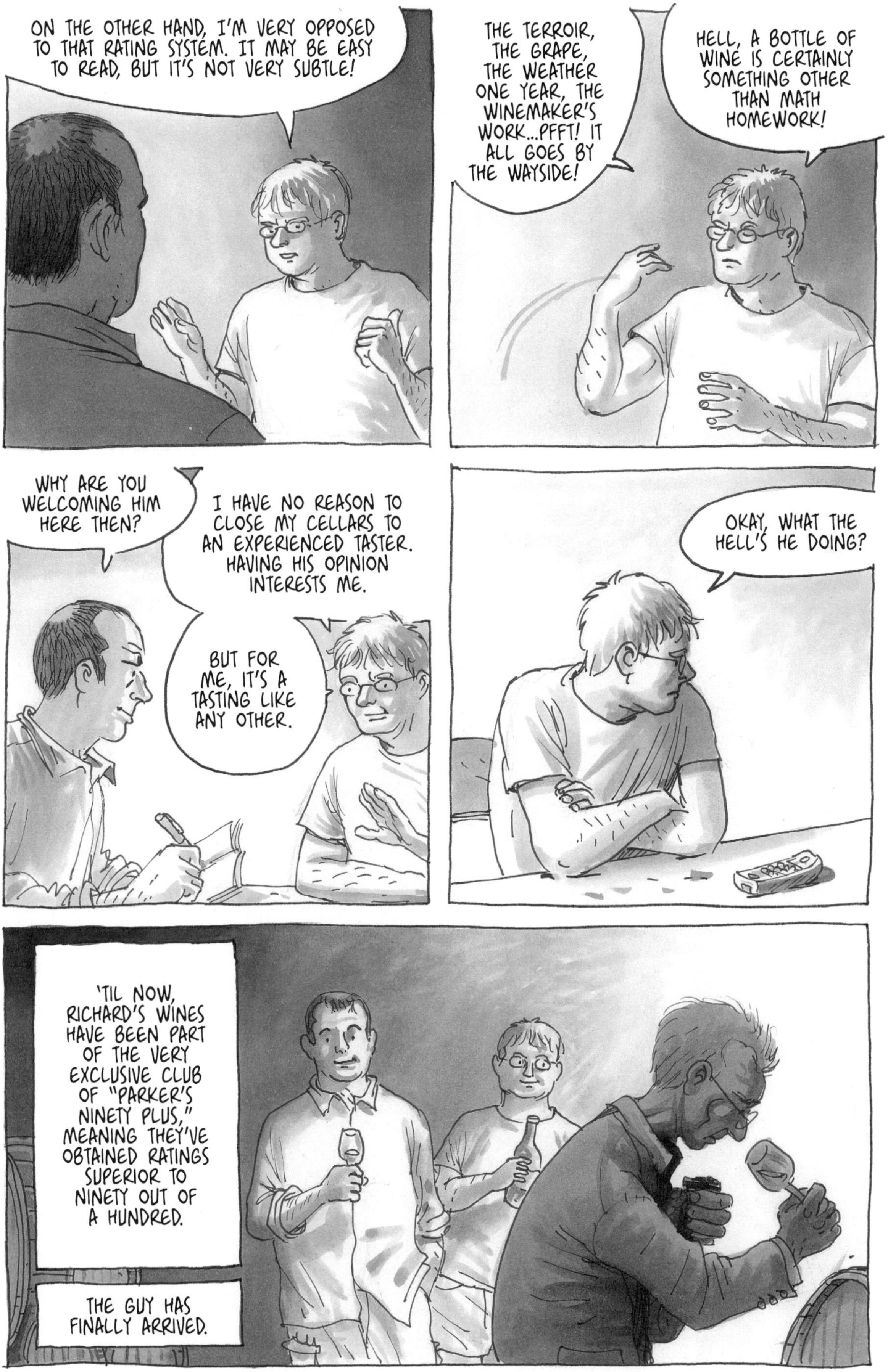
ON THE OTHER HAND, I'M VERY OPPOSED TO THAT RATING SYSTEM. IT MAY BE EASY TO READ, BUT IT'S NOT VERY SUBTLE!
THE TERROIR, THE GRAPE, THE WEATHER ONE YEAR, THE WINEMAKER'S WORK...PFFT! IT ALL GOES BY THE WAYSIDE!
HELL, A BOTTLE OF WINE IS CERTAINLY SOMETHING OTHER THAN MATH HOMEWORK!
WHY ARE YOU WELCOMING HIM HERE THEN?
I HAVE NO REASON TO CLOSE MY CELLARS TO AN EXPERIENCED TASTER. HAVING HIS OPINION INTERESTS ME.
BUT FOR ME, IT'S A TASTING LIKE ANY OTHER.
OKAY, WHAT THE HELL'S HE DOING?
'TIL NOW, RICHARD'S WINES HAVE BEEN PART OF THE VERY EXCLUSIVE CLUB OF "PARKER'S NINETY PLUS," MEANING THEY'VE OBTAINED RATINGS SUPERIOR TO NINETY OUT OF A HUNDRED.
THE GUY HAS FINALLY ARRIVED.

BETWEEN EACH GLASS, HE ISOLATES HIMSELF IN THE BACK OF THE CELLAR, AND MURMURS HIS COMMENTS, IN ENGLISH, INTO HIS DICTAPHONE.

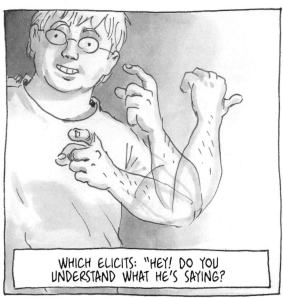

WHICH ELICITS: "HEY! DO YOU UNDERSTAND WHAT HE'S SAYING?"

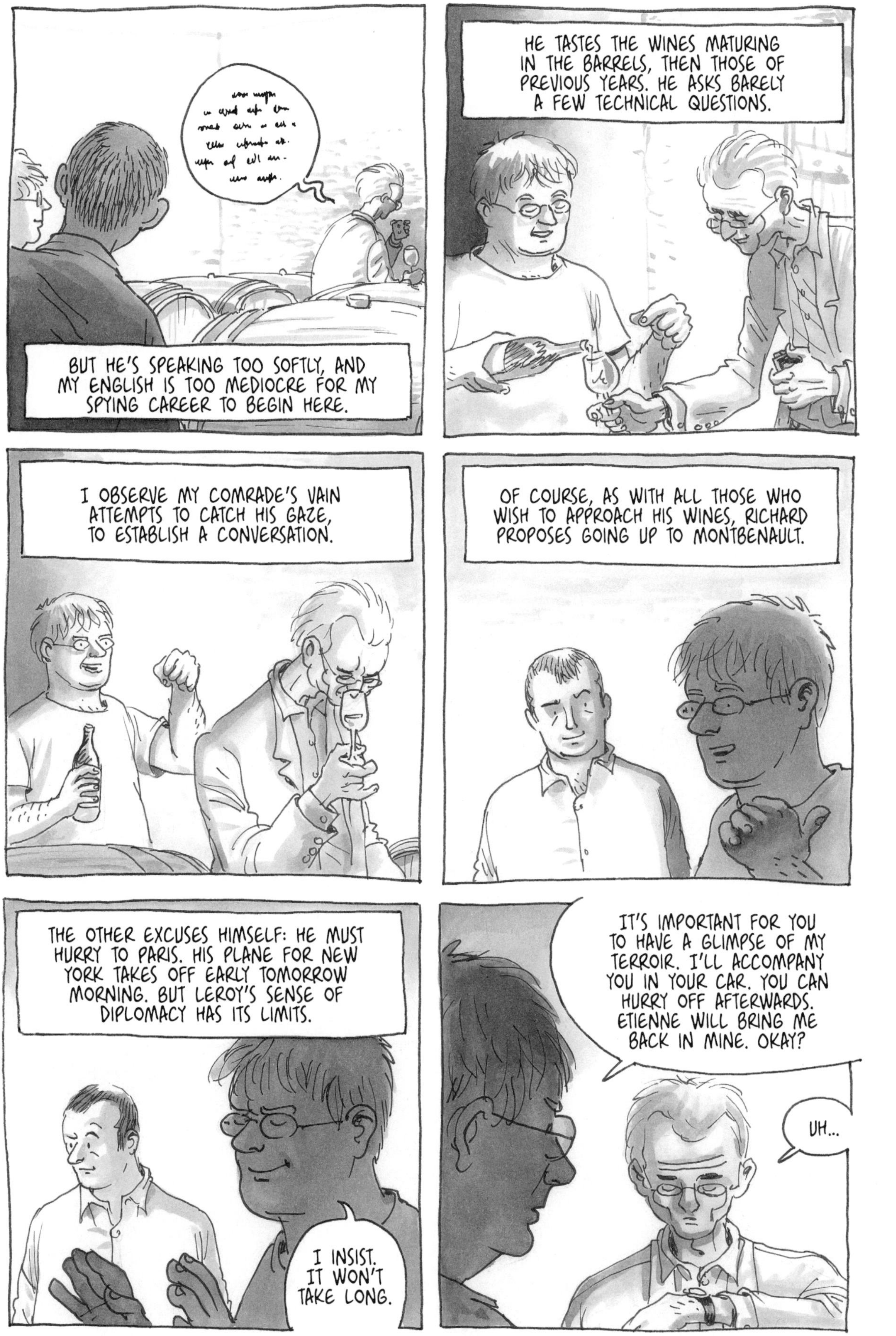
BUT HE'S SPEAKING TOO SOFTLY, AND MY ENGLISH IS TOO MEDIOCRE FOR MY SPYING CAREER TO BEGIN HERE.
HE TASTES THE WINES MATURING IN THE BARRELS, THEN THOSE OF PREVIOUS YEARS. HE ASKS BARELY A FEW TECHNICAL QUESTIONS.
I OBSERVE MY COMRADE'S VAIN ATTEMPTS TO CATCH HIS GAZE, TO ESTABLISH A CONVERSATION.
OF COURSE, AS WITH ALL THOSE WHO WISH TO APPROACH HIS WINES, RICHARD PROPOSES GOING UP TO MONTBENAULT.
THE OTHER EXCUSES HIMSELF: HE MUST HURRY TO PARIS. HIS PLANE FOR NEW YORK TAKES OFF EARLY TOMORROW MORNING. BUT LEROY'S SENSE OF DIPLOMACY HAS ITS LIMITS.
I INSIST. IT WON'T TAKE LONG.
IT'S IMPORTANT FOR YOU TO HAVE A GLIMPSE OF MY TERROIR. I'LL ACCOMPANY YOU IN YOUR CAR. YOU CAN HURRY OFF AFTERWARDS. ETIENNE WILL BRING ME BACK IN MINE. OKAY?
UH...

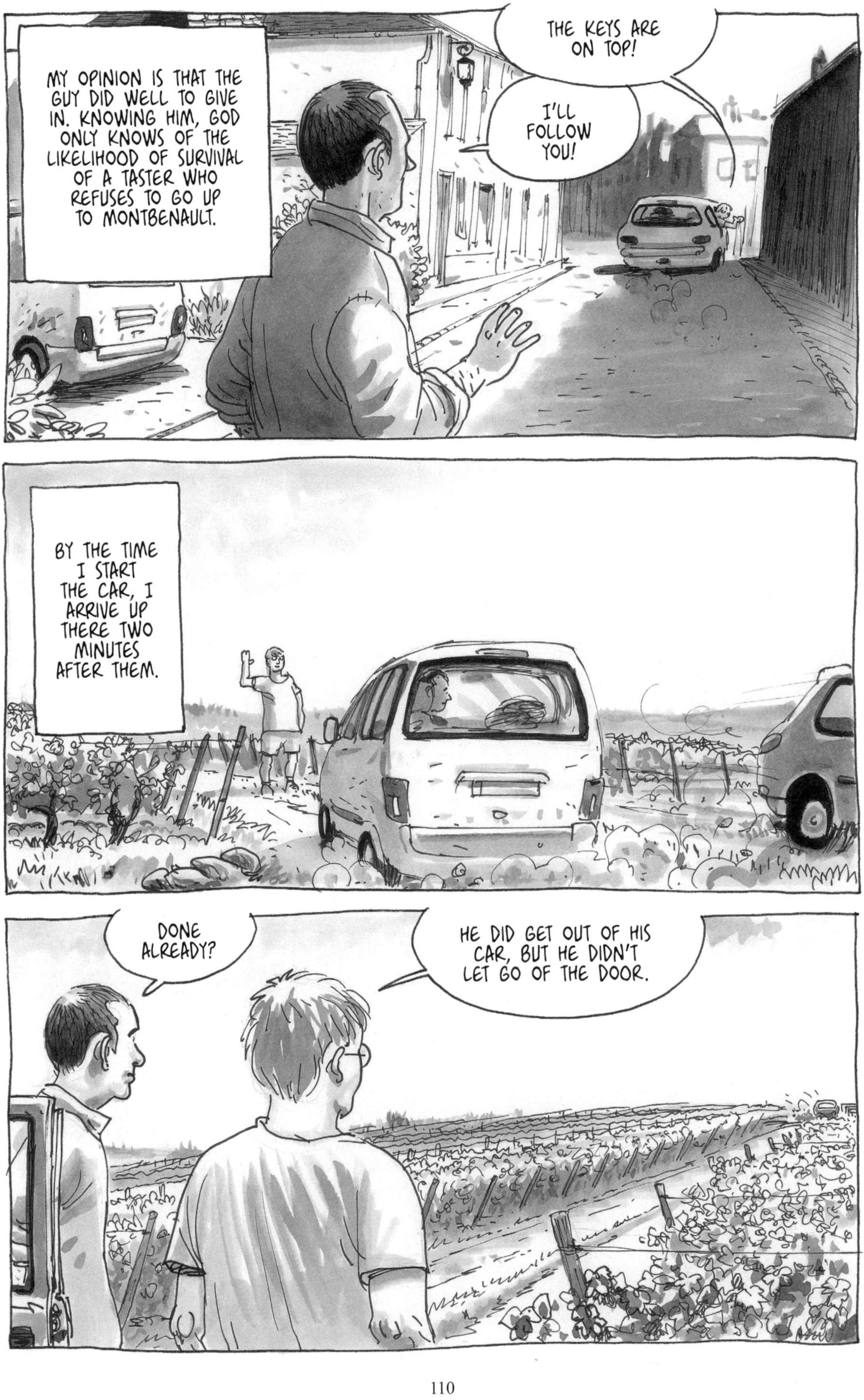
MY OPINION IS THAT THE GUY DID WELL TO GIVE IN. KNOWING HIM, GOD ONLY KNOWS OF THE LIKELIHOOD OF SURVIVAL OF A TASTER WHO REFUSES TO GO UP TO MONTBENAULT.
THE KEYS ARE ON TOP!
I'LL FOLLOW YOU!
BY THE TIME I START THE CAR, I ARRIVE UP THERE TWO MINUTES AFTER THEM.
DONE ALREADY?
HE DID GET OUT OF HIS CAR, BUT HE DIDN'T LET GO OF THE DOOR.

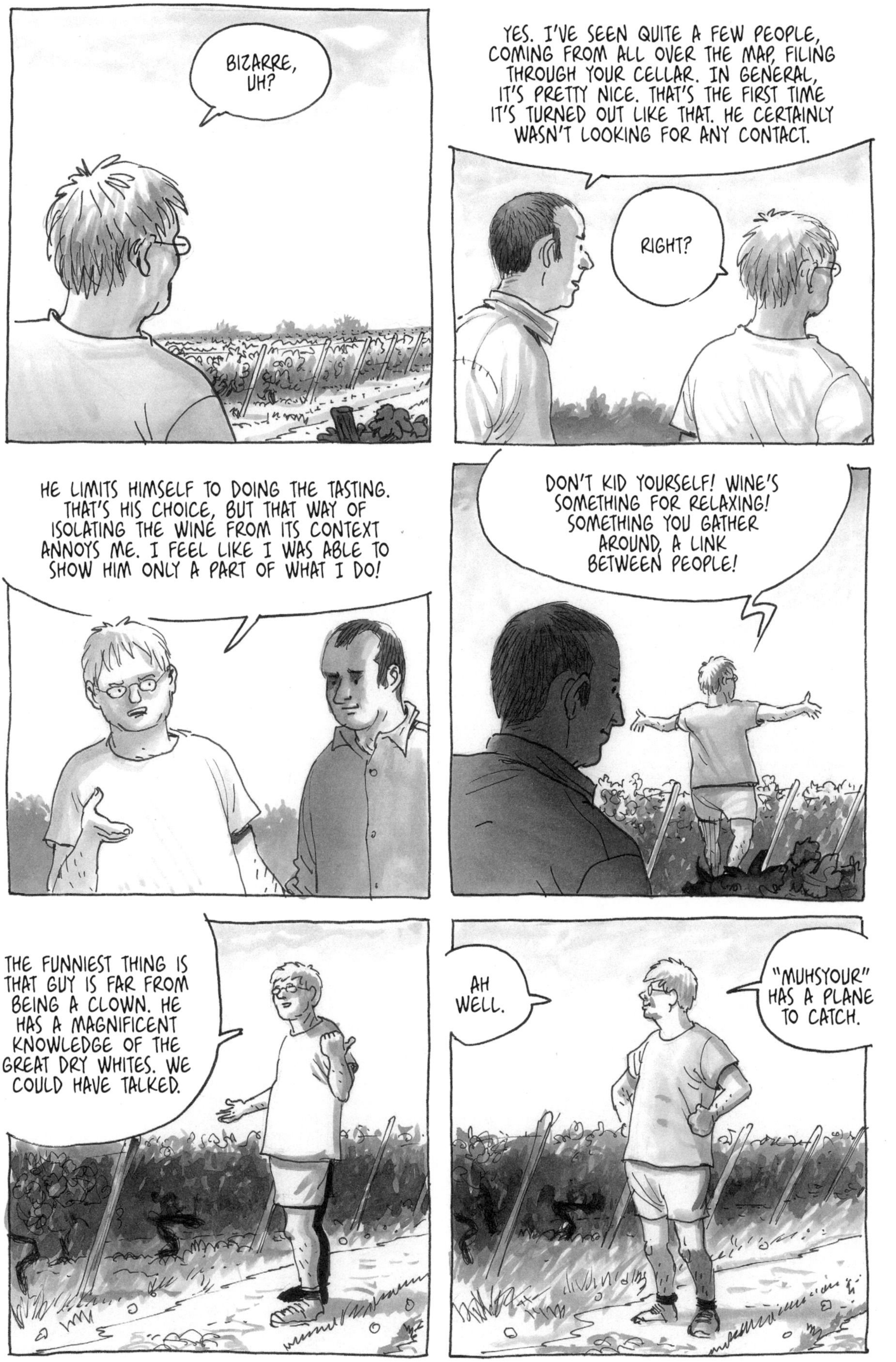
BIZARRE, UH?
YES. I'VE SEEN QUITE A FEW PEOPLE, COMING FROM ALL OVER THE MAP, FILING THROUGH YOUR CELLAR. IN GENERAL, IT'S PRETTY NICE. THAT'S THE FIRST TIME IT'S TURNED OUT LIKE THAT. HE CERTAINLY WASN'T LOOKING FOR ANY CONTACT.
RIGHT?
HE LIMITS HIMSELF TO DOING THE TASTING. THAT'S HIS CHOICE, BUT THAT WAY OF ISOLATING THE WINE FROM ITS CONTEXT ANNOYS ME. I FEEL LIKE I WAS ABLE TO SHOW HIM ONLY A PART OF WHAT I DO!
DON'T KID YOURSELF! WINE'S SOMETHING FOR RELAXING! SOMETHING YOU GATHER AROUND, A LINK BETWEEN PEOPLE!
THE FUNNIEST THING IS THAT GUY IS FAR FROM BEING A CLOWN. HE HAS A MAGNIFICENT KNOWLEDGE OF THE GREAT DRY WHITES. WE COULD HAVE TALKED.
AH WELL.
"MUHSYOUR" HAS A PLANE TO CATCH.

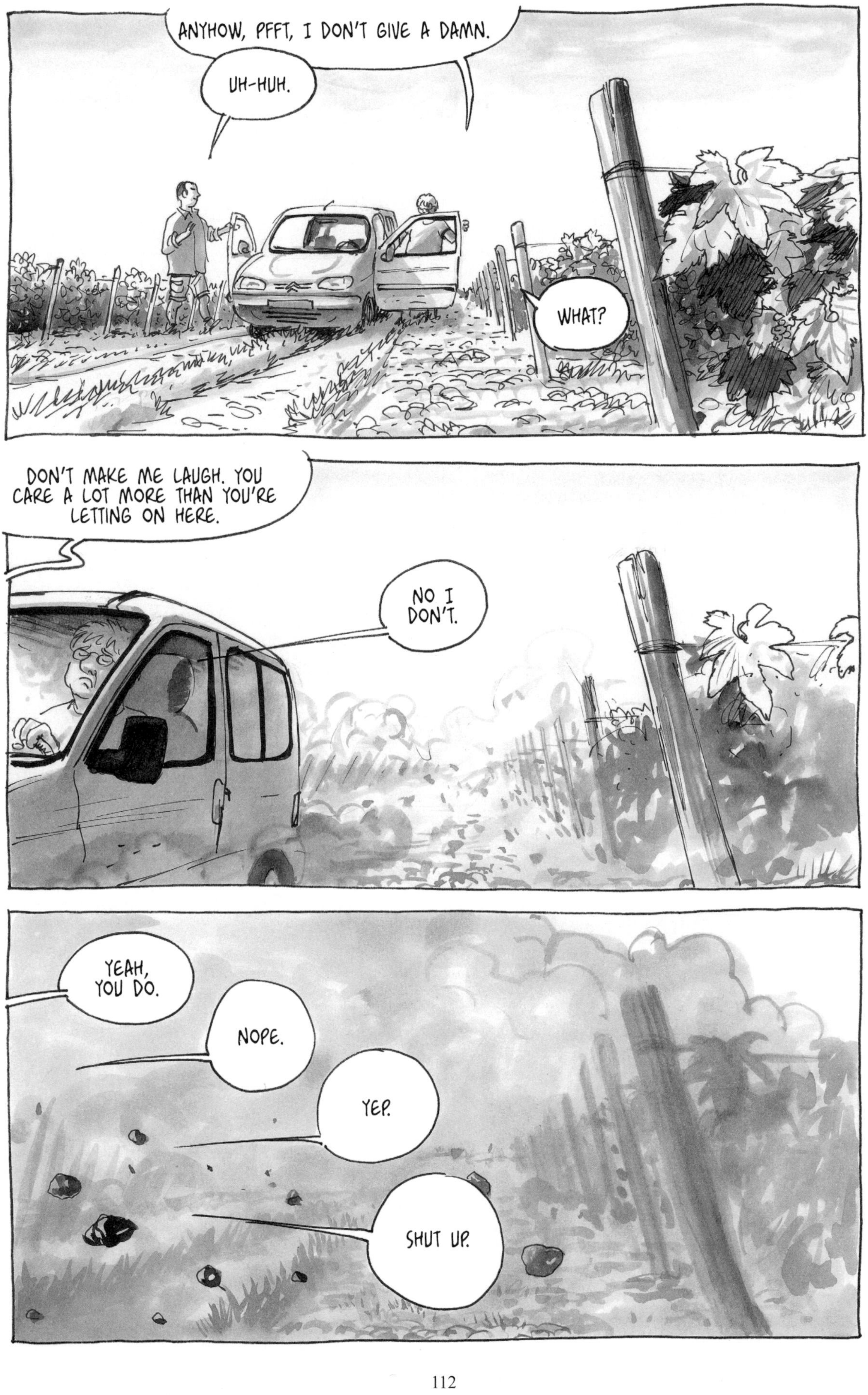
ANYHOW, PFFT, I DON'T GIVE A DAMN.
UH-HUH.
WHAT?
DON'T MAKE ME LAUGH. YOU CARE A LOT MORE THAN YOU'RE LETTING ON HERE.
NO I DON'T.
YEAH, YOU DO.
NOPE.
YEP.
SHUT UP.

CHAPTER NINE   SAYING SOMETHING
STUPID:
(SOMETIMES)
A GOOD IDEA

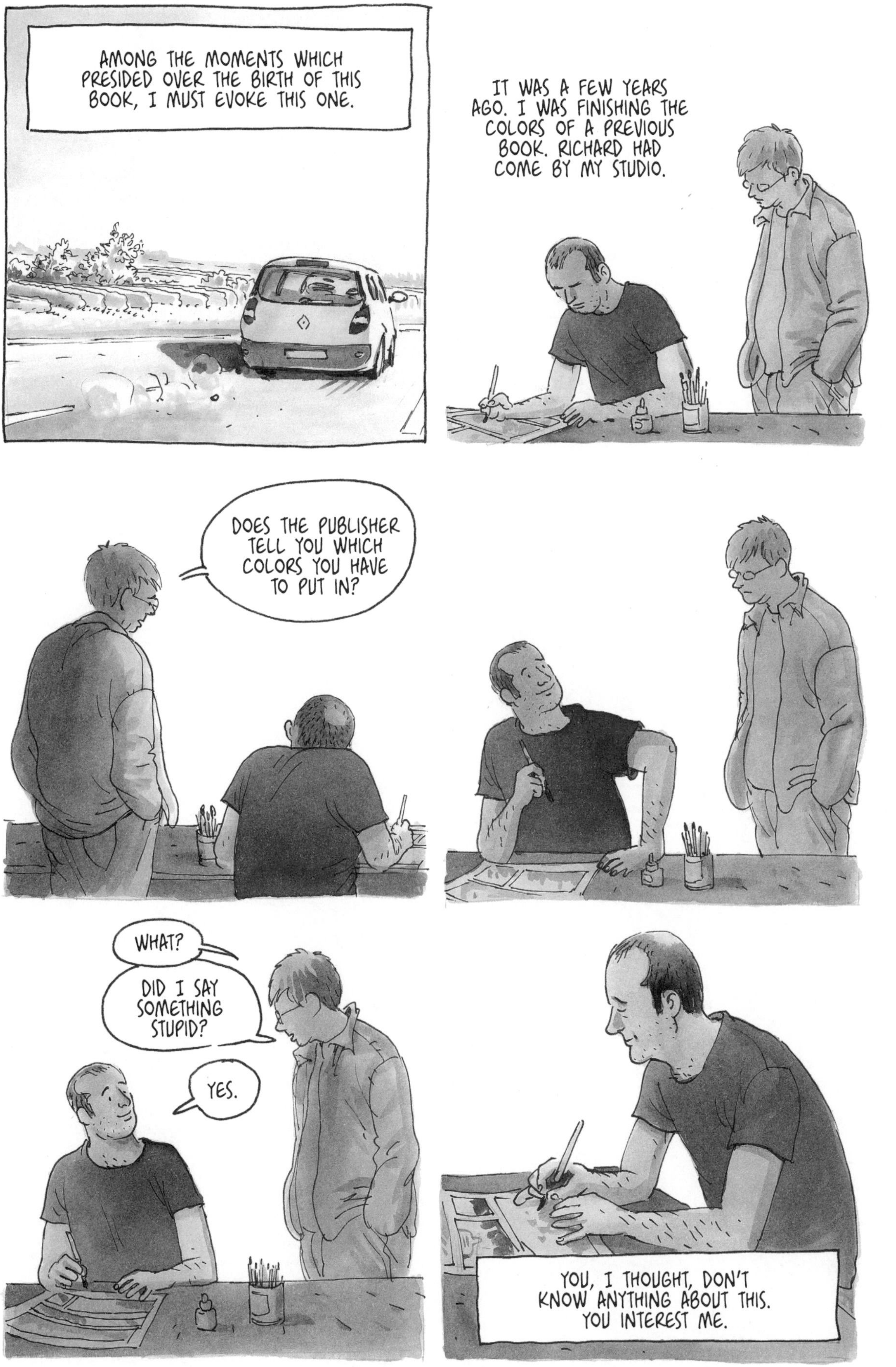

AMONG THE MOMENTS WHICH PRESIDED OVER THE BIRTH OF THIS BOOK, I MUST EVOKE THIS ONE.
IT WAS A FEW YEARS AGO. I WAS FINISHING THE COLORS OF A PREVIOUS BOOK. RICHARD HAD COME BY MY STUDIO.
DOES THE PUBLISHER TELL YOU WHICH COLORS YOU HAVE TO PUT IN?
WHAT?
DID I SAY SOMETHING STUPID?
YES.
YOU, I THOUGHT, DON'T KNOW ANYTHING ABOUT THIS. YOU INTEREST ME.

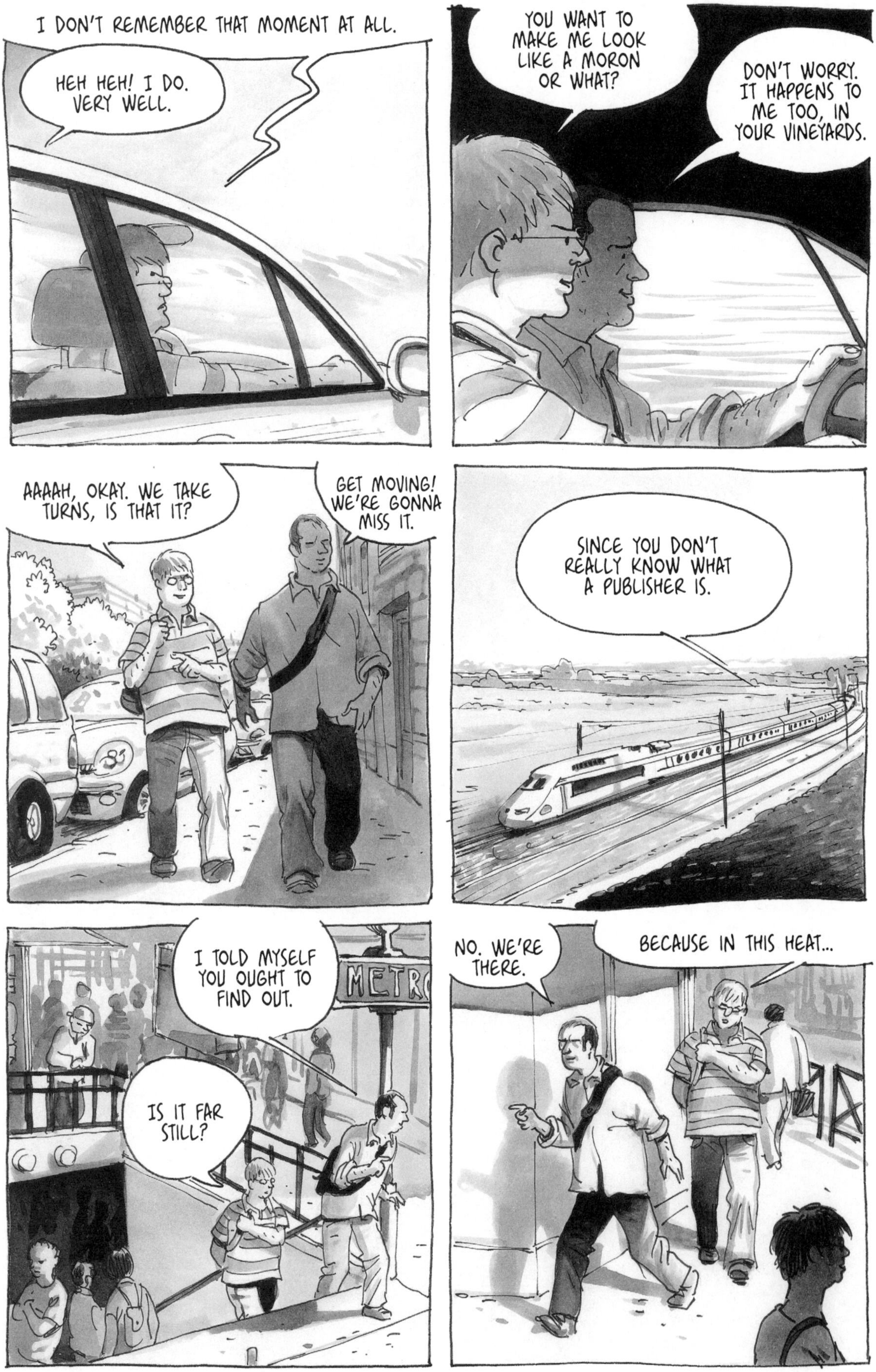
I DON'T REMEMBER THAT MOMENT AT ALL.
HEH HEH! I DO. VERY WELL.
YOU WANT TO MAKE ME LOOK LIKE A MORON OR WHAT?
DON'T WORRY. IT HAPPENS TO ME TOO, IN YOUR VINEYARDS.
AAAAH, OKAY. WE TAKE TURNS, IS THAT IT?
GET MOVING! WE'RE GONNA MISS IT.
SINCE YOU DON'T REALLY KNOW WHAT A PUBLISHER IS.
I TOLD MYSELF YOU OUGHT TO FIND OUT.
METRO
IS IT FAR STILL?
NO. WE'RE THERE.
BECAUSE IN THIS HEAT...

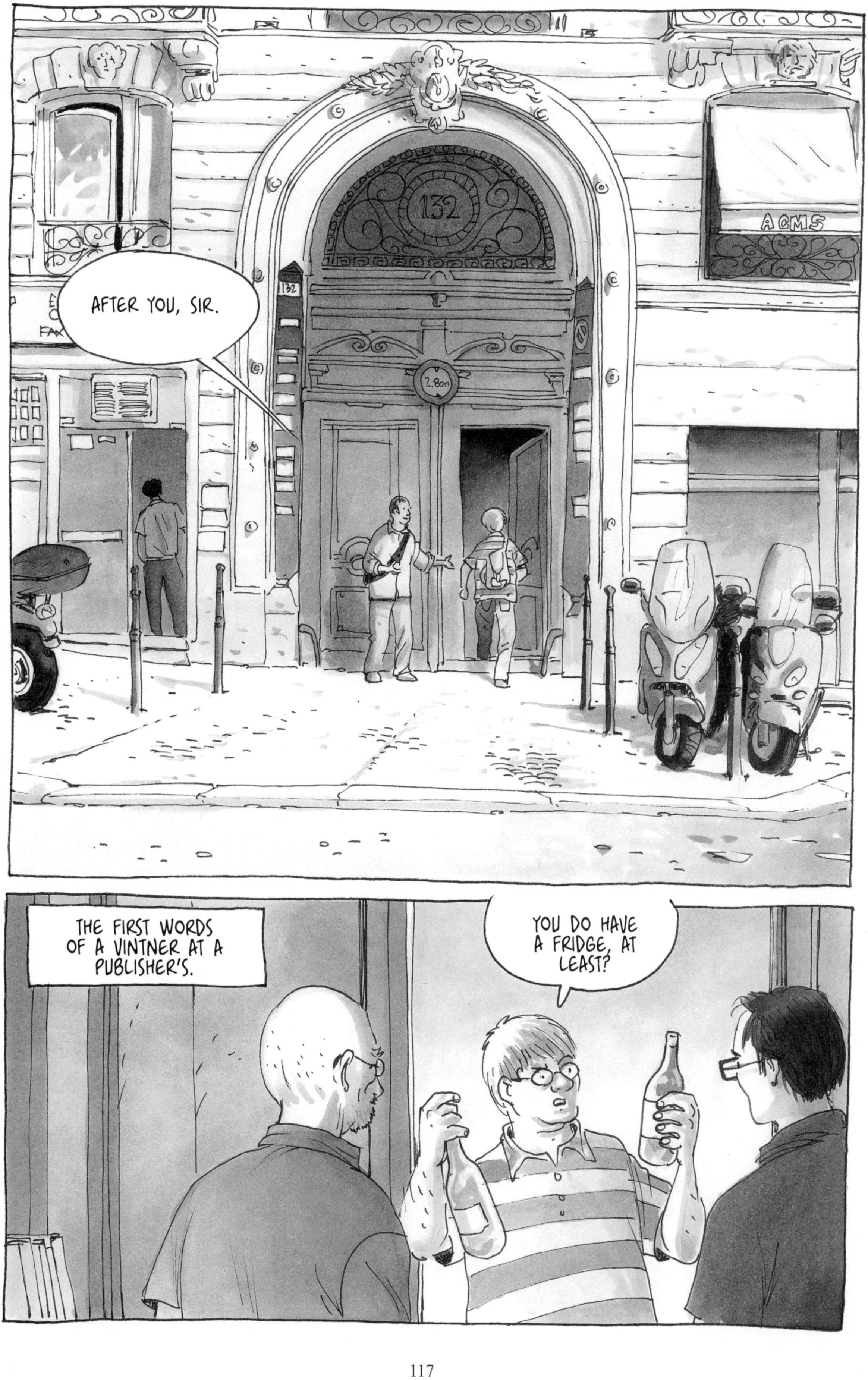
132
AFTER YOU, SIR.
THE FIRST WORDS OF A VINTNER AT A PUBLISHER'S.
YOU DO HAVE A FRIDGE, AT LEAST?

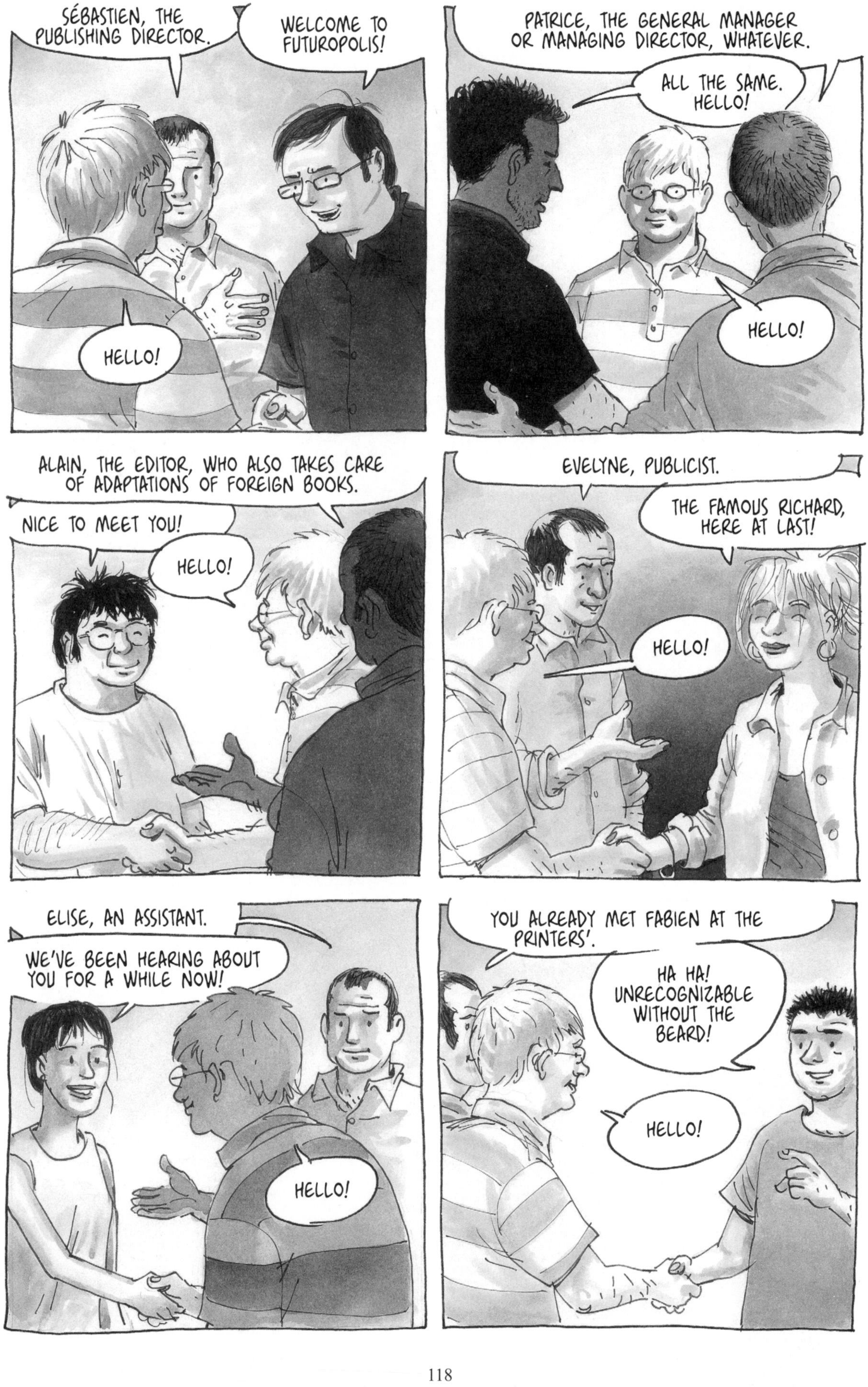
SÉBASTIEN, THE PUBLISHING DIRECTOR.
WELCOME TO FUTUROPOLIS!
HELLO!
PATRICE, THE GENERAL MANAGER OR MANAGING DIRECTOR, WHATEVER.
ALL THE SAME. HELLO!
HELLO!
ALAIN, THE EDITOR, WHO ALSO TAKES CARE OF ADAPTATIONS OF FOREIGN BOOKS.
NICE TO MEET YOU!
HELLO!
EVELYNE, PUBLICIST.
THE FAMOUS RICHARD, HERE AT LAST!
HELLO!
ELISE, AN ASSISTANT.
WE'VE BEEN HEARING ABOUT YOU FOR A WHILE NOW!
HELLO!
YOU ALREADY MET FABIEN AT THE PRINTERS'.
HA HA! UNRECOGNIZABLE WITHOUT THE BEARD!
HELLO!

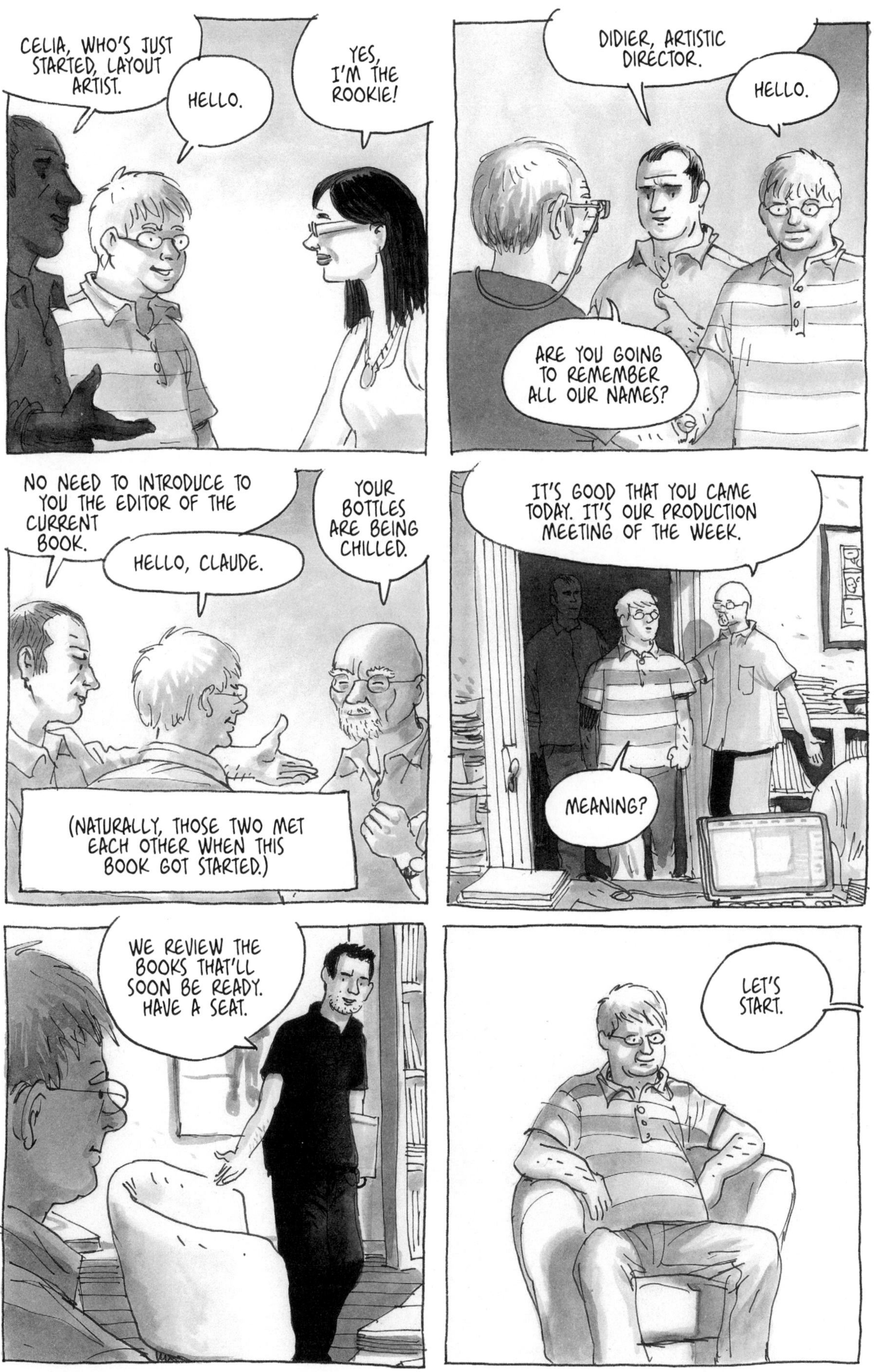
CELIA, WHO'S JUST STARTED, LAYOUT ARTIST.
HELLO.
YES, I'M THE ROOKIE!
DIDIER, ARTISTIC DIRECTOR.
HELLO.
ARE YOU GOING TO REMEMBER ALL OUR NAMES?
NO NEED TO INTRODUCE TO YOU THE EDITOR OF THE CURRENT BOOK.
HELLO, CLAUDE.
YOUR BOTTLES ARE BEING CHILLED.
(NATURALLY, THOSE TWO MET EACH OTHER WHEN THIS BOOK GOT STARTED.)
IT'S GOOD THAT YOU CAME TODAY. IT'S OUR PRODUCTION MEETING OF THE WEEK.
MEANING?
WE REVIEW THE BOOKS THAT'LL SOON BE READY. HAVE A SEAT.
LET'S START.

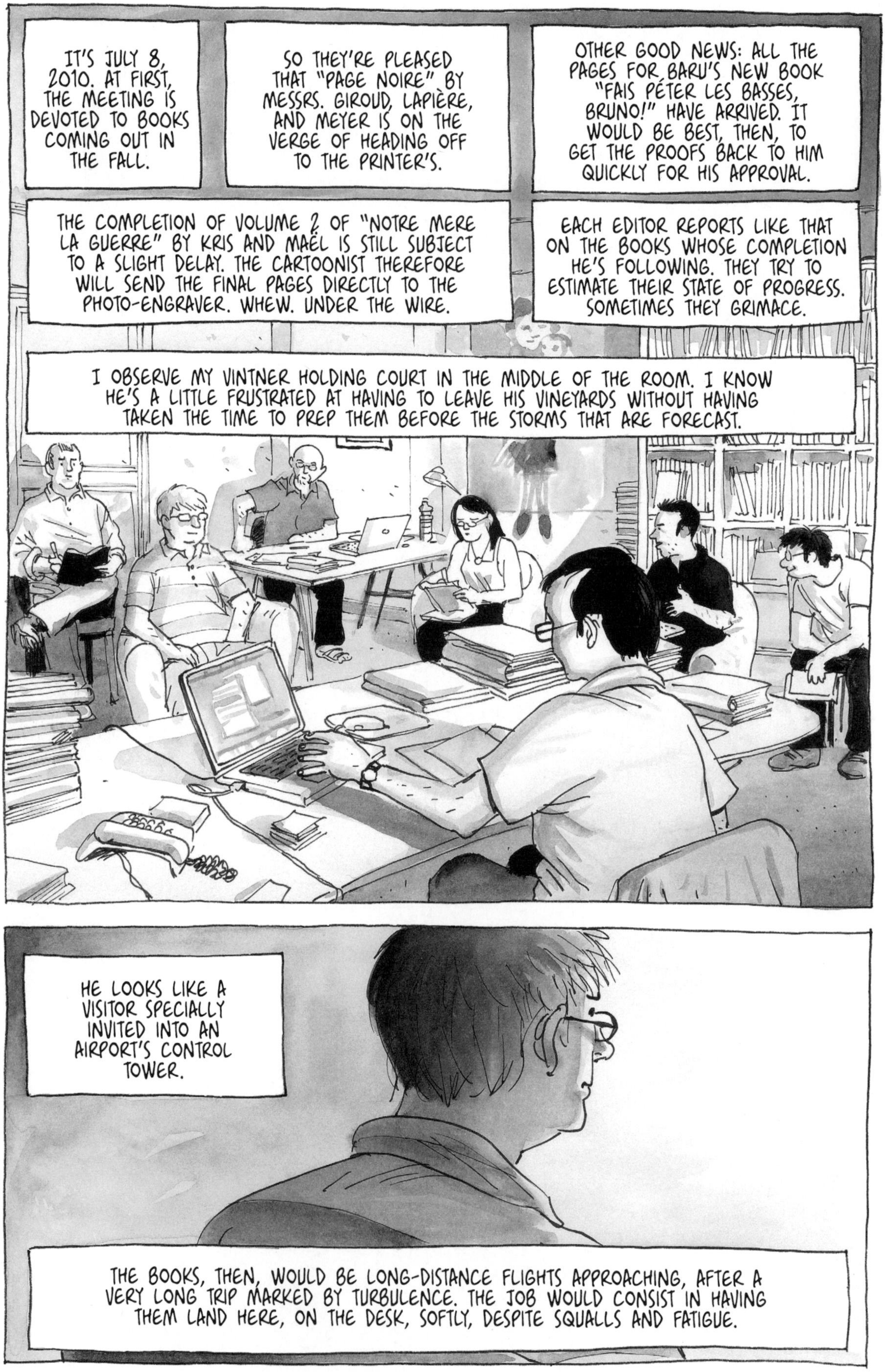
IT'S JULY 8, 2010. AT FIRST, THE MEETING IS DEVOTED TO BOOKS COMING OUT IN THE FALL.
SO THEY'RE PLEASED THAT "PAGE NOIRE" BY MESSRS. GIROUD, LAPIÈRE, AND MEYER IS ON THE VERGE OF HEADING OFF TO THE PRINTER'S.
OTHER GOOD NEWS: ALL THE PAGES FOR BARU'S NEW BOOK "FAIS PÉTER LES BASSES, BRUNO!" HAVE ARRIVED. IT WOULD BE BEST, THEN, TO GET THE PROOFS BACK TO HIM QUICKLY FOR HIS APPROVAL.
THE COMPLETION OF VOLUME 2 OF "NOTRE MERE LA GUERRE" BY KRIS AND MAËL IS STILL SUBJECT TO A SLIGHT DELAY. THE CARTOONIST THEREFORE WILL SEND THE FINAL PAGES DIRECTLY TO THE PHOTO-ENGRAVER. WHEW. UNDER THE WIRE.
EACH EDITOR REPORTS LIKE THAT ON THE BOOKS WHOSE COMPLETION HE'S FOLLOWING. THEY TRY TO ESTIMATE THEIR STATE OF PROGRESS. SOMETIMES THEY GRIMACE.
I OBSERVE MY VINTNER HOLDING COURT IN THE MIDDLE OF THE ROOM. I KNOW HE'S A LITTLE FRUSTRATED AT HAVING TO LEAVE HIS VINEYARDS WITHOUT HAVING TAKEN THE TIME TO PREP THEM BEFORE THE STORMS THAT ARE FORECAST.
HE LOOKS LIKE A VISITOR SPECIALLY INVITED INTO AN AIRPORT'S CONTROL TOWER.
THE BOOKS, THEN, WOULD BE LONG-DISTANCE FLIGHTS APPROACHING, AFTER A VERY LONG TRIP MARKED BY TURBULENCE. THE JOB WOULD CONSIST IN HAVING THEM LAND HERE, ON THE DESK, SOFTLY, DESPITE SQUALLS AND FATIGUE.

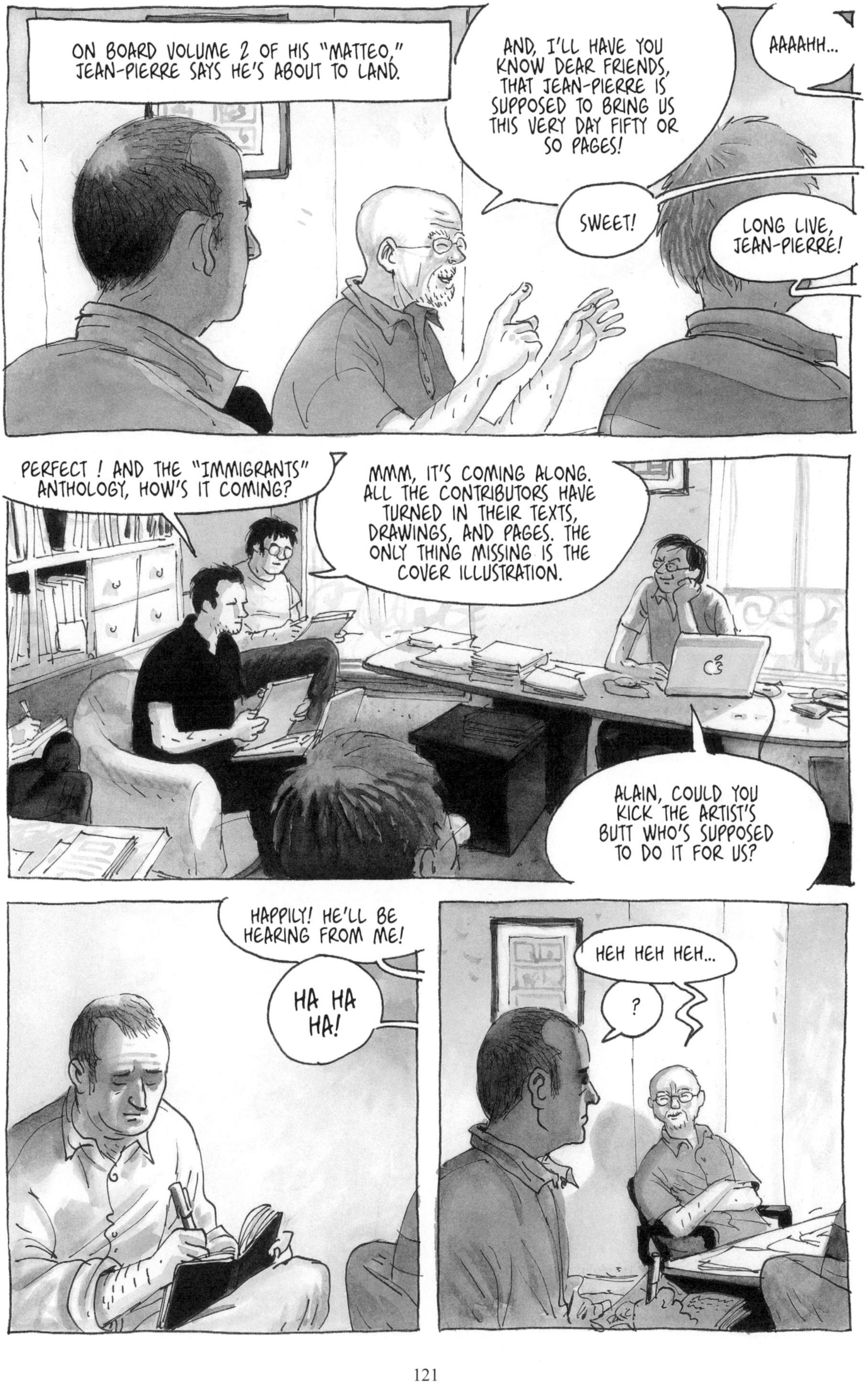
ON BOARD VOLUME 2 OF HIS "MATTEO," JEAN-PIERRE SAYS HE'S ABOUT TO LAND.
AND, I'LL HAVE YOU KNOW DEAR FRIENDS, THAT JEAN-PIERRE IS SUPPOSED TO BRING US THIS VERY DAY FIFTY OR SO PAGES!
AAAAHH...
SWEET!
LONG LIVE, JEAN-PIERRE!
PERFECT ! AND THE "IMMIGRANTS" ANTHOLOGY, HOW'S IT COMING?
MMM, IT'S COMING ALONG. ALL THE CONTRIBUTORS HAVE TURNED IN THEIR TEXTS, DRAWINGS, AND PAGES. THE ONLY THING MISSING IS THE COVER ILLUSTRATION.
ALAIN, COULD YOU KICK THE ARTIST'S BUTT WHO'S SUPPOSED TO DO IT FOR US?
HAPPILY! HE'LL BE HEARING FROM ME!
HA HA HA!
HEH HEH HEH...
?

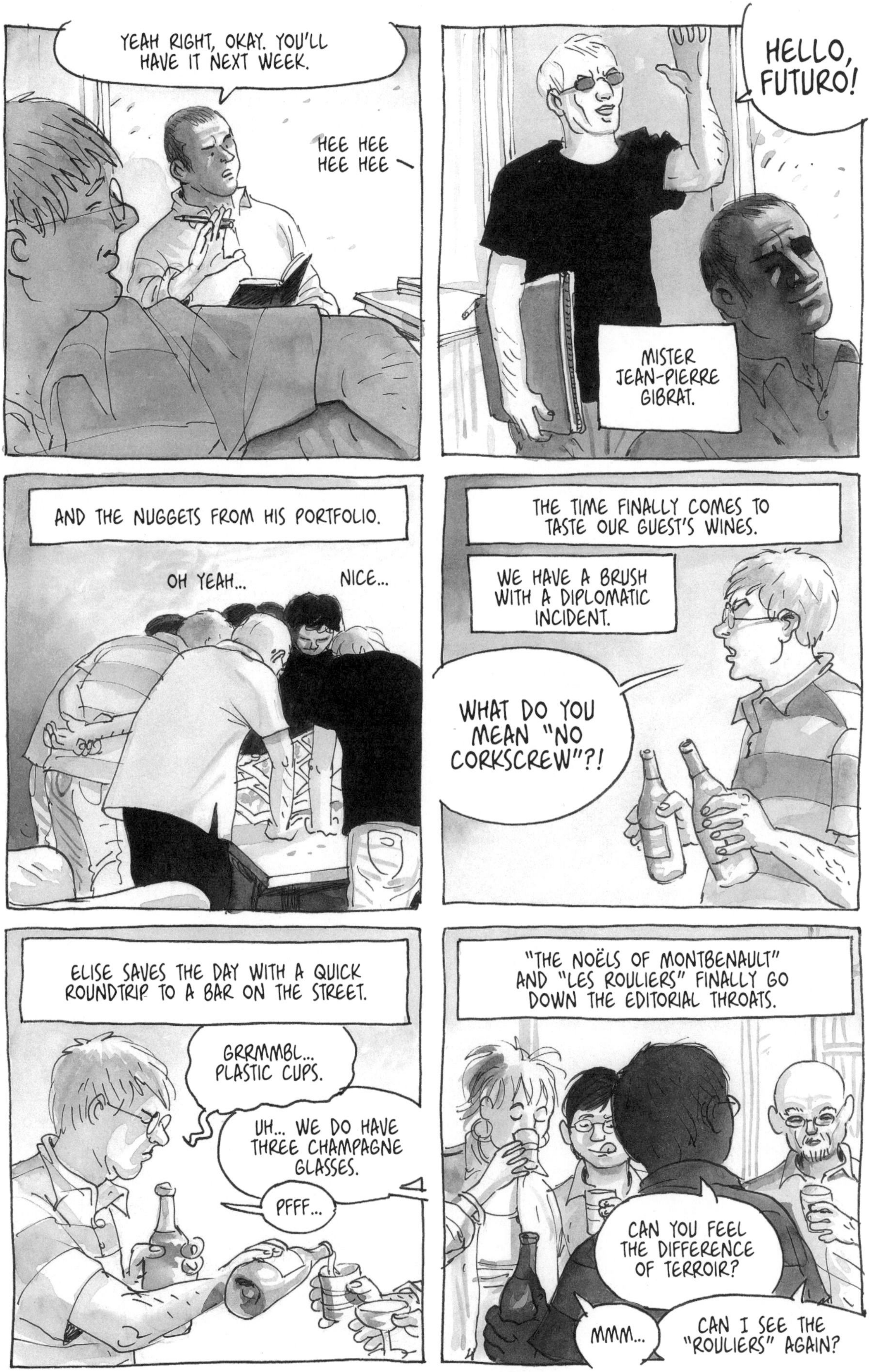
YEAH RIGHT, OKAY. YOU'LL HAVE IT NEXT WEEK.
HEE HEE HEE HEE
HELLO, FUTURO!
MISTER JEAN-PIERRE GIBRAT.
AND THE NUGGETS FROM HIS PORTFOLIO.
OH YEAH...
NICE...
THE TIME FINALLY COMES TO TASTE OUR GUEST'S WINES.
WE HAVE A BRUSH WITH A DIPLOMATIC INCIDENT.
WHAT DO YOU MEAN "NO CORKSCREW"?!
ELISE SAVES THE DAY WITH A QUICK ROUNDTRIP TO A BAR ON THE STREET.
GRRMMBL... PLASTIC CUPS.
UH... WE DO HAVE THREE CHAMPAGNE GLASSES.
PFFF...
"THE NOËLS OF MONTBENAULT" AND "LES ROULIERS" FINALLY GO DOWN THE EDITORIAL THROATS.
CAN YOU FEEL THE DIFFERENCE OF TERROIR?
MMM...
CAN I SEE THE "ROULIERS" AGAIN?

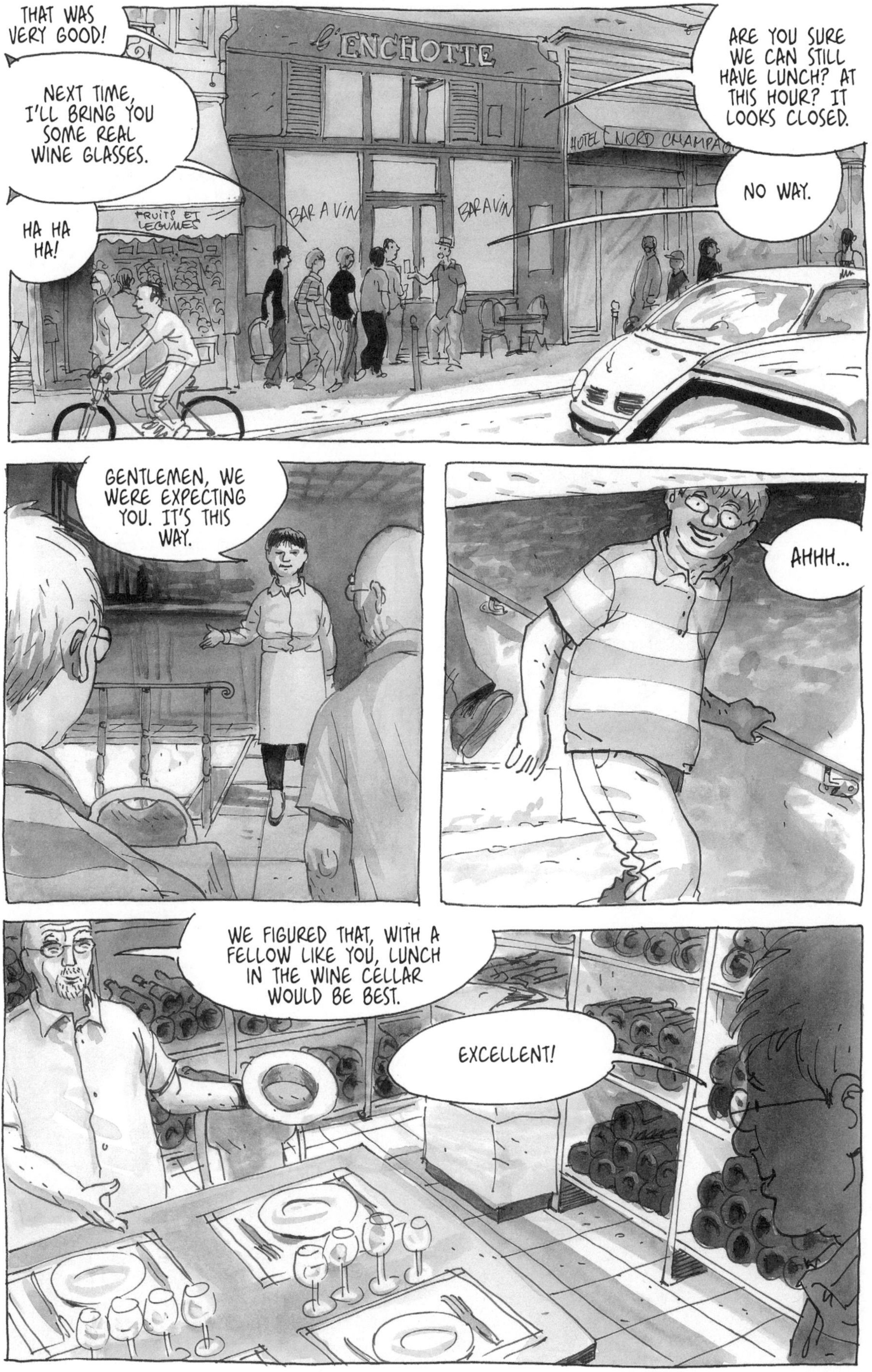
THAT WAS VERY GOOD!
L'ENCHOTTE
NEXT TIME, I'LL BRING YOU SOME REAL WINE GLASSES.
HA HA HA!
FRUITS ET LEGUMES
BAR A VIN
BAR A VIN
ARE YOU SURE WE CAN STILL HAVE LUNCH? AT THIS HOUR? IT LOOKS CLOSED.
NO WAY.
GENTLEMEN, WE WERE EXPECTING YOU. IT'S THIS WAY.
AHHH...
WE FIGURED THAT, WITH A FELLOW LIKE YOU, LUNCH IN THE WINE CELLAR WOULD BE BEST.
EXCELLENT!

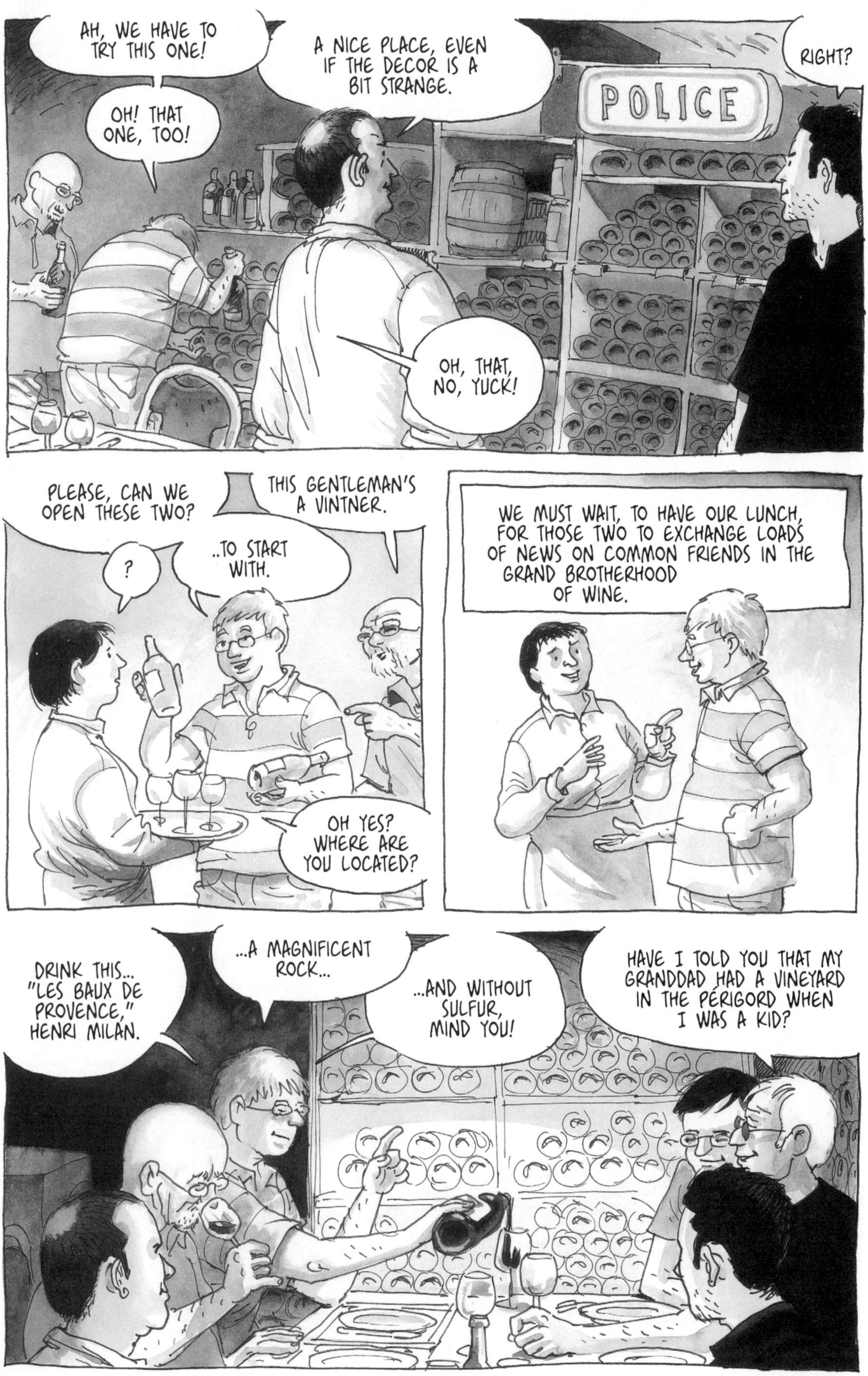
AH, WE HAVE TO TRY THIS ONE!
OH! THAT ONE, TOO!
A NICE PLACE, EVEN IF THE DECOR IS A BIT STRANGE.
POLICE
RIGHT?
OH, THAT, NO, YUCK!
PLEASE, CAN WE OPEN THESE TWO?
?
..TO START WITH.
THIS GENTLEMAN'S A VINTNER.
OH YES? WHERE ARE YOU LOCATED?
WE MUST WAIT, TO HAVE OUR LUNCH, FOR THOSE TWO TO EXCHANGE LOADS OF NEWS ON COMMON FRIENDS IN THE GRAND BROTHERHOOD OF WINE.
DRINK THIS... "LES BAUX DE PROVENCE," HENRI MILAN.
...A MAGNIFICENT ROCK...
...AND WITHOUT SULFUR, MIND YOU!
HAVE I TOLD YOU THAT MY GRANDDAD HAD A VINEYARD IN THE PÉRIGORD WHEN I WAS A KID?

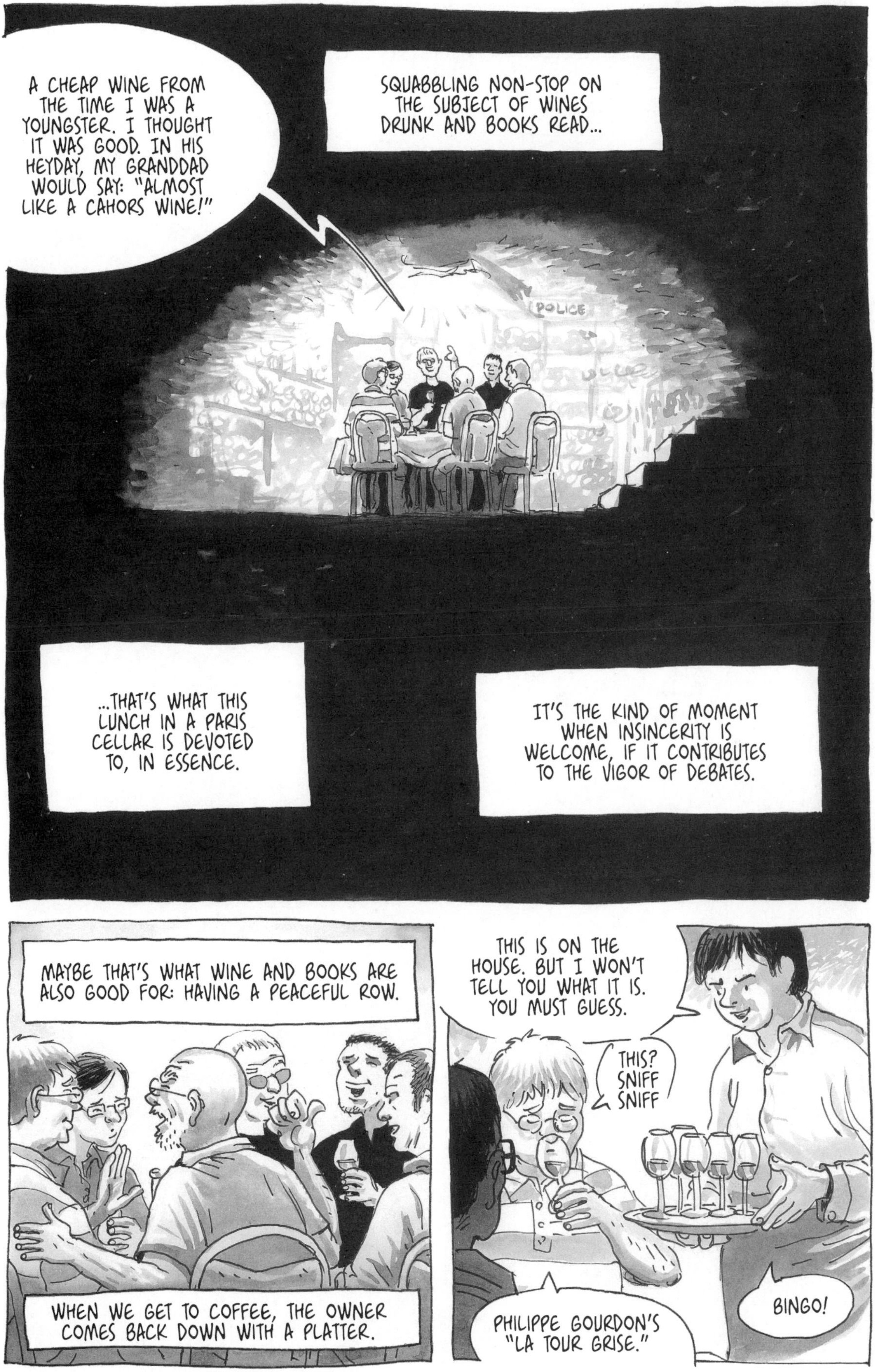
A CHEAP WINE FROM THE TIME I WAS A YOUNGSTER. I THOUGHT IT WAS GOOD. IN HIS HEYDAY, MY GRANDDAD WOULD SAY: "ALMOST LIKE A CAHORS WINE!"
SQUABBLING NON-STOP ON THE SUBJECT OF WINES DRUNK AND BOOKS READ...
POLICE
...THAT'S WHAT THIS LUNCH IN A PARIS CELLAR IS DEVOTED TO, IN ESSENCE.
IT'S THE KIND OF MOMENT WHEN INSINCERITY IS WELCOME, IF IT CONTRIBUTES TO THE VIGOR OF DEBATES.
MAYBE THAT'S WHAT WINE AND BOOKS ARE ALSO GOOD FOR: HAVING A PEACEFUL ROW.
WHEN WE GET TO COFFEE, THE OWNER COMES BACK DOWN WITH A PLATTER.
THIS IS ON THE HOUSE. BUT I WON'T TELL YOU WHAT IT IS. YOU MUST GUESS.
THIS? SNIFF SNIFF
PHILIPPE GOURDON'S "LA TOUR GRISE."
BINGO!

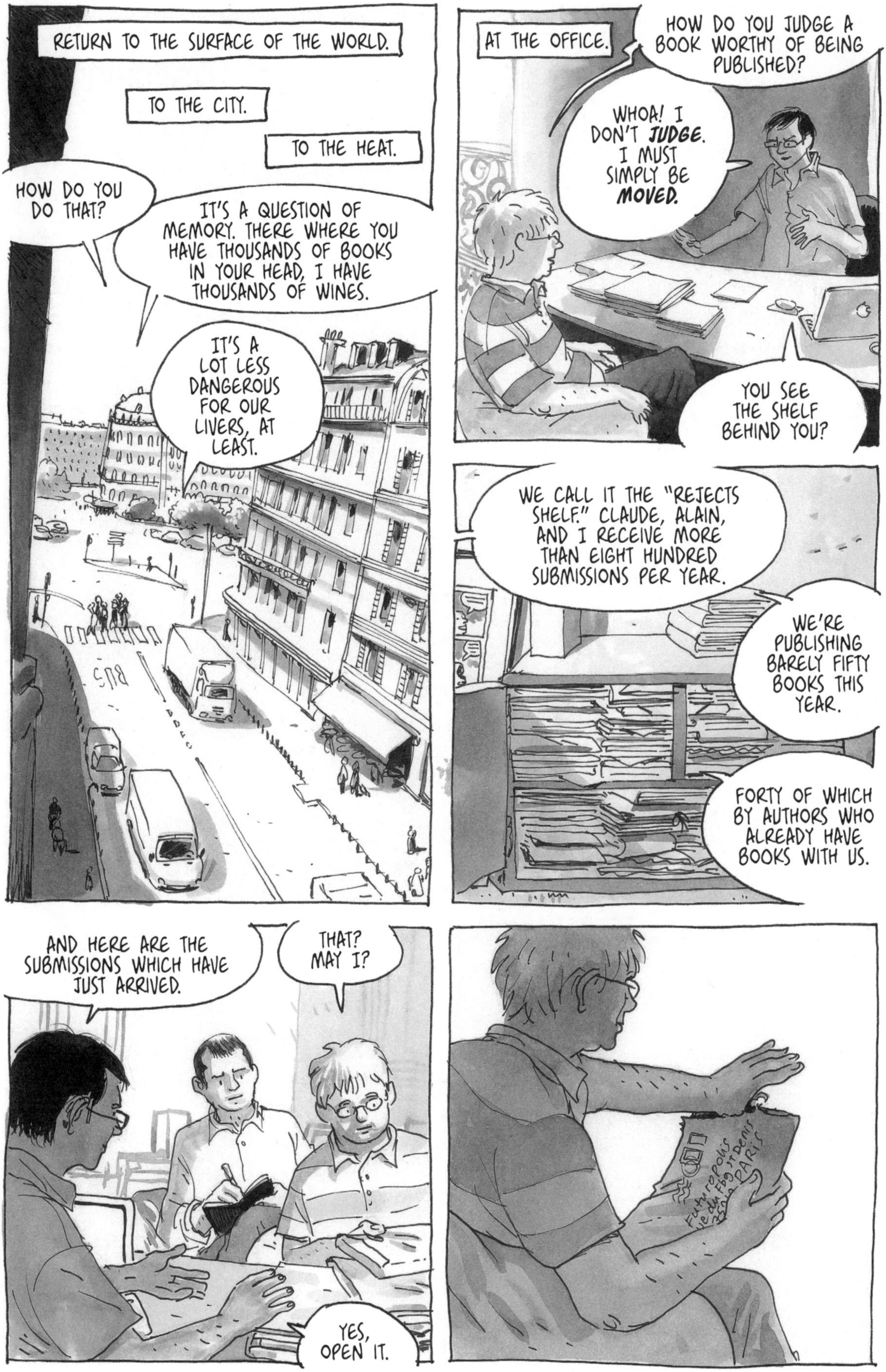
RETURN TO THE SURFACE OF THE WORLD.
TO THE CITY.
TO THE HEAT.
HOW DO YOU DO THAT?
IT'S A QUESTION OF MEMORY. THERE WHERE YOU HAVE THOUSANDS OF BOOKS IN YOUR HEAD, I HAVE THOUSANDS OF WINES.
IT'S A LOT LESS DANGEROUS FOR OUR LIVERS, AT LEAST.
AT THE OFFICE.
HOW DO YOU JUDGE A BOOK WORTHY OF BEING PUBLISHED?
WHOA! I DON'T **JUDGE**. I MUST SIMPLY BE **MOVED**.
YOU SEE THE SHELF BEHIND YOU?
WE CALL IT THE "REJECTS SHELF." CLAUDE, ALAIN, AND I RECEIVE MORE THAN EIGHT HUNDRED SUBMISSIONS PER YEAR.
WE'RE PUBLISHING BARELY FIFTY BOOKS THIS YEAR.
FORTY OF WHICH BY AUTHORS WHO ALREADY HAVE BOOKS WITH US.
AND HERE ARE THE SUBMISSIONS WHICH HAVE JUST ARRIVED.
THAT? MAY I?
YES, OPEN IT.
Futuropolis
PARIS

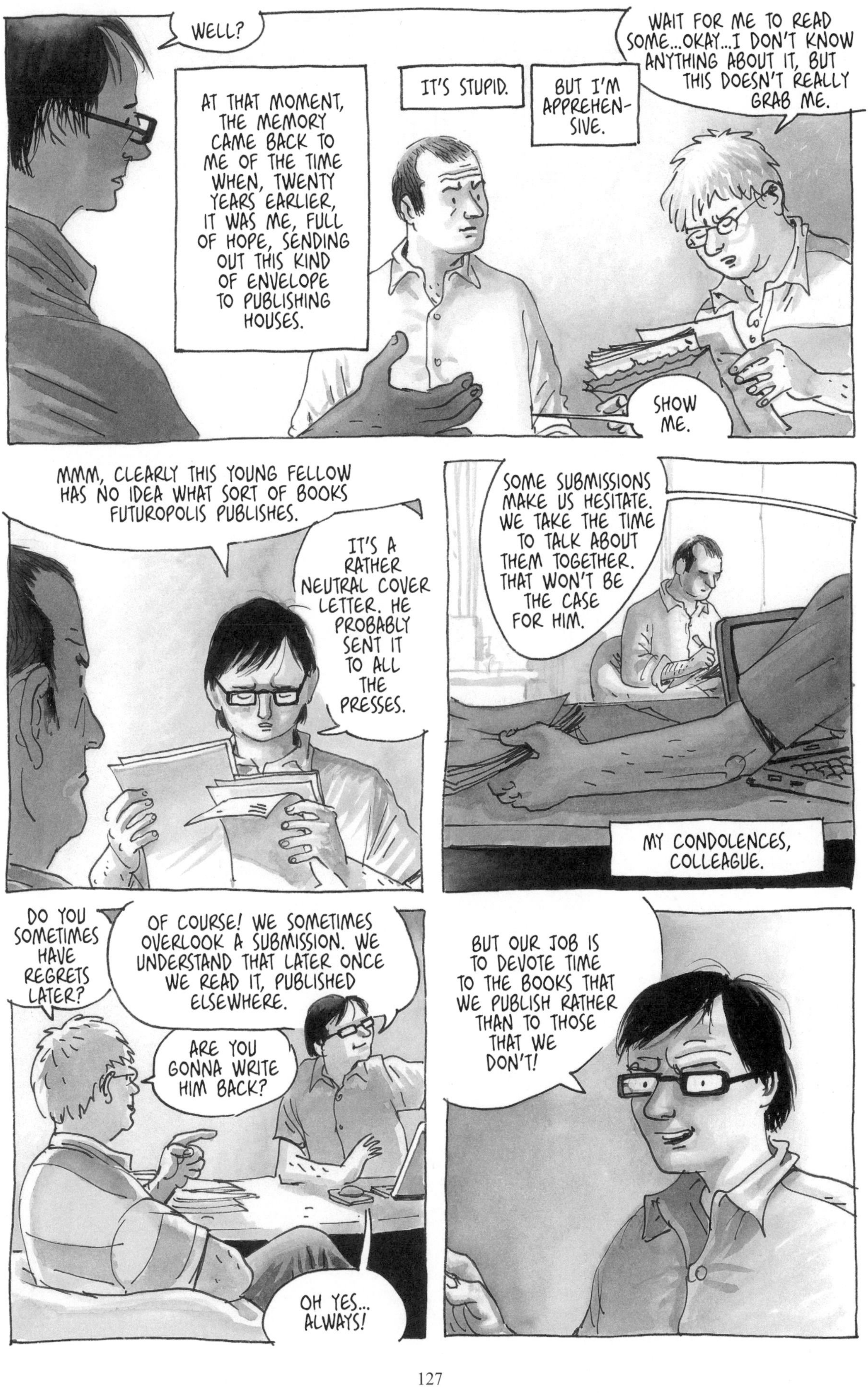

WELL?
AT THAT MOMENT, THE MEMORY CAME BACK TO ME OF THE TIME WHEN, TWENTY YEARS EARLIER, IT WAS ME, FULL OF HOPE, SENDING OUT THIS KIND OF ENVELOPE TO PUBLISHING HOUSES.
IT'S STUPID.
BUT I'M APPREHEN-SIVE.
WAIT FOR ME TO READ SOME...OKAY...I DON'T KNOW ANYTHING ABOUT IT, BUT THIS DOESN'T REALLY GRAB ME.
SHOW ME.
MMM, CLEARLY THIS YOUNG FELLOW HAS NO IDEA WHAT SORT OF BOOKS FUTUROPOLIS PUBLISHES.
IT'S A RATHER NEUTRAL COVER LETTER. HE PROBABLY SENT IT TO ALL THE PRESSES.
SOME SUBMISSIONS MAKE US HESITATE. WE TAKE THE TIME TO TALK ABOUT THEM TOGETHER. THAT WON'T BE THE CASE FOR HIM.
MY CONDOLENCES, COLLEAGUE.
DO YOU SOMETIMES HAVE REGRETS LATER?
OF COURSE! WE SOMETIMES OVERLOOK A SUBMISSION. WE UNDERSTAND THAT LATER ONCE WE READ IT, PUBLISHED ELSEWHERE.
ARE YOU GONNA WRITE HIM BACK?
OH YES... ALWAYS!
BUT OUR JOB IS TO DEVOTE TIME TO THE BOOKS THAT WE PUBLISH RATHER THAN TO THOSE THAT WE DON'T!

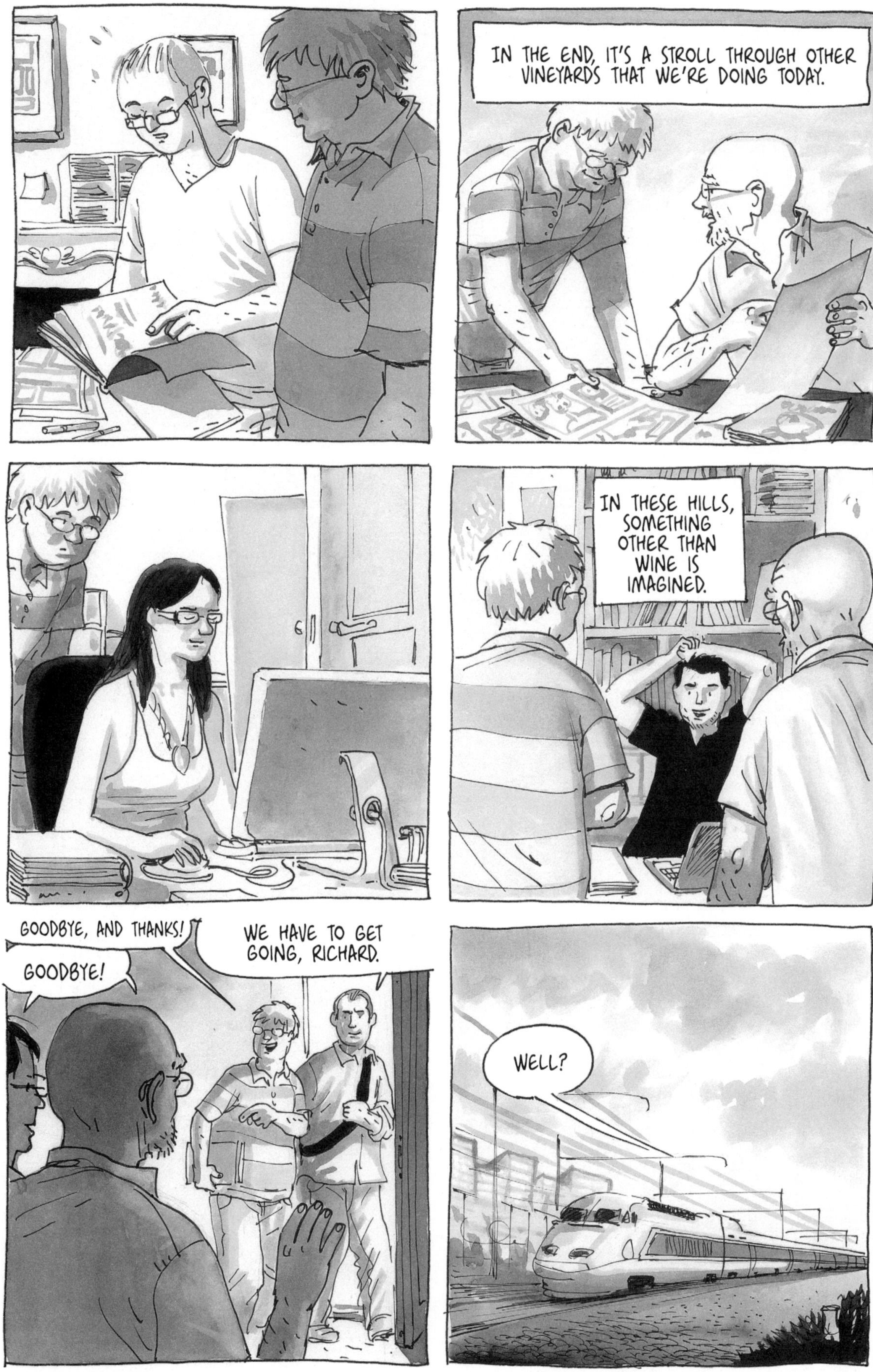
IN THE END, IT'S A STROLL THROUGH OTHER VINEYARDS THAT WE'RE DOING TODAY.
IN THESE HILLS, SOMETHING OTHER THAN WINE IS IMAGINED.
GOODBYE, AND THANKS!
WE HAVE TO GET GOING, RICHARD.
GOODBYE!
WELL?

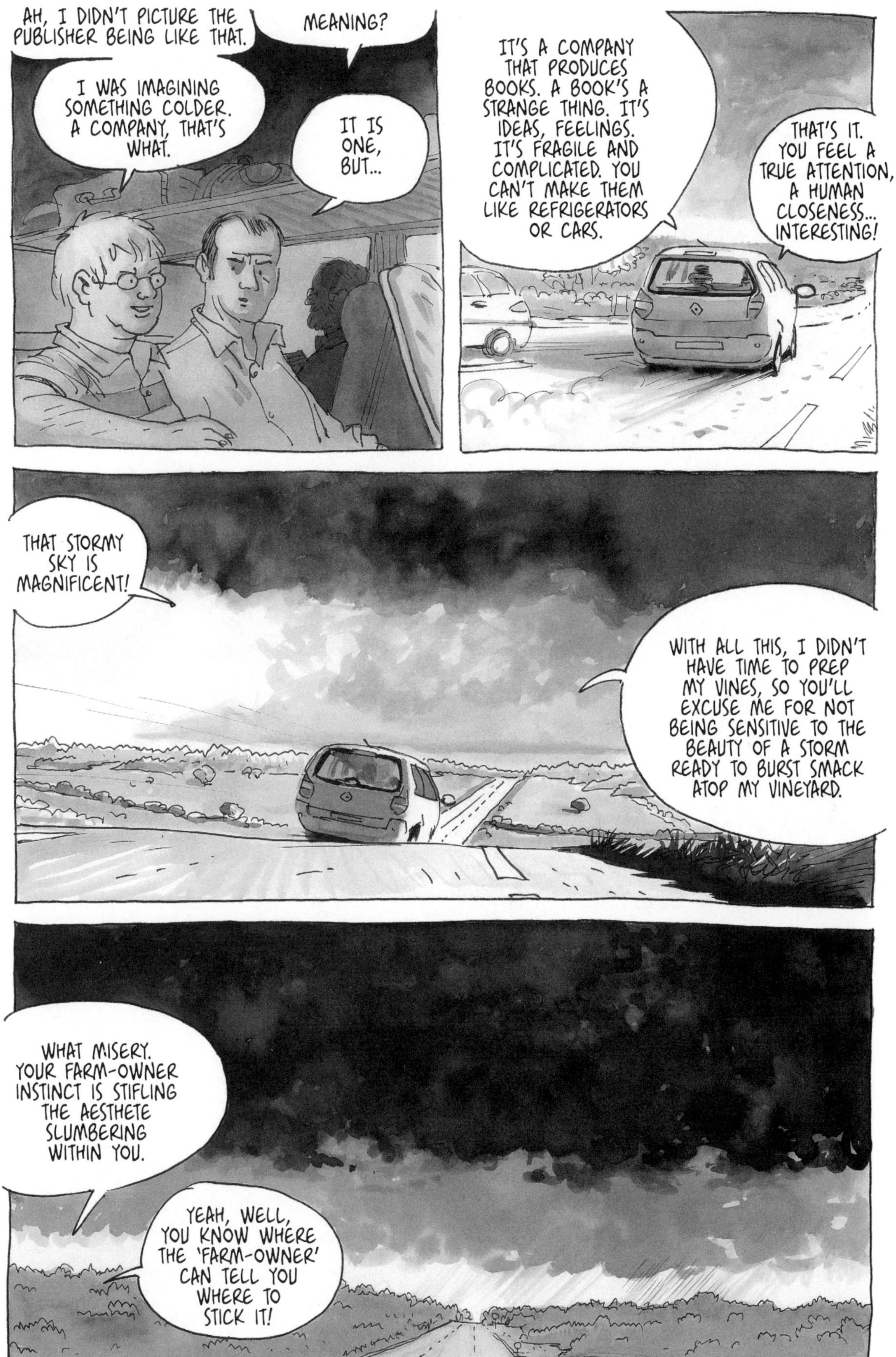
AH, I DIDN'T PICTURE THE PUBLISHER BEING LIKE THAT.
MEANING?
I WAS IMAGINING SOMETHING COLDER. A COMPANY, THAT'S WHAT.
IT IS ONE, BUT...
IT'S A COMPANY THAT PRODUCES BOOKS. A BOOK'S A STRANGE THING. IT'S IDEAS, FEELINGS. IT'S FRAGILE AND COMPLICATED. YOU CAN'T MAKE THEM LIKE REFRIGERATORS OR CARS.
THAT'S IT. YOU FEEL A TRUE ATTENTION, A HUMAN CLOSENESS... INTERESTING!
THAT STORMY SKY IS MAGNIFICENT!
WITH ALL THIS, I DIDN'T HAVE TIME TO PREP MY VINES, SO YOU'LL EXCUSE ME FOR NOT BEING SENSITIVE TO THE BEAUTY OF A STORM READY TO BURST SMACK ATOP MY VINEYARD.
WHAT MISERY. YOUR FARM-OWNER INSTINCT IS STIFLING THE AESTHETE SLUMBERING WITHIN YOU.
YEAH, WELL, YOU KNOW WHERE THE 'FARM-OWNER' CAN TELL YOU WHERE TO STICK IT!

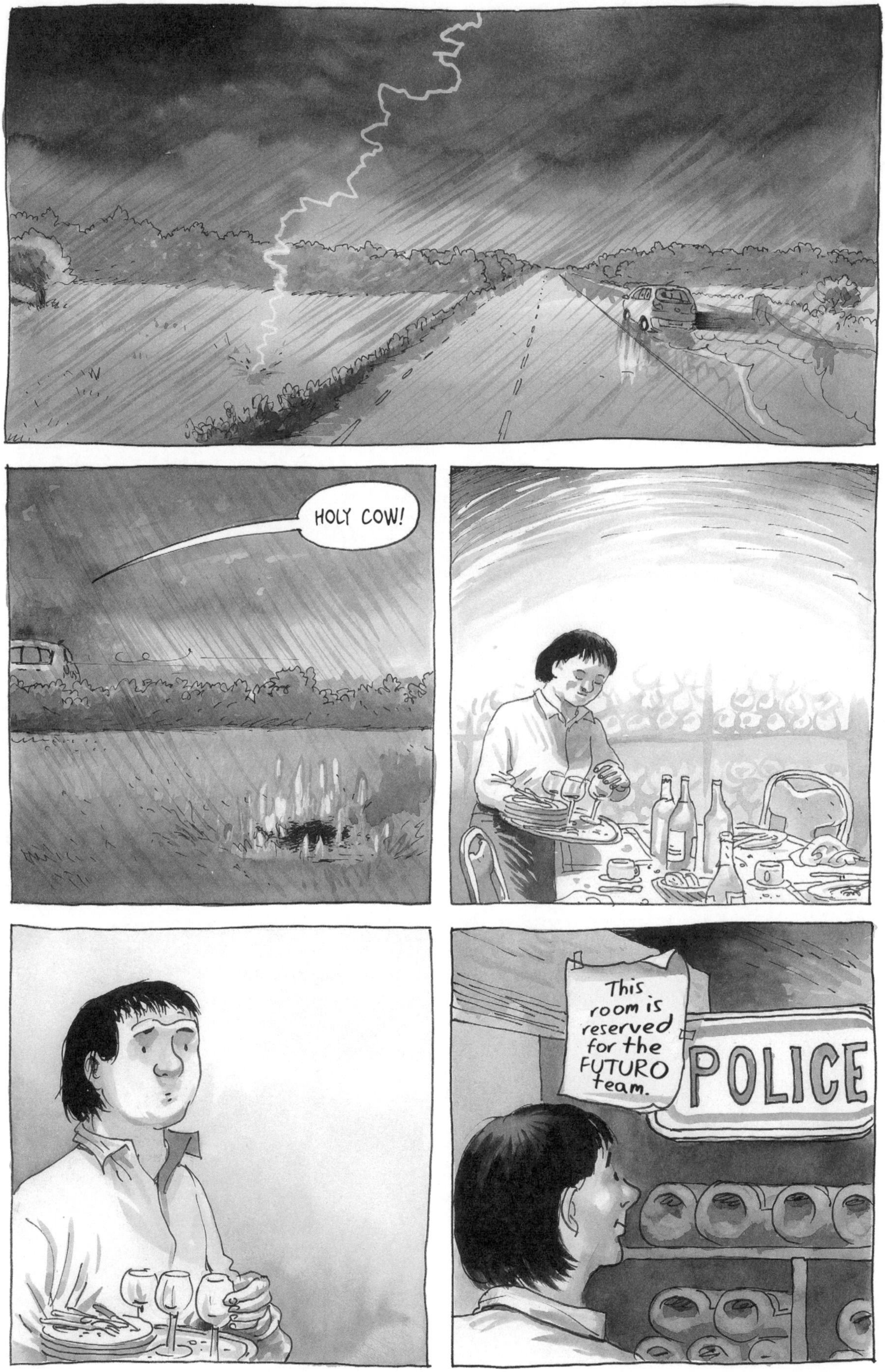
HOLY COW!
This room is reserved for the FUTURO team.
POLICE

CHAPTER TEN   THE BLUNDER

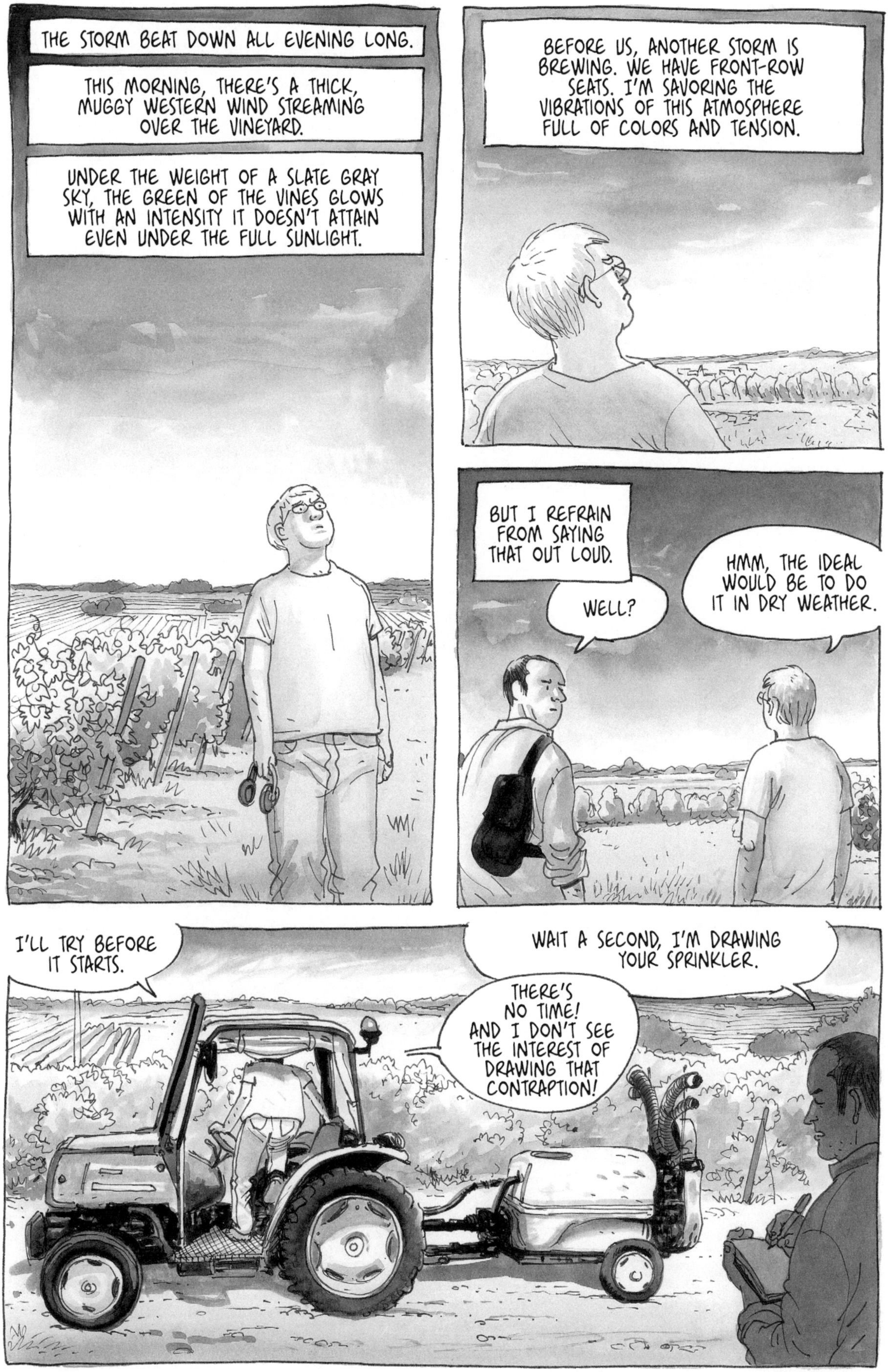

THE STORM BEAT DOWN ALL EVENING LONG.
THIS MORNING, THERE'S A THICK, MUGGY WESTERN WIND STREAMING OVER THE VINEYARD.
UNDER THE WEIGHT OF A SLATE GRAY SKY, THE GREEN OF THE VINES GLOWS WITH AN INTENSITY IT DOESN'T ATTAIN EVEN UNDER THE FULL SUNLIGHT.
BEFORE US, ANOTHER STORM IS BREWING. WE HAVE FRONT-ROW SEATS. I'M SAVORING THE VIBRATIONS OF THIS ATMOSPHERE FULL OF COLORS AND TENSION.
BUT I REFRAIN FROM SAYING THAT OUT LOUD.
WELL?
HMM, THE IDEAL WOULD BE TO DO IT IN DRY WEATHER.
I'LL TRY BEFORE IT STARTS.
WAIT A SECOND, I'M DRAWING YOUR SPRINKLER.
THERE'S NO TIME! AND I DON'T SEE THE INTEREST OF DRAWING THAT CONTRAPTION!

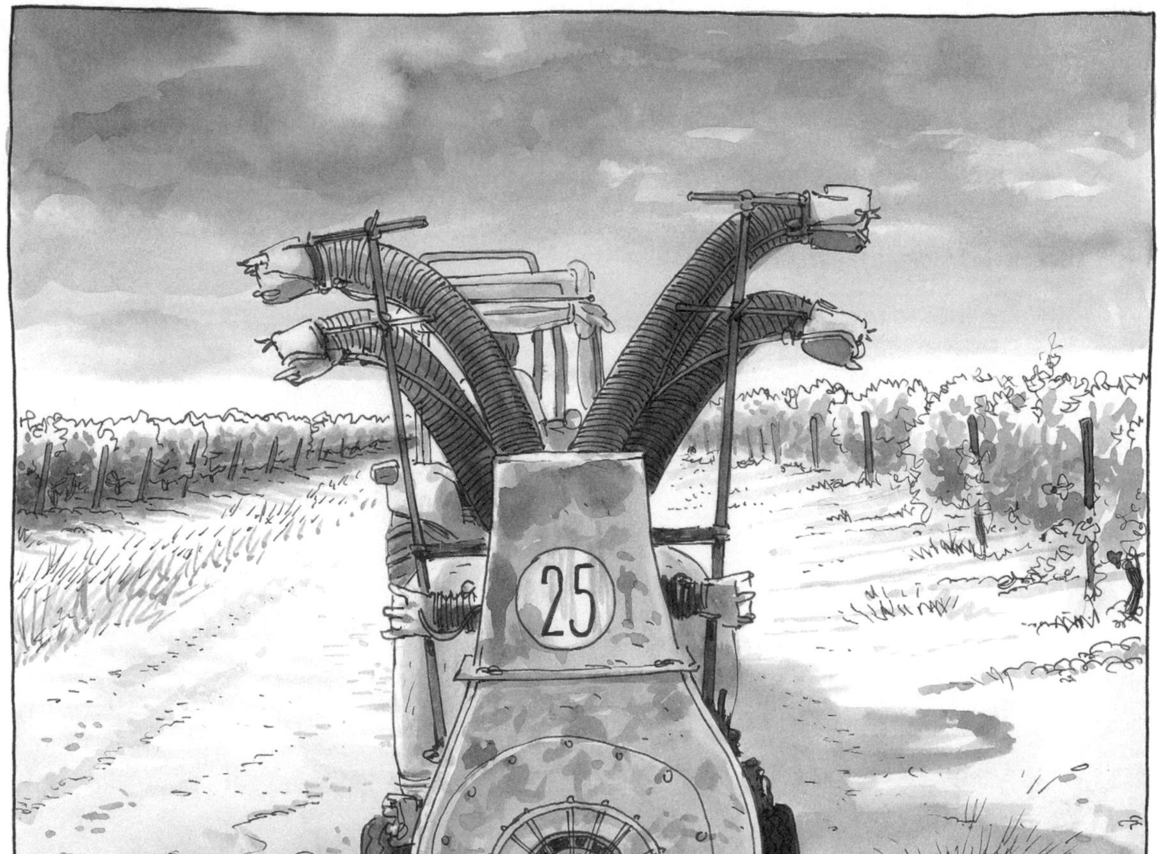
25
ONE MIGHT WANT TO DRAW THIS "CONTRAPTION" BECAUSE IT'S BEAUTIFUL LIKE ONE OF MARCEL DUCHAMP'S READYMADES.

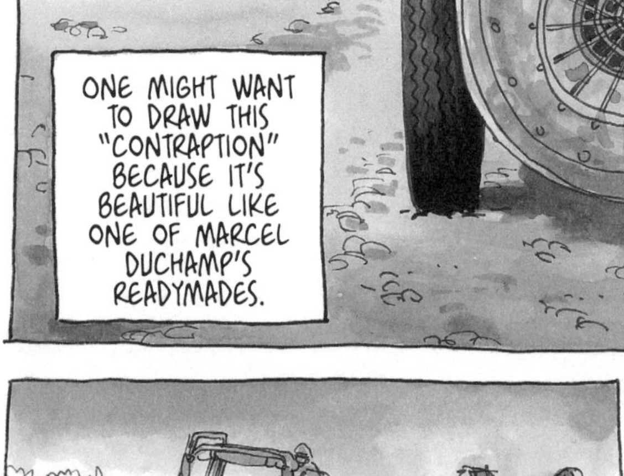
ALAS, THAT FORMAL ELEGANCE EVAPORATES ONCE THE SPRAYER SETS IN MOTION.

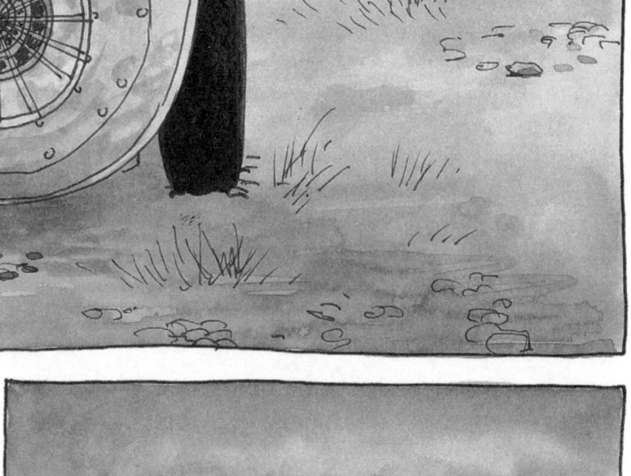
THEN IT BECOMES WHAT IT HAS ALWAYS BEEN: A BIG, STUPID, SERVILE GOOSE, SPITTING WITH RAGE WHILE PONDEROUSLY WADDLING ALONG BEHIND ITS BOSS.

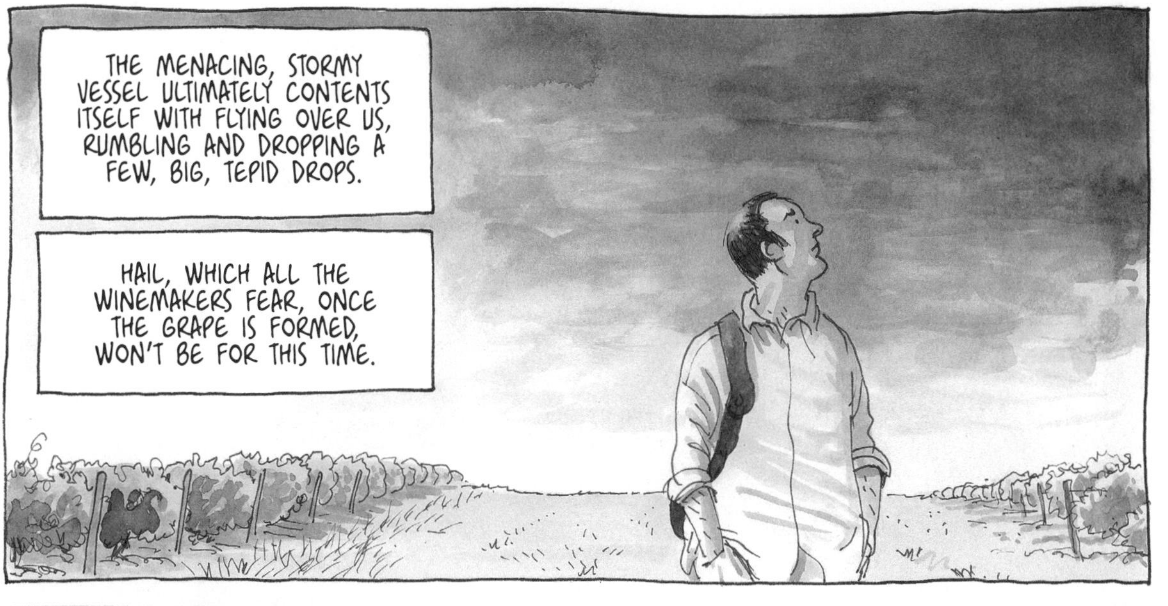
THE MENACING, STORMY VESSEL ULTIMATELY CONTENTS ITSELF WITH FLYING OVER US, RUMBLING AND DROPPING A FEW, BIG, TEPID DROPS.
HAIL, WHICH ALL THE WINEMAKERS FEAR, ONCE THE GRAPE IS FORMED, WON'T BE FOR THIS TIME.

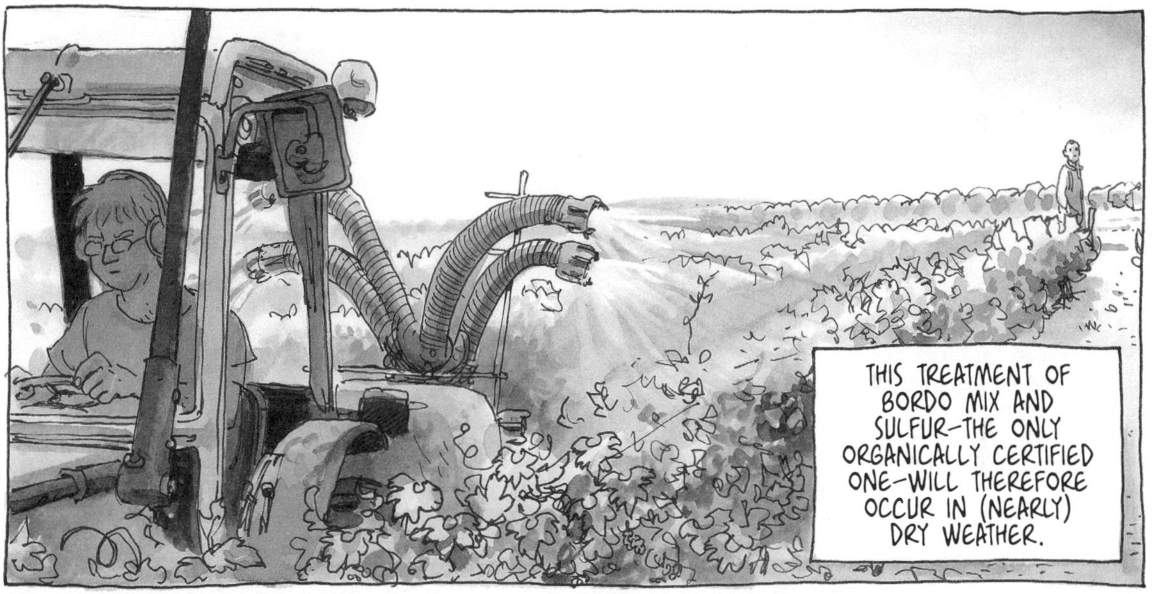
THIS TREATMENT OF BORDO MIX AND SULFUR—THE ONLY ORGANICALLY CERTIFIED ONE—WILL THEREFORE OCCUR IN (NEARLY) DRY WEATHER.

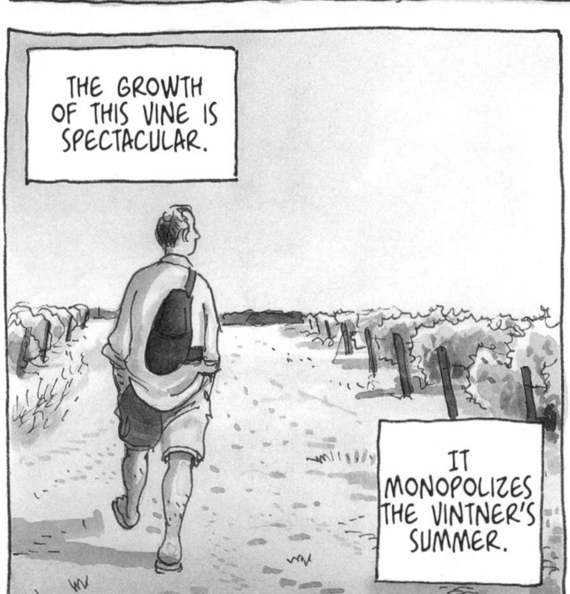
THE GROWTH OF THIS VINE IS SPECTACULAR.
IT MONOPOLIZES THE VINTNER'S SUMMER.

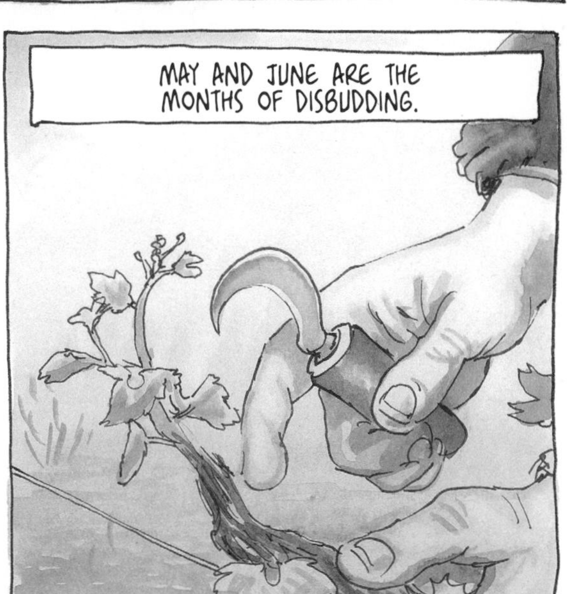
MAY AND JUNE ARE THE MONTHS OF DISBUDDING.

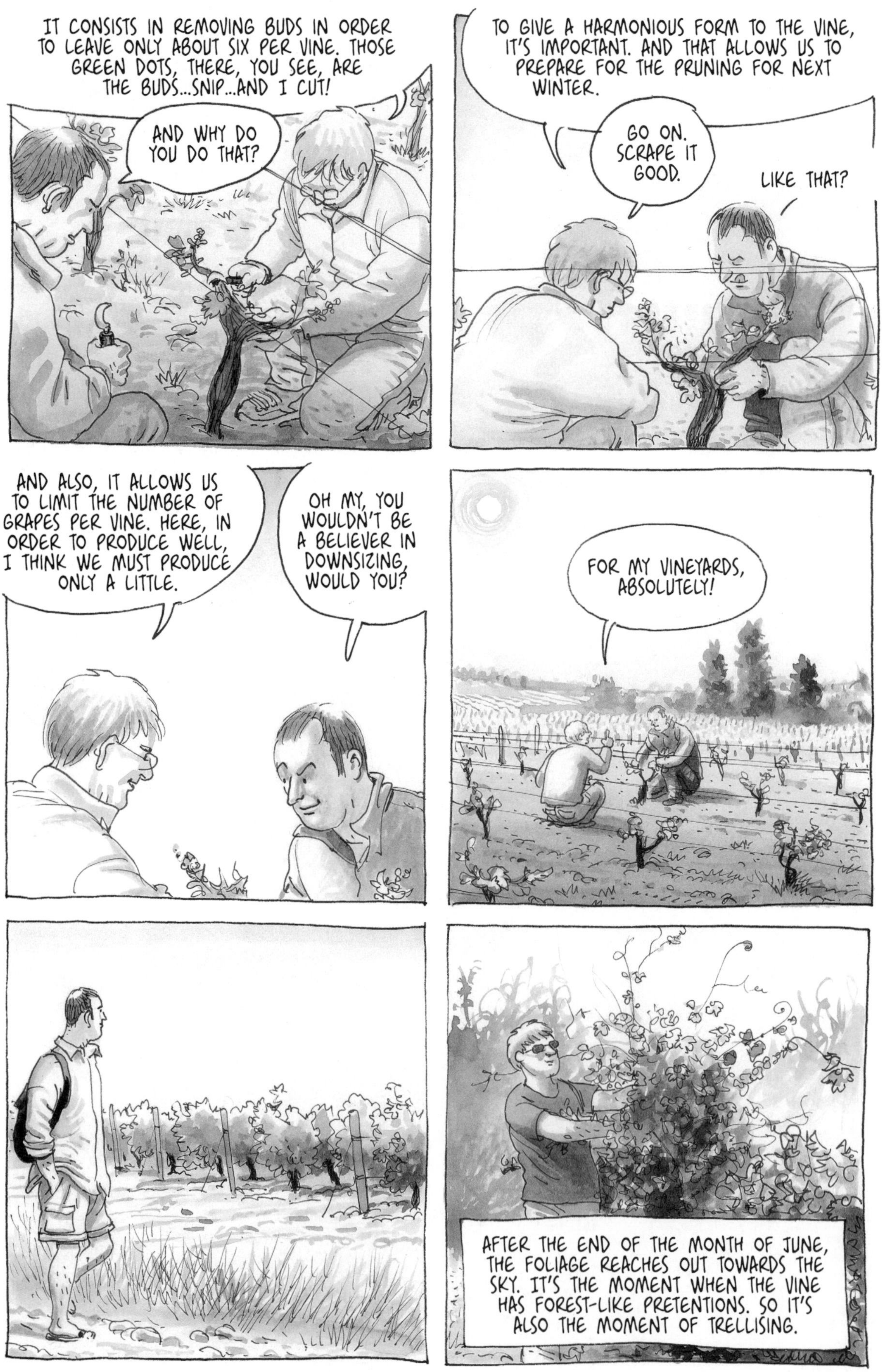
IT CONSISTS IN REMOVING BUDS IN ORDER TO LEAVE ONLY ABOUT SIX PER VINE. THOSE GREEN DOTS, THERE, YOU SEE, ARE THE BUDS...SNIP...AND I CUT!
AND WHY DO YOU DO THAT?
TO GIVE A HARMONIOUS FORM TO THE VINE, IT'S IMPORTANT. AND THAT ALLOWS US TO PREPARE FOR THE PRUNING FOR NEXT WINTER.
GO ON. SCRAPE IT GOOD.
LIKE THAT?
AND ALSO, IT ALLOWS US TO LIMIT THE NUMBER OF GRAPES PER VINE. HERE, IN ORDER TO PRODUCE WELL, I THINK WE MUST PRODUCE ONLY A LITTLE.
OH MY, YOU WOULDN'T BE A BELIEVER IN DOWNSIZING, WOULD YOU?
FOR MY VINEYARDS, ABSOLUTELY!
AFTER THE END OF THE MONTH OF JUNE, THE FOLIAGE REACHES OUT TOWARDS THE SKY. IT'S THE MOMENT WHEN THE VINE HAS FOREST-LIKE PRETENTIONS. SO IT'S ALSO THE MOMENT OF TRELLISING.

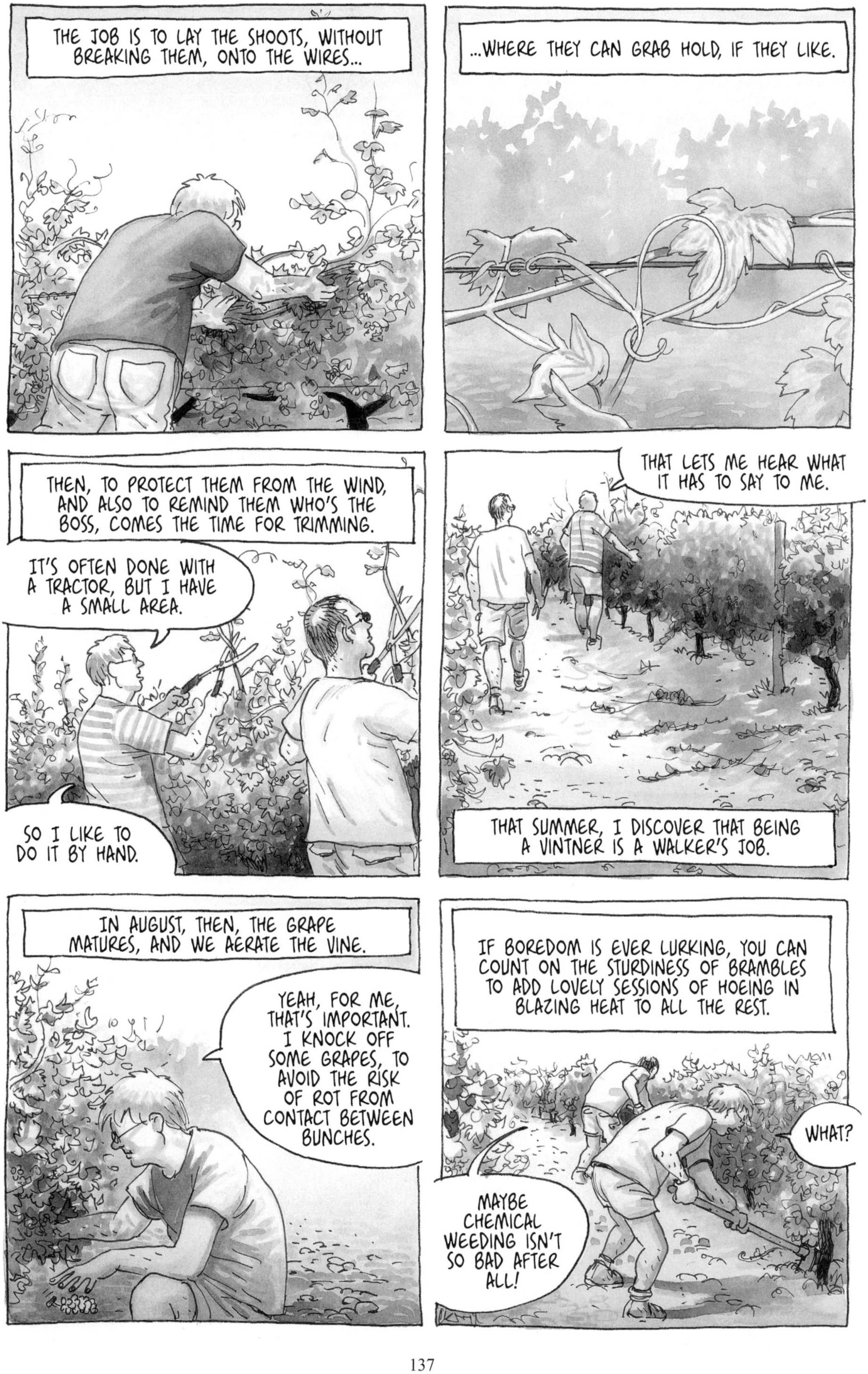
THE JOB IS TO LAY THE SHOOTS, WITHOUT BREAKING THEM, ONTO THE WIRES...
...WHERE THEY CAN GRAB HOLD, IF THEY LIKE.
THEN, TO PROTECT THEM FROM THE WIND, AND ALSO TO REMIND THEM WHO'S THE BOSS, COMES THE TIME FOR TRIMMING.
IT'S OFTEN DONE WITH A TRACTOR, BUT I HAVE A SMALL AREA.
SO I LIKE TO DO IT BY HAND.
THAT LETS ME HEAR WHAT IT HAS TO SAY TO ME.
THAT SUMMER, I DISCOVER THAT BEING A VINTNER IS A WALKER'S JOB.
IN AUGUST, THEN, THE GRAPE MATURES, AND WE AERATE THE VINE.
YEAH, FOR ME, THAT'S IMPORTANT. I KNOCK OFF SOME GRAPES, TO AVOID THE RISK OF ROT FROM CONTACT BETWEEN BUNCHES.
IF BOREDOM IS EVER LURKING, YOU CAN COUNT ON THE STURDINESS OF BRAMBLES TO ADD LOVELY SESSIONS OF HOEING IN BLAZING HEAT TO ALL THE REST.
MAYBE CHEMICAL WEEDING ISN'T SO BAD AFTER ALL!
WHAT?

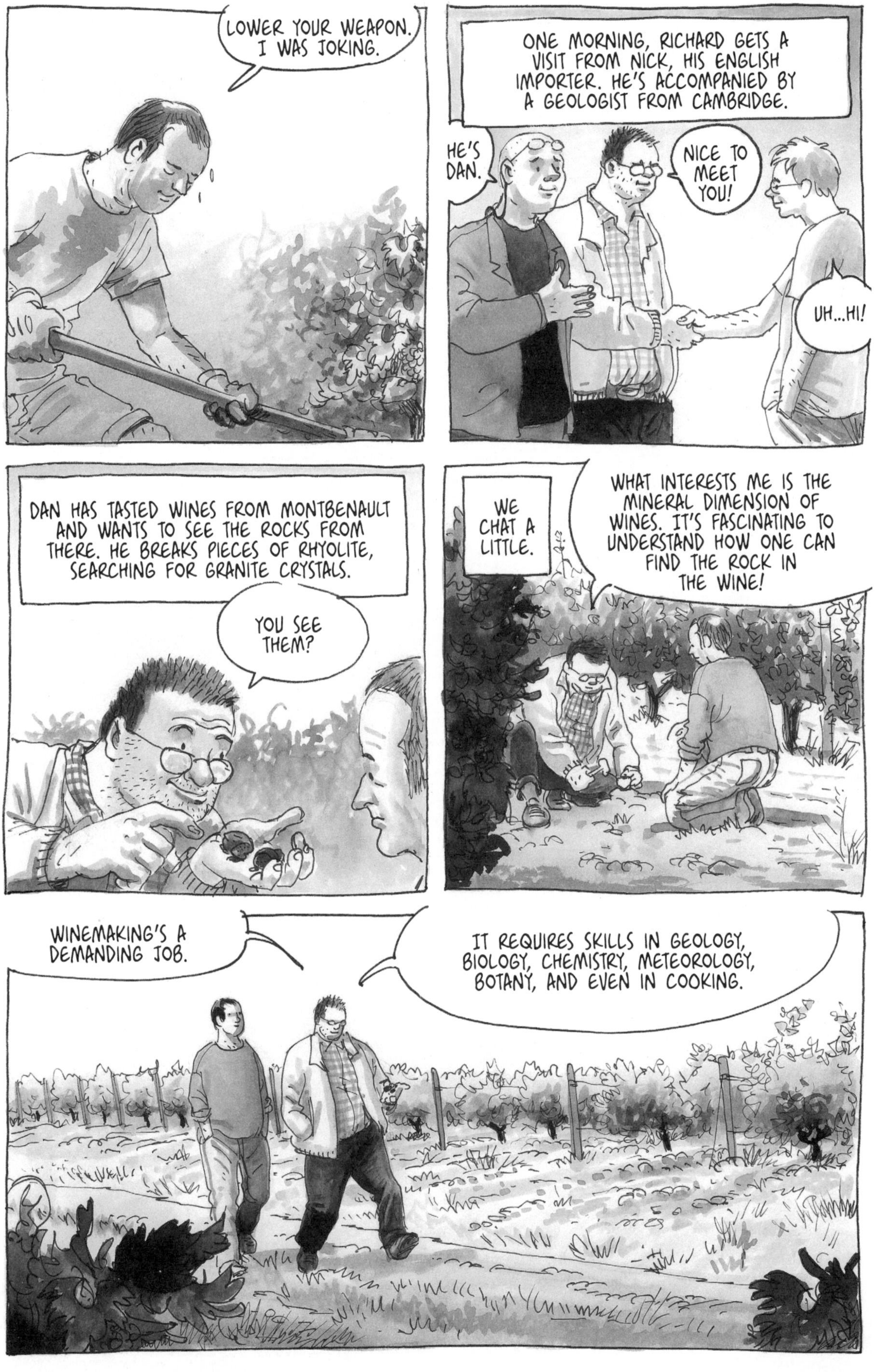
LOWER YOUR WEAPON. I WAS JOKING.
ONE MORNING, RICHARD GETS A VISIT FROM NICK, HIS ENGLISH IMPORTER. HE'S ACCOMPANIED BY A GEOLOGIST FROM CAMBRIDGE.
HE'S DAN.
NICE TO MEET YOU!
UH...HI!
DAN HAS TASTED WINES FROM MONTBENAULT AND WANTS TO SEE THE ROCKS FROM THERE. HE BREAKS PIECES OF RHYOLITE, SEARCHING FOR GRANITE CRYSTALS.
YOU SEE THEM?
WE CHAT A LITTLE.
WHAT INTERESTS ME IS THE MINERAL DIMENSION OF WINES. IT'S FASCINATING TO UNDERSTAND HOW ONE CAN FIND THE ROCK IN THE WINE!
WINEMAKING'S A DEMANDING JOB.
IT REQUIRES SKILLS IN GEOLOGY, BIOLOGY, CHEMISTRY, METEOROLOGY, BOTANY, AND EVEN IN COOKING.

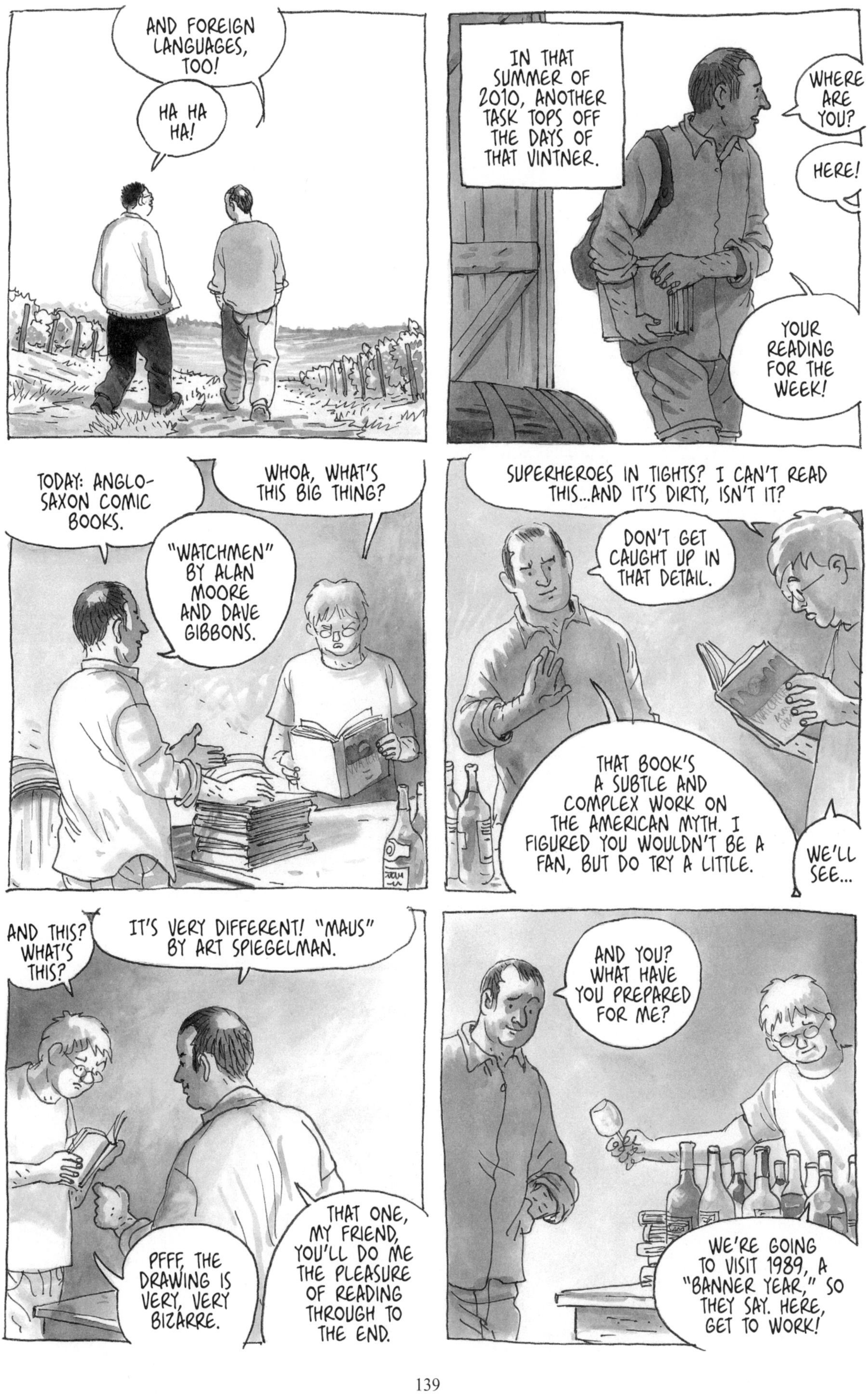
AND FOREIGN LANGUAGES, TOO!
HA HA HA!
IN THAT SUMMER OF 2010, ANOTHER TASK TOPS OFF THE DAYS OF THAT VINTNER.
WHERE ARE YOU?
HERE!
YOUR READING FOR THE WEEK!
TODAY: ANGLO-SAXON COMIC BOOKS.
WHOA, WHAT'S THIS BIG THING?
"WATCHMEN" BY ALAN MOORE AND DAVE GIBBONS.
SUPERHEROES IN TIGHTS? I CAN'T READ THIS...AND IT'S DIRTY, ISN'T IT?
DON'T GET CAUGHT UP IN THAT DETAIL.
THAT BOOK'S A SUBTLE AND COMPLEX WORK ON THE AMERICAN MYTH. I FIGURED YOU WOULDN'T BE A FAN, BUT DO TRY A LITTLE.
WE'LL SEE...
AND THIS? WHAT'S THIS?
IT'S VERY DIFFERENT! "MAUS" BY ART SPIEGELMAN.
PFFF, THE DRAWING IS VERY, VERY BIZARRE.
THAT ONE, MY FRIEND, YOU'LL DO ME THE PLEASURE OF READING THROUGH TO THE END.
AND YOU? WHAT HAVE YOU PREPARED FOR ME?
WE'RE GOING TO VISIT 1989, A "BANNER YEAR," SO THEY SAY. HERE, GET TO WORK!

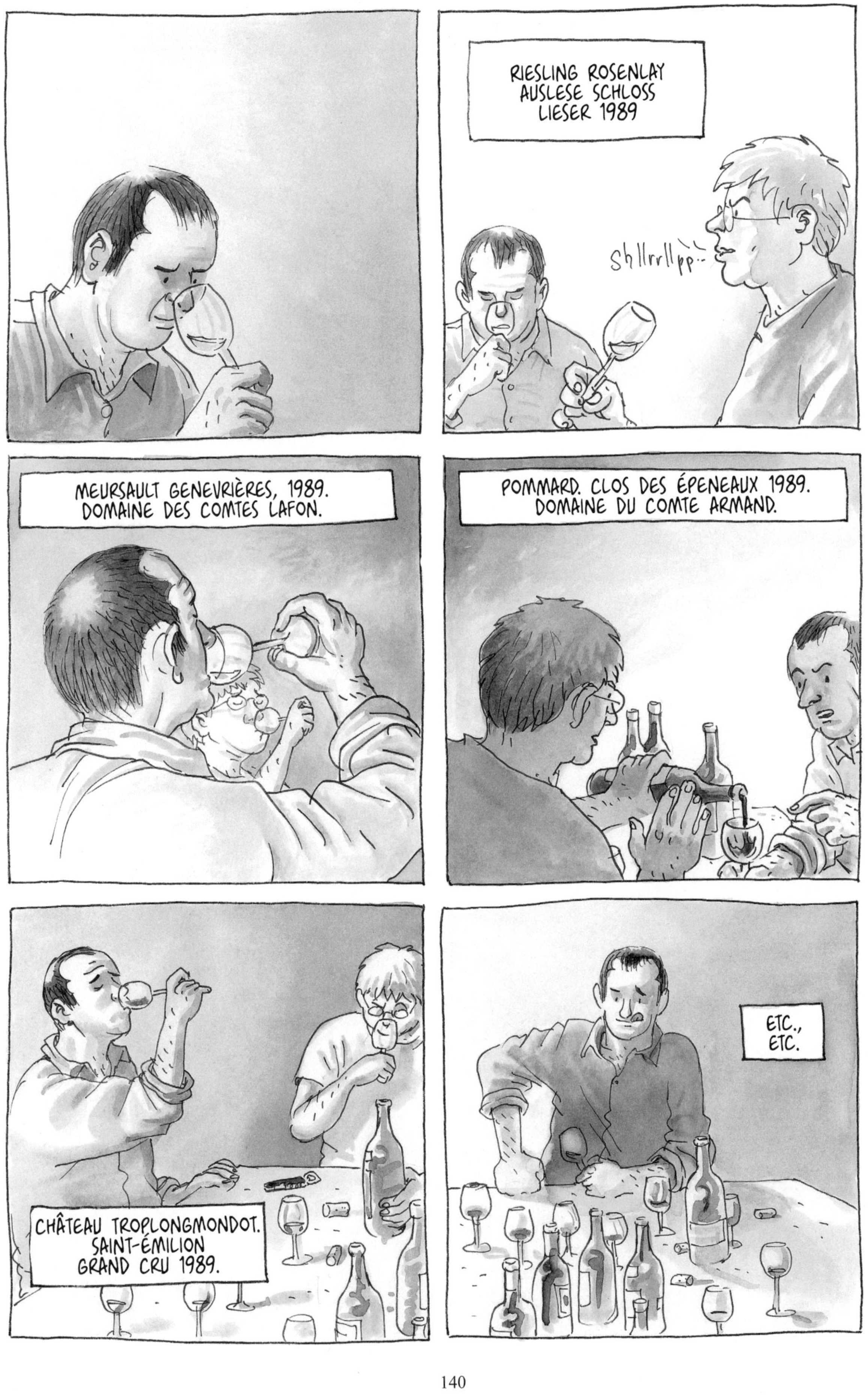
RIESLING ROSENLAY AUSLESE SCHLOSS LIESER 1989
Shllrrllpp..
MEURSAULT GENEVRIÈRES, 1989. DOMAINE DES COMTES LAFON.
POMMARD. CLOS DES ÉPENEAUX 1989. DOMAINE DU COMTE ARMAND.
CHÂTEAU TROPLONGMONDOT. SAINT-ÉMILION GRAND CRU 1989.
ETC., ETC.

WELL?

AH, QUITE A NICE TASTING!

APART FROM A FEW EXCEPTIONS, LIKE THE MEURSAULT AND THE POMMARD, WHICH WERE PRECURSORS IN BIODYNAMICS, IT ALL WAS MADE WITHOUT WORKING THE SOIL, UH.

IN 1989, NOT MANY HAD BEGUN THAT.

THIS ONE APPEALS TO ME LESS.

THAT ONE? DON'T BOTHER. POUR IT DOWN THE SINK.

OH WELL NO.

YES, GO AHEAD.

HA HA HA HA HA!

WHAT?

THAT'S WHAT'S GREAT ABOUT PEOPLE WHO DON'T KNOW ANYTHING. FOR LOTS OF "CONNOISSEURS," WHAT YOU JUST DID WAS SACRILEGIOUS!

REALLY?

AND HOW! I KNOW PEOPLE READY TO SACRIFICE QUITE A LOT TO DRINK THAT WINE. AT THE AUCTIONS, THEY'RE TALKING HUNDREDS OF EUROS. WHAT'S INTERESTING IS THAT YOU, UNAWARE, ALLOW YOURSELF TO NOT LIKE IT.

NOT KNOWING IS BEING FREE? A PARADOX!

HERE. TASTE THIS ONE.

WHAT IS IT?

NO QUESTIONS! TASTE!

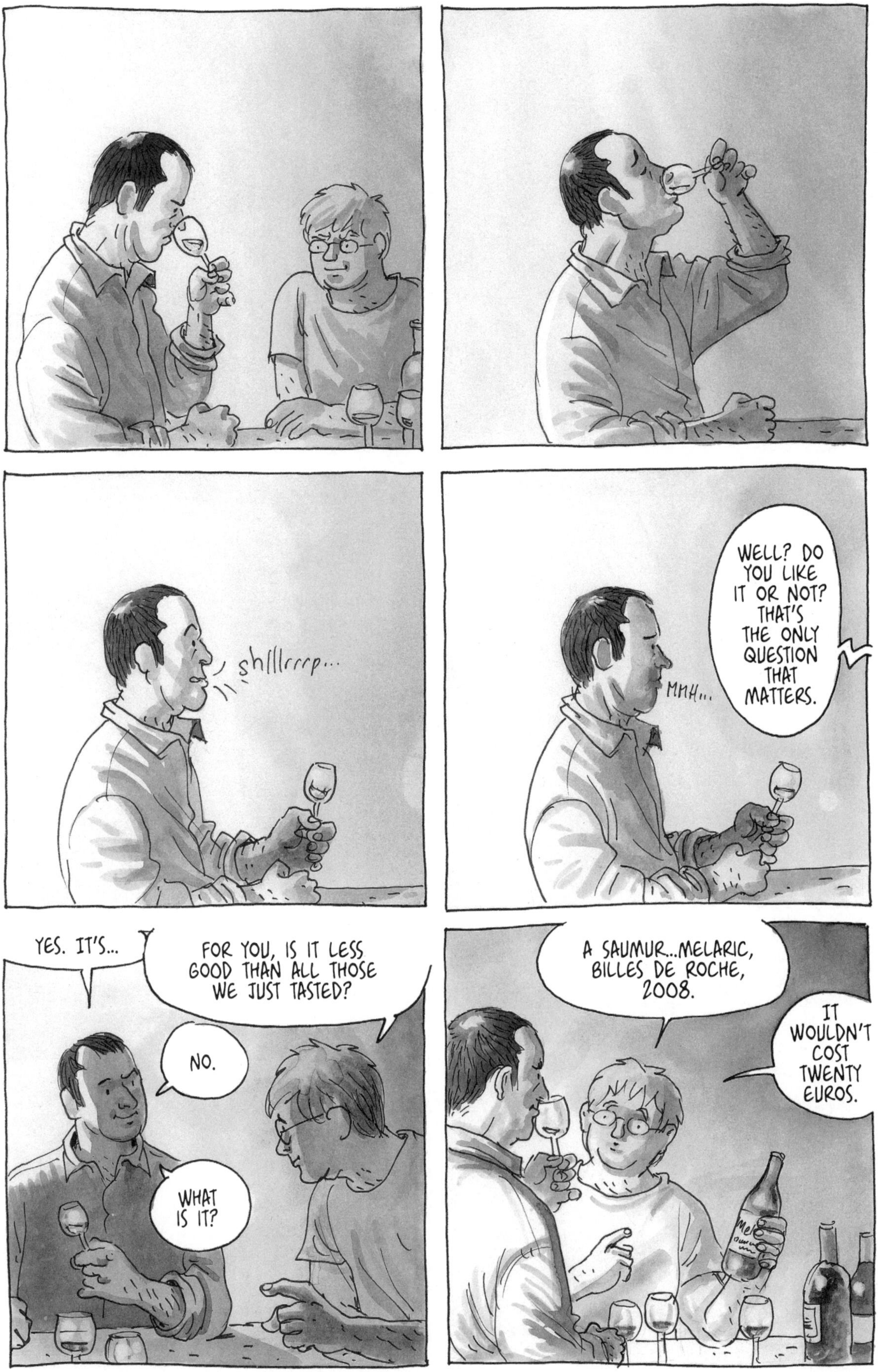
shllllrrrp...
MMH...
WELL? DO YOU LIKE IT OR NOT? THAT'S THE ONLY QUESTION THAT MATTERS.
YES. IT'S...
FOR YOU, IS IT LESS GOOD THAN ALL THOSE WE JUST TASTED?
NO.
WHAT IS IT?
A SAUMUR...MELARIC, BILLES DE ROCHE, 2008.
IT WOULDN'T COST TWENTY EUROS.

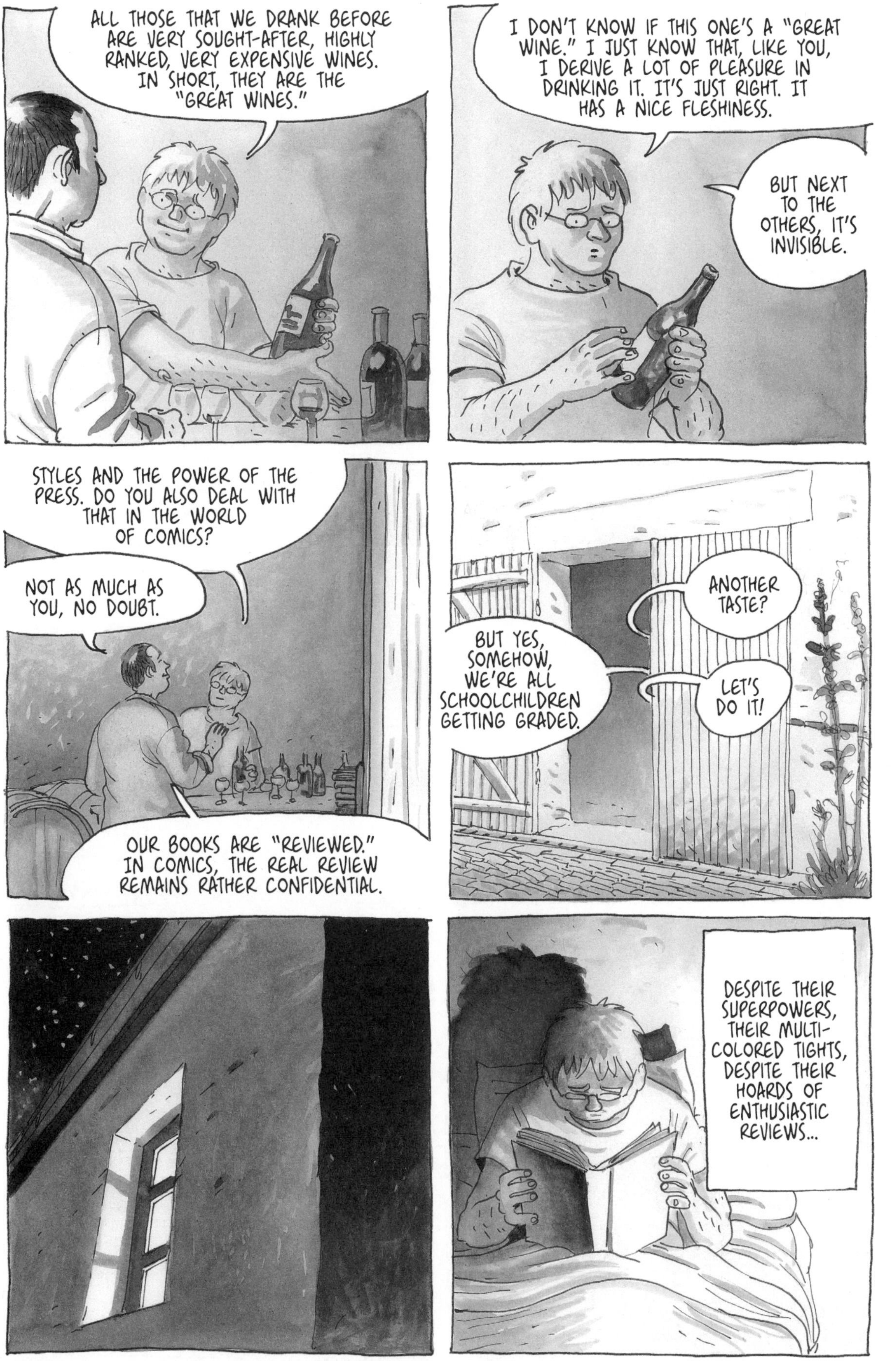
ALL THOSE THAT WE DRANK BEFORE ARE VERY SOUGHT-AFTER, HIGHLY RANKED, VERY EXPENSIVE WINES. IN SHORT, THEY ARE THE "GREAT WINES."
I DON'T KNOW IF THIS ONE'S A "GREAT WINE." I JUST KNOW THAT, LIKE YOU, I DERIVE A LOT OF PLEASURE IN DRINKING IT. IT'S JUST RIGHT. IT HAS A NICE FLESHINESS.
BUT NEXT TO THE OTHERS, IT'S INVISIBLE.
STYLES AND THE POWER OF THE PRESS. DO YOU ALSO DEAL WITH THAT IN THE WORLD OF COMICS?
NOT AS MUCH AS YOU, NO DOUBT.
OUR BOOKS ARE "REVIEWED." IN COMICS, THE REAL REVIEW REMAINS RATHER CONFIDENTIAL.
ANOTHER TASTE?
BUT YES, SOMEHOW, WE'RE ALL SCHOOLCHILDREN GETTING GRADED.
LET'S DO IT!
DESPITE THEIR SUPERPOWERS, THEIR MULTI-COLORED TIGHTS, DESPITE THEIR HOARDS OF ENTHUSIASTIC REVIEWS...

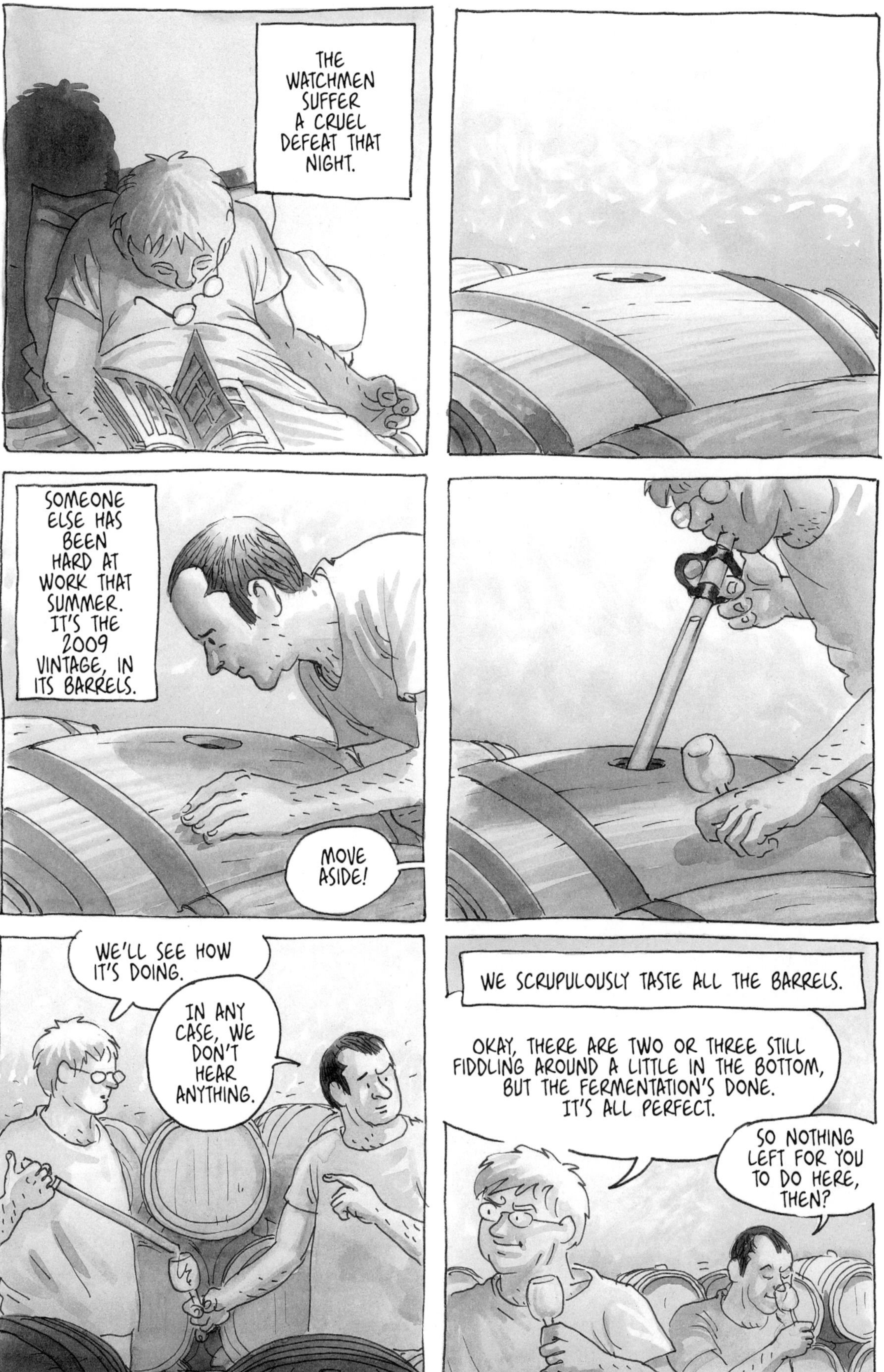
THE WATCHMEN SUFFER A CRUEL DEFEAT THAT NIGHT.
SOMEONE ELSE HAS BEEN HARD AT WORK THAT SUMMER. IT'S THE 2009 VINTAGE, IN ITS BARRELS.
MOVE ASIDE!
WE'LL SEE HOW IT'S DOING.
IN ANY CASE, WE DON'T HEAR ANYTHING.
WE SCRUPULOUSLY TASTE ALL THE BARRELS.
OKAY, THERE ARE TWO OR THREE STILL FIDDLING AROUND A LITTLE IN THE BOTTOM, BUT THE FERMENTATION'S DONE. IT'S ALL PERFECT.
SO NOTHING LEFT FOR YOU TO DO HERE, THEN?

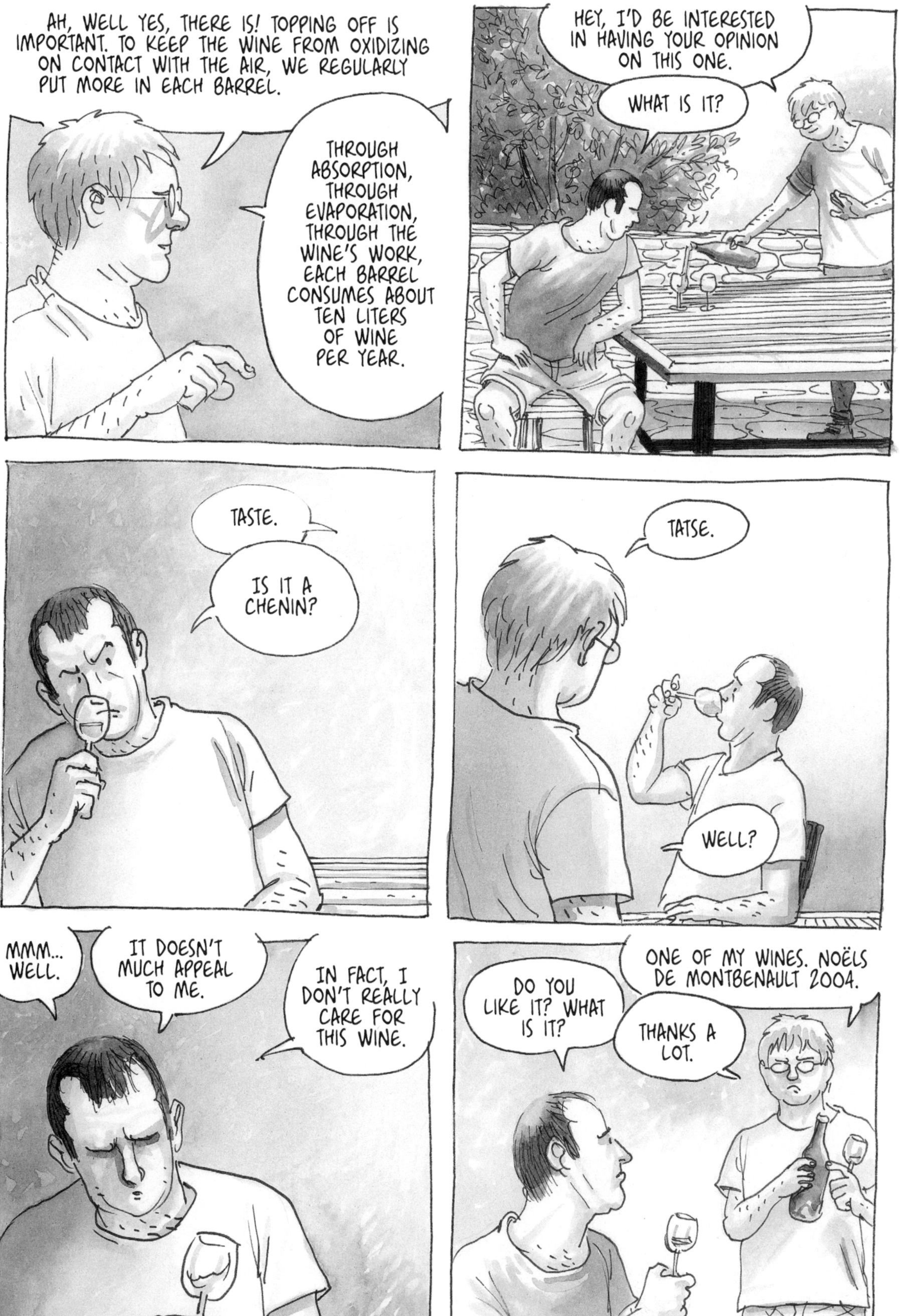

AH, WELL YES, THERE IS! TOPPING OFF IS IMPORTANT. TO KEEP THE WINE FROM OXIDIZING ON CONTACT WITH THE AIR, WE REGULARLY PUT MORE IN EACH BARREL.
THROUGH ABSORPTION, THROUGH EVAPORATION, THROUGH THE WINE'S WORK, EACH BARREL CONSUMES ABOUT TEN LITERS OF WINE PER YEAR.
HEY, I'D BE INTERESTED IN HAVING YOUR OPINION ON THIS ONE.
WHAT IS IT?
TASTE.
IS IT A CHENIN?
TATSE.
WELL?
MMM... WELL.
IT DOESN'T MUCH APPEAL TO ME.
IN FACT, I DON'T REALLY CARE FOR THIS WINE.
DO YOU LIKE IT? WHAT IS IT?
ONE OF MY WINES. NOËLS DE MONTBENAULT 2004.
THANKS A LOT.

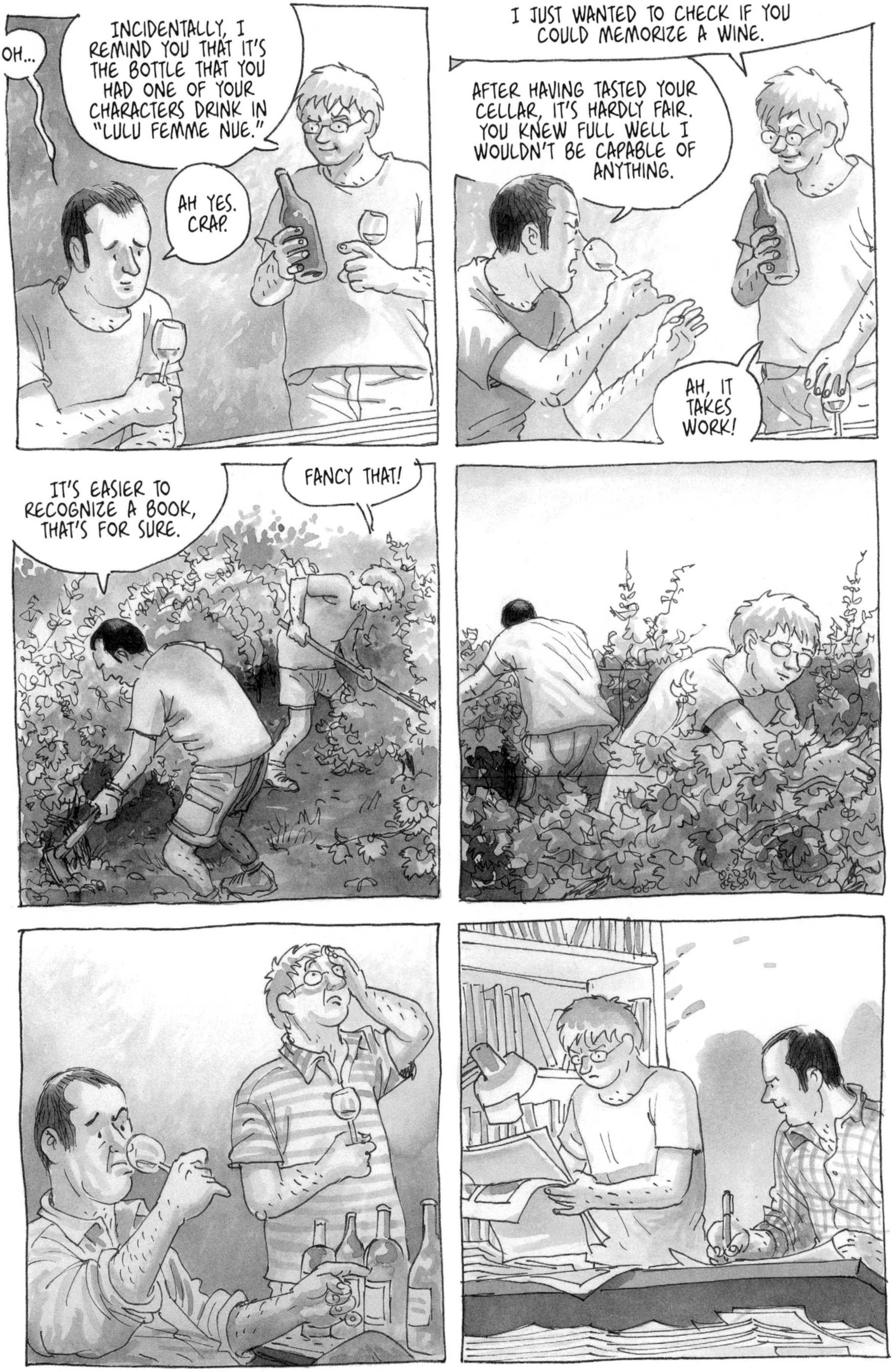
OH...
INCIDENTALLY, I REMIND YOU THAT IT'S THE BOTTLE THAT YOU HAD ONE OF YOUR CHARACTERS DRINK IN "LULU FEMME NUE."
AH YES. CRAP.
I JUST WANTED TO CHECK IF YOU COULD MEMORIZE A WINE.
AFTER HAVING TASTED YOUR CELLAR, IT'S HARDLY FAIR. YOU KNEW FULL WELL I WOULDN'T BE CAPABLE OF ANYTHING.
AH, IT TAKES WORK!
IT'S EASIER TO RECOGNIZE A BOOK, THAT'S FOR SURE.
FANCY THAT!

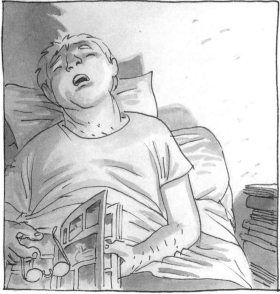

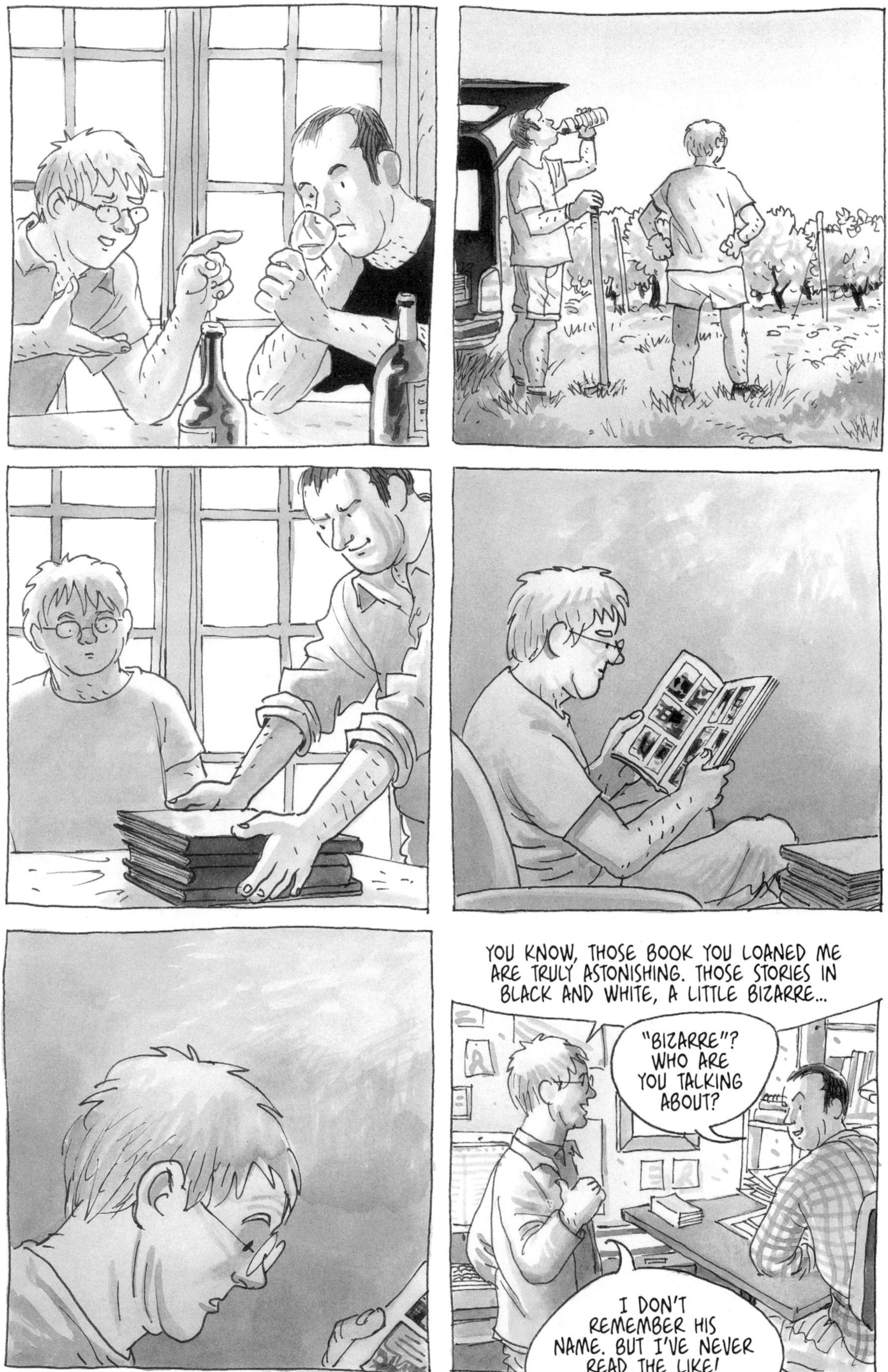
YOU KNOW, THOSE BOOK YOU LOANED ME ARE TRULY ASTONISHING. THOSE STORIES IN BLACK AND WHITE, A LITTLE BIZARRE...
"BIZARRE"? WHO ARE YOU TALKING ABOUT?
I DON'T REMEMBER HIS NAME. BUT I'VE NEVER READ THE LIKE!

CHAPTER ELEVEN BLACKS AND WHITES

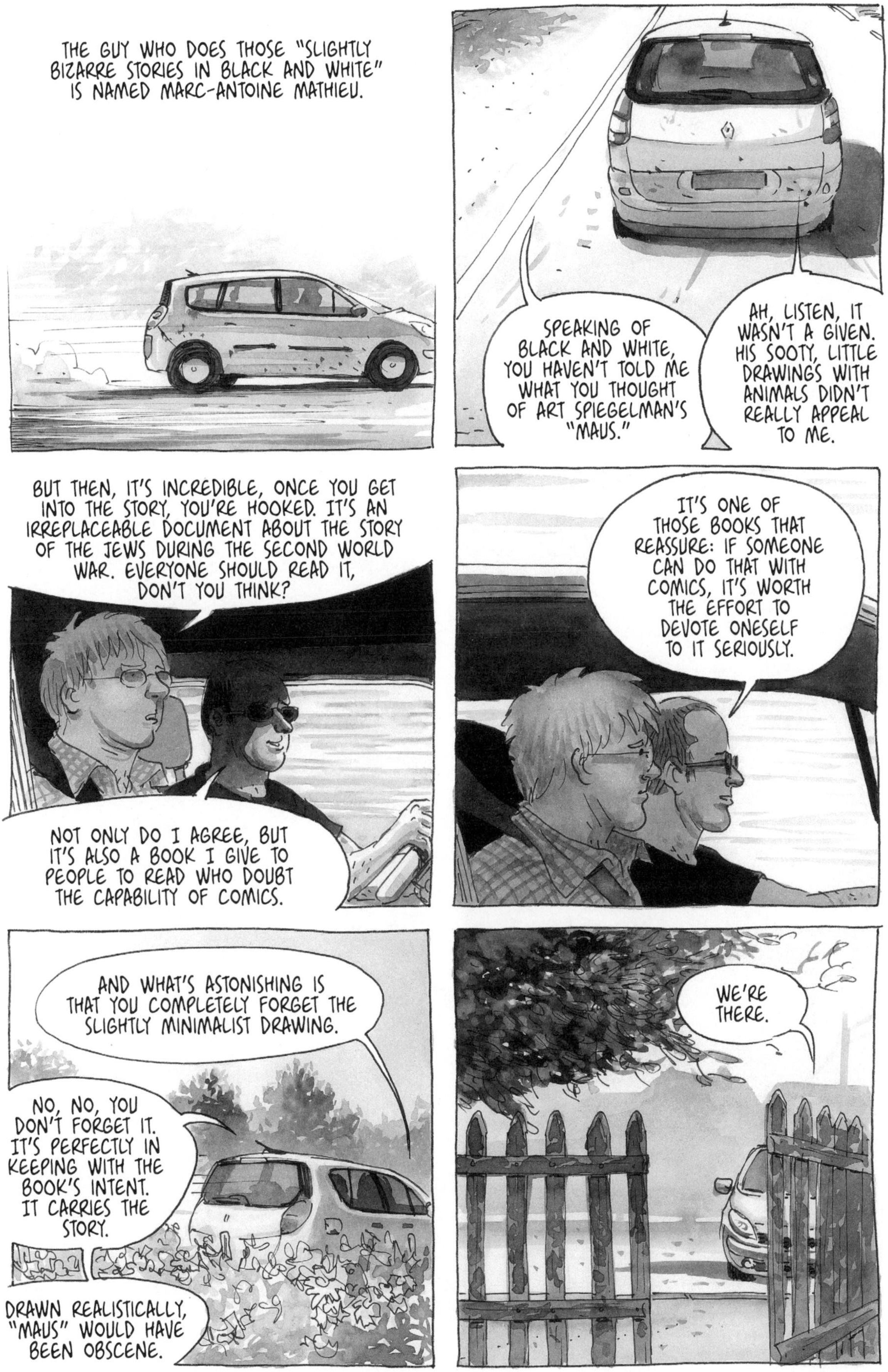
THE GUY WHO DOES THOSE "SLIGHTLY BIZARRE STORIES IN BLACK AND WHITE" IS NAMED MARC-ANTOINE MATHIEU.
SPEAKING OF BLACK AND WHITE, YOU HAVEN'T TOLD ME WHAT YOU THOUGHT OF ART SPIEGELMAN'S "MAUS."
AH, LISTEN, IT WASN'T A GIVEN. HIS SOOTY, LITTLE DRAWINGS WITH ANIMALS DIDN'T REALLY APPEAL TO ME.
BUT THEN, IT'S INCREDIBLE, ONCE YOU GET INTO THE STORY, YOU'RE HOOKED. IT'S AN IRREPLACEABLE DOCUMENT ABOUT THE STORY OF THE JEWS DURING THE SECOND WORLD WAR. EVERYONE SHOULD READ IT, DON'T YOU THINK?
NOT ONLY DO I AGREE, BUT IT'S ALSO A BOOK I GIVE TO PEOPLE TO READ WHO DOUBT THE CAPABILITY OF COMICS.
IT'S ONE OF THOSE BOOKS THAT REASSURE: IF SOMEONE CAN DO THAT WITH COMICS, IT'S WORTH THE EFFORT TO DEVOTE ONESELF TO IT SERIOUSLY.
AND WHAT'S ASTONISHING IS THAT YOU COMPLETELY FORGET THE SLIGHTLY MINIMALIST DRAWING.
NO, NO, YOU DON'T FORGET IT. IT'S PERFECTLY IN KEEPING WITH THE BOOK'S INTENT. IT CARRIES THE STORY.
DRAWN REALISTICALLY, "MAUS" WOULD HAVE BEEN OBSCENE.
WE'RE THERE.

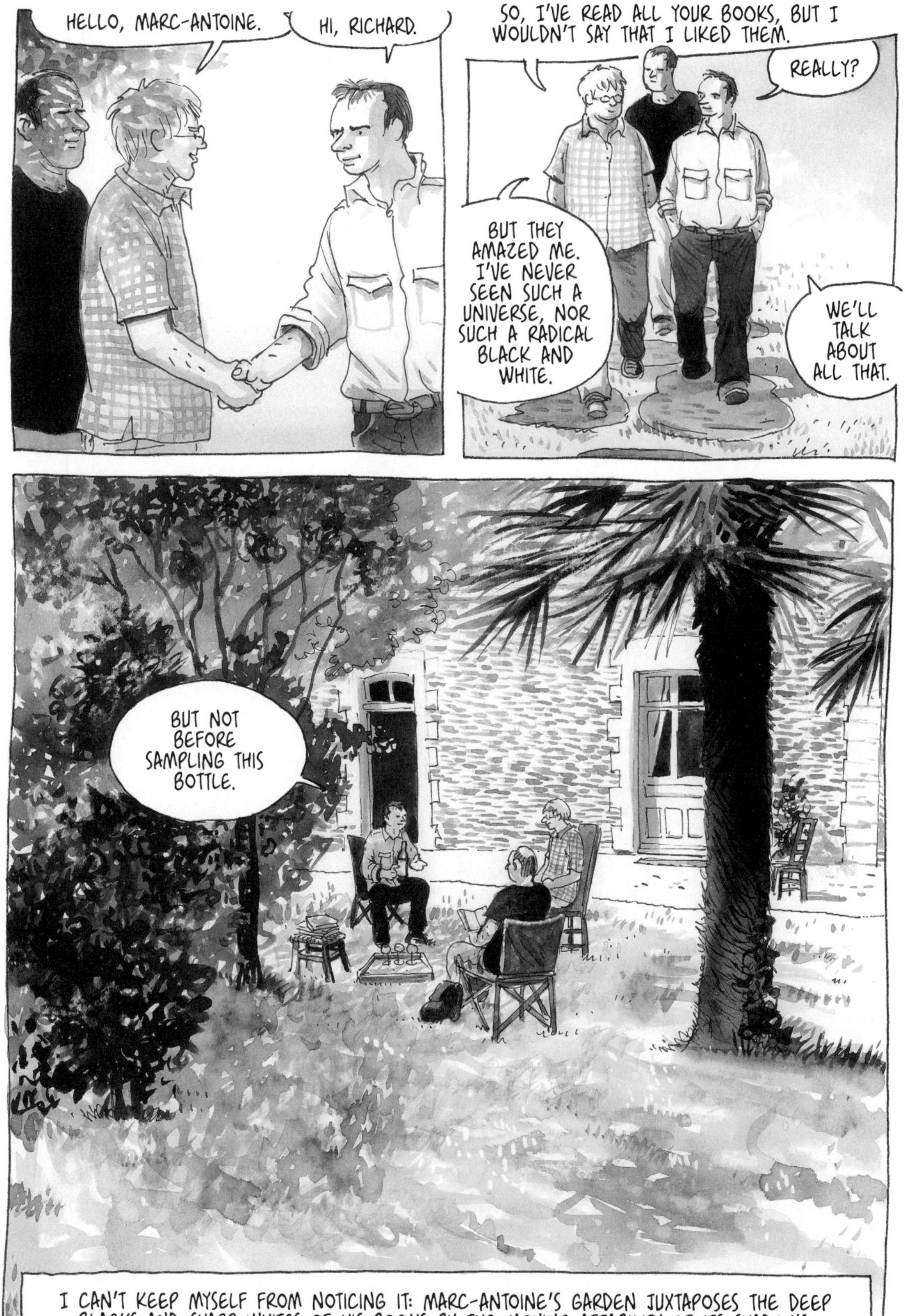

HELLO, MARC-ANTOINE.
HI, RICHARD.
SO, I'VE READ ALL YOUR BOOKS, BUT I WOULDN'T SAY THAT I LIKED THEM.
REALLY?
BUT THEY AMAZED ME. I'VE NEVER SEEN SUCH A UNIVERSE, NOR SUCH A RADICAL BLACK AND WHITE.
WE'LL TALK ABOUT ALL THAT.
BUT NOT BEFORE SAMPLING THIS BOTTLE.
I CAN'T KEEP MYSELF FROM NOTICING IT: MARC-ANTOINE'S GARDEN JUXTAPOSES THE DEEP BLACKS AND SHARP WHITES OF HIS BOOKS BY THE MOVING AFFABILITY OF ITS SHADOWS.

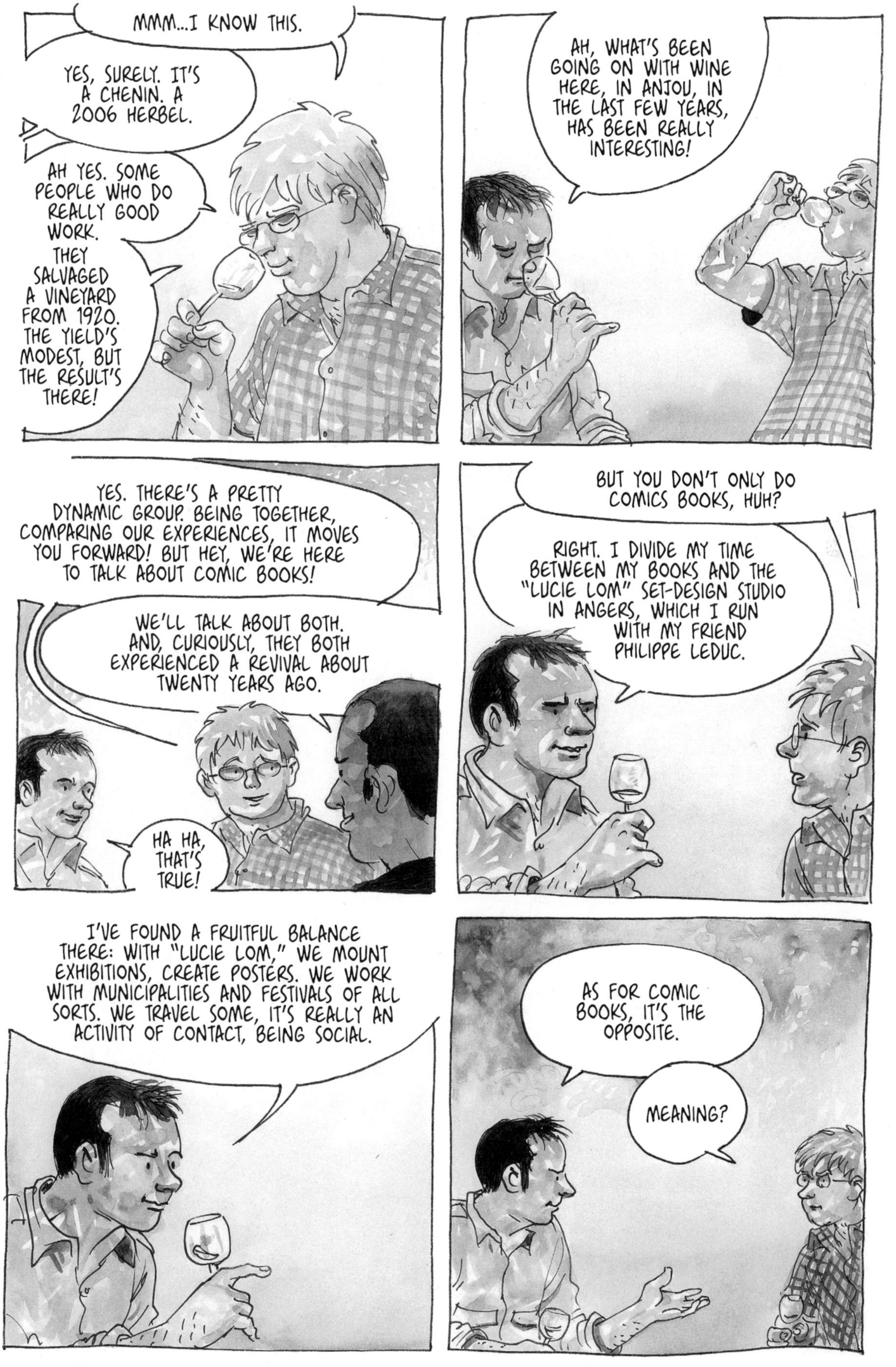
MMM...I KNOW THIS.
YES, SURELY. IT'S A CHENIN. A 2006 HERBEL.
AH YES. SOME PEOPLE WHO DO REALLY GOOD WORK.
THEY SALVAGED A VINEYARD FROM 1920. THE YIELD'S MODEST, BUT THE RESULT'S THERE!
AH, WHAT'S BEEN GOING ON WITH WINE HERE, IN ANJOU, IN THE LAST FEW YEARS, HAS BEEN REALLY INTERESTING!
YES. THERE'S A PRETTY DYNAMIC GROUP. BEING TOGETHER, COMPARING OUR EXPERIENCES, IT MOVES YOU FORWARD! BUT HEY, WE'RE HERE TO TALK ABOUT COMIC BOOKS!
WE'LL TALK ABOUT BOTH. AND, CURIOUSLY, THEY BOTH EXPERIENCED A REVIVAL ABOUT TWENTY YEARS AGO.
HA HA, THAT'S TRUE!
BUT YOU DON'T ONLY DO COMICS BOOKS, HUH?
RIGHT. I DIVIDE MY TIME BETWEEN MY BOOKS AND THE "LUCIE LOM" SET-DESIGN STUDIO IN ANGERS, WHICH I RUN WITH MY FRIEND PHILIPPE LEDUC.
I'VE FOUND A FRUITFUL BALANCE THERE: WITH "LUCIE LOM," WE MOUNT EXHIBITIONS, CREATE POSTERS. WE WORK WITH MUNICIPALITIES AND FESTIVALS OF ALL SORTS. WE TRAVEL SOME, IT'S REALLY AN ACTIVITY OF CONTACT, BEING SOCIAL.
AS FOR COMIC BOOKS, IT'S THE OPPOSITE.
MEANING?

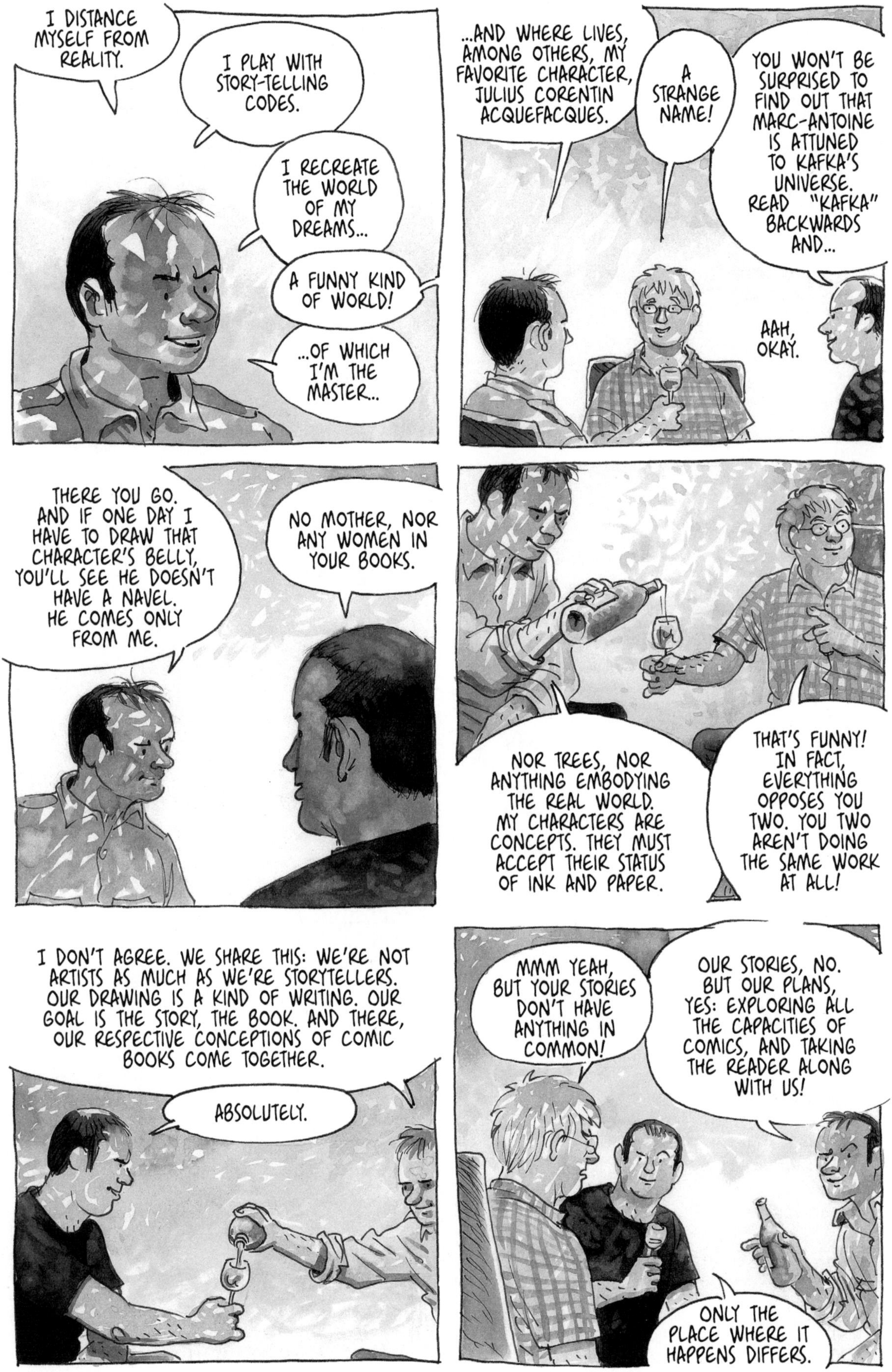
I DISTANCE MYSELF FROM REALITY.
I PLAY WITH STORY-TELLING CODES.
I RECREATE THE WORLD OF MY DREAMS...
A FUNNY KIND OF WORLD!
...OF WHICH I'M THE MASTER..
...AND WHERE LIVES, AMONG OTHERS, MY FAVORITE CHARACTER, JULIUS CORENTIN ACQUEFACQUES.
A STRANGE NAME!
YOU WON'T BE SURPRISED TO FIND OUT THAT MARC-ANTOINE IS ATTUNED TO KAFKA'S UNIVERSE. READ "KAFKA" BACKWARDS AND...
AAH, OKAY.
THERE YOU GO. AND IF ONE DAY I HAVE TO DRAW THAT CHARACTER'S BELLY, YOU'LL SEE HE DOESN'T HAVE A NAVEL. HE COMES ONLY FROM ME.
NO MOTHER, NOR ANY WOMEN IN YOUR BOOKS.
NOR TREES, NOR ANYTHING EMBODYING THE REAL WORLD. MY CHARACTERS ARE CONCEPTS. THEY MUST ACCEPT THEIR STATUS OF INK AND PAPER.
THAT'S FUNNY! IN FACT, EVERYTHING OPPOSES YOU TWO. YOU TWO AREN'T DOING THE SAME WORK AT ALL!
I DON'T AGREE. WE SHARE THIS: WE'RE NOT ARTISTS AS MUCH AS WE'RE STORYTELLERS. OUR DRAWING IS A KIND OF WRITING. OUR GOAL IS THE STORY, THE BOOK. AND THERE, OUR RESPECTIVE CONCEPTIONS OF COMIC BOOKS COME TOGETHER.
ABSOLUTELY.
MMM YEAH, BUT YOUR STORIES DON'T HAVE ANYTHING IN COMMON!
OUR STORIES, NO. BUT OUR PLANS, YES: EXPLORING ALL THE CAPACITIES OF COMICS, AND TAKING THE READER ALONG WITH US!
ONLY THE PLACE WHERE IT HAPPENS DIFFERS.

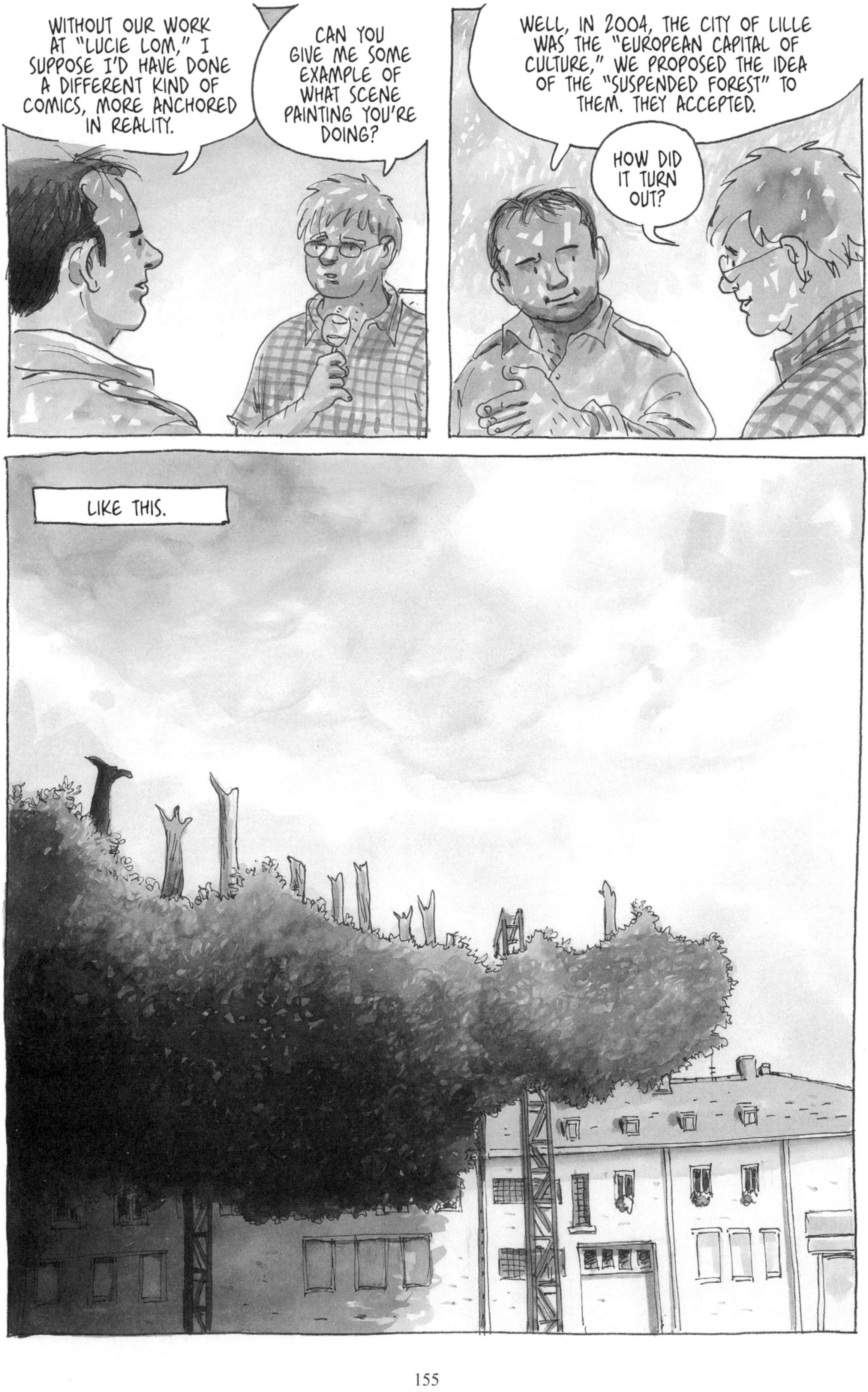
WITHOUT OUR WORK AT "LUCIE LOM," I SUPPOSE I'D HAVE DONE A DIFFERENT KIND OF COMICS, MORE ANCHORED IN REALITY.
CAN YOU GIVE ME SOME EXAMPLE OF WHAT SCENE PAINTING YOU'RE DOING?
WELL, IN 2004, THE CITY OF LILLE WAS THE "EUROPEAN CAPITAL OF CULTURE," WE PROPOSED THE IDEA OF THE "SUSPENDED FOREST" TO THEM. THEY ACCEPTED.
HOW DID IT TURN OUT?
LIKE THIS.

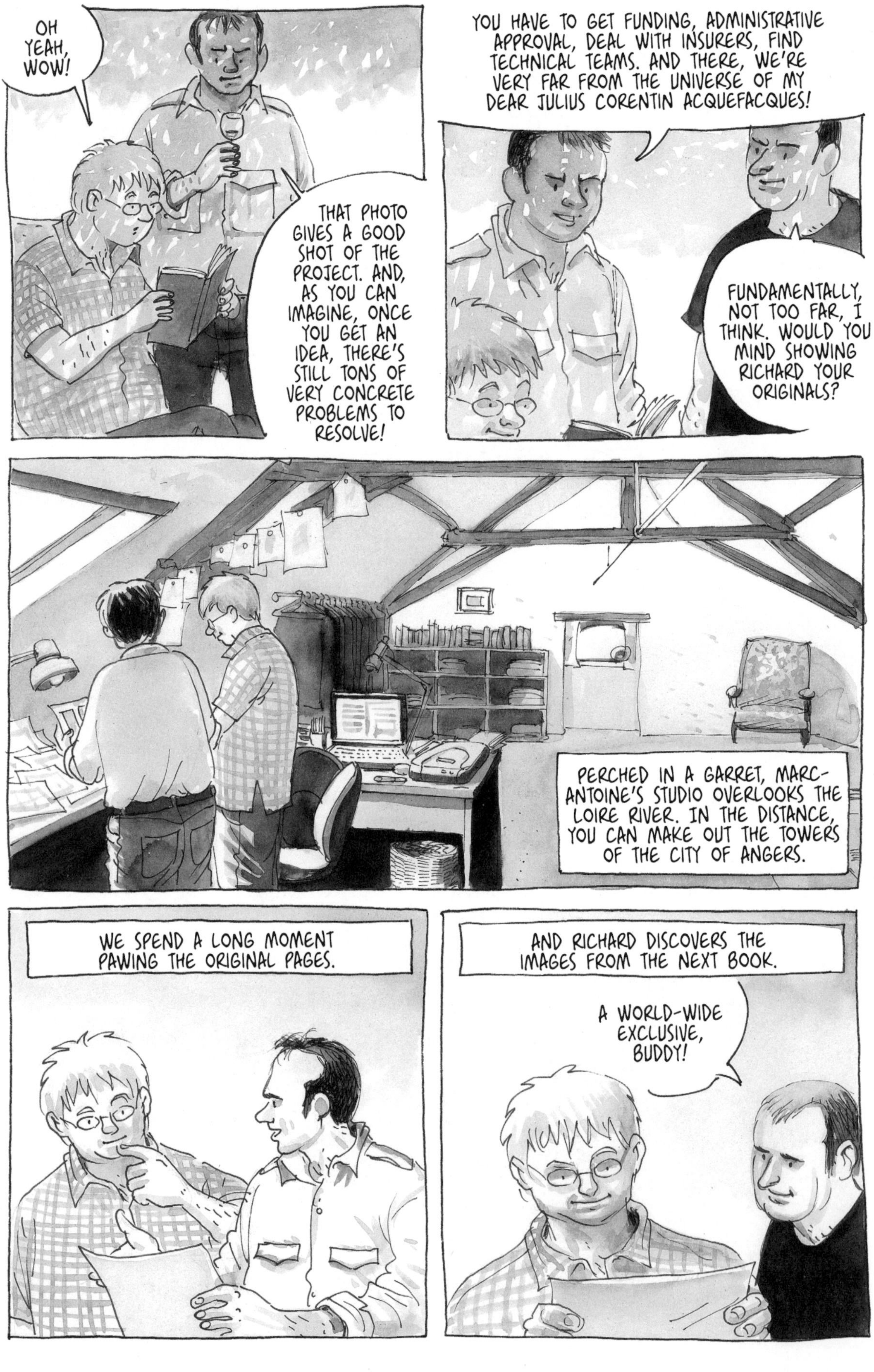
OH YEAH, WOW!
THAT PHOTO GIVES A GOOD SHOT OF THE PROJECT. AND, AS YOU CAN IMAGINE, ONCE YOU GET AN IDEA, THERE'S STILL TONS OF VERY CONCRETE PROBLEMS TO RESOLVE!
YOU HAVE TO GET FUNDING, ADMINISTRATIVE APPROVAL, DEAL WITH INSURERS, FIND TECHNICAL TEAMS. AND THERE, WE'RE VERY FAR FROM THE UNIVERSE OF MY DEAR JULIUS CORENTIN ACQUEFACQUES!
FUNDAMENTALLY, NOT TOO FAR, I THINK. WOULD YOU MIND SHOWING RICHARD YOUR ORIGINALS?
PERCHED IN A GARRET, MARC-ANTOINE'S STUDIO OVERLOOKS THE LOIRE RIVER. IN THE DISTANCE, YOU CAN MAKE OUT THE TOWERS OF THE CITY OF ANGERS.
WE SPEND A LONG MOMENT PAWING THE ORIGINAL PAGES.
AND RICHARD DISCOVERS THE IMAGES FROM THE NEXT BOOK.
A WORLD-WIDE EXCLUSIVE, BUDDY!

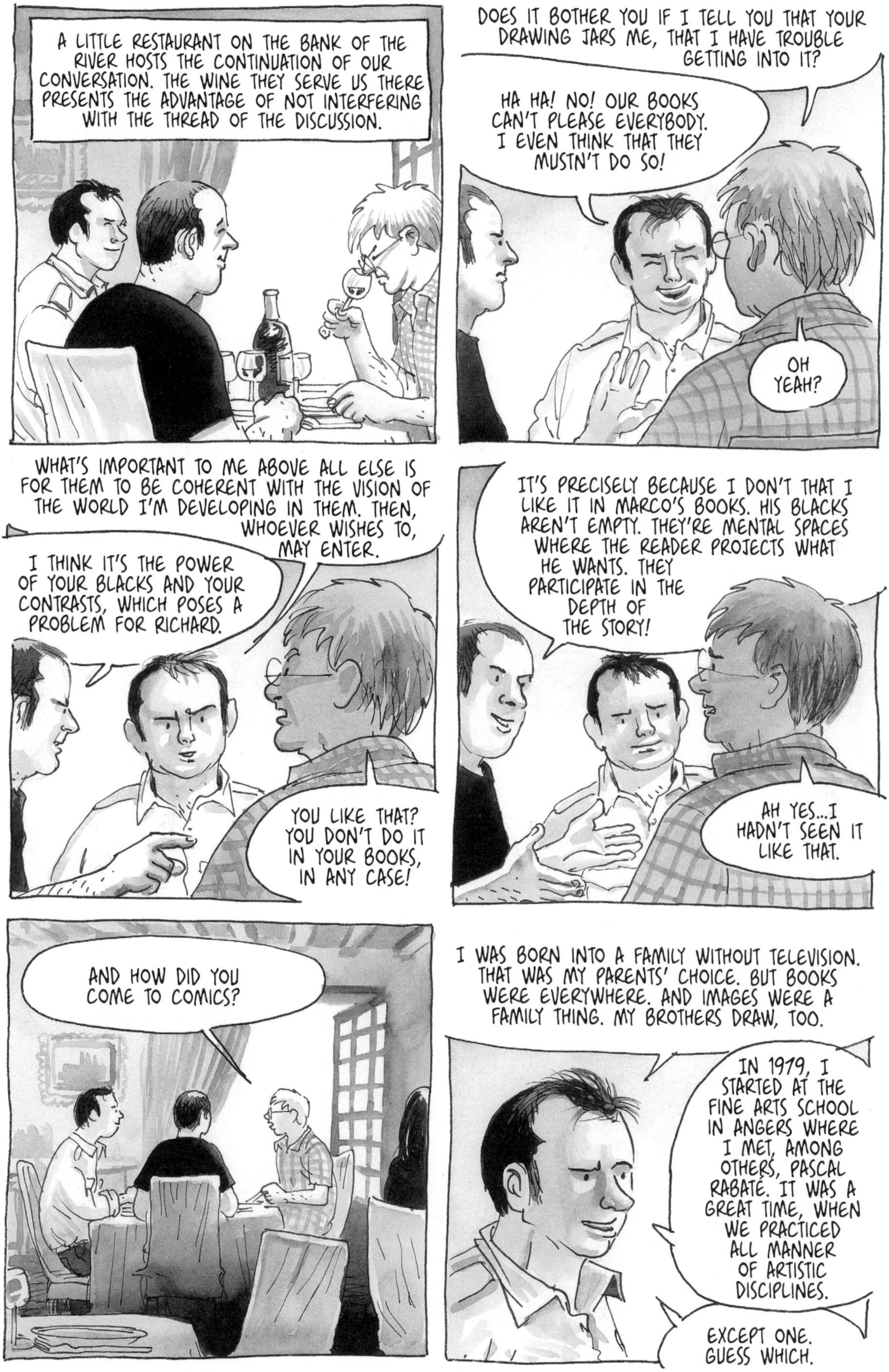
A LITTLE RESTAURANT ON THE BANK OF THE RIVER HOSTS THE CONTINUATION OF OUR CONVERSATION. THE WINE THEY SERVE US THERE PRESENTS THE ADVANTAGE OF NOT INTERFERING WITH THE THREAD OF THE DISCUSSION.
DOES IT BOTHER YOU IF I TELL YOU THAT YOUR DRAWING JARS ME, THAT I HAVE TROUBLE GETTING INTO IT?
HA HA! NO! OUR BOOKS CAN'T PLEASE EVERYBODY. I EVEN THINK THAT THEY MUSTN'T DO SO!
OH YEAH?
WHAT'S IMPORTANT TO ME ABOVE ALL ELSE IS FOR THEM TO BE COHERENT WITH THE VISION OF THE WORLD I'M DEVELOPING IN THEM. THEN, WHOEVER WISHES TO, MAY ENTER.
I THINK IT'S THE POWER OF YOUR BLACKS AND YOUR CONTRASTS, WHICH POSES A PROBLEM FOR RICHARD.
YOU LIKE THAT? YOU DON'T DO IT IN YOUR BOOKS, IN ANY CASE!
IT'S PRECISELY BECAUSE I DON'T THAT I LIKE IT IN MARCO'S BOOKS. HIS BLACKS AREN'T EMPTY. THEY'RE MENTAL SPACES WHERE THE READER PROJECTS WHAT HE WANTS. THEY PARTICIPATE IN THE DEPTH OF THE STORY!
AH YES...I HADN'T SEEN IT LIKE THAT.
AND HOW DID YOU COME TO COMICS?
I WAS BORN INTO A FAMILY WITHOUT TELEVISION. THAT WAS MY PARENTS' CHOICE. BUT BOOKS WERE EVERYWHERE. AND IMAGES WERE A FAMILY THING. MY BROTHERS DRAW, TOO.
IN 1979, I STARTED AT THE FINE ARTS SCHOOL IN ANGERS WHERE I MET, AMONG OTHERS, PASCAL RABATÉ. IT WAS A GREAT TIME, WHEN WE PRACTICED ALL MANNER OF ARTISTIC DISCIPLINES.
EXCEPT ONE. GUESS WHICH.

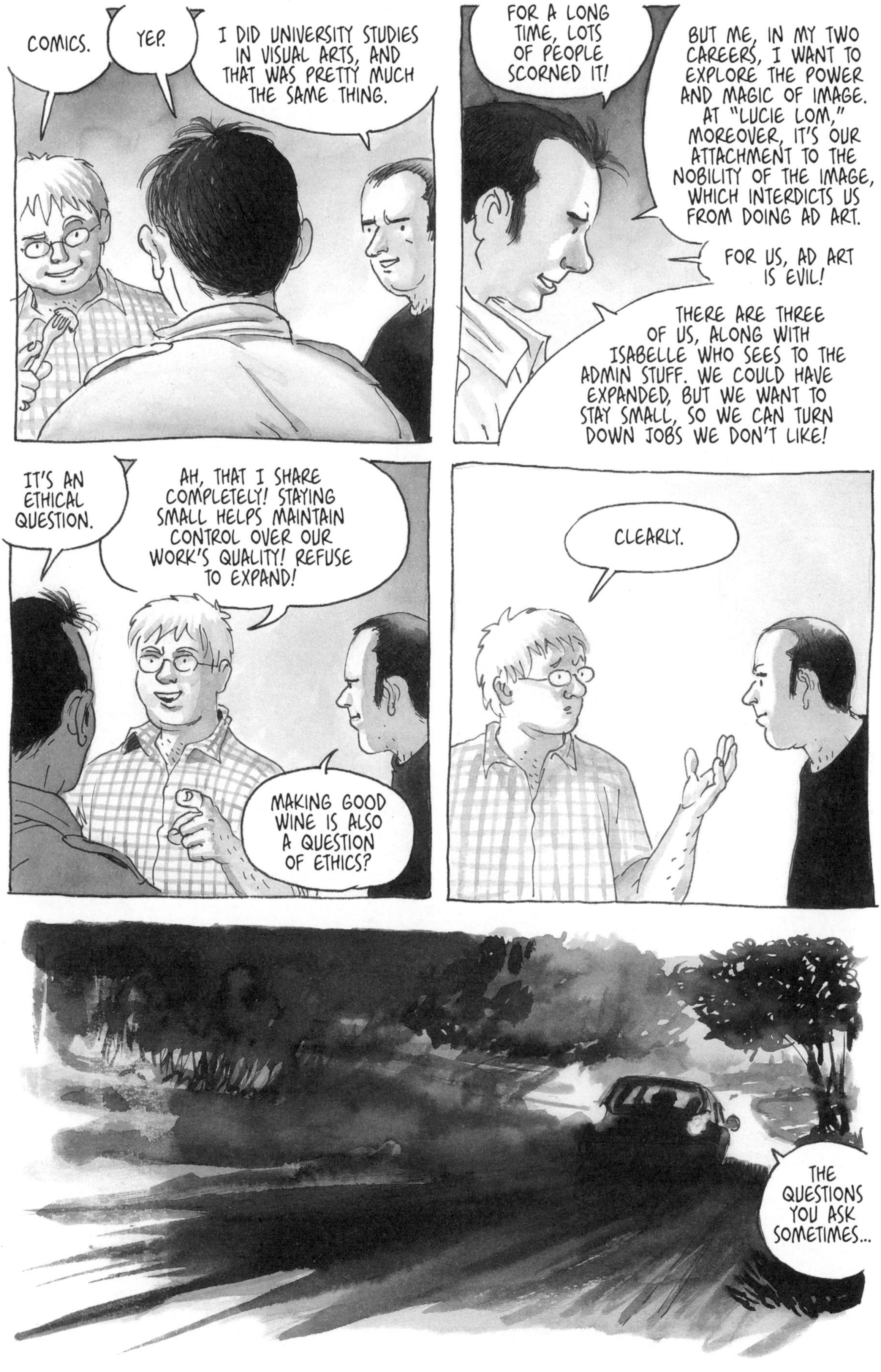

COMICS.
YEP.
I DID UNIVERSITY STUDIES IN VISUAL ARTS, AND THAT WAS PRETTY MUCH THE SAME THING.
FOR A LONG TIME, LOTS OF PEOPLE SCORNED IT!
BUT ME, IN MY TWO CAREERS, I WANT TO EXPLORE THE POWER AND MAGIC OF IMAGE. AT "LUCIE LOM," MOREOVER, IT'S OUR ATTACHMENT TO THE NOBILITY OF THE IMAGE, WHICH INTERDICTS US FROM DOING AD ART.
FOR US, AD ART IS EVIL!
THERE ARE THREE OF US, ALONG WITH ISABELLE WHO SEES TO THE ADMIN STUFF. WE COULD HAVE EXPANDED, BUT WE WANT TO STAY SMALL, SO WE CAN TURN DOWN JOBS WE DON'T LIKE!
IT'S AN ETHICAL QUESTION.
AH, THAT I SHARE COMPLETELY! STAYING SMALL HELPS MAINTAIN CONTROL OVER OUR WORK'S QUALITY! REFUSE TO EXPAND!
MAKING GOOD WINE IS ALSO A QUESTION OF ETHICS?
CLEARLY.
THE QUESTIONS YOU ASK SOMETIMES...

CHAPTER TWELVE   WHEREIN,
WHEN CERTAIN
VINTNERS SUFFER
SULFUR.

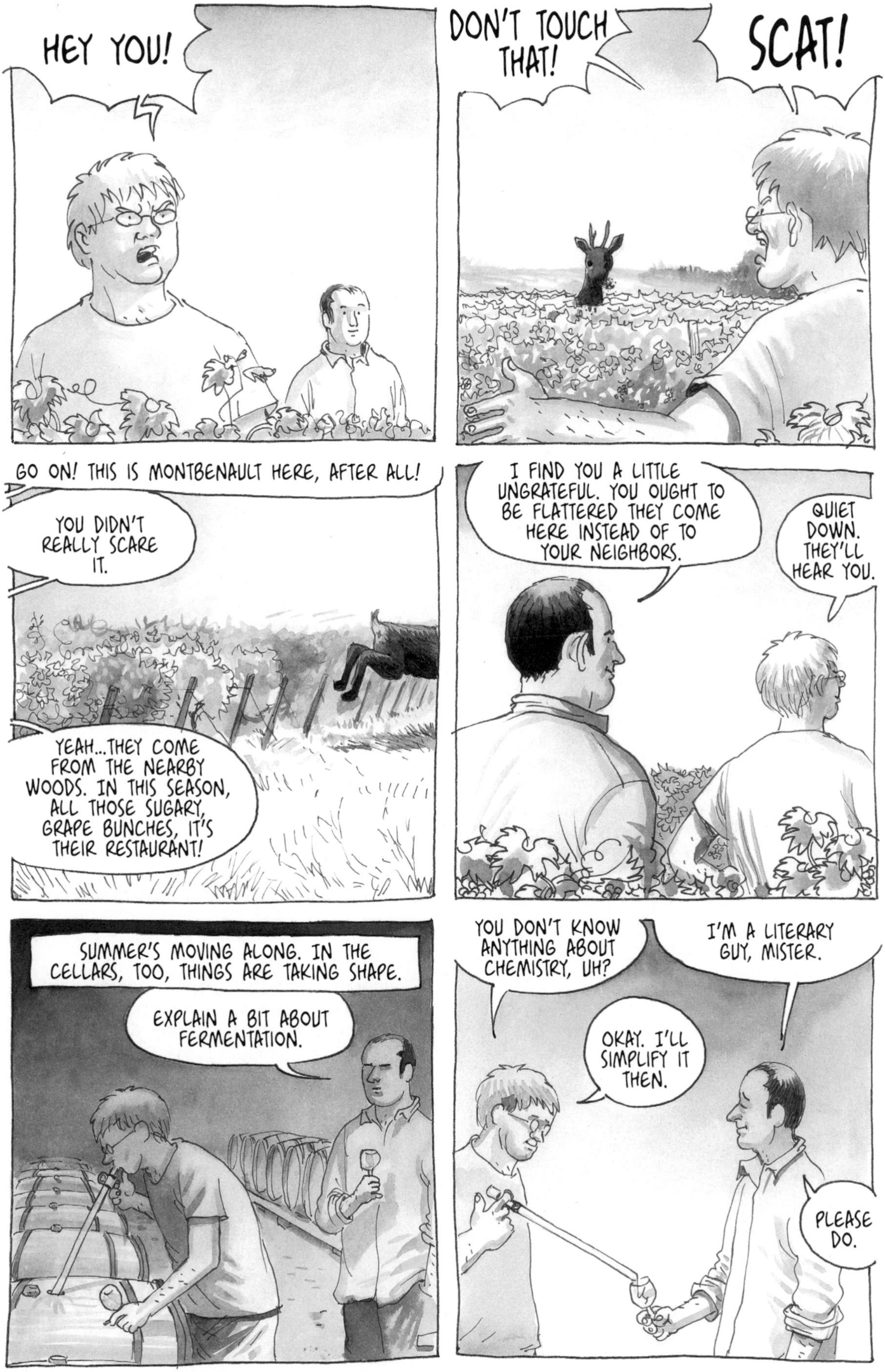
HEY YOU!
DON'T TOUCH THAT!
SCAT!
GO ON! THIS IS MONTBENAULT HERE, AFTER ALL!
YOU DIDN'T REALLY SCARE IT.
YEAH...THEY COME FROM THE NEARBY WOODS. IN THIS SEASON, ALL THOSE SUGARY, GRAPE BUNCHES, IT'S THEIR RESTAURANT!
I FIND YOU A LITTLE UNGRATEFUL. YOU OUGHT TO BE FLATTERED THEY COME HERE INSTEAD OF TO YOUR NEIGHBORS.
QUIET DOWN. THEY'LL HEAR YOU.
SUMMER'S MOVING ALONG. IN THE CELLARS, TOO, THINGS ARE TAKING SHAPE.
EXPLAIN A BIT ABOUT FERMENTATION.
YOU DON'T KNOW ANYTHING ABOUT CHEMISTRY, UH?
I'M A LITERARY GUY, MISTER.
OKAY. I'LL SIMPLIFY IT THEN.
PLEASE DO.

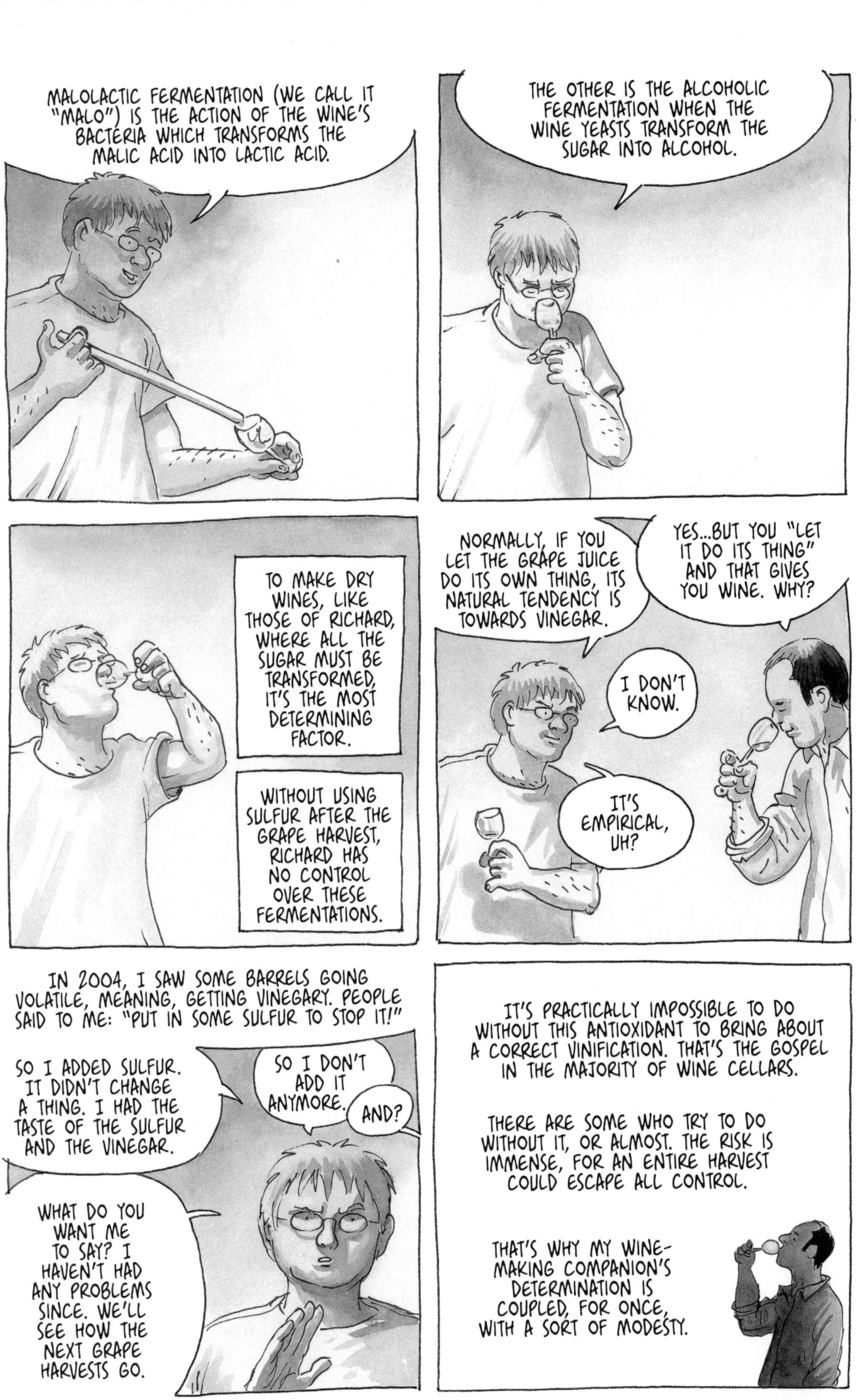
MALOLACTIC FERMENTATION (WE CALL IT "MALO") IS THE ACTION OF THE WINE'S BACTERIA WHICH TRANSFORMS THE MALIC ACID INTO LACTIC ACID.
THE OTHER IS THE ALCOHOLIC FERMENTATION WHEN THE WINE YEASTS TRANSFORM THE SUGAR INTO ALCOHOL.
TO MAKE DRY WINES, LIKE THOSE OF RICHARD, WHERE ALL THE SUGAR MUST BE TRANSFORMED, IT'S THE MOST DETERMINING FACTOR.
WITHOUT USING SULFUR AFTER THE GRAPE HARVEST, RICHARD HAS NO CONTROL OVER THESE FERMENTATIONS.
NORMALLY, IF YOU LET THE GRAPE JUICE DO ITS OWN THING, ITS NATURAL TENDENCY IS TOWARDS VINEGAR.
YES...BUT YOU "LET IT DO ITS THING" AND THAT GIVES YOU WINE. WHY?
I DON'T KNOW.
IT'S EMPIRICAL, UH?
IN 2004, I SAW SOME BARRELS GOING VOLATILE, MEANING, GETTING VINEGARY. PEOPLE SAID TO ME: "PUT IN SOME SULFUR TO STOP IT!"
SO I ADDED SULFUR. IT DIDN'T CHANGE A THING. I HAD THE TASTE OF THE SULFUR AND THE VINEGAR.
SO I DON'T ADD IT ANYMORE.
AND?
WHAT DO YOU WANT ME TO SAY? I HAVEN'T HAD ANY PROBLEMS SINCE. WE'LL SEE HOW THE NEXT GRAPE HARVESTS GO.
IT'S PRACTICALLY IMPOSSIBLE TO DO WITHOUT THIS ANTIOXIDANT TO BRING ABOUT A CORRECT VINIFICATION. THAT'S THE GOSPEL IN THE MAJORITY OF WINE CELLARS.
THERE ARE SOME WHO TRY TO DO WITHOUT IT, OR ALMOST. THE RISK IS IMMENSE, FOR AN ENTIRE HARVEST COULD ESCAPE ALL CONTROL.
THAT'S WHY MY WINE-MAKING COMPANION'S DETERMINATION IS COUPLED, FOR ONCE, WITH A SORT OF MODESTY.

DOIN' OKAY?

YEAH! IT'S MY FAVORITE MOMENT OF THE YEAR!

SEPTEMBER IS AT HAND.

THE WINE'S READY. THE TIME'S COME FOR IT TO LEAVE THE COZY BARREL FOR THE VAT, THEN THE BOTTLE. IT'S THE BEGINNING OF THE VOYAGE.

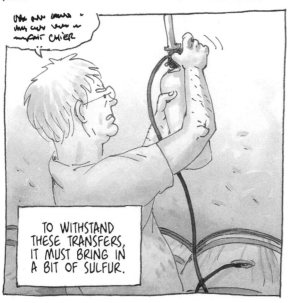

TO WITHSTAND THESE TRANSFERS, IT MUST BRING IN A BIT OF SULFUR.

IS IT REALLY NECESSARY TO DRAW THIS?

I'M JUST TAKING NOTES. YOU CAN'T DO WITHOUT IT, IF IT ANNOYS YOU TO THAT EXTENT?

HEY! IT'S NOT THAT SIMPLE!

I DON'T YET DARE DO THE BOTTLING WITHOUT SULFUR, BECAUSE, AT THAT MOMENT, THE WINE IS IN CONTACT WITH THE AIR. WITHOUT SULFUR, IT TRULY RISKS GOING BAD.

HOW MUCH DO YOU PUT IN?

I DO A TOTAL OF AROUND 30 MILLIGRAMS OF SULFUR PER LITER.

(AFTER ANALYSIS, 34, EXACTLY.).

MEANS NOTHING TO ME. IS THAT A LOT?

WITH ORGANICS, THE AUTHORIZED DOSE IS 120. WITH NON-ORGANIC, 210.

I'M TRYING TO HEAD TOWARDS ZERO.

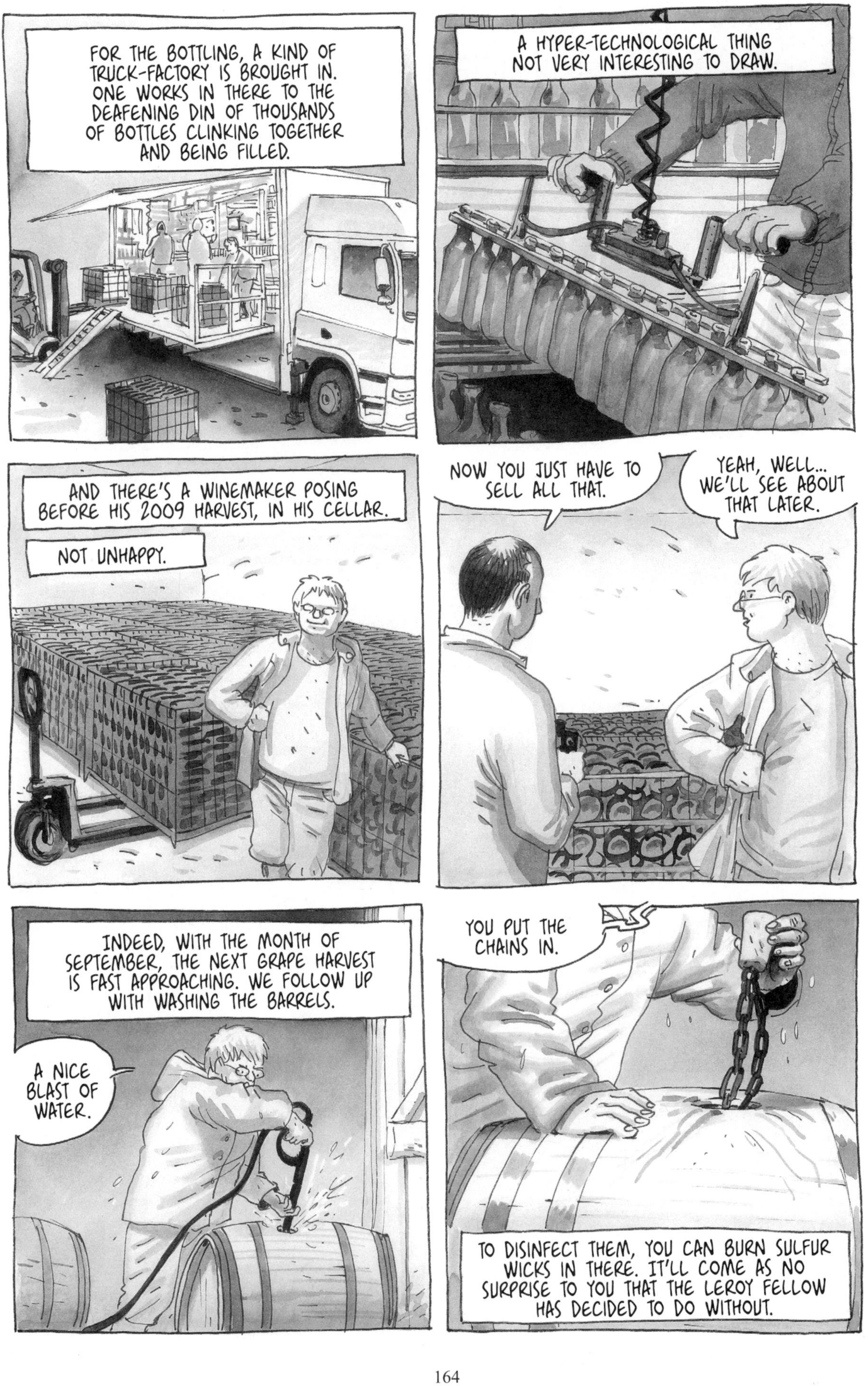
FOR THE BOTTLING, A KIND OF TRUCK-FACTORY IS BROUGHT IN. ONE WORKS IN THERE TO THE DEAFENING DIN OF THOUSANDS OF BOTTLES CLINKING TOGETHER AND BEING FILLED.
A HYPER-TECHNOLOGICAL THING NOT VERY INTERESTING TO DRAW.
AND THERE'S A WINEMAKER POSING BEFORE HIS 2009 HARVEST, IN HIS CELLAR.
NOT UNHAPPY.
NOW YOU JUST HAVE TO SELL ALL THAT.
YEAH, WELL... WE'LL SEE ABOUT THAT LATER.
INDEED, WITH THE MONTH OF SEPTEMBER, THE NEXT GRAPE HARVEST IS FAST APPROACHING. WE FOLLOW UP WITH WASHING THE BARRELS.
A NICE BLAST OF WATER.
YOU PUT THE CHAINS IN.
TO DISINFECT THEM, YOU CAN BURN SULFUR WICKS IN THERE. IT'LL COME AS NO SURPRISE TO YOU THAT THE LEROY FELLOW HAS DECIDED TO DO WITHOUT.

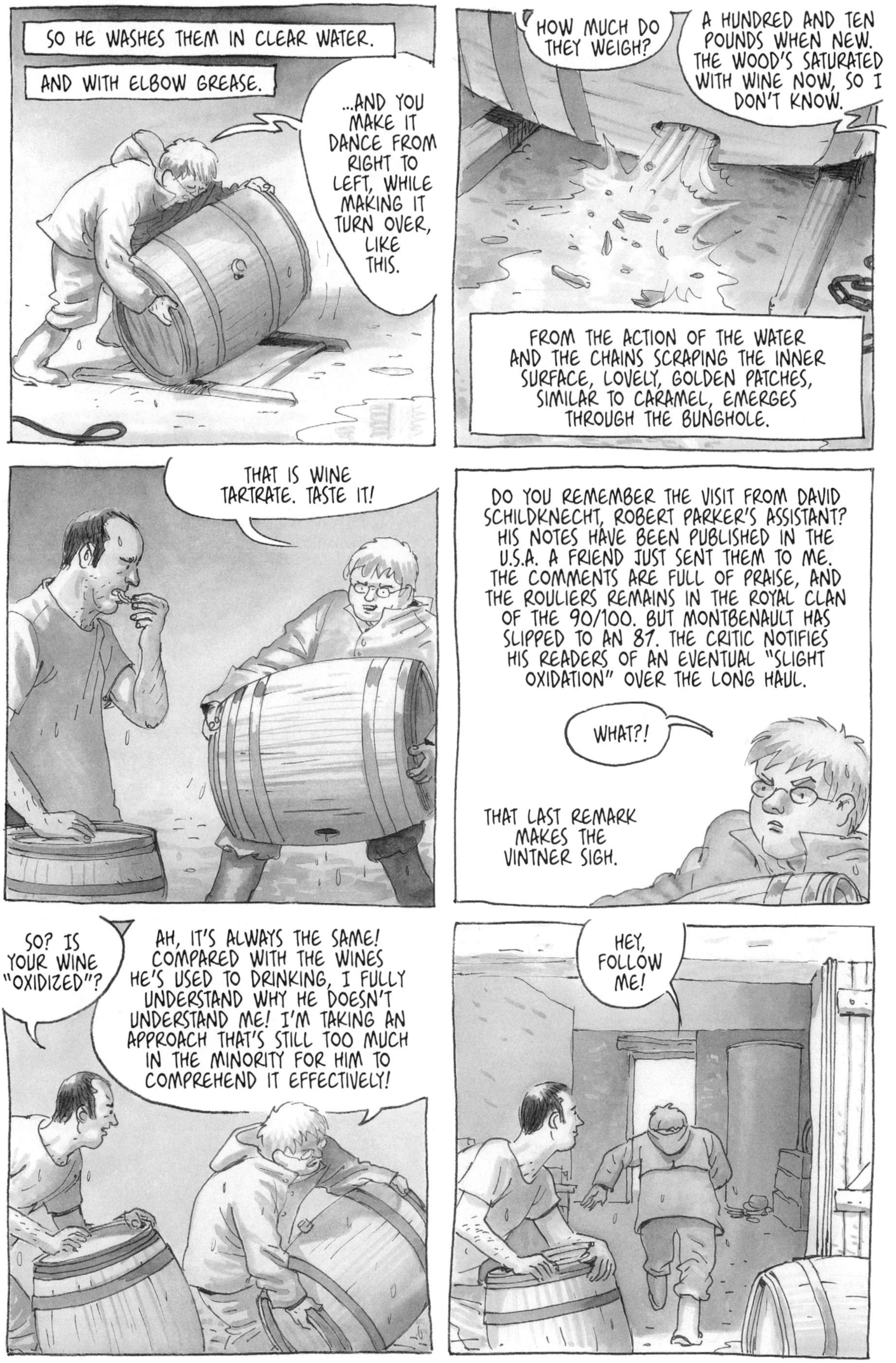
SO HE WASHES THEM IN CLEAR WATER.
AND WITH ELBOW GREASE.
...AND YOU MAKE IT DANCE FROM RIGHT TO LEFT, WHILE MAKING IT TURN OVER, LIKE THIS.
HOW MUCH DO THEY WEIGH?
A HUNDRED AND TEN POUNDS WHEN NEW. THE WOOD'S SATURATED WITH WINE NOW, SO I DON'T KNOW.
FROM THE ACTION OF THE WATER AND THE CHAINS SCRAPING THE INNER SURFACE, LOVELY, GOLDEN PATCHES, SIMILAR TO CARAMEL, EMERGES THROUGH THE BUNGHOLE.
THAT IS WINE TARTRATE. TASTE IT!
DO YOU REMEMBER THE VISIT FROM DAVID SCHILDKNECHT, ROBERT PARKER'S ASSISTANT? HIS NOTES HAVE BEEN PUBLISHED IN THE U.S.A. A FRIEND JUST SENT THEM TO ME. THE COMMENTS ARE FULL OF PRAISE, AND THE ROULIERS REMAINS IN THE ROYAL CLAN OF THE 90/100. BUT MONTBENAULT HAS SLIPPED TO AN 87. THE CRITIC NOTIFIES HIS READERS OF AN EVENTUAL "SLIGHT OXIDATION" OVER THE LONG HAUL.
WHAT?!
THAT LAST REMARK MAKES THE VINTNER SIGH.
SO? IS YOUR WINE "OXIDIZED"?
AH, IT'S ALWAYS THE SAME! COMPARED WITH THE WINES HE'S USED TO DRINKING, I FULLY UNDERSTAND WHY HE DOESN'T UNDERSTAND ME! I'M TAKING AN APPROACH THAT'S STILL TOO MUCH IN THE MINORITY FOR HIM TO COMPREHEND IT EFFECTIVELY!
HEY, FOLLOW ME!

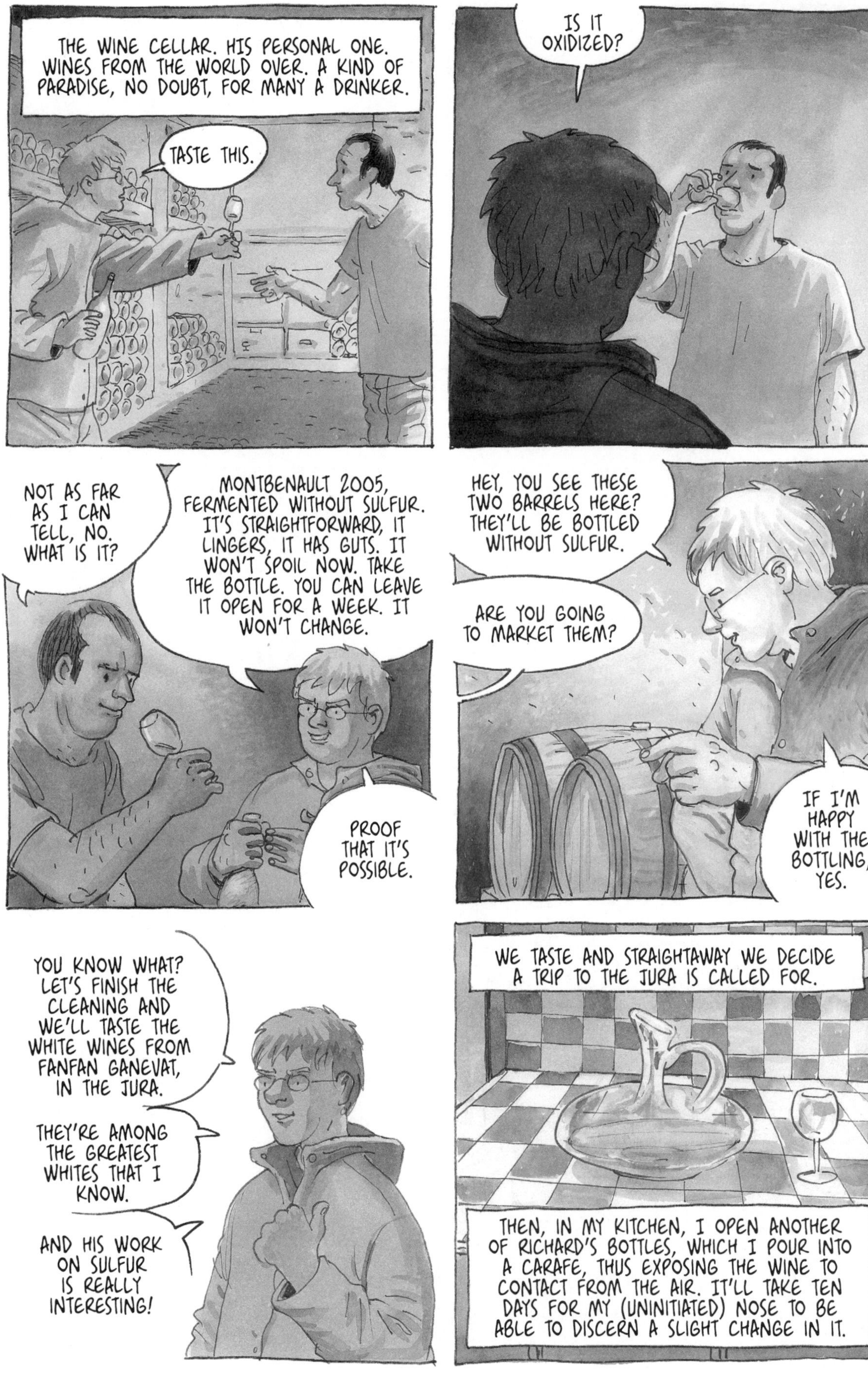
THE WINE CELLAR. HIS PERSONAL ONE. WINES FROM THE WORLD OVER. A KIND OF PARADISE, NO DOUBT, FOR MANY A DRINKER.
TASTE THIS.
IS IT OXIDIZED?
NOT AS FAR AS I CAN TELL, NO. WHAT IS IT?
MONTBENAULT 2005, FERMENTED WITHOUT SULFUR. IT'S STRAIGHTFORWARD, IT LINGERS, IT HAS GUTS. IT WON'T SPOIL NOW. TAKE THE BOTTLE. YOU CAN LEAVE IT OPEN FOR A WEEK. IT WON'T CHANGE.
PROOF THAT IT'S POSSIBLE.
HEY, YOU SEE THESE TWO BARRELS HERE? THEY'LL BE BOTTLED WITHOUT SULFUR.
ARE YOU GOING TO MARKET THEM?
IF I'M HAPPY WITH THE BOTTLING, YES.
YOU KNOW WHAT? LET'S FINISH THE CLEANING AND WE'LL TASTE THE WHITE WINES FROM FANFAN GANEVAT, IN THE JURA.
THEY'RE AMONG THE GREATEST WHITES THAT I KNOW.
AND HIS WORK ON SULFUR IS REALLY INTERESTING!
WE TASTE AND STRAIGHTAWAY WE DECIDE A TRIP TO THE JURA IS CALLED FOR.
THEN, IN MY KITCHEN, I OPEN ANOTHER OF RICHARD'S BOTTLES, WHICH I POUR INTO A CARAFE, THUS EXPOSING THE WINE TO CONTACT FROM THE AIR. IT'LL TAKE TEN DAYS FOR MY (UNINITIATED) NOSE TO BE ABLE TO DISCERN A SLIGHT CHANGE IN IT.

CHAPTER THIRTEEN BUCKET!

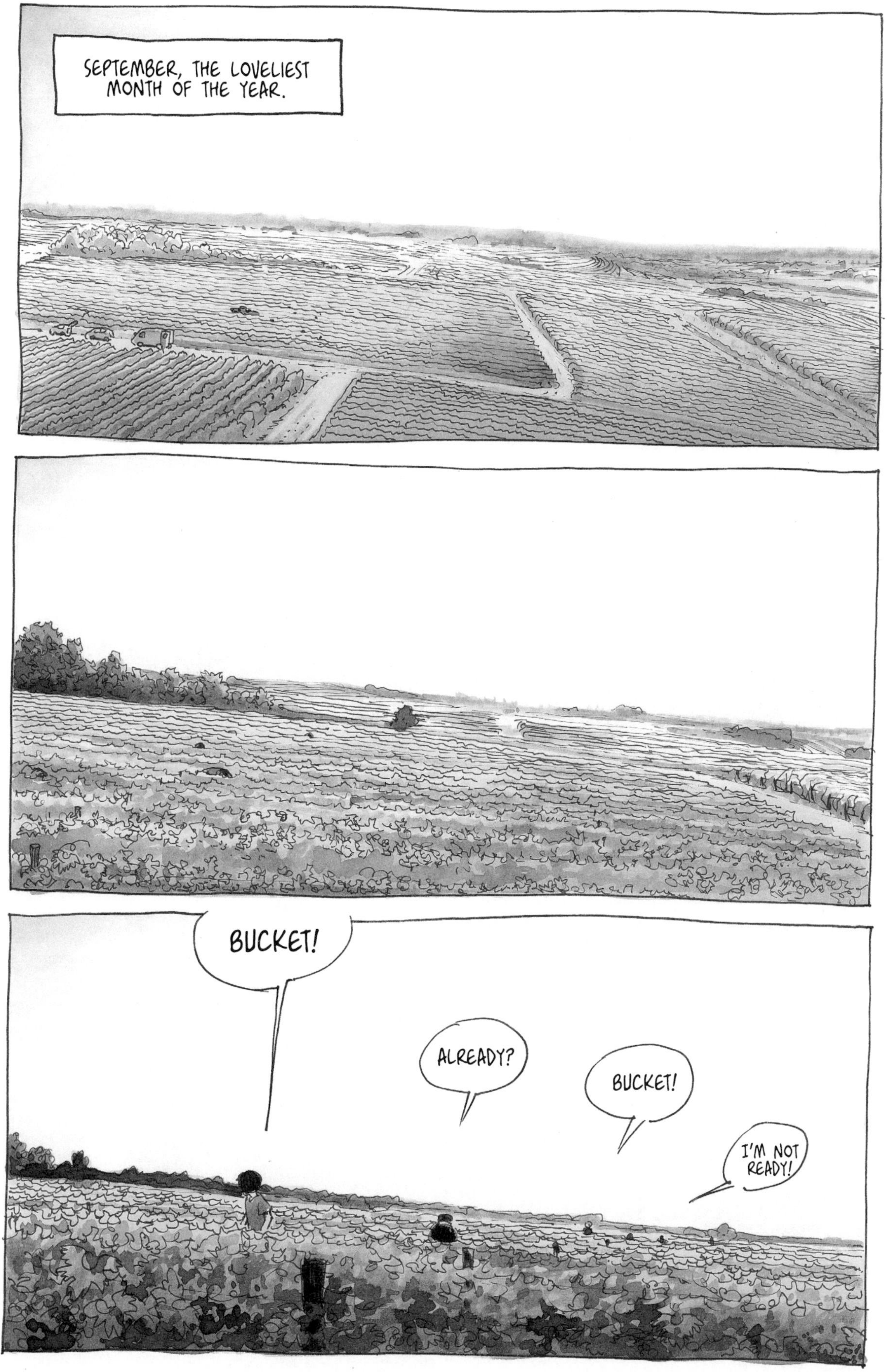
SEPTEMBER, THE LOVELIEST MONTH OF THE YEAR.
BUCKET!
ALREADY?
BUCKET!
I'M NOT READY!

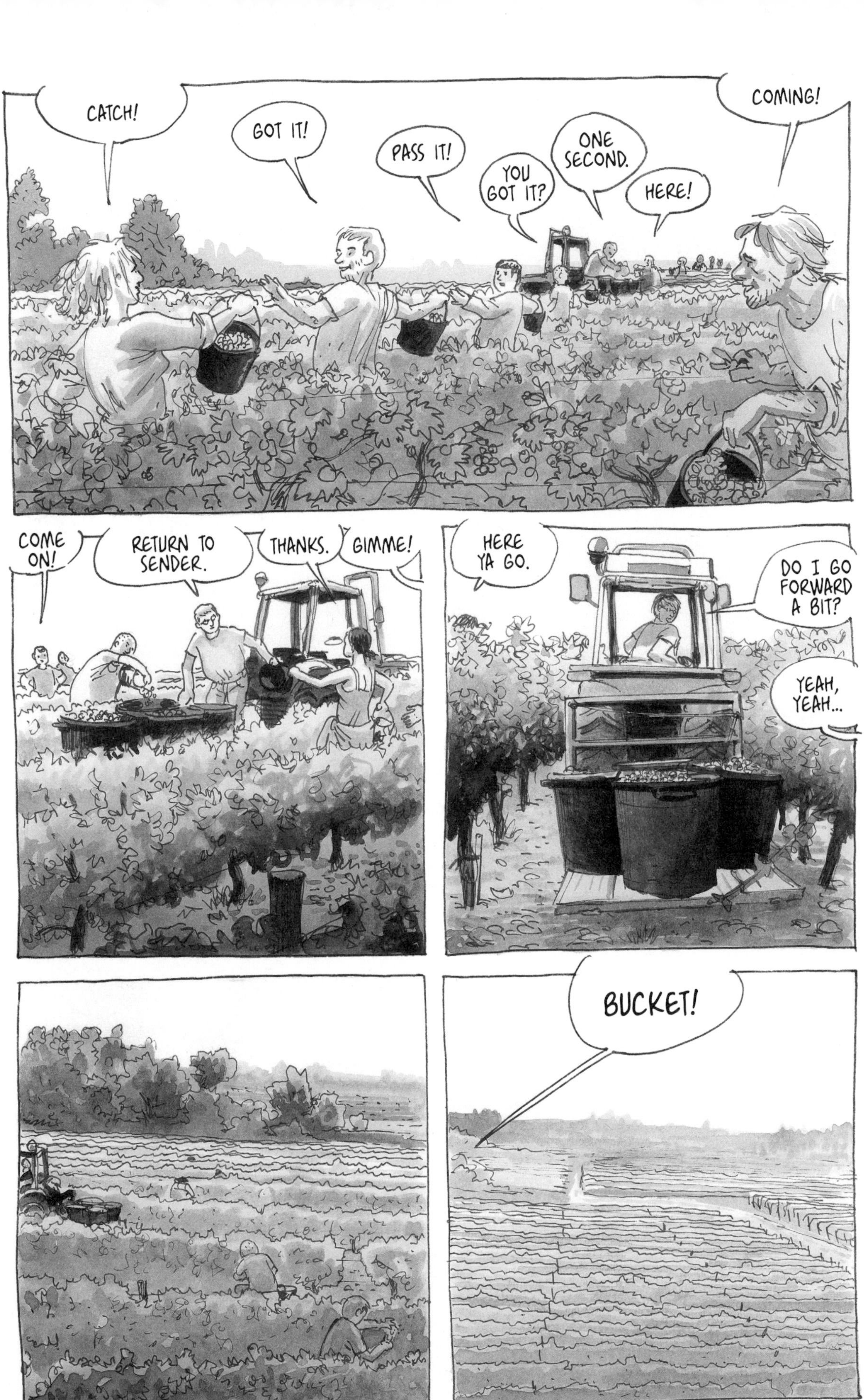
CATCH!
GOT IT!
PASS IT!
YOU GOT IT?
ONE SECOND.
HERE!
COMING!
COME ON!
RETURN TO SENDER.
THANKS.
GIMME!
HERE YA GO.
DO I GO FORWARD A BIT?
YEAH, YEAH...
BUCKET!

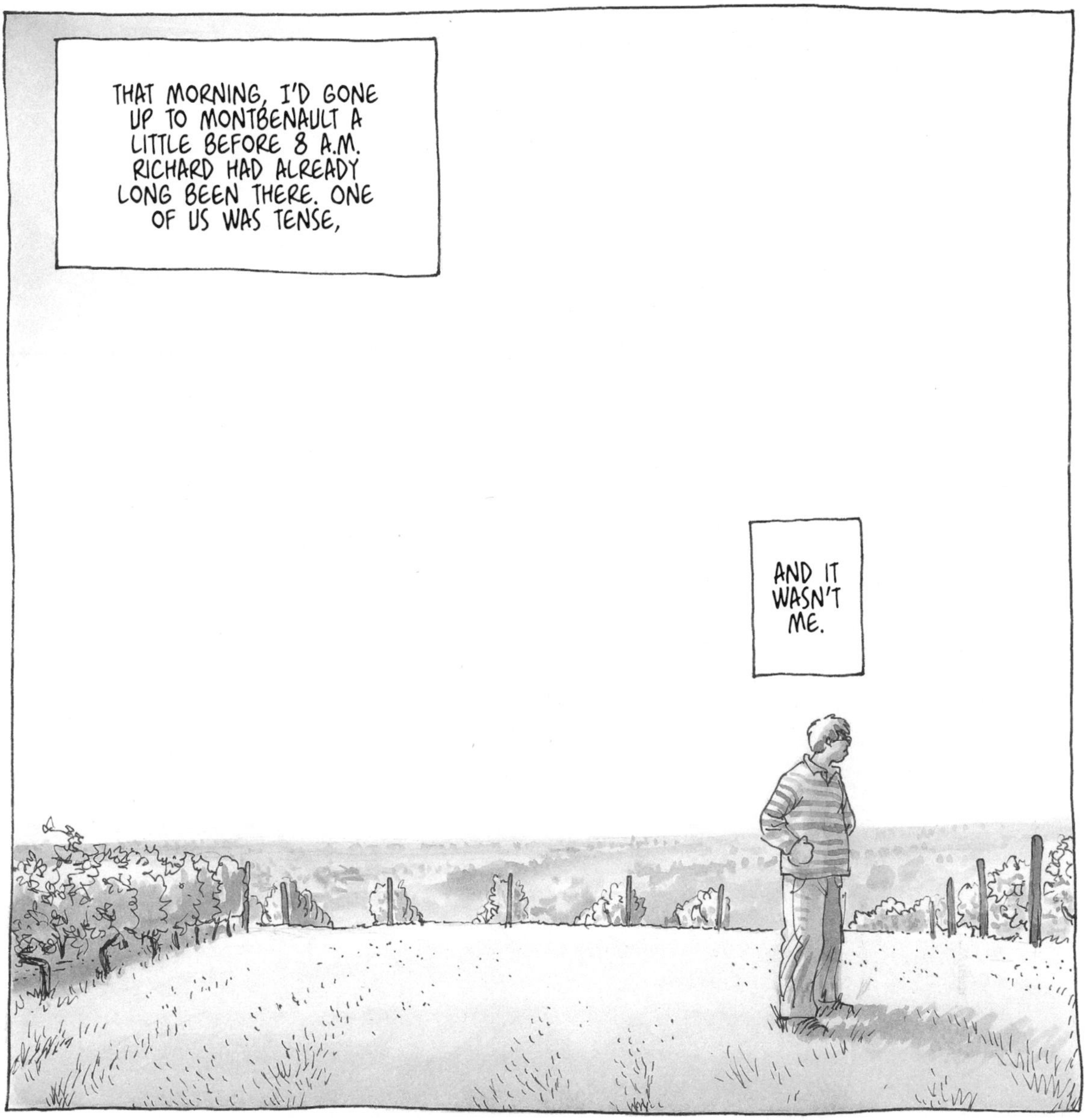
THAT MORNING, I'D GONE UP TO MONTBENAULT A LITTLE BEFORE 8 A.M. RICHARD HAD ALREADY LONG BEEN THERE. ONE OF US WAS TENSE,
AND IT WASN'T ME.

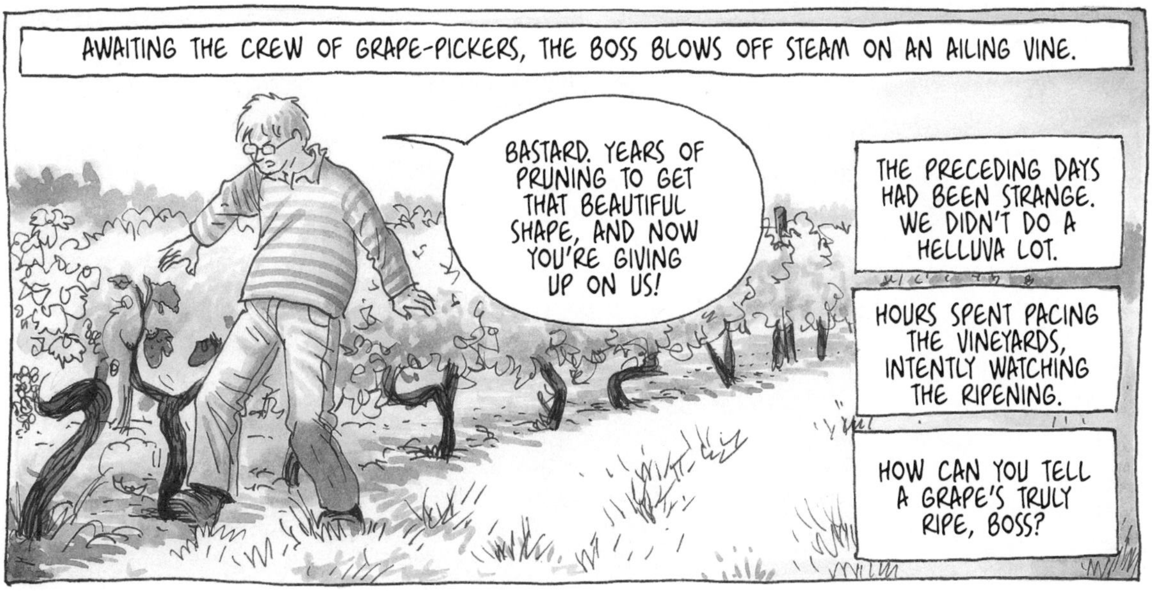
AWAITING THE CREW OF GRAPE-PICKERS, THE BOSS BLOWS OFF STEAM ON AN AILING VINE.
BASTARD. YEARS OF PRUNING TO GET THAT BEAUTIFUL SHAPE, AND NOW YOU'RE GIVING UP ON US!
THE PRECEDING DAYS HAD BEEN STRANGE. WE DIDN'T DO A HELLUVA LOT.
HOURS SPENT PACING THE VINEYARDS, INTENTLY WATCHING THE RIPENING.
HOW CAN YOU TELL A GRAPE'S TRULY RIPE, BOSS?

FROM ONE PLOT TO THE OTHER, ONE WINEMAKER TO ANOTHER, IT REALLY DEPENDS ON THE TERROIR, ON THE SOIL'S WORK, AND THE WORK FROM THE WHOLE YEAR.

I HAVE ONLY ONE CRITERION.

I TASTE THE GRAPE.

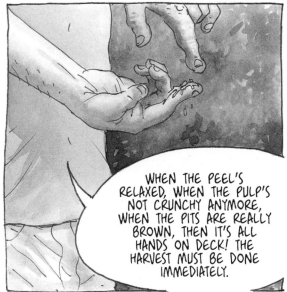

WHEN THE PEEL'S RELAXED, WHEN THE PULP'S NOT CRUNCHY ANYMORE, WHEN THE PITS ARE REALLY BROWN, THEN IT'S ALL HANDS ON DECK! THE HARVEST MUST BE DONE IMMEDIATELY.

THE DAY AFTER THAT IS IDEAL.

AND NOW?

WHAT DO YOU THINK?

ALL HANDS ON DECK.

THAT MORNING, THEN.

HERE WE ARE!

DAMN, RICHARD, YOU'VE GOT SOME NICE BOTRYTIS ON SOME OF YOUR GRAPE BUNCHES. YOU COULD MAKE SOME COTEAUX-DU-LAYON WINES!

WELL, YEAH, BUT NO.

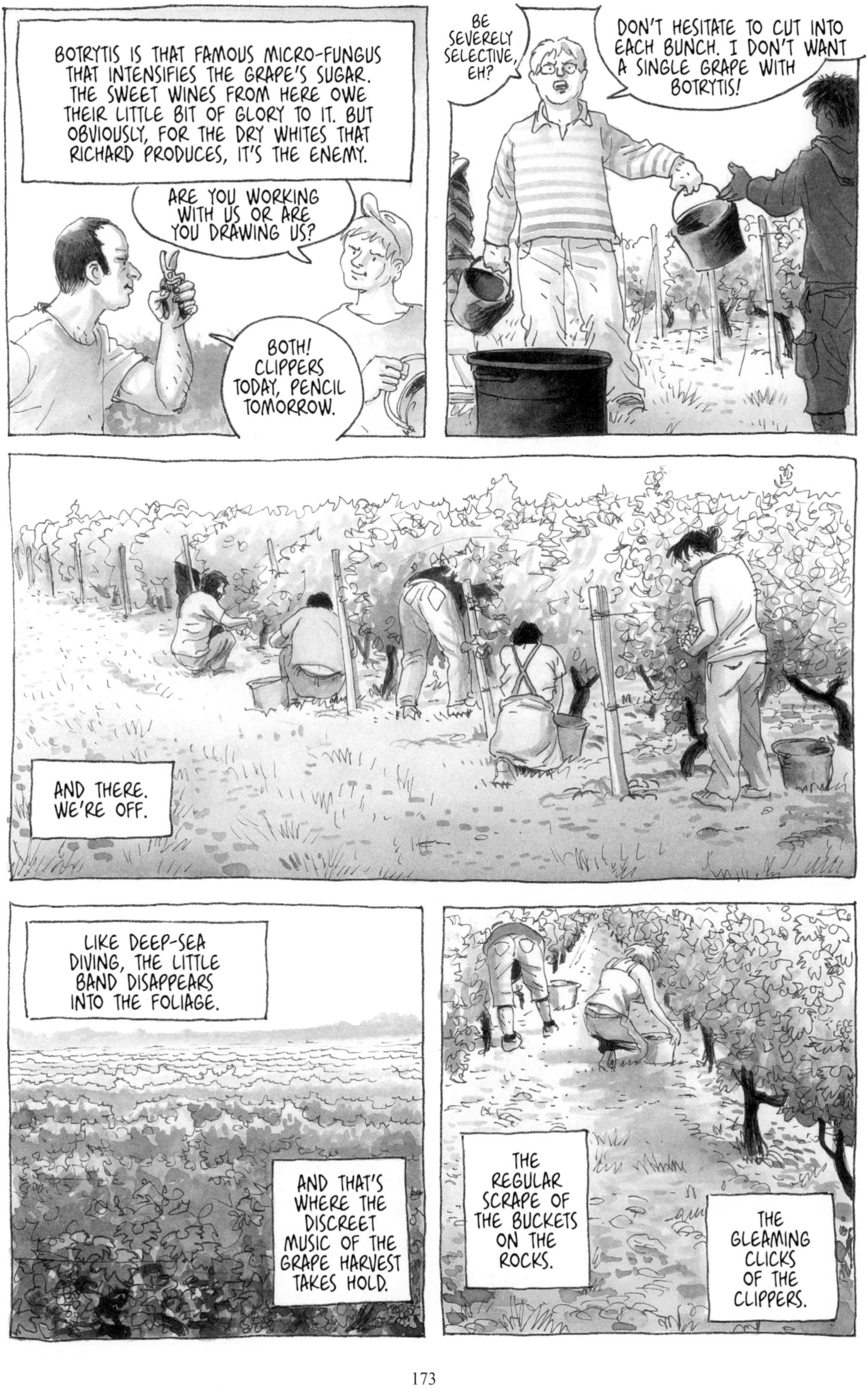
BOTRYTIS IS THAT FAMOUS MICRO-FUNGUS THAT INTENSIFIES THE GRAPE'S SUGAR. THE SWEET WINES FROM HERE OWE THEIR LITTLE BIT OF GLORY TO IT. BUT OBVIOUSLY, FOR THE DRY WHITES THAT RICHARD PRODUCES, IT'S THE ENEMY.
ARE YOU WORKING WITH US OR ARE YOU DRAWING US?
BOTH! CLIPPERS TODAY, PENCIL TOMORROW.
BE SEVERELY SELECTIVE, EH?
DON'T HESITATE TO CUT INTO EACH BUNCH. I DON'T WANT A SINGLE GRAPE WITH BOTRYTIS!
AND THERE. WE'RE OFF.
LIKE DEEP-SEA DIVING, THE LITTLE BAND DISAPPEARS INTO THE FOLIAGE.
AND THAT'S WHERE THE DISCREET MUSIC OF THE GRAPE HARVEST TAKES HOLD.
THE REGULAR SCRAPE OF THE BUCKETS ON THE ROCKS.
THE GLEAMING CLICKS OF THE CLIPPERS.

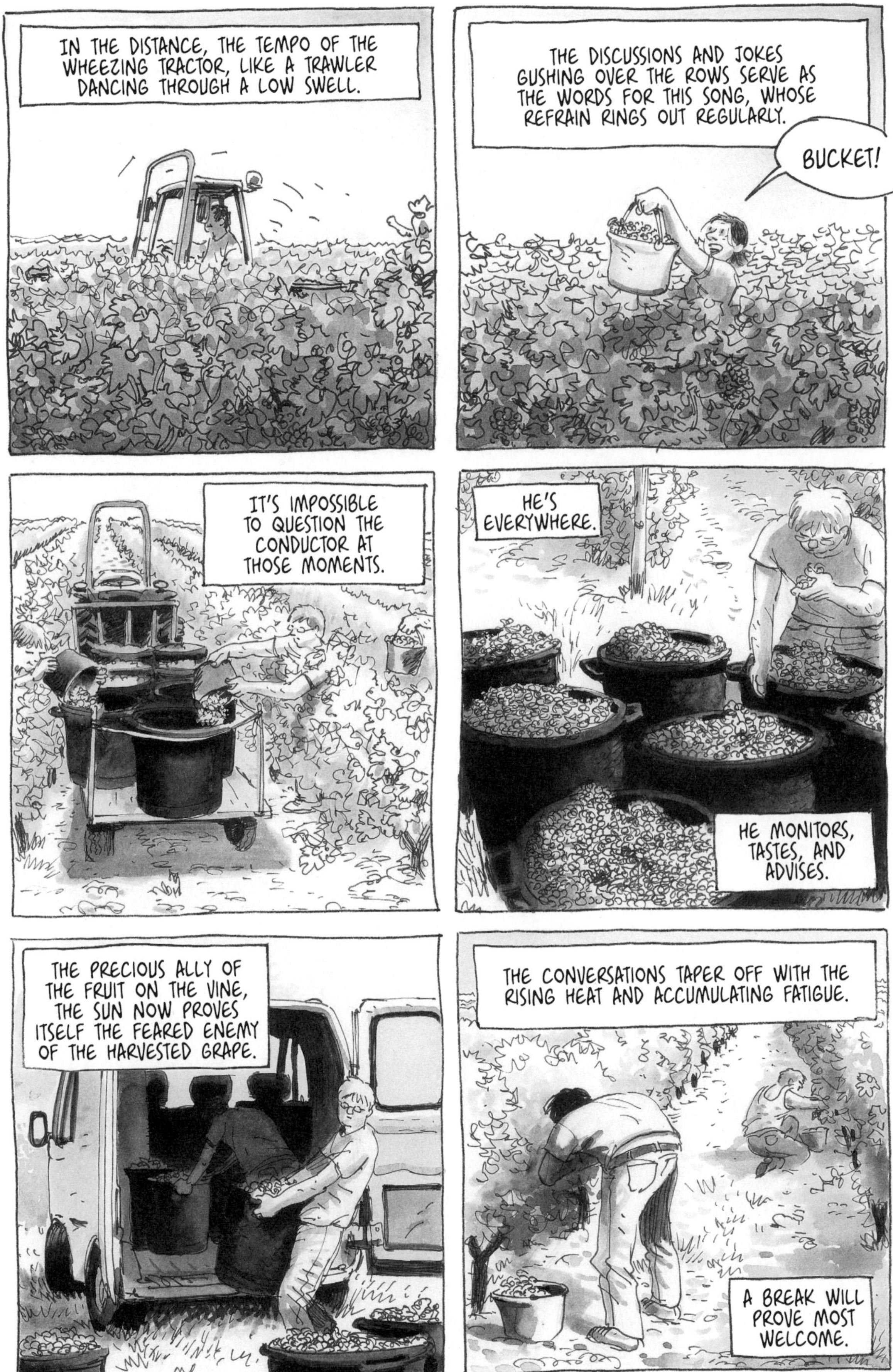
IN THE DISTANCE, THE TEMPO OF THE WHEEZING TRACTOR, LIKE A TRAWLER DANCING THROUGH A LOW SWELL.
THE DISCUSSIONS AND JOKES GUSHING OVER THE ROWS SERVE AS THE WORDS FOR THIS SONG, WHOSE REFRAIN RINGS OUT REGULARLY.
BUCKET!
IT'S IMPOSSIBLE TO QUESTION THE CONDUCTOR AT THOSE MOMENTS.
HE'S EVERYWHERE.
HE MONITORS, TASTES, AND ADVISES.
THE PRECIOUS ALLY OF THE FRUIT ON THE VINE, THE SUN NOW PROVES ITSELF THE FEARED ENEMY OF THE HARVESTED GRAPE.
THE CONVERSATIONS TAPER OFF WITH THE RISING HEAT AND ACCUMULATING FATIGUE.
A BREAK WILL PROVE MOST WELCOME.

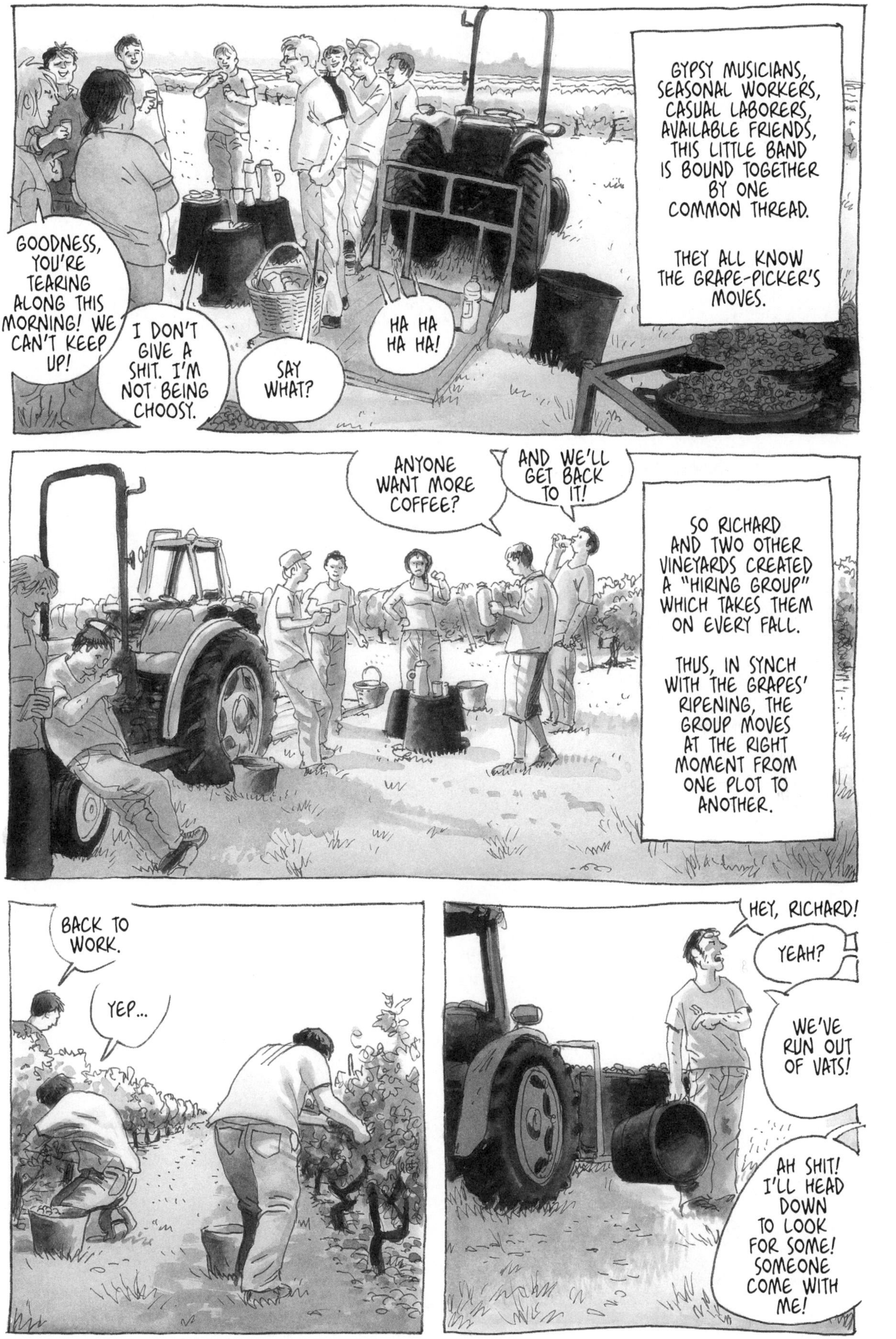
GOODNESS, YOU'RE TEARING ALONG THIS MORNING! WE CAN'T KEEP UP!
I DON'T GIVE A SHIT. I'M NOT BEING CHOOSY.
SAY WHAT?
HA HA HA HA!
GYPSY MUSICIANS, SEASONAL WORKERS, CASUAL LABORERS, AVAILABLE FRIENDS, THIS LITTLE BAND IS BOUND TOGETHER BY ONE COMMON THREAD.
THEY ALL KNOW THE GRAPE-PICKER'S MOVES.
ANYONE WANT MORE COFFEE?
AND WE'LL GET BACK TO IT!
SO RICHARD AND TWO OTHER VINEYARDS CREATED A "HIRING GROUP" WHICH TAKES THEM ON EVERY FALL.
THUS, IN SYNCH WITH THE GRAPES' RIPENING, THE GROUP MOVES AT THE RIGHT MOMENT FROM ONE PLOT TO ANOTHER.
BACK TO WORK.
YEP...
HEY, RICHARD!
YEAH?
WE'VE RUN OUT OF VATS!
AH SHIT! I'LL HEAD DOWN TO LOOK FOR SOME! SOMEONE COME WITH ME!

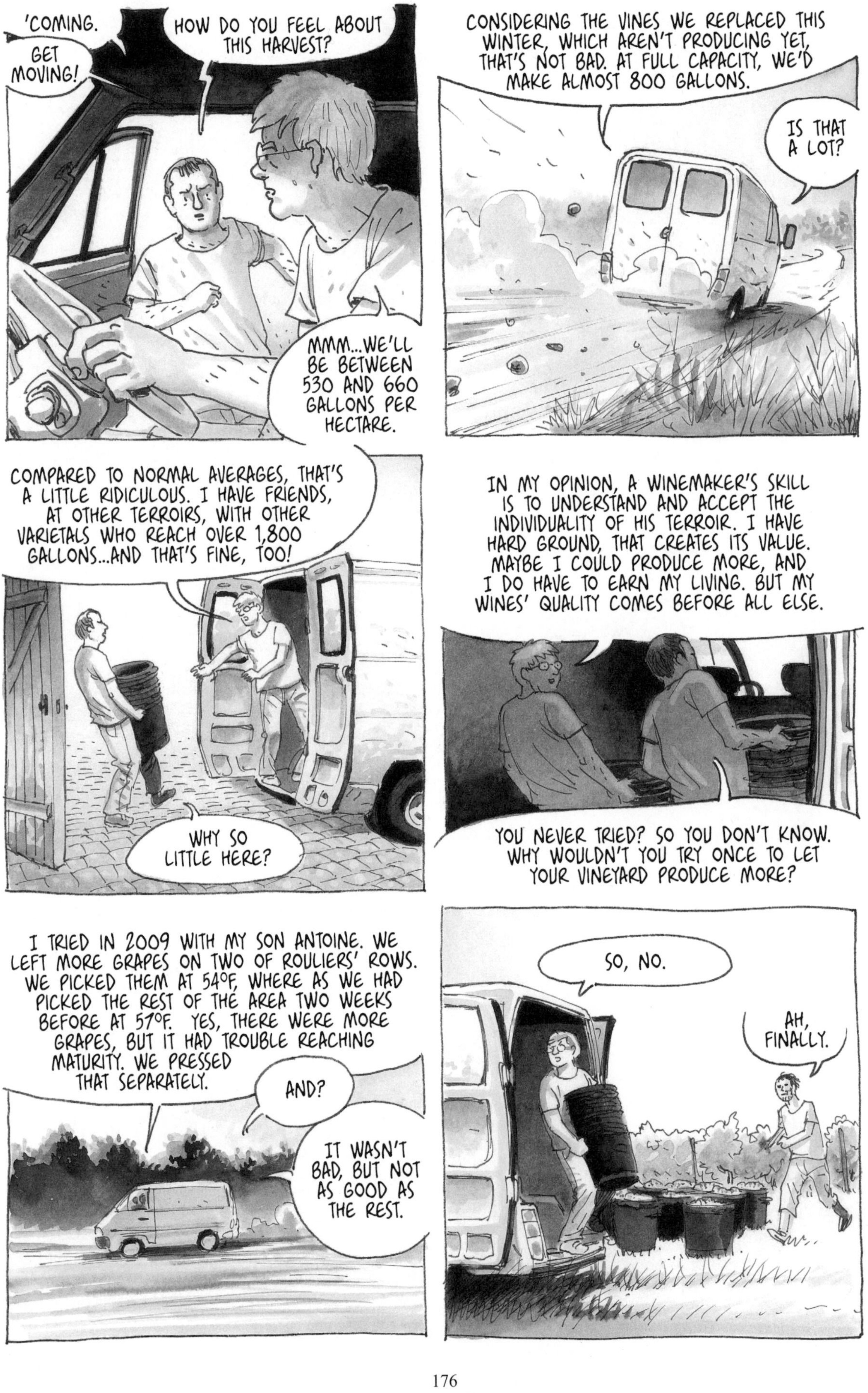
'COMING.
GET MOVING!
HOW DO YOU FEEL ABOUT THIS HARVEST?
MMM...WE'LL BE BETWEEN 530 AND 660 GALLONS PER HECTARE.
CONSIDERING THE VINES WE REPLACED THIS WINTER, WHICH AREN'T PRODUCING YET, THAT'S NOT BAD. AT FULL CAPACITY, WE'D MAKE ALMOST 800 GALLONS.
IS THAT A LOT?
COMPARED TO NORMAL AVERAGES, THAT'S A LITTLE RIDICULOUS. I HAVE FRIENDS, AT OTHER TERROIRS, WITH OTHER VARIETALS WHO REACH OVER 1,800 GALLONS...AND THAT'S FINE, TOO!
WHY SO LITTLE HERE?
IN MY OPINION, A WINEMAKER'S SKILL IS TO UNDERSTAND AND ACCEPT THE INDIVIDUALITY OF HIS TERROIR. I HAVE HARD GROUND, THAT CREATES ITS VALUE. MAYBE I COULD PRODUCE MORE, AND I DO HAVE TO EARN MY LIVING. BUT MY WINES' QUALITY COMES BEFORE ALL ELSE.
YOU NEVER TRIED? SO YOU DON'T KNOW. WHY WOULDN'T YOU TRY ONCE TO LET YOUR VINEYARD PRODUCE MORE?
I TRIED IN 2009 WITH MY SON ANTOINE. WE LEFT MORE GRAPES ON TWO OF ROULIERS' ROWS. WE PICKED THEM AT 54ºF, WHERE AS WE HAD PICKED THE REST OF THE AREA TWO WEEKS BEFORE AT 57ºF. YES, THERE WERE MORE GRAPES, BUT IT HAD TROUBLE REACHING MATURITY. WE PRESSED THAT SEPARATELY.
AND?
IT WASN'T BAD, BUT NOT AS GOOD AS THE REST.
SO, NO.
AH, FINALLY.

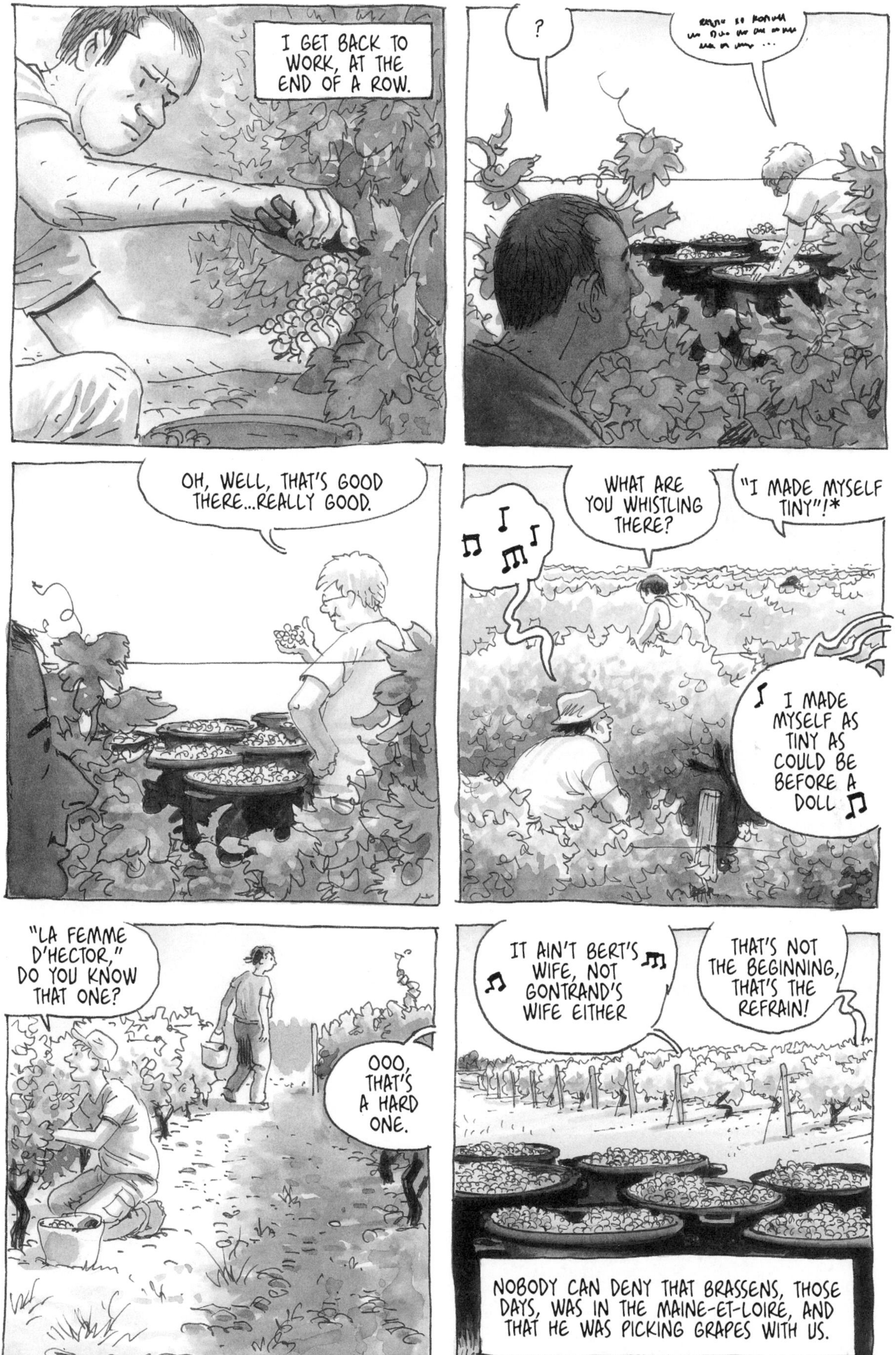
I GET BACK TO WORK, AT THE END OF A ROW.
?
OH, WELL, THAT'S GOOD THERE...REALLY GOOD.
WHAT ARE YOU WHISTLING THERE?
"I MADE MYSELF TINY"!*
I MADE MYSELF AS TINY AS COULD BE BEFORE A DOLL
"LA FEMME D'HECTOR," DO YOU KNOW THAT ONE?
OOO, THAT'S A HARD ONE.
IT AIN'T BERT'S WIFE, NOT GONTRAND'S WIFE EITHER
THAT'S NOT THE BEGINNING, THAT'S THE REFRAIN!
NOBODY CAN DENY THAT BRASSENS, THOSE DAYS, WAS IN THE MAINE-ET-LOIRE, AND THAT HE WAS PICKING GRAPES WITH US.

*THESE LINES COME FROM TWO OF GEORGE BRASSENS' SONGS: "JE ME SUIS FAIT TOUT PETIT" AND "LA FEMME D'HECTOR."

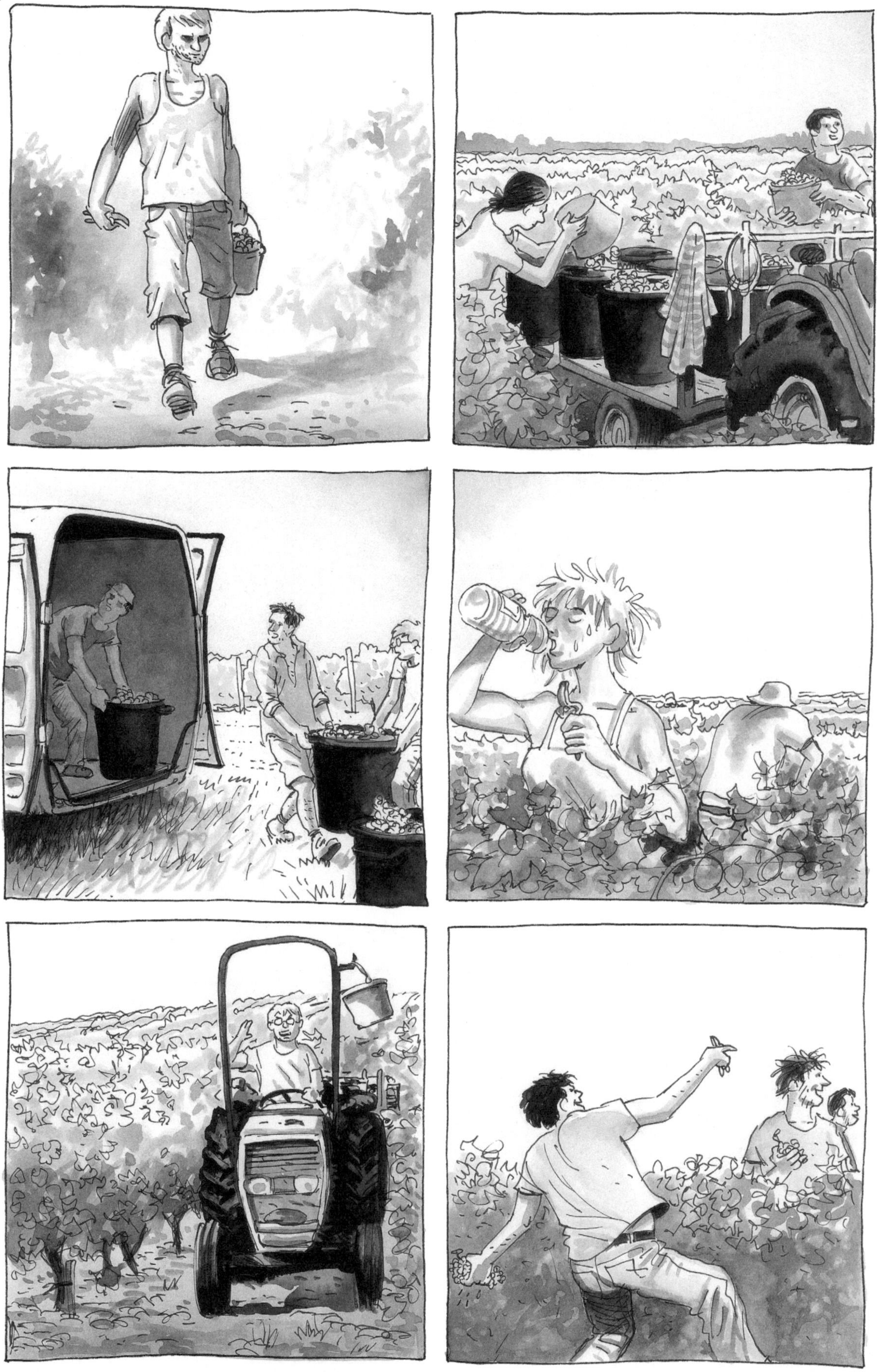

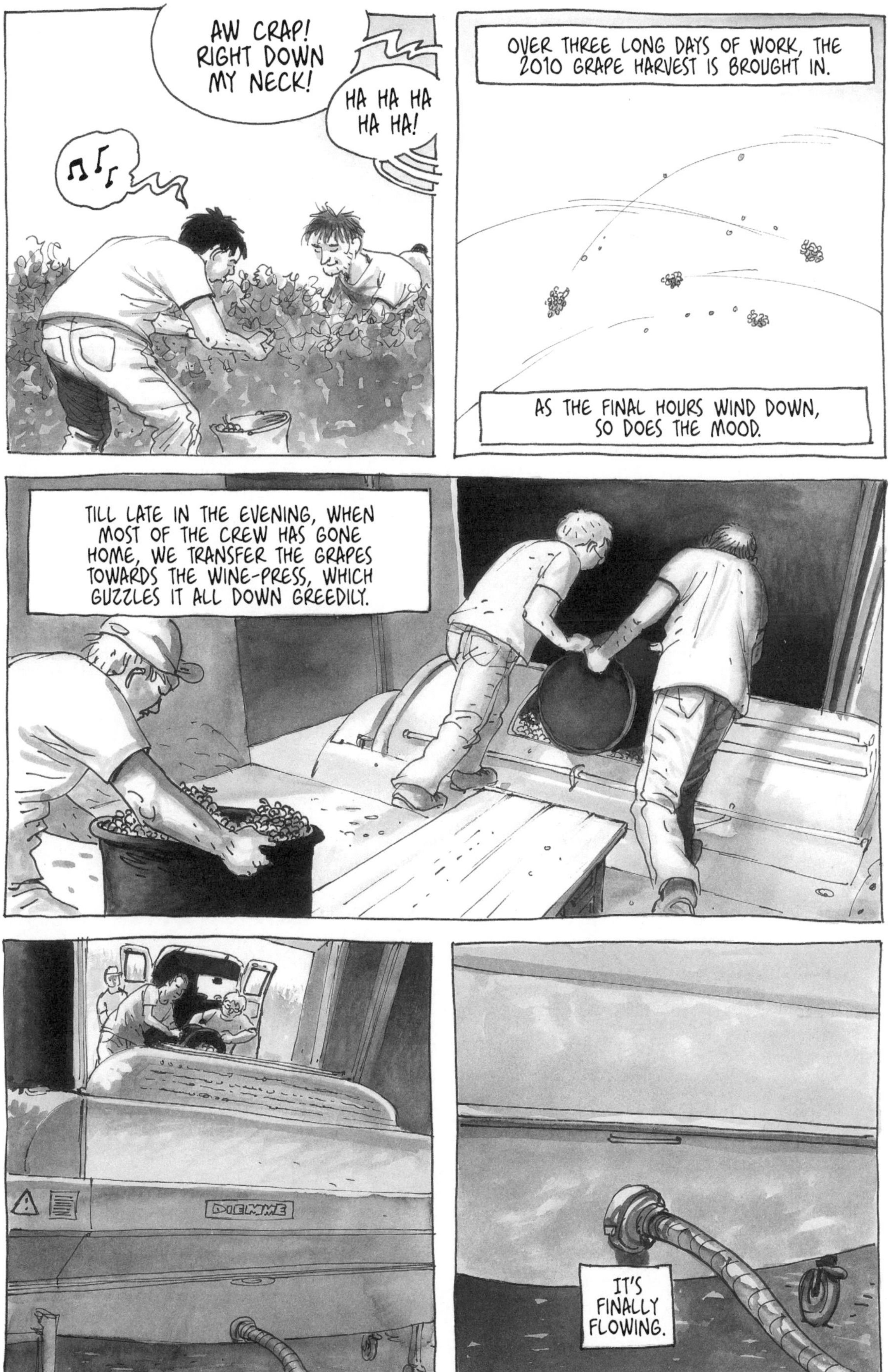
AW CRAP! RIGHT DOWN MY NECK!
HA HA HA HA HA!
OVER THREE LONG DAYS OF WORK, THE 2010 GRAPE HARVEST IS BROUGHT IN.
AS THE FINAL HOURS WIND DOWN, SO DOES THE MOOD.
TILL LATE IN THE EVENING, WHEN MOST OF THE CREW HAS GONE HOME, WE TRANSFER THE GRAPES TOWARDS THE WINE-PRESS, WHICH GUZZLES IT ALL DOWN GREEDILY.
DIEMME
IT'S FINALLY FLOWING.

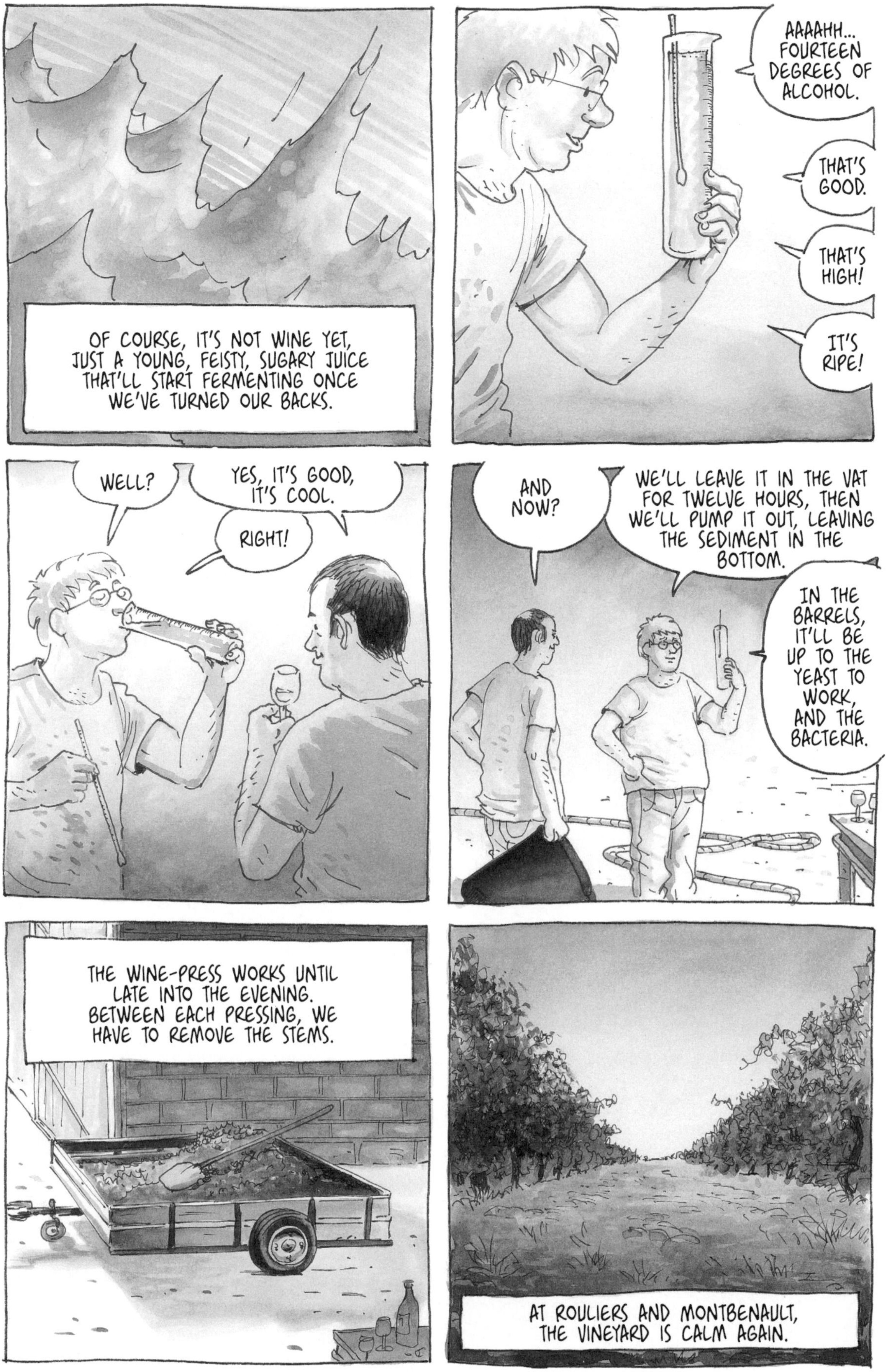
OF COURSE, IT'S NOT WINE YET, JUST A YOUNG, FEISTY, SUGARY JUICE THAT'LL START FERMENTING ONCE WE'VE TURNED OUR BACKS.
AAAAHH... FOURTEEN DEGREES OF ALCOHOL.
THAT'S GOOD.
THAT'S HIGH!
IT'S RIPE!
WELL?
YES, IT'S GOOD, IT'S COOL.
RIGHT!
AND NOW?
WE'LL LEAVE IT IN THE VAT FOR TWELVE HOURS, THEN WE'LL PUMP IT OUT, LEAVING THE SEDIMENT IN THE BOTTOM.
IN THE BARRELS, IT'LL BE UP TO THE YEAST TO WORK, AND THE BACTERIA.
THE WINE-PRESS WORKS UNTIL LATE INTO THE EVENING. BETWEEN EACH PRESSING, WE HAVE TO REMOVE THE STEMS.
AT ROULIERS AND MONTBENAULT, THE VINEYARD IS CALM AGAIN.

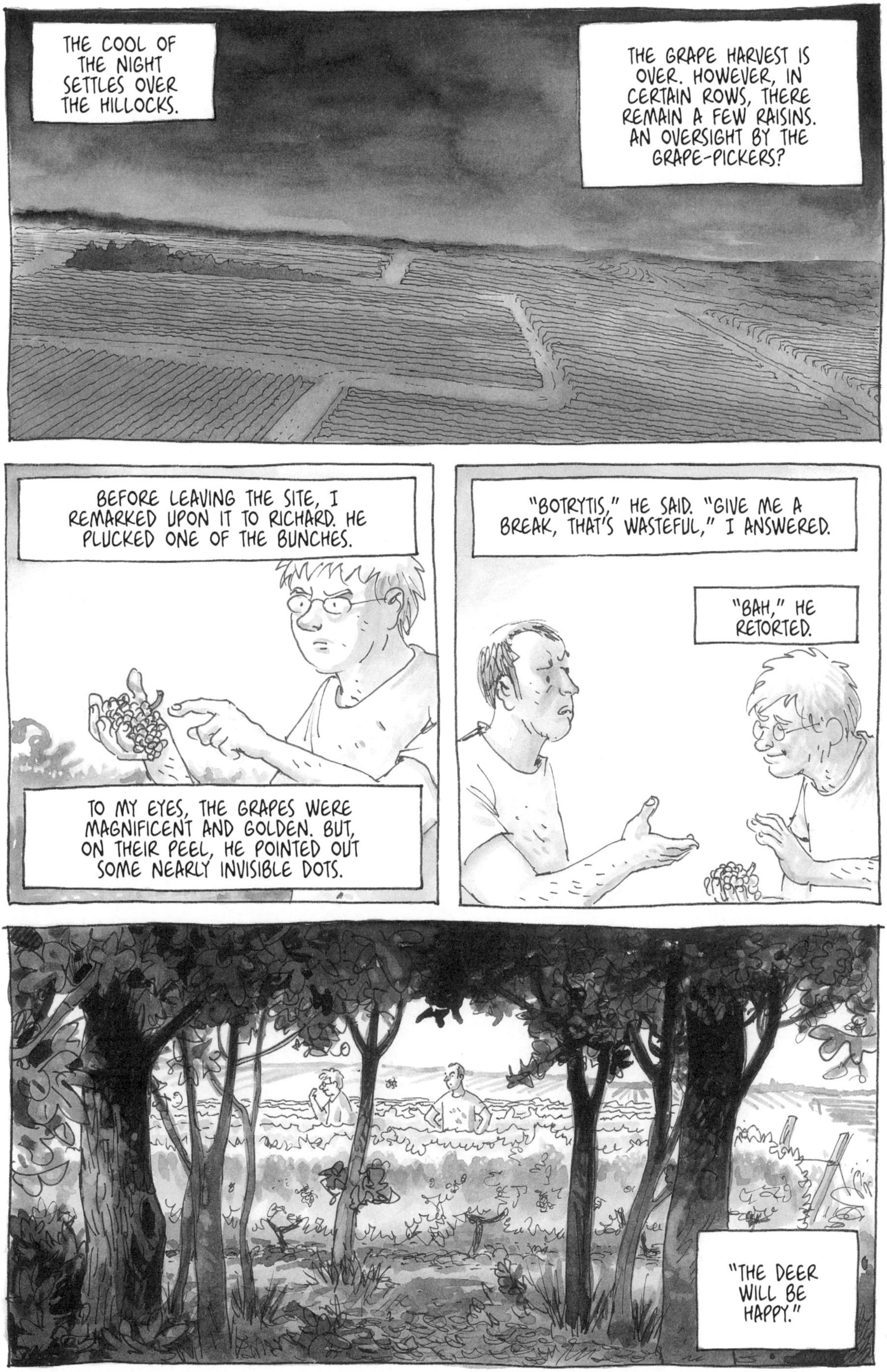
THE COOL OF THE NIGHT SETTLES OVER THE HILLOCKS.
THE GRAPE HARVEST IS OVER. HOWEVER, IN CERTAIN ROWS, THERE REMAIN A FEW RAISINS. AN OVERSIGHT BY THE GRAPE-PICKERS?
BEFORE LEAVING THE SITE, I REMARKED UPON IT TO RICHARD. HE PLUCKED ONE OF THE BUNCHES.
TO MY EYES, THE GRAPES WERE MAGNIFICENT AND GOLDEN. BUT, ON THEIR PEEL, HE POINTED OUT SOME NEARLY INVISIBLE DOTS.
"BOTRYTIS," HE SAID. "GIVE ME A BREAK, THAT'S WASTEFUL," I ANSWERED.
"BAH," HE RETORTED.
"THE DEER WILL BE HAPPY."

CHAPTER FOURTEEN   LABEL DRINKERS

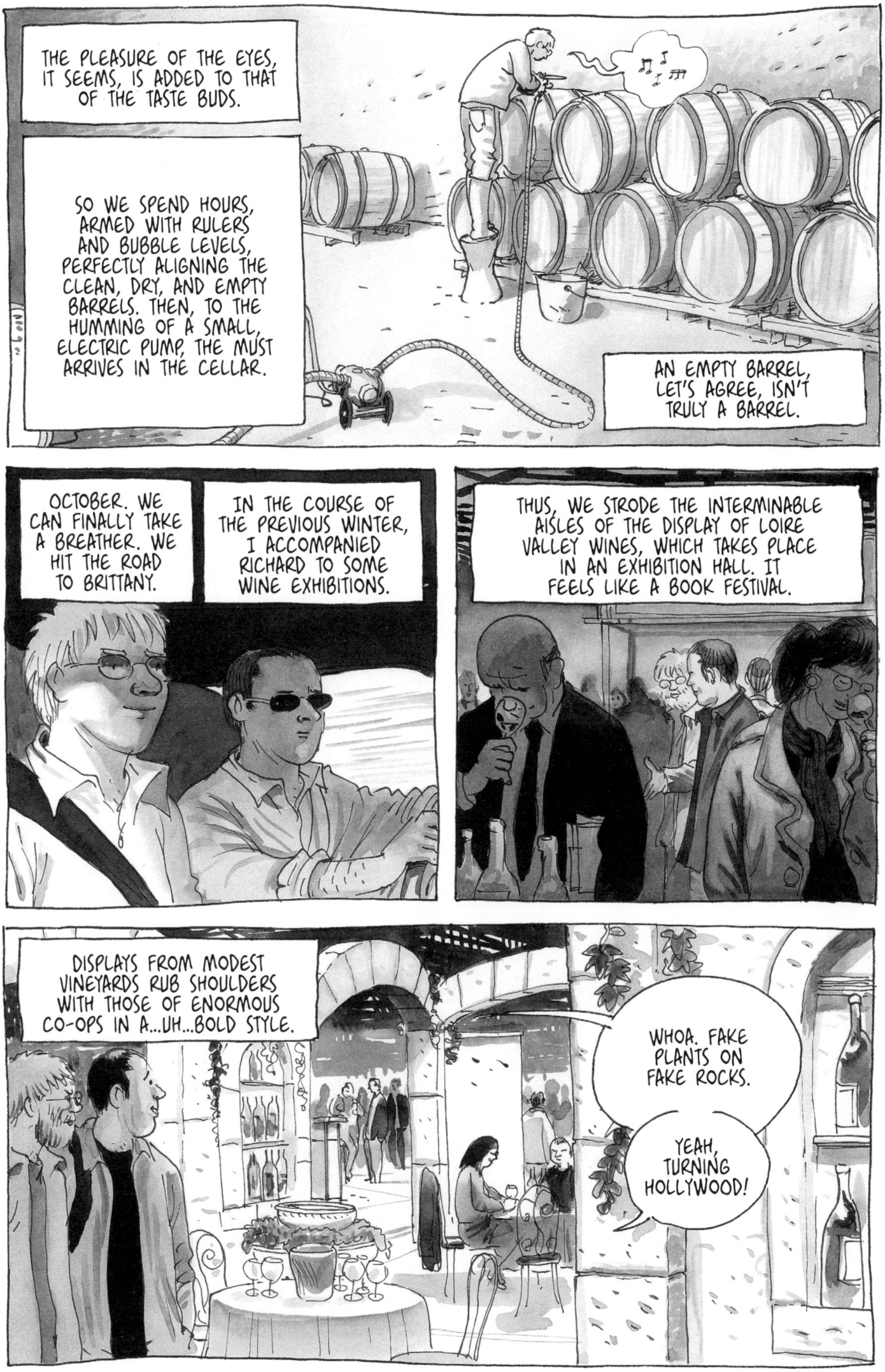
THE PLEASURE OF THE EYES, IT SEEMS, IS ADDED TO THAT OF THE TASTE BUDS.
SO WE SPEND HOURS, ARMED WITH RULERS AND BUBBLE LEVELS, PERFECTLY ALIGNING THE CLEAN, DRY, AND EMPTY BARRELS. THEN, TO THE HUMMING OF A SMALL, ELECTRIC PUMP, THE MUST ARRIVES IN THE CELLAR.
AN EMPTY BARREL, LET'S AGREE, ISN'T TRULY A BARREL.
OCTOBER. WE CAN FINALLY TAKE A BREATHER. WE HIT THE ROAD TO BRITTANY.
IN THE COURSE OF THE PREVIOUS WINTER, I ACCOMPANIED RICHARD TO SOME WINE EXHIBITIONS.
THUS, WE STRODE THE INTERMINABLE AISLES OF THE DISPLAY OF LOIRE VALLEY WINES, WHICH TAKES PLACE IN AN EXHIBITION HALL. IT FEELS LIKE A BOOK FESTIVAL.
DISPLAYS FROM MODEST VINEYARDS RUB SHOULDERS WITH THOSE OF ENORMOUS CO-OPS IN A...UH...BOLD STYLE.
WHOA. FAKE PLANTS ON FAKE ROCKS.
YEAH, TURNING HOLLYWOOD!

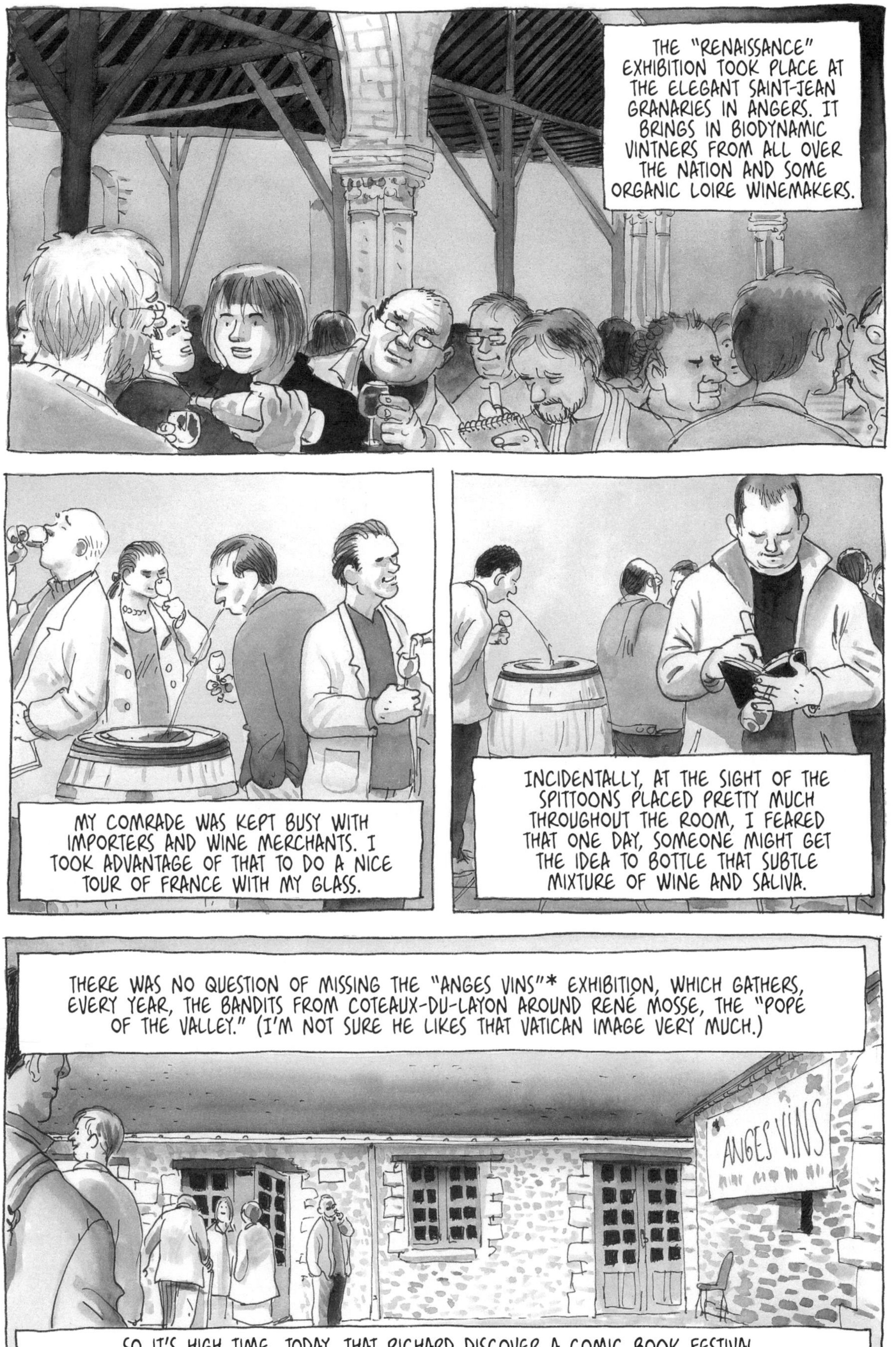
THE "RENAISSANCE" EXHIBITION TOOK PLACE AT THE ELEGANT SAINT-JEAN GRANARIES IN ANGERS. IT BRINGS IN BIODYNAMIC VINTNERS FROM ALL OVER THE NATION AND SOME ORGANIC LOIRE WINEMAKERS.
MY COMRADE WAS KEPT BUSY WITH IMPORTERS AND WINE MERCHANTS. I TOOK ADVANTAGE OF THAT TO DO A NICE TOUR OF FRANCE WITH MY GLASS.
INCIDENTALLY, AT THE SIGHT OF THE SPITTOONS PLACED PRETTY MUCH THROUGHOUT THE ROOM, I FEARED THAT ONE DAY, SOMEONE MIGHT GET THE IDEA TO BOTTLE THAT SUBTLE MIXTURE OF WINE AND SALIVA.
THERE WAS NO QUESTION OF MISSING THE "ANGES VINS"* EXHIBITION, WHICH GATHERS, EVERY YEAR, THE BANDITS FROM COTEAUX-DU-LAYON AROUND RENÉ MOSSE, THE "POPE OF THE VALLEY." (I'M NOT SURE HE LIKES THAT VATICAN IMAGE VERY MUCH.)
ANGES VINS
SO IT'S HIGH TIME, TODAY, THAT RICHARD DISCOVER A COMIC BOOK FESTIVAL.

*"ANGEVIN" IS THE ADJECTIVE FOR THINGS FROM ANJOU AND ANGERS IN FRANCE. BROKEN INTO TWO WORDS, IT HERE MEANS "ANGEL WINES."

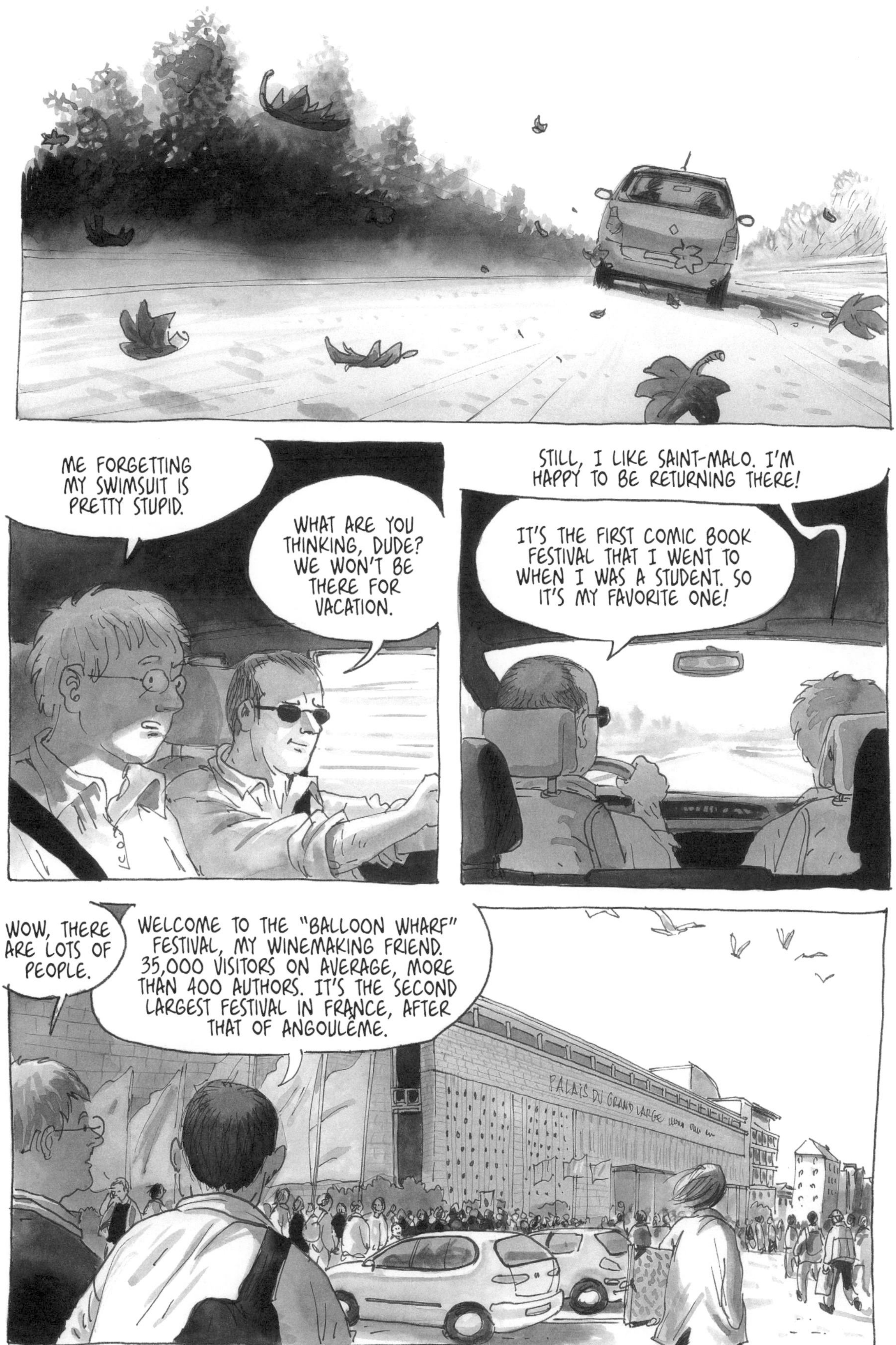
ME FORGETTING MY SWIMSUIT IS PRETTY STUPID.
WHAT ARE YOU THINKING, DUDE? WE WON'T BE THERE FOR VACATION.
STILL, I LIKE SAINT-MALO. I'M HAPPY TO BE RETURNING THERE!
IT'S THE FIRST COMIC BOOK FESTIVAL THAT I WENT TO WHEN I WAS A STUDENT. SO IT'S MY FAVORITE ONE!
WOW, THERE ARE LOTS OF PEOPLE.
WELCOME TO THE "BALLOON WHARF" FESTIVAL, MY WINEMAKING FRIEND. 35,000 VISITORS ON AVERAGE, MORE THAN 400 AUTHORS. IT'S THE SECOND LARGEST FESTIVAL IN FRANCE, AFTER THAT OF ANGOULÊME.
PALAIS DU GRAND LARGE

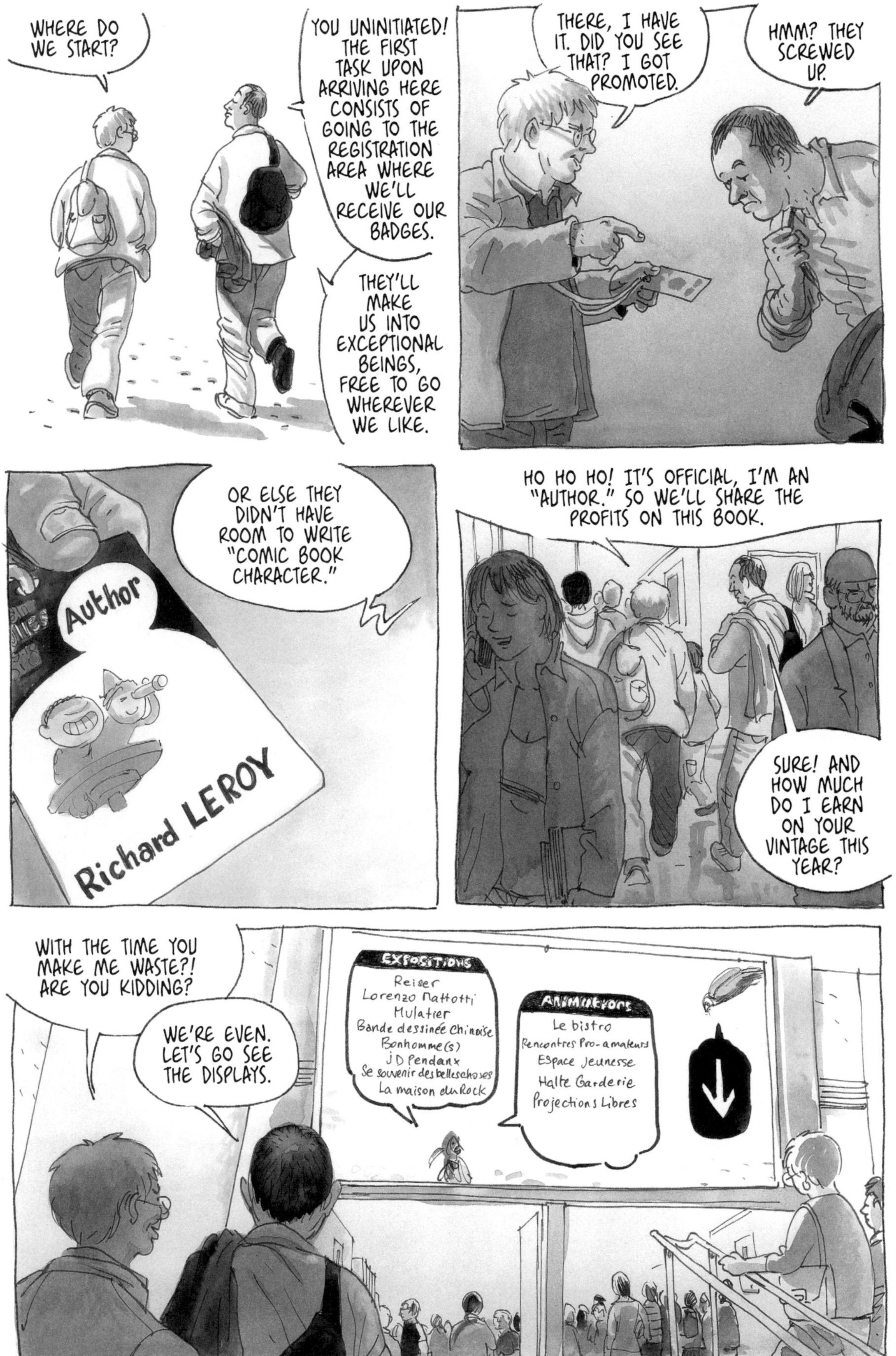
WHERE DO WE START?
YOU UNINITIATED! THE FIRST TASK UPON ARRIVING HERE CONSISTS OF GOING TO THE REGISTRATION AREA WHERE WE'LL RECEIVE OUR BADGES.
THEY'LL MAKE US INTO EXCEPTIONAL BEINGS, FREE TO GO WHEREVER WE LIKE.
THERE, I HAVE IT. DID YOU SEE THAT? I GOT PROMOTED.
HMM? THEY SCREWED UP.
Author
Richard LEROY
OR ELSE THEY DIDN'T HAVE ROOM TO WRITE "COMIC BOOK CHARACTER."
HO HO HO! IT'S OFFICIAL, I'M AN "AUTHOR." SO WE'LL SHARE THE PROFITS ON THIS BOOK.
SURE! AND HOW MUCH DO I EARN ON YOUR VINTAGE THIS YEAR?
WITH THE TIME YOU MAKE ME WASTE?! ARE YOU KIDDING?
WE'RE EVEN. LET'S GO SEE THE DISPLAYS.
EXPOSITIONS
Reiser
Lorenzo Mattotti
Mulatier
Bande dessinée Chinoise
Bonhomme(s)
J D Pendanx
Se souvenir des belles choses
La maison du Rock
ANIMATIONS
Le bistro
Rencontres Pro-amateurs
Espace Jeunesse
Halte Garderie
Projections Libres

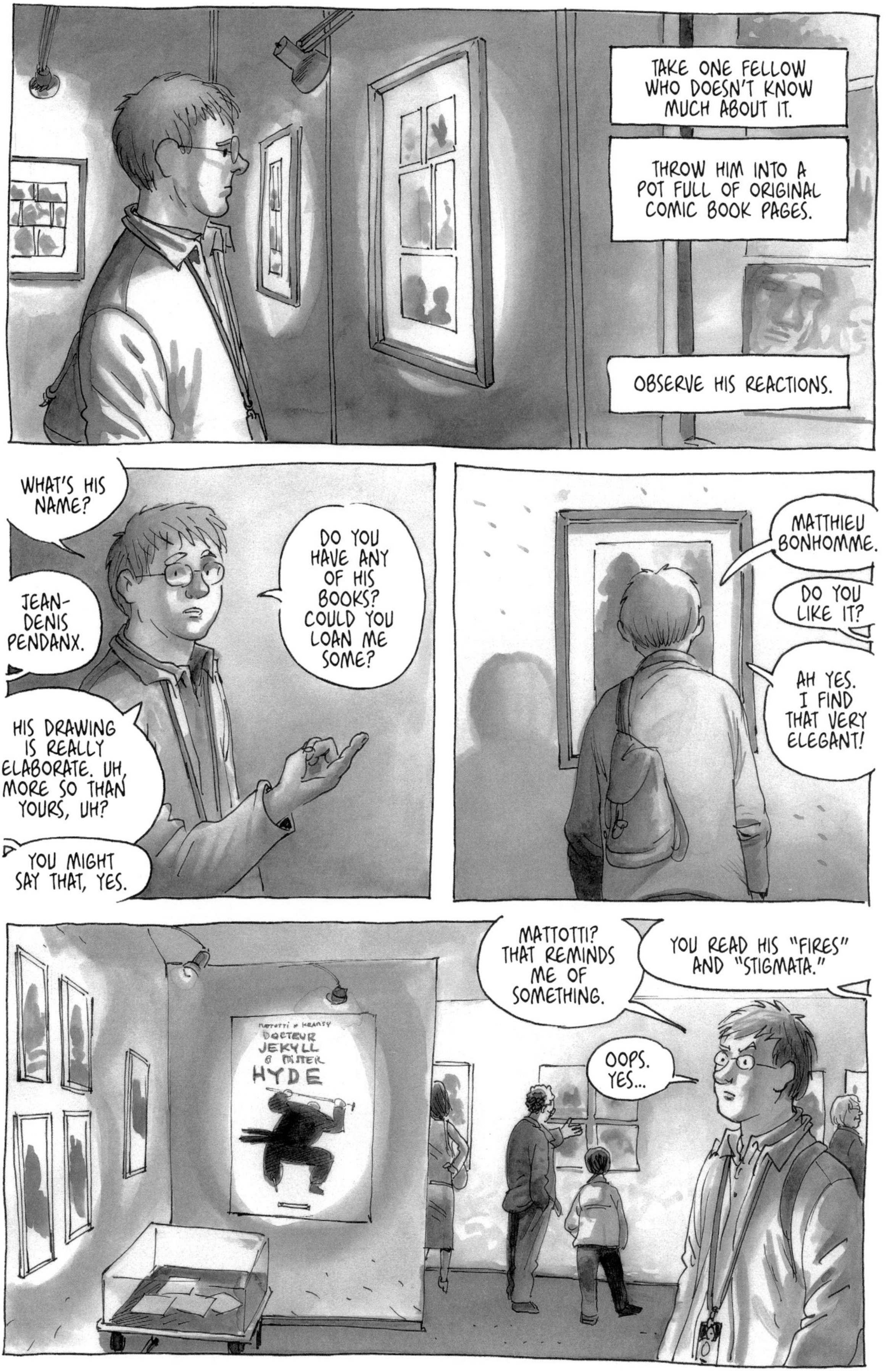
TAKE ONE FELLOW WHO DOESN'T KNOW MUCH ABOUT IT.
THROW HIM INTO A POT FULL OF ORIGINAL COMIC BOOK PAGES.
OBSERVE HIS REACTIONS.
WHAT'S HIS NAME?
JEAN-DENIS PENDANX.
DO YOU HAVE ANY OF HIS BOOKS? COULD YOU LOAN ME SOME?
HIS DRAWING IS REALLY ELABORATE. UH, MORE SO THAN YOURS, UH?
YOU MIGHT SAY THAT, YES.
MATTHIEU BONHOMME.
DO YOU LIKE IT?
AH YES. I FIND THAT VERY ELEGANT!
DOCTEUR JEKYLL & MISTER HYDE
MATTOTTI? THAT REMINDS ME OF SOMETHING.
YOU READ HIS "FIRES" AND "STIGMATA."
OOPS. YES...

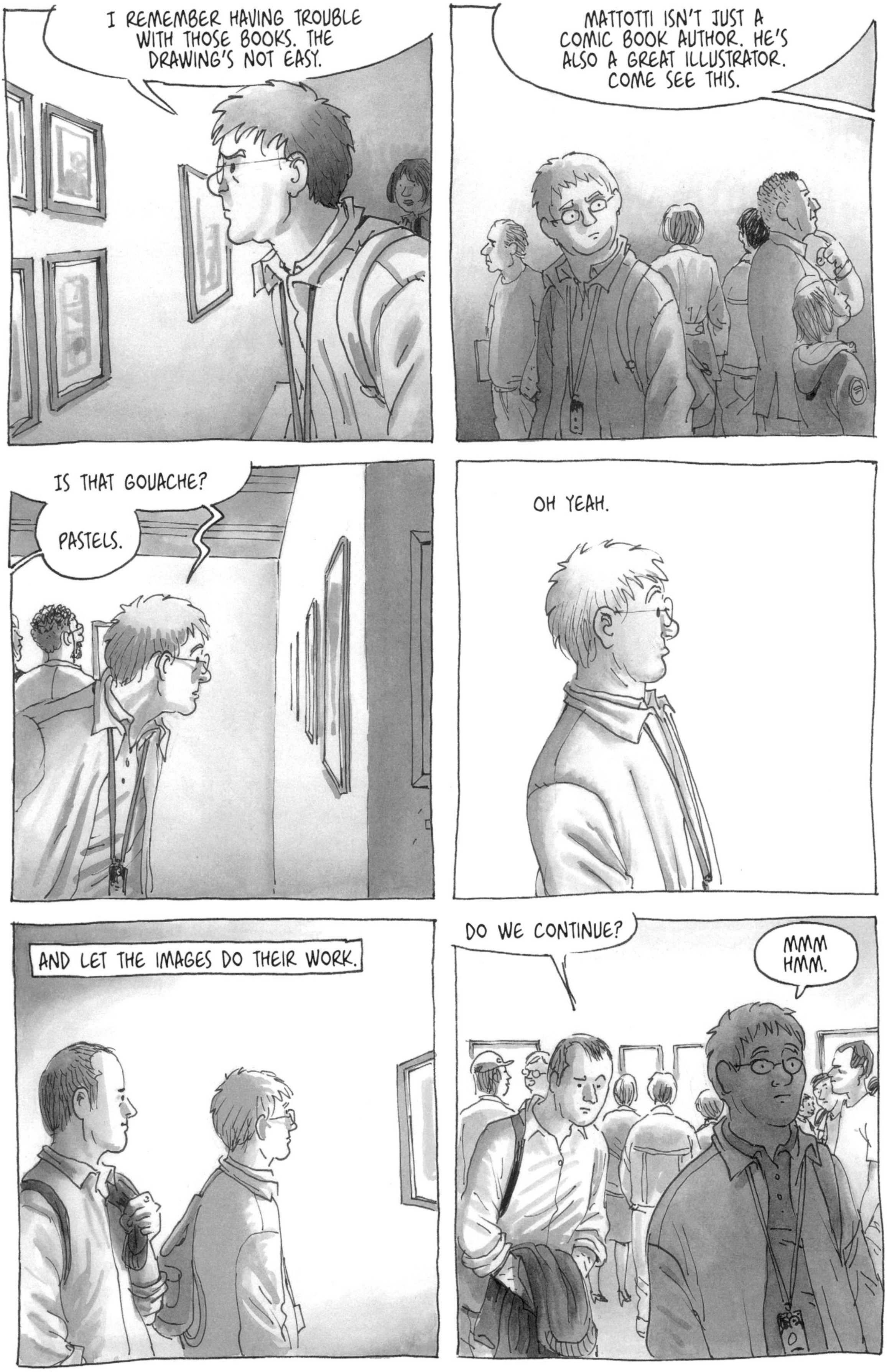
I REMEMBER HAVING TROUBLE WITH THOSE BOOKS. THE DRAWING'S NOT EASY.
MATTOTTI ISN'T JUST A COMIC BOOK AUTHOR. HE'S ALSO A GREAT ILLUSTRATOR. COME SEE THIS.
IS THAT GOUACHE?
PASTELS.
OH YEAH.
AND LET THE IMAGES DO THEIR WORK.
DO WE CONTINUE?
MMM HMM.

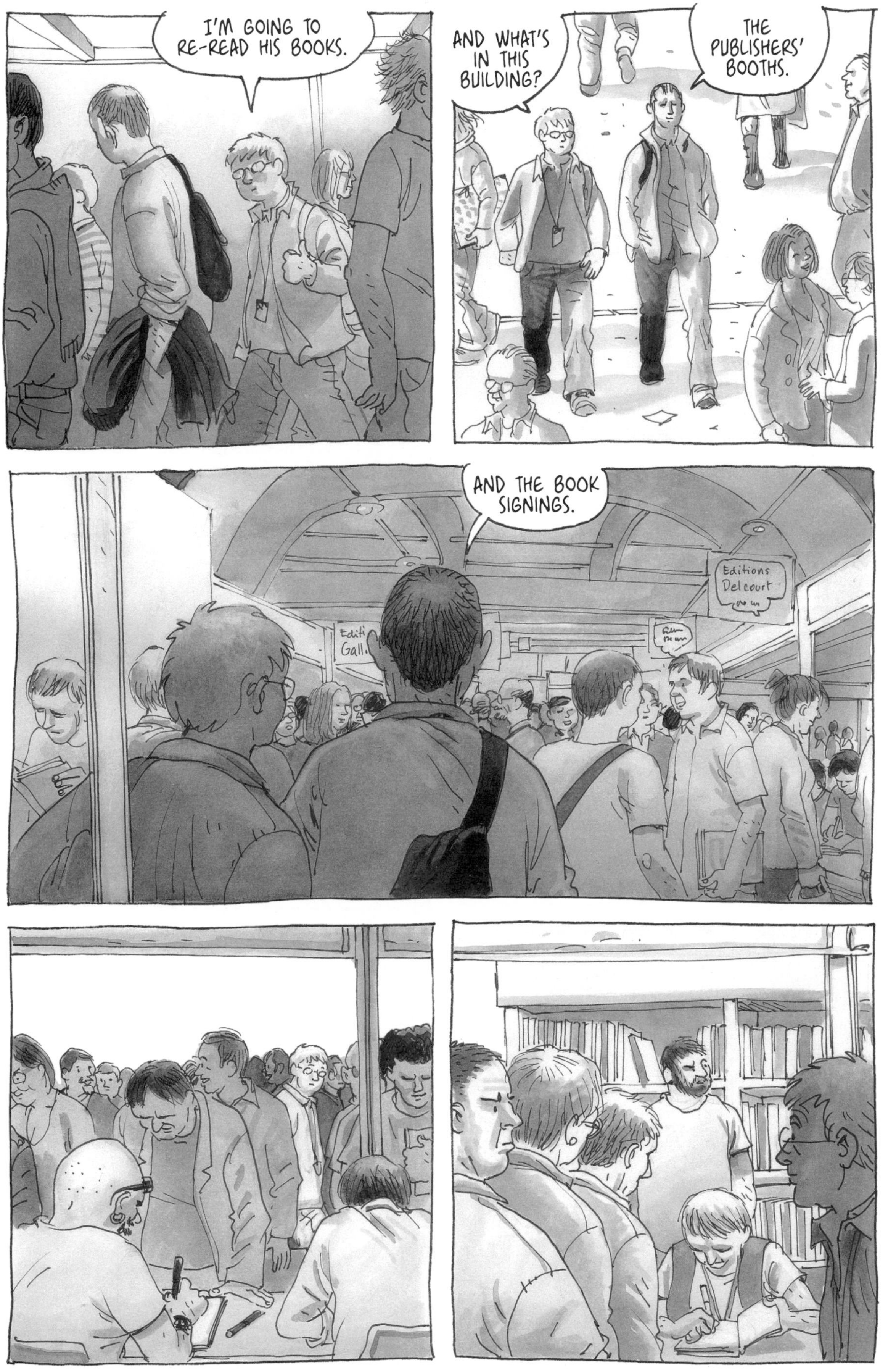
I'M GOING TO RE-READ HIS BOOKS.
AND WHAT'S IN THIS BUILDING?
THE PUBLISHERS' BOOTHS.
AND THE BOOK SIGNINGS.
Editions Delcourt

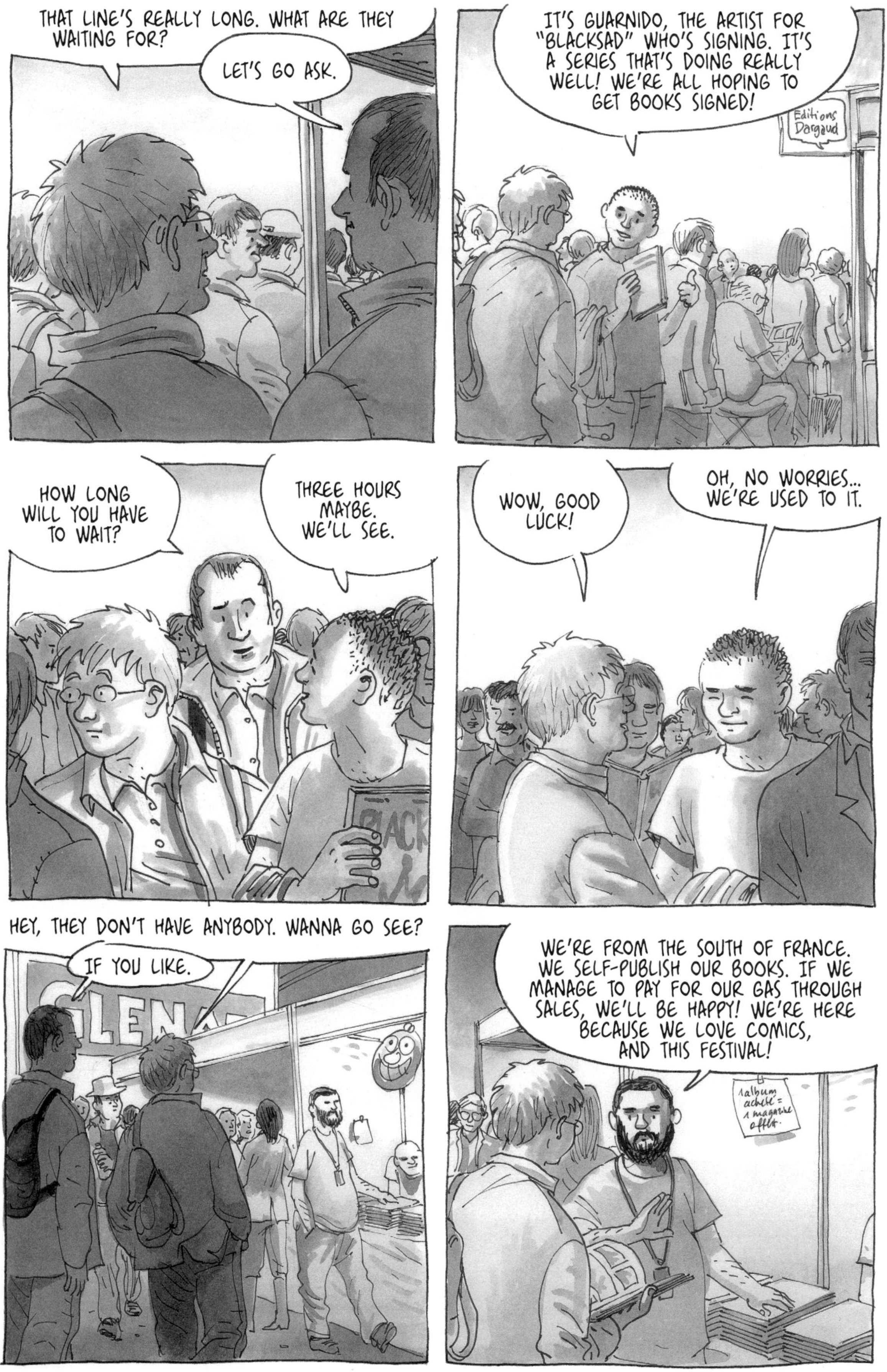
THAT LINE'S REALLY LONG. WHAT ARE THEY WAITING FOR?
LET'S GO ASK.
IT'S GUARNIDO, THE ARTIST FOR "BLACKSAD" WHO'S SIGNING. IT'S A SERIES THAT'S DOING REALLY WELL! WE'RE ALL HOPING TO GET BOOKS SIGNED!
Editions Dargaud
HOW LONG WILL YOU HAVE TO WAIT?
THREE HOURS MAYBE. WE'LL SEE.
WOW, GOOD LUCK!
OH, NO WORRIES... WE'RE USED TO IT.
HEY, THEY DON'T HAVE ANYBODY. WANNA GO SEE?
IF YOU LIKE.
WE'RE FROM THE SOUTH OF FRANCE. WE SELF-PUBLISH OUR BOOKS. IF WE MANAGE TO PAY FOR OUR GAS THROUGH SALES, WE'LL BE HAPPY! WE'RE HERE BECAUSE WE LOVE COMICS, AND THIS FESTIVAL!
1 album acheté = 1 magazine offert

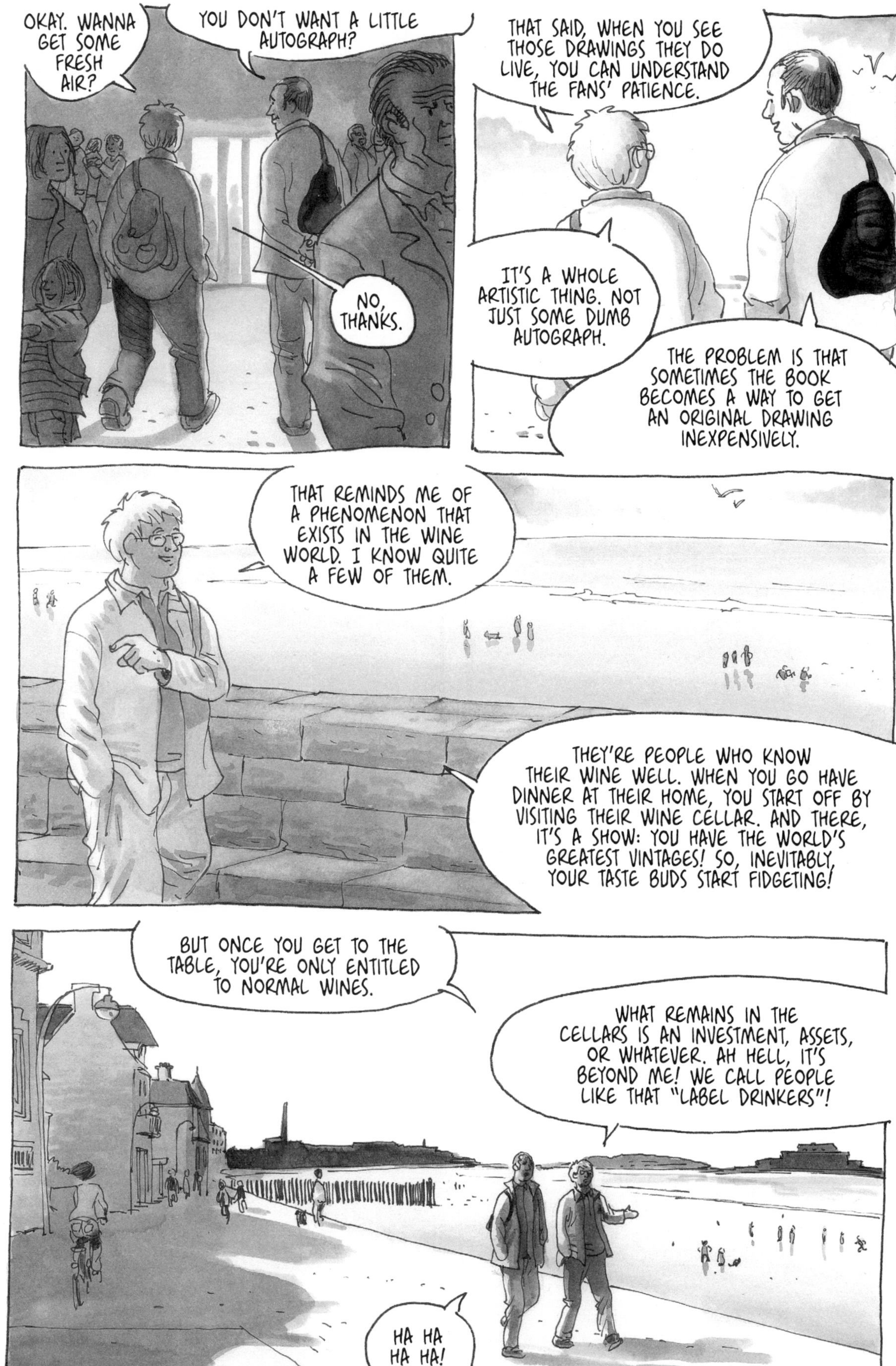
OKAY. WANNA GET SOME FRESH AIR?
YOU DON'T WANT A LITTLE AUTOGRAPH?
NO, THANKS.
THAT SAID, WHEN YOU SEE THOSE DRAWINGS THEY DO LIVE, YOU CAN UNDERSTAND THE FANS' PATIENCE.
IT'S A WHOLE ARTISTIC THING. NOT JUST SOME DUMB AUTOGRAPH.
THE PROBLEM IS THAT SOMETIMES THE BOOK BECOMES A WAY TO GET AN ORIGINAL DRAWING INEXPENSIVELY.
THAT REMINDS ME OF A PHENOMENON THAT EXISTS IN THE WINE WORLD. I KNOW QUITE A FEW OF THEM.
THEY'RE PEOPLE WHO KNOW THEIR WINE WELL. WHEN YOU GO HAVE DINNER AT THEIR HOME, YOU START OFF BY VISITING THEIR WINE CELLAR. AND THERE, IT'S A SHOW: YOU HAVE THE WORLD'S GREATEST VINTAGES! SO, INEVITABLY, YOUR TASTE BUDS START FIDGETING!
BUT ONCE YOU GET TO THE TABLE, YOU'RE ONLY ENTITLED TO NORMAL WINES.
WHAT REMAINS IN THE CELLARS IS AN INVESTMENT, ASSETS, OR WHATEVER. AH HELL, IT'S BEYOND ME! WE CALL PEOPLE LIKE THAT "LABEL DRINKERS"!
HA HA HA HA!

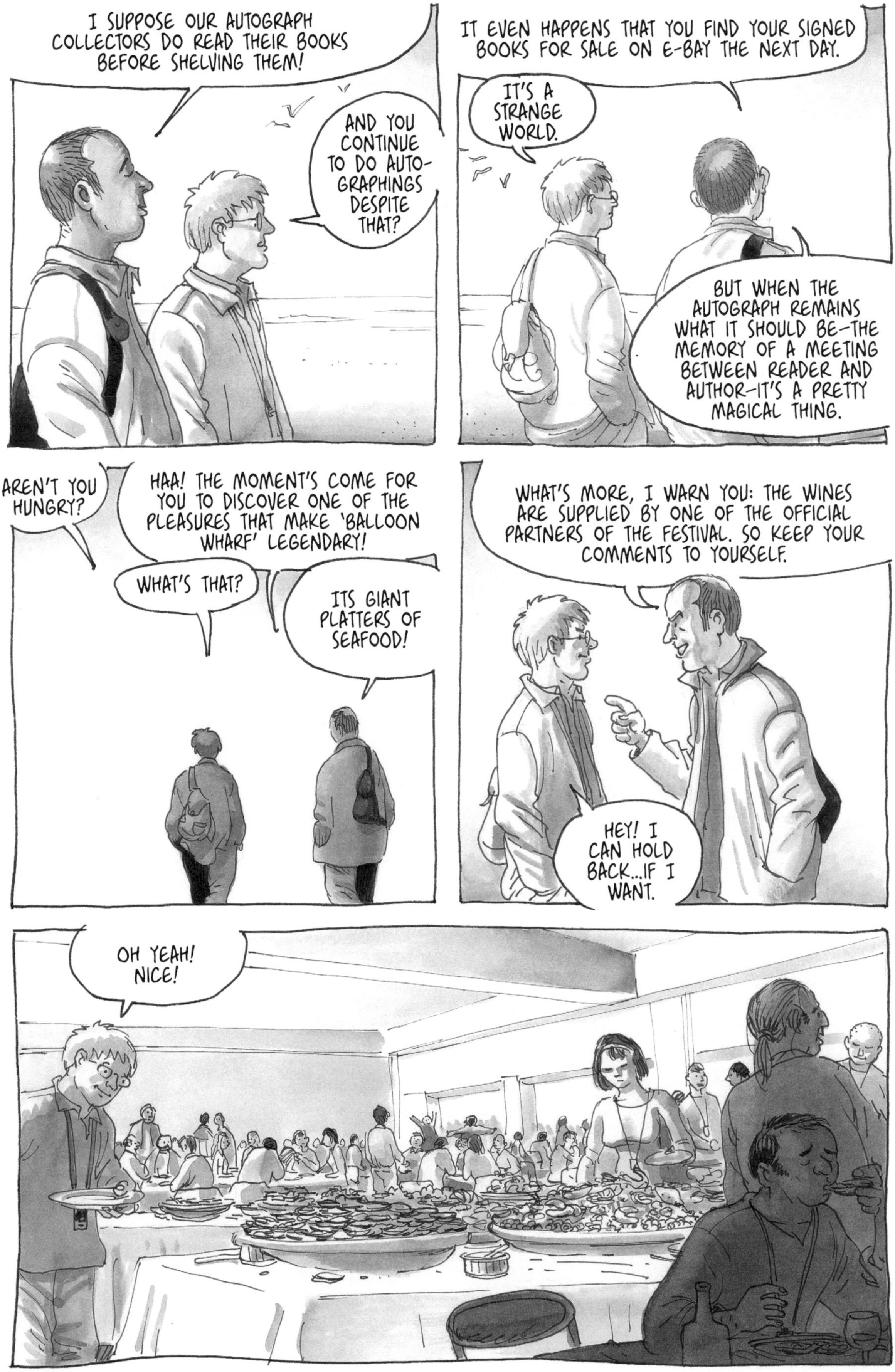
I SUPPOSE OUR AUTOGRAPH COLLECTORS DO READ THEIR BOOKS BEFORE SHELVING THEM!
AND YOU CONTINUE TO DO AUTO-GRAPHINGS DESPITE THAT?
IT EVEN HAPPENS THAT YOU FIND YOUR SIGNED BOOKS FOR SALE ON E-BAY THE NEXT DAY.
IT'S A STRANGE WORLD.
BUT WHEN THE AUTOGRAPH REMAINS WHAT IT SHOULD BE—THE MEMORY OF A MEETING BETWEEN READER AND AUTHOR—IT'S A PRETTY MAGICAL THING.
AREN'T YOU HUNGRY?
HAA! THE MOMENT'S COME FOR YOU TO DISCOVER ONE OF THE PLEASURES THAT MAKE 'BALLOON WHARF' LEGENDARY!
WHAT'S THAT?
ITS GIANT PLATTERS OF SEAFOOD!
WHAT'S MORE, I WARN YOU: THE WINES ARE SUPPLIED BY ONE OF THE OFFICIAL PARTNERS OF THE FESTIVAL. SO KEEP YOUR COMMENTS TO YOURSELF.
HEY! I CAN HOLD BACK...IF I WANT.
OH YEAH! NICE!

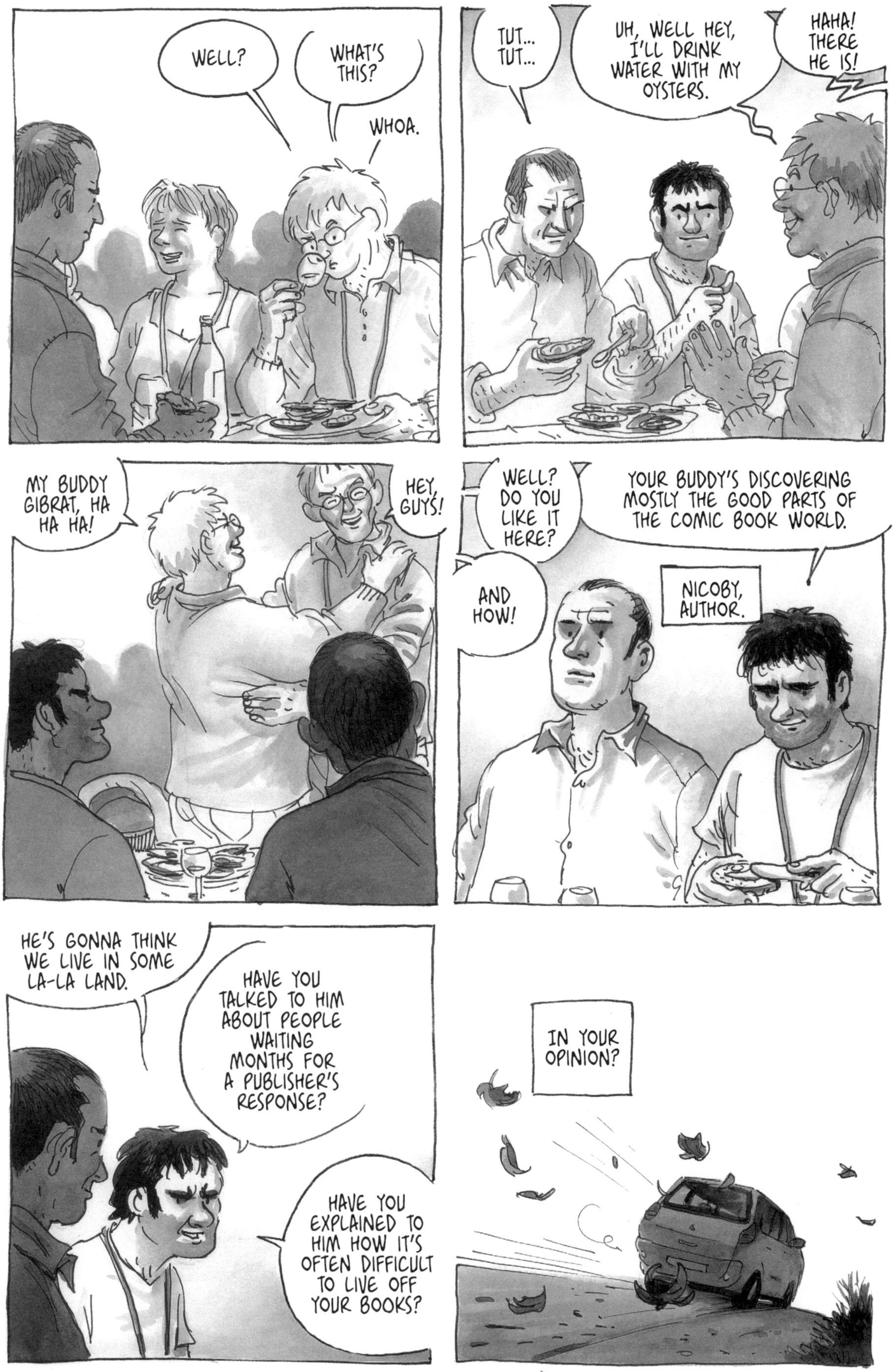
WELL?
WHAT'S THIS?
WHOA.
TUT... TUT...
UH, WELL HEY, I'LL DRINK WATER WITH MY OYSTERS.
HAHA! THERE HE IS!
MY BUDDY GIBRAT, HA HA HA!
HEY, GUYS!
WELL? DO YOU LIKE IT HERE?
AND HOW!
YOUR BUDDY'S DISCOVERING MOSTLY THE GOOD PARTS OF THE COMIC BOOK WORLD.
NICOBY, AUTHOR.
HE'S GONNA THINK WE LIVE IN SOME LA-LA LAND.
HAVE YOU TALKED TO HIM ABOUT PEOPLE WAITING MONTHS FOR A PUBLISHER'S RESPONSE?
HAVE YOU EXPLAINED TO HIM HOW IT'S OFTEN DIFFICULT TO LIVE OFF YOUR BOOKS?
IN YOUR OPINION?

CHAPTER FIFTEEN   MONTBENAULT
PARIS
KABUL

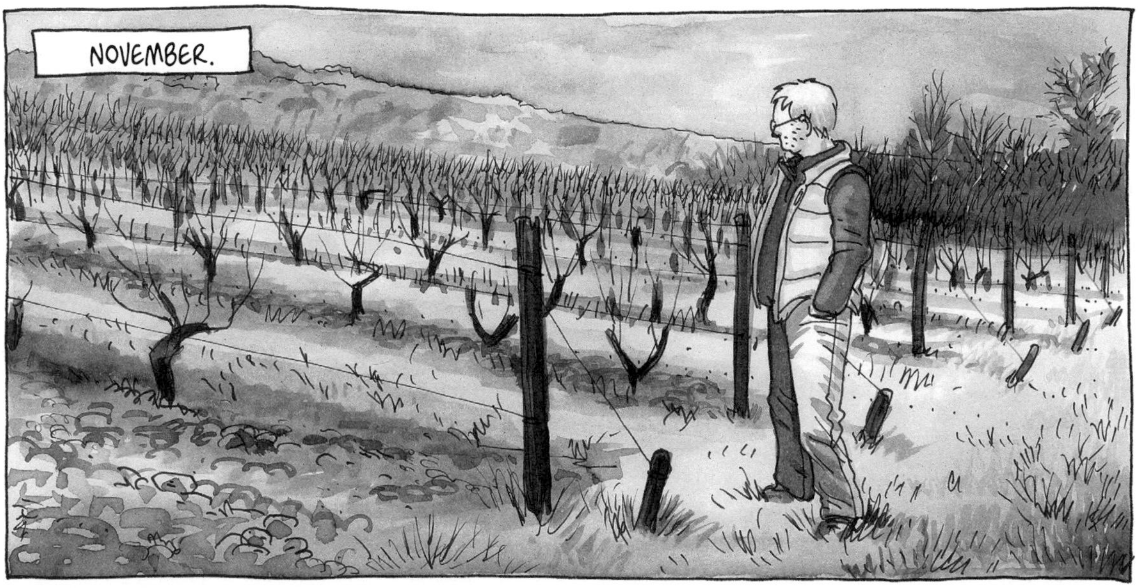
NOVEMBER.

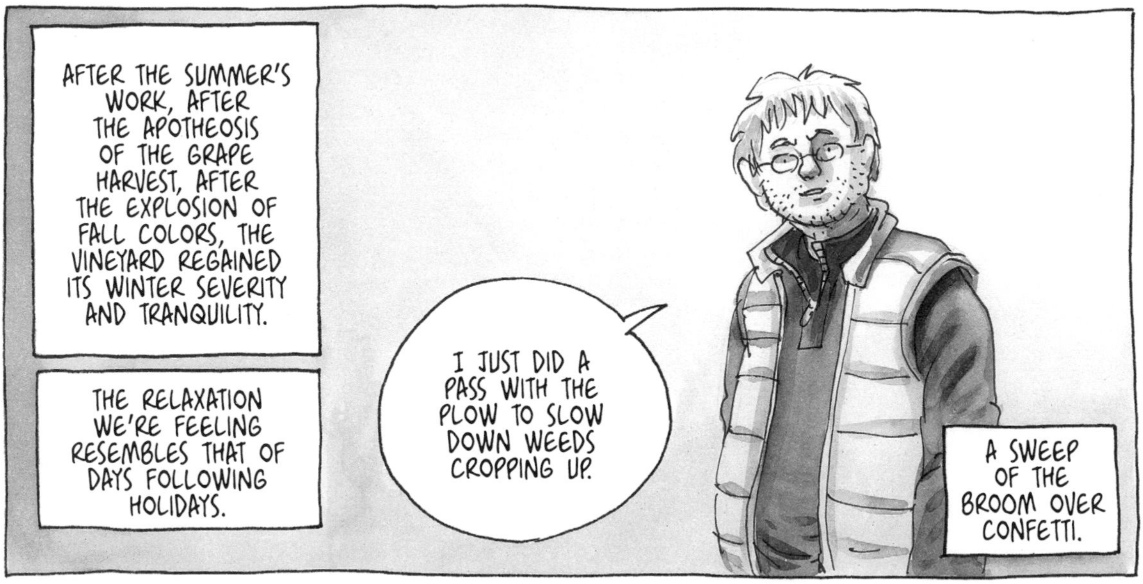
AFTER THE SUMMER'S WORK, AFTER THE APOTHEOSIS OF THE GRAPE HARVEST, AFTER THE EXPLOSION OF FALL COLORS, THE VINEYARD REGAINED ITS WINTER SEVERITY AND TRANQUILITY.
THE RELAXATION WE'RE FEELING RESEMBLES THAT OF DAYS FOLLOWING HOLIDAYS.
I JUST DID A PASS WITH THE PLOW TO SLOW DOWN WEEDS CROPPING UP.
A SWEEP OF THE BROOM OVER CONFETTI.

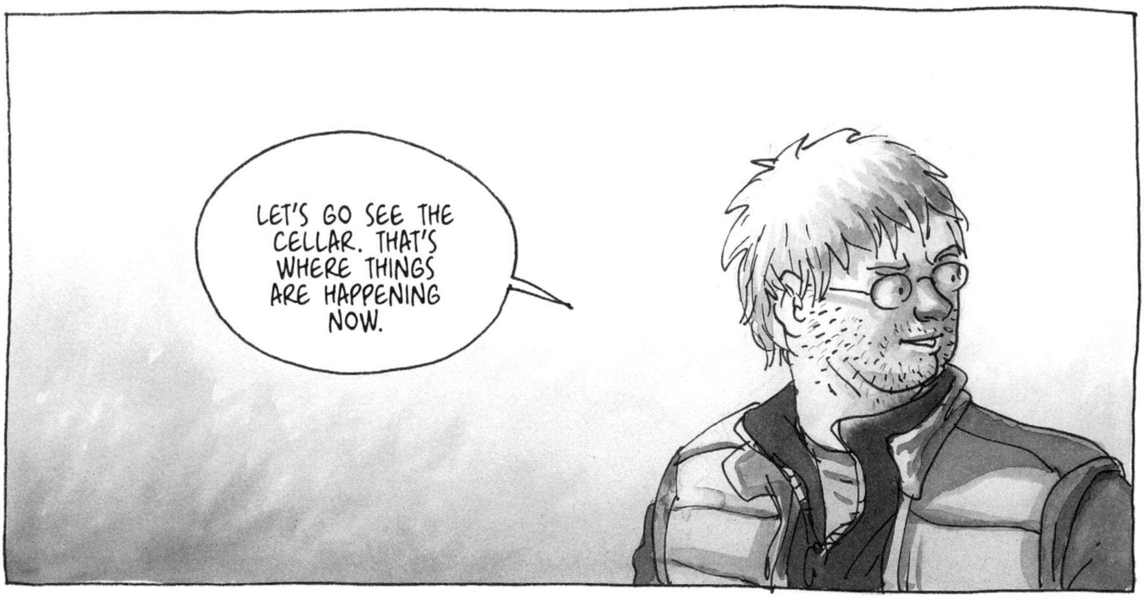
LET'S GO SEE THE CELLAR. THAT'S WHERE THINGS ARE HAPPENING NOW.

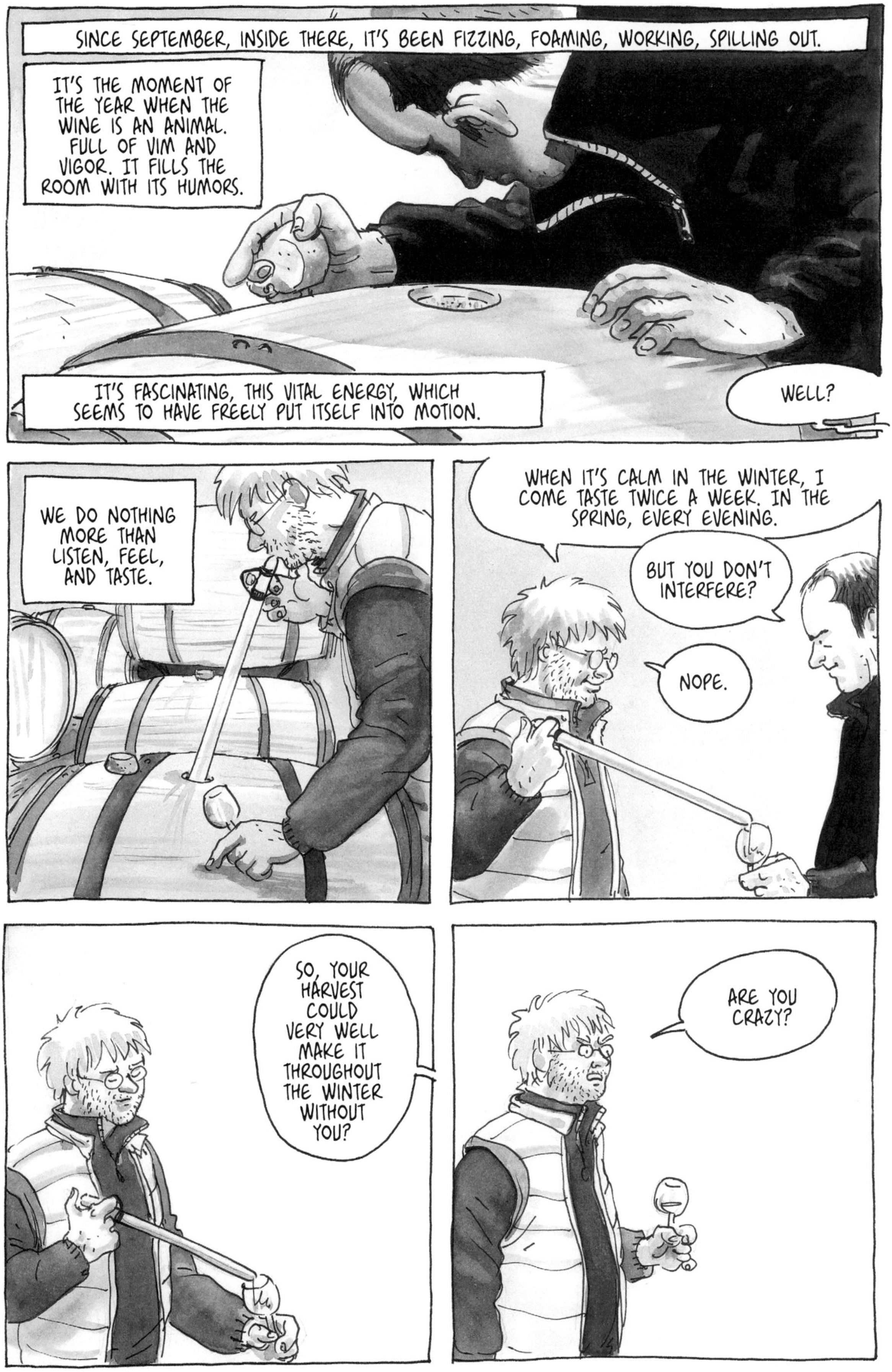
SINCE SEPTEMBER, INSIDE THERE, IT'S BEEN FIZZING, FOAMING, WORKING, SPILLING OUT.
IT'S THE MOMENT OF THE YEAR WHEN THE WINE IS AN ANIMAL. FULL OF VIM AND VIGOR. IT FILLS THE ROOM WITH ITS HUMORS.
IT'S FASCINATING, THIS VITAL ENERGY, WHICH SEEMS TO HAVE FREELY PUT ITSELF INTO MOTION.
WELL?
WE DO NOTHING MORE THAN LISTEN, FEEL, AND TASTE.
WHEN IT'S CALM IN THE WINTER, I COME TASTE TWICE A WEEK. IN THE SPRING, EVERY EVENING.
BUT YOU DON'T INTERFERE?
NOPE.
SO, YOUR HARVEST COULD VERY WELL MAKE IT THROUGHOUT THE WINTER WITHOUT YOU?
ARE YOU CRAZY?

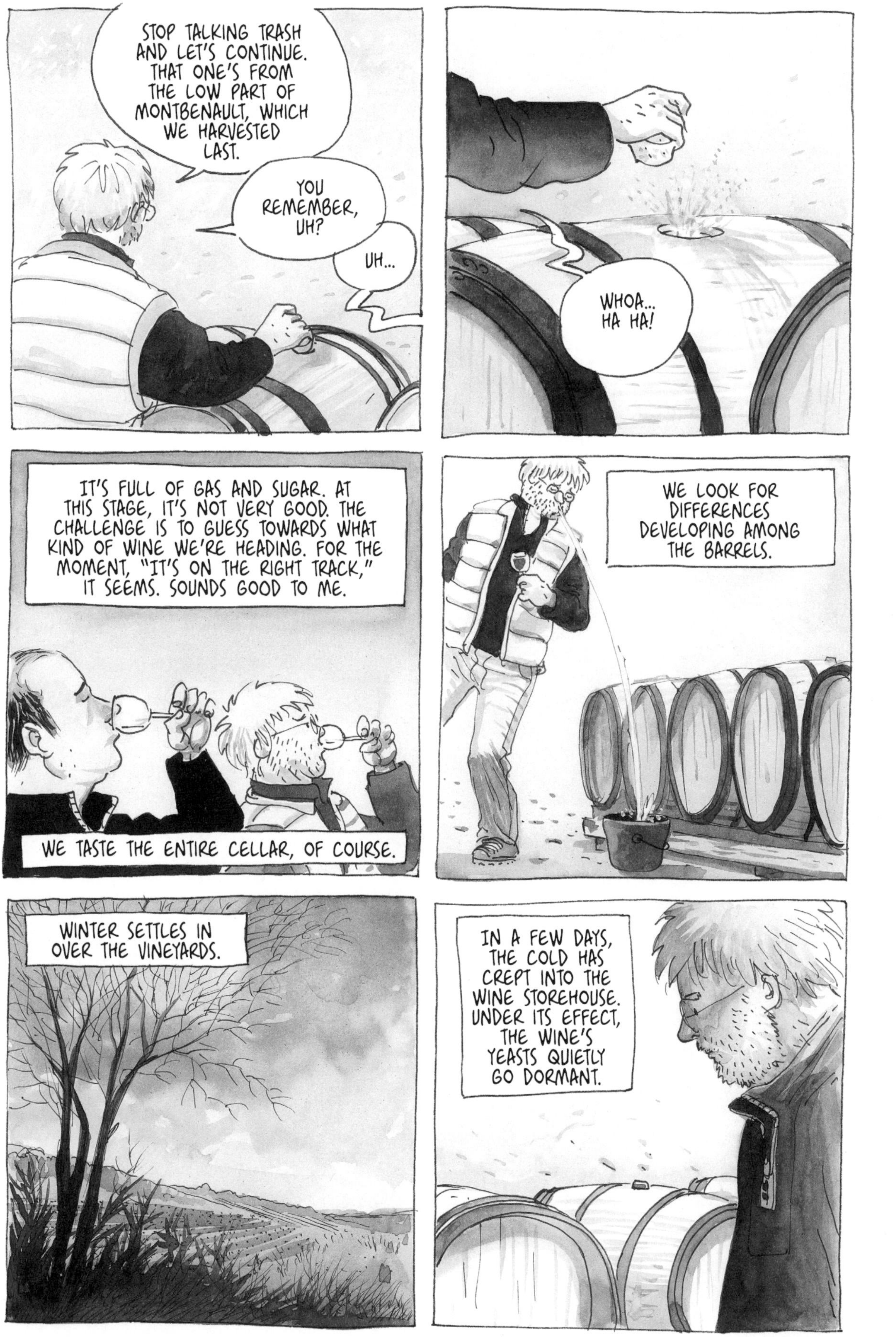
STOP TALKING TRASH AND LET'S CONTINUE. THAT ONE'S FROM THE LOW PART OF MONTBENAULT, WHICH WE HARVESTED LAST.
YOU REMEMBER, UH?
UH...
WHOA... HA HA!
IT'S FULL OF GAS AND SUGAR. AT THIS STAGE, IT'S NOT VERY GOOD. THE CHALLENGE IS TO GUESS TOWARDS WHAT KIND OF WINE WE'RE HEADING. FOR THE MOMENT, "IT'S ON THE RIGHT TRACK," IT SEEMS. SOUNDS GOOD TO ME.
WE TASTE THE ENTIRE CELLAR, OF COURSE.
WE LOOK FOR DIFFERENCES DEVELOPING AMONG THE BARRELS.
WINTER SETTLES IN OVER THE VINEYARDS.
IN A FEW DAYS, THE COLD HAS CREPT INTO THE WINE STOREHOUSE. UNDER ITS EFFECT, THE WINE'S YEASTS QUIETLY GO DORMANT.

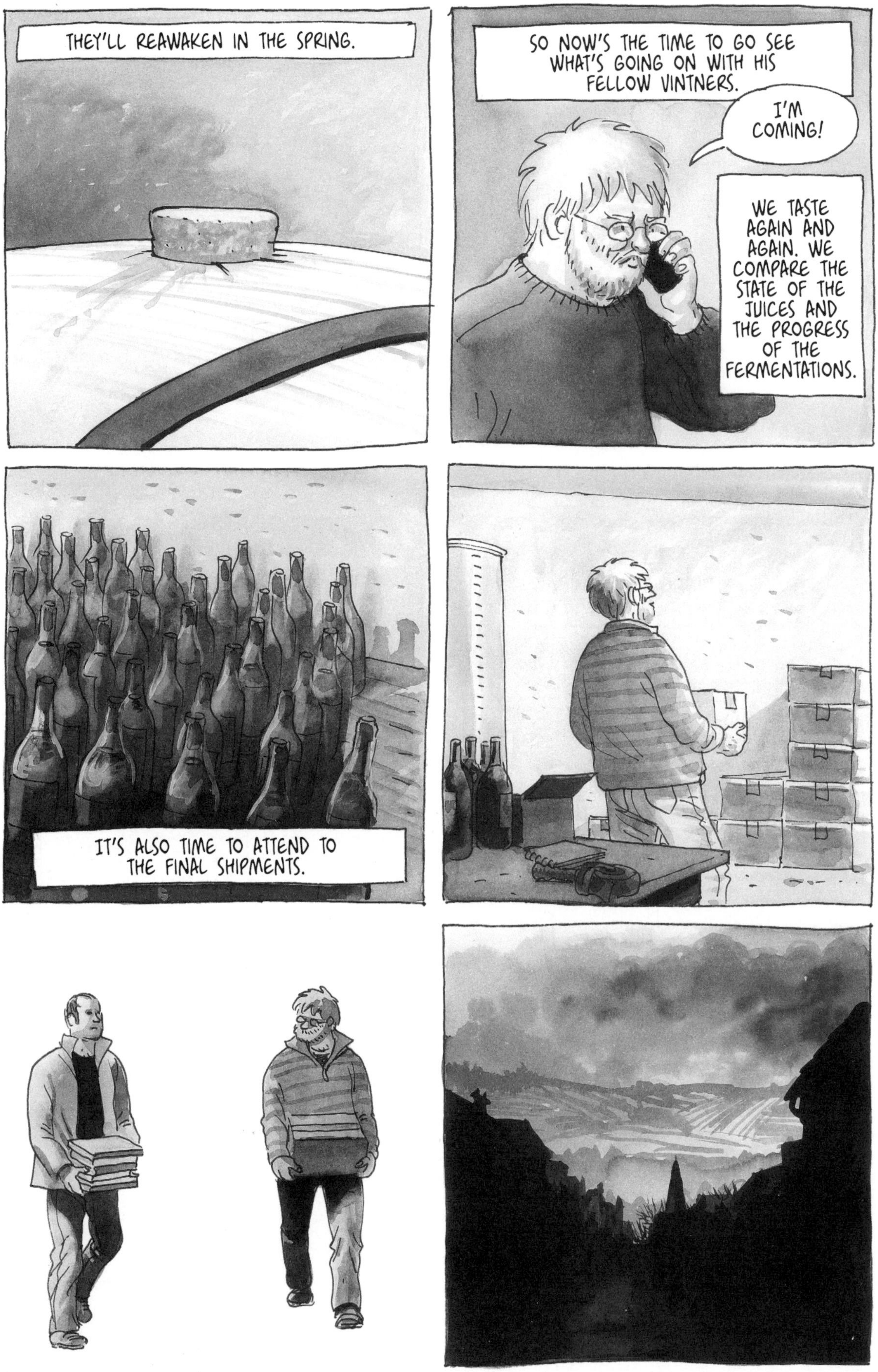
THEY'LL REAWAKEN IN THE SPRING.
SO NOW'S THE TIME TO GO SEE WHAT'S GOING ON WITH HIS FELLOW VINTNERS.
I'M COMING!
WE TASTE AGAIN AND AGAIN. WE COMPARE THE STATE OF THE JUICES AND THE PROGRESS OF THE FERMENTATIONS.
IT'S ALSO TIME TO ATTEND TO THE FINAL SHIPMENTS.

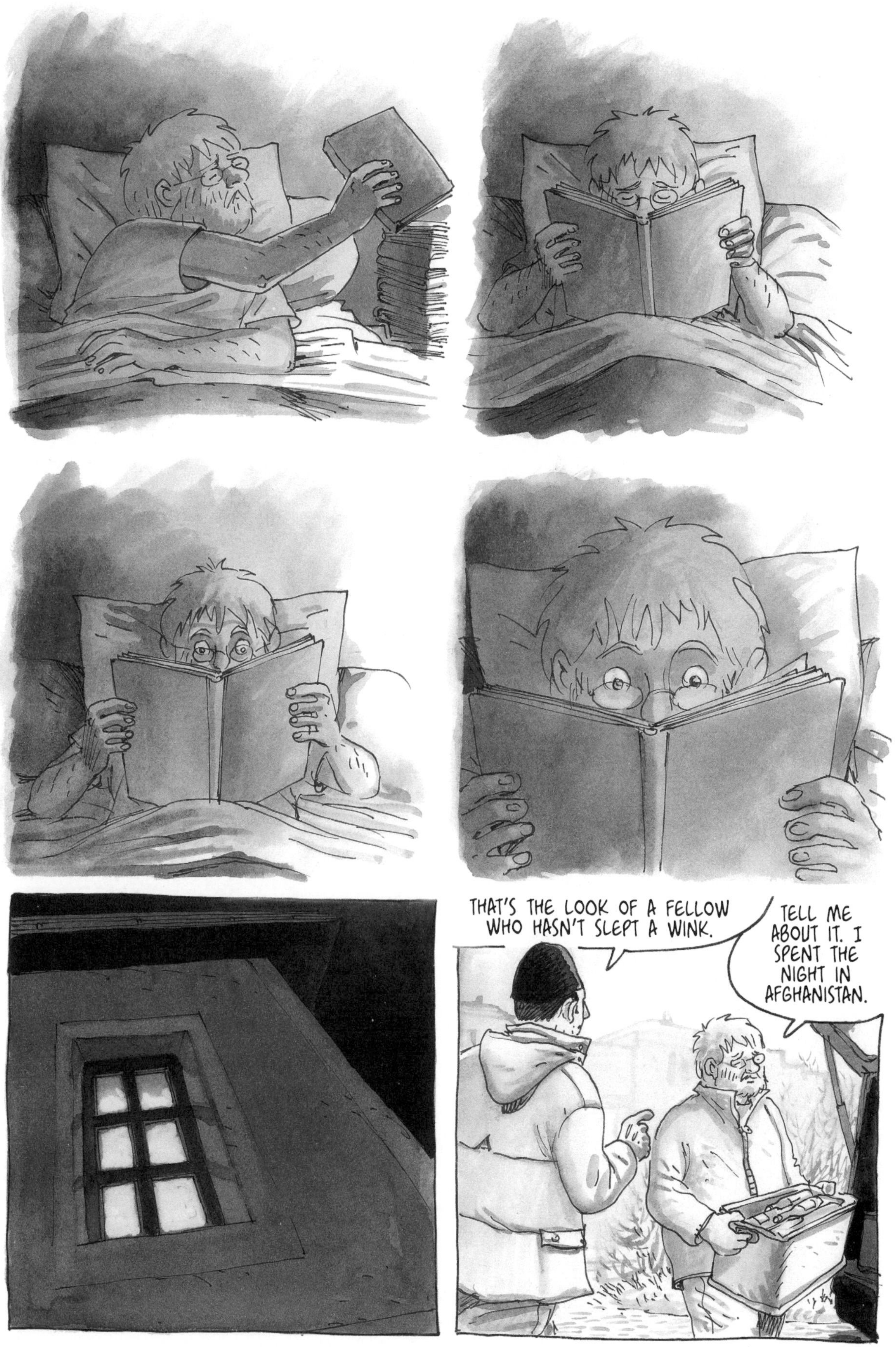
THAT'S THE LOOK OF A FELLOW WHO HASN'T SLEPT A WINK.
TELL ME ABOUT IT. I SPENT THE NIGHT IN AFGHANISTAN.

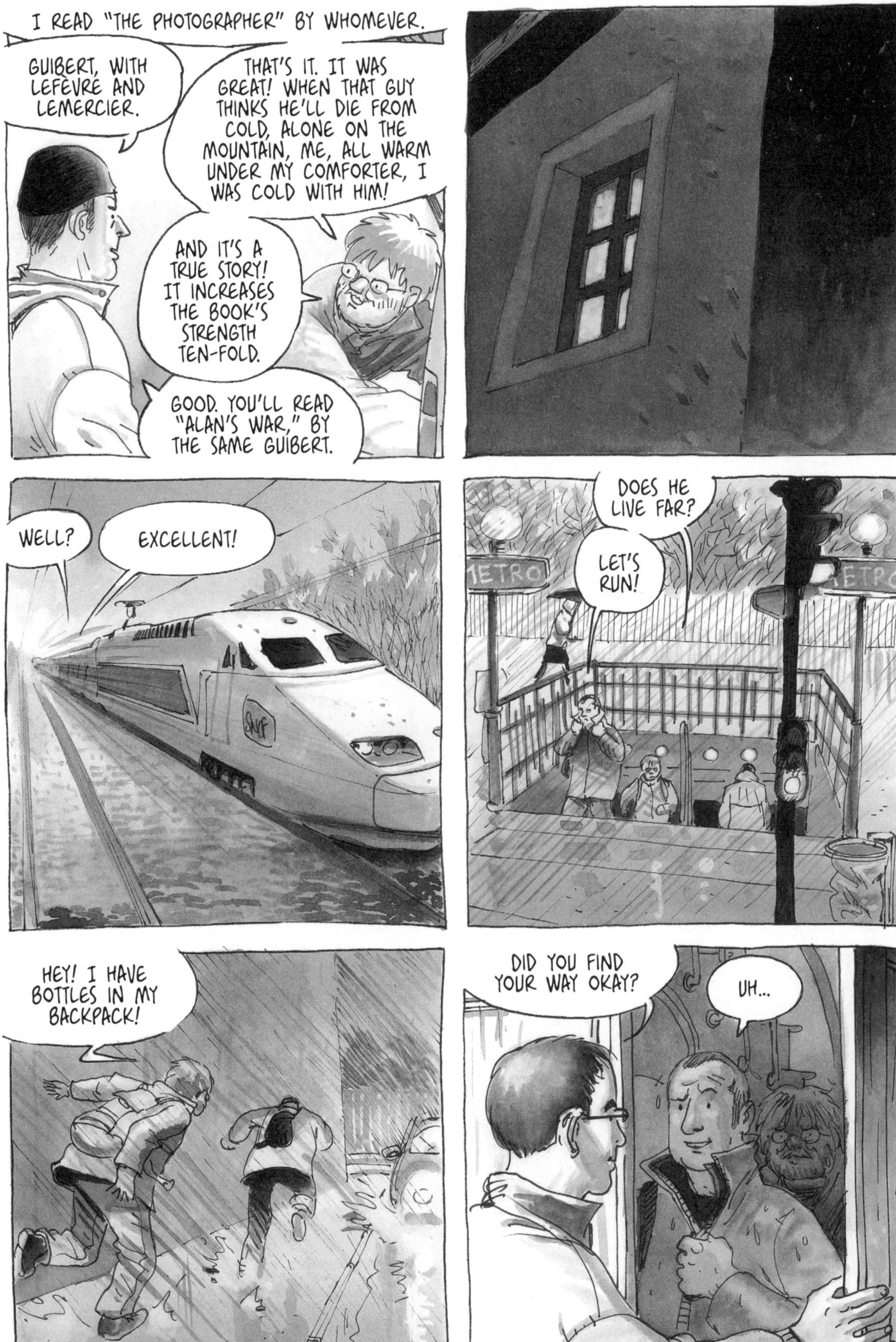
I READ "THE PHOTOGRAPHER" BY WHOMEVER.
GUIBERT, WITH LEFÈVRE AND LEMERCIER.
THAT'S IT. IT WAS GREAT! WHEN THAT GUY THINKS HE'LL DIE FROM COLD, ALONE ON THE MOUNTAIN, ME, ALL WARM UNDER MY COMFORTER, I WAS COLD WITH HIM!
AND IT'S A TRUE STORY! IT INCREASES THE BOOK'S STRENGTH TEN-FOLD.
GOOD. YOU'LL READ "ALAN'S WAR," BY THE SAME GUIBERT.
WELL?
EXCELLENT!
SNCF
METRO
METRO
DOES HE LIVE FAR?
LET'S RUN!
HEY! I HAVE BOTTLES IN MY BACKPACK!
DID YOU FIND YOUR WAY OKAY?
UH...

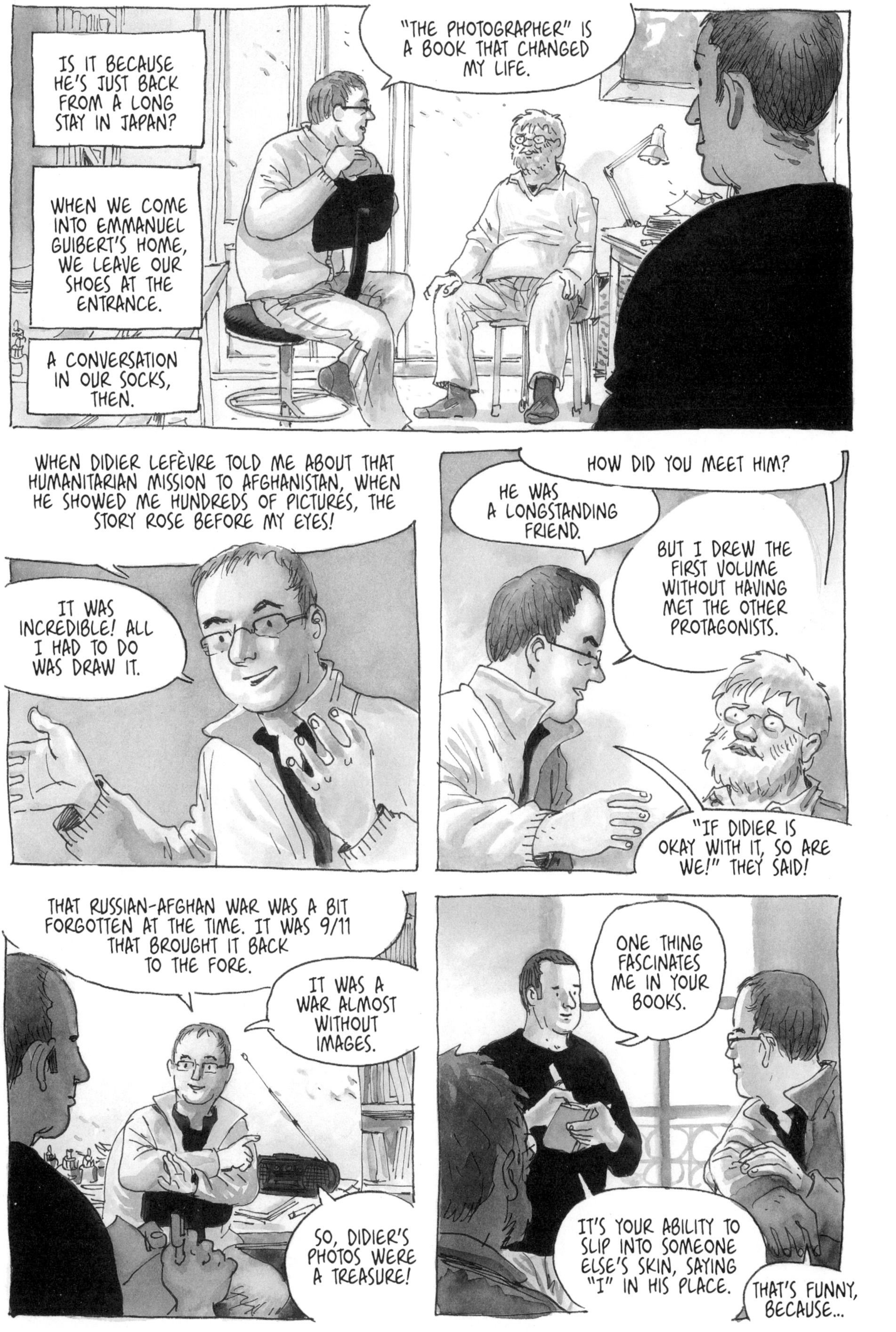
IS IT BECAUSE HE'S JUST BACK FROM A LONG STAY IN JAPAN?
"THE PHOTOGRAPHER" IS A BOOK THAT CHANGED MY LIFE.
WHEN WE COME INTO EMMANUEL GUIBERT'S HOME, WE LEAVE OUR SHOES AT THE ENTRANCE.
A CONVERSATION IN OUR SOCKS, THEN.
WHEN DIDIER LEFÈVRE TOLD ME ABOUT THAT HUMANITARIAN MISSION TO AFGHANISTAN, WHEN HE SHOWED ME HUNDREDS OF PICTURES, THE STORY ROSE BEFORE MY EYES!
IT WAS INCREDIBLE! ALL I HAD TO DO WAS DRAW IT.
HOW DID YOU MEET HIM?
HE WAS A LONGSTANDING FRIEND.
BUT I DREW THE FIRST VOLUME WITHOUT HAVING MET THE OTHER PROTAGONISTS.
"IF DIDIER IS OKAY WITH IT, SO ARE WE!" THEY SAID!
THAT RUSSIAN-AFGHAN WAR WAS A BIT FORGOTTEN AT THE TIME. IT WAS 9/11 THAT BROUGHT IT BACK TO THE FORE.
IT WAS A WAR ALMOST WITHOUT IMAGES.
SO, DIDIER'S PHOTOS WERE A TREASURE!
ONE THING FASCINATES ME IN YOUR BOOKS.
IT'S YOUR ABILITY TO SLIP INTO SOMEONE ELSE'S SKIN, SAYING "I" IN HIS PLACE.
THAT'S FUNNY, BECAUSE...

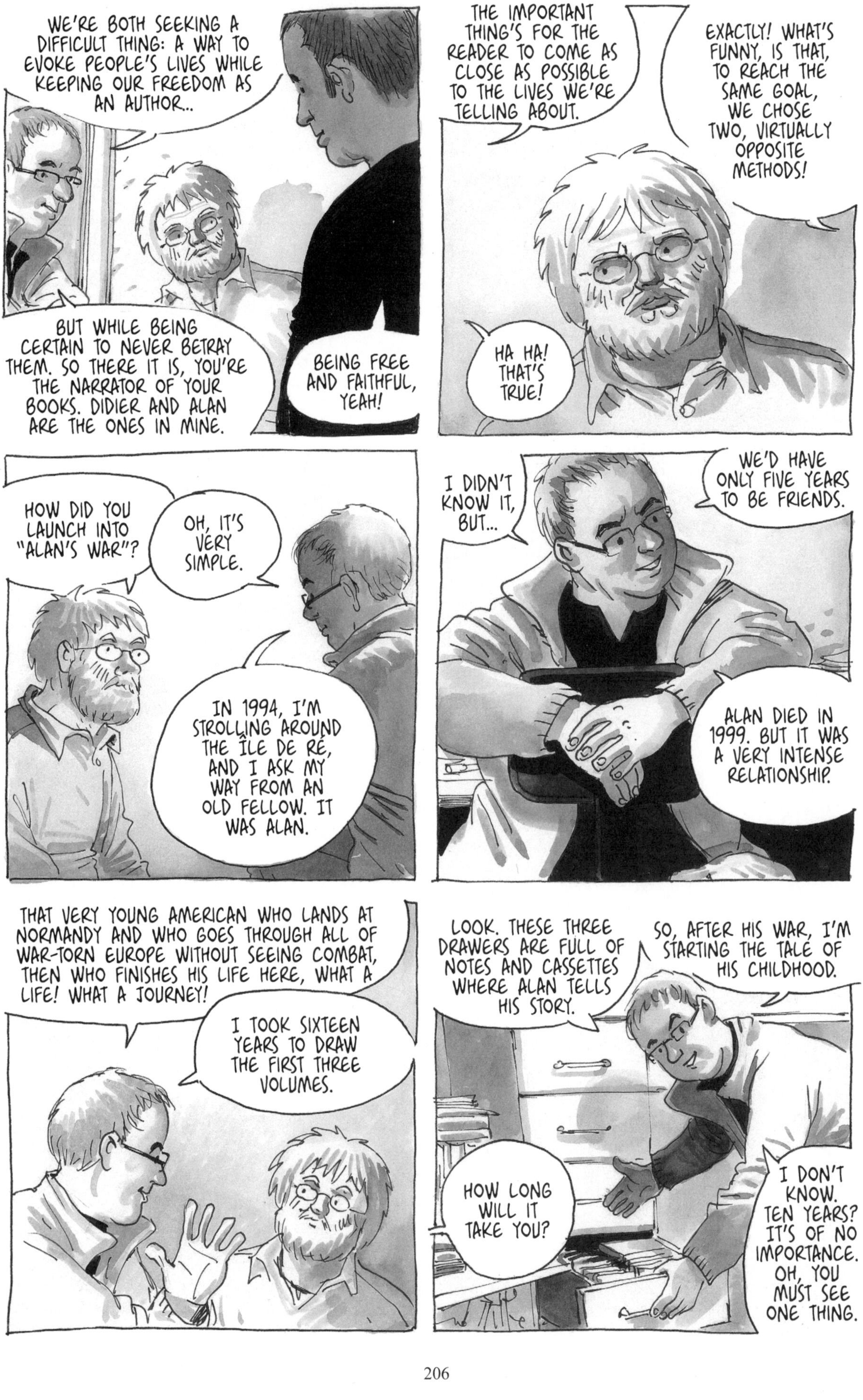
WE'RE BOTH SEEKING A DIFFICULT THING: A WAY TO EVOKE PEOPLE'S LIVES WHILE KEEPING OUR FREEDOM AS AN AUTHOR...
BUT WHILE BEING CERTAIN TO NEVER BETRAY THEM. SO THERE IT IS, YOU'RE THE NARRATOR OF YOUR BOOKS. DIDIER AND ALAN ARE THE ONES IN MINE.
BEING FREE AND FAITHFUL, YEAH!
THE IMPORTANT THING'S FOR THE READER TO COME AS CLOSE AS POSSIBLE TO THE LIVES WE'RE TELLING ABOUT.
EXACTLY! WHAT'S FUNNY, IS THAT, TO REACH THE SAME GOAL, WE CHOSE TWO, VIRTUALLY OPPOSITE METHODS!
HA HA! THAT'S TRUE!
HOW DID YOU LAUNCH INTO "ALAN'S WAR"?
OH, IT'S VERY SIMPLE.
IN 1994, I'M STROLLING AROUND THE ÎLE DE RÉ, AND I ASK MY WAY FROM AN OLD FELLOW. IT WAS ALAN.
I DIDN'T KNOW IT, BUT...
WE'D HAVE ONLY FIVE YEARS TO BE FRIENDS.
ALAN DIED IN 1999. BUT IT WAS A VERY INTENSE RELATIONSHIP.
THAT VERY YOUNG AMERICAN WHO LANDS AT NORMANDY AND WHO GOES THROUGH ALL OF WAR-TORN EUROPE WITHOUT SEEING COMBAT, THEN WHO FINISHES HIS LIFE HERE, WHAT A LIFE! WHAT A JOURNEY!
I TOOK SIXTEEN YEARS TO DRAW THE FIRST THREE VOLUMES.
LOOK. THESE THREE DRAWERS ARE FULL OF NOTES AND CASSETTES WHERE ALAN TELLS HIS STORY.
SO, AFTER HIS WAR, I'M STARTING THE TALE OF HIS CHILDHOOD.
HOW LONG WILL IT TAKE YOU?
I DON'T KNOW. TEN YEARS? IT'S OF NO IMPORTANCE. OH, YOU MUST SEE ONE THING.

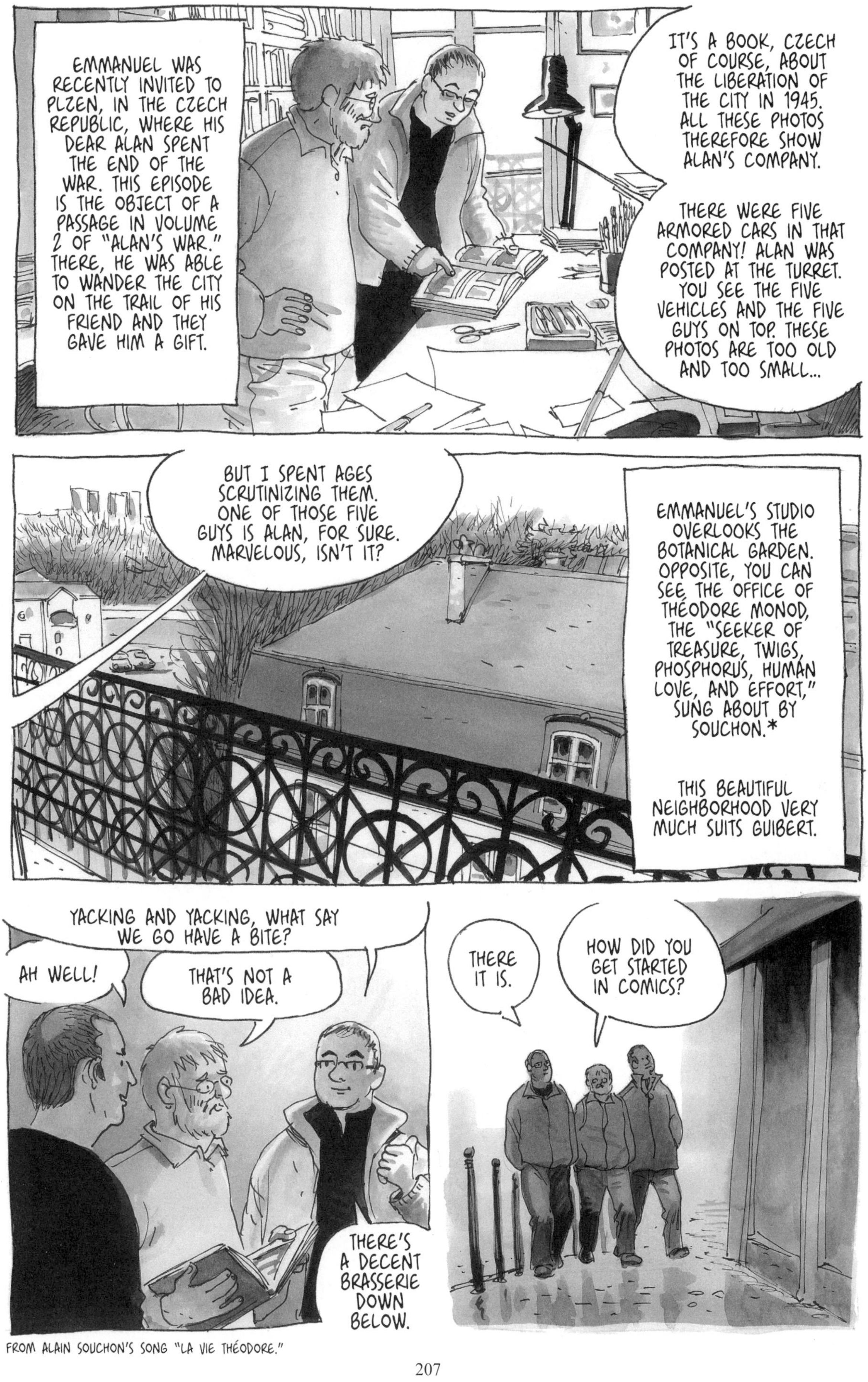
EMMANUEL WAS RECENTLY INVITED TO PLZEN, IN THE CZECH REPUBLIC, WHERE HIS DEAR ALAN SPENT THE END OF THE WAR. THIS EPISODE IS THE OBJECT OF A PASSAGE IN VOLUME 2 OF "ALAN'S WAR." THERE, HE WAS ABLE TO WANDER THE CITY ON THE TRAIL OF HIS FRIEND AND THEY GAVE HIM A GIFT.
IT'S A BOOK, CZECH OF COURSE, ABOUT THE LIBERATION OF THE CITY IN 1945. ALL THESE PHOTOS THEREFORE SHOW ALAN'S COMPANY.
THERE WERE FIVE ARMORED CARS IN THAT COMPANY! ALAN WAS POSTED AT THE TURRET. YOU SEE THE FIVE VEHICLES AND THE FIVE GUYS ON TOP. THESE PHOTOS ARE TOO OLD AND TOO SMALL...
BUT I SPENT AGES SCRUTINIZING THEM. ONE OF THOSE FIVE GUYS IS ALAN, FOR SURE. MARVELOUS, ISN'T IT?
EMMANUEL'S STUDIO OVERLOOKS THE BOTANICAL GARDEN. OPPOSITE, YOU CAN SEE THE OFFICE OF THÉODORE MONOD, THE "SEEKER OF TREASURE, TWIGS, PHOSPHORUS, HUMAN LOVE, AND EFFORT," SUNG ABOUT BY SOUCHON.*
THIS BEAUTIFUL NEIGHBORHOOD VERY MUCH SUITS GUIBERT.
YACKING AND YACKING, WHAT SAY WE GO HAVE A BITE?
AH WELL!
THAT'S NOT A BAD IDEA.
THERE'S A DECENT BRASSERIE DOWN BELOW.
THERE IT IS.
HOW DID YOU GET STARTED IN COMICS?

* FROM ALAIN SOUCHON'S SONG "LA VIE THÉODORE."

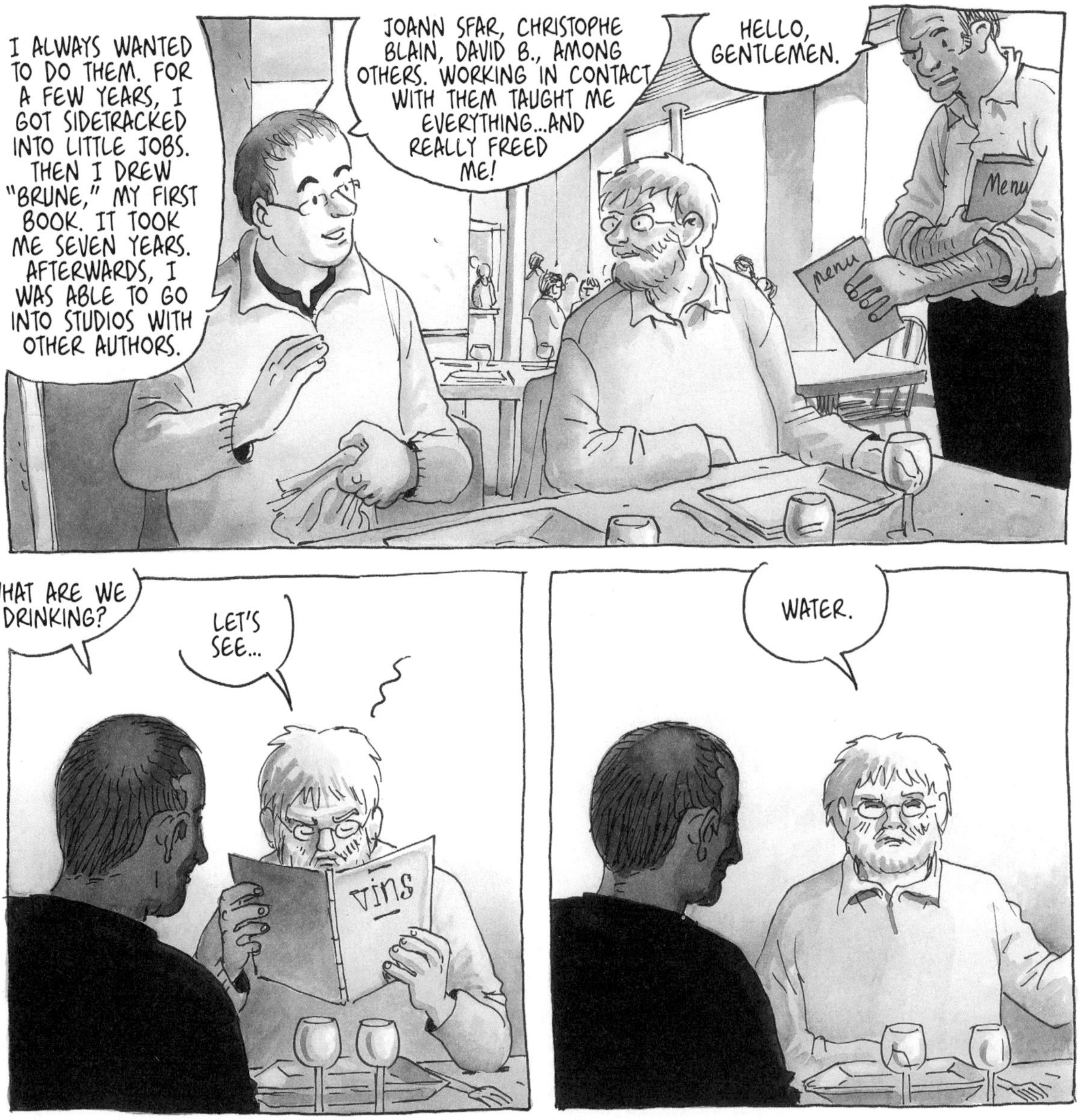
I ALWAYS WANTED TO DO THEM. FOR A FEW YEARS, I GOT SIDETRACKED INTO LITTLE JOBS. THEN I DREW "BRUNE," MY FIRST BOOK. IT TOOK ME SEVEN YEARS. AFTERWARDS, I WAS ABLE TO GO INTO STUDIOS WITH OTHER AUTHORS.
JOANN SFAR, CHRISTOPHE BLAIN, DAVID B., AMONG OTHERS. WORKING IN CONTACT WITH THEM TAUGHT ME EVERYTHING...AND REALLY FREED ME!
HELLO, GENTLEMEN.
Menu
menu
WHAT ARE WE DRINKING?
LET'S SEE...
vins
WATER.

FROM AFGHANISTAN TO THE SECOND WORLD WAR, FROM EMMANUEL'S NEXT BOOK, ABOUT GYPSIES, WITH ALAIN KELER, ANOTHER PHOTOGRAPHER, TO HIS COLLECTION OF ILLUSTRATIONS DRAWN IN JAPAN, THAT LITTLE RESTAURANT TABLE, WITH OR WITHOUT WINE, PROVES AS BIG AS THE WORLD.

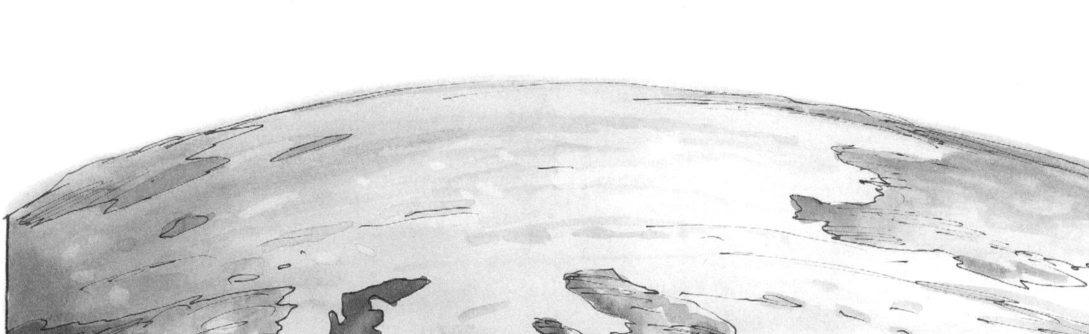

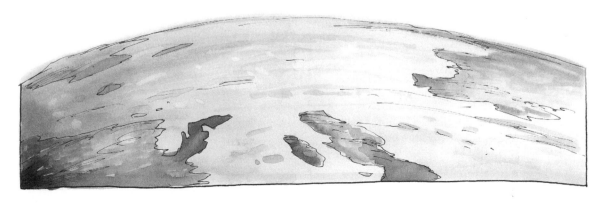

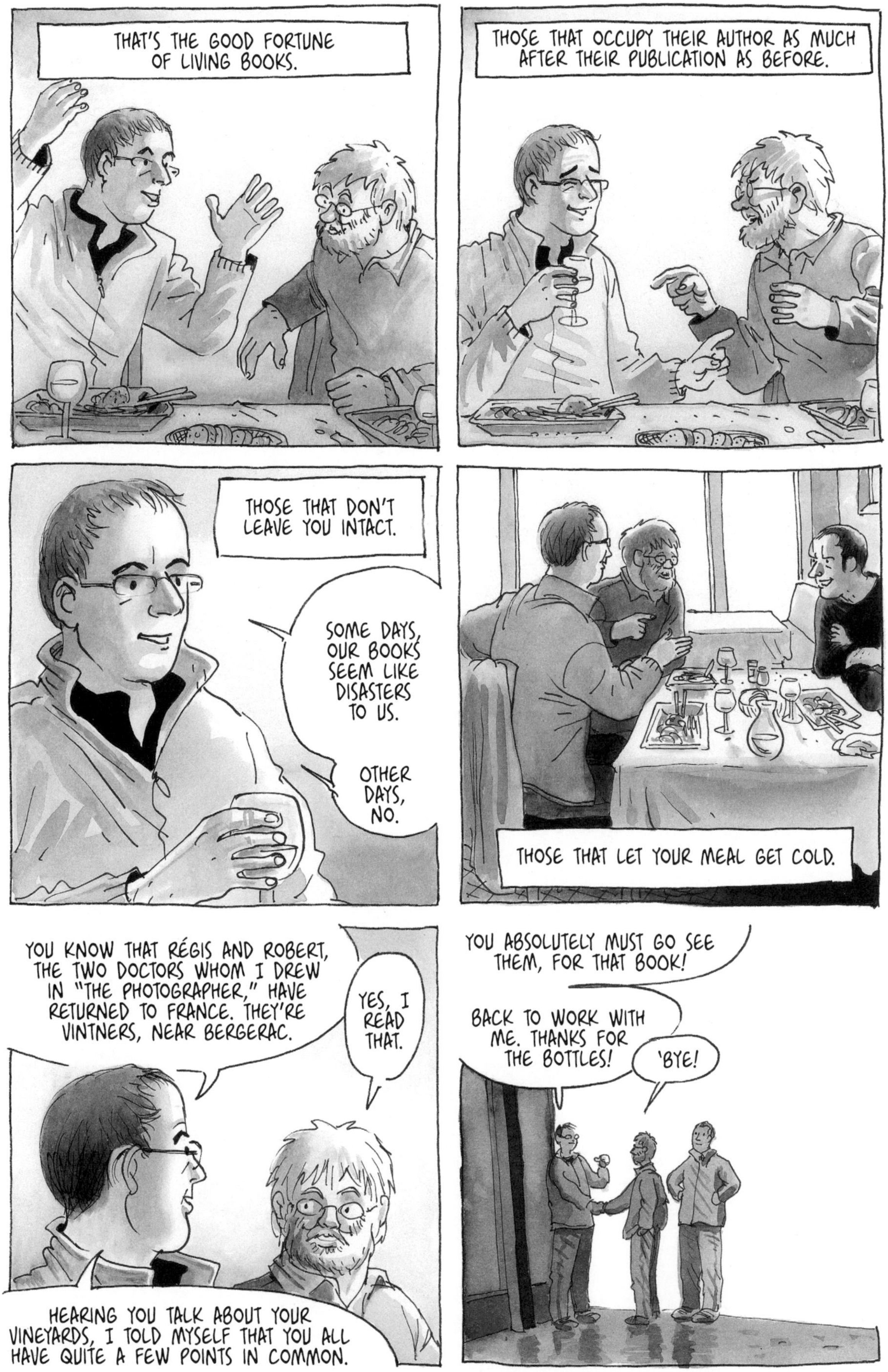
THAT'S THE GOOD FORTUNE OF LIVING BOOKS.
THOSE THAT OCCUPY THEIR AUTHOR AS MUCH AFTER THEIR PUBLICATION AS BEFORE.
THOSE THAT DON'T LEAVE YOU INTACT.
SOME DAYS, OUR BOOKS SEEM LIKE DISASTERS TO US.
OTHER DAYS, NO.
THOSE THAT LET YOUR MEAL GET COLD.
YOU KNOW THAT RÉGIS AND ROBERT, THE TWO DOCTORS WHOM I DREW IN "THE PHOTOGRAPHER," HAVE RETURNED TO FRANCE. THEY'RE VINTNERS, NEAR BERGERAC.
YES, I READ THAT.
HEARING YOU TALK ABOUT YOUR VINEYARDS, I TOLD MYSELF THAT YOU ALL HAVE QUITE A FEW POINTS IN COMMON.
YOU ABSOLUTELY MUST GO SEE THEM, FOR THAT BOOK!
BACK TO WORK WITH ME. THANKS FOR THE BOTTLES!
'BYE!

CHAPTER SIXTEEN   A TEETERING
STATUE

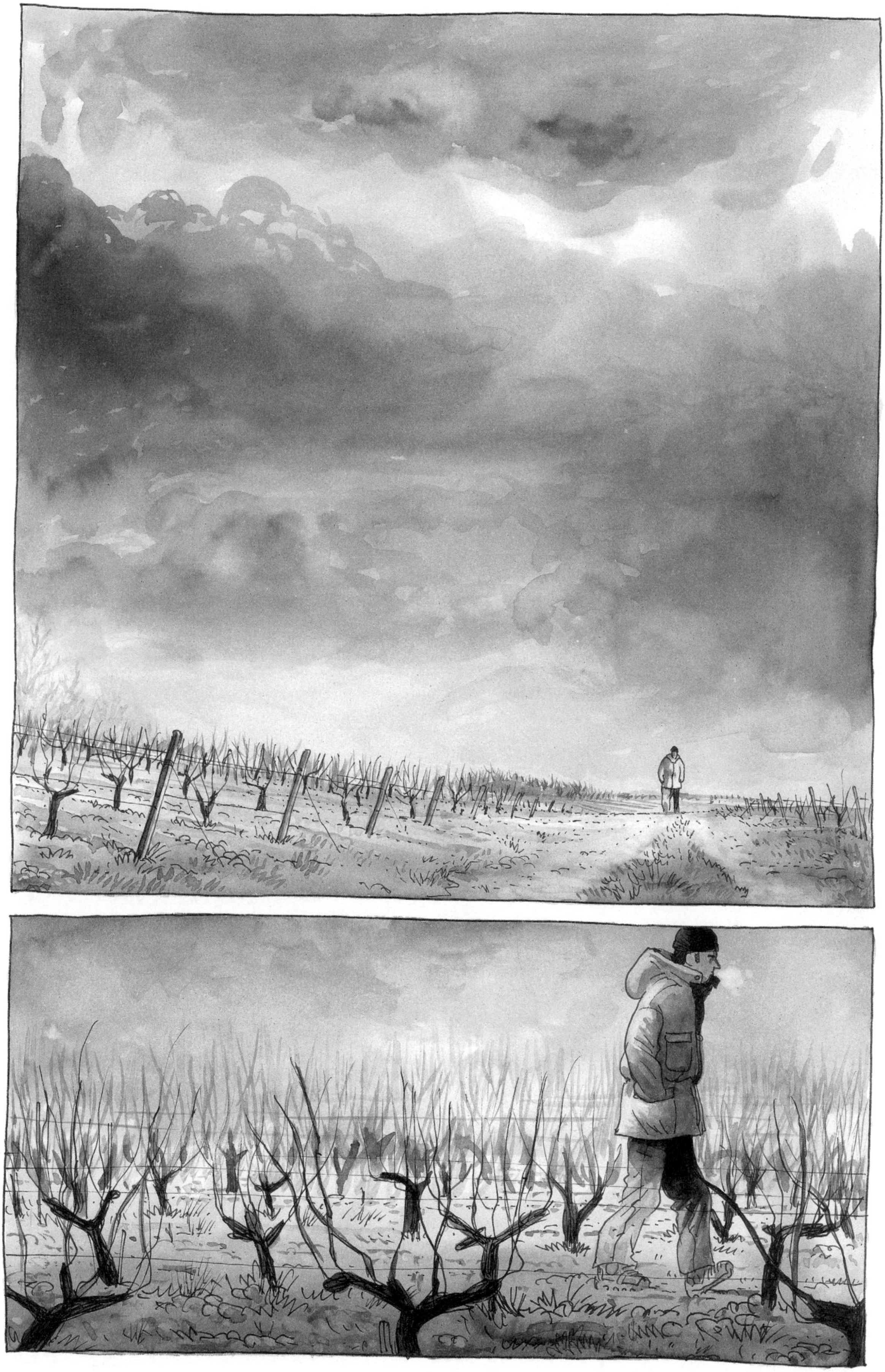

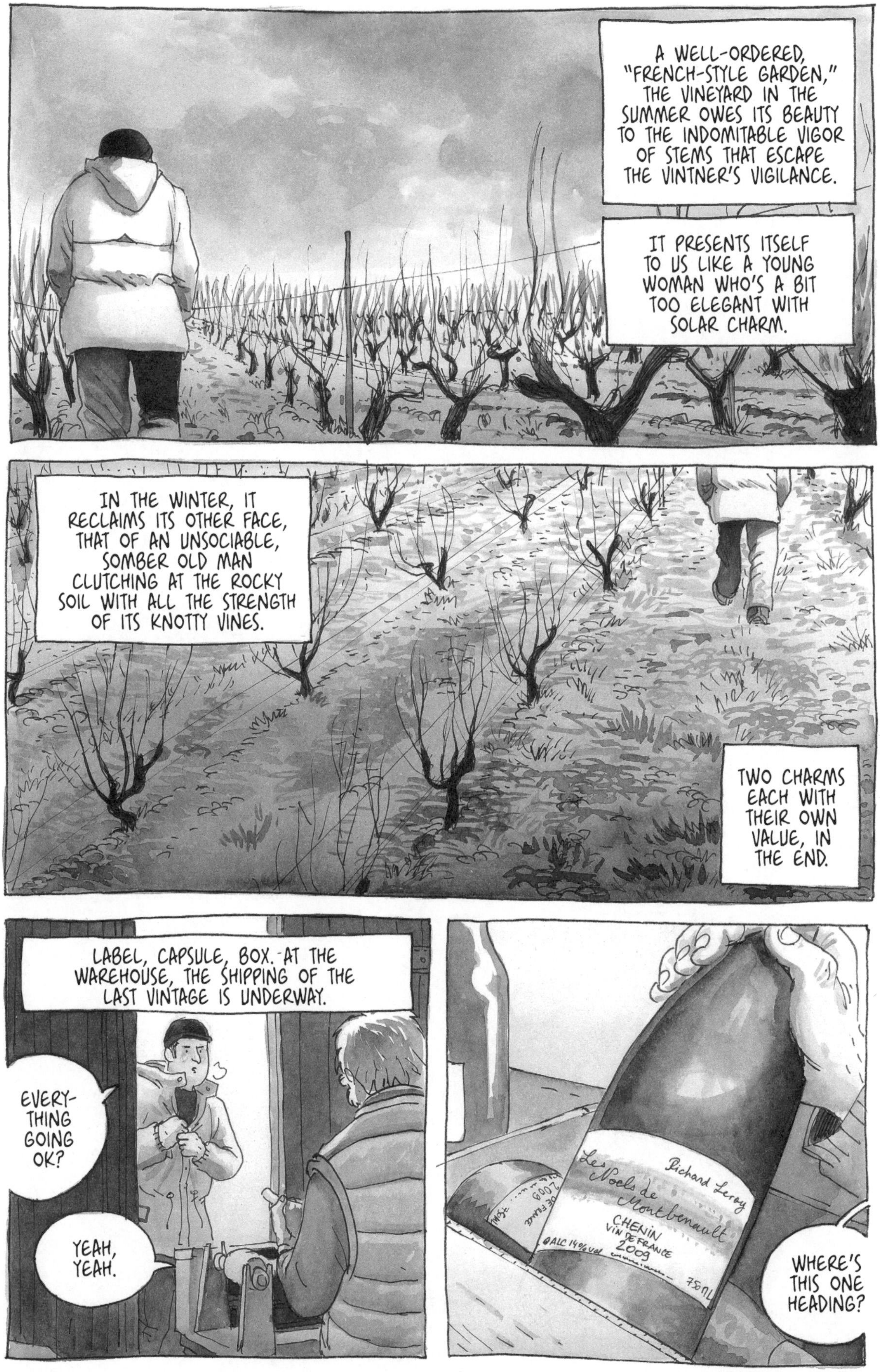
A WELL-ORDERED, "FRENCH-STYLE GARDEN," THE VINEYARD IN THE SUMMER OWES ITS BEAUTY TO THE INDOMITABLE VIGOR OF STEMS THAT ESCAPE THE VINTNER'S VIGILANCE.
IT PRESENTS ITSELF TO US LIKE A YOUNG WOMAN WHO'S A BIT TOO ELEGANT WITH SOLAR CHARM.
IN THE WINTER, IT RECLAIMS ITS OTHER FACE, THAT OF AN UNSOCIABLE, SOMBER OLD MAN CLUTCHING AT THE ROCKY SOIL WITH ALL THE STRENGTH OF ITS KNOTTY VINES.
TWO CHARMS EACH WITH THEIR OWN VALUE, IN THE END.
LABEL, CAPSULE, BOX. AT THE WAREHOUSE, THE SHIPPING OF THE LAST VINTAGE IS UNDERWAY.
EVERY-THING GOING OK?
YEAH, YEAH.
Richard Leroy
Les Noels de Montbenault
CHENIN
VIN DE FRANCE
2009
WHERE'S THIS ONE HEADING?

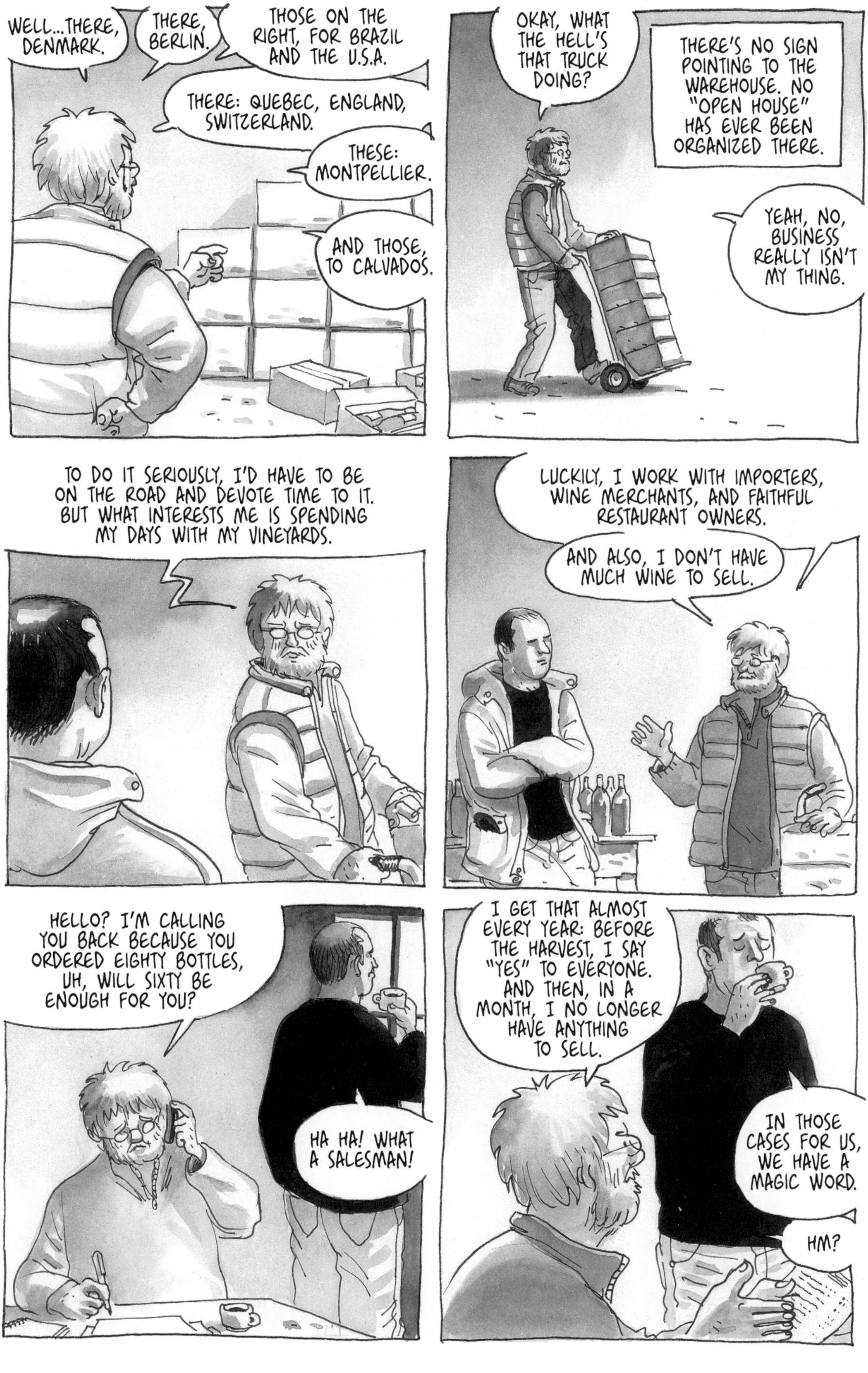

WELL...THERE, DENMARK.
THERE, BERLIN.
THOSE ON THE RIGHT, FOR BRAZIL AND THE U.S.A.
THERE: QUEBEC, ENGLAND, SWITZERLAND.
THESE: MONTPELLIER.
AND THOSE, TO CALVADOS.
OKAY, WHAT THE HELL'S THAT TRUCK DOING?
THERE'S NO SIGN POINTING TO THE WAREHOUSE. NO "OPEN HOUSE" HAS EVER BEEN ORGANIZED THERE.
YEAH, NO, BUSINESS REALLY ISN'T MY THING.
TO DO IT SERIOUSLY, I'D HAVE TO BE ON THE ROAD AND DEVOTE TIME TO IT. BUT WHAT INTERESTS ME IS SPENDING MY DAYS WITH MY VINEYARDS.
LUCKILY, I WORK WITH IMPORTERS, WINE MERCHANTS, AND FAITHFUL RESTAURANT OWNERS.
AND ALSO, I DON'T HAVE MUCH WINE TO SELL.
HELLO? I'M CALLING YOU BACK BECAUSE YOU ORDERED EIGHTY BOTTLES, UH, WILL SIXTY BE ENOUGH FOR YOU?
HA HA! WHAT A SALESMAN!
I GET THAT ALMOST EVERY YEAR: BEFORE THE HARVEST, I SAY "YES" TO EVERYONE. AND THEN, IN A MONTH, I NO LONGER HAVE ANYTHING TO SELL.
IN THOSE CASES FOR US, WE HAVE A MAGIC WORD.
HM?

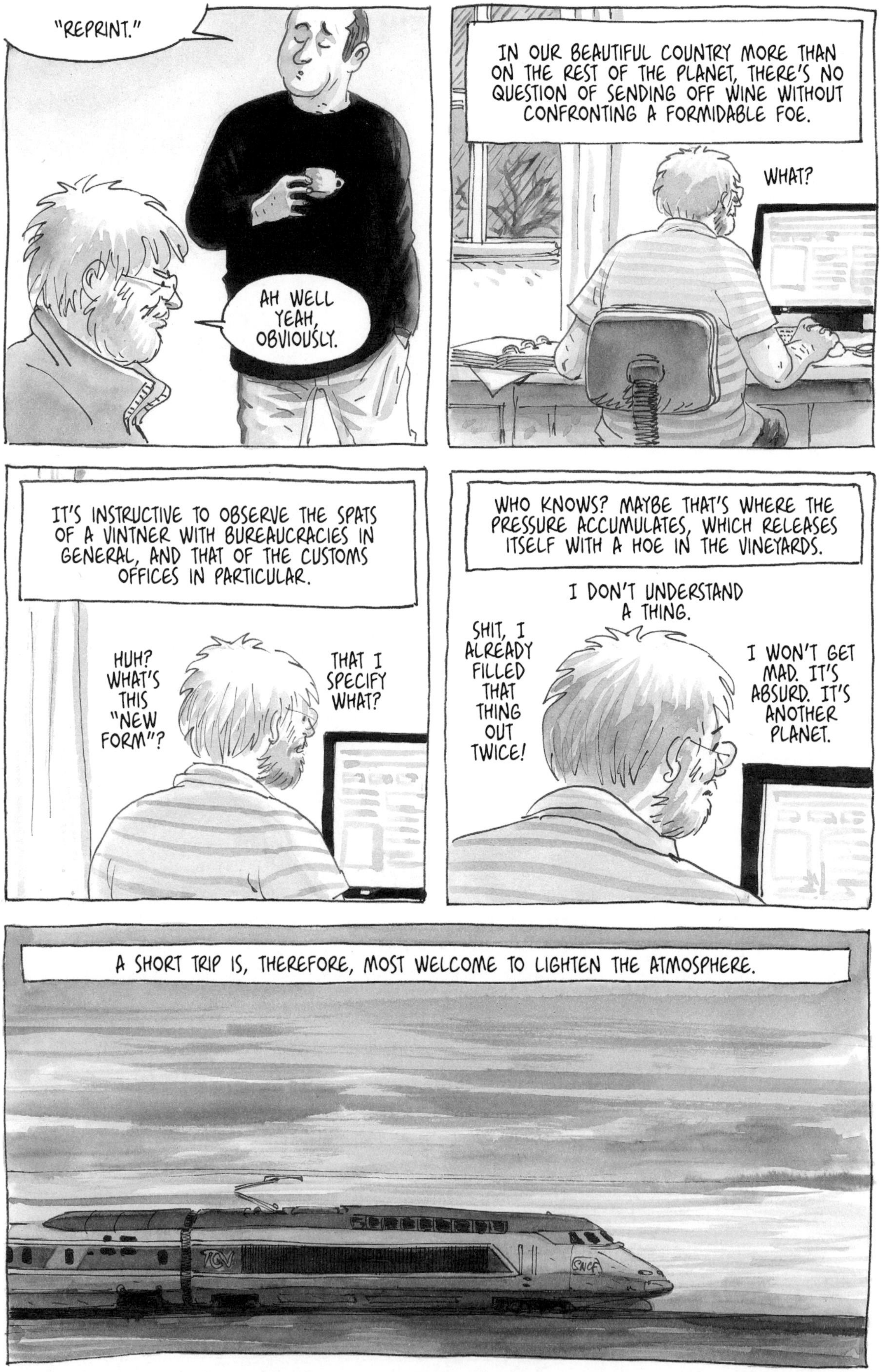
"REPRINT."
AH WELL YEAH, OBVIOUSLY.
IN OUR BEAUTIFUL COUNTRY MORE THAN ON THE REST OF THE PLANET, THERE'S NO QUESTION OF SENDING OFF WINE WITHOUT CONFRONTING A FORMIDABLE FOE.
WHAT?
IT'S INSTRUCTIVE TO OBSERVE THE SPATS OF A VINTNER WITH BUREAUCRACIES IN GENERAL, AND THAT OF THE CUSTOMS OFFICES IN PARTICULAR.
HUH? WHAT'S THIS "NEW FORM"?
THAT I SPECIFY WHAT?
WHO KNOWS? MAYBE THAT'S WHERE THE PRESSURE ACCUMULATES, WHICH RELEASES ITSELF WITH A HOE IN THE VINEYARDS.
I DON'T UNDERSTAND A THING.
SHIT, I ALREADY FILLED THAT THING OUT TWICE!
I WON'T GET MAD. IT'S ABSURD. IT'S ANOTHER PLANET.
A SHORT TRIP IS, THEREFORE, MOST WELCOME TO LIGHTEN THE ATMOSPHERE.

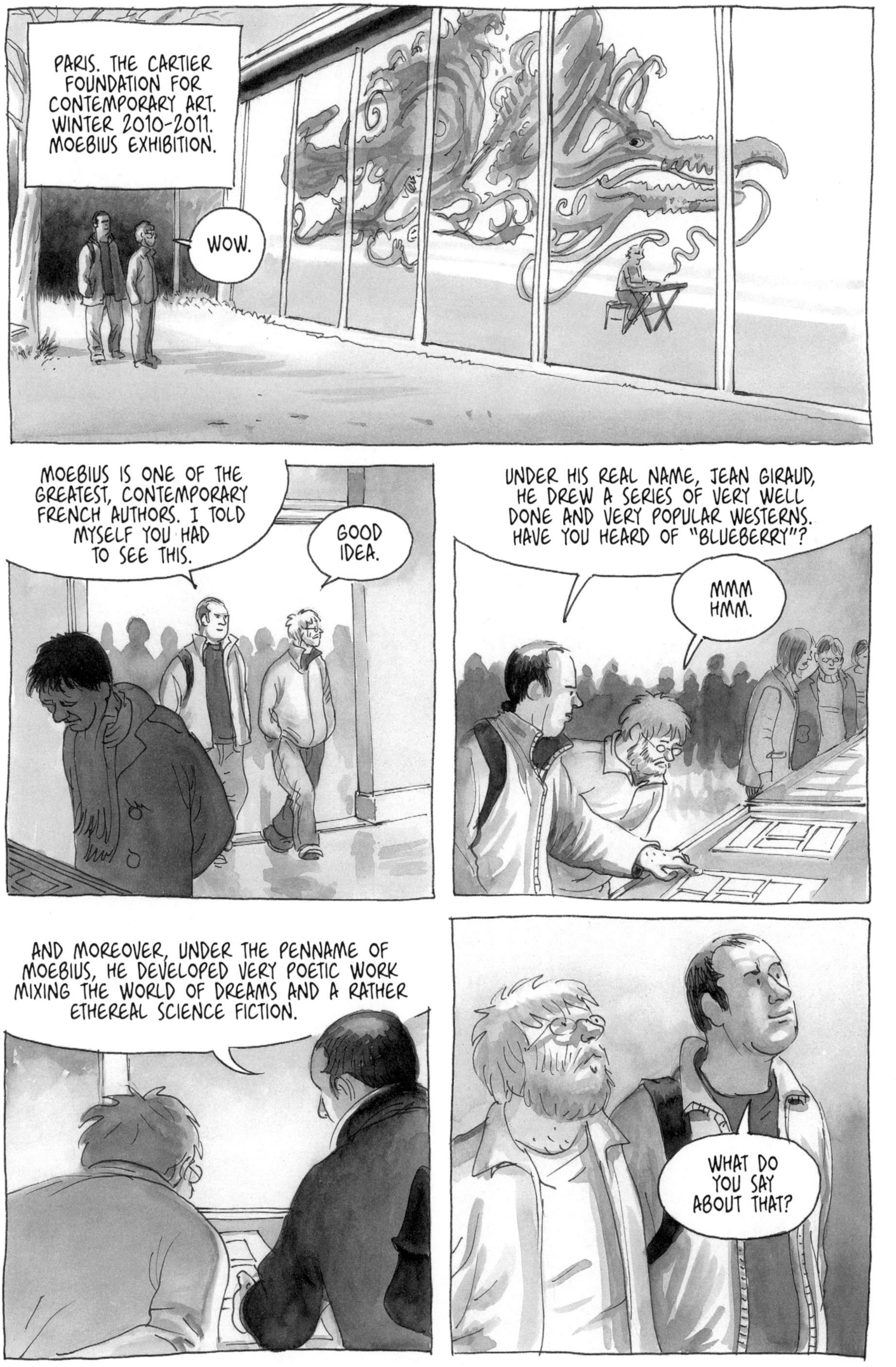
PARIS. THE CARTIER FOUNDATION FOR CONTEMPORARY ART. WINTER 2010-2011. MOEBIUS EXHIBITION.
WOW.
MOEBIUS IS ONE OF THE GREATEST, CONTEMPORARY FRENCH AUTHORS. I TOLD MYSELF YOU HAD TO SEE THIS.
GOOD IDEA.
UNDER HIS REAL NAME, JEAN GIRAUD, HE DREW A SERIES OF VERY WELL DONE AND VERY POPULAR WESTERNS. HAVE YOU HEARD OF "BLUEBERRY"?
MMM HMM.
AND MOREOVER, UNDER THE PENNAME OF MOEBIUS, HE DEVELOPED VERY POETIC WORK MIXING THE WORLD OF DREAMS AND A RATHER ETHEREAL SCIENCE FICTION.
WHAT DO YOU SAY ABOUT THAT?

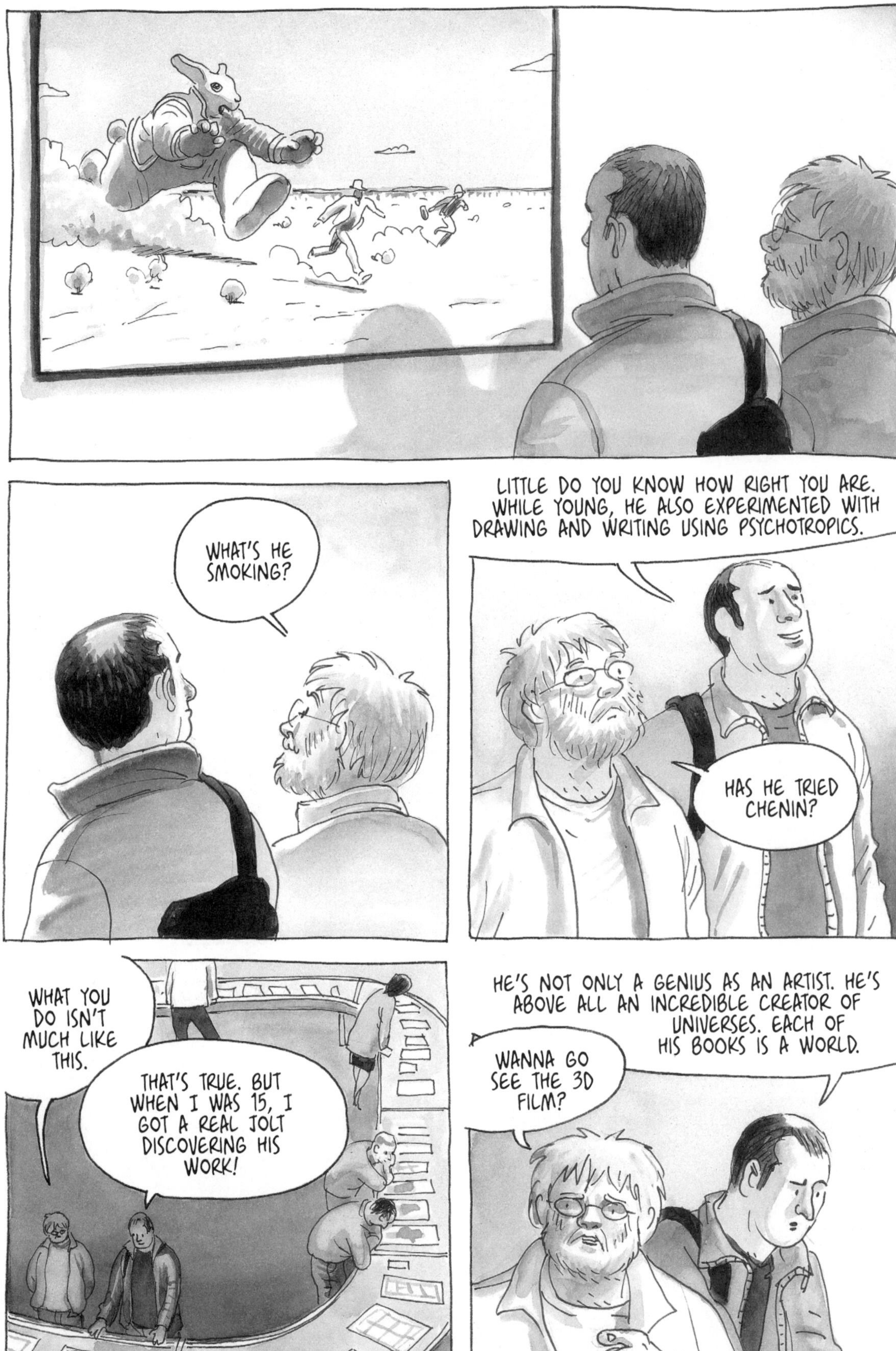
WHAT'S HE SMOKING?
LITTLE DO YOU KNOW HOW RIGHT YOU ARE. WHILE YOUNG, HE ALSO EXPERIMENTED WITH DRAWING AND WRITING USING PSYCHOTROPICS.
HAS HE TRIED CHENIN?
WHAT YOU DO ISN'T MUCH LIKE THIS.
THAT'S TRUE. BUT WHEN I WAS 15, I GOT A REAL JOLT DISCOVERING HIS WORK!
HE'S NOT ONLY A GENIUS AS AN ARTIST. HE'S ABOVE ALL AN INCREDIBLE CREATOR OF UNIVERSES. EACH OF HIS BOOKS IS A WORLD.
WANNA GO SEE THE 3D FILM?

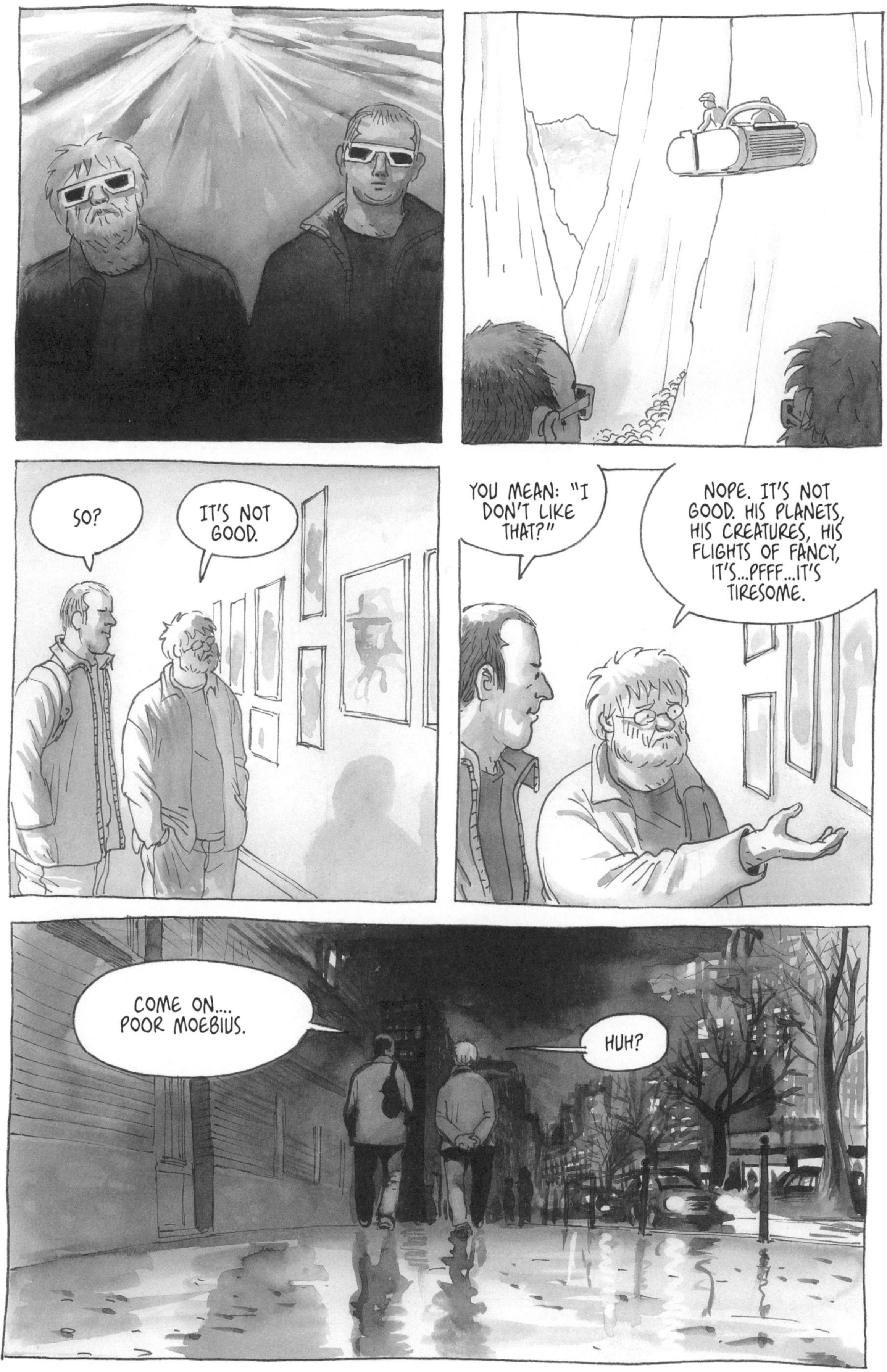
SO?
IT'S NOT GOOD.
YOU MEAN: "I DON'T LIKE THAT?"
NOPE. IT'S NOT GOOD. HIS PLANETS, HIS CREATURES, HIS FLIGHTS OF FANCY, IT'S...PFFF...IT'S TIRESOME.
COME ON.... POOR MOEBIUS.
HUH?

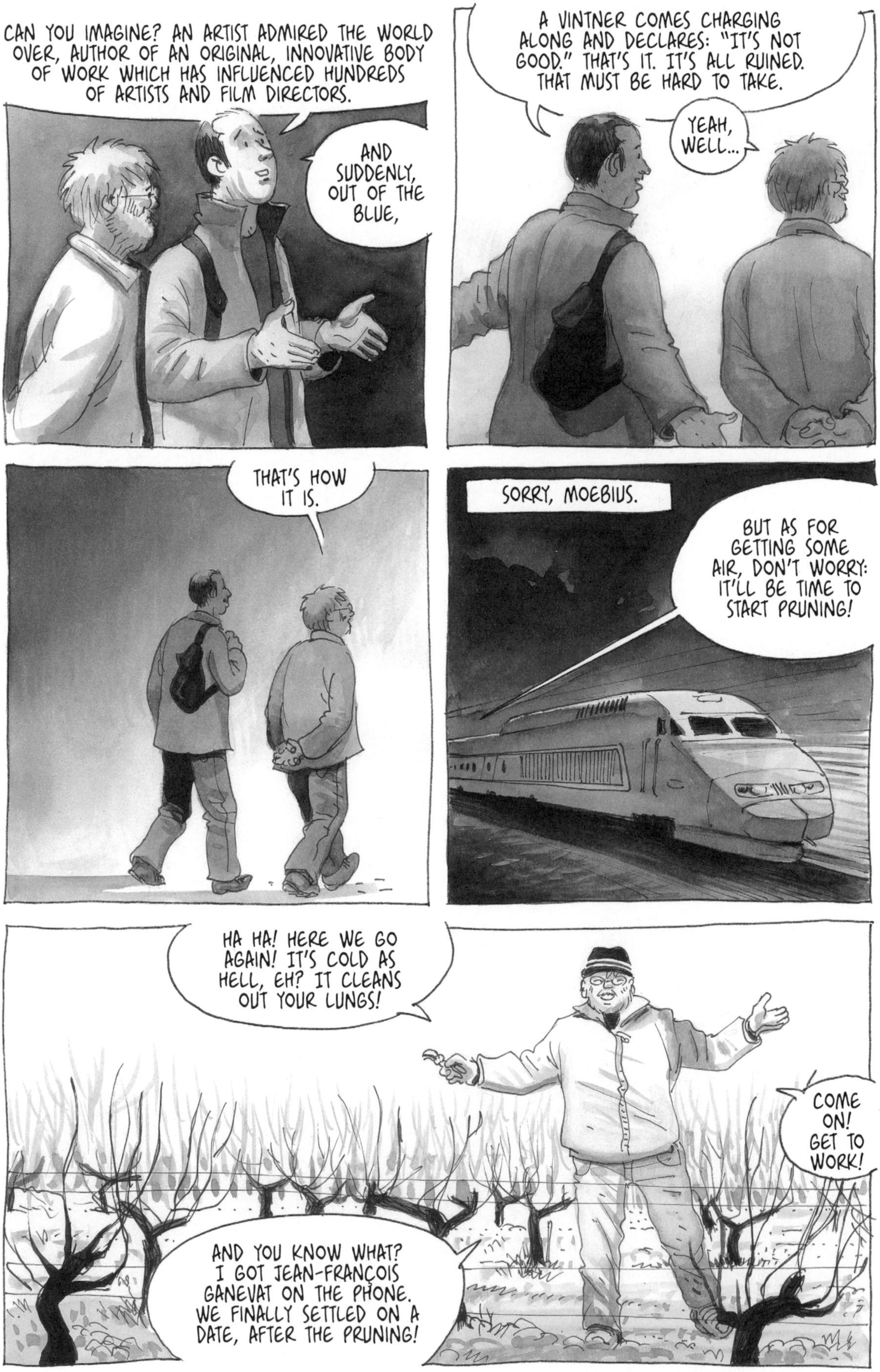
CAN YOU IMAGINE? AN ARTIST ADMIRED THE WORLD OVER, AUTHOR OF AN ORIGINAL, INNOVATIVE BODY OF WORK WHICH HAS INFLUENCED HUNDREDS OF ARTISTS AND FILM DIRECTORS.
AND SUDDENLY, OUT OF THE BLUE,
A VINTNER COMES CHARGING ALONG AND DECLARES: "IT'S NOT GOOD." THAT'S IT. IT'S ALL RUINED. THAT MUST BE HARD TO TAKE.
YEAH, WELL...
THAT'S HOW IT IS.
SORRY, MOEBIUS.
BUT AS FOR GETTING SOME AIR, DON'T WORRY: IT'LL BE TIME TO START PRUNING!
HA HA! HERE WE GO AGAIN! IT'S COLD AS HELL, EH? IT CLEANS OUT YOUR LUNGS!
COME ON! GET TO WORK!
AND YOU KNOW WHAT? I GOT JEAN-FRANCOIS GANEVAT ON THE PHONE. WE FINALLY SETTLED ON A DATE, AFTER THE PRUNING!

CHAPTER SEVENTEEN   SAVAGNINS,
POULSARDS,
AND COMPANY

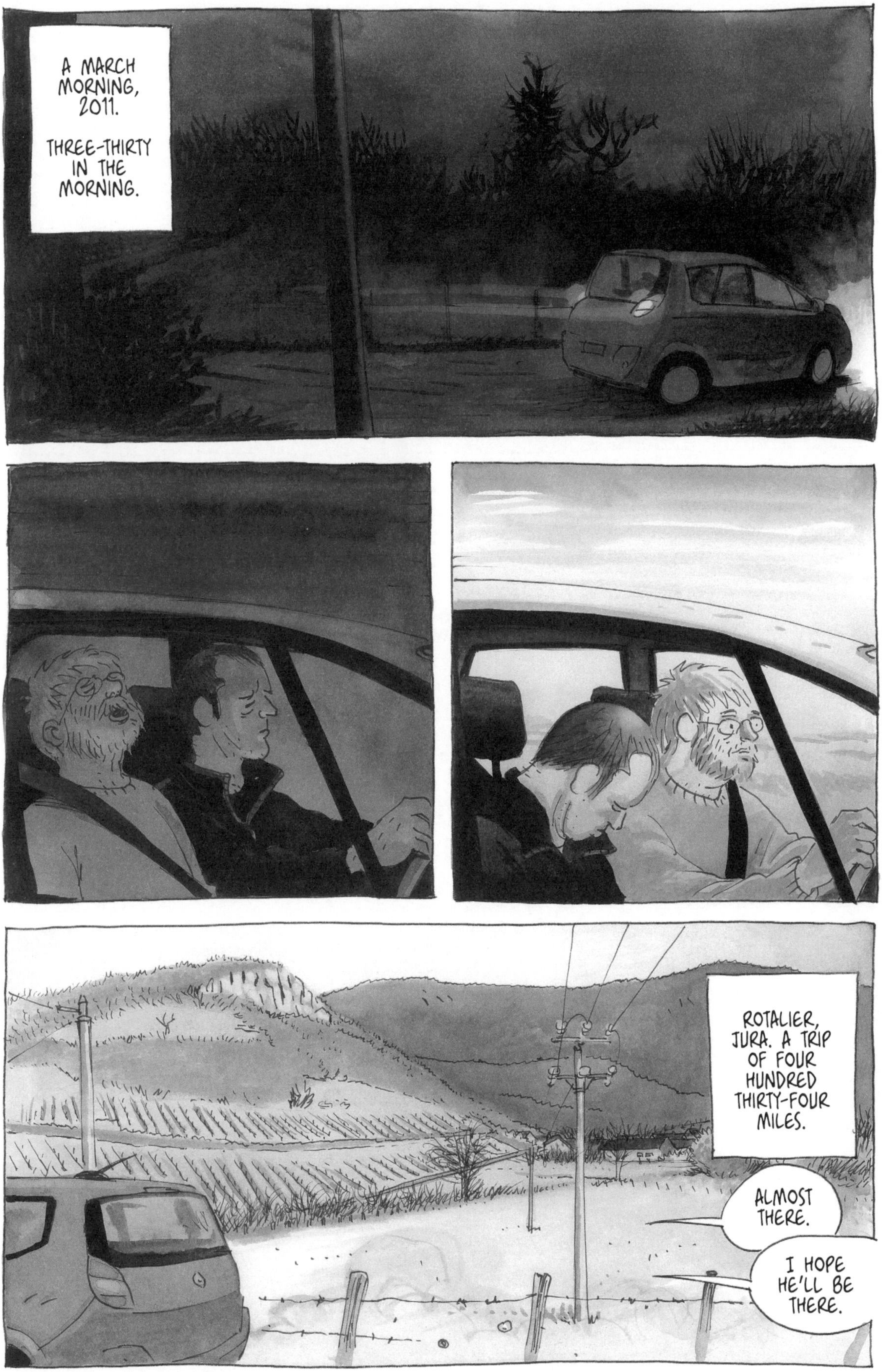
A MARCH MORNING, 2011.
THREE-THIRTY IN THE MORNING.
ROTALIER, JURA. A TRIP OF FOUR HUNDRED THIRTY-FOUR MILES.
ALMOST THERE.
I HOPE HE'LL BE THERE.

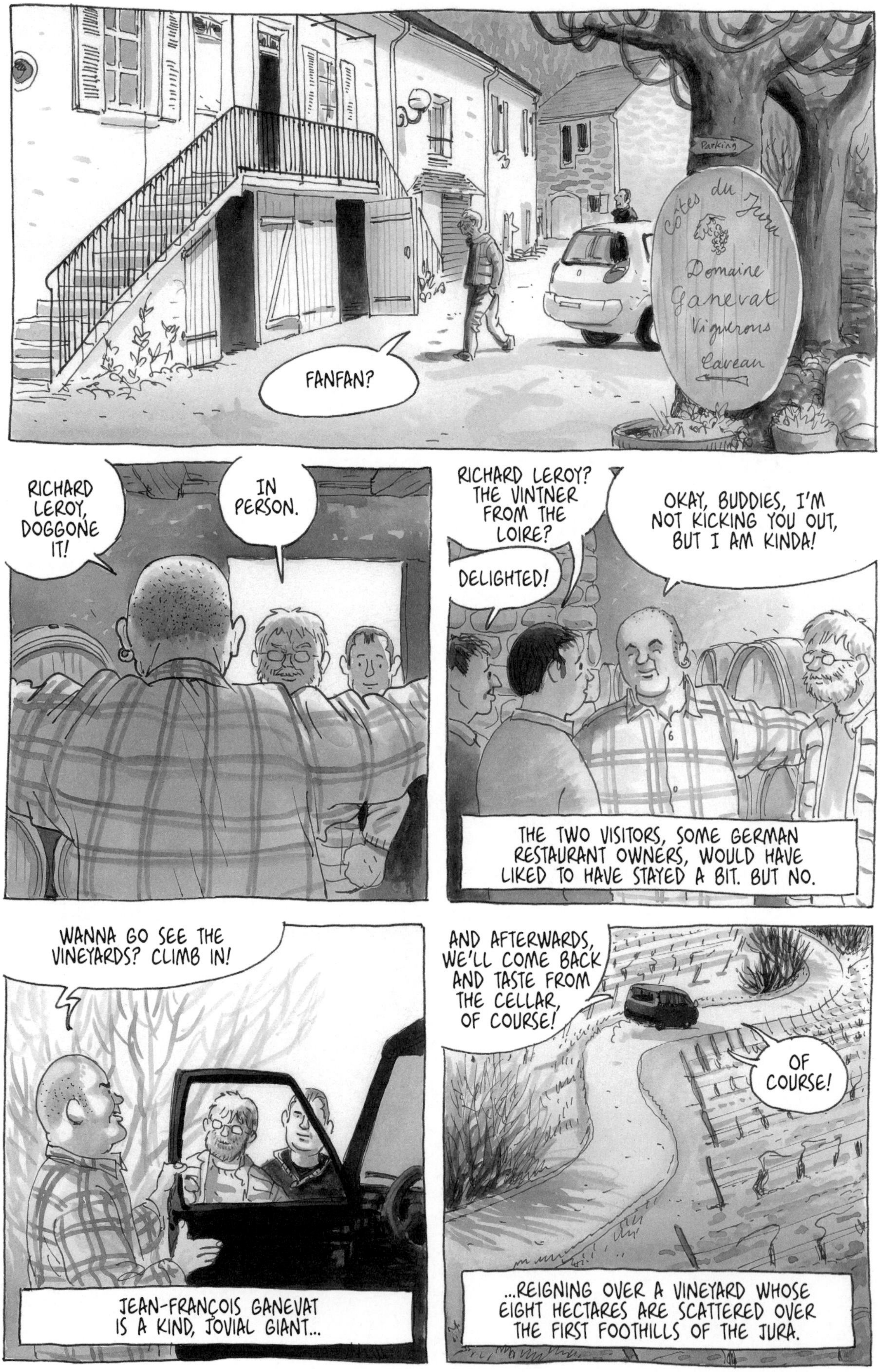
FANFAN?
Cotes du Jura
Domaine Ganevat Vignerons Caveau
Parking
RICHARD LEROY, DOGGONE IT!
IN PERSON.
RICHARD LEROY? THE VINTNER FROM THE LOIRE?
DELIGHTED!
OKAY, BUDDIES, I'M NOT KICKING YOU OUT, BUT I AM KINDA!
THE TWO VISITORS, SOME GERMAN RESTAURANT OWNERS, WOULD HAVE LIKED TO HAVE STAYED A BIT. BUT NO.
WANNA GO SEE THE VINEYARDS? CLIMB IN!
JEAN-FRANÇOIS GANEVAT IS A KIND, JOVIAL GIANT...
AND AFTERWARDS, WE'LL COME BACK AND TASTE FROM THE CELLAR, OF COURSE!
OF COURSE!
...REIGNING OVER A VINEYARD WHOSE EIGHT HECTARES ARE SCATTERED OVER THE FIRST FOOTHILLS OF THE JURA.

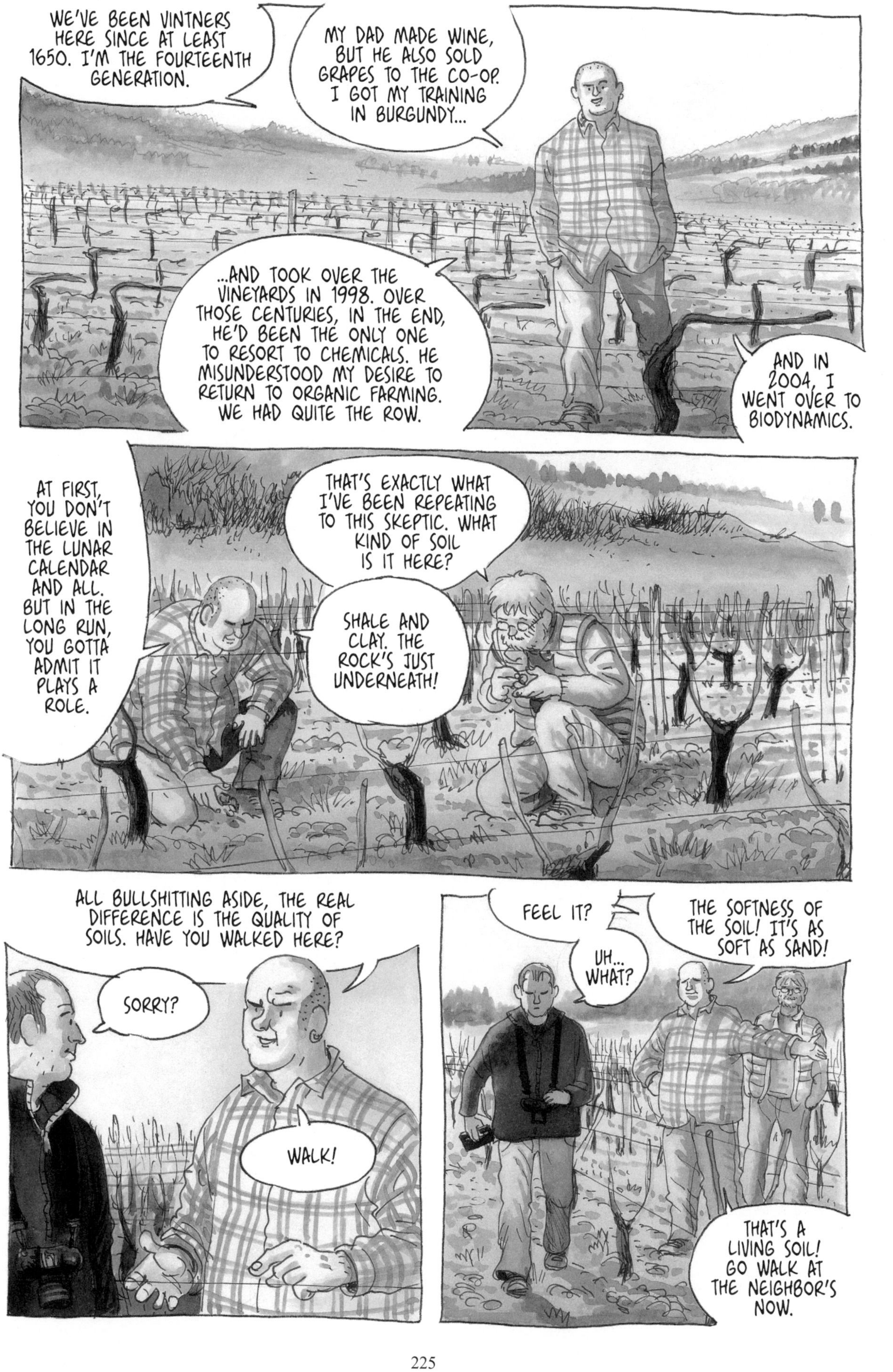
WE'VE BEEN VINTNERS HERE SINCE AT LEAST 1650. I'M THE FOURTEENTH GENERATION.
MY DAD MADE WINE, BUT HE ALSO SOLD GRAPES TO THE CO-OP. I GOT MY TRAINING IN BURGUNDY...
...AND TOOK OVER THE VINEYARDS IN 1998. OVER THOSE CENTURIES, IN THE END, HE'D BEEN THE ONLY ONE TO RESORT TO CHEMICALS. HE MISUNDERSTOOD MY DESIRE TO RETURN TO ORGANIC FARMING. WE HAD QUITE THE ROW.
AND IN 2004, I WENT OVER TO BIODYNAMICS.
AT FIRST, YOU DON'T BELIEVE IN THE LUNAR CALENDAR AND ALL. BUT IN THE LONG RUN, YOU GOTTA ADMIT IT PLAYS A ROLE.
THAT'S EXACTLY WHAT I'VE BEEN REPEATING TO THIS SKEPTIC. WHAT KIND OF SOIL IS IT HERE?
SHALE AND CLAY. THE ROCK'S JUST UNDERNEATH!
ALL BULLSHITTING ASIDE, THE REAL DIFFERENCE IS THE QUALITY OF SOILS. HAVE YOU WALKED HERE?
SORRY?
WALK!
FEEL IT?
UH... WHAT?
THE SOFTNESS OF THE SOIL! IT'S AS SOFT AS SAND!
THAT'S A LIVING SOIL! GO WALK AT THE NEIGHBOR'S NOW.

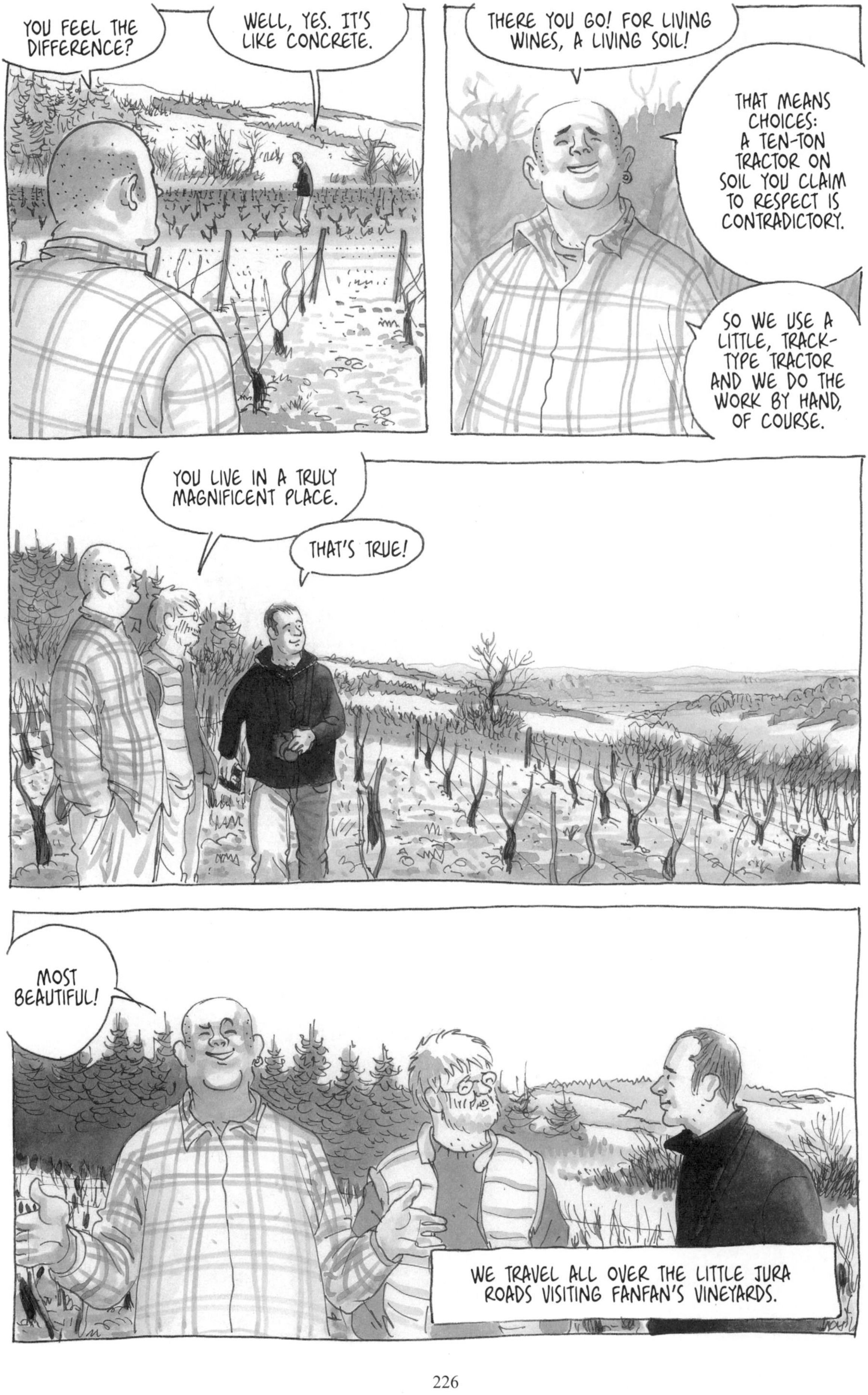
YOU FEEL THE DIFFERENCE?
WELL, YES. IT'S LIKE CONCRETE.
THERE YOU GO! FOR LIVING WINES, A LIVING SOIL!
THAT MEANS CHOICES: A TEN-TON TRACTOR ON SOIL YOU CLAIM TO RESPECT IS CONTRADICTORY.
SO WE USE A LITTLE, TRACK-TYPE TRACTOR AND WE DO THE WORK BY HAND, OF COURSE.
YOU LIVE IN A TRULY MAGNIFICENT PLACE.
THAT'S TRUE!
MOST BEAUTIFUL!
WE TRAVEL ALL OVER THE LITTLE JURA ROADS VISITING FANFAN'S VINEYARDS.

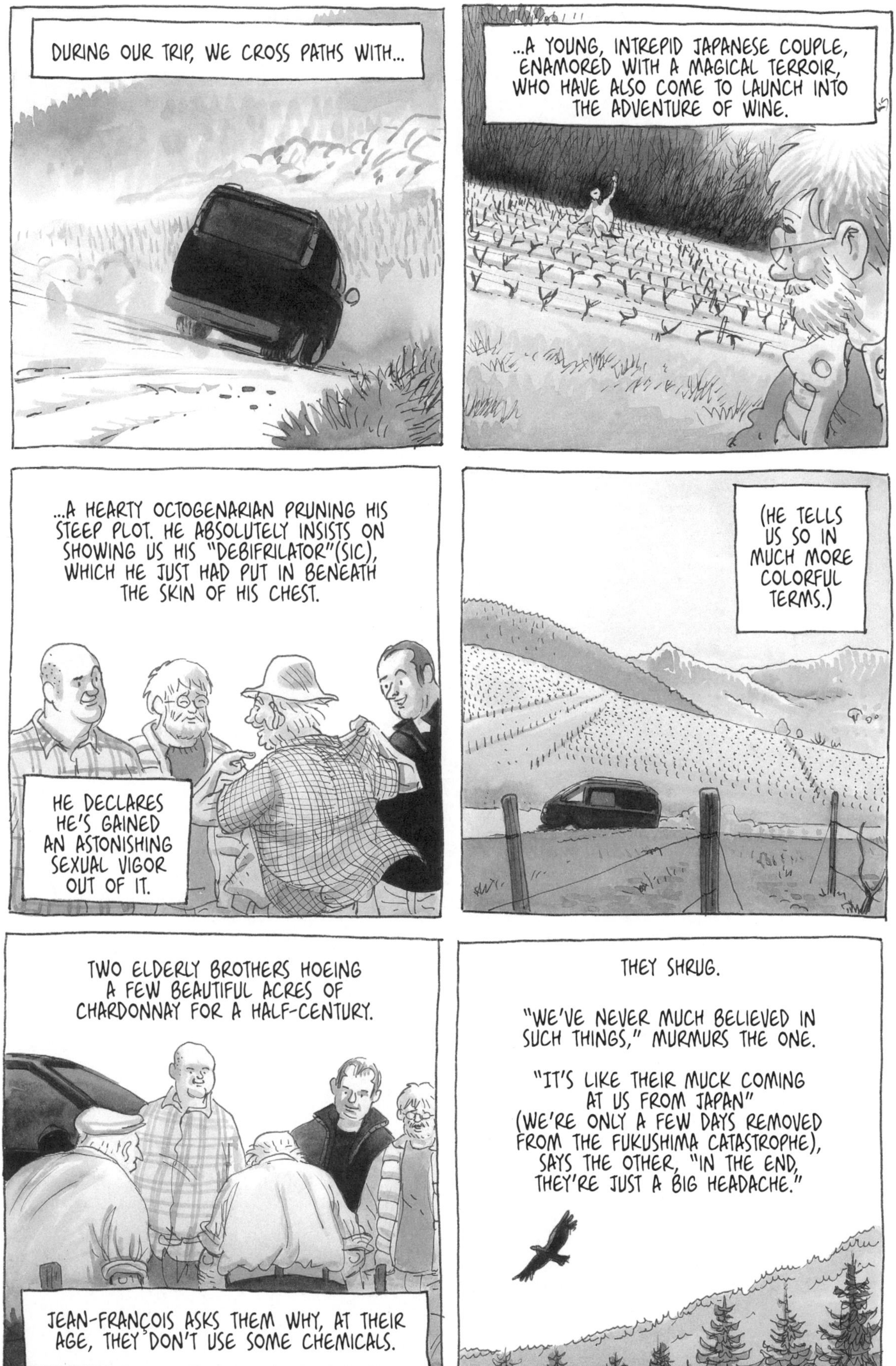
DURING OUR TRIP, WE CROSS PATHS WITH...
...A YOUNG, INTREPID JAPANESE COUPLE, ENAMORED WITH A MAGICAL TERROIR, WHO HAVE ALSO COME TO LAUNCH INTO THE ADVENTURE OF WINE.
...A HEARTY OCTOGENARIAN PRUNING HIS STEEP PLOT. HE ABSOLUTELY INSISTS ON SHOWING US HIS "DEBIFRILATOR"(SIC), WHICH HE JUST HAD PUT IN BENEATH THE SKIN OF HIS CHEST.
HE DECLARES HE'S GAINED AN ASTONISHING SEXUAL VIGOR OUT OF IT.
(HE TELLS US SO IN MUCH MORE COLORFUL TERMS.)
TWO ELDERLY BROTHERS HOEING A FEW BEAUTIFUL ACRES OF CHARDONNAY FOR A HALF-CENTURY.
JEAN-FRANÇOIS ASKS THEM WHY, AT THEIR AGE, THEY DON'T USE SOME CHEMICALS.
THEY SHRUG.
"WE'VE NEVER MUCH BELIEVED IN SUCH THINGS," MURMURS THE ONE.
"IT'S LIKE THEIR MUCK COMING AT US FROM JAPAN" (WE'RE ONLY A FEW DAYS REMOVED FROM THE FUKUSHIMA CATASTROPHE), SAYS THE OTHER, "IN THE END, THEY'RE JUST A BIG HEADACHE."

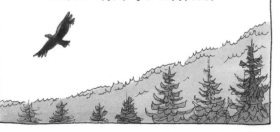

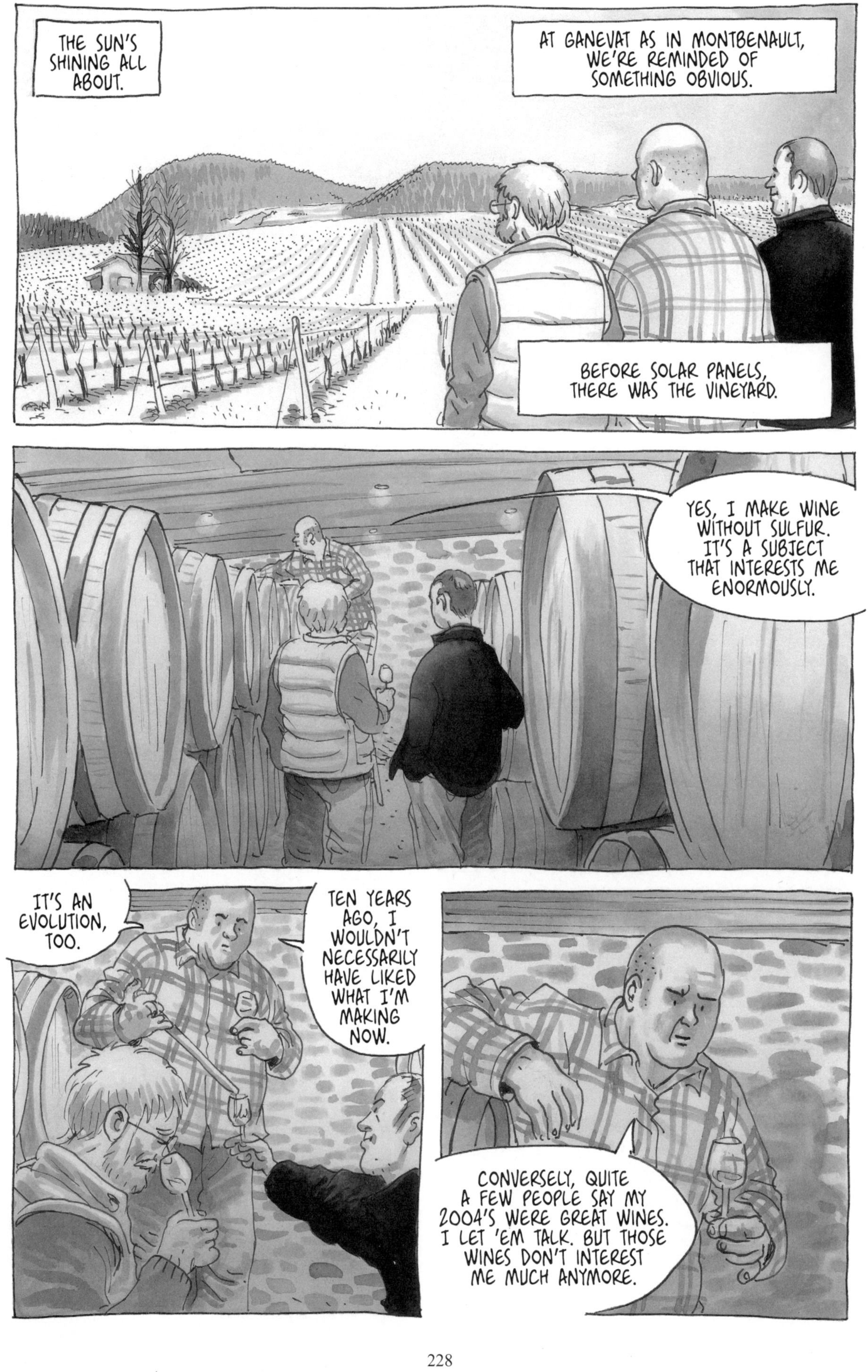
THE SUN'S SHINING ALL ABOUT.
AT GANEVAT AS IN MONTBENAULT, WE'RE REMINDED OF SOMETHING OBVIOUS.
BEFORE SOLAR PANELS, THERE WAS THE VINEYARD.
YES, I MAKE WINE WITHOUT SULFUR. IT'S A SUBJECT THAT INTERESTS ME ENORMOUSLY.
IT'S AN EVOLUTION, TOO.
TEN YEARS AGO, I WOULDN'T NECESSARILY HAVE LIKED WHAT I'M MAKING NOW.
CONVERSELY, QUITE A FEW PEOPLE SAY MY 2004'S WERE GREAT WINES. I LET 'EM TALK. BUT THOSE WINES DON'T INTEREST ME MUCH ANYMORE.

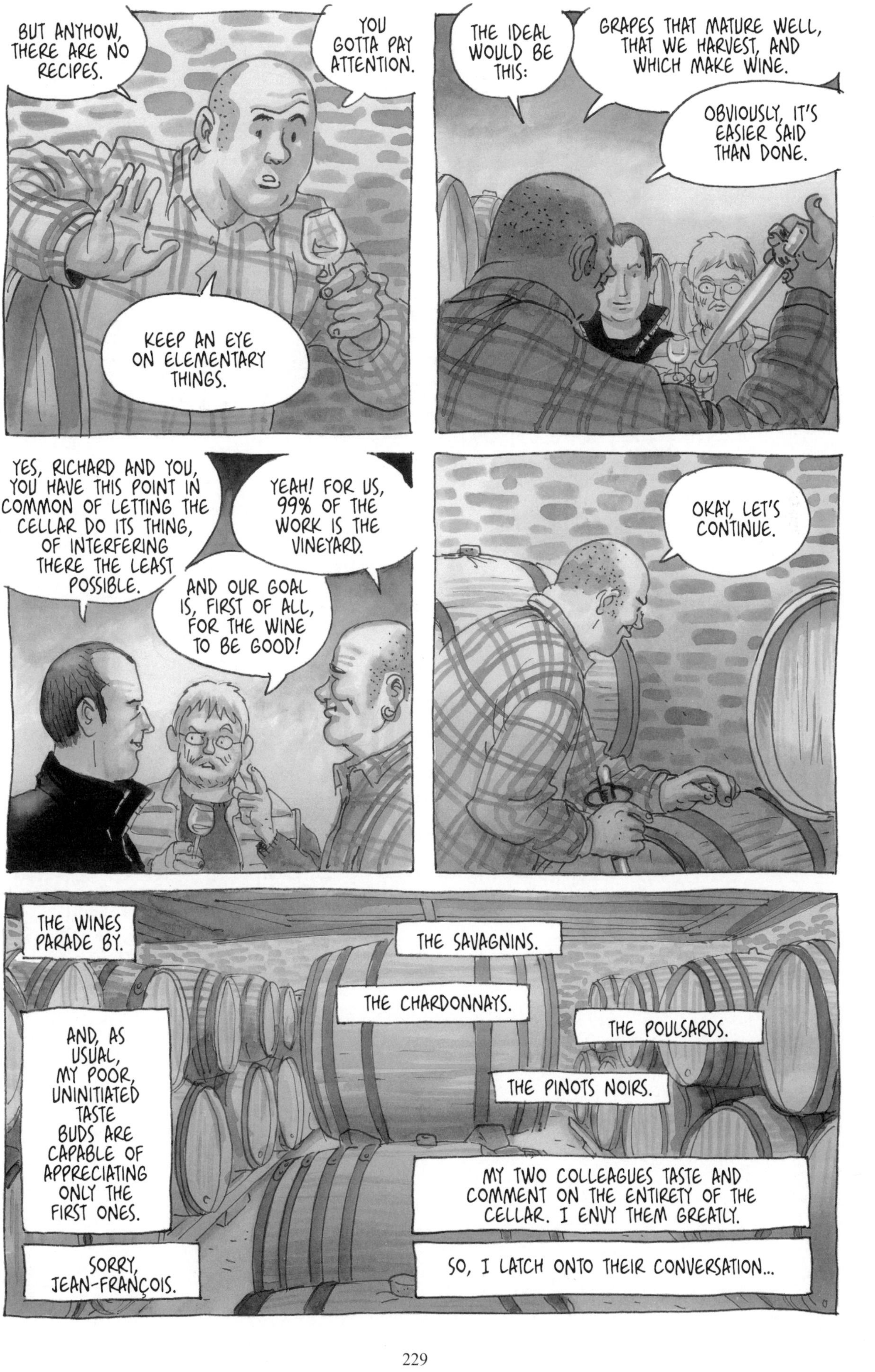
BUT ANYHOW, THERE ARE NO RECIPES.
YOU GOTTA PAY ATTENTION.
KEEP AN EYE ON ELEMENTARY THINGS.
THE IDEAL WOULD BE THIS:
GRAPES THAT MATURE WELL, THAT WE HARVEST, AND WHICH MAKE WINE.
OBVIOUSLY, IT'S EASIER SAID THAN DONE.
YES, RICHARD AND YOU, YOU HAVE THIS POINT IN COMMON OF LETTING THE CELLAR DO ITS THING, OF INTERFERING THERE THE LEAST POSSIBLE.
YEAH! FOR US, 99% OF THE WORK IS THE VINEYARD.
AND OUR GOAL IS, FIRST OF ALL, FOR THE WINE TO BE GOOD!
OKAY, LET'S CONTINUE.
THE WINES PARADE BY.
THE SAVAGNINS.
THE CHARDONNAYS.
THE POULSARDS.
THE PINOTS NOIRS.
AND, AS USUAL, MY POOR, UNINITIATED TASTE BUDS ARE CAPABLE OF APPRECIATING ONLY THE FIRST ONES.
MY TWO COLLEAGUES TASTE AND COMMENT ON THE ENTIRETY OF THE CELLAR. I ENVY THEM GREATLY.
SORRY, JEAN-FRANÇOIS.
SO, I LATCH ONTO THEIR CONVERSATION...

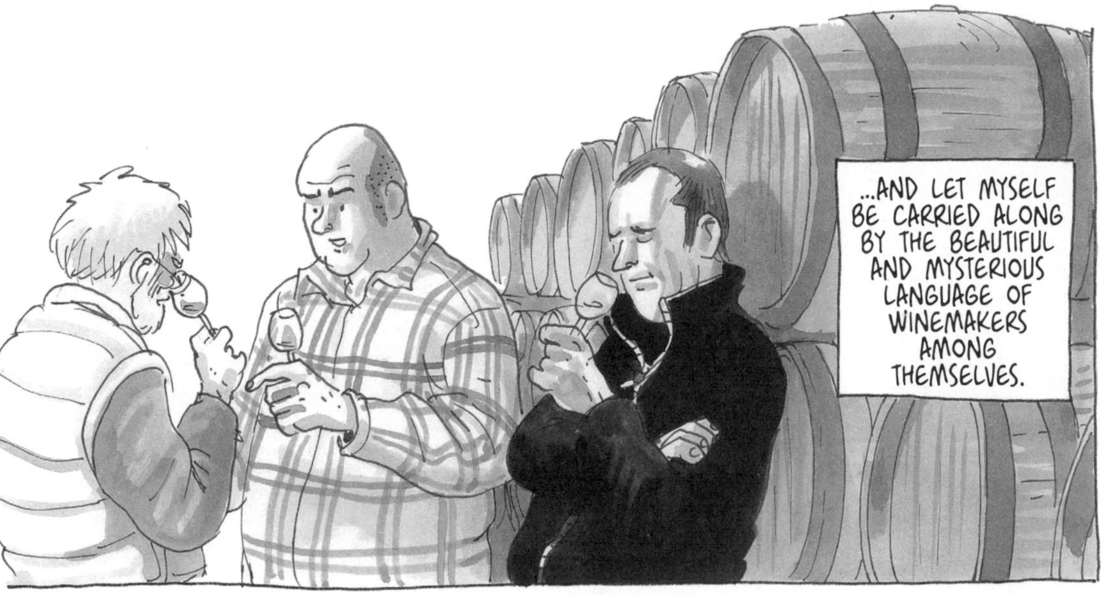
...AND LET MYSELF BE CARRIED ALONG BY THE BEAUTIFUL AND MYSTERIOUS LANGUAGE OF WINEMAKERS AMONG THEMSELVES.

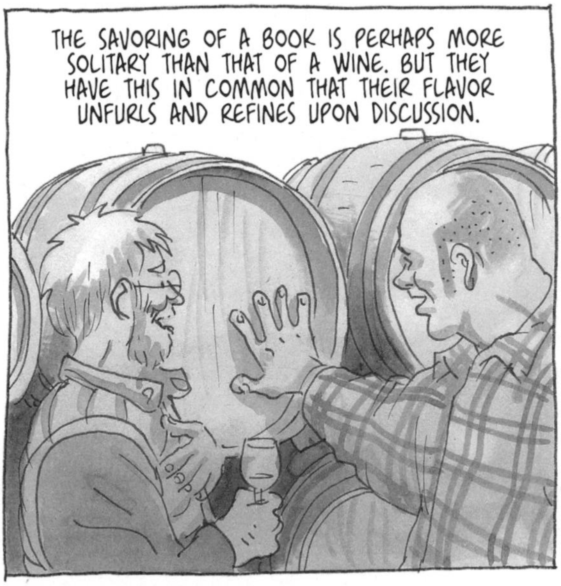
THE SAVORING OF A BOOK IS PERHAPS MORE SOLITARY THAN THAT OF A WINE. BUT THEY HAVE THIS IN COMMON THAT THEIR FLAVOR UNFURLS AND REFINES UPON DISCUSSION.

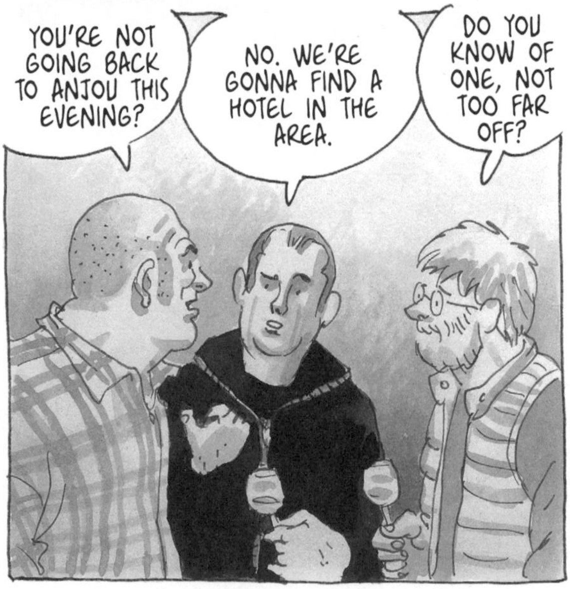
YOU'RE NOT GOING BACK TO ANJOU THIS EVENING?
NO. WE'RE GONNA FIND A HOTEL IN THE AREA.
DO YOU KNOW OF ONE, NOT TOO FAR OFF?

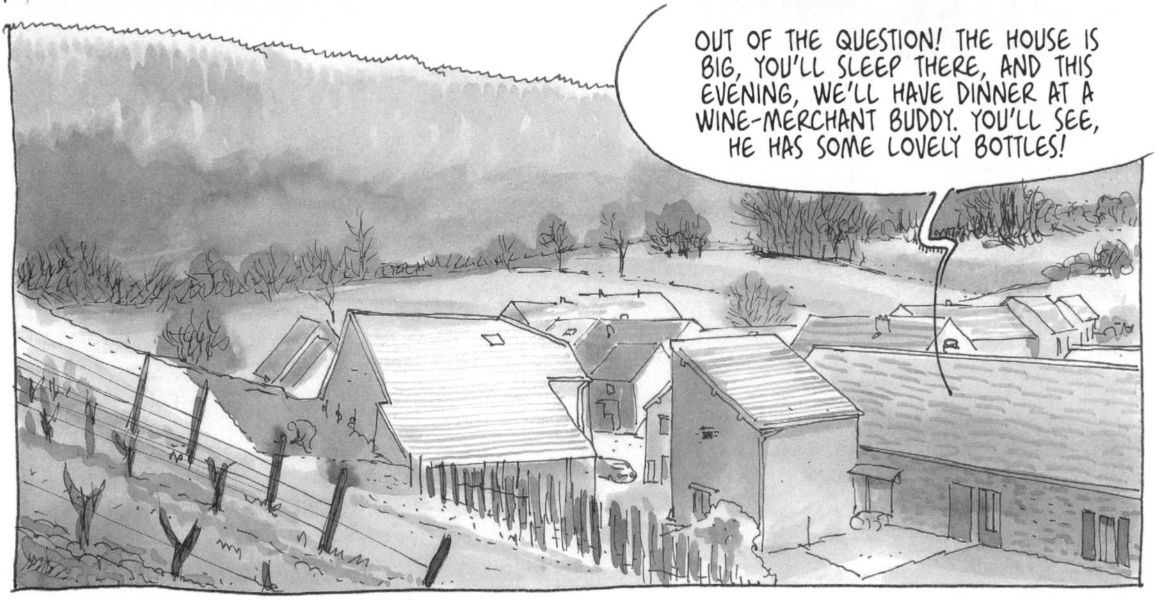
OUT OF THE QUESTION! THE HOUSE IS BIG, YOU'LL SLEEP THERE, AND THIS EVENING, WE'LL HAVE DINNER AT A WINE-MERCHANT BUDDY. YOU'LL SEE, HE HAS SOME LOVELY BOTTLES!

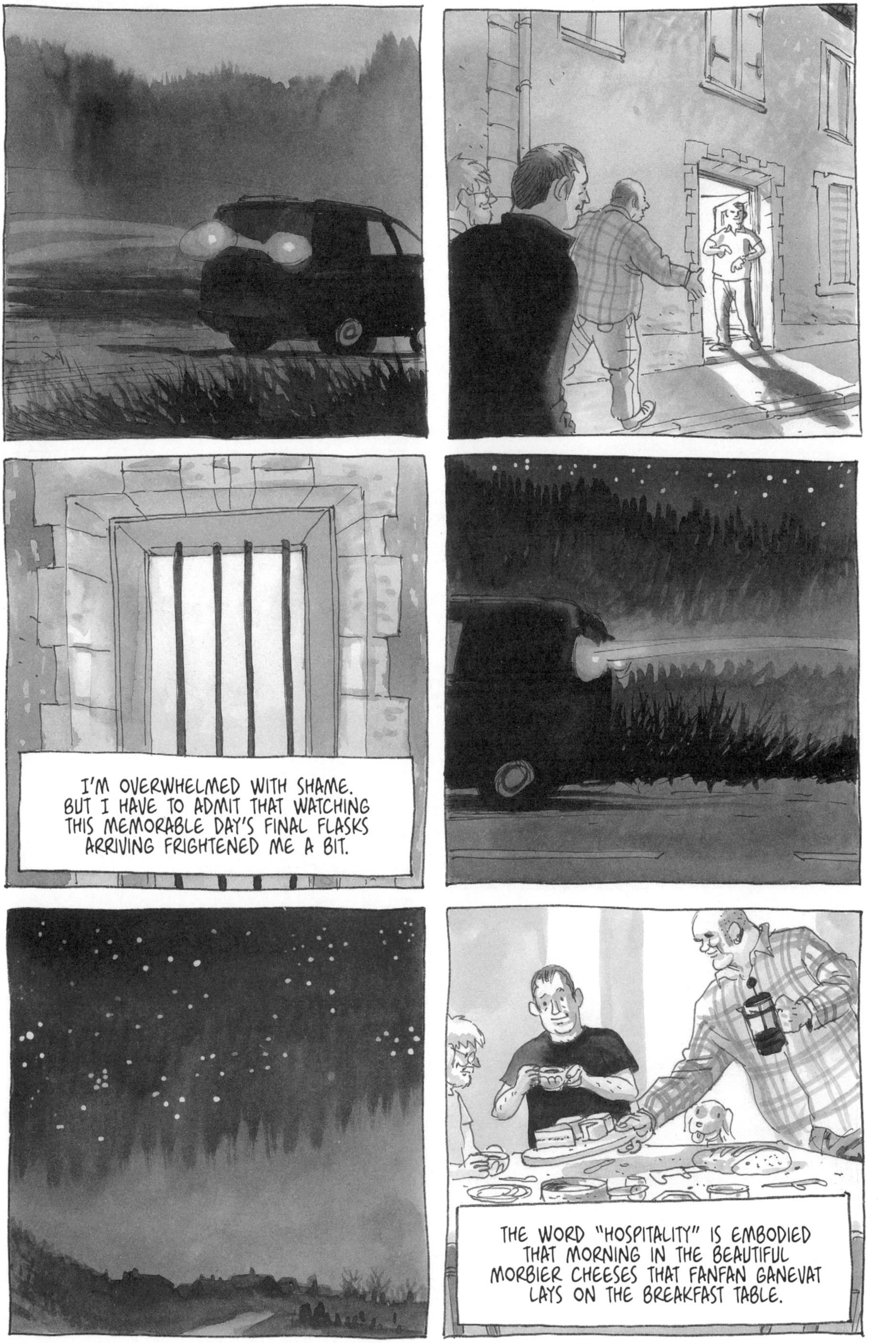
I'M OVERWHELMED WITH SHAME. BUT I HAVE TO ADMIT THAT WATCHING THIS MEMORABLE DAY'S FINAL FLASKS ARRIVING FRIGHTENED ME A BIT.
THE WORD "HOSPITALITY" IS EMBODIED THAT MORNING IN THE BEAUTIFUL MORBIER CHEESES THAT FANFAN GANEVAT LAYS ON THE BREAKFAST TABLE.

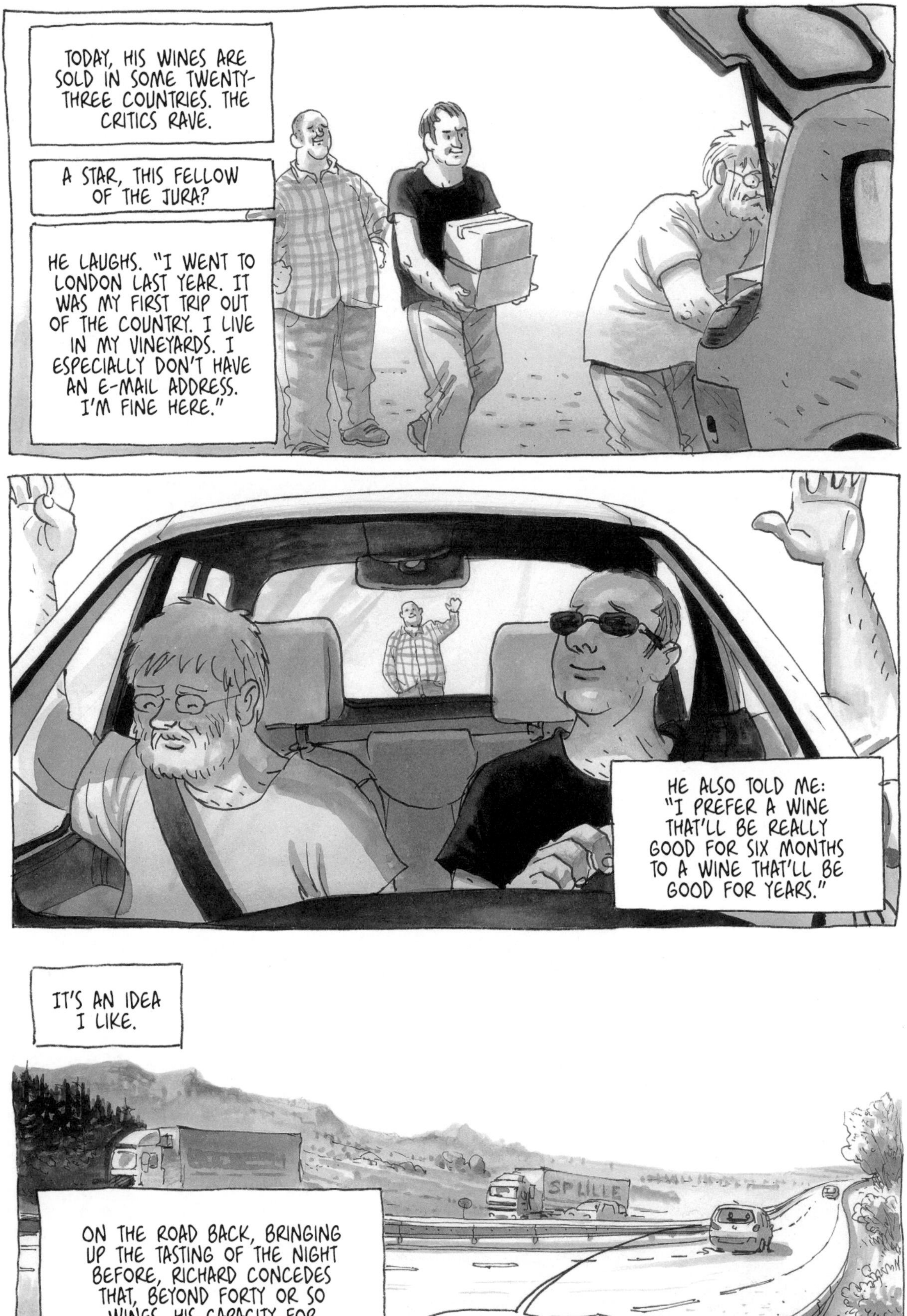

TODAY, HIS WINES ARE SOLD IN SOME TWENTY-THREE COUNTRIES. THE CRITICS RAVE.
A STAR, THIS FELLOW OF THE JURA?
HE LAUGHS. "I WENT TO LONDON LAST YEAR. IT WAS MY FIRST TRIP OUT OF THE COUNTRY. I LIVE IN MY VINEYARDS. I ESPECIALLY DON'T HAVE AN E-MAIL ADDRESS. I'M FINE HERE."
HE ALSO TOLD ME: "I PREFER A WINE THAT'LL BE REALLY GOOD FOR SIX MONTHS TO A WINE THAT'LL BE GOOD FOR YEARS."
IT'S AN IDEA I LIKE.
ON THE ROAD BACK, BRINGING UP THE TASTING OF THE NIGHT BEFORE, RICHARD CONCEDES THAT, BEYOND FORTY OR SO WINES, HIS CAPACITY FOR TASTING DECLINES A BIT.
AMATEUR!

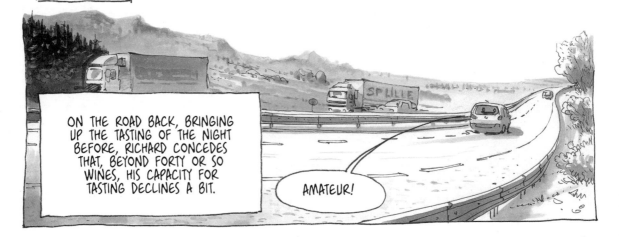

CHAPTER EIGHTEEN

NIELLUCCIO, VERMENTINU, BIANCO GENTILE AND OUBAPO

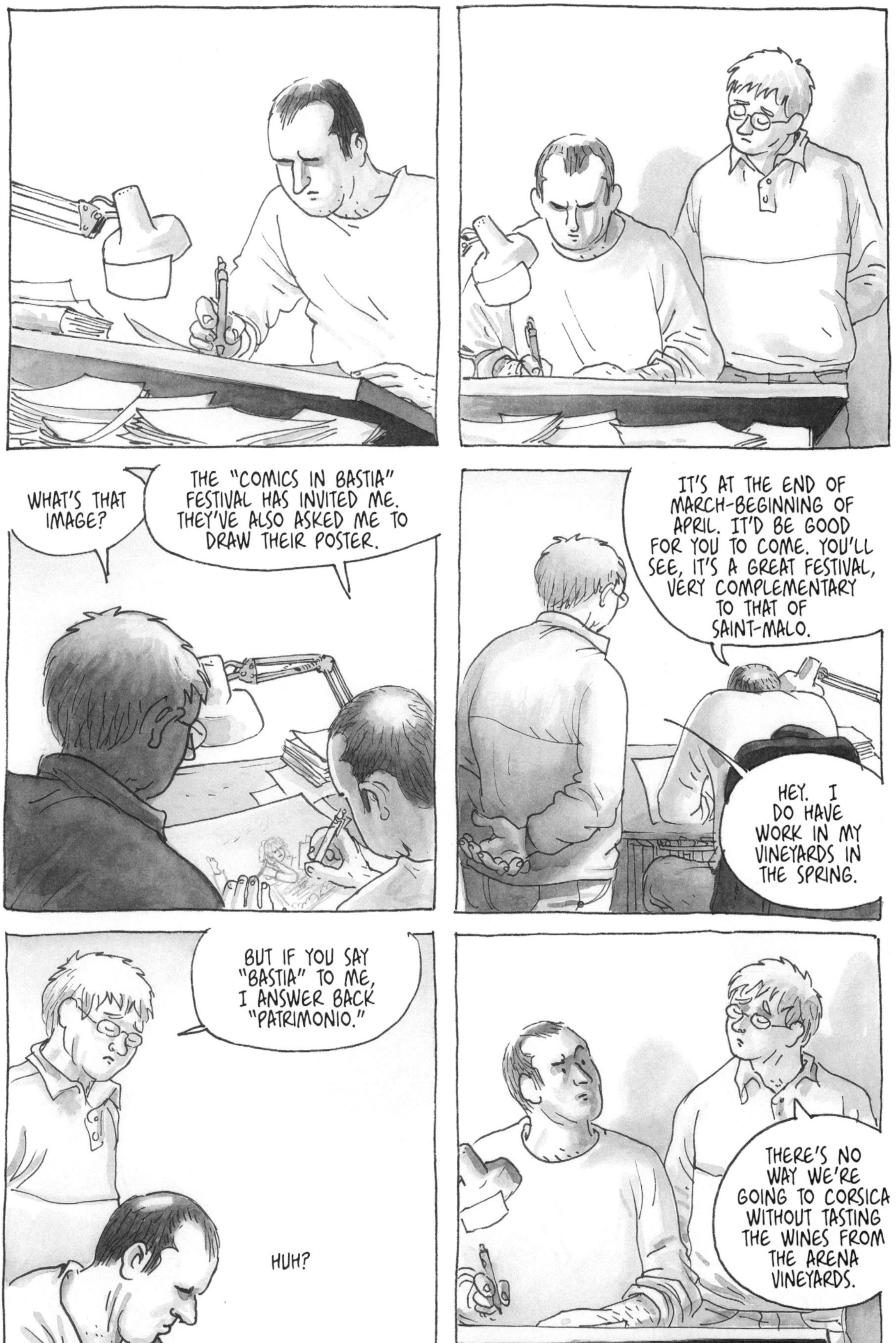
WHAT'S THAT IMAGE?
THE "COMICS IN BASTIA" FESTIVAL HAS INVITED ME. THEY'VE ALSO ASKED ME TO DRAW THEIR POSTER.
IT'S AT THE END OF MARCH-BEGINNING OF APRIL. IT'D BE GOOD FOR YOU TO COME. YOU'LL SEE, IT'S A GREAT FESTIVAL, VERY COMPLEMENTARY TO THAT OF SAINT-MALO.
HEY. I DO HAVE WORK IN MY VINEYARDS IN THE SPRING.
BUT IF YOU SAY "BASTIA" TO ME, I ANSWER BACK "PATRIMONIO."
HUH?
THERE'S NO WAY WE'RE GOING TO CORSICA WITHOUT TASTING THE WINES FROM THE ARENA VINEYARDS.

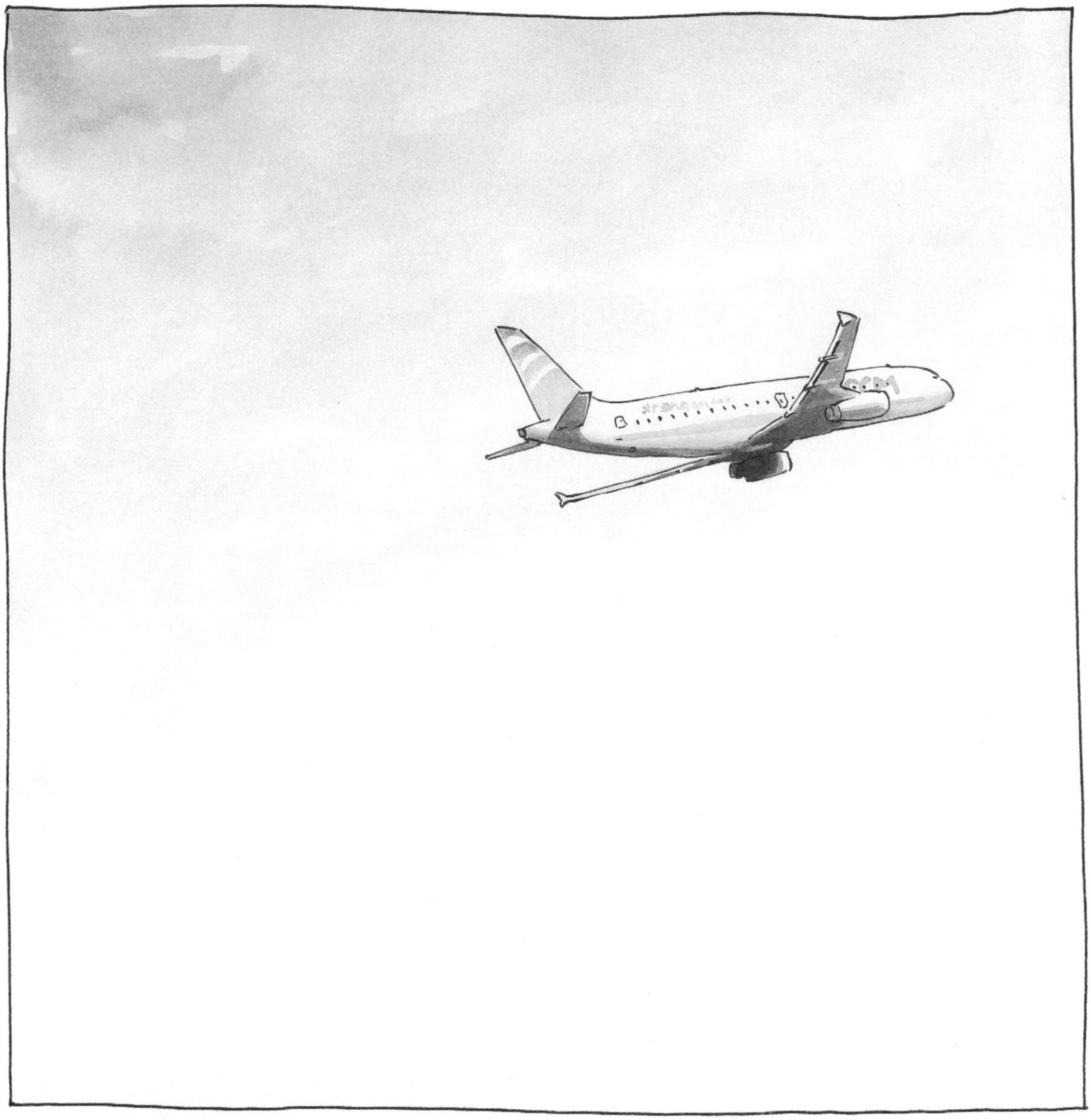

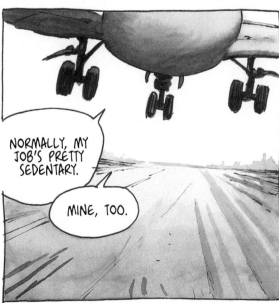

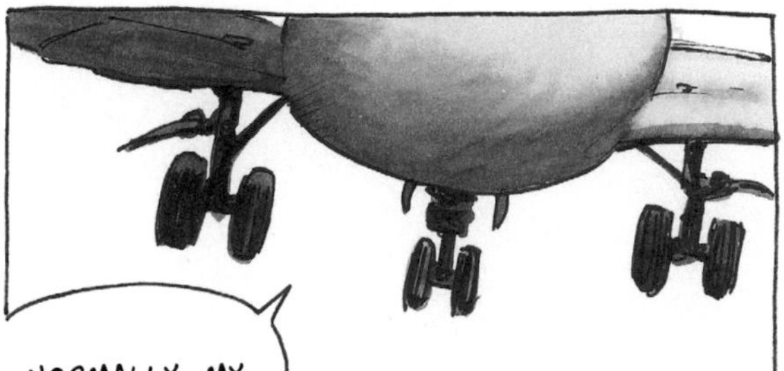
NORMALLY, MY JOB'S PRETTY SEDENTARY.
MINE, TOO.

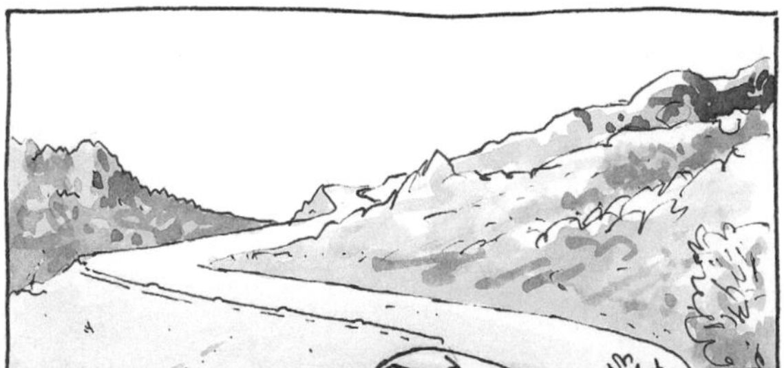

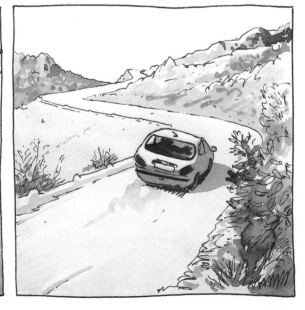

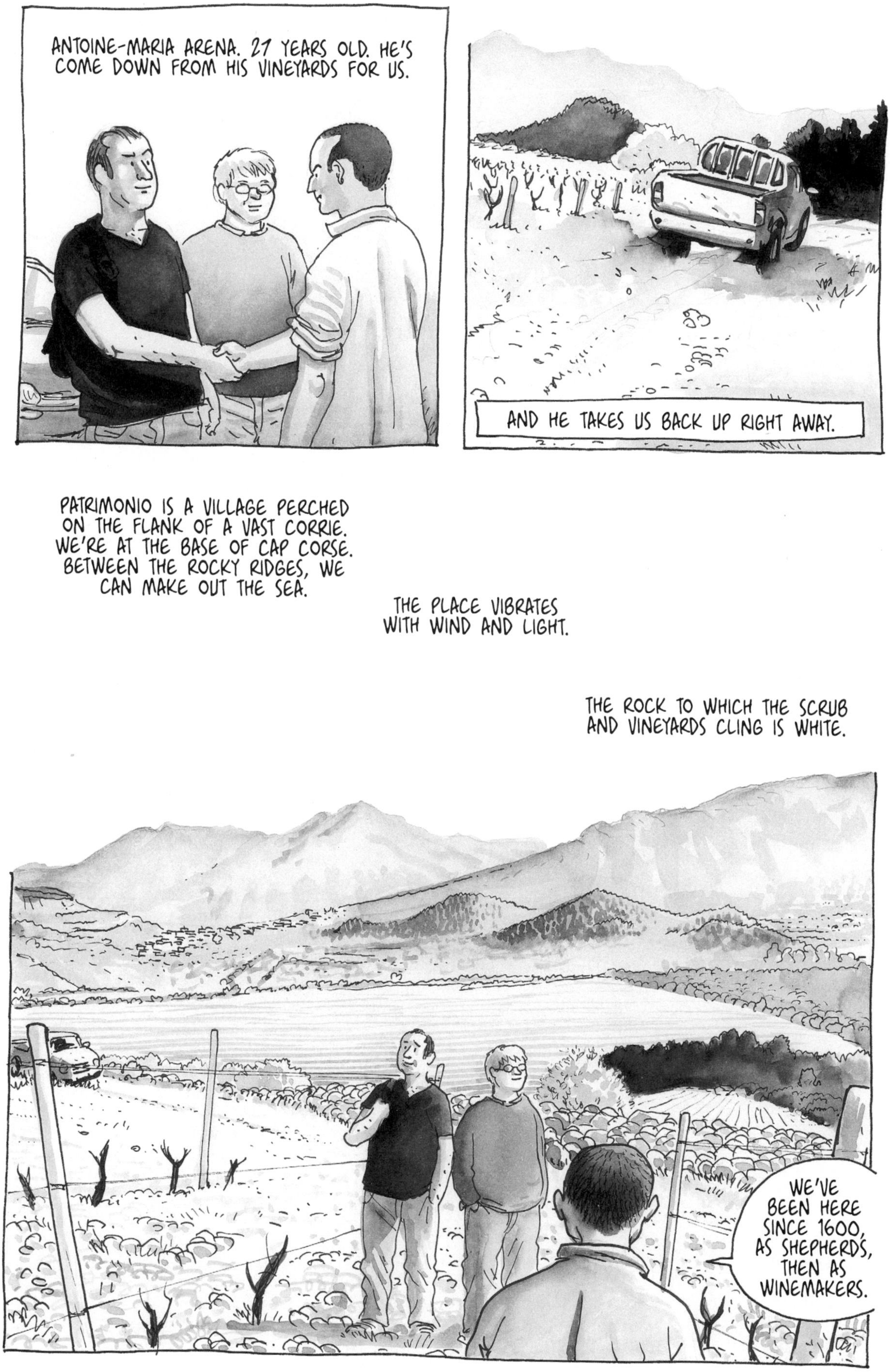
ANTOINE-MARIA ARENA. 27 YEARS OLD. HE'S COME DOWN FROM HIS VINEYARDS FOR US.
AND HE TAKES US BACK UP RIGHT AWAY.
PATRIMONIO IS A VILLAGE PERCHED ON THE FLANK OF A VAST CORRIE. WE'RE AT THE BASE OF CAP CORSE. BETWEEN THE ROCKY RIDGES, WE CAN MAKE OUT THE SEA.
THE PLACE VIBRATES WITH WIND AND LIGHT.
THE ROCK TO WHICH THE SCRUB AND VINEYARDS CLING IS WHITE.
WE'VE BEEN HERE SINCE 1600, AS SHEPHERDS, THEN AS WINEMAKERS.

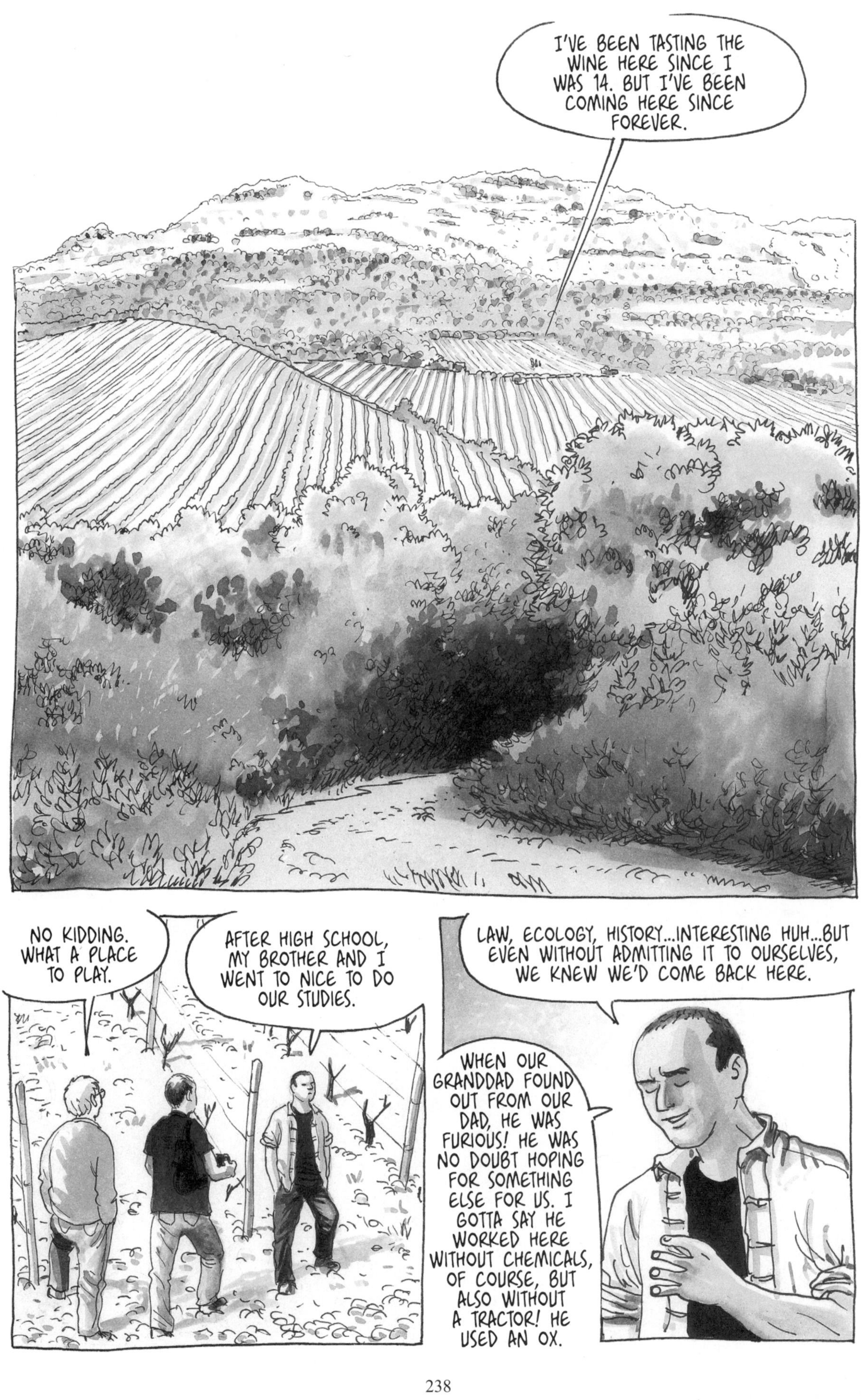

I'VE BEEN TASTING THE WINE HERE SINCE I WAS 14. BUT I'VE BEEN COMING HERE SINCE FOREVER.
NO KIDDING. WHAT A PLACE TO PLAY.
AFTER HIGH SCHOOL, MY BROTHER AND I WENT TO NICE TO DO OUR STUDIES.
LAW, ECOLOGY, HISTORY...INTERESTING HUH...BUT EVEN WITHOUT ADMITTING IT TO OURSELVES, WE KNEW WE'D COME BACK HERE.
WHEN OUR GRANDDAD FOUND OUT FROM OUR DAD, HE WAS FURIOUS! HE WAS NO DOUBT HOPING FOR SOMETHING ELSE FOR US. I GOTTA SAY HE WORKED HERE WITHOUT CHEMICALS, OF COURSE, BUT ALSO WITHOUT A TRACTOR! HE USED AN OX.

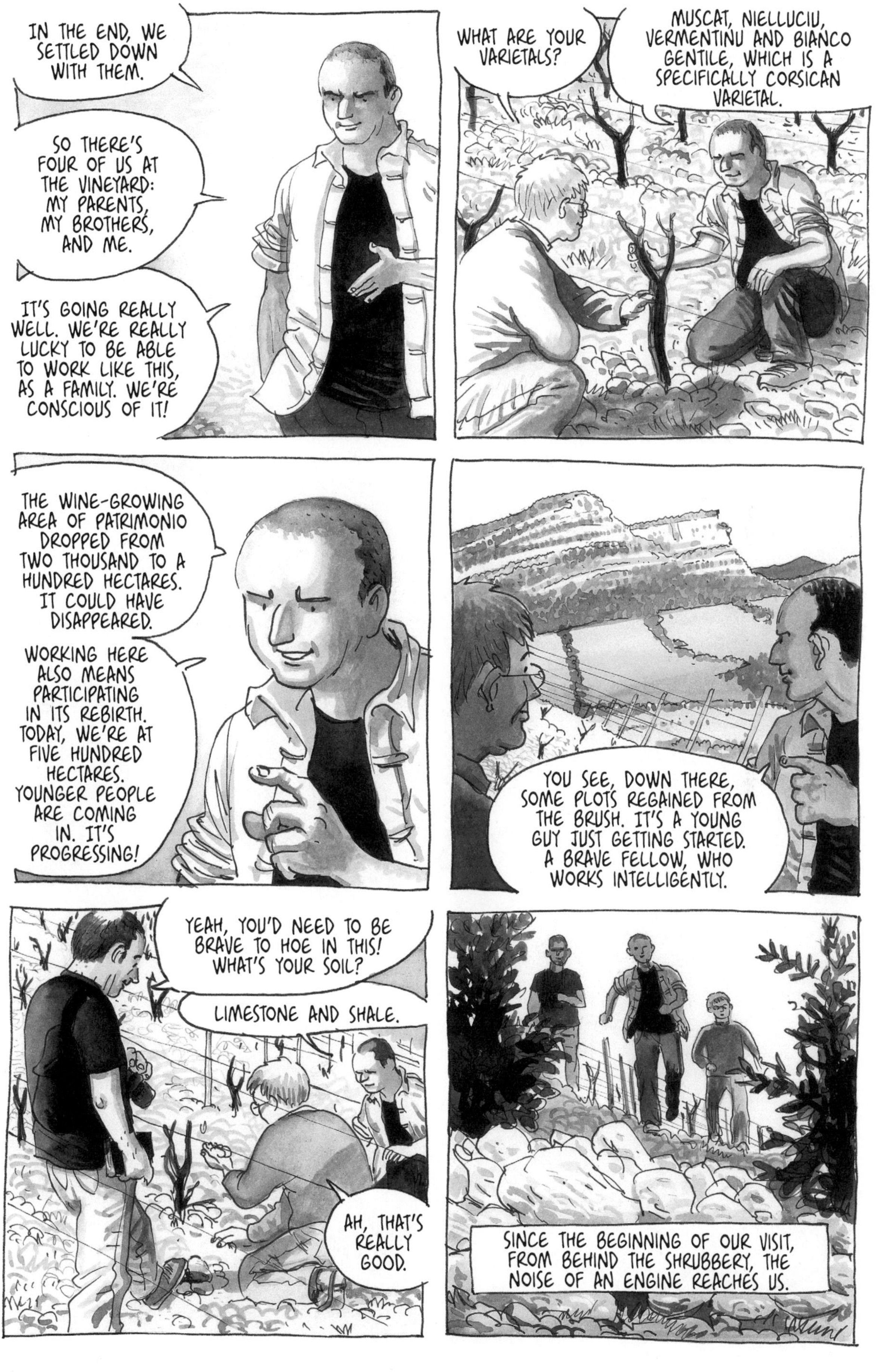
IN THE END, WE SETTLED DOWN WITH THEM.
SO THERE'S FOUR OF US AT THE VINEYARD: MY PARENTS, MY BROTHERS, AND ME.
IT'S GOING REALLY WELL. WE'RE REALLY LUCKY TO BE ABLE TO WORK LIKE THIS, AS A FAMILY. WE'RE CONSCIOUS OF IT!
WHAT ARE YOUR VARIETALS?
MUSCAT, NIELLUCIU, VERMENTINU AND BIANCO GENTILE, WHICH IS A SPECIFICALLY CORSICAN VARIETAL.
THE WINE-GROWING AREA OF PATRIMONIO DROPPED FROM TWO THOUSAND TO A HUNDRED HECTARES. IT COULD HAVE DISAPPEARED.
WORKING HERE ALSO MEANS PARTICIPATING IN ITS REBIRTH. TODAY, WE'RE AT FIVE HUNDRED HECTARES. YOUNGER PEOPLE ARE COMING IN. IT'S PROGRESSING!
YOU SEE, DOWN THERE, SOME PLOTS REGAINED FROM THE BRUSH. IT'S A YOUNG GUY JUST GETTING STARTED. A BRAVE FELLOW, WHO WORKS INTELLIGENTLY.
YEAH, YOU'D NEED TO BE BRAVE TO HOE IN THIS! WHAT'S YOUR SOIL?
LIMESTONE AND SHALE.
AH, THAT'S REALLY GOOD.
SINCE THE BEGINNING OF OUR VISIT, FROM BEHIND THE SHRUBBERY, THE NOISE OF AN ENGINE REACHES US.

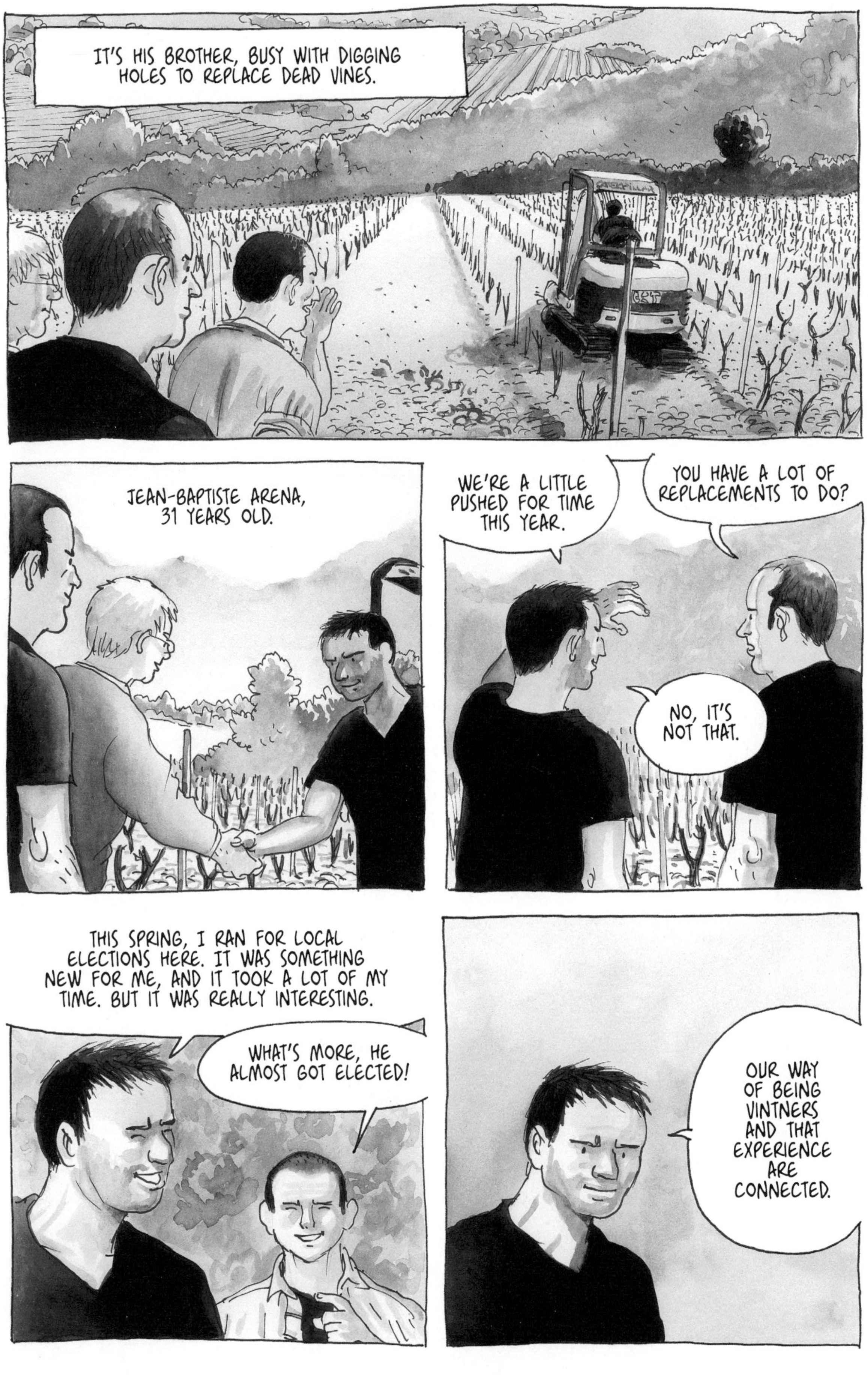
IT'S HIS BROTHER, BUSY WITH DIGGING HOLES TO REPLACE DEAD VINES.
JEAN-BAPTISTE ARENA, 31 YEARS OLD.
WE'RE A LITTLE PUSHED FOR TIME THIS YEAR.
YOU HAVE A LOT OF REPLACEMENTS TO DO?
NO, IT'S NOT THAT.
THIS SPRING, I RAN FOR LOCAL ELECTIONS HERE. IT WAS SOMETHING NEW FOR ME, AND IT TOOK A LOT OF MY TIME. BUT IT WAS REALLY INTERESTING.
WHAT'S MORE, HE ALMOST GOT ELECTED!
OUR WAY OF BEING VINTNERS AND THAT EXPERIENCE ARE CONNECTED.

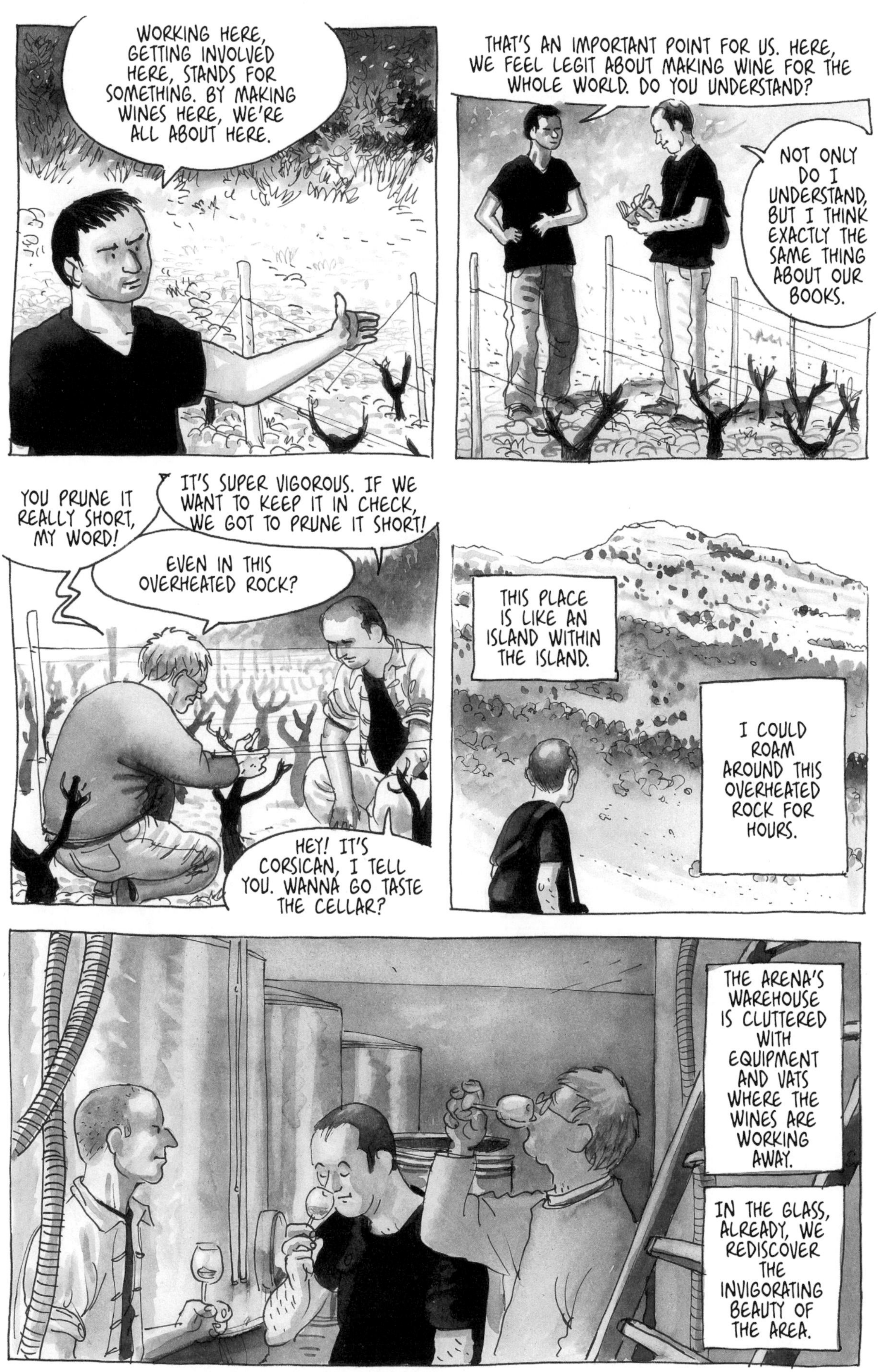
WORKING HERE, GETTING INVOLVED HERE, STANDS FOR SOMETHING. BY MAKING WINES HERE, WE'RE ALL ABOUT HERE.
THAT'S AN IMPORTANT POINT FOR US. HERE, WE FEEL LEGIT ABOUT MAKING WINE FOR THE WHOLE WORLD. DO YOU UNDERSTAND?
NOT ONLY DO I UNDERSTAND, BUT I THINK EXACTLY THE SAME THING ABOUT OUR BOOKS.
YOU PRUNE IT REALLY SHORT, MY WORD!
IT'S SUPER VIGOROUS. IF WE WANT TO KEEP IT IN CHECK, WE GOT TO PRUNE IT SHORT!
EVEN IN THIS OVERHEATED ROCK?
HEY! IT'S CORSICAN, I TELL YOU. WANNA GO TASTE THE CELLAR?
THIS PLACE IS LIKE AN ISLAND WITHIN THE ISLAND.
I COULD ROAM AROUND THIS OVERHEATED ROCK FOR HOURS.
THE ARENA'S WAREHOUSE IS CLUTTERED WITH EQUIPMENT AND VATS WHERE THE WINES ARE WORKING AWAY.
IN THE GLASS, ALREADY, WE REDISCOVER THE INVIGORATING BEAUTY OF THE AREA.

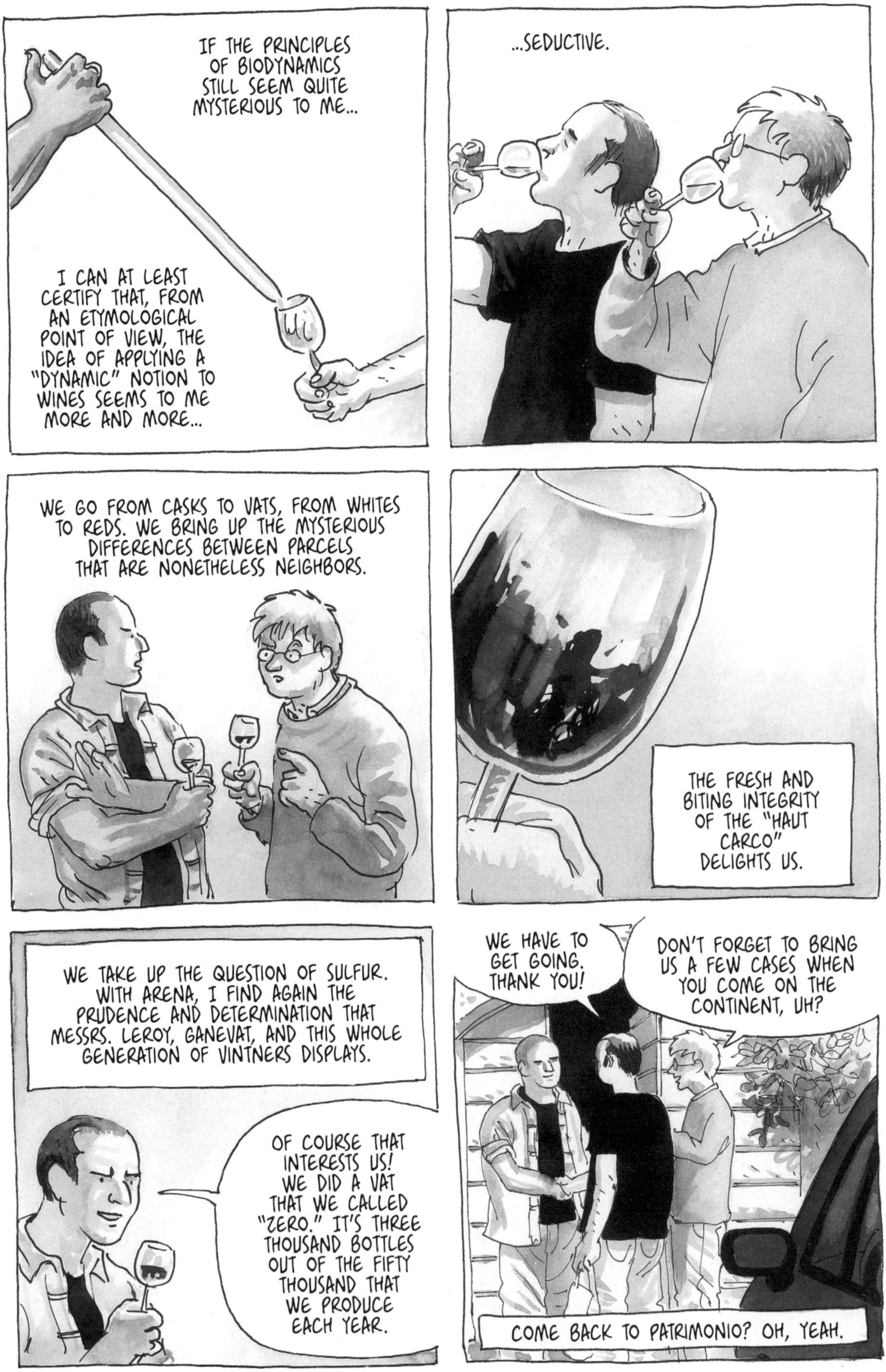
IF THE PRINCIPLES OF BIODYNAMICS STILL SEEM QUITE MYSTERIOUS TO ME...
I CAN AT LEAST CERTIFY THAT, FROM AN ETYMOLOGICAL POINT OF VIEW, THE IDEA OF APPLYING A "DYNAMIC" NOTION TO WINES SEEMS TO ME MORE AND MORE...
...SEDUCTIVE.
WE GO FROM CASKS TO VATS, FROM WHITES TO REDS. WE BRING UP THE MYSTERIOUS DIFFERENCES BETWEEN PARCELS THAT ARE NONETHELESS NEIGHBORS.
THE FRESH AND BITING INTEGRITY OF THE "HAUT CARCO" DELIGHTS US.
WE TAKE UP THE QUESTION OF SULFUR. WITH ARENA, I FIND AGAIN THE PRUDENCE AND DETERMINATION THAT MESSRS. LEROY, GANEVAT, AND THIS WHOLE GENERATION OF VINTNERS DISPLAYS.
OF COURSE THAT INTERESTS US! WE DID A VAT THAT WE CALLED "ZERO." IT'S THREE THOUSAND BOTTLES OUT OF THE FIFTY THOUSAND THAT WE PRODUCE EACH YEAR.
WE HAVE TO GET GOING. THANK YOU!
DON'T FORGET TO BRING US A FEW CASES WHEN YOU COME ON THE CONTINENT, UH?
COME BACK TO PATRIMONIO? OH, YEAH.

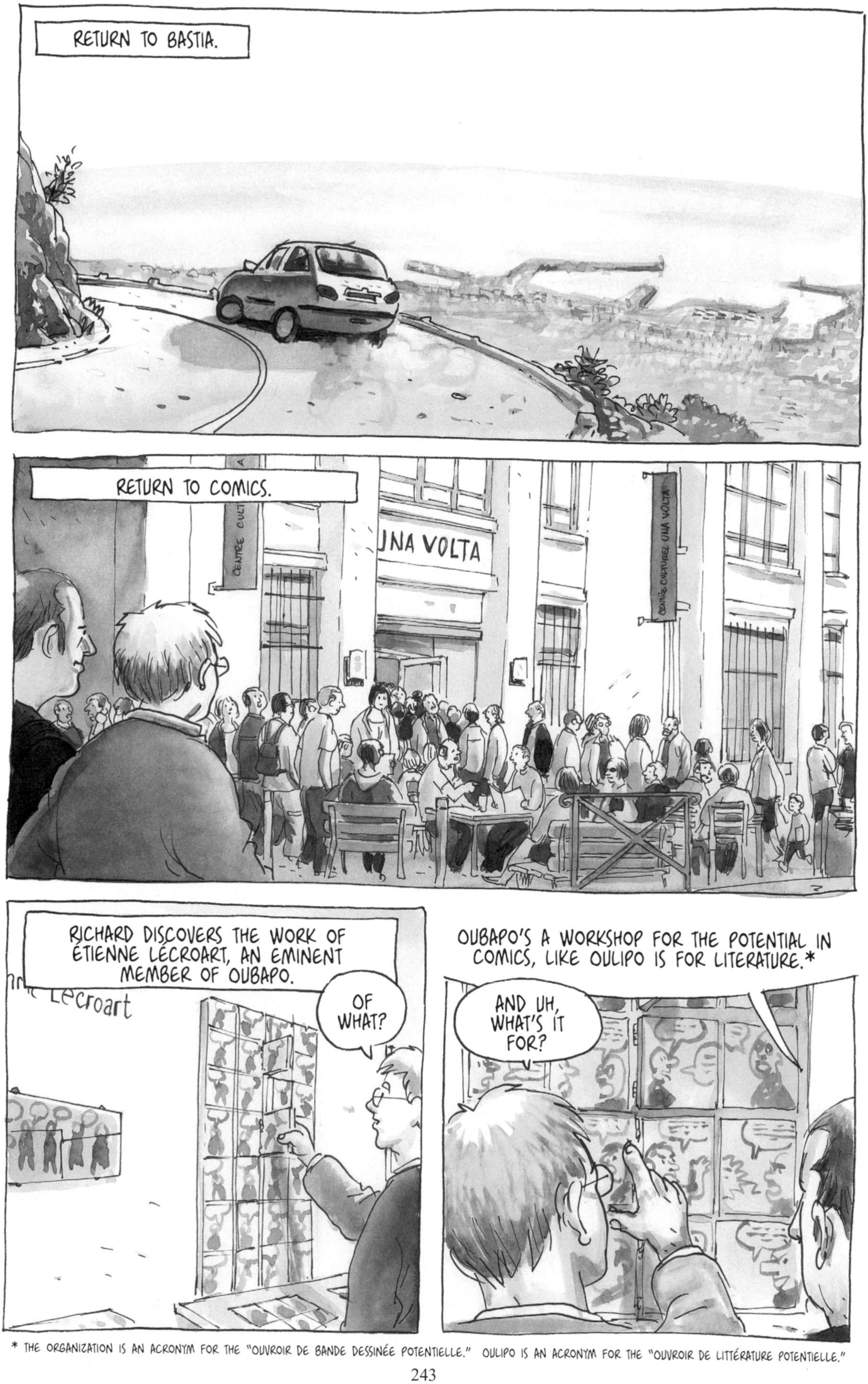
RETURN TO BASTIA.
RETURN TO COMICS.
UNA VOLTA
CENTRE CULTUREL UNA VOLTA
RICHARD DISCOVERS THE WORK OF ÉTIENNE LÉCROART, AN EMINENT MEMBER OF OUBAPO.
OF WHAT?
OUBAPO'S A WORKSHOP FOR THE POTENTIAL IN COMICS, LIKE OULIPO IS FOR LITERATURE.*
AND UH, WHAT'S IT FOR?

* THE ORGANIZATION IS AN ACRONYM FOR THE "OUVROIR DE BANDE DESSINÉE POTENTIELLE." OULIPO IS AN ACRONYM FOR THE "OUVROIR DE LITTÉRATURE POTENTIELLE."

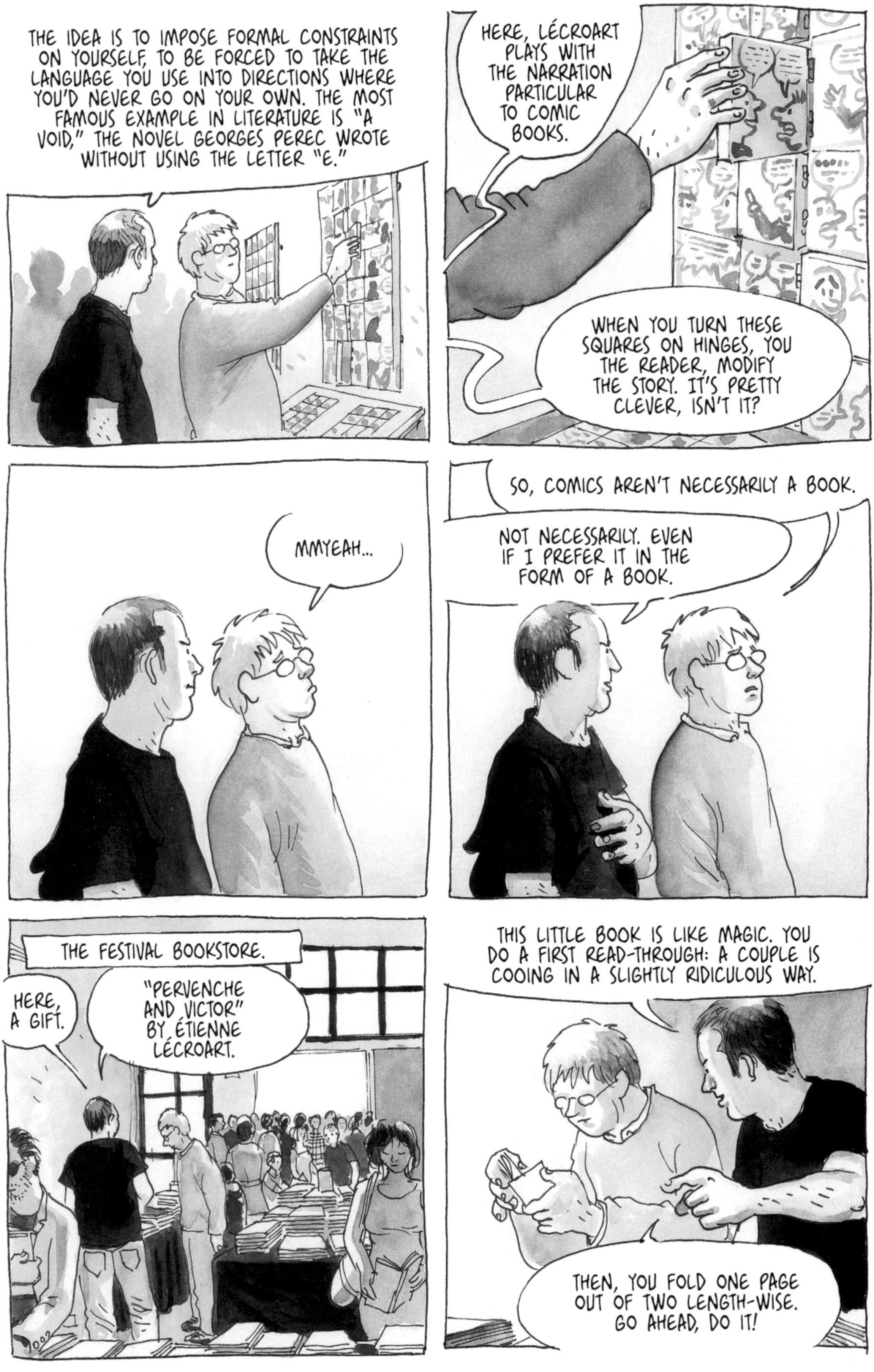
THE IDEA IS TO IMPOSE FORMAL CONSTRAINTS ON YOURSELF, TO BE FORCED TO TAKE THE LANGUAGE YOU USE INTO DIRECTIONS WHERE YOU'D NEVER GO ON YOUR OWN. THE MOST FAMOUS EXAMPLE IN LITERATURE IS "A VOID," THE NOVEL GEORGES PEREC WROTE WITHOUT USING THE LETTER "E."
HERE, LÉCROART PLAYS WITH THE NARRATION PARTICULAR TO COMIC BOOKS.
WHEN YOU TURN THESE SQUARES ON HINGES, YOU THE READER, MODIFY THE STORY. IT'S PRETTY CLEVER, ISN'T IT?
MMYEAH...
SO, COMICS AREN'T NECESSARILY A BOOK.
NOT NECESSARILY. EVEN IF I PREFER IT IN THE FORM OF A BOOK.
THE FESTIVAL BOOKSTORE.
HERE, A GIFT.
"PERVENCHE AND VICTOR" BY ÉTIENNE LÉCROART.
THIS LITTLE BOOK IS LIKE MAGIC. YOU DO A FIRST READ-THROUGH: A COUPLE IS COOING IN A SLIGHTLY RIDICULOUS WAY.
THEN, YOU FOLD ONE PAGE OUT OF TWO LENGTH-WISE. GO AHEAD, DO IT!

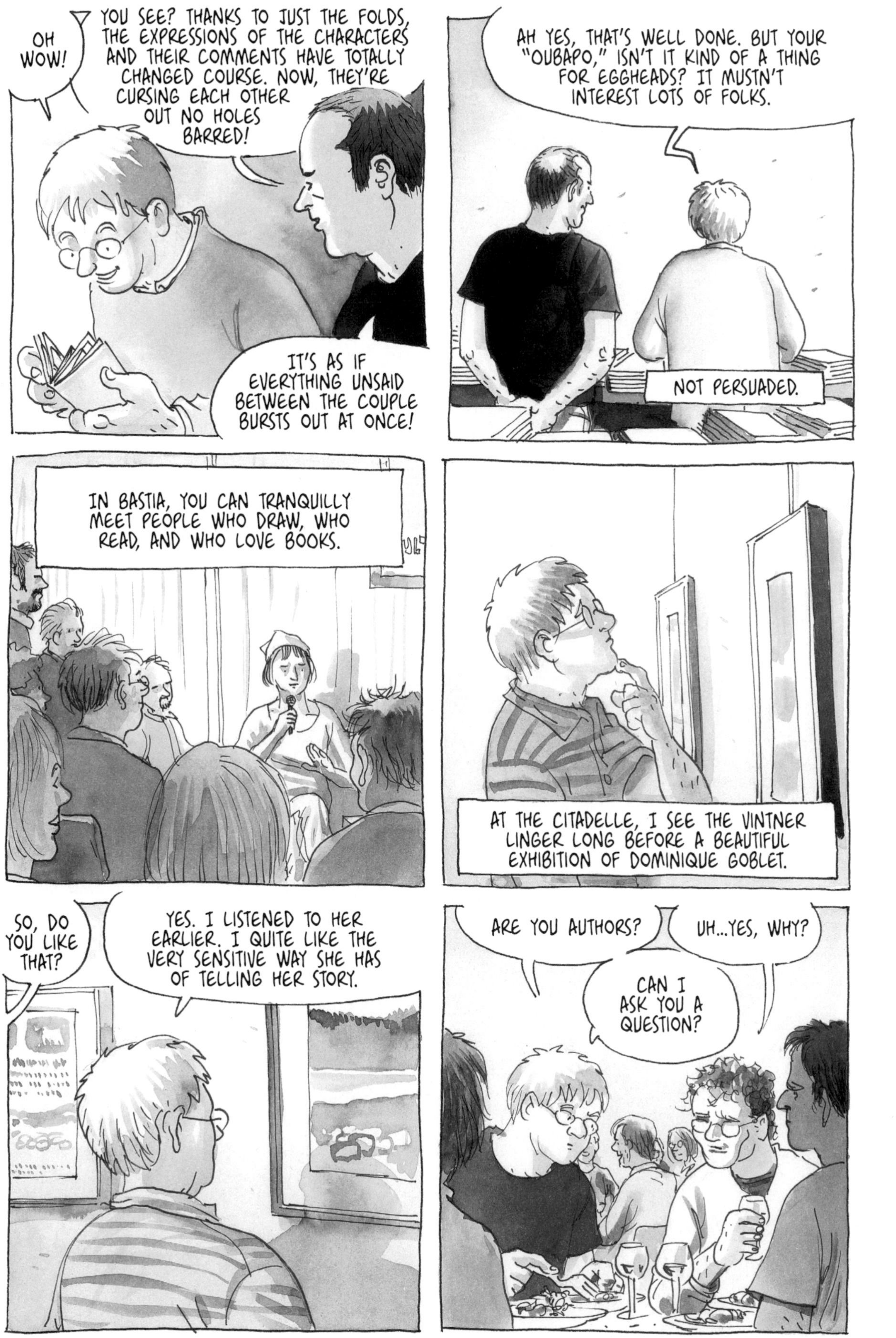
OH WOW!
YOU SEE? THANKS TO JUST THE FOLDS, THE EXPRESSIONS OF THE CHARACTERS AND THEIR COMMENTS HAVE TOTALLY CHANGED COURSE. NOW, THEY'RE CURSING EACH OTHER OUT NO HOLES BARRED!
IT'S AS IF EVERYTHING UNSAID BETWEEN THE COUPLE BURSTS OUT AT ONCE!
AH YES, THAT'S WELL DONE. BUT YOUR "OUBAPO," ISN'T IT KIND OF A THING FOR EGGHEADS? IT MUSTN'T INTEREST LOTS OF FOLKS.
NOT PERSUADED.
IN BASTIA, YOU CAN TRANQUILLY MEET PEOPLE WHO DRAW, WHO READ, AND WHO LOVE BOOKS.
AT THE CITADELLE, I SEE THE VINTNER LINGER LONG BEFORE A BEAUTIFUL EXHIBITION OF DOMINIQUE GOBLET.
SO, DO YOU LIKE THAT?
YES. I LISTENED TO HER EARLIER. I QUITE LIKE THE VERY SENSITIVE WAY SHE HAS OF TELLING HER STORY.
ARE YOU AUTHORS?
UH...YES, WHY?
CAN I ASK YOU A QUESTION?

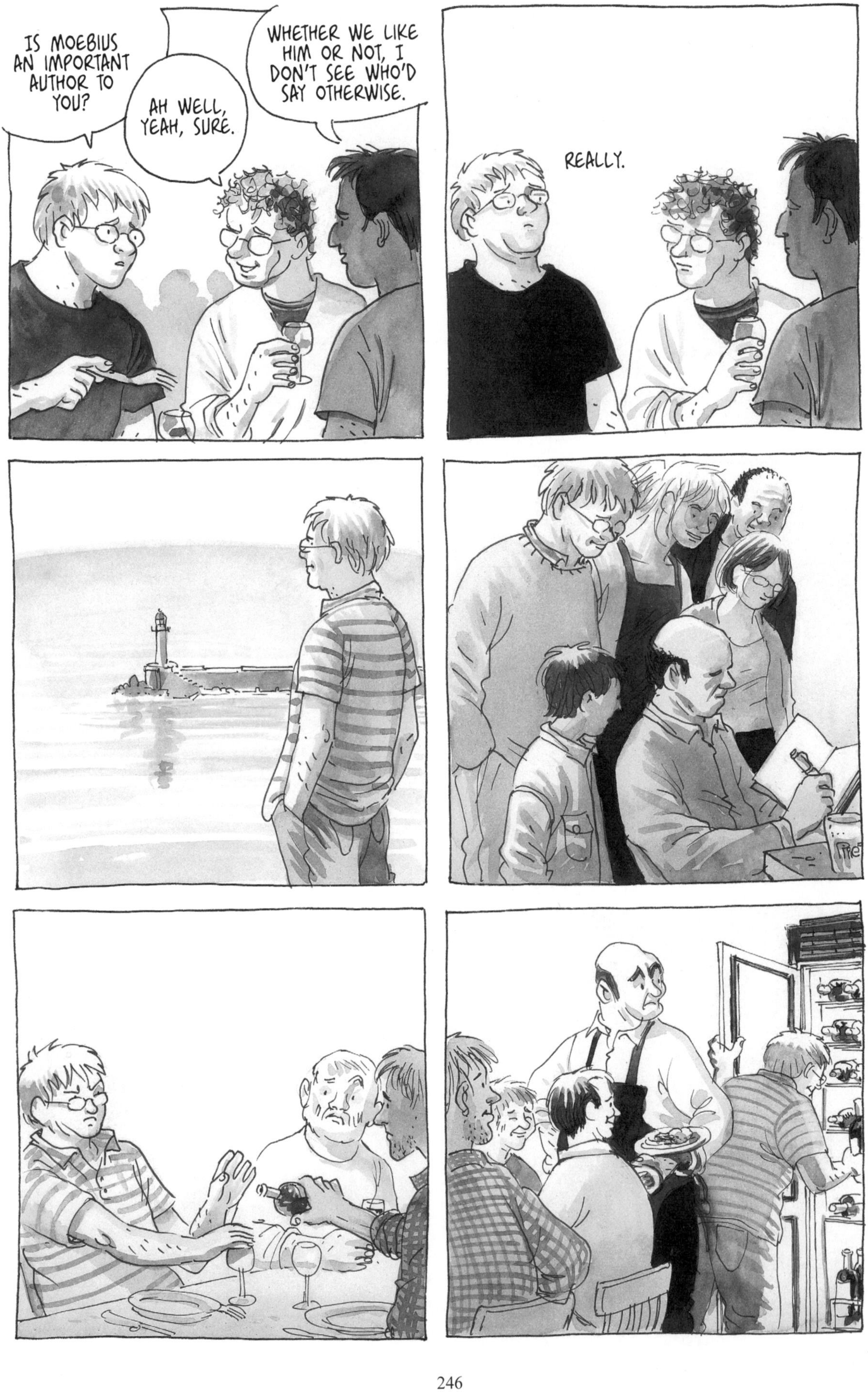
IS MOEBIUS AN IMPORTANT AUTHOR TO YOU?
AH WELL, YEAH, SURE.
WHETHER WE LIKE HIM OR NOT, I DON'T SEE WHO'D SAY OTHERWISE.
REALLY.

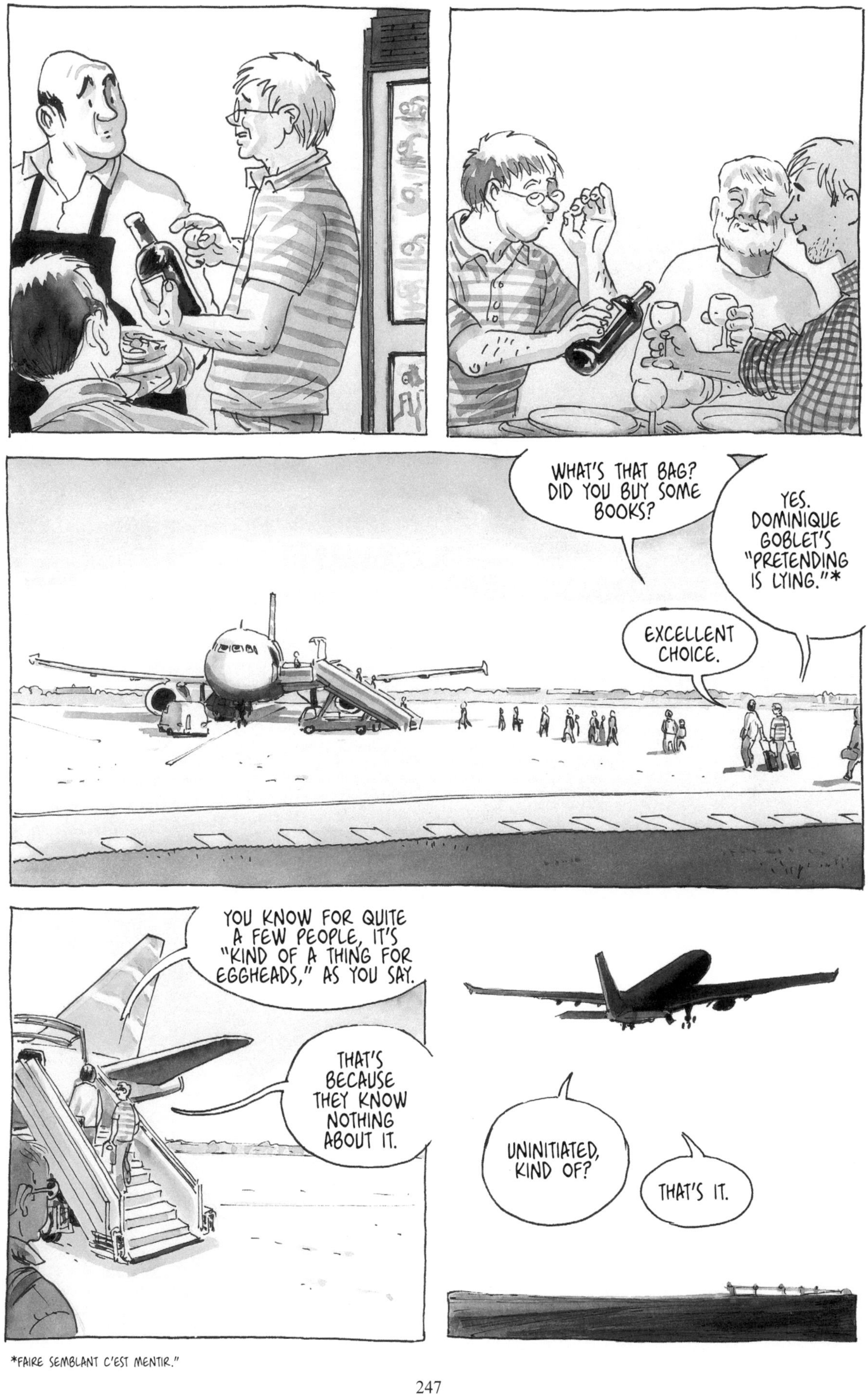
WHAT'S THAT BAG? DID YOU BUY SOME BOOKS?
YES. DOMINIQUE GOBLET'S "PRETENDING IS LYING."*
EXCELLENT CHOICE.
YOU KNOW FOR QUITE A FEW PEOPLE, IT'S "KIND OF A THING FOR EGGHEADS," AS YOU SAY.
THAT'S BECAUSE THEY KNOW NOTHING ABOUT IT.
UNINITIATED, KIND OF?
THAT'S IT.

*FAIRE SEMBLANT C'EST MENTIR."

CHAPTER NINETEEN FINAL REVELATIONS
UNDER A CHERRY
TREE

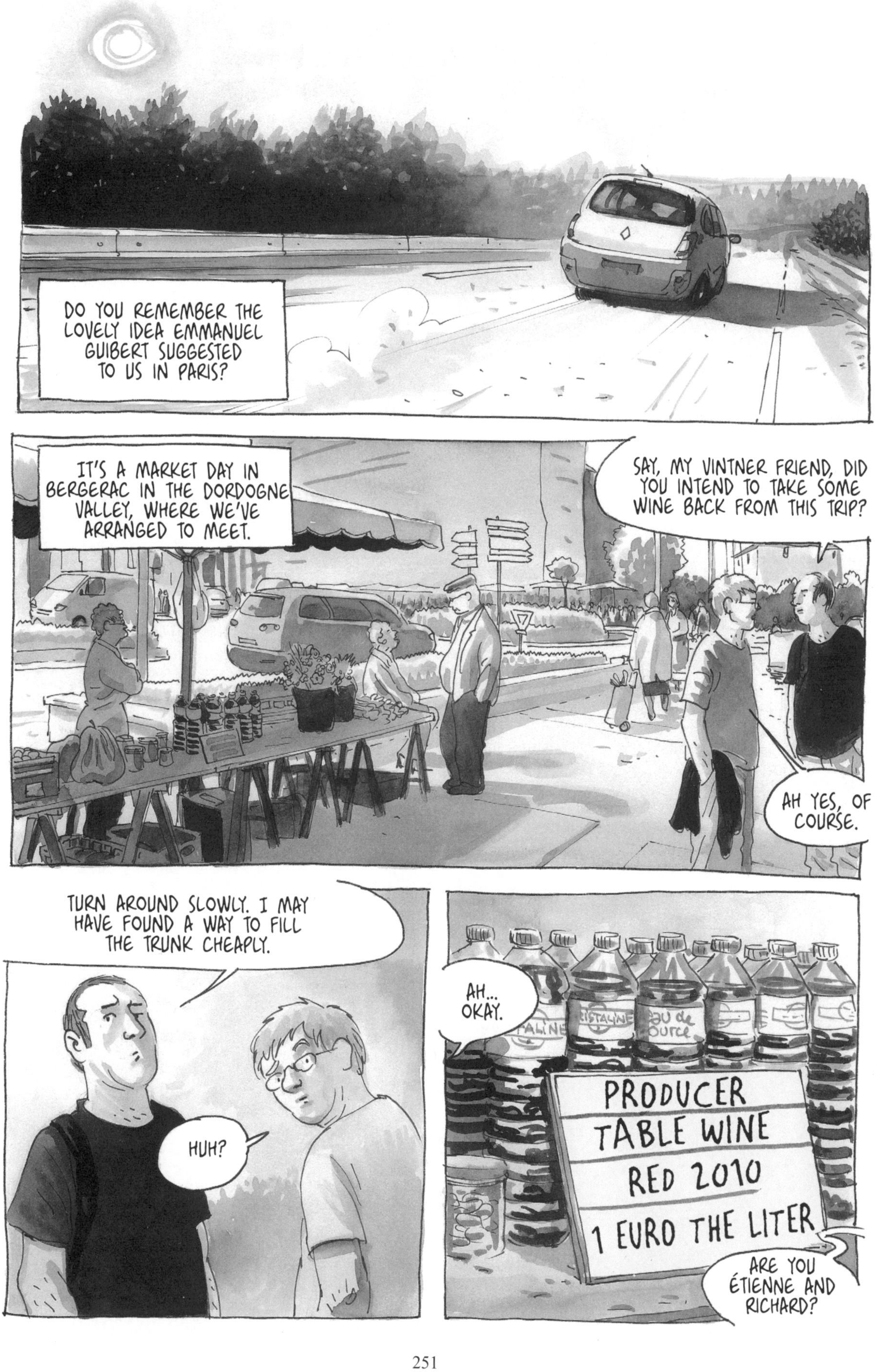
DO YOU REMEMBER THE LOVELY IDEA EMMANUEL GUIBERT SUGGESTED TO US IN PARIS?
IT'S A MARKET DAY IN BERGERAC IN THE DORDOGNE VALLEY, WHERE WE'VE ARRANGED TO MEET.
SAY, MY VINTNER FRIEND, DID YOU INTEND TO TAKE SOME WINE BACK FROM THIS TRIP?
AH YES, OF COURSE.
TURN AROUND SLOWLY. I MAY HAVE FOUND A WAY TO FILL THE TRUNK CHEAPLY.
HUH?
AH... OKAY.
PRODUCER
TABLE WINE
RED 2010
1 EURO THE LITER
ARE YOU ÉTIENNE AND RICHARD?

I'M RÉGIS.

HI.

ROBERT'S AWAITING US AT THE RESTAURANT. SHALL WE?

CRAP. NO TIME TO MAKE ANY PURCHASES.

SO, IN "THE PHOTOGRAPHER" DRAWN BY EMMANUEL, WE DISCOVER THE INCREDIBLE SAGA OF A TEAM OF "DOCTORS WITHOUT BORDERS" IN A WAR-TORN AFGHANISTAN IN 1986.

APRIL 2011. ROBERT, SALÉON-TERRAS AND RÉGIS LANSADE, MEMBERS OF THAT HEROIC BAND, ARE SEATED BEFORE US.

THE WAITRESS HAS JUST PUT ONE OF THEIR BOTTLES ON THE TABLE.

HOW DID YOU SETTLE DOWN HERE?

AH, IT'S A LONG STORY.

FOR ME, THE VINEYARD IS, FIRST OF ALL, A CHILDHOOD MEMORY: MY GRANDFATHER RAN ONE. I ALWAYS LOVED THAT.

IN THE SEVENTIES, DURING MY MEDICAL STUDIES, I WORKED IN A VINEYARD IN VOSNE-ROMANÉE IN BURGUNDY.

AFTER AFGHANISTAN, IN 1990, I SET UP MY MEDICAL PRACTICE IN THE ARDÈCHE.

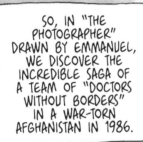

WE CAME BACK TO FRANCE AT THE SAME TIME. I DID STUDIES IN ENOLOGY. THEN I BECAME AN "ENOLOGIST-COUNSELOR," HERE, IN BERGERAC.

MY FATHER WAS A WINEMAKER. HE RIPPED OUT HIS VINEYARD IN THE SIXTIES. I HAD MY OWN CELLAR WHEN I WAS 17!

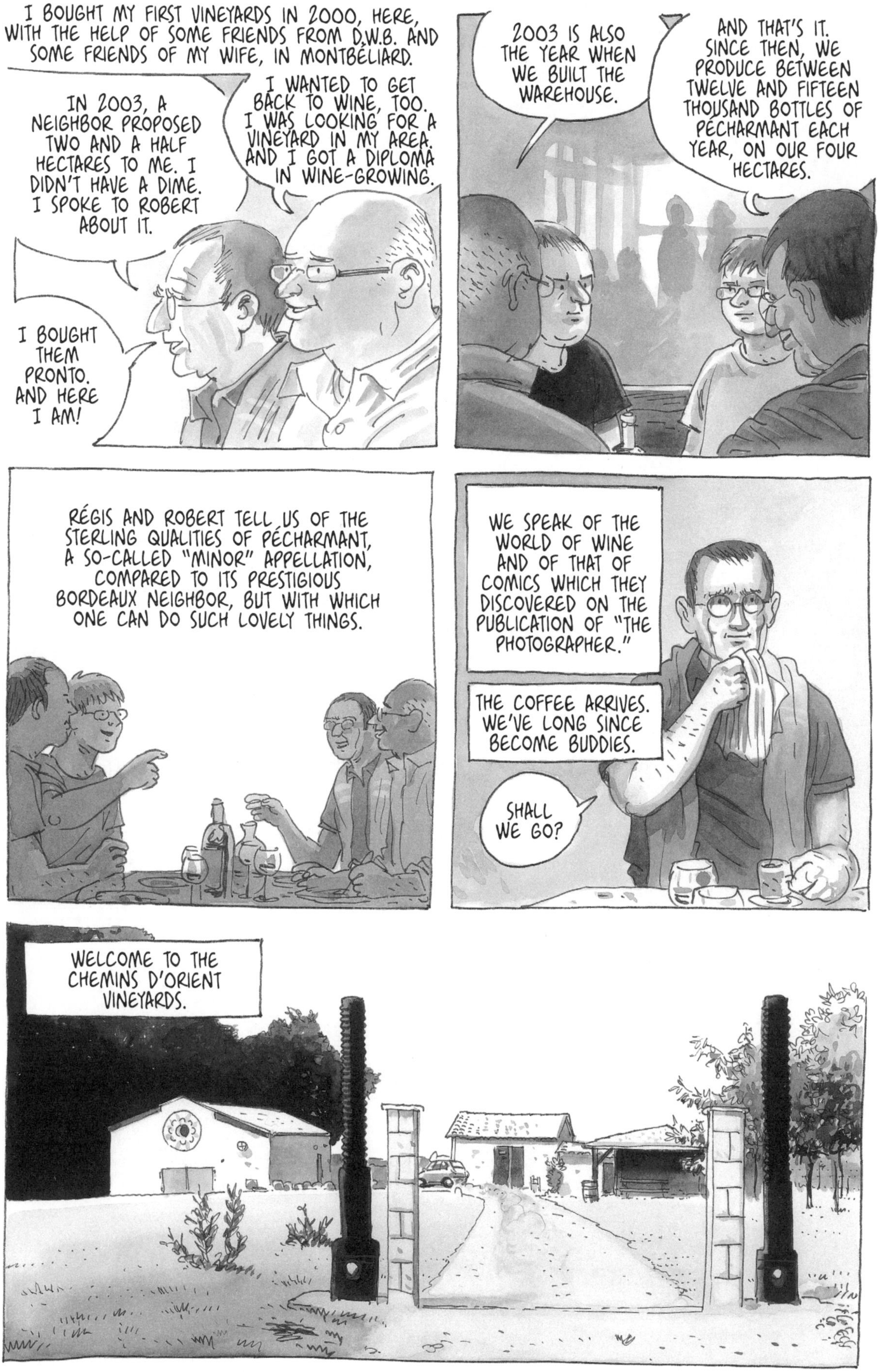
I BOUGHT MY FIRST VINEYARDS IN 2000, HERE, WITH THE HELP OF SOME FRIENDS FROM D.W.B. AND SOME FRIENDS OF MY WIFE, IN MONTBÉLIARD.
IN 2003, A NEIGHBOR PROPOSED TWO AND A HALF HECTARES TO ME. I DIDN'T HAVE A DIME. I SPOKE TO ROBERT ABOUT IT.
I WANTED TO GET BACK TO WINE, TOO. I WAS LOOKING FOR A VINEYARD IN MY AREA. AND I GOT A DIPLOMA IN WINE-GROWING.
I BOUGHT THEM PRONTO. AND HERE I AM!
2003 IS ALSO THE YEAR WHEN WE BUILT THE WAREHOUSE.
AND THAT'S IT. SINCE THEN, WE PRODUCE BETWEEN TWELVE AND FIFTEEN THOUSAND BOTTLES OF PÉCHARMANT EACH YEAR, ON OUR FOUR HECTARES.
RÉGIS AND ROBERT TELL US OF THE STERLING QUALITIES OF PÉCHARMANT, A SO-CALLED "MINOR" APPELLATION, COMPARED TO ITS PRESTIGIOUS BORDEAUX NEIGHBOR, BUT WITH WHICH ONE CAN DO SUCH LOVELY THINGS.
WE SPEAK OF THE WORLD OF WINE AND OF THAT OF COMICS WHICH THEY DISCOVERED ON THE PUBLICATION OF "THE PHOTOGRAPHER."
THE COFFEE ARRIVES. WE'VE LONG SINCE BECOME BUDDIES.
SHALL WE GO?
WELCOME TO THE CHEMINS D'ORIENT VINEYARDS.

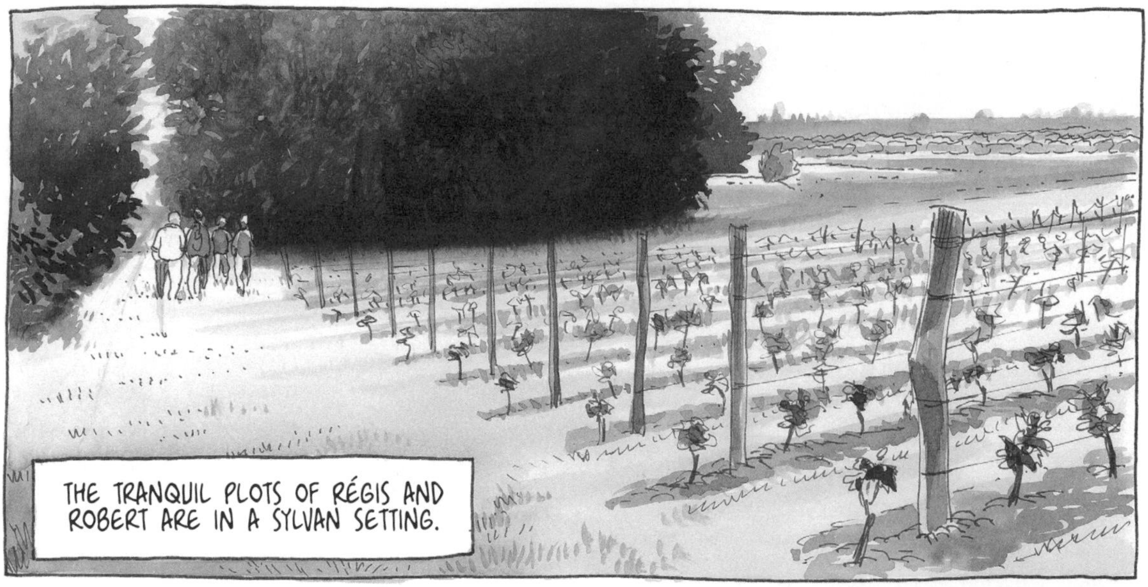
THE TRANQUIL PLOTS OF RÉGIS AND ROBERT ARE IN A SYLVAN SETTING.

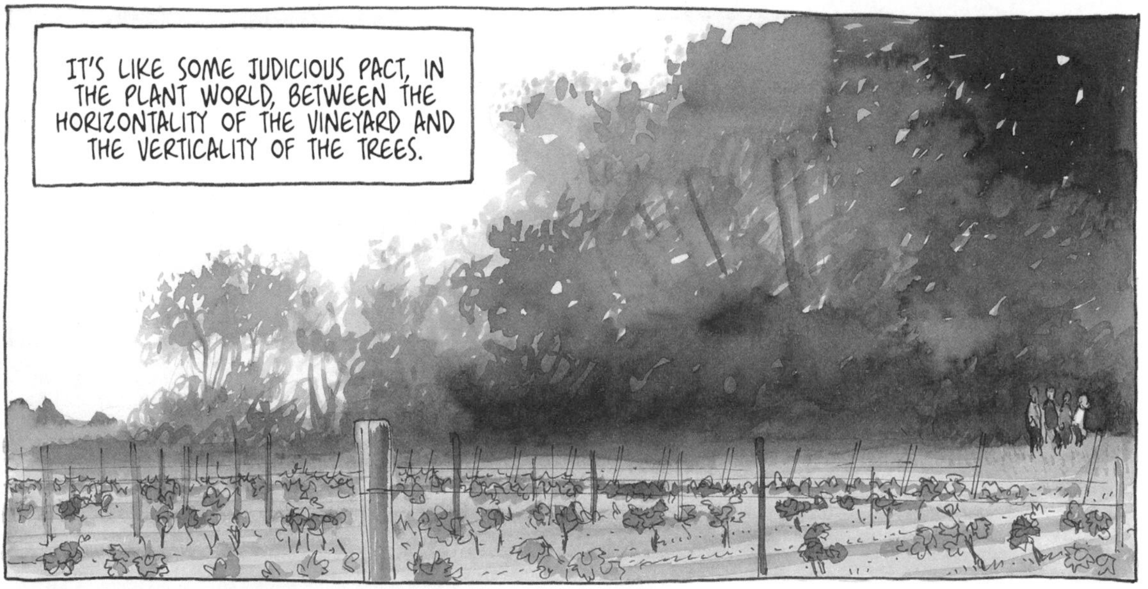
IT'S LIKE SOME JUDICIOUS PACT, IN THE PLANT WORLD, BETWEEN THE HORIZONTALITY OF THE VINEYARD AND THE VERTICALITY OF THE TREES.

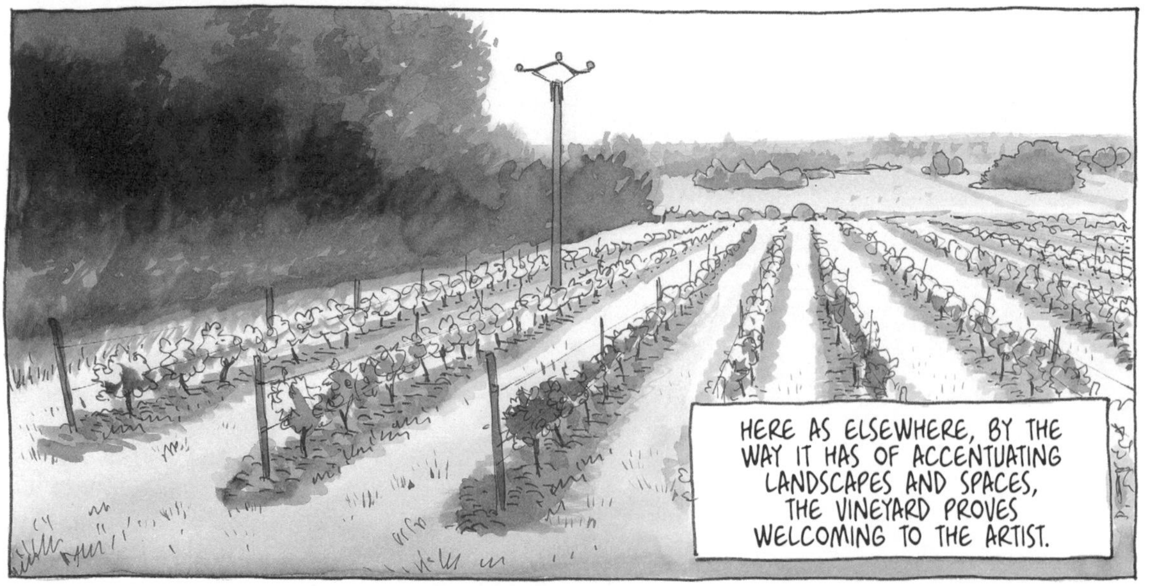
HERE AS ELSEWHERE, BY THE WAY IT HAS OF ACCENTUATING LANDSCAPES AND SPACES, THE VINEYARD PROVES WELCOMING TO THE ARTIST.

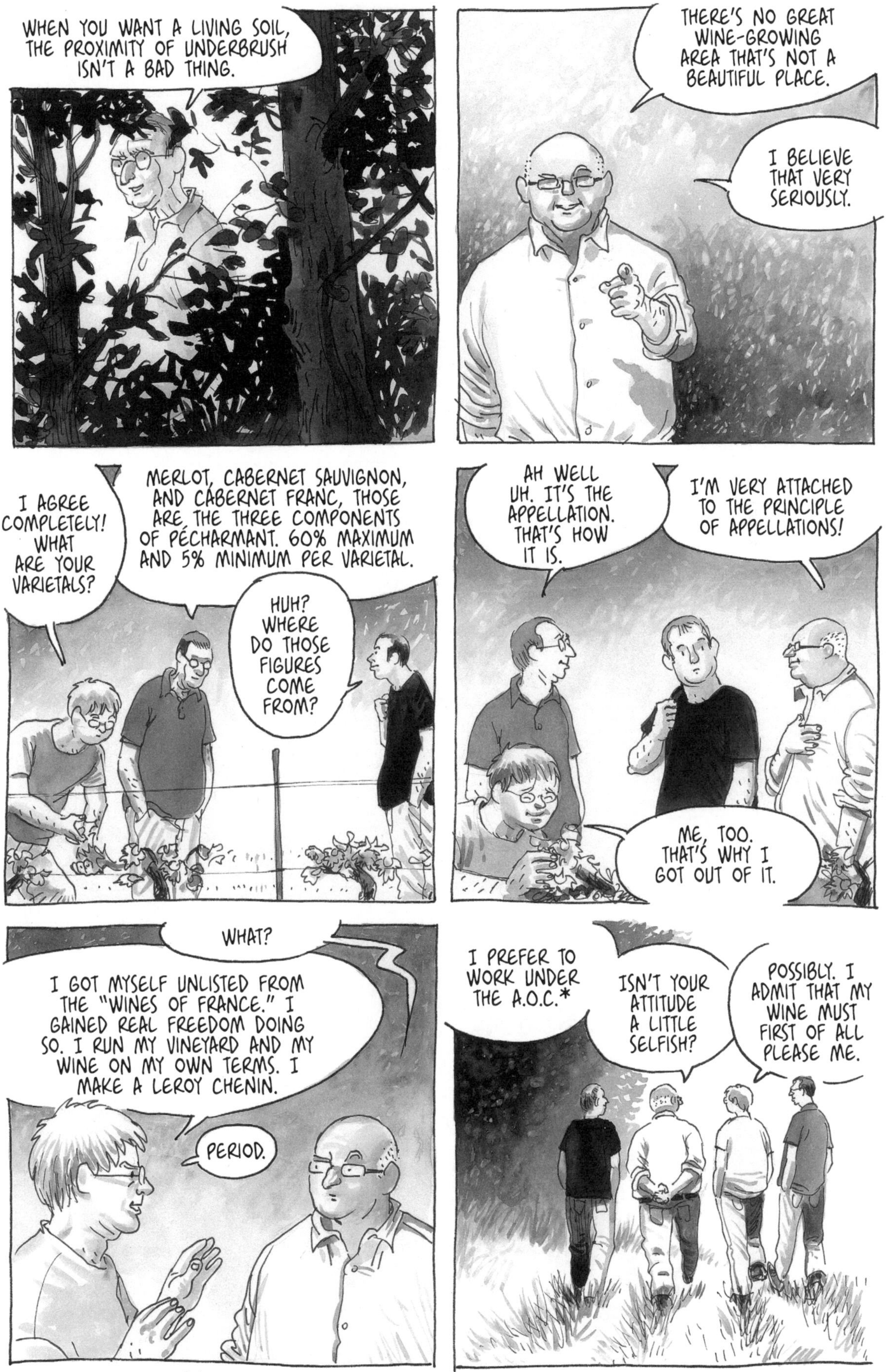
WHEN YOU WANT A LIVING SOIL, THE PROXIMITY OF UNDERBRUSH ISN'T A BAD THING.
THERE'S NO GREAT WINE-GROWING AREA THAT'S NOT A BEAUTIFUL PLACE.
I BELIEVE THAT VERY SERIOUSLY.
I AGREE COMPLETELY! WHAT ARE YOUR VARIETALS?
MERLOT, CABERNET SAUVIGNON, AND CABERNET FRANC, THOSE ARE THE THREE COMPONENTS OF PÉCHARMANT. 60% MAXIMUM AND 5% MINIMUM PER VARIETAL.
HUH? WHERE DO THOSE FIGURES COME FROM?
AH WELL UH. IT'S THE APPELLATION. THAT'S HOW IT IS.
I'M VERY ATTACHED TO THE PRINCIPLE OF APPELLATIONS!
ME, TOO. THAT'S WHY I GOT OUT OF IT.
WHAT?
I GOT MYSELF UNLISTED FROM THE "WINES OF FRANCE." I GAINED REAL FREEDOM DOING SO. I RUN MY VINEYARD AND MY WINE ON MY OWN TERMS. I MAKE A LEROY CHENIN.
PERIOD.
I PREFER TO WORK UNDER THE A.O.C.*
ISN'T YOUR ATTITUDE A LITTLE SELFISH?
POSSIBLY. I ADMIT THAT MY WINE MUST FIRST OF ALL PLEASE ME.

* "APPELLATION D'ORIGINE CONTRÔLÉE," THE FRENCH GOVERNMENT'S MECHANISM FOR CONTROLLING THE DESIGNATION OF ORIGIN FOR WINES AND OTHER PRODUCTS THROUGH CLEARLY DEFINED STANDARDS.

WANNA A TASTE?

SURE.

I KNOW THAT IMAGE.

THAT'S A PHOTO OF YOUR FRIEND DIDIER LEVÈFRE, ISN'T IT? IT'S REPRODUCED IN "THE PHOTOGRAPHER."

DIDIER DIED IN 2001, AT ALMOST 50 YEARS OF AGE, THREE DAYS AFTER RECEIVING A PRIZE AT THE ANGOULÊME FESTIVAL.

OUR 2001 VINTAGE BEARS HIS NAME.

A TOAST TO YOU, DIDIER LEFÈVRE.

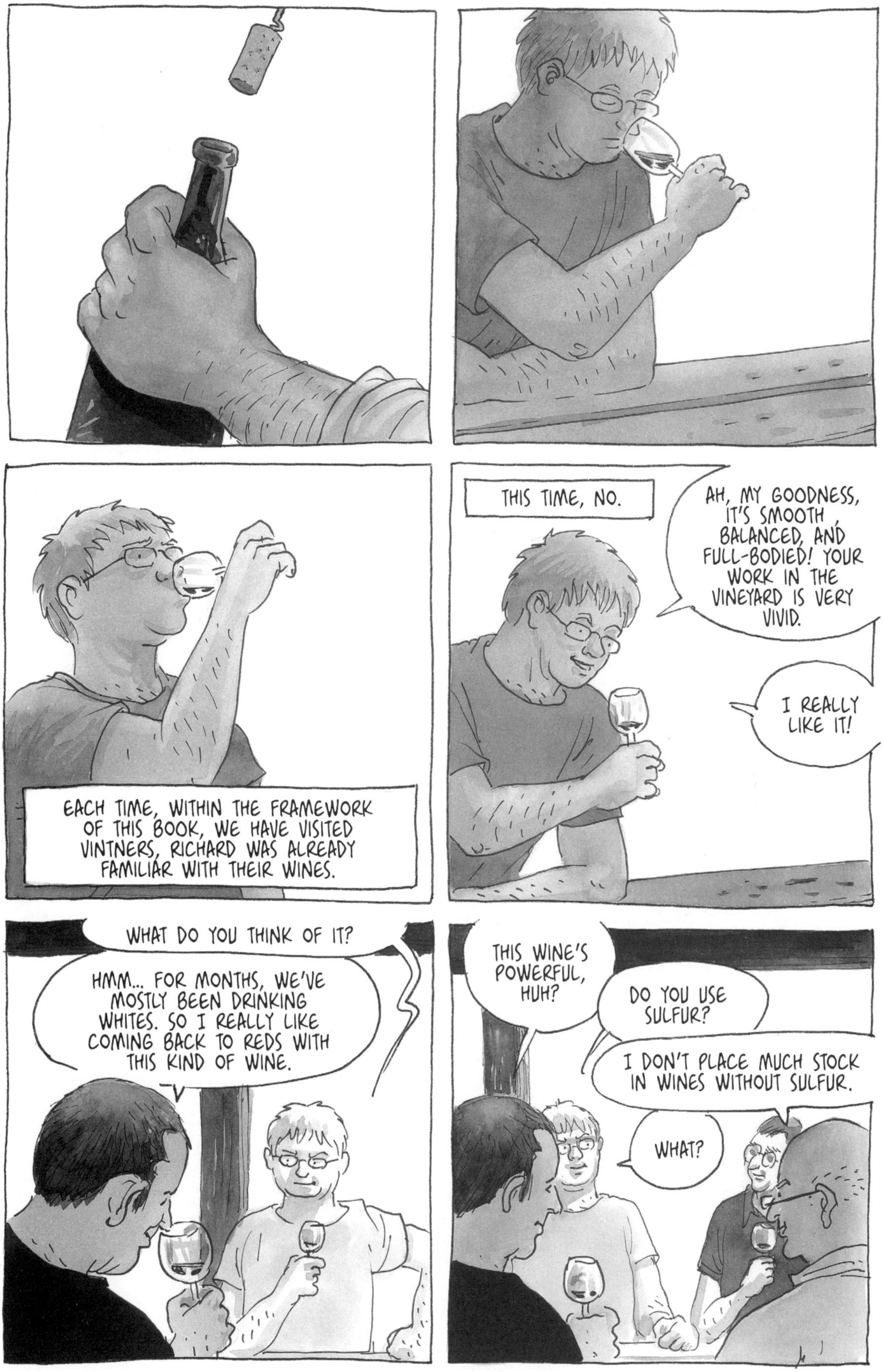
EACH TIME, WITHIN THE FRAMEWORK OF THIS BOOK, WE HAVE VISITED VINTNERS, RICHARD WAS ALREADY FAMILIAR WITH THEIR WINES.
THIS TIME, NO.
AH, MY GOODNESS, IT'S SMOOTH, BALANCED, AND FULL-BODIED! YOUR WORK IN THE VINEYARD IS VERY VIVID.
I REALLY LIKE IT!
WHAT DO YOU THINK OF IT?
HMM... FOR MONTHS, WE'VE MOSTLY BEEN DRINKING WHITES. SO I REALLY LIKE COMING BACK TO REDS WITH THIS KIND OF WINE.
THIS WINE'S POWERFUL, HUH?
DO YOU USE SULFUR?
I DON'T PLACE MUCH STOCK IN WINES WITHOUT SULFUR.
WHAT?

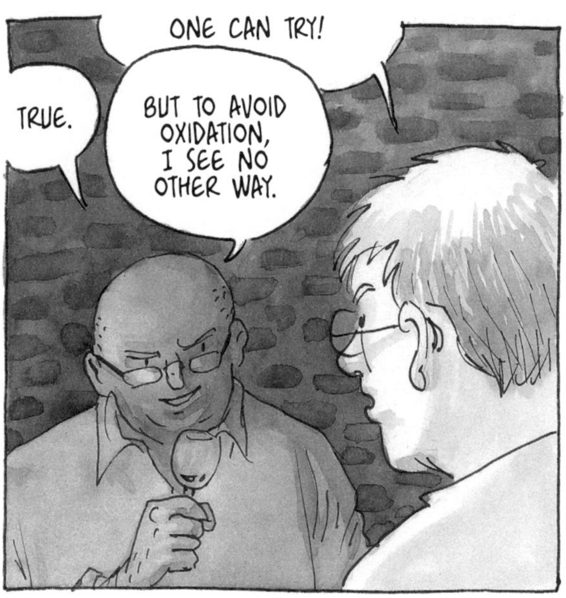
ONE CAN TRY!
TRUE.
BUT TO AVOID OXIDATION, I SEE NO OTHER WAY.

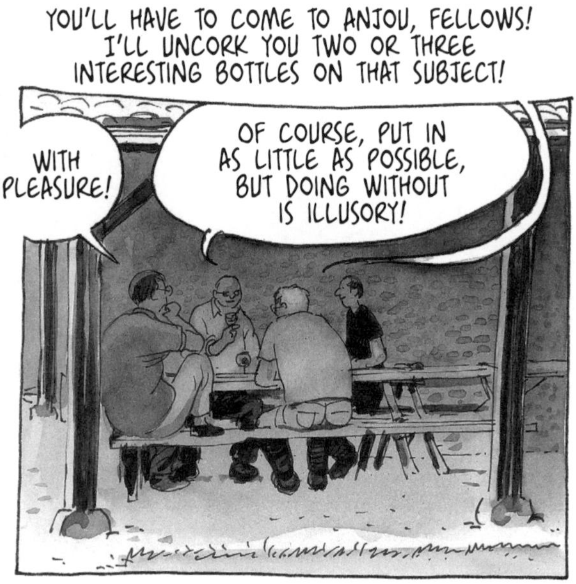
YOU'LL HAVE TO COME TO ANJOU, FELLOWS! I'LL UNCORK YOU TWO OR THREE INTERESTING BOTTLES ON THAT SUBJECT!
WITH PLEASURE!
OF COURSE, PUT IN AS LITTLE AS POSSIBLE, BUT DOING WITHOUT IS ILLUSORY!

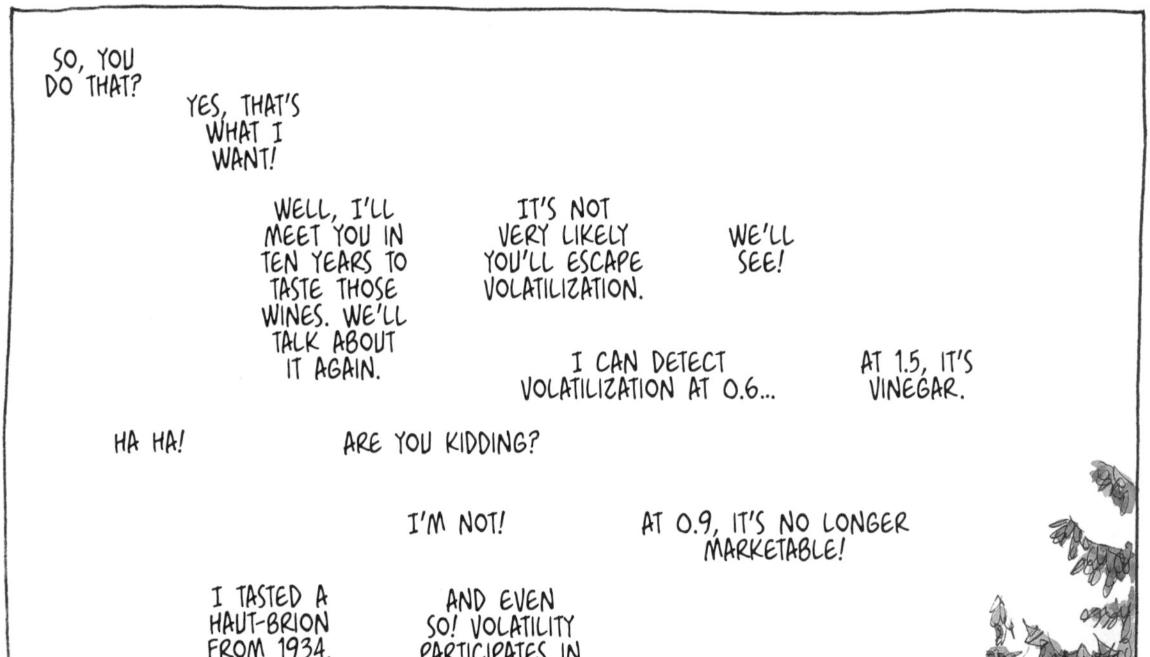
SO, YOU DO THAT?
YES, THAT'S WHAT I WANT!
WELL, I'LL MEET YOU IN TEN YEARS TO TASTE THOSE WINES. WE'LL TALK ABOUT IT AGAIN.
IT'S NOT VERY LIKELY YOU'LL ESCAPE VOLATILIZATION.
WE'LL SEE!
I CAN DETECT VOLATILIZATION AT 0.6...
AT 1.5, IT'S VINEGAR.
HA HA!
ARE YOU KIDDING?
I'M NOT!
AT 0.9, IT'S NO LONGER MARKETABLE!
I TASTED A HAUT-BRION FROM 1934. THERE WASN'T ANY VOLATILITY!
AND EVEN SO! VOLATILITY PARTICIPATES IN THE COMPLEXITY OF A WINE!

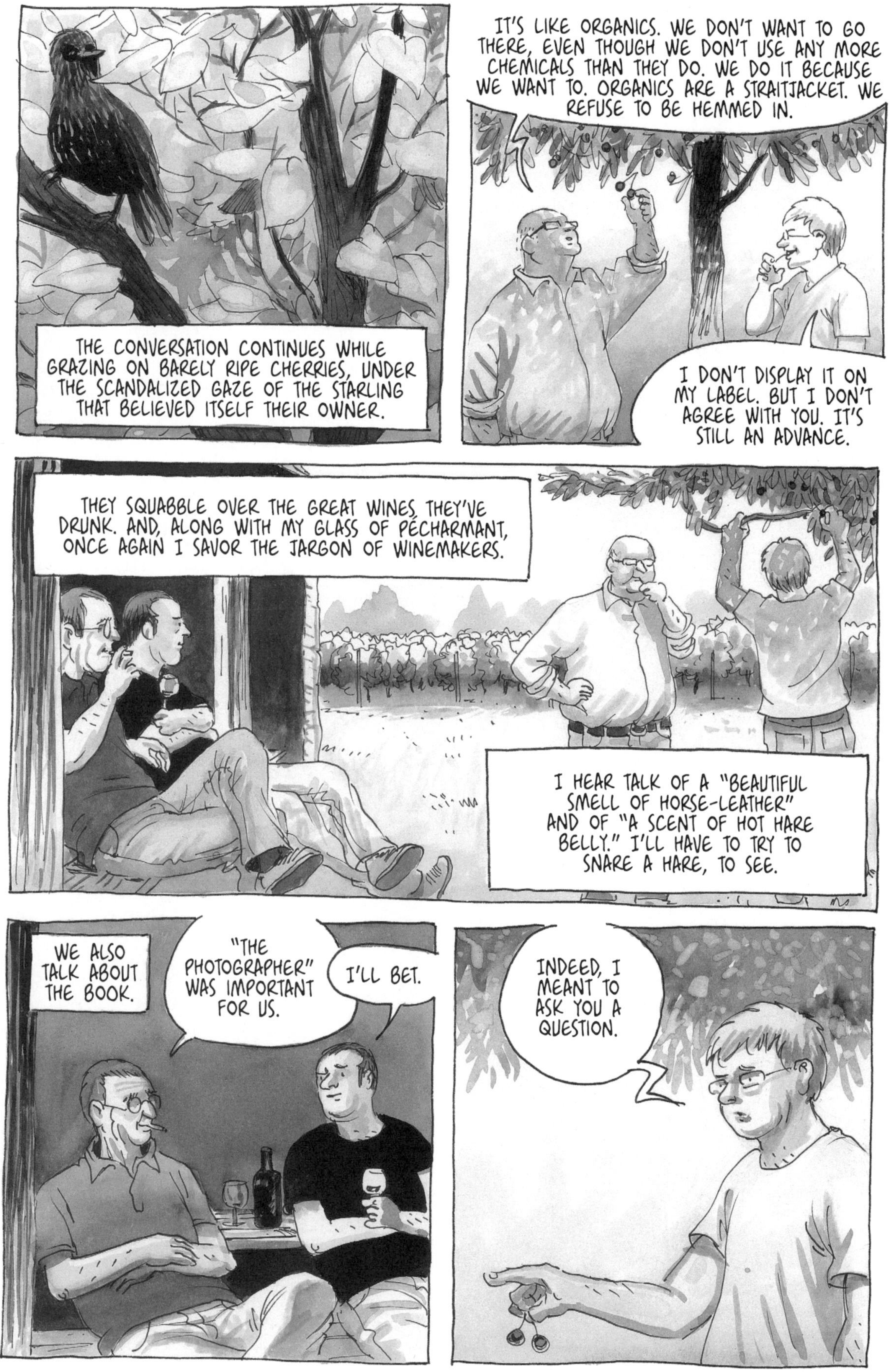
THE CONVERSATION CONTINUES WHILE GRAZING ON BARELY RIPE CHERRIES, UNDER THE SCANDALIZED GAZE OF THE STARLING THAT BELIEVED ITSELF THEIR OWNER.
IT'S LIKE ORGANICS. WE DON'T WANT TO GO THERE, EVEN THOUGH WE DON'T USE ANY MORE CHEMICALS THAN THEY DO. WE DO IT BECAUSE WE WANT TO. ORGANICS ARE A STRAITJACKET. WE REFUSE TO BE HEMMED IN.
I DON'T DISPLAY IT ON MY LABEL. BUT I DON'T AGREE WITH YOU. IT'S STILL AN ADVANCE.
THEY SQUABBLE OVER THE GREAT WINES THEY'VE DRUNK. AND, ALONG WITH MY GLASS OF PÉCHARMANT, ONCE AGAIN I SAVOR THE JARGON OF WINEMAKERS.
I HEAR TALK OF A "BEAUTIFUL SMELL OF HORSE-LEATHER" AND OF "A SCENT OF HOT HARE BELLY." I'LL HAVE TO TRY TO SNARE A HARE, TO SEE.
WE ALSO TALK ABOUT THE BOOK.
"THE PHOTOGRAPHER" WAS IMPORTANT FOR US.
I'LL BET.
INDEED, I MEANT TO ASK YOU A QUESTION.

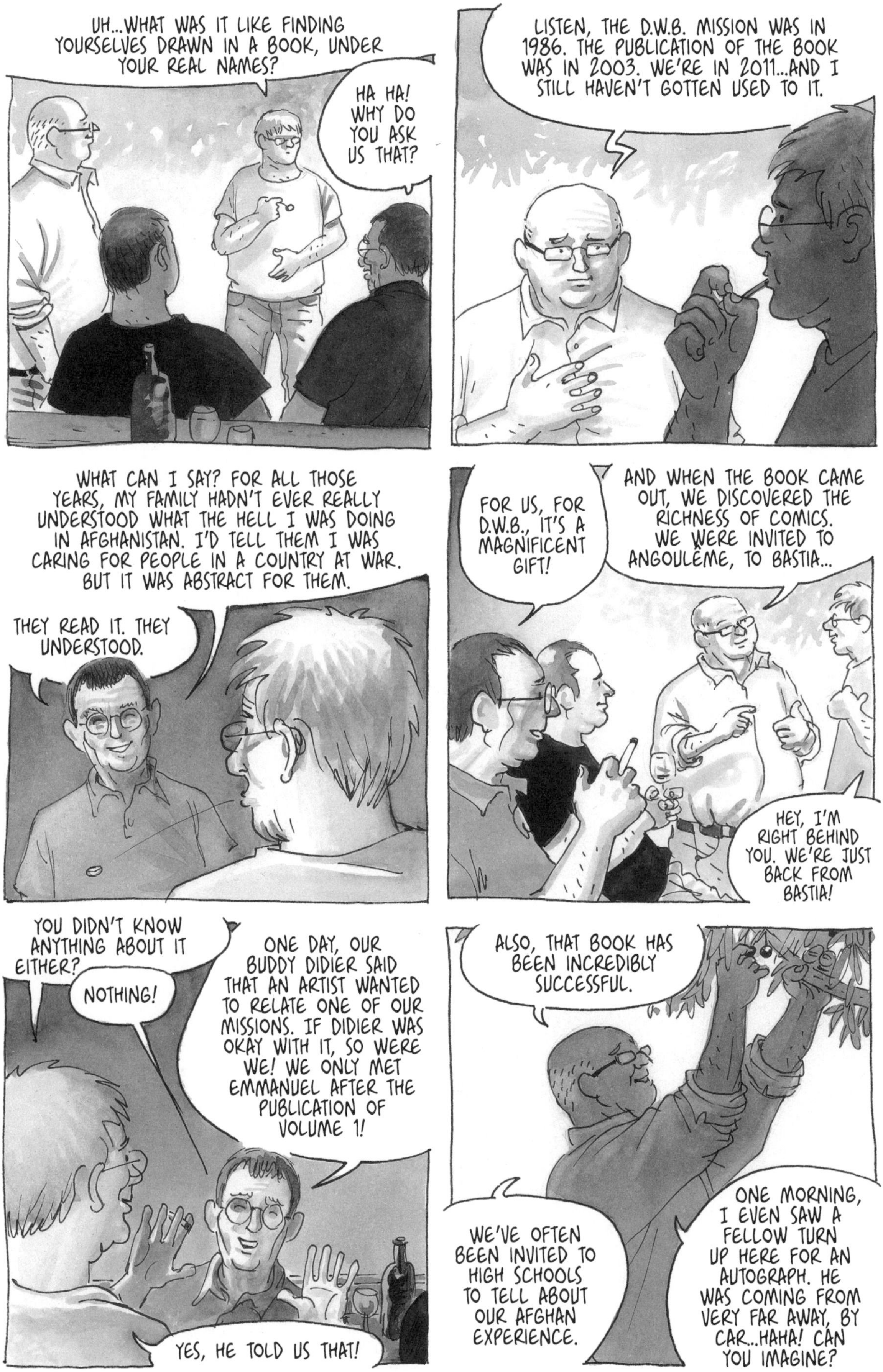
UH...WHAT WAS IT LIKE FINDING YOURSELVES DRAWN IN A BOOK, UNDER YOUR REAL NAMES?
HA HA! WHY DO YOU ASK US THAT?
LISTEN, THE D.W.B. MISSION WAS IN 1986. THE PUBLICATION OF THE BOOK WAS IN 2003. WE'RE IN 2011...AND I STILL HAVEN'T GOTTEN USED TO IT.
WHAT CAN I SAY? FOR ALL THOSE YEARS, MY FAMILY HADN'T EVER REALLY UNDERSTOOD WHAT THE HELL I WAS DOING IN AFGHANISTAN. I'D TELL THEM I WAS CARING FOR PEOPLE IN A COUNTRY AT WAR. BUT IT WAS ABSTRACT FOR THEM.
THEY READ IT. THEY UNDERSTOOD.
FOR US, FOR D.W.B., IT'S A MAGNIFICENT GIFT!
AND WHEN THE BOOK CAME OUT, WE DISCOVERED THE RICHNESS OF COMICS. WE WERE INVITED TO ANGOULÊME, TO BASTIA...
HEY, I'M RIGHT BEHIND YOU. WE'RE JUST BACK FROM BASTIA!
YOU DIDN'T KNOW ANYTHING ABOUT IT EITHER?
NOTHING!
ONE DAY, OUR BUDDY DIDIER SAID THAT AN ARTIST WANTED TO RELATE ONE OF OUR MISSIONS. IF DIDIER WAS OKAY WITH IT, SO WERE WE! WE ONLY MET EMMANUEL AFTER THE PUBLICATION OF VOLUME 1!
YES, HE TOLD US THAT!
ALSO, THAT BOOK HAS BEEN INCREDIBLY SUCCESSFUL.
WE'VE OFTEN BEEN INVITED TO HIGH SCHOOLS TO TELL ABOUT OUR AFGHAN EXPERIENCE.
ONE MORNING, I EVEN SAW A FELLOW TURN UP HERE FOR AN AUTOGRAPH. HE WAS COMING FROM VERY FAR AWAY, BY CAR...HAHA! CAN YOU IMAGINE?

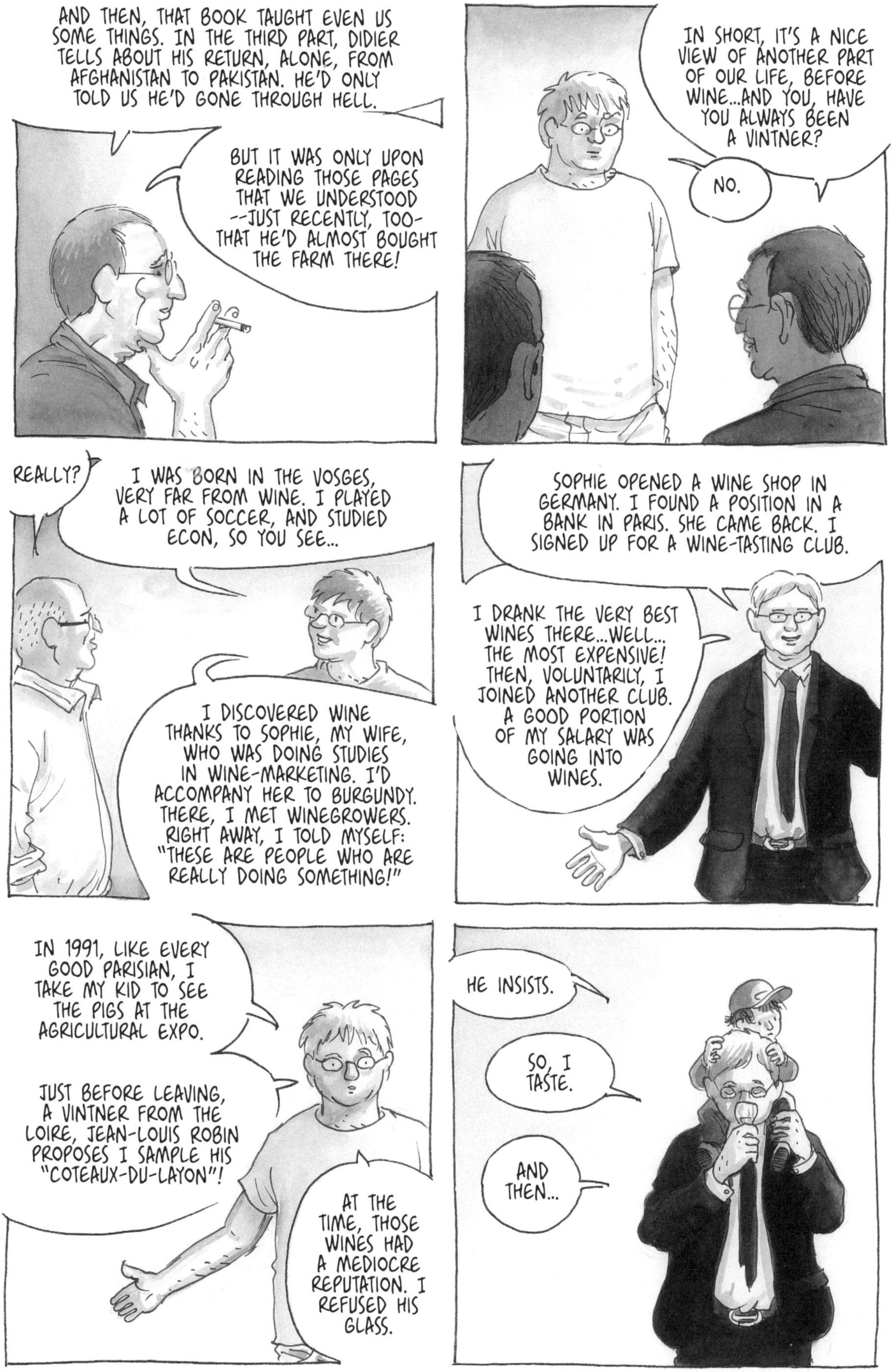
AND THEN, THAT BOOK TAUGHT EVEN US SOME THINGS. IN THE THIRD PART, DIDIER TELLS ABOUT HIS RETURN, ALONE, FROM AFGHANISTAN TO PAKISTAN. HE'D ONLY TOLD US HE'D GONE THROUGH HELL.
BUT IT WAS ONLY UPON READING THOSE PAGES THAT WE UNDERSTOOD --JUST RECENTLY, TOO-THAT HE'D ALMOST BOUGHT THE FARM THERE!
IN SHORT, IT'S A NICE VIEW OF ANOTHER PART OF OUR LIFE, BEFORE WINE...AND YOU, HAVE YOU ALWAYS BEEN A VINTNER?
NO.
REALLY?
I WAS BORN IN THE VOSGES, VERY FAR FROM WINE. I PLAYED A LOT OF SOCCER, AND STUDIED ECON, SO YOU SEE...
I DISCOVERED WINE THANKS TO SOPHIE, MY WIFE, WHO WAS DOING STUDIES IN WINE-MARKETING. I'D ACCOMPANY HER TO BURGUNDY. THERE, I MET WINEGROWERS. RIGHT AWAY, I TOLD MYSELF: "THESE ARE PEOPLE WHO ARE REALLY DOING SOMETHING!"
SOPHIE OPENED A WINE SHOP IN GERMANY. I FOUND A POSITION IN A BANK IN PARIS. SHE CAME BACK. I SIGNED UP FOR A WINE-TASTING CLUB.
I DRANK THE VERY BEST WINES THERE...WELL... THE MOST EXPENSIVE! THEN, VOLUNTARILY, I JOINED ANOTHER CLUB. A GOOD PORTION OF MY SALARY WAS GOING INTO WINES.
IN 1991, LIKE EVERY GOOD PARISIAN, I TAKE MY KID TO SEE THE PIGS AT THE AGRICULTURAL EXPO.
JUST BEFORE LEAVING, A VINTNER FROM THE LOIRE, JEAN-LOUIS ROBIN PROPOSES I SAMPLE HIS "COTEAUX-DU-LAYON"!
AT THE TIME, THOSE WINES HAD A MEDIOCRE REPUTATION. I REFUSED HIS GLASS.
HE INSISTS.
SO, I TASTE.
AND THEN...

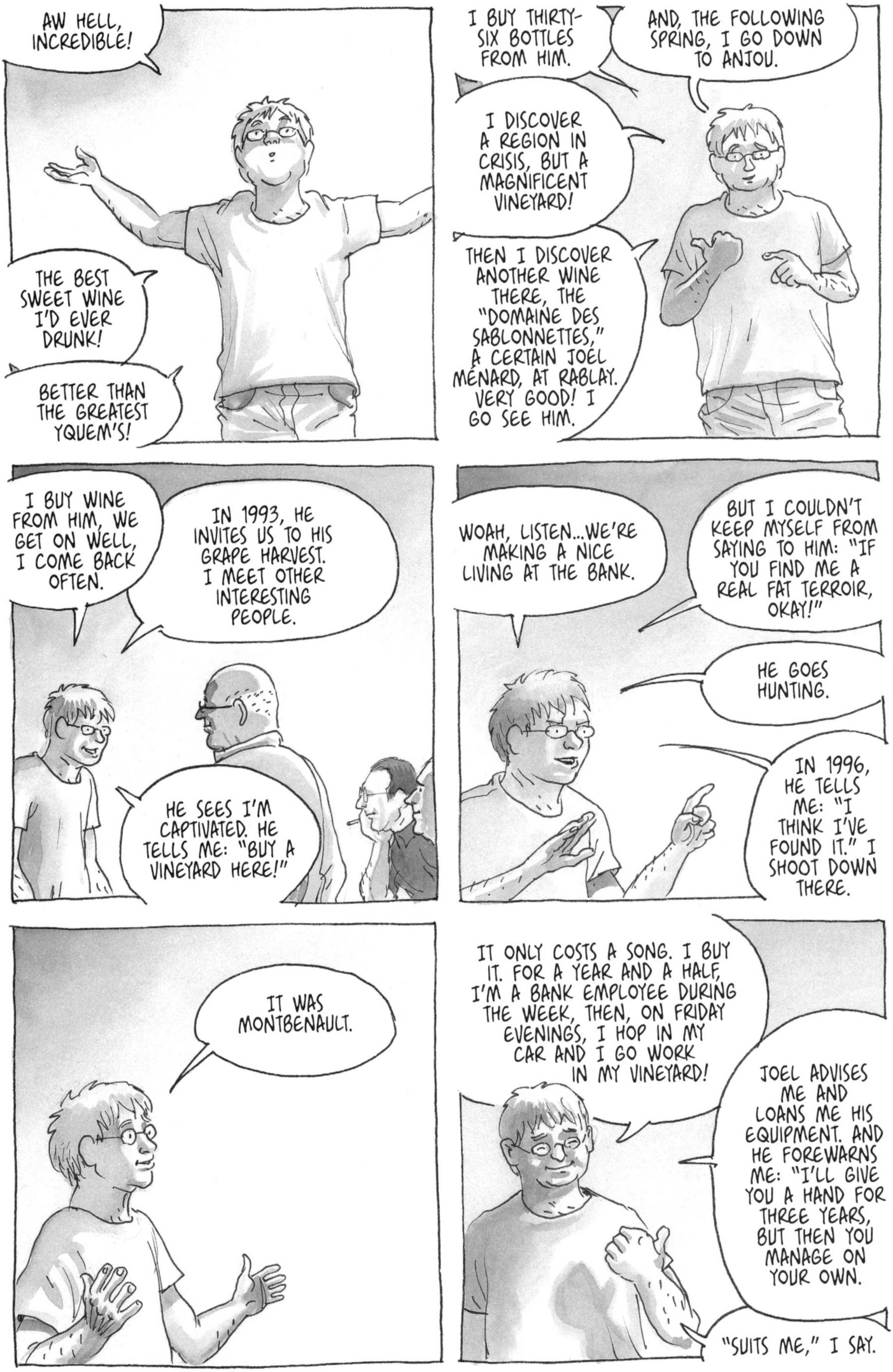
AW HELL, INCREDIBLE!
THE BEST SWEET WINE I'D EVER DRUNK!
BETTER THAN THE GREATEST YQUEM'S!
I BUY THIRTY-SIX BOTTLES FROM HIM.
AND, THE FOLLOWING SPRING, I GO DOWN TO ANJOU.
I DISCOVER A REGION IN CRISIS, BUT A MAGNIFICENT VINEYARD!
THEN I DISCOVER ANOTHER WINE THERE, THE "DOMAINE DES SABLONNETTES," A CERTAIN JOEL MÉNARD, AT RABLAY. VERY GOOD! I GO SEE HIM.
I BUY WINE FROM HIM, WE GET ON WELL, I COME BACK OFTEN.
IN 1993, HE INVITES US TO HIS GRAPE HARVEST. I MEET OTHER INTERESTING PEOPLE.
HE SEES I'M CAPTIVATED. HE TELLS ME: "BUY A VINEYARD HERE!"
WOAH, LISTEN...WE'RE MAKING A NICE LIVING AT THE BANK.
BUT I COULDN'T KEEP MYSELF FROM SAYING TO HIM: "IF YOU FIND ME A REAL FAT TERROIR, OKAY!"
HE GOES HUNTING.
IN 1996, HE TELLS ME: "I THINK I'VE FOUND IT." I SHOOT DOWN THERE.
IT WAS MONTBENAULT.
IT ONLY COSTS A SONG. I BUY IT. FOR A YEAR AND A HALF, I'M A BANK EMPLOYEE DURING THE WEEK, THEN, ON FRIDAY EVENINGS, I HOP IN MY CAR AND I GO WORK IN MY VINEYARD!
JOEL ADVISES ME AND LOANS ME HIS EQUIPMENT. AND HE FOREWARNS ME: "I'LL GIVE YOU A HAND FOR THREE YEARS, BUT THEN YOU MANAGE ON YOUR OWN.
"SUITS ME," I SAY.

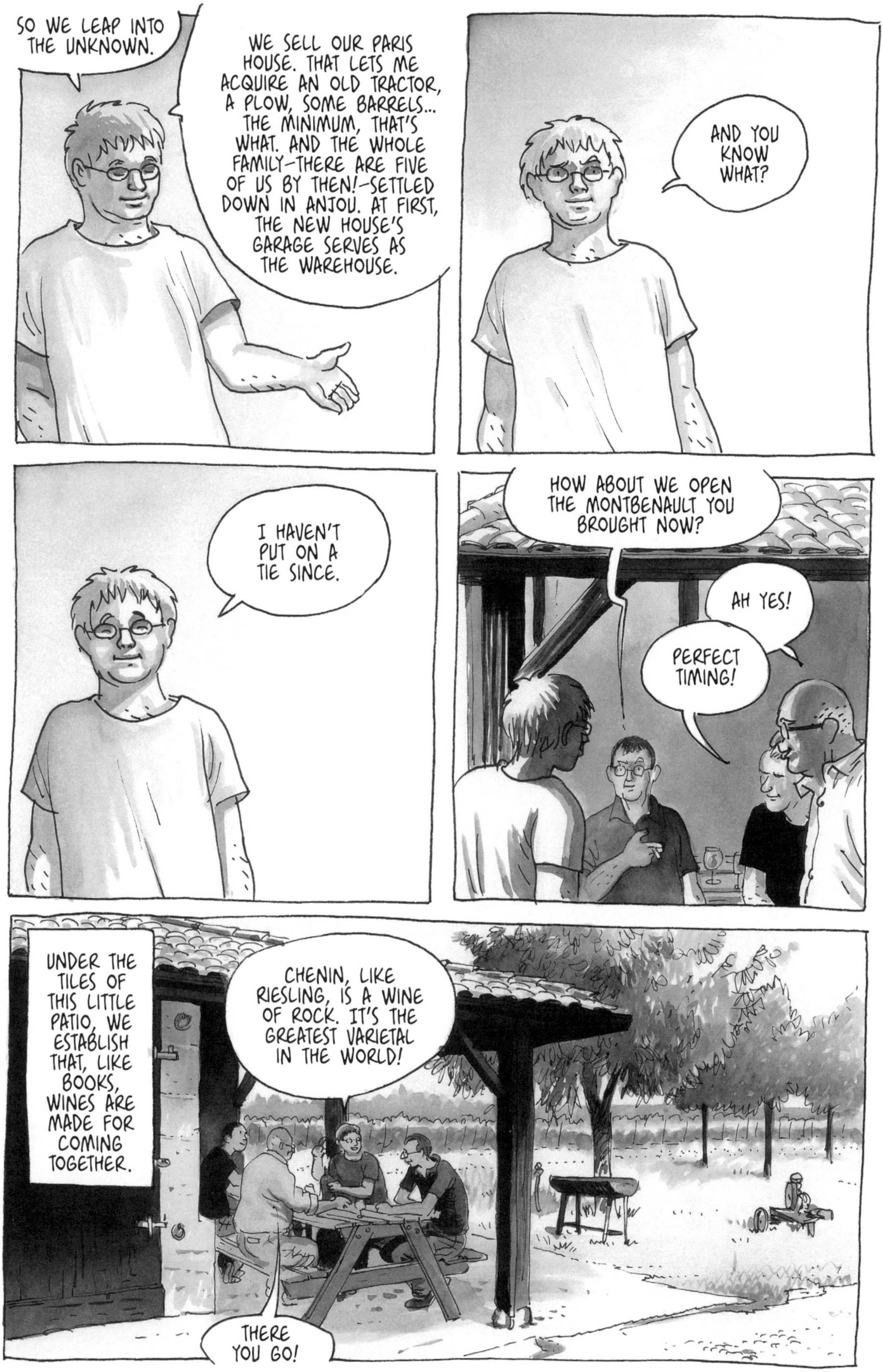
SO WE LEAP INTO THE UNKNOWN.
WE SELL OUR PARIS HOUSE. THAT LETS ME ACQUIRE AN OLD TRACTOR, A PLOW, SOME BARRELS... THE MINIMUM, THAT'S WHAT. AND THE WHOLE FAMILY—THERE ARE FIVE OF US BY THEN!—SETTLED DOWN IN ANJOU. AT FIRST, THE NEW HOUSE'S GARAGE SERVES AS THE WAREHOUSE.
AND YOU KNOW WHAT?
I HAVEN'T PUT ON A TIE SINCE.
HOW ABOUT WE OPEN THE MONTBENAULT YOU BROUGHT NOW?
AH YES!
PERFECT TIMING!
UNDER THE TILES OF THIS LITTLE PATIO, WE ESTABLISH THAT, LIKE BOOKS, WINES ARE MADE FOR COMING TOGETHER.
CHENIN, LIKE RIESLING, IS A WINE OF ROCK. IT'S THE GREATEST VARIETAL IN THE WORLD!
THERE YOU GO!

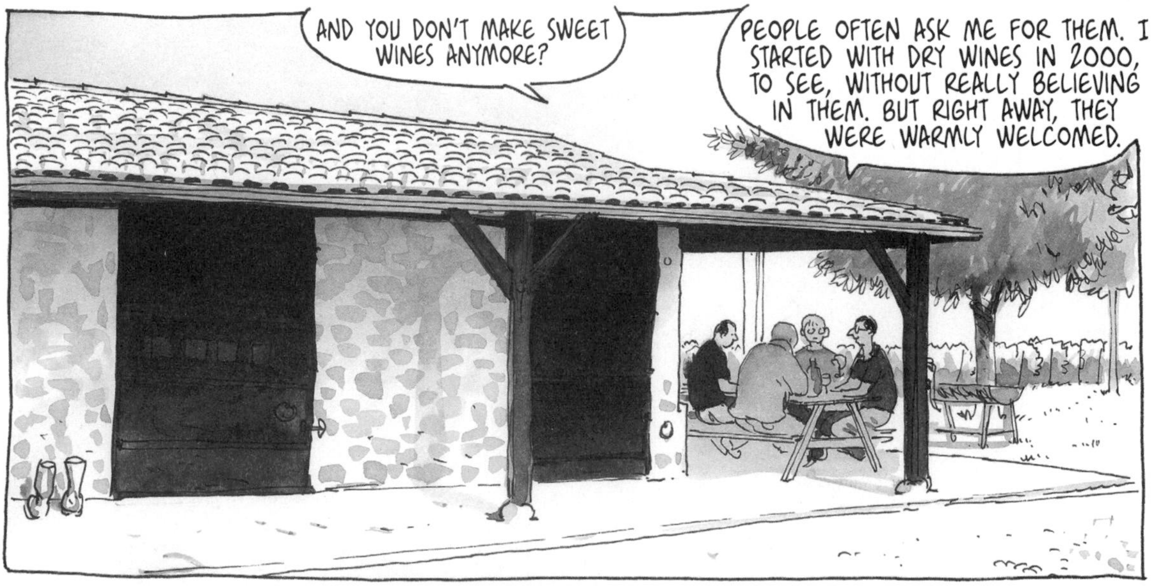
AND YOU DON'T MAKE SWEET WINES ANYMORE?
PEOPLE OFTEN ASK ME FOR THEM. I STARTED WITH DRY WINES IN 2000, TO SEE, WITHOUT REALLY BELIEVING IN THEM. BUT RIGHT AWAY, THEY WERE WARMLY WELCOMED.

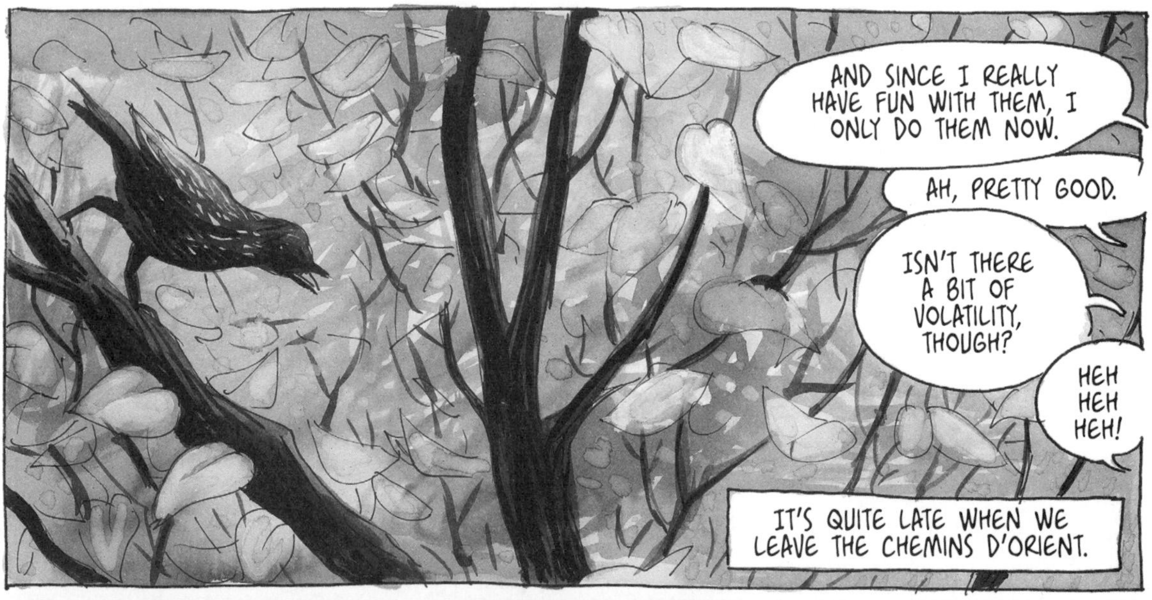
AND SINCE I REALLY HAVE FUN WITH THEM, I ONLY DO THEM NOW.
AH, PRETTY GOOD.
ISN'T THERE A BIT OF VOLATILITY, THOUGH?
HEH HEH HEH!
IT'S QUITE LATE WHEN WE LEAVE THE CHEMINS D'ORIENT.

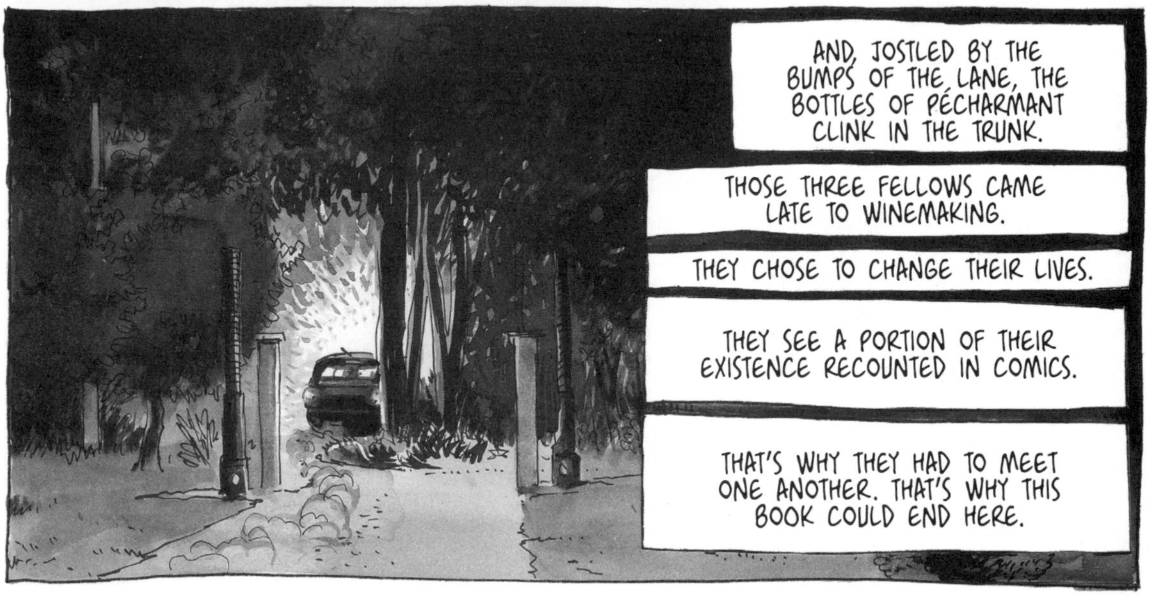
AND, JOSTLED BY THE BUMPS OF THE LANE, THE BOTTLES OF PÉCHARMANT CLINK IN THE TRUNK.
THOSE THREE FELLOWS CAME LATE TO WINEMAKING.
THEY CHOSE TO CHANGE THEIR LIVES.
THEY SEE A PORTION OF THEIR EXISTENCE RECOUNTED IN COMICS.
THAT'S WHY THEY HAD TO MEET ONE ANOTHER. THAT'S WHY THIS BOOK COULD END HERE.

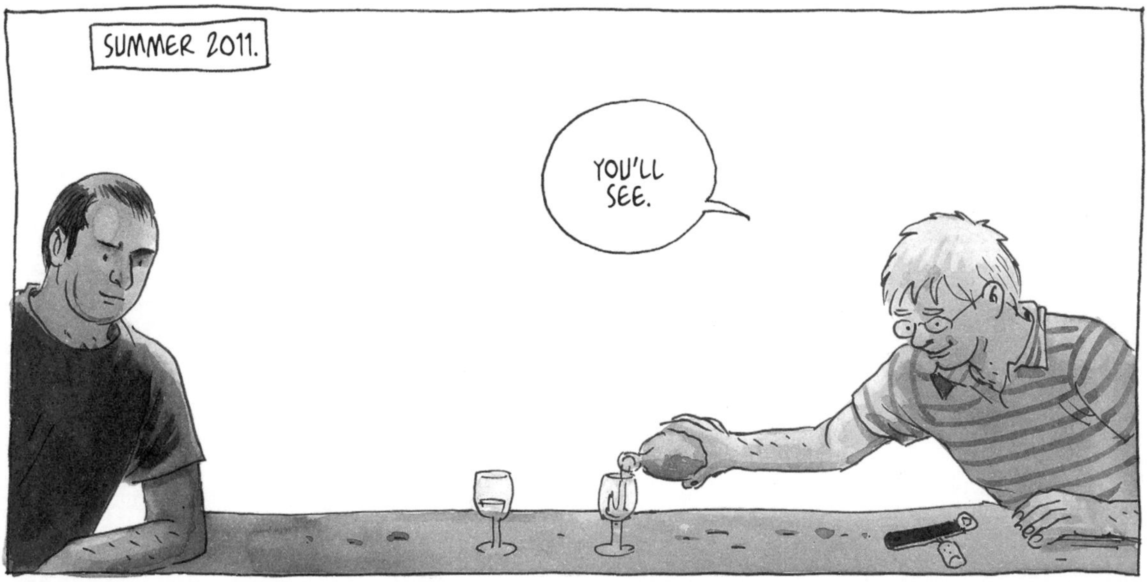
SUMMER 2011.
YOU'LL SEE.

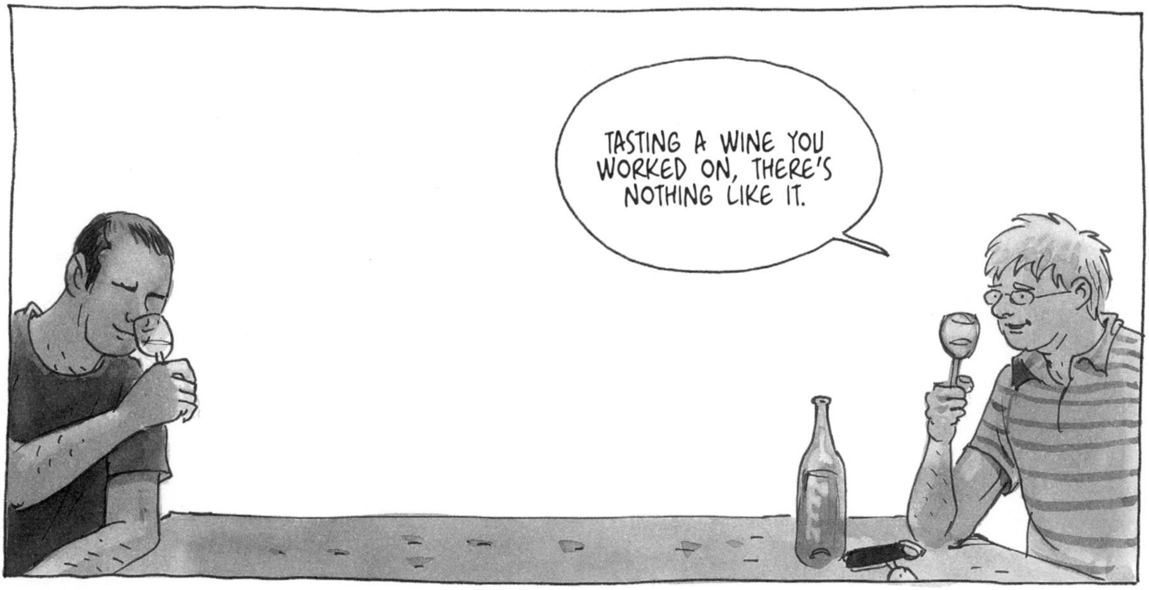
TASTING A WINE YOU WORKED ON, THERE'S NOTHING LIKE IT.

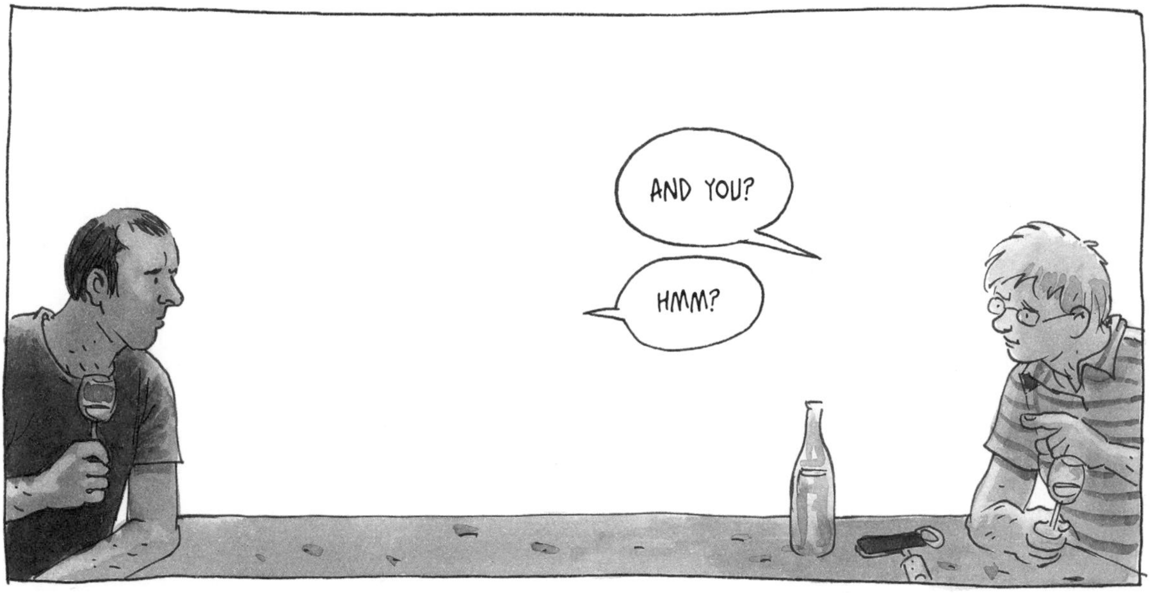
AND YOU?
HMM?

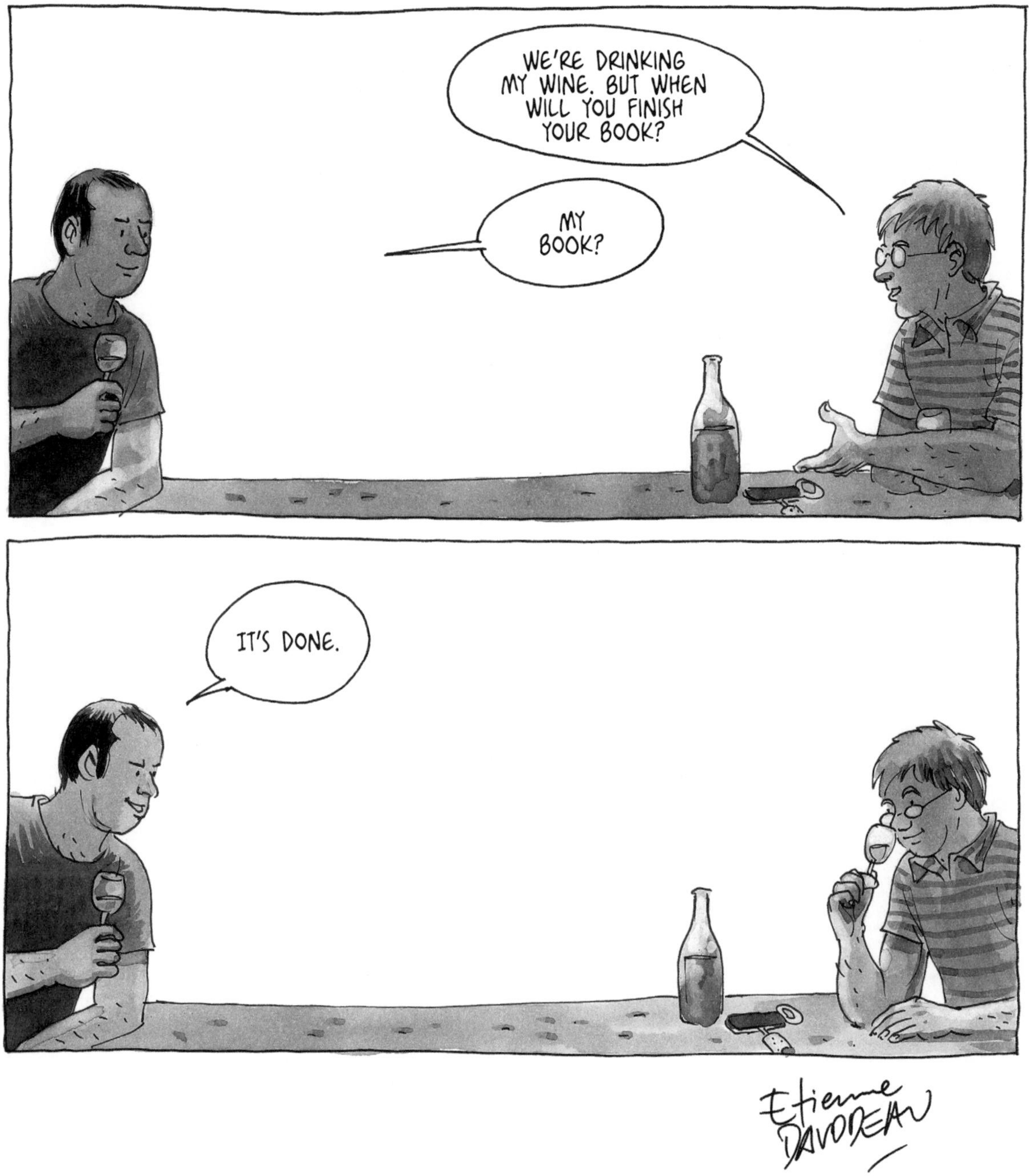
WE'RE DRINKING MY WINE. BUT WHEN WILL YOU FINISH YOUR BOOK?
MY BOOK?
IT'S DONE.
Etienne DAVODEAU

DRUNK READ

Cuvée Marguerite 2008, côtes-du-jura, Jean-François Ganevat	*Mattéo*, Jean-Pierre Gibrat (Futuropolis)
Grotte Di Sole 2008, patrimonio, Domaine Arena	*L'Origine*, Marc-Antoine Mathieu (Delcourt)
Cuvée Noshak 2008, pécharmant, Les Chemins de l'Orient	*The Photographer*, Emmanuel Guibert, Didier Lefèvre, and Frédéric Leme
Le Volagré 2005, montlouis-sur-loire, Stéphane Cossais	(Dupuis, First Second)
Meursault-Genevièvres 1989, Domaine des Comtes Lafon	*Approximate Continuum Comics*, Lewis Trondheim (Cornélius, Fantagrap
Côte-Rôtie La Mouiline 1991, Guigal	*L'Enragé*, Baru (Dupuis)
Marienburg Raffes Mosel 2008, Riesling, Clemens Busch	*Le Filet de Saint-Pierre*, Jean-Pierre Autheman (Glénat)
Vin de France 2008 "no sulfur added," Domaine Henri Milan	*À la recherche de Peter Pan*, Cosey (Le Lombard)
Château Beauséjour Bécot, saint-émilion grand cru 1990	*La Bouille*, Troubs (Rackham)
Barbaresco Pajé 2004, Luca Roagna	*Fraise et Chocolat*, Aurélia Aurita (Les Impressions Nouvelles)
Clef de sol 2009, touraine-amboise, Domaine de la Grange Tiphaine	*Rebetiko*, David Prudhomme (Futuropolis, Abrams)
Châteauneuf-du-Pape 2004, Laurent Charvin	*Léon la came*, Nicolas de Crécy and Sylvain Chomet (Casterman)
La Chappelle Hermitage 1990, Paul Jaboulet Aîné	*Exit Wounds*, Rutu Modan (Actes Sud, Drawn & Quarterly)
Clos Rougeard Les Poyeux 2005, saumur-champigny, G. A. E. C. Foucault	*Maus*, Art Spiegelman (Pantheon)
Initials B. B. 2008, anjou, Agnès & René Mosse	*Lupus*, Frederik Peeters (Atrabile)
Pouilly-vinzelles Vieilles Vignes 2007, Domaine Valette	*It Was the War of the Trenches*, Jacques Tardi (Casterman, Fantagraphic
Les Pierres Noires 2009, Domaine de l'Anglore	*Le Baron noir*, Yves Got and René Pétillon (Drugstore)
Les Coteaux Kanté 2009, grolleau, Bruno Richard	*The Speed Abater*, Christophe Blain (Dupuis, NBM Publishing)
Bourgueil 1971, Domaine de la Lande	*Journal*, Fabrice Neaud (Ego comme X)
Château Margaux 1982	*L'ombre aux tableaux et autres histoires*, Jean-C. Denis (Drugstore)
Le Vilain Canard 2005, coteaux-du-layon, Domaine des Sablonettes	*Le Val des ânes*, Matthieu Blanchin (Ego comme X)
Réserve du Pigeonnier 2005, saumur, Château de Fosse-Sèche	*Stigmata*, Lorenzo Mattotti and Claudio Persanti (Casterman, Fantagrap
Les Pucelles 2002, puligny-montrachet, Domaine Leflaive	*Le temps des bombes*, Emmanuel Moynot (Delcourt)
Vin de France Chenin 2007, Les vignes Herbel	*Faire semblant, c'est mentir*, Dominique Goblet (L'Association)
Graviers 2006, saint-nicolas-de-bourgueil, Domaine du Mortier	*Calvin and Hobbes*, Bill Watterson (Andrews McMeel Publishing)
Cuvée Haitza 2007, irouléguy, Domaine Arretxea	*Corps à corps*, Grégory Mardon (Dupuis)
Nuits d'ivresse 2008, bourgueil, Domaine Pierre Breton	*The Blue Notebook*, André Juillard (Casterman, NBM Publishing)
Château Sociando-Malet, haut-médoc, 1996	*Yukiko's Spinach*, Frédéric Boilet (Ego comme X, Fanfare/Ponent Mon)
Meursault-Perrières 1994, Jean-François Coche-Dury	*Livret de phamille*, Jean-Christophe Menu (l'Association)
Billes de Roche 2008, saumur, Melaric	*Agrippine*, Claire Bretecher (Dargaud)
Mazis-Chambertin 1993, Dom. Laurent.	*Boucherie charcuterie même combat*, Bruno Heitz (Le Seuil)
Châteauneuf-du-Pape 2004, Domaine Pierre André.	*Arrugas*, Paco Roca (Astiberri)
Fonterenza 2006, Brunelo Di Montalcino, Francesca et Margherita Padovani	*Ibicus*, Pascal Rabaté (Vents d'Ouest)
Pommard Clos des Epeneaux 1989, Comte Armand	*Palestine*, Joe Sacco (Fantagraphics)
La Mémé 2008, côtes-du-rhône, Domaine Gramenon	*Deux Tueurs*, Mezzo and Pirus (Delcourt)
Charmes-Chambertin 1998, Domaine Dugat-Py	*Domu, A Child's Dream*, Katsuhiro Otomo (Dark Horse)
Château Bel Air-Marquis d'Aligre Margaux 1970	*5,000 Kilometers per Second*, Manuele Fior (Atrabile, Fantagraphics)
Bézigon 2006, anjou, Jean-Christophe Garnier	*Les Aveugles*, F'Murrr (Casterman)
Morgan Côte du Py 2008, Domaine Jean Foillard	*A Distant Neighborhood*, Jiro Taniguchi (Fanfare/Ponent Mon)
Grand vin de l'Altenberg 2004, Domaine Marcel Deiss	*Jolies Ténèbres*, Kerascoët and Fabien Vehlmann (Dupuis)
Jadis 2004, faugères, Domaine Léon Barral	*Shenzhen*, Guy Delisle (L'Association, Drawn and Quarterly)
Chinon Vieilles Vignes 2004, Philippe Alliet	*Muchacho*, Emmanuel Lepage (Dupuis)

Thanks for agreeing to appear in this book:
To Jean-Pierre Gibrat, Bruno Richard,
David Schildknecht, Marc-Antoine Mathieu, Nicoby,
Emmanual Guibert, Jean-François Ganevat, Antoine-Marie Arena,
Jean-Baptiste Arena, Robert Saléon-Terras and Régis Lansade.

Thanks to Lewis Trondheim for his theory of the beak.

Thanks to Angélique Duveillier and the Lesaffre printing co.
(Tournai), as well as Philippe Fitam and to the cooperage of
Adour (Plaisance du Gers) for their welcome.

Thanks to the Futuropolis staff for its participation.
In the vineyards, they will long keep the memory
of that summer day when you all came
to hoe Montbenault's brambles and to taste from its cellar.

Thanks to the Quai des Bulles Festival (Saint-Malo),
to Dominique Matteï and his entire staff at the
Una Volta cultural center (Bastia).

Thanks to Joub, and to Sophie Leroy
for their attentive reading.

In one way or another, thanks to the following who equally
contributed to the production of this book:
Imanol Garay, Pascal Marquet, Thierry Atzori,
Antoine Arena, Marc & François Delaunay, Nady Foucault,
René Mosse, Mark Angeli, Joël Ménard, and the whole band of
2010 grape-pickers, including those who
mangled Brassens' songs a little.

The image of the "suspended forest" from the Lucie Lom agency,
page 155, was executed from a photo by Jeff Rabillon.

Thanks to Claude Gendrot, a vintage editor.

Again and always, thanks to Françoise Roy
for her indispensable support.

And, of course, thanks to Richard Leroy,
who played the game far beyond my expectations.

É. D.

RICHARD LEROY

Comicslit is an imprint
and trademark of

NANTIER • BEALL • MINOUSTCHINE
Publishing inc.
new york